Woodrow Wilson

LIFE AND LETTERS

*Books on Woodrow Wilson
by Ray Stannard Baker*

◇◇◇◇◇◇◇◇◇◇◇◇◇◇◇◇◇◇◇◇◇◇◇◇◇◇◇◇◇

WHAT WILSON DID AT PARIS, 1919

WOODROW WILSON AND WORLD SETTLE-
MENT, AN ACCOUNT OF THE PEACE CON-
FERENCE AT PARIS, IN THREE VOLUMES,
1923

WOODROW WILSON, LIFE AND LETTERS,
1927–1939

THE PUBLIC PAPERS OF WOODROW WILSON,
AUTHORIZED EDITION, SIX VOLUMES, ED-
ITED, WITH WILLIAM E. DODD, 1925–1927

WOODROW WILSON, 1918

Woodrow Wilson

LIFE AND LETTERS

War Leader

April 6, 1917 — February 28, 1918

BY

RAY STANNARD BAKER

Illustrated

VOLUME SEVEN

New York

DOUBLEDAY, DORAN & COMPANY, INC.

1939

PRINTED AT THE *Country Life Press*, GARDEN CITY, N. Y., U. S. A.

CONTENTS

VOLUME VII

PAGE

CHAPTER I. WILSON PREPARES FOR ACTIVE WAR . 1
(April, May, June, 1917)

First American troops arrive in France.
The President orders six American destroyers to the submarine zone; backs a program to give America supremacy in the air.
He makes a militant address on Flag Day—"The war was begun by the military masters of Germany"; sends a friendly commission to the newest democracy, Russia.
Balfour, in a private letter, sends copies of several secret treaties to the President.

CHAPTER II. "SURELY WE ARE LIVING IN A MAD WORLD" 139
(July, August, September, 1917)

Wilson repudiates idea of congressional committee on conduct of the war—"a millstone around my neck"; rejects the Pope's peace proposal: "We cannot take the word of the present rulers of Germany."
Drafts Hoover and Garfield to head the food and coal organizations; appoints a War Industries Board.
Suffragettes bedevil the White House.

PAGE

Labor troubles spread on the west coast, in Arizona, in New York.

CHAPTER III. INSISTS UPON A "UNIFIED CONDUCT OF THE WAR" 288
(October, November, December, 1917)

The President sends Colonel House to the Allied War Conference—"Take the whip hand. We not only accede to the plan for a unified conduct of the war but insist upon it"; demands a Supreme War Council; guides "Inquiry" in preparing information for use at a future peace conference—"what we . . . are seeking is a basis which will be fair to all."

Takes over the railroads of the country; asks Congress for war with Austria-Hungary and is greeted by a roar of enthusiasm.

The Bolsheviks seize power, but Wilson has "not lost faith in the Russian outcome."

Italy falters—disaster at Caporetto.

American troops get into the trenches.

CHAPTER IV. "A RAMPAGING MOOD OF HOSTILE CRITICISM" 442
(January, February, 1918)

America begins to feel the pinch of war—heatless, meatless, wheatless, sweetless days.

Wilson brands Senator Chamberlain's charges of military inefficiency as "an astonishing and absolutely unjustifiable distortion of the truth"; backs Garfield's bitterly resented coal order—"We must just bow our heads and let the storm beat."

*He states his Fourteen Points—"a summing up
of all that I have been thinking recently";
replies to the Austrian Emperor's suggestion
of a direct exchange of views on peace, asking
him to be more explicit.*

*Secretary Baker meets criticism of the War De-
partment before a Senate Committee. Ollie
James reports to the President: "He's eating
'em up!"*

Index 575

LIST OF ILLUSTRATIONS

Woodrow Wilson, 1918 . . . . . Frontispiece

FACING PAGE

Edward M. House 32

Arthur J. Balfour 32

General Pershing Arriving in France 108

American Soldiers in the Trenches 144

General Pershing Inspecting the French Front Line
Accompanied by General Franchet d'Esperey . 144

Josephus Daniels, Secretary of the Navy . . . 244

Newton D. Baker, Secretary of War 244

American Troops Going Over the Top in One of
Their Early Battles 340

Rear-Admiral William S. Sims 428

General John J. Pershing 428

American Troops—The 166th Infantry in a Wintry
March to the French Front 508

LIST OF FACSIMILES

PAGE

The President's War Program 9

Wilson and the Russian Commission 18

President Wilson Calls an Army into Being . . 103

For More Vigorous Naval Warfare 146

Wilson Answers the Pope 221

An Intimate Personal Letter 238

Lloyd George Writes a Personal Letter to Wilson . 278

The President's Interest in the Armenians and
    Syrians 332

"Take the Whip Hand!" 359

President Wilson's Interest in the Mooney Case . 490

Letter to Herbert Hoover 557

Reply to the Emperor of Austria 573

INTRODUCTION

W ITH THIS volume of *The Life and Letters of Woodrow Wilson* the author takes his courage in his hands and ventures a radical change of method. Previous volumes have been divided into chapters according to the subjects treated; in this the presentation is strictly chronological.

One of the greatest temptations of the biographer, as of the historian, is over-simplification: the itch to fit his subject neatly into preconceived categories. Discussion by subject is primarily such a simplification, an artificial device to make clear what the man was by exhibiting him in action in some limited or familiar field.

Carlyle's study of Cromwell, after long consideration, resolved itself into the chronological publication, with the necessary "elucidations," of Cromwell's letters.

". . . these words," he wrote, "authentically spoken and written by the chief actor in the business, must be of prime moment for [the] understanding of it. These are the words this man found suitable to represent the Things themselves, around him, and in him, of which we seek a History. . . ."

It was possible, perhaps, in the earlier years of Woodrow Wilson's political career, to interpret him best by watching him meet the momentous problems already well understood by the American people. His attitude toward boss politics, for example, the knowledge of which is bred in the bone of every American, invited a ready comparison with former leadership in the same field and made for a sound, if limited, estimate of the man himself. A similarly instinctive popular understanding could be counted upon by the biographer in exploring the President's strategy, as well as his tactics, on the familiar battlegrounds of tariff reform, the control of monopolies, the labor problem, woman suffrage and the like. We soon discovered what kind of an American Woodrow Wilson was.

When the Great War broke upon the world, an entirely new problem presented itself. The field, which had hitherto been narrowly domestic, now included the entire world. Everything was in flux. In the earlier period the President could act, with the coöperation of Congress, upon forces which he could control. When the war broke, he must act upon forces which were mostly beyond his control. He must continually extemporize both policy and action. He had suddenly become a world leader, and must be tested by new standards.

When the author began to study, day by day, the war record of the President, watching the development of the ominous problems which continuously confronted him— however clear now to us, still obscure to him—reading the astonishingly sharp, clear, often drily brief letters, largely devoid of the literary graces he earlier cultivated, written, as Carlyle said of Cromwell's, "in the very flame and conflagration of a revolutionary struggle and with an eye to the despatch of indispensable pressing business alone," he felt himself attaining a vitally new understanding of the man. Here was Woodrow Wilson, probably the foremost, certainly the most powerful and significant, statesman of his times, meeting the stupendous responsibilities thrust upon him, making day after day decisions of momentous importance.

"Take the whip hand. We not only accede to the plan for a unified conduct of the war but insist upon it."

In the light of the daily record—no previous American

administration is as completely documented as his—we can watch the most difficult of controversial issues quite simply and naturally unfolding themselves. We know not only what he was saying, but what he was thinking; his own preparatory notes are there for our reading. We can follow his reluctant awakening to the gravity of the problem of Russia; we see why and how censorship of communications and the press inevitably grew up in an atmosphere traditionally hostile to it; we can trace the curious history of American knowledge of the secret treaties of Europe, and their sinister aftermath: and above all, we can achieve an understanding, such as no general summary could give us, of the President's patient, unremitting struggle to find an opening toward peace, and his developing thought as to what the terms of that peace should be. His vision of a League of Nations was not invented, it grew. It grew in the travail of many minds working, for the first time, upon the vast catastrophe of a world war. We see it vividly day by day in these letters and documents: we are able to estimate more justly the vital part that Woodrow Wilson played in its growth.

One other vast advantage of reading a day-by-day chronicle, rather than a discussion by subject which so easily warps an understanding of the relative importance of any one element of a problem, is the appreciation of the immense significance, in this war as in no former one, of the economic, industrial and mechanical factors. They intrude everywhere, overshadowing the generals, forcing the hands of politicians and orators: we see it here in brilliant relief. Oil, coal, steel, money, bread! It was, as the President himself said, a war of resources no less than of men.

We see him working for days upon the unromantic problem of the prices of bunker coal, conferring with striking workers and disgruntled employers, presently taking over the control of all the railroads of the United States—and all this at a time when he was struggling week after week with a Congress that begrudged giving him the power he urgently required.

During the period covered by this volume there were, indeed, no separate subjects; there was only one vast, overwhelming, irresistible purpose: war. Every domestic issue, however acute in former years, was subdued to the passion and toil of that task. Political partisanship was transmuted: industrial and labor controversies, so troublesome in times of peace, were reduced, though not always easily, to a semblance of harmony.

The biographer, like the novelist, often succeeds best in heightening the reader's sense of reality by presenting his character against a background of common scenes, in the familiar atmosphere of his daily life. Thus we may watch, in the daily records, Woodrow Wilson's intimate goings and comings, his hours of labor, his method of rest and recreation, his visits to the theater or the art gallery, his golf, his rides in the country; when he had breakfast, whom he entertained at luncheon or dinner, and the people—we know most of them familiarly by name—who came to see him. We may watch him, the quiet, steady, dependable leader, sitting there in the White House at the calm center of the vast organization of a nation at war. He knew well that the "greatest need in every direction" was "coördination and unification," and we see how, day after day, by conference, by correspondence, by public addresses, he secured it. It is probable that it was never before possible to make so complete a record of the daily life of an American president as the one here presented.

In order to complete the understanding of the President's daily activities, and contribute to a clear realization of the immense importance of them, the biographer has presented day by day enough of the background of current events, both at home and abroad, to give some conception of the world-wide problems he was continually facing. If the Germans were winning a battle on the French front, if food was short in London, if there were strikes of discontented workers in Italy, the news, reaching the President first of all, intimately affected his daily decisions. Significant incidents have been drawn from the memoirs and diaries of the time, and from newspapers, magazines and other sources; all as critically studied as the letters themselves.

Woodrow Wilson's daily record rests chiefly upon the authority of two diaries of appointments, one kept in Secretary Tumulty's office in the executive department, the other, and far more intimate, kept by the chief usher of the White House. Neither is complete, since certain visitors were not recorded in either diary, and the narrative has therefore been augmented or corrected from references in letters, or private diaries placed in the author's hands, and from other sources. Here, as elsewhere, selection has been imperative, names of mere casual callers, such as groups of constituents presented by Congressmen, having been omitted.

Many of the addresses quoted are from *The Public Papers of Woodrow Wilson*, edited in six volumes by Ray Stannard Baker and William E. Dodd. In several instances in which brief addresses were omitted from the original collection, they have, where the subject seemed of sufficient importance, been reproduced or liberally quoted in this volume.

The biographer need not here repeat his description of the documentation upon which this narrative as a whole depends, since it is given in full in the introduction of Volume I of the *Life and Letters*. Suffice it to say that the private papers of Woodrow Wilson, placed in his hands in 1925, have been vastly augmented by documents, letters, diaries and other material supplied by the President's associates and friends. In the fourteen years since this work was begun, there has been a steady flow of biographies, histories and memoirs, both American and foreign, many of which, quoted or referred to in this volume, have been of great value to the writer.

Since the basis of the record here presented is wholly chronological, especial efforts have been made to provide an index more than ordinarily comprehensive, thus enabling the reader to ascertain speedily the President's record in any particular field. An immense amount of collateral material is made available by references in the footnotes.

In the preparation of this volume the author is under the deepest obligations to Katharine E. Brand, who has been his assistant since the beginning of his task, and whose knowledge of the documents, as well as the collateral material relating to the Wilson period, is unequaled. The work, as it stands, so dependent upon the accuracy of its context, could not have been completed without her loyal assistance. Inez C. Fuller and Roberta E. Bourne have greatly helped in the preparation of the copy and the reading of proofs.

The author feels beggared when considering his innumerable other obligations to friends who have assisted him, or authorities with whom he has corresponded. No writer could ever have had more generous assistance from those who knew the President or were interested in the ideals he set forth, or the work he did. They have helped to make this volume, more than any of the previous ones, a truly coöperative enterprise, committed to seeking a better understanding of Woodrow Wilson. The author must content himself with references to many of these friends in the text or footnotes of this volume.

Three special obligations, however, should be here acknowledged: To Bernard M. Baruch, for his more than generous assistance in securing for the use of this biographer important letters and documents. To Colonel House, who furnished the author with copies of a number of the President's letters of which no carbon copies exist, since they were written on his own typewriter; and to the Library of Yale University for permission to use many unpublished extracts from the letters of Colonel House there deposited as a part of the House Collection.

A remarkable series of scrapbooks, made by John Randolph Bolling for the President and Mrs. Wilson, dating from October 7, 1915, has been of real assistance.

Most important of all, Mrs. Woodrow Wilson throughout the years has been a loyal friend and a helpful critic.

Woodrow Wilson
LIFE AND LETTERS

Woodrow Wilson

LIFE AND LETTERS

CHAPTER I

WILSON PREPARES FOR ACTIVE WAR

(April, May, June, 1917)

First American troops arrive in France.

The President orders six American destroyers to the submarine zone; backs a program to give America supremacy in the air.

He makes a militant address on Flag Day—"The war was begun by the military masters of Germany"; sends a friendly commission to the newest democracy, Russia.

Balfour, in a private letter, sends copies of several secret treaties to the President.

Friday, April 6, 1917.

AT NOON on Friday, the 6th of April, Woodrow Wilson signed the formal proclamation that brought the United States into the World War. Four days previously, on the 2nd, he had delivered his address to the Houses of Congress asking immediate action. Debate in the Senate had lasted for thirteen hours and in the House still longer. The war resolution, as finally passed, with the Vice-President's signature still fresh upon it, reached the White House while the President and Mrs. Wilson were at luncheon. They arose at once and, accompanied by the President's cousin, Miss Helen Bones, went directly to the usher's office, just off the main entrance of the White House. Rudolph Forster, veteran executive secretary, was waiting with the parchment document in his hand. The little family group, accompanied only by Colonel Starling of the Secret Service, and Mr. Hoover, the head usher, watched silently while the President affixed his signature to the momentous document. A moment later he signed the formal proclamation of war.

Preparations had been made for the instant communication of the news. Before the President had risen from his chair a navy officer wigwagged from a window in the Executive Office, and a few seconds later the wireless station at Arlington was notifying our ships in harbor and at sea—as well as the whole world—that America was at war.

Half an hour later the President appeared at the Executive Office where he found Senator Smith of South Carolina and a group of anxious business men waiting to discuss the shortage of nitrates in the South. The President replied that he would make inquiry, and wrote to Denman of the Shipping Board the next day, expressing the hope that "it will be possible to do something promptly to relieve a situation which threatens the food supply as well as the clothing supply of the country and of the world." Fifteen minutes later Representative Garrett of Tennessee called.

At 2:30 the cabinet met, according to schedule. Gregory had already ordered the arrest of some sixty persons suspected of having designs upon the security of the United States. Houston discussed the mobilizing of the economic resources of the country. The President read aloud a message to the effect that the British wished to send a commission to the United States, and expressed his desire to avoid such visits if possible.

The President's official day ended when the cabinet meeting broke up. "Evening [recorded the head usher in his diary] in private room."

> The President issued a public statement approving the selective draft legislation which the War Department had presented to the Military Committee of the Senate and House, explaining that it was intended to apply for the period of the war only. He issued also an appeal in behalf of the Red Cross.[1]
>
> Control of all radio stations was taken by the government.[2]
>
> Ninety-one German vessels lying in American ports were taken into custody; and the officers and crews turned over to the immigration authorities.

[1] New York *Times*, April 7, 1917, for both papers. The President himself gave $500 to the Red Cross on April 16th.

[2] *Foreign Relations*, 1917, Supp. 2, Vol. II, pp. 1230–1231.

In Europe, the situation was growing increasingly difficult. Germany had settled herself stubbornly in defense of her "Hindenburg line." The French, faced with a black mood among the weary troops, were more concerned at the moment with restoration of discipline and confidence than with further attack.[1] The British were on the point of undertaking their summer offensive, but without the coöperation of a sweeping French offensive.[2] Russia, broken by revolution, was temporarily out of the battle.

To Colonel House, who had sent the President, on the 5th, a telegram just received, proposing that Balfour head a commission of British experts to the United States to place at the disposal of this government the experience gained by England in the war:

MY DEAR HOUSE,

Of course there is nothing for it but to reply to Drummond that we shall be glad to receive such a commission and to see Mr. Balfour at the head of it.

The plan has its manifest dangers. I do not think that all of the country will understand or relish. A great many will look upon the mission as an attempt to in some degree take charge of us as an assistant to Great Britain, particularly if the Secretary of State for Foreign Affairs heads the commission. But, on the other hand, it will serve a great many useful purposes and perhaps save a good deal of time in getting together.

In great haste,

Affectionately,

WOODROW WILSON[3]

---

[1] A. H. Frazier of the American Embassy in Paris had written almost two months before that the French had "nearly reached the limit," and all through May and June their troubles multiplied. By the end of July, however, under the wise direction of Pétain the spirit had greatly improved. Cruttwell, *A History of the Great War,* p. 415.

[2] Palmer, *Newton D. Baker,* Vol. I, pp. 150–151.

[3] House replied to Drummond on the 9th that the President was "greatly pleased" that Balfour would come. *The Intimate Papers of Colonel House,* edited by Charles Seymour, Vol. III, p. 36. Hereafter called *Intimate Papers.*

The French also proposed to send a commission. *Foreign Relations,* 1917, Supp. 2,

To his secretary, Tumulty, who had presented a query from Otto H. Kahn, as to whether opera in German, sung by German artists, should continue at the Metropolitan Opera House during the war:

"I think you are right. It would not be wise to express an opinion in regard to this matter, and yet personally I should hate to see them stop German opera. . . . I have no doubt that I can trust to the good sense and moderation of the directors of the Metropolitan Opera Company not to take any extreme or unnecessary action."

Saturday, April 7th.

The President and Mrs. Wilson played golf on a Virginia course. It was the President's custom, whenever possible, to make Saturday a day of change, or at least of freedom from routine engagements. ". . . Saturdays and Sundays are the only days I have," he wrote a few weeks after this, "on which to keep the spark of life in me going and I really feel that I ought to avoid serious engagements on those days . . ."[1] After luncheon he closeted himself in his study for the afternoon. It may well have been at this time that he worked out, on the typewriter which stood in a corner of his study, the notes headed "7 Apr. '17" (see facsimile on p. 9). In the evening the President and Miss Bones, his cousin, went to Keith's Theater.[2]

Vol. I, p. 8. ". . . . I have studied this problem from various angles," Lansing wrote the President on the 6th, "and have sought a way to avoid these visits without causing offense, since you so expressed your desire at Cabinet meeting today, but I am afraid there is no way which will not cause ill-feeling and at the present time that must be avoided at all hazards. . . ." On the 8th Ambassadors Page and Sharp were instructed to notify the British and French governments that the proposed commissions would be "most welcome." *Ibid.*, pp. 14–15.

[1]To Secretary Lane, June 16, 1917.

[2]During the next months of great responsibility and strain, the President felt more than ever the necessity for regular periods in the outdoor air—golf, horseback rides now and then, walks, drives—and for the relaxation which an evening at the theater always afforded him. Day after day he drove, usually with Mrs. Wilson or Dr. Grayson, to one of the golf courses near by, often leaving before official Washington was abroad in the morning. Sometimes as often as two or three times a week, he went to the theater with Mrs. Wilson, or Miss Bones, or some other member of the family. Dr. Grayson, his personal friend and physician, not only approved this program, but insisted upon it, knowing better than anyone else the tremendous concentration with which the President attacked his work, and the weariness of mind and body which was the in-

The Council of National Defense voted that Herbert Hoover be requested to take the chairmanship of a committee on food supply and prices; and that Daniel Willard be requested "to call upon the railroads so to organize their business as to lead to the greatest expedition in the movement of freight."

Secretary Burleson suspended mail service to Germany for the duration of the war.

The New York *Times* reported that the steel men of the country had agreed to furnish the army and navy with all the structural steel they needed for defense purposes for the coming year at a reduction of about $18,000,000 from the current market price.

Editorial reaction from the press of the nation was already overwhelmingly favorable to the President's course. Letters and telegrams of congratulation and endless offers of assistance began to tax the clerical facilities of the White House.[1]

Cuba declared war on Germany.

To Dr. Charles W. Eliot:

"I feel . . . that it is not wise or opportune now to choose a permanent system for the country in the matter of our military defense, because we must not delay our immediate preparation for the purpose of making plans which cannot be wisely made until we know what the future policy of the world is going to be, but I agree with you that when the time of the choice comes there is a vast deal to learn from the experience of Switzerland and I am sure I among others will be glad to learn it."

To Elihu Root:

". . . I am glad that you see what seemed to me to be the implication of my action but what most of the news-

evitable result. These activities are not here recorded in every case, since they constituted a part of the President's daily routine, and the mere repetition would become wearisome.

[1] President Wilson said to his brother-in-law, later, that "America was never so beautiful as in the spring, summer and autumn of 1917 when people were stirred by a passion in common, forgot themselves and political differences in an urge to put all they had, all they were, to use in a great purpose." Stockton Axson to the author.

papers have missed, that instead of abrogating the Monroe Doctrine the position I have taken plants it more securely than ever upon the very principles upon which the whole world is invited to act."

To J. P. Morgan:

"Your letter . . . is certainly a most generous one and I want to express my warm appreciation of the spirit of service in which it is written. I am sure I can count upon you and your associates in this emergency."

To William Jennings Bryan, who had resigned as Secretary of State because he feared that the President's policies would lead to war, and who had telegraphed on April 6th: "Believing it to be the duty of the citizen to bear his part of the burdens of war and his share of its perils I hereby tender my services to the government. Please enroll me as a private whenever I am needed and assign me to any work that I can do until called to the colors. I shall through the Red Cross contribute to the comfort of soldiers in the hospitals and through the Y.M.C.A. aid in safeguarding the morals of the men in camp." The President replied by wire:

"Thank you very warmly for your telegram. I am sure that the whole country will believe that you are ready to serve in any way that may set its interests forward."

To Francis B. Sayre, the President's son-in-law:
MY DEAR FRANK:

Bless your heart for your letter . . . Of course, I knew how you would feel and how ready you would stand to do anything that you could do in this time of the country's need for every man who can think straight and act effectively. I do not now see just what advice to give you, but you may be sure that I will keep your offer in my mind as I do in my heart.

I long very constantly to see dear Jessie and you and the baby. I am sure you do not need to be told how constantly I am thinking of you and how warmly I love you all.

In necessary haste, with deep love for all,

Affectionately yours,

WOODROW WILSON.

PROFESSOR FRANCIS B. SAYRE
Williamstown, Massachusetts.

To M. W. Jacobus, an old friend of the Princeton days:
"MY DEAR FRIEND:

"Your letter . . . sounds a very deep and a very true note about the present interests and problems of the world. You are undoubtedly right in thinking that at bottom there lies the spiritual problem which is the spring of life. Your letter has moved me very deeply and I thank you for it with all my heart."

Easter Sunday, April 8th.

Mrs. Wilson went alone to an early service at St. Margaret's Episcopal Church; at 11 o'clock she went again, this time accompanied by the President. Representative Adamson, chairman of the House Committee on Interstate and Foreign Commerce, called in the early afternoon to discuss the drafting of a bill authorizing government control and operation during the war of all railroad, telegraph and telephone lines of the country.[1] As soon as this conference was concluded, the President and Mrs. Wilson and Mrs. Wilson's brother went for one of the long Sunday drives which they so much enjoyed. They returned at 5:20, in time for the President to confer with T. W. Gregory and the Assistant Attorney General as to German activities in this country and in Central and South America. The evening was quietly spent, with no appointments.

The Council of National Defense made public a statement by its sub-committee on labor, signed by Samuel Gompers and his fellow members on the committee, which urged both capital and labor to unite in common support of the

---

[1] On April 12th Adamson sent the President a completed draft of such a bill.

nation, setting aside for the duration of the war any plans for changes in labor standards.

The shout of welcome in Europe at America's entry into the war began to be heard in the United States. "It is a red-letter day for us! . . ." exulted Premier Ribot of France. The London *Times* referred, with more than ordinary enthusiasm, to "an event which is certain to influence the destiny of mankind on both sides of the Atlantic for a generation to come."[1] Lloyd George's message to the American people was widely published.[2] The Italian, Russian and Belgian press rang with words of approval. The civil population of Rheims was ordered to evacuate, while German shells continued their destruction of the city.

Monday, April 9th.

The President spent the entire morning at work in his study. Mrs. Wilson's secretary, Miss Benham, remained for luncheon as she often did, and Secretary McAdoo was also a guest.[3] In the afternoon the President conferred with Representative Dent, chairman of the House Committee on Military Affairs, who had been summoned to discuss the conscription feature of the army bill. ". . . an hour's conference developed a sharp difference in views."[4] The Secretary of the Navy called at 4:45.

Formal announcement was delivered to the State Department that Austria-Hungary had severed diplomatic relations with the United States.[5]

[1] *Literary Digest*, April 14, 1917.

[2] *Current History*, May, 1917, p. 224.

[3] During all of Woodrow Wilson's life, whether at the small house at Wesleyan, or the more pretentious president's house at Princeton, or the White House at Washington, relatives came and went freely, always welcome. The President made an effort to keep his table free from discussion of business, politics, affairs of state; meals were to be quiet, homelike periods in a busy life. (McAdoo, being a member of the cabinet as well as a member of the family, sometimes broke over this rule, to the President's irritation!) There were surprisingly few days which did not find at least one extra member of the family at the luncheon or dinner table. Miss Helen Bones, of course, lived at the White House part of the time, the McAdoos were frequently there, and occasionally James Woodrow, the President's nephew, his brother Joseph R. Wilson with his wife and daughter, and others. Mrs. Wilson's mother, Mrs. W. H. Bolling, her sister, Miss Bertha, and her brother, John Randolph Bolling (in later years Mr. Wilson's private secretary), were frequent guests. Those who lived farther away kept in touch through short visits—the Sayres, Miss Margaret Wilson, Dr. Axson, the Misses Hoyt, John Wilson of Pennsylvania, George Howe.

[4] New York *Times*, April 10, 1917.

[5] *Foreign Relations*, 1917, Supp. 1, pp. 594-595.

PROGRAMME. *7 Apr. '17*

Measures for war:

    The Additional Forces Bill,

    The additional navy Bill,

    And all legislation needed to
put the country in a thorough state of defense and
preparation for action.

Bills for the safeguarding of the
nation:

    These include the bills re-
centcy submitted to the Judiciary Committee by the Department of Justice.

    Some further suggestions,
affecting, for example, various
restrictions on trading with
the enemy, will presently be
forthcoming from the Council
for National Defense.

Webb Bill.

Amendments to Shipping Bill.

Amendments to Federal Reserve Act.

Strike legislation, particularly
control of the Railroads for
military purposes and the increase of the Interstate Commerce Commission.

THE PRESIDENT'S WAR PROGRAM

On the day after President Wilson signed the American Declaration
of War he wrote out on his own typewriter this "Programme" for
vigorous new legislation to carry it on.

9

Senator Weeks of Massachusetts and Representative Madden
of Illinois, both Republicans, simultaneously introduced
resolutions providing for a joint committee of Congress
on the prosecution of the war.[1]

Admiral Sims arrived in Liverpool.[2]

Elihu Root, speaking at the Republican Club in New York,
said:

"We must have no criticism now. The fate of our country is involved. . . .

"We need no coalition Government to make us loyal.
We will make a coalition ourselves with every Democrat
in the country. . . ."[3]

The Provisional government of Russia put out a statement
on war aims: ". . . free Russia does not aim to dominate
other peoples and deprive them of their national patri-
mony, to occupy foreign territories by force, but to establish a firm peace on the foundation of the right of peoples
to determine their own destiny. . . ."[4]

At dawn the British began their great offensive on a 12-mile
front north and south of Arras, Canadian troops gaining an
"heroic success" in the capture of Vimy Ridge. Nearly
6,000 prisoners were taken in the first onset.

To Carter Glass, who had written: "My two sons are enlisted
for the war; and, having voted in Congress to impose this
obligation of service on them, I cannot endure the thought of
standing by and doing nothing. It would make me very unhappy: hence I earnestly request that the age limit be waived
in my case in order that I may be assigned to active duty
somewhere.":

"I beg that you will not think of enlisting in the Army.
You are one of the men I shall most depend upon to keep

[1]This was not the first move toward "coalition" control of the conduct of the war,
nor by any means the last. On the day of the declaration of war, Senator Smith of
Michigan, Republican, had pointed out in the Senate that the President would find
many able men for his cabinet or for other purposes in the Republican ranks.

[2]*Naval Investigation Hearings*, 1920, Vol. I, p. 2, Sims to Daniels, January 7, 1920.
For Admiral Sims's description of the conditions he found, see *ibid.*; also *The Victory
at Sea*, pp. 5 *et seq.*

[3]New York *Times*, April 10, 1917.

[4]*Foreign Relations*, 1918, *Russia*, Vol. I, pp. 39–40. Transmitted to Lansing May 3rd.
This volume, p. 46. During the intervening month there was much uneasiness lest
Russia make a separate peace.

the counsels of the country steady and the Congress efficient in the performance of its fundamental and all-important duties. Surely, you are just as much serving the colors there as you could be in the ranks of the Army. . . ."[1]

Tuesday, April 10th.

At noon Theodore Roosevelt arrived, vigorous and hearty, full of enthusiasm about his great project for recruiting and leading a division of volunteers to the front in France. "Mr. Tumulty received a hearty slap on the back," and the President shook hands cordially. At the close of the conference the crowd of newspaper men who had been hungrily waiting outside pounced upon the smiling Colonel. ". . . . The President received me with the utmost courtesy and consideration, and, doubtless, in his own good time will come to a decision. . . ."[2]

After luncheon the President went to the Executive Office, where he received Representative Anthony of Kansas. At 2:30 the cabinet met. The session was a long one, with much discussion of the policy to be adopted toward the interned German ships. Secretary Lansing laid before the President a draft of an executive order creating a War Trade Committee. Late in the afternoon the President received Governor Stuart of Virginia and Representative Carter Glass.

> Admirals of the United States, Great Britain and France conferred at Fortress Monroe, Hampton Roads, in regard to coöperation in the naval war.[3]
>
> Ambassador Francis telegraphed from Russia to Secretary Lansing: ". . . . Allies have binding agreement to negotiate no separate peace and also probably agreements as to nature of that peace and perhaps specific agreements or understandings between some of Allies concerning territory

---

[1]During the early part of the war the President wrote a good many similar letters to senators, congressmen and those in other branches of service who felt it their duty to resign and go into the army. His advice was much the same in every case.

[2]New York *Times*, April 11, 1917; also Huston Thompson, in the *Dearborn Independent*, May 22, 1926; for George Creel's account, based upon a talk with the President three days later, see *The War, the World and Wilson*, pp. 78 *et seq.* Creel writes: ". . . . My keenest impression at the time was the President's appreciation of Mr. Roosevelt's intense virility, picturesque personality, and love of fighting. . . ."

[3]*Naval Investigation Hearings*, 1920, Vol. II, p. 2086; also Daniels, *Our Navy at War*, pp. 45 *et seq.*

and other subjects which endeavoring discreetly to learn definitely. . . ."[1]

The British advance continued, in spite of heavy snowstorms and bitterly cold weather.

To Secretary Lansing, a letter written on the President's own typewriter:

MY DEAR MR. SECRETARY,

The recent debates on the war resolution in Congress lead me to suggest that you send the following confidential message to Ambassador Page in London:

"Take an early opportunity in conversation with the Prime Minister to convey to him in the most confidential manner the information that the only circumstance which seems now to stand in the way of an absolutely cordial cooperation with Great Britain by practically all Americans who are not influenced by ties of blood directly associating them with Germany is the failure so far to find a satisfactory method of self-government for Ireland. This appeared very strikingly in the recent debates in Congress upon the war resolution and appeared in the speeches of opponents of that resolution who were not themselves Irishmen or representatives of constituencies in which Irish voters were influential, notably several members from the South. If the people of the United States could feel that there was an early prospect of the establishment for Ireland of substantial self-government a very great element of satisfaction and enthusiasm would be added to the cooperation now about to be organized between this country and Great Britain. Convey this information unofficially of course but as having no little significance. Successful action now would absolutely divorce our

---

[1]*Foreign Relations*, 1917, Supp. 2, Vol. I, pp. 18–19. A reference, of course, to certain of the secret treaties. Nothing has been found to indicate that this hint was ever replied to or followed up by the Department of State. It is not known, moreover, whether or not the President ever saw it.

citizens of Irish birth and sympathy from the German sympathizers here with whom many of them have been inclined to make common cause."

Page now knows the Prime Minister well enough to know how to say these things to him frankly, and if a way could be found now to grant Ireland what she has so often been promised, it would be felt that the real programme of government by the consent of the governed had been adopted everywhere in the anti-Prussian world.

Faithfully Yours,
W. W.[1]

To Representative Claude Kitchin, written at the suggestion of Secretary McAdoo:[2]

"I have been in constant consultation with the Secretary of the Treasury with regard to the suggestions he has made to the Committee of Ways and Means about the financial legislation necessary for the conduct of the war and concerning the methods of raising the necessary funds, and write you this line to say that those suggestions have my entire approval.

"May I express the hope that the Committee may accept these suggestions in substance as embodying the best thought of the administration, and that it may be able to present this legislation at an early date to the Congress?"

Wednesday, April 11th.

At 11:30 the Attorney General and Frank L. Polk, Counselor of the Department of State, called, and half an hour later the

---

[1]In a letter of May 4th to the President, Page wrote that he had invited Lloyd George to dinner a short time before. ". . . after dinner, I took him to a corner of the drawing room and delivered your message to him about Ireland. 'God knows, I'm trying,' he replied. 'Tell the President that. And tell him to talk to Balfour.' Presently he broke out, 'Madmen, madmen—I never saw any such task,' and he pointed across the room to Sir Edward Carson, his First Lord of the Admiralty—'madmen.' 'But the President's right. We've got to settle it and we've got to settle it now.' . . ." *The Life and Letters of Walter H. Page*, Vol. II, pp. 259–260.

[2]McAdoo attended, on the afternoon of the 10th, a session of the House Committee on Ways and Means, during which "the greatest single bond issue in the history of the world" was agreed upon. New York *Times*, April 11, 1917.

President went over to the Capitol, where he spent an hour or so in the Speaker's room, conferring with Clark and with Majority Leader Kitchin. Afternoon engagements had been made with: Frank B. Noyes, president of the Associated Press; Senator Swanson of Virginia; Representative Lever, who discussed the problem of increasing the production of food in the country; Chairman Denman of the Shipping Board; the Secretary of War.

> Executives of the leading railroads of the country, meeting in Washington at the call of the Council of National Defense, named a Railroads War Board of five men to direct the operation of American railways during the war. Daniel Willard was chairman *ex officio*.[1]
>
> The New York *Times* contained an editorial protesting against the press censorship section of the Espionage bill —one of the early guns fired in this controversial issue.
>
> Thomas Nelson Page, ambassador to Italy, wrote the President that his war address had been "delivered in Austria by the Italian aeroplanes as good ammunition for countries fighting for Democracy and peace." ". . . . There is talk also of having the address posted in every commune in Italy. . . ."
>
> Brazil severed relations with Germany.
>
> The food situation in Great Britain was admitted to be critical—within a week London was observing its first meatless day.

To Secretary Baker, a letter written on the President's own typewriter:

". . . . We are in danger of creating too much machinery. . . .

"It seems to me much more practical to use the few officers we have in getting troops ready here and creating the materials for cooperation than to send them parleying to England and France. I would like to have a personal talk with you about this."

---

[1]Clarkson, *Industrial America in the World War*, p. 81; New York *Times*, April 12, 1917.

To General G. W. Goethals:

"... I have given my approval to the plan of the United States Shipping Board for the construction of a large emergency wooden fleet to assist in the carriage of supplies and munitions to the Allies and for other services during the war. When this undertaking was conceived, the Board entertained the hope that they might have the use of your directing genius in the marshaling of the resources of the country for the rapid construction of the tonnage required; indeed it was in part upon that hope that they formed the plan....

"I personally would like to see the weight of your connection with this enterprise added to the answer which we will thus be giving to the challenge of the submarine."

To H. A. Garfield:

".... I hope with all my heart that my address to the Congress has convinced you that I had good reasons and that the course I pursued was not pursued either in haste or in vexation. I should not like to feel that I was going against the judgment of a man whose judgment I so highly and sincerely value."

To Professor Harry Fielding Reid, an old friend, of Johns Hopkins University. Mrs. Reid corresponded with the President for many years:

".... It renders me not a little uneasy to learn that you are going to venture upon the seas at this time. I wish I knew of some way of adding to your security.

"It is generous of you to ask whether there is anything I can suggest that you could do.... I shall trust to your own knowledge of affairs and of the opportunity to find out the things that will be of greatest service....

"Please give my warm regards to Mrs. Reid.

"It is very lonely sometimes when I must go for so long without seeing my friends, but my absorption just now is so great that fortunately I do not have time to think of my bereavement."

Thursday, April 12th.

President Wilson remained in his study until almost 12 o'clock, when he joined Mrs. Wilson and her brother in a drive before luncheon. Afternoon callers were: Senator Paul O. Husting, who discussed the question of conscription versus volunteering, and put forward a suggestion for a compromise plan; Senators King of Utah, Shafroth of Colorado, and Kendrick of Wyoming, all Democrats; the Secretary of War. Mr. and Mrs. Wilson went together for a short walk in the late afternoon; and the President and Miss Bones spent the evening at the National Theater.

> Charles E. Hughes, speaking in New York, said: ". . . . All thoughts of partisanship are laid aside. . . ."[1]
>
> Lloyd George, speaking before the American Luncheon Club in London: ". . . . The road to victory, the guarantee of victory, the absolute assurance of victory, has to be found in one word, 'ships,' and a second word, 'ships,' and a third word, 'ships.' . . . ."[2]

To Secretary Lansing, who, on April 9th, had sent the President a memorandum suggesting a commission to Russia. On the 11th he had written again on the same subject, saying: ". . . . I wish we could do something to prevent the socialistic element in Russia from carrying out any plan which would destroy the efficiency of the Allied Powers. . . ." The President's reply was written on his own typewriter:

"The suggestion of a commission to Russia has come to me from a number of quarters and I am inclined to think that it would be a good plan to send one, and send it practically at once.

"The important, perhaps the all-important thing is the personnel. Men of large view, tested discretion, and a sympathetic appreciation of just what it is they have been

---

[1] New York *Times*, April 13, 1917.
[2] *Ibid.*

sent over for are the sort we need; and is it necessary, besides, that they should *look* the part? . . . .

"We must find the right men, and they must not all be Democrats,—need not any of them be Democrats,—but should all be genuinely enthusiastic for the success of the Russian revolution."

To the Marquis de Lafayette, who had telegraphed on April 8th: "I respectfully salute the champion of individual and world wide liberty," the President telegraphed:

"Your message is doubly gratifying coming from one of the illustrious race revered and honored by all liberty-loving Americans."

Friday, April 13th.

At 12:30 the French ambassador called; and before the regular biweekly cabinet meeting George Creel came in for a talk. It was at this time, probably, that the President "talked freely and interestedly" of Theodore Roosevelt's visit, "giving a very vivid picture of the meeting."[1] At the cabinet meeting which followed, it was determined to ask Congress to give the President "power to establish embargoes." Houston, just back from an agricultural conference in St. Louis, was full of his subject.[2] After an appointment in the late afternoon with Representative H. F. Fisher, a new Democratic member of the House, the President spent the evening with his family.

Secretary Baker explained to Roosevelt why his plan for raising a division was not acceptable.[3]
Bolivia severed relations with Germany.
General Haig reported that the British were "astride the Hindenburg line."

To Secretary Lansing, written on the President's own typewriter:

" . . . the more I think the matter over the more I am convinced that this is a good time to go forward with our

[1] Creel, *The War, the World and Wilson*, p. 78. See this volume, p. 11.
[2] Houston, *Eight Years With Wilson's Cabinet*, Vol. I, p. 263.
[3] Palmer, *Newton D. Baker*, Vol. I, p. 201.

THE SECRETARY OF STATE,
WASHINGTON

April 12, 1917.

My dear Mr. President:

I have your note of today in relation to the suggested Russian Commission and have been thinking over the personnel of such Commission.   I think we may agree that

Samuel Gompers is as available a man as we could get.   In
regard to Oscar Straus I should doubt very much the advisability of sending another Jew and I believe there is
a measure of danger in overplaying the Jew element.   I
do not think Willard Straight is the man at all for the
place and I doubt very much from my acquaintance with Dr.
Wheeler whether he would be suitable.

I should think we ought to have, in addition to a
labor leader, such a man as Doctor John R. Mott; a busi-
nessman like Cyrus McCormick or Howard Elliott; a finan-
cier like Bertrand; and a lawyer of prominence.

In regard to Professor Harper of Chicago, I have heard
from several different sources that he is not as popular
as I had supposed in Russia.   I am therefore afraid to ad-

vise his

The President,
    The White House.

18

vise his selection. Of course I assume Mr. Crane would

be joined to any Commission that might be sent.

As soon as you determine upon the make-up of the

commission I will take it up with the individuals if you

so desire, or, possibly, it would be more effective if

you communicated directly with them.

Faithfully yours,

Robert Lansing

WILSON AND THE RUSSIAN COMMISSION

Letter from Secretary Lansing to President Wilson, April 12, 1917, with lists in the President's handwriting of possible members of the Commission to Russia. Secretary Lansing probably drew the design—he often sketched absent-mindedly while he talked, using whatever paper happened to be before him. The Russian Commission, as finally chosen, was as follows: Elihu Root; Charles R. Crane; John R. Mott; Cyrus H. McCormick; S. R. Bertron; James Duncan; Charles Edward Russell.

Pan-American treaty with such countries as are able to come in. There would be a rather substantial advantage in having Brazil come in first, for the German influence has been supposed to be stronger there, and the German plans for immigration and control more definite, than anywhere else in Latin America. . . ."

To Secretary Baker, who had sent over to the White House a letter from ex-President Taft, in which Taft referred to the decision of the President and Baker to "follow the recommendations of the General Staff and of your military advisers, to increase your army only by recruiting the regular army and the National Guard, and by a conscription system," and not to send abroad an army until a million men could be trained, under the conscription system, for that purpose. Taft commented: ". . . . I am so profoundly convinced of the correctness of your conclusions, and the wisdom of what you propose, that I can not refrain from writing you to felicitate you. . . ."

"MY DEAR BAKER:

". . . . President Taft is certainly acting in a mighty big way . . ."

Saturday, April 14th.

In the morning the President remained closeted in his study, hard at work. He even had a table set up in his room, and Mrs. Wilson and Miss Bones joined him there for a quiet luncheon. After a call from Mr. Whitehouse (probably J. Howard Whitehouse, Liberal member of Parliament) at two o'clock, he again closed his study door, Mrs. Wilson remaining with him. In the evening the family went together to the Belasco Theater.

> President Wilson signed an executive order creating the Committee on Public Information; and named George Creel as chairman, the other members being Lansing, Baker and Daniels.[1]

---

[1]Secretaries Lansing, Baker and Daniels, in their joint letter of April 13th to the President in regard to such a committee, had said:

". . . . It is our opinion that the two functions—censorship and publicity—can be

Admiral Sims sent his first two telegrams to the Navy Department: the first a statement regarding the serious situation of the war at sea, and an outline of the help needed from America; the second emphasizing the first and adding that the information therein was "not even known to the majority of British officials."[1]

It was reported that Austrians and Germans were throwing peace propaganda into the Russian trenches.

Sunday, April 15th.

President and Mrs. Wilson did not, as was their usual custom, go to church in the morning, but remained in the private part of the White House. A group of relatives were guests at luncheon and the whole party went for a drive in the afternoon. At 8:35 in the evening Secretary Baker called for a short conference. No official letters were written, since it was Mr. Wilson's custom, whenever possible, to keep Sunday in the old-fashioned way.

A plan for a mine barrage across the North Sea was presented by the Bureau of Ordnance.[2]

Monday, April 16th.

The President spent the first part of the morning at work in his study. At ten o'clock William J. Bryan called, and, after the interview, declared that he intended to support the government in any war plans decided upon. ". . . . In war time the President speaks for the whole country and there should be no division or dissension. . . ." The Assistant Secretary of State, William Phillips, called toward noon. Afternoon appointments:

joined in honesty and with profit, and we recommend the creation of a Committee on Public Information. . . ."

George Creel wrote later: "In no degree was the Committee an agency of censorship, a machinery of concealment or repression. . . . In all things, from first to last . . . it was a plain publicity proposition . . ." Creel, *How We Advertised America*, p. 4.

Controversy is still raging over the functions of the "Com. Pub." as it came to be called. Lansing comments on Creel with caustic pen (*War Memoirs of Robert Lansing*, pp. 322–323); Will Irwin, who assumed the direction of the Foreign Section in the spring of 1918, gives an extremely favorable account (*Propaganda and the News*, pp. 184 *et seq.*). Other reports vary in the same way.

[1] *Foreign Relations*, 1917, Supp. 2, Vol. I, pp. 23–25; *Naval Investigation Hearings*, 1920, Vol. I, pp. 29, 38–39.

[2] *Naval Investigation Hearings*, 1920, Vol. II, p. 2027. The main features of the project as adopted and carried out were included in this early plan.

the ambassador from Chile, who presented his credentials; Senator Hughes of New Jersey; Representative Doremus of Michigan; Senators Chamberlain of Oregon and Phelan of California; Senators Fletcher and Ransdell, and Representative Small, who discussed the need of a river and harbor bill. President and Mrs. Wilson went out for a short drive before dinner; the head usher's diary records: "Evening with family."

> The President issued an appeal to the people: ". . . . The supreme test of the Nation has come. We must all speak, act, and serve together!"[1]

> Secretary Daniels, "with the President's hearty approval," telegraphed Admiral Sims, asking whether it was not "practicable to blockade German coast efficiently and completely, thus making practically impossible the egress and ingress of submarines."[2]

> The Emergency Fleet Corporation was organized "with a capital stock of $50,000,000, all of which was subscribed for by the United States Shipping Board."[3] G. W. Goethals was made general manager.

> It was announced from Paris that General Nivelle had launched an offensive on a 25-mile front between Soissons and Rheims.

To William Dahne of Laporte, Indiana:

"Your telegram . . . gave me the deepest gratification. I have never at any time, as you know, doubted the unhesitating loyalty of our fellow-citizens of German extraction, but such expressions of loyalty and of devotion to the service of the country . . . are none the less gratifying and inspiriting."

To Richard Lloyd Jones of the *Wisconsin State Journal:*

"My attention has from time to time been called to the admirable editorials you have been publishing in support

---

[1] *The Public Papers of Woodrow Wilson*, edited by Ray Stannard Baker and William E. Dodd, Vol. V, pp. 22–27. Hereafter called *Public Papers.*

[2] *Naval Investigation Hearings*, 1920, Vol. I, p. 186; also Daniels, "Wilson, Master Strategist," in the *American Legion Monthly*, December, 1926. Sims replied on the 18th that such a plan had been found "wholly impracticable." *Foreign Relations*, 1917, Supp. 2, Vol. I, pp. 28–29.

[3] Hurley, *The Bridge to France*, p. 24.

of the administration in the present emergency, and I cannot deny myself the pleasure of dropping you a line to say how deeply and sincerely they have been appreciated. Such things make it worth while to be a public servant."

To his daughter, Margaret Woodrow Wilson, a telegram:

"All of us join in sending you birthday greetings and more love than the wires can carry. May you have not only many happy returns but may each year bring greater and greater happiness. We will celebrate when you get back."

Tuesday, April 17th.

The President and Dr. Grayson drove to the Suburban Club in the morning for two hours of golf. Before the regular cabinet meeting the President received the Mexican ambassador, Señor Bonillas, who presented his credentials. In response to the ambassador's words, the President made a short address.[1] At 2:15 he received Representative Meeker and Mrs. Alice V. Redmore. After the members of the cabinet had left, Representative Dent, who had been summoned by the President, arrived to continue the discussion on conscription. Representatives Mann and Lenroot, both Republicans, had also been summoned on the same subject; they saw the President at 5:30. The evening Mr. Wilson spent quietly with his family.

The President signed the General Deficiency Appropriation bill which placed at his disposal $100,000,000 for "national security and defense."

The British offensive on the Western Front was reported halted for a time because of continued rain and snow; but the French were still advancing.

---

[1]"The close neighborhood of the United States and Mexico makes it most desirable that there should be between the two countries relations of friendly trust and confidence. It has been my endeavor in these years of unrest and strife in Mexico to impress upon the Mexican people that the United States has none but the best interests of Mexico at heart, and has no wish more selfish than to see its people placed in the enjoyment of the blessings of peace, happiness, and prosperity by the establishment of a constitutional and stable government capable, among other things, of affording due protection to American citizens and property and of meeting all other international requirements. . . .

"The United States asks no more, and can, of course, accept no less." *New York Times,* April 18, 1917.

To Senator Lee S. Overman, in regard to the nomination of Lester H. Woolsey as Solicitor for the Department of State:

". . . Mr. Woolsey is and has for some time been one of the Secretary's right-hand, indispensable men. He is a genuine expert. He has worked up through the ranks to his present position of confidence and trust in the department, and I am so much interested to have the State Department operated at a maximum of efficiency that I would not dare to put in a new man from the outside. . . ."

Wednesday, April 18th.

The President spent the entire morning in his study. At noon he went over to the Senate building for an hour's conference with various senators, chiefly about the proposed committee on the conduct of the war, of which he disapproved. During the afternoon he received: Representative Fitzgerald of New York; Senator Simmons of North Carolina and Mr. Hugh MacRae; Representative Crisp of Georgia and Judge Whipple; Senators Owen of Oklahoma and Hoke Smith of Georgia.

Both Houses of the British Parliament passed a resolution of welcome upon America's entry into the war.

Ambassador Page in London reported to the Department of State that the Prime Ministers of Great Britain and France were to go to Italy for a conference about possible peace with Austria.[1]

Thursday, April 19th.

The President spent the morning in his study; and just before luncheon the Attorney General called. Afternoon appointments: the minister from the Netherlands, to discuss proposals pending in Congress for the limitation of exports from the United States;[2] Secretary Lane; Senator Phelan of California and Rudolph Spreckels; Secretary McAdoo and William Denman of the Shipping Board.

The American steamship *Mongolia* fired the first American gun of the war, at a German submarine, sinking it, it was believed.

[1] *Foreign Relations,* 1917, Supp. 2, Vol. I, p. 28.
[2] See *ibid.,* Vol. II, p. 1117.

A conference was held at St. Jean de Maurienne (Lloyd George, Ribot, Sonnino) which represented secret diplomacy within secret diplomacy. ". . . . The chief subjects for discussion, forming the ostensible object of the conference," writes Lloyd George, "were Italy's aspirations in Asia Minor, and the question of Greece. [This portion of the conference resulted in one of the secret treaties.] When these had been dealt with, we proceeded to talk about the prospects of an early peace with Austria . . ." [The Prince Sixte negotiations, unknown to Sonnino, and not revealed to him at this time.][1]

Paris reported that the French, under General Nivelle, were still gaining.

To Secretary Lansing:

"I would be very much obliged if you would be kind enough to let me see the report on Japanese activities in China made by Consul General Baker in August last. I want to get a better grasp on things over there than I feel that I have now."

To Secretary Lansing, who had written on the 18th: "It is with increasing anxiety that I have seen the trend of recent reports from Mexico. It appears to me that the military party in the Mexican Government is controlling its policies and that that party is intensely pro-German or at least anti-American. . . .

"The danger spots of course are Tampico and the border, and possibly the Tehuantapec railway which I believe is English owned and operated. The trouble will very likely arise over Mexico's alleged effort to enforce neutrality by denying Mexican ports to American naval vessels and those of Great Britain and France. This will be a very plausible ground for demanding that any naval vessels at Tampico be withdrawn. Technically they will have right on their side, but from a practical point of view we cannot respect Mexican neutrality so far as Tampico is concerned. Our refusal to withdraw our protection from the oil wells, which I assume will be your view, may result in an open declaration of war or in an ultimatum

---

[1] *War Memoirs of David Lloyd George*, Vol. IV, pp. 236 *et seq.*

which will result in war. . . ." The President's reply was written on his own typewriter:

MY DEAR MR. SECRETARY,

I do not know what to make out of the despatches from Mexico. It is by no means clear (matching the information of the War Department from General Pershing with the information of the State Department) which is the Anti-American party, Carranza's or that which is forming under the leadership of disaffected military men. We shall have to await developments before we come to a conclusion about that.

Carranza will, no doubt, in any case, be stiff and technical in insisting upon his authority to enforce neutrality, and will in all likelihood, as you anticipate, demand the removal of any armed ships we may have within Mexican territorial waters. All of our larger ships lie, of necessity, beyond the three mile limit.

The United States cannot afford to be too "practical." She is the leading champion of the right of self-government and of political independence everywhere. Only the most extraordinary circumstances of arbitrary injustice on the part of the Mexican government would make me feel that we had the right to take control at Tampico or at the Tehuantapec R.R.

As I suggested, in a previous letter on this subject, there is reason to believe that the government at Mexico City is not in real control of the Tampico district itself and that English influences are. The same may be true at Tehuantapec. . . .

I would be very much obliged if you would confer very fully with the British Ambassador about this whole situation.[1] There is absolutely no breach of the Monroe Doc-

---

[1]Lansing saw the British ambassador the same day, and again on April 24th, regarding the Mexican oil fields. At the meeting on the 24th Bonillas assured Lansing that "his government did not contemplate an embargo on oil." *War Memoirs of Robert Lansing*, pp. 314–316.

trine in allowing the British to exercise an influence there which anti-American sentiment in Mexico for the time prevents our exercising. After you have ascertained the British plans and intentions thereabout we should have a conference (you and I) about what we may and can do,— I mean can consistently with our principles and with our predominant influence just now in Latin America.

Faithfully Yours,
W. W.

To Secretary Lansing, who had written on the 17th, saying that Da Gama was ill, and absent from Washington, so that the Pan-American treaty had not yet been taken up with him. The enforced delay, Lansing added, had given him time to think the matter over carefully, and certain difficulties had occurred to him. The President's reply was written on his own typewriter:

"The answers to the important questions you here raise are reasonably clear to me. . . .

"If any one of the signatories to our proposed Pan-American treaty should become an ally of Germany against her European enemies, we would undoubtedly be bound to protect her against any loss of territory or any curtailment of her political independence that any of the Entente group might attempt; but we would be obliged to do that in any case, under the Monroe Doctrine.

"Should any one of the signatories permit its territory to be used as a base of military or naval operations against us, it would manifestly be acting in contravention of the patent meaning of the pact and we would be free to act as if there were no pact.

"As for 'influences' and propaganda, we could not prevent them, any more than Great Britain has been able to prevent them in the United States, where they were very formidable, though they of course did not have the countenance of the Government.

"I do not see that the other signatories would in the present circumstances be obligated to declare war on Germany. They would be obligated to come to our assistance with arms only when our political independence or territorial integrity were evidently and immediately threatened.

"These questions do not seem to me to constitute difficulties of practical importance. If we can meet Brazil's wishes sufficiently to get her adherence to the pact, I shall feel warranted in pressing on. It seems to me that this is the very time when such a league would make the deepest impression and have the greatest moral effect on both sides of the water."

To Secretary Lansing, a letter written on the President's own typewriter:

MY DEAR MR. SECRETARY,

I have been thinking a great deal about the personnel of the Russian Commission. I hope that in your conference with him to-day you will find Mr. Root a real friend of the revolution. If you do, the Commission that has framed itself in my mind would be as follows:

Elihu Root, New York,
John R. Mott, New York,
Charles R. Crane,
Cyrus H. McCormick, Chicago,
Eugene Meyer, jr., New York,
S. R. Bertron, New York,
John F. Stevens, New York,

and a representative of Labour whom I would suggest that we choose in this way: seek the advice of Mr. Gompers as to whom we could send whom the Socialists over there would not regard as an active opponent of Socialism. Gompers himself and the leaders immediately associated with him are known to be pronounced opponents of Socialism and would hardly be influential in the present ruling circles of labour at Petrograd. And yet we shall have to be careful, if we are to send a real representative of American Labour, not to send a Socialist.

Faithfully Yours,

W. W.

If you see no objections to this list, from an international or from a Russian point of view, I will be glad to write to these gentlemen and ask them to serve.

W. W.

To Samuel Gompers:

"I am ashamed to say that the truth is that amidst the pressure of other things I have not been able to give the attention it deserves to the question of voluntary supplemental aid to the dependents of men in the military and naval forces, but my general idea is that it would be wise to concentrate everything of this sort in a very few channels and my suggestion would be that you confer with Miss Boardman as to the practicability of affiliating the efforts you are generously thinking of making in this matter with the work of the Red Cross. I am sure she would be able to make some very valuable and practical suggestions."

To J. Milton Waldron, a colored minister of Washington, who had written that while the colored people were loyal citizens, few of them were enthusiastic in their support of the President and his administration. A "few words of reassurance"—that the country needed the loyal support of all, that there would be no discrimination—he felt would be helpful:

"Thank you sincerely for writing me. Your letter was the first notice I had that many of the members of the colored race were not enthusiastic in their support of the Government in this crisis. I am sure their conduct throughout this great emergency will show that there is little if any basis for a statement of this sweeping character. . . ."

To Representative Guy T. Helvering, who had asked the President to express his views on the subject of a selective draft, since that term was not generally understood by the people:

"I welcome the inquiry of your letter . . . because I have realized the truth of what you say from my own observation . . .

"The process of the draft is, I think, very clearly set forth in the bill drafted by the War Department and which I so earnestly hope the Congress will adopt, but it is worth while to state the idea which underlies the bill a little more fully.

"I took occasion the other day in an address to the people of the country[1] to point out the many forms of patriotic service that were open to them and to emphasize the fact that the military part of the service was by no means the only part, and perhaps, all things considered, not the most vital part. Our object is a mobilization of all the productive and active forces of the nation and their development to the highest point of coöperation and efficiency, and the idea of the selective draft is that those should be chosen for service in the Army who can be most readily spared from the prosecution of the other activities which the country must engage in and to which it must devote a great deal of its best energy and capacity.

"The volunteer system does not do this. When men choose themselves, they sometimes choose without due regard to their other responsibilities. Men may come from the farms or from the mines or from the factories or centers of business who ought not to come but ought to stand back of the armies in the field and see that they get everything that they need and that the people of the country are sustained in the meantime.

"The principle of the selective draft, in short, has at its heart this idea, that there is a universal obligation to

---

[1] April 16th. See this volume, p. 22.

serve and that a public authority should choose those upon whom the obligation of military service shall rest, and also in a sense choose those who shall do the rest of the nation's work. The bill if adopted will do more, I believe, than any other single instrumentality to create the impression of universal service in the Army and out of it, and if properly administered will be a great source of stimulation.

"Those who feel that we are turning away altogether from the voluntary principle seem to forget that some 600,000 men will be needed to fill the ranks of the Regular Army and the National Guard and that a very great field of individual enthusiasm lies there wide open."

To Representative John H. Small:
"I have your letter . . . and have read it with not a little sympathy. I am sure that whatever we do with regard to the refugee German ships, and under whatever form of law we do it, we should be careful that the real owners suffer no injuries. I have been in consultation with the Attorney General as to the form and have not received his final advice."

Friday, April 20th.

At 2:30 the regular cabinet meeting was held, the matter of regulating food exports to the northern neutrals of Europe in order to prevent food from reaching Germany being one of the subjects under discussion.[1] George Creel called at 4:30, and at 5 o'clock, Dr. John R. Mott. The President and Mrs. Wilson went for a short drive before dinner.

Great Britain celebrated widely the entrance of the United States into the war: an American flag flew over the Houses of Parliament, and a solemn service was held in St. Paul's Cathedral.

Turkey severed relations with the United States.

[1]On the 20th, probably after the cabinet discussion, Lansing telegraphed Minister Egan in Denmark, saying that the legislation under consideration in regard to exports was not intended to "produce burdensome restrictions upon or interruptions in our

To Secretary Lansing, who had sent the President a suggested list of contraband, saying in part: ". . . . We ought to issue a list of contraband. We are receiving inquiries in regard to the matter and are unable to answer. . . .":

"I agree with you that this form is the best in which to announce our list of contraband and that we should make an immediate announcement;[1] but I am not clear as to the meaning of all of the enclosed statement. . . ."[2]

Saturday, April 21st.

Shortly before luncheon the President walked over to the War Department, returning in half an hour. The latter part of the day afforded real relaxation—he took a long drive with Mrs. Wilson in the afternoon, and went to Keith's with Miss Bones in the evening.

The New York *Times* reported that the British Mission had arrived on American soil "at a place . . . which cannot be named"—one of the first noticeable evidences of self-imposed censorship.

A committee headed by Cleveland H. Dodge was named to take charge of the Red Cross campaign.

Herbert Hoover sent from London a report on the alarming shipping conditions: ". . . it is urgently necessary to create at once a committee that will undertake all chartering both for neutral and Allied tonnage for account commercial and governmental purposes, forbidding absolutely any private chartering except through such committee. . . ."[3]

Sunday, April 22nd.

President and Mrs. Wilson went to the Central Presbyterian Church in the morning;[4] and in the afternoon they took a long drive.

---

commerce with neutral countries," and instructing him to "take occasion to allay public alarm relative to its injurious effects on Danish commerce." *Foreign Relations*, Supp. 2, Vol. II, pp. 806–807.

[1]Such an announcement was made on June 30, 1917, in the Instructions for the Navy. See this volume, p. 138.

[2]For Lansing's letter and for the President's letter entire, see Savage, *Policy of the United States Toward Maritime Commerce in War*, Vol. II, pp. 597–598.

[3]*Foreign Relations*, 1917, Supp. 2, Vol. I, pp. 594–595.

[4]Mrs. Wilson was a member of St. Margaret's Episcopal Church, the President a

ARTHUR J. BALFOUR

EDWARD M. HOUSE

The members of the British Mission, headed by A. J. Balfour, arrived in Washington and were met at the train by Secretary Lansing. Thousands lined the streets along which they were driven.[1]

Monday, April 23rd.

At 9:30 the President received Senator Atlee Pomerene of Ohio; at 10 o'clock, Secretary Daniels and the Board of Visitors to the Naval Academy; and at 11, Mr. Balfour, head of the British Mission, accompanied by Secretary Lansing. The head usher's diary records: "8 aides present; received in blue room where private conference was held lasting three quarters of an hour." During the afternoon the President received: the minister from Belgium, M. de Cartier de Marchienne, who presented his credentials; Robert McCormick of the Chicago *Tribune*; Senator Smith of South Carolina. In the late afternoon the President and Mrs. Wilson managed to get away for a short drive together; and that evening a dinner was given at the White House in honor of the British Mission. "8.00 Dinner, covers for 52; guests received in East Room . . . . coffee and cigars at table; no music at dinner. Guests left 11:10."

A Shipping Committee of the Council of National Defense was named, William Denman, chairman of the Shipping Board, as its head.

It was announced from The Hague that German military authorities were placing munition factories under martial law to prevent strikes and counteract Socialistic propaganda.

Presbyterian. Their custom was, for a number of years, to go together on one Sunday to the Episcopal Church; on the next Sunday, to the Central Presbyterian Church.

[1] For further details of their reception, see: New York *Times*, April 23, 1917; *War Memoirs of Robert Lansing*, p. 273. Colonel House had seen Balfour in New York on the morning of the 22nd, afterwards writing to the President: ". . . . I told Balfour that unless you advised to the contrary I thought it would be well to minimize the importance of his visit here to the extent of a denial that it was for the purpose of forming some sort of agreement with the Allies. [Balfour made a statement to this effect on the 25th.] I find there is a feeling that this country is about to commit itself to a secret alliance with them.

"Such men as Lippmann and Croly [Walter Lippmann and Herbert Croly, both of the *New Republic*] have been to see me, and I could not convince them that the object of the visit of the British and French was not for this purpose."

The Colonel also added: "I hope you will agree with me that the best policy now is to avoid a discussion of peace settlements. Balfour concurs in this. If the Allies begin to discuss terms among themselves, they will soon hate one another worse than they do Germany . . ."

Tuesday, April 24th.

At noon William Denman called to see the President. Colonel Edward T. Brown, an old friend who was frequently a visitor at the White House, made one of the family at luncheon. At 2:30 in the afternoon the regular cabinet meeting was held, methods for increasing the supply of food and for transporting produce to Europe being among the subjects discussed. Immediately afterward the President went to the War Department for a few minutes. He returned in time to receive Assistant Secretary Phillips of the State Department; while in another part of the White House Mr. Balfour was calling upon Mrs. Wilson. In the late afternoon the President and Mrs. Wilson managed a short drive together; and about 10:30 that night the President spent fifteen minutes at the Pan-American Building, where a reception was being held in honor of the British Mission.

The President signed the bond bill, providing for a total issue of $7,000,000,000 of Treasury obligations.

A flotilla of American destroyers sailed for Queenstown, under sealed orders. Admiral Sims had telegraphed on the same day: "Situation continues critical. Nine vessels sunk yesterday. Recommend that all destroyers now available be sent earliest possible date . . ."[1]

Desperate fighting was reported in the Arras sector. ". . . attack and counter-attack go on all day . . ."

To his secretary, Tumulty, who called attention to a resolution adopted by the Just Government League of Maryland asking the President to send a message to the governor and General Assembly of the state, endorsing a bill to confer suffrage upon the women of Maryland:

"The real answer to this letter I think it would perhaps be better for you to write than me. It is that I believe that such action as they suggest would do the cause more harm than good. As a one-time member of the Jersey Legislature, I think you can yourself imagine how you would feel about a letter from the President of the United States

[1]Daniels, *The Navy and the Nation,* p. xi; *Naval Investigation Hearings,* 1920, Vol. I, p. 40.

urging action by the State Legislature in the way of domestic policy of this sort. I am sure you will know how to intimate this difficulty to these ladies."

Wednesday, April 25th.

After a round of golf with Mrs. Wilson, the President returned to the White House to meet Dr. John R. Mott at 11:30. Dudley Field Malone, Collector of the Port of New York and a friend of some years' standing, was one of the luncheon guests. After a conference in the early afternoon—with William Denman and B. M. Baruch, a member of the Advisory Committee of the Council of National Defense—Mr. and Mrs. Wilson and Dr. Grayson went for a horseback ride.

The French Mission arrived in Washington, the enthusiastic reception given them by the waiting crowds centering about the figure of General Joffre.[1]

The United States government made a loan of $200,000,000 to the British government.

The American Newspaper Publishers Association, in annual convention, passed a resolution urging the elimination of the press censorship provision from the pending Espionage bill; and a resolution in support of the President.[2]

German U-boat activity was reported by the British to have been, in the last week, the greatest since the beginning of the submarine campaign. Lord Devonport, British food controller, admitted that the situation was serious.

---

[1] Newton D. Baker, discussing the visits of the British and French Missions some years later said: ". . . . The military and naval aides and members . . . were sent respectively to the War and Navy Departments. I received the military men with the Chief of Staff and after the formal reception was over, the Chief of Staff presented all the military members to members of our General Staff. They were then paired off with members of our General Staff having the same functions. . . . I had personal conferences with Marshal Joffre and General Bridges and reports were made to me by the General Staff covering the conferences and the results.

"In a general way, I communicated these conference proceedings to the President verbally, but in one or two instances, I sent him written reports. Daniels did the same thing with the British and French navy men and his own bureau of operations. I think their finance people conducted similar conferences in the Treasury Department. . . ." Baker to the author.

The activities and discussions of the various commissions are not included here, except in cases where the President touched them directly.

[2] New York *Times*, April 26, 1917; M. E. Stone, *Fifty Years a Journalist*, p. 325.

To Arthur Brisbane:

"I sincerely appreciate the frankness of your interesting letter . . . with reference to the so-called Espionage Bill now awaiting action of the Congress.

"I approve of this legislation but I need not assure you and those interested in it that, whatever action the Congress may decide upon, so far as I am personally concerned, I shall not expect or permit any part of this law to apply to me or any of my official acts, or in any way to be used as a shield against criticism.

"I can imagine no greater disservice to the country than to establish a system of censorship that would deny to the people of a free republic like our own their indisputable right to criticise their own public officials. While exercising the great powers of the office I hold, I would regret in a crisis like the one through which we are now passing to lose the benefit of patriotic and intelligent criticism.

"In these trying times one can feel certain only of his motives, which he must strive to purge of selfishness of every kind, and await with patience for the judgment of a calmer day to vindicate the wisdom of the course he has tried conscientiously to follow.

"Thank you for having written me."

To George S. Johns, editor of the St. Louis *Post-Dispatch:*

"Thank you for your letter . . . It certainly warmed my heart, my dear fellow. The approval of old friends is mighty dear to me just now.

"From present indications, I think we will win with the fight in the House, and there is no doubt we shall win it in the Senate for the selective draft. Your suggestion about a Congressional commission to go abroad and study the matter is a very interesting one and in ordinary circumstances I should not hesitate to suggest it to the leaders in Congress, but in the actual circumstances it is so imperative that we should get to work at once to raise and drill an army that I am afraid there isn't time for it. We must do the most practicable thing and do it quickly . . ."

Thursday, April 26th.

At 9:30 Elihu Root called upon the President presumably to discuss his appointment to the Russian Commission. At 11 o'clock the members of the French Mission arrived and were presented by Secretary Lansing. The reception took place in the Blue Room, eight aides being present at the ceremony.

The President told Colonel House, who had come to Washington at the President's request, that his conversation with Mr. Balfour had not been "satisfactory," and asked: "How would it be to invite him to a family dinner, you being present, and go into a conference afterwards?" House again argued against discussing peace terms with the Allies, but the President "thought it would be a pity to have Balfour go home without a discussion of the subject." House then advanced the theory that "there was no harm in discussing it between themselves if it was distinctly understood and could be said, that there was no official discussion of the subject, and if neither Government would discuss peace terms with any of the other Allies." It was agreed that this should be done. House was commissioned to invite Mr. Balfour to dinner, "thus preserving the desired atmosphere" of informality; later it was decided that House should first discuss with Balfour the "general problem of war aims and ask him about the secret treaties."[1] In the late afternoon the President and Mrs. Wilson and Dr. Grayson went for a horseback ride. At a quarter of eight Secretary Baker called; at 8 o'clock a dinner was given at the White House in honor of the members of the French Mission—"covers for 62." General Joffre sat next to Mrs. Wilson, and when the Virginia ham was served he was much taken with it, saying to his hostess that he wished Madame Joffre could have a piece. Mrs. Wilson

---

[1] *Intimate Papers*, Vol. III, pp. 39–41. Balfour, in a handwritten note of the 26th, accepting the President's invitation, said in part: ". . . . Nothing will give me greater pleasure than enjoying your hospitality under the proposed condition; and in addition to the pleasure, I cannot doubt that much advantage will be gained from conversation carried on with Colonel House and yourself in informal fashion." From original copy in Woodrow Wilson's *Scrapbook*, Vol. I, p. 23, prepared by John Randolph Bolling.

immediately promised to send a Virginia ham to Madame Joffre as a souvenir! This she did, to the delight of all concerned.

L. S. Rowe, for the American commissioners, transmitted to the President the report of the American-Mexican Joint Commission; and on the same day Carranza's election to the presidency was declared official in Mexico.[1]

The General Railroad Board of the Council of National Defense gave orders directing the country's railroads to give coal and iron ore preference over all other traffic.

Friday, April 27th.

At the regular Friday cabinet meeting there was discussion of the information presented by the French and British Missions in regard to the need for food, railway rolling stock, oil, steel, coal and money; and above all, ships. While the cabinet was in session Mrs. Wilson and Dr. Grayson had started on a horseback ride; as soon as the President was free, he joined them.

Guatemala severed relations with Germany.

To Professor Walter Williams, who had invited the President to attend a "Made-in-Japan" banquet at the University of Missouri:

". . . . Just as the ancient Greeks held it to be a pledge of indissoluble friendship to eat salt together, so it would seem that to partake in the United States of a banquet made in Japan, which symbolically at least, would bring Americans and Japanese together around a common board, ought to add strength to the tie of friendship between the two nations which has become historic.

"In this critical hour when the United States takes its place alongside of Japan and her allies in the battle for righteousness and civilization, increased significance is given to such a covenant . . .

"It is often nothing more than lack of acquaintance that leads to international misunderstanding. . . ."

---

[1] *Foreign Relations,* 1917, pp. 916–938.

To Cyrus H. McCormick:

"You may have seen in the papers that we are thinking of sending a commission to Russia. I am very anxious that the commission should be really representative of what we are and of what we are thinking and I am writing to ask if it will not be possible for you to be a member of the commission. I hope most sincerely that it will be, for I believe that your cooperation will be of the highest value.

"The plan would be for the commission to start as soon as its members could get ready for the journey and to take a government vessel at San Francisco and proceed directly to Vladivostok.

"This route has been adopted not merely because it is the safer route, but also because it is thought that the impression made in Russia would be all the deeper if the commission crossed Siberia where the most dramatic effects of the recent revolution have been witnessed.

"The object of the commission is, primarily, to show our interest and sympathy at this critical juncture in Russian affairs and, secondly, to associate ourselves in counsel and in all friendly service with the present Government of Russia. It is the opinion of those best acquainted with Russia that the time is most opportune for a visit of this sort from commissioners of the United States and that the effect of it will be in every way helpful and stimulating."[1]

Saturday, April 28th.

The President spent most of the morning in his study. Secretary McAdoo came in at 11:30 to discuss the conditions under which foreign loans should be made. At 12:40 ex-President Taft called, for a conference on Red Cross affairs. After a horseback ride in the afternoon, the President presided over a family dinner, John Randolph Bolling and Rolfe E. Bolling being present, as well as Colonel House, who was a

[1]Similar letters were sent to: Eugene Meyer, Jr., S. R. Bertron, James Duncan, William English Walling. Invitations to Elihu Root, who was to head the commission, and to John R. Mott, were probably delivered orally.

guest at the White House. In the evening the President, Miss
Bones and Colonel House went to the National Theater.

> Colonel House and Mr. Balfour conferred for an hour and a
> half, at the President's request, on the subject of peace
> terms.[1]
>
> Ambassador Page telegraphed to Secretary Lansing from
> London that there was "reason for the greatest alarm
> concerning the issue of the war caused by the increasing
> success of the German submarines," and recommended
> "the immediate sending of every destroyer and all other
> craft that can be of anti-submarine use."[2]
>
> Censorship was established over submarine cables, telegraph
> and telephone lines, by executive order.[3]
>
> Secretary Lansing issued a statement announcing that all the
> Latin-American republics, with the exception of Mexico,
> Chile and Argentina, had now supported the stand of the
> United States.

To Miss Lillian D. Wald, who sent the President a petition urging him to make a statement reminding the country "of the
peculiar obligation devolving upon all Americans in this war to
uphold in every way our constitutional rights and liberties.":

"The letter signed by yourself and others . . . has, of
course, chimed in with my own feelings and sentiments.

---

[1]They discussed the secret treaties to some extent, and House wrote out a brief and
unsatisfactory memorandum of their conversation. See *Intimate Papers*, Vol. III,
pp. 42–46. Balfour produced a map, upon which were written (according to House's
later statement) the lines of the secret treaties. The map has disappeared entirely;
Colonel House wrote to the author, on January 13, 1922: ". . . he [Balfour] explained
the secret treaties the Allies had made during the war. In looking over some maps
which he had brought with him he indicated the territory involved in these treaties.
I was not particularly interested for the reason that it seemed to me much more important to bend all energies to the winning of the war, and I finally told Mr. Balfour
that they were dividing the bearskin before the bear had been killed.

"He did not have copies of the secret treaties with him, but I suggested it would
be well to have them sent for the information of the President and the State Department. Whether this was done I do not know, but Mr. Balfour was entirely frank in
discussing the treaties and showed no inclination whatever to conceal any of the
facts. . . ."

This account should be read in connection with Balfour's letter to the President of
May 18th, this volume, pp. 74–75.

[2]*Foreign Relations*, 1917, Supp. 2, Vol. I, pp. 46–47; see also *The Life and Letters of
Walter H. Page*, Vol. II, pp. 277–278; Sims, *The Victory at Sea*, pp. 48–49.

[3]*Foreign Relations*, 1917, Supp. 2, Vol. II, pp. 1233–1234.

I do not know what steps it will be practicable to take in the immediate future to safeguard the things which I agree with you in thinking ought in any circumstances to be safeguarded, but you may be sure I will have the matter in mind and will act, I hope, at the right time in the spirit of your suggestion."

To William Denman, chairman of the Shipping Board:

"Since we are all working together for a common end, may I not urge that as fast as the German ships can be put in repair, crews be obtained for them and the necessary equipment, and they be put at once into operation in the trans-Atlantic transportation? I have no doubt at all that Congress will give me the necessary authority in this matter and that they will understand and approve my acting in the meantime if their action should be in any way delayed.

"May I not suggest also that, besides sending the COLUMBIA to Honolulu to bring back the German ships lying there, the Shipping Board if practicable send six sea-going tugs also to Honolulu to assist so that we may at the very earliest possible date get the ships there also into operation?

"It seems to me highly important, also, that the exact condition of the German ships lying in the harbors of the Philippines should be ascertained as soon as possible and whether it would be practicable to bring them to the United States in the tow of tugs. It has occurred to me that it might perhaps be feasible to bring them home with a certain amount of freight aboard and so contribute to defray the expenses of the operation.

"I think it advisable that the Board should apply as promptly as possible and with as exact specifications as possible to the Navy Department with a view to securing the proper and necessary armaments for the ships that are to take part in the trans-Atlantic traffic.

"If you will be kind enough to communicate with the Secretary of the Treasury as the work of repair on the vessels is completed, he will issue the necessary orders for their delivery into the hands of the representatives of the Board."

To Rabbi Stephen S. Wise, who urged the President not to appoint Elihu Root to the Russian Commission. ". . . why should a man be singled out for this great opportunity of service to a fellow-democracy in the making who is not of your mind, who is not a sharer of your own spirit touching the fundamental issues of democracy? . . . .":

"Before your letter about Mr. Root came, I had already asked him to serve as the head of the commission we are about to send to Russia. Before doing so I convinced myself that he was genuinely and heartily in sympathy with the revolution in Russia, and his experience is such, his tact so great, and his appreciation of the object of the commission so clear that I cannot but feel that he will prove to have been an admirable choice.

"I, of course, appreciate the considerations which you urge and indeed had them in mind before making the choice, but I believe, all things weighed together, my choice has been the wise one. It distresses me that your judgment should be different."

Sunday, April 29th.

The President and Mrs. Wilson went to St. Margaret's Episcopal Church in the morning and returned to the White House for a quiet luncheon together. In the afternoon they took a long drive. Colonel House joined them at dinner, writing in his diary afterward: ". . . . After dinner we went to the upstairs sitting room and talked upon general subjects for awhile. The President read several chapters from Oliver's 'Ordeal by Battle.' . . . .

"The President declared his intention of writing some things which were on his mind, after he retired from office . . . . He said he had no notion of writing about his administration, but expressed a desire to write one book which he has long had in mind and which he thought might have an influence for good.[1]

"He said, 'I write with difficulty and it takes everything out of me.' . . . I asked how long it took him to write his April 2nd Address to Congress. He said ten hours . . ."[2]

Monday, April 30th.

At 9:40 in the morning Secretary Baker called, probably in regard to the draft bill then pending. At 10 o'clock M. Jusserand, the French ambassador, arrived with M. Viviani, head of the French Mission. It is probable that at this time the President broached to Viviani the subject of bases of peace, and found himself sharply brought up by Viviani's statement of the French point of view.[3] At 12:30 Secretary Daniels called, remaining for luncheon at the White House. Afternoon appointments were few: a committee from the G.A.R., to extend an invitation; Chairman Harris of the Federal Trade Commission; Oliver P. Newman, one of the commissioners of the District of Columbia. Mr. Balfour was a guest at an informal dinner in the evening, the only others at the table being Mrs. Wilson, Miss Bones and Colonel House. ". . . . The President did most of the talking. . . . The conversation was along general lines, mostly educational, historical and architectural. The President told several stories of Lincoln, and Balfour listened with interest. . . .

"We took our coffee in the oval sitting room and when it was finished we went to the President's study and began a conference, the importance of which cannot be over-estimated. The President continued to do most of the talking. It was evident to me that he was keyed up for this conference, as he had been resting most of the afternoon . . .

"The ground we covered was exactly the same as Balfour and I had covered in our conference Saturday. . . .

---

[1] "P.o.P."? See *Woodrow Wilson, Life and Letters*, Vol. II, *Princeton*, pp. 119–120.

[2] *Intimate Papers*, Vol. III, pp. 46–47.

[3] Writing to Colonel House on July 21st, the President said in part:

". . . . England and France *have not the same views with regard to peace that we have* by any means. When the war is over we can force them to our way of thinking, because by that time they will, among other things, be financially in our hands; but we cannot force them now, and any attempt to speak for them or to speak our common mind would bring on disagreements which would inevitably come to the surface in public . . . I saw this all too plainly in a conversation with Viviani. . . ."

"The discussion ran from shortly before eight o'clock until half past ten, when the President was due at a reception given by the Secretary of State to the members of Congress to meet the British and French Missions.

"I asked Balfour again about the Allies' treaties with each other and the desirability of his giving copies to the President. He again agreed to do so. . . .

"Before I left, the President had returned and we had a few minutes further conversation. He was delighted at Balfour's comments, and seemed happy over the result of the evening's work."[1]

Secretary Baker reported to the President "the first instance of destruction in any of our Government arsenals which is obviously malicious"—an accident to an engine at the Springfield Arsenal, due to emery in the bearings.

Admiral Jellico informed Rear-Admiral Sims that the convoy system was to be tried out.[2]

A military commission arrived from Cuba to discuss coördination of Cuban forces and resources with those of the United States.

Tuesday, May 1st.

After a morning horseback ride with Mrs. Wilson and Dr. Grayson, the President spent several hours in his study. At

---

[1]*Intimate Papers*, Vol. III, pp. 47–49. Balfour himself, writing of this conference in his little book called *Retrospect*, says: ". . . . I think the question of the secret treaties was raised by the President after we had left the dinner-table. There were no secrets between us then or afterwards, on any of the many subjects that came up for discussion. . . ." (P. 243.) Colonel House returned to Washington on the night of April 30th. Dr. Seymour writes: ". . . at Wilson's suggestion arrangements were made for him to continue conversations with members of the Allied Missions. What the President chiefly desired was an understanding regarding the tone of public statements that might be issued with the purpose of affecting opinion in Germany. It was also important to discuss the general sense of any replies that might be made to future peace proposals. He did not intend to bind himself to approve Allied policies, but he did wish to know what was in the minds of the British and French. . . .

"On all these matters agreement between the President and House was so complete that he knew that his own point of view would be clearly explained by Colonel House to Mr. Balfour, and the conference would have the advantage of being entirely unofficial." *Ibid.*, pp. 54–55. For comment upon Wilson's "strange and unclear relationship" with House, see *Woodrow Wilson, Life and Letters*, Vol. V, *Neutrality*, p. 50 and Vol. VI, *Facing War*, p. 129.

[2]The first convoy arrived in good condition, May 20th. Sims, *The Victory at Sea*, p. 114. According to Josephus Daniels, the President said to him "early in the war": "Daniels, why don't the British convoy their merchant ships and thus protect them from submarines?" Daniels, *Our Navy at War*, p. 144.

2 o'clock the Swiss minister called; half an hour later the cabinet assembled. Mrs. Wilson received the members of the French Commission in the late afternoon. The remainder of the day was spent quietly, with no engagements except a call from William Denman of the Shipping Board about eight o'clock in the evening.

> Secretary Lansing telegraphed Ambassador Francis, announcing a commission to Russia, under the leadership of Elihu Root, "a most distinguished statesman, who is devoted to the cause of political liberty and to the sovereign rights of the people." "It is the primary purpose of this commission to convey to the Russian Government the friendship and good will of this nation and to express the confident hope that the Russian people, having developed a political system founded on the principle of democracy, will join with the free people of America in resisting with firmness and fortitude the ambitious designs of the German Government . . . The commission will further be charged with the duty of finding the most efficient means of cooperating with the Russian Government in the prosecution of the war . . ."[1]
>
> The French were reported to have taken over 21,000 prisoners since April 16th; but it was admitted in Paris that German attacks were succeeding along the Aisne, near Chemin-des-Dames.

To John Nevin Sayre, a brother of Francis B. Sayre, who had written the President urging exemption for individual conscientious objectors:

". . . I can assure you that the point you raise as to individual conscientious scruple has by no means been overlooked. I know it has been called to the attention of the two Houses more than once and it has seemed impossible to make the exceptions apply to individuals because it would open the door to so much that was unconscientious on the part of persons who wished to escape service. I think you can see how that would be. At any

---

[1] *Foreign Relations,* 1917, Supp. 2, Vol. I, p. 51.

rate, the committees felt the difficulty insuperable and thought the arrangement they did make the best feasible."

Wednesday, May 2nd.

At noon Cleveland H. Dodge and a committee called to discuss plans for the creation of a Red Cross War Council. M. Viviani, head of the French Commission, and M. Hovelaque, counselor, were luncheon guests. At 2 o'clock Secretary Baker presented representatives of the State Councils of National Defense, then in conference at Washington.[1] ". . . . My function," said the President to his callers, "has not of recent days been to give advice but to get things coordinated so that there will not be any, or at any rate too much, lost motion, and in order that things should not be done twice by different bodies or done in conflict. . . ."[2] Later in the afternoon the President received Marshal Joffre, and Colonel Cosby who acted as interpreter. ". . . . It is thought," said the New York *Times* report, "that both M. Viviani and Marshal Joffre expressed again France's desire that the American division be sent" to carry the American flag at the front.

A $2,000,000,000 Liberty Loan was announced by Secretary McAdoo.

Thursday, May 3rd.

The President's afternoon callers were: Senator E. S. Johnson of South Dakota, in regard to the construction of a nitrate plant; Senators Underwood and Bankhead of Alabama, and Governor Harding of the Federal Reserve Board, also of Alabama; Senator Martin of Virginia. In the late afternoon Lady Lester Kaye and Mrs. George Vanderbilt called upon the President and Mrs. Wilson.

Herbert Hoover landed in the United States.
The Russian chargé, Onou, transmitted to Secretary Lansing the Russian Provisional government's statement of April

---

[1]That morning Secretary Lane had startled the conference by telling in pessimistic terms of the U-boat dangers. New York *Times*, May 3, 1917. ". . . Secretary Lane," writes Grosvenor Clarkson, ". . . cut loose and told the actual truth about submarine losses at that time. . . . The next morning it was the story of the day in the newspapers . . ." Quoted in *The Life and Letters of Franklin K. Lane*, pp. 249–250.

[2]For entire address, see *Public Papers*, Vol. V, pp. 28–29.

9th,[1] accompanying it by order of the Minister of Foreign Affairs of the Provisional government, with certain "remarks":

". . . the Provisional Government's declarations cannot of course afford the slightest ground for the deduction that the collapse of the old edifice means a lesser share taken by Russia in the common struggle of all the Allies . . . . the Provisional Government . . . will continue the strict observance of the engagements assumed toward Russia's allies. . . ."[2]

"Another day of close, fierce, difficult fighting . . ." on the battle front at Arras.[3]

To Secretary Lansing, who had urged censorship of the mails. Burleson had written that censorship was unnecessary, since it would be a "duplication of work that is being better performed by our allies." Forwarding his statement to Lansing, the President wrote a covering letter on his own typewriter:

". . . . I have given the matter a great deal of thought and have discussed it with a number of persons who are familiar with the circumstances of our communications by post with the countries to the south of us, and I fully agree with the conclusions of the Postmaster General. At any rate for the present. Circumstances which we do not know may come to light and existing circumstances may change."[4]

To Secretary Baker, who had reported, on the 2nd, a long conference with General Bridges of the British Mission. They had decided upon: the extension of medical aid to the British forces on the French front by the dispatch of hospital units, doctors,

---

[1]See this volume, p. 10.

[2]The note was sent also to the Allied governments. *Foreign Relations,* 1918, *Russia,* Vol. I, pp. 38–40. These "remarks," so satisfying to the nations at war against Germany, caused angry reverberations in Russia. Lenin, who had returned to Russia secretly in April, seized the opportunity to make trouble. Crowds marched in the streets with banners calling for the resignation of the Ministers of Foreign Affairs and of War and Navy. "New Government passing through trying ordeal . . ." telegraphed Ambassador Francis on May 4th. *Ibid.,* p. 40.

[3]Philip Gibbs, in *Current History,* June, 1917, p. 409.

[4]Lansing replied on the 5th urging censorship to Latin-American countries at least, and saying that Balfour strongly agreed.

and nurses, "with the understanding that these units are to be subject to collection as a part of our own military forces as they may be needed"; similar arrangements with the British as to air squadrons; and with the French as to ambulance service. The question of aid from America in the operation of English and French railroads in France was taken up, but not settled. The President's reply was on his own typewriter:

"I have your letter of yesterday in which you give me . . . the topics of your discussion with General Bridges . . .

"As you say, we have already agreed with regard to all but one of them, namely, the advisability of active and immediate cooperation in the maintenance and operation of the railways of France which are being used for the support of the armies at the front. I approve of the plan proposed for such cooperation and hope that one of the first things done will be to carry it out."

To Secretary Baker, in reply to a second letter quoting General Bridges regarding Roosevelt's request for authority to raise a division. Bridges said "that this is too serious a kind of warfare for untrained men or amateurs of any sort, and that he had taken the liberty of telegraphing to the Chief of the British Staff and protesting against any favor being shown from them toward the organization of any form of volunteer group from America for such an expedition. He thought the Germans would ridicule a hastily-organized expedition of non-professionals and that both the British and French would be depressed by such an expedition as an evidence of our failing to appreciate the seriousness of the situation; but that if such an expedition were made up of regulars and led by one of our professional soldiers, it would command instant respect in spite of being small. . . ." The President's reply was written on his own typewriter:

". . . . I had a similar conversation with General Joffre. I entirely agree with the conclusions arrived at, and I allowed General Joffre to take it for granted that such a force would be sent just as soon as we could send it."

To Andrew D. White, who had urged "selective conscription"—taking for foreign service, for example, Theodore Roosevelt, and men "such as were the riflemen, sharpshooters and ranchmen with whom Andrew Jackson won the battle of New Orleans.":

". . . . I could not venture . . . to act upon any advice but that of the professional soldiers who have either witnessed or taken part in the struggle. It is their unanimous advice that any other course than that which we are pursuing in our preparations for securing an Army would be a fatal mistake, a mistake registered in dead men, in unnecessary and cruel loss of life. My recent conversations with the military men accompanying the two commissions from France and England have confirmed me in this conviction, and I must act upon it."

To John D. Sprunt, an old friend of the President's father, who had written from England on April 5th telling of the death of two of his sons at the front:

MY DEAR FRIEND:

It was a source of very great gratification to me to receive your letter. Tragical as the story is which it conveys, there is a touch of steadfastness and heroism about the whole thing which touches me very deeply. It shows in you in these latter days of supreme trial the same quality that I used to perceive in you when I was a youngster and shared my dear father's admiration for all the sterling traits which we perceived in you. My thoughts often go back to the days in Wilmington and no figure of those days is more distinct than your own.

We have ourselves now gone into this grim and terrible war and there will be many a home no doubt in this country to which the same sort of story will come that has pulled at my heartstrings as I have read your letter. God grant that the common experience may breed steadfast, common purposes!

My heart goes out to you.

Cordially and sincerely yours,
WOODROW WILSON

To Senator Paul O. Husting, who had urged the advantages of his compromise plan for combining the best features of the volunteer and conscription systems:

"I feel very derelict in not having replied sooner to your interesting and important letter . . . but I am sure you will understand and forgive when I say that I was so rushed from one thing to another that it was only when the debate on the Army Bill was nearing its conclusion I was able to turn to your letter and give it the attention which it deserved. If I had known its subject matter, I would, of course, have sacrificed something else and read it sooner.

"I am sure, my dear Senator, that the initial supposition upon which what you urge is based is a mistaken one. I think that later consideration of the matter and a fuller plan with regard to the methods to be adopted have convinced the War Department that it will not take anything like so long as they had at first supposed to effect the enrollment and the draft. As a matter of fact, it can probably be effected quite as fast as camps and materials can be supplied.

"It is important to remember that in addition to the force of 500,000 men which we have principally been discussing, it will be necessary to raise a force of over 600,000 men to bring the Regular Army and the National Guard up to the authorized war strength. These men must be taken care of as well as the 500,000 and I dare say (though in this matter I have not yet conferred with the Secretary of War) that it may not be possible prudently to call the additional 500,000 men into camp for training at once.

"My own feeling and position has been simply this: We are undertaking the grimmest business of war that the world has ever known, the Congress has authorized me to put the whole force and power of the United States into this war, and I would not dare in the circumstances to turn away from the unanimous advice of our own trained soldiers and of the soldiers who have been through the extraordinary experiences of the last three years in France and England. Their advice is unanimously in favor of the plan proposed to the Congress by the War Department and I feel that I have no choice in the matter but to follow experts in a war of experts.

"I share the sentiments expressed in your letter and the predilections, but stern experience is an inexorable tutor."

Friday, May 4th.

The President spent the morning in his study. In addition to the regular cabinet meeting in the afternoon, he had appointments with: James P. Munroe, who was presented by Secretary Redfield; Senators Phelan of California and Walsh of Montana.

> Subscriptions to the Liberty Loan poured into the Treasury Department during the day at the rate of nearly $20,000,000 an hour.
>
> The six American destroyers which had sailed on April 24th reached Queenstown; and commenced operations in the submarine area within a few days.[1]
>
> The New York *Times* was publishing almost daily editorials against the censorship provision in the Espionage bill. ".... Let the attempt to suppress freedom of speech, in whatever guise it appears, be defeated unanimously. While we are warring to make democracy safe in the world, let us keep it safe in the United States."[2]
>
> Herbert Hoover arrived in Washington for conferences with various cabinet members.[3]

---

[1]*Foreign Relations*, 1917, Supp. 2, Vol. I, p. 77; Sims, *The Victory at Sea*, pp. 50–52, 118.

[2]May 4, 1917. On this very day the House passed the Espionage bill with a somewhat modified censorship provision.

[3]Colonel House, who had seen Hoover the day he landed in New York, wrote to the President: ".... I trust Houston will give him full powers as to food control. He knows it better than anyone in the world and would inspire confidence both in Europe and here. Unless Houston does give him full control I am afraid he will be unwilling to undertake the job for he is the kind of man that has to have complete control in order to do the thing well."

To Mrs. George Bass, who wrote that she had been holding conferences with Miss Jane Addams, Miss Lillian D. Wald and others, and that they had agreed to waive their objection to conscription and "follow you wherever you had to lead them." But, added Mrs. Bass, they had asked her to obtain certain assurances:

". . . . I have not for a moment lost sight of the danger of the breaking down of the standards of labor, the risk of a relaxation of the enforcement of the Child Labor Law, or the preservation in general of the social structure during hostilities. On the contrary, I think that the Draft Act affords me an unusual power to see that the unfortunate things these ladies dread do not occur, because the idea of the draft is not only the drawing of men into the military service of the Government, but the virtual assigning of men to the necessary labor of the country. Its central idea was to disturb the industrial and social structure of the country just as little as possible. . . ."

Saturday, May 5th.

At noon the President and Mrs. Wilson went to the Capitol to hear Mr. Balfour address the House of Representatives— the President thereby breaking a long-established precedent. They slipped in with their party, unannounced, and were not noticed for some time by anyone but Ambassador Jusserand, who rose. Gradually others discovered the President, and the galleries joined in applause. When the British Mission arrived, they too were warmly greeted. After the address the President went downstairs and joined the line of congressmen as they filed past to shake hands with Mr. Balfour and others of the mission.

A commission on training camp activities was announced, Raymond B. Fosdick, chairman.

The British plan for a League to Enforce Peace, as drawn up by Lord Bryce's committee, was made public about this time.[1]

---

[1] For an outline of the plan, see New York *Times,* May 6, 1917.

To Braxton D. Gibson:

". . . . I do not know that I can give you the best advice about attending the meeting of the League to Enforce Peace, but I may say that I think that the activities of the League are based upon a very much too definite programme which I myself have been very careful not to subscribe to. The general idea of the League I have publicly endorsed in an address at one of the banquets given by the League, but further than that I cannot go and I think it would be very unwise to go at the present time. The agitation conducted by the League has not always been wise, but in view of my concurrence with the general idea they have advocated, I have never felt at liberty to criticise them."

Sunday, May 6th.

The President and Mrs. Wilson attended the Central Presbyterian Church in the morning, returning to the White House for a quiet luncheon, with no guests. In the early afternoon the President conferred with Justice Brandeis and probably with Senator Martin in regard to the amendment to the Espionage bill materially limiting the embargo powers conferred on the Executive. He persuaded Martin that the amendment was unwise.[1]

Monday, May 7th.

At 11:30 in the morning the President conferred with William Denman. Afternoon appointments: Dr. Ray L. Wilbur of Stanford University, who probably discussed the critical oil situation in California; S. R. Bertron, who was to be a member of the Commission to Russia; Commissioners Hall and Clark of the Interstate Commerce Commission; and the Secretary of Labor.

Herbert Hoover appeared before the House Committee on Agriculture and discussed (behind closed doors, at his own request) the necessity for the conservation and distribution of foodstuffs under government direction.

[1]The following day Martin moved a reconsideration of the amendment, and on the 8th a provision was adopted which gave the President "full and elastic powers of embargo."

An order from Secretary Lansing was distributed among State Department officials instructing them not to talk with newspaper men "even on insignificant matters of fact or detail."

200,000 men were ready to go to France with Roosevelt, announced New York *Times* headlines.

To Secretary Lansing, who wrote on May 5th that Balfour and Lord Percy had called attention "to the large amount of commercial information which the British Government had collected in regard to firms doing business in the neutral countries of Europe—information which the British Government was using in discriminating between persons in those countries to whom goods might safely be allowed to be shipped, and another class of persons who were merely channels of trade with Germany." In order to put this information at the service of the United States, Balfour suggested that someone be designated to represent the United States in the War Trade Intelligence Department in London. The President replied, using his own typewriter:

"The practicability and wisdom of carrying out this very useful suggestion depends, as in so many other cases, upon finding the right man,—a really capable man who will be equally able and well poised and sensible, not likely to swell with importance and instruct us every day by cable. Have you such a man in mind, or do you think you could find one?"

To Secretary Lansing, who, in forwarding a letter just received from Elihu Root, wrote: ". . . . I judge from his letter that he feels that the usefulness and importance of his commission will be weakened by having in Russia contemporaneously another commission [the railroad commission[1]] dealing with the technical side of a topic which he believes he is to discuss with the Russian Government. . . ." The President's reply was written on his own typewriter:

"I think that Mr. Root's mistake about the character and functions of the commission of railway experts is a

---

[1]Which left for Russia on May 9th. See this volume, p. 61.

very natural one, but that it will be removed when Mr. Bertron repeats to him a conversation he (Mr. B) and I had this afternoon.

"This is my understanding of the mission of the railway experts: It bears no resemblance to that of the Commission of which Mr. Root is to act as chairman. It is not going to ask What can the United States do for Russia? but only to say We have been sent here to put ourselves at your disposal to do anything we can to assist in the working out of your transportation problem. They are to report nothing back to us. They are delegated to do nothing but serve Russia on the ground, if she wishes to use them, as I understand she does.

"There would, therefore, be no propriety in making them subsidiary to the Commission or in giving them any connection with it of any kind.

"If this is not clear to all concerned, I will of course take any course that may seem wise to make it clear."

To Colonel House, who had reported a talk with General Goethals regarding the shipbuilding program. ". . . . He is very much disturbed over the delay in getting . . . started. . . .

"The tonnage required cannot be built wholly of timber because, in the first place, there is not enough seasoned timber in the country to anywhere near meet the requirements, and the wooden ships cannot be built as quickly as the steel nor are they as effective when built. . . ."

MY DEAR HOUSE,

My whole day, nearly, has been devoted to the shipping problem, or, rather, to the ship-building problem. Denman has stated it to me, together with the views of General Goethals, several times, in a series of conferences. It will not be possible to follow General Goethals' program in all its length but I have had Denman on "the Hill" to-day laying the whole situation before the men up there upon whom we shall have to depend and I am arranging for conferences in which I shall take part and use my influence in this all-important matter to the utmost. I think that General Goethals may rest assured that substantially the program he outlines in the memorandum just received in your letter of yesterday will be adopted by the Congress and carried out.

The Shipping Board have prepared a bill which is now ready for introduction and upon it, I think, we can build action which will enable us to do the utmost that our shipyards can do now and can be expanded to do and can be assisted by the structural steel men to accomplish with steel and workmen taken for the time being from bridge work and work on sky-scrapers, with a steady output of standardized freighters.

The English representatives have already agreed to let their contracts with the yards be taken over or thrust aside, and the way is clearing.

This is only a line to say that General Goethals may be sure that I am on the job and that the way will be cleared as fast as possible for what I realize to be immediately and imperatively necessary. I have recently bought some 80,000 tons of Austrian shipping and hope soon to buy as much more; and we are getting the German ships in repair as fast as the shops can repair them.

By the way, we are going to name the two German raiders which were interned here and which have naturally fallen into our possession The STEUBEN and the DeKALB. That seemed to me to have a poetic propriety about it!

Faithfully Yours,
Woodrow Wilson

All of us unite in the most affectionate messages.

W. W.

To Breckinridge Long, Third Assistant Secretary of State, who reported the desire of M. Bakhméteff, retiring ambassador from Russia, to call upon the President before leaving Washington:

"May I not say that I should like very much to be excused from the necessity of seeing Mr. Bakhmeteff? I would be very much obliged if you would advise me as to whether it is diplomatically necessary that I should in the circumstances.

"The circumstances are these, as you know: Mr. Bakhmeteff resigned his position as Ambassador from Russia, saying that he had no sympathy whatever with the things that have recently been happening in Russia, whereas I have the greatest sympathy with them. I do not understand that he has formal letters of recall to present and if he has not, I do not see any necessity for my receiving him. I would very much like your advice and the advice of the department."

Tuesday, May 8th.

The President worked in his study until 12:30, when he received John F. Stevens and members of the railroad commission to Russia. During the afternoon, in addition to the regular cabinet meeting, he received: Dr. Jones and Governor Lister of Washington state; Representative J. A. Elston of California; Senator P. G. Gerry of Rhode Island; Senator D. U. Fletcher of Florida; the British Labor Commissioners, accompanied by the Secretary of Labor and representatives of the American Federation of Labor. "Evening with family."

Secretary Lansing announced to the press that any subordinate giving out information conveying a criticism of the department's policies would be dismissed.[1]

Herbert Hoover appeared before the Senate Committee on Agriculture, urging a separate department of the government to deal with the food question.

Liberia severed diplomatic relations with Germany.

---

[1]The New York *Times* commented: "The attitude of the State Department and the Department of Justice is provoking more and more criticism in Congress and in the country." (May 9th.) Tumulty wrote, this same day, pointing out the danger inherent in the policy being adopted with regard to censorship: ". . . . I know how strongly you feel on the matter of a strict censorship but I would not be doing my full duty to you and the Administration if I did not say to you that there is gradually growing a feeling of bitter resentment against the whole business, which is daily spreading. . . ."

To Secretary Lansing, who had written to inquire what policy was to be followed regarding the treaty of 1799 with Prussia, which provided that "merchants of either country then residing in the other, shall be allowed to remain nine months to collect their debts and settle their affairs, and may depart freely, carrying off all their effects (*biens*), without molestation or hindrance." The treaty if kept, Lansing pointed out, would conflict with the treatment of enemy aliens under the President's proclamation of April 6th:

"I am sorry not to have sent you sooner an answer to the very important question stated in the enclosed letter. The fact of the matter is that it has given me not a little trouble to arrive at a right solution of the quandary, if, indeed, I have arrived at such a solution.

"It is clear to me, as it is to you, that we cannot arbitrarily ignore this treaty. It was made for war, not for peace,—for just such relations between ourselves and Germany as have now arisen; and I do not feel that Germany's playing fast and loose with the obligations of this treaty, as of all others, affords, *for us* who are proud to observe obligations and would like to set an example, a sufficient ground for repudiating our own promises under it.

"At the same time, it is clear to me that the treaty cannot have had in its contemplation any subjects of Germany living in this country except those whose conduct and purpose were peaceable and consistent (so far as they were concerned) with the peace and security of the United States. It cannot have been intended to extend privileges to those who might from any reasonable point of view be thought to be plotting or intending mischief against us.

"I should say, therefore, that it was our duty to allow all German citizens resident in this country the full nine months stipulated in which 'to collect their debts and settle their affairs' and to permit them to 'depart freely, carrying off all their effects without molestation or hindrance'; but that it was our privilege to discriminate amongst them just as we are discriminating amongst those alien enemies who remain in residence here, distinguishing and restraining those whom we have reason to believe to entertain purposes hostile or inimical to the United States. Such persons ought not to be permitted to leave our territory freely or to carry their effects into a neighbouring country where it is known that they will in all probability have a better opportunity to do us harm than they would have if they remained here. This line will be hard to draw, no doubt, but it will be as practicable to draw it amongst those leaving the country as amongst those who remain in it."[1]

To Mrs. Carrie Chapman Catt:

"I am sure you will believe that I have as much interest as even you can have not only in putting nothing in the way of the women of Russia, but also in aiding them in any way to the full realization of their rights under the new order of things there; but I have had some pretty intimate glimpses of the situation over there recently and the thing that stands out most clearly to my mind is that they would at the present juncture of affairs not only be very sensitive to any attempt at their political guidance on our part, but would resent it and react from it in a way that would be very detrimental to the interests of the country and to the relations of Russia and the United States.

"I am trying to put men on the commission whose popular sympathies and catholic view of human rights will be recognized (at any rate, in the case of most of them), but they are going, not to offer advice or to attempt guidance, but only to express the deep sympathy of the United States, its readiness to assist Russia in every way that can wisely be planned, and our desire to learn how

[1]*Foreign Relations*, 1918, Supp. 2, pp. 169–171, for both letters.

the cooperation between the two countries can be most intimate and effective in the present war."

To Representative E. S. Candler:

".... Some instinct tells me that I ought for the present absolutely to refrain from speech-making and, therefore, I feel not only that I must stick to my duties here and deny myself the pleasure of attending the unveiling of the Confederate monument in Shiloh National Park, but also that perhaps I had better not write anything, because if I undertook to write a letter which would be worth reading it would have to be more than a perfunctory compliment. I don't know whether I am right or wrong in following my instinct in this matter, and I need not tell you that it has nothing whatever to do with a thought of the issues between North and South,—there is no longer any trouble in the thought of the country there,—but only with the judgment that since all sorts of extravagant inferences are drawn from everything anyone in authority says, it is just as well not to give the newspapers an opportunity to exercise their ingenuity. . . ."

Wednesday, May 9th.

At 11:30 the President conferred with a group of senators and representatives whom he had summoned to discuss shipbuilding plans: Senators Lodge, Hitchcock, Underwood, Martin, James, Walsh, Jones, Knox, Smoot, Gallinger, Wolcott, King, Swanson and Warren; Representatives Padgett, Kahn, Speaker Clark, Flood, Gillett, Sherley, Green, Fitzgerald, Alexander, Lenroot. The New York *Times* account said, in part: "The President, who seemed bent on taking his hearers into his full confidence regarding his plan for an effective merchant marine, said that he wanted the appropriation provisions to be inserted in the Urgent Deficiency bill now pending in the Senate . . . and that he wanted it accompanied by powers for the Government to commandeer shipyards and construction agencies of all sorts, as may be done for naval work." Mrs. Charles R. Crane and Mrs. Richard Crane were guests at luncheon. At 2 o'clock Herbert Hoover called upon the President. On leaving the White House he was asked whether he would accept a place as food dictator if one were created. "I don't want to be food dictator for the American people," he replied. "The man who accepts such a position will die on the barbed wire of the first line entrenchments." Other afternoon conferences: Representative Sherley of Kentucky; Senator Swanson of Virginia; Senator Calder of New York. The President and Mrs. Wilson had tea in the Red Room late in the afternoon, with Mrs. Thomas L. Chadbourne and Mrs. McAdoo as guests.

A loan of $75,000,000 to the French and Belgian governments was announced by Hoover, to be used by the American-Belgian Relief Commission in purchasing food for Belgium and Northern France.

The United States railroad commission, John F. Stevens at its head, left for Petrograd.

Thursday, May 10th.

The President worked in his study until 12:45. There were a number of afternoon appointments: Representatives Lever of South Carolina and Haugen of Iowa and Secretary Houston, to discuss the administration Food bill, the President urging immediate passage; the Attorney General; Senators Nelson and Kellogg of Minnesota.

The President announced the creation of a Red Cross War Council.[1]

The *Official Bulletin*, published by the Committee on Public Information, made its first appearance.[2]

To Secretary Lansing, in regard to the Russian Commission:
"I think our list is now complete, namely:
"Mr. Elihu Root,
"Mr. Charles R. Crane,
"Dr. John R. Mott,

[1] For entire announcement, see *Official Bulletin*, May 11, 1917. For the President's letter of the 10th to Eliot Wadsworth, announcing the creation of such a council, and for his letter to H. P. Davison, asking him to accept the chairmanship, see *Public Papers*, Vol. V, pp. 30, 31.

[2] George Creel writes that he himself was not at first in favor of the publication, but that the President insisted upon it. Creel, *How We Advertised America*, p. 208.

"Mr. Cyrus H. McCormick,

"Mr. S. R. Bertron,

"Mr. James Duncan, as the representative of labor,

"Mr. Charles Edward Russell.

"I have only just learned of the willingness of Mr. Russell to serve and am sending him a note today to learn the earliest hour at which he would be ready to leave. I think it would be wise now to give out the names of the Commissioners and supply the Press with as full information as they desire about the several members. I am enclosing the account of Mr. Russell from Who's Who."[1]

To Secretary Baker, who wrote, on the 8th, that he was notifying Pershing to report in person to Washington. ". . . . When he arrives here, I shall have him go to France at once . . . the expeditionary force which in the meantime will be assembled, consisting of about 12,000 men . . . will be embarked even before General Pershing arrives in France . . .

"It has been determined that the force shall cooperate with the French land forces."[2] The President's reply was written on his own typewriter:

"I have already had the pleasure of speaking with you over the telephone concerning the enclosed, but I am sending this memorandum to express in a more permanent form my approval of the programme here outlined, so far as it refers to the immediate despatch of General Pershing and the despatch so soon as possible thereafter of the Division which he is to command in France."

[1]The list of members included a statesman, a Y.M.C.A. leader, a retired business man, a prominent banker, a representative of the American Federation of Labor, a Socialist. Major General Hugh L. Scott and Rear-Admiral James H. Glennon were also included, representing the army and navy. Stanley Washburn was secretary. The make-up of the group caused considerable difficulty. As has been shown (this volume, p. 42), the choice of Root was questioned. A Jewish member was decided upon, and Eugene Meyer consented to serve, but he was later tactfully asked to withdraw because of the extreme bitterness toward the Jews which still existed in Russia. Gompers himself was asked to serve as the labor member, but refused, suggesting that James Duncan, first vice-president of the American Federation of Labor, be chosen. *Seventy Years of Life and Labor*, Vol. II, p. 398.

[2]Palmer, *Newton D. Baker*, Vol. I, p. 167.

To William H. Taft:

"Since I had the pleasure of seeing you, I have had several talks with the other men most active in the Red Cross and with one voice and very earnestly they protest against your retiring from the chairmanship of the Executive Committee. My own preference and instinct, as you know, is to the same effect, and I am going to take the liberty of asking you to reconsider your request to me and accede to the desire which we all entertain, and entertain most earnestly, that you should retain that position. We all think that it would be a very serious detriment to the Red Cross if you should retire from that post of leadership."[1]

To Theodore H. Price of New York, business man and writer on economic subjects who had suggested an unofficial commission (men like Lord Bryce, Joseph H. Choate, Maximilian Harden and others) to meet in a neutral country and "paint a word picture" of a democratized world at peace and politically confederated for the maintenance of human rights:

"I . . . wish I could share your hope that the suggestion . . . would, if adopted, lead to an early contemplation of peace, but I must say that in contact with the grim realities of the situation from day to day it is a hope I cannot share.

"I am none the less obliged to you for your thoughtfulness in sending me the public-spirited dream you have had."

To Representative John N. Garner:

"Your letter of today has given me a good deal of distress, for two reasons:

"In the first place, because of the feeling you evidently have that the services, the most loyal and active and constant services, you have rendered the administration in Congress have not been appreciated at their true value,

---

[1] President Taft replied that he would "of course" yield to the President's suggestion.

or, rather, have not been in any public way recognized. I can assure you that that impression on your part is entirely unfounded. I have kept in close touch, as you know, with what was going on in Congress and I have valued your assistance all the more highly because you were giving it in circumstances of personal discouragement and without the slightest expectation of any other recognition than the enhanced reputation you were gaining, and worthily gaining, as a loyal servant of your state and of the country.

"In the second place, I must protest very earnestly against the construction you place upon the selection of the gentleman from Tennessee for the Boundary Commission. He has been urged upon the Secretary of State by many other persons than the Senator to whom you allude, and I think the Secretary of State would be as incapable as I am sure you know I would be of making any such appointment for purely political reasons.

"I must admit that I have not been able to pay as much personal attention to appointments of any kind during the last few months as I formerly endeavored to pay, for reasons which I am sure will be obvious to you, but I have known enough of this particular case to be able to exonerate the Secretary of State absolutely.

"I wish, my dear Mr. Garner, that you could know what is really in my mind and heart in all matters of this sort. I am sure that if you did, you would not feel that there has been any lack of appreciation or of genuine admiration for the course you have pursued."

Friday, May 11th.

Returning from his regular golf game with Dr. Grayson, the President spent two hours in his study before luncheon. At a quarter past two Senator Robinson and former Representative Cravens of Arkansas called; at 2:30 the cabinet met. The project for concentrating, in one commission, authority over the purchase and shipment to Europe of war supplies for the allied nations was discussed.

> Secretary Daniels telegraphed Admiral Sims: "Much opinion here is in favor of concerted efforts by the Allies to establish a complete barrier across the North Sea, Norway, and Scotland . . . Make full report."[1]

To Secretary Lansing, who had sent the President a copy of a letter from Balfour which reported the decision of the French Socialist minority to send a representative to the Stockholm conference. If the French government allowed this, Balfour thought, pressure would probably be exerted toward the same end by the British Socialist group. He understood that there was also "a question as regards delegates from the United States." The President's reply was written on his own typewriter:

". . . I do not like the movement among the Socialists to confer about international affairs. They are likely to make a deal of mischief, especially in connection with affairs in Russia. I think our own people would warmly resent any encouragement by our government of the American Socialists who may seek to take part, especially after their recent almost treasonable utterances in their convention (at St. Louis, was it not?). It is their own lookout what they do. We should neither give them leave nor seek to restrain them. My own view is, that they will make themselves either hated or ridiculous."

To Governor William D. Stephens of California, telegram:

"I hope that in view of certain international aspects which the case has assumed you will not deem me impertinent or beyond my rights if I very warmly and earnestly urge upon you the wisdom and desirability of commuting the sentence of Mooney or at least suspending its execution until the charges of perjury lodged against the witnesses in the case are judicially probed to the bottom. Such an action on your part would I can assure you have the

---

[1] *Naval Investigation Hearings,* 1920, Vol. I, p. 188.

widest and most beneficial results and greatly relieve some critical situations outside the United States."[1]

Saturday, May 12th.

The President spent a number of hours in his study before luncheon. At 3:20 he and Mrs. Wilson left for Continental Hall, where the President made an address at the dedication of the Red Cross building.[2] ". . . the heart of the country is in this war . . . We have gone in with no special grievance of our own, because we have always said that we were the friends and servants of mankind.

"We look for no profit. We look for no advantage. We will accept no advantage out of this war. We go because we believe that the very principles upon which the American Republic was founded are now at stake and must be vindicated. . . ."

After his address the President took a short drive with Mrs. Wilson, returning in time to confer with Secretary Baker before dinner. At nine o'clock in the evening he touched a button which opened the Actors' Fund Bazaar in New York.

Italian forces, under General Cadorna, began a furious 18-day drive against the Austrian troops, fighting among the mountains and in the desolate Carso plateau.

Sunday, May 13th.

The President and Mrs. Wilson went to the Central Presbyterian Church in the morning. Dr. E. P. Davis, an old friend from Philadelphia, Dr. and Mrs. Grayson, and Mrs. Wilson's brother, John Randolph Bolling, were luncheon guests; in the afternoon Mr. and Mrs. Wilson and Mr. Bolling took a long drive. Herbert Hoover called to see the President at 6:30.

Colonel House and Mr. Balfour conferred, at House's apartment in New York, on the possible inauguration of peace measures. ". . . . Germany at any time might make a tentative offer. . . ." Reporting the conference to the President, House said they had agreed on the wisdom of a small peace conference; of certain concessions to Turkey and Austria

---

[1]Governor Stephens replied the same day by wire that Mooney's sentence was "stayed indefinitely by appeal pending in state supreme court." The President wrote a note of thanks on the 14th. ". . . . It relieves a rather serious anxiety."

[2]*Public Papers*, Vol. V, pp. 32–35.

if they could be persuaded to break away from Germany
or force Germany to make peace; of not insisting upon
punishment for the makers of the war before even a
tentative discussion of the settlement.[1]

Monday, May 14th.

The President worked in his study until 12:30, when he received Ambassador Jusserand and M. Viviani, the interview
having been arranged at Jusserand's request. After luncheon he
conferred with: Representative Helvering of Kansas; J. A. H.
Hopkins and a committee containing representatives of "each
of the liberal Parties"—Progressive, Woman's, Independent
Republican, Independent Democratic, Labor, Socialist, Prohibition.[2] They urged the passage of the Susan B. Anthony
amendment as a part of the war program at the existing session
of Congress. The President told them he felt that the introduction of the question just at that time might complicate matters;
though he made them feel his conviction that the war had put
the woman suffrage question on a new basis.[3] Elihu Root and
other members of the Commission to Russia called sometime
during the day. In the evening the President and Miss Bones
went to Ringling's Circus.

> Terrific fighting was reported from the Chemin des Dames
> and the neighboring points of the Aisne heights—one of
> the "most awful parts of the battle line in France . . .
> where mutual bombardments never cease and infantry
> fighting goes on continuously."[4]

To Senator Charles A. Culberson, chairman of the Senate Judiciary Committee:[5]

"I am taking the liberty of sending to you with the
earnest hope that it may commend itself to your com-

---

[1] See *Intimate Papers,* Vol. III, pp. 55–57. A footnote states that the President
answered House's letter by telephone, and "approved its general tenor."

[2] The committee had been appointed in pursuance of a resolution adopted by the
National Progressive Convention at St. Louis in April.

[3] I. H. Irwin, *The Story of the Woman's Party,* p. 300.

[4] G. H. Perris, London *Daily Chronicle* correspondent with the French army, in
Current History, June, 1917, p. 415.

[5] Sent also to Senator F. G. Newlands, chairman of the Interstate Commerce Committee of the Senate; and to Representatives Webb and Adamson, chairmen of the
same committees of the House.

mittee and to the Senate a Joint Resolution authorizing me to direct that certain kinds of traffic or particular shipments shall from time to time have preference or priority in transportation by common carriers by railroad or water. The exercise of such authority has become imperatively necessary because there is at present no authority in existence by which such decisions can be made. The railroads of the country have in a very practical and patriotic way consented to the formation under the guidance of the Council of National Defense of an Executive Committee presided over by Mr. Daniel Willard, through which they undertake to serve the interests of the Government and of the country in the best and most effective way possible under our guidance. Of course, one department thinks the shipments in which it is most interested the most important and deserving of immediate transportation, while another department thinks it an imperative necessity that other shipments should take priority. What this resolution would provide, if adopted, would be some authority by which competitive questions of this sort could be determined. It would cause no friction, indeed, it would remove it, and it would relieve a very great embarrassment arising out of the existing conditions. . . .

"Inasmuch as I had some doubt as to the committee jurisdiction in this matter, I have taken the liberty of communicating to the same effect with Senator Newlands."

To Representative E. W. Pou, a letter written at the suggestion of Mrs. H. H. Gardener:

"My attention has been called to the question as to whether it was desirable to appoint a Committee on Woman Suffrage in the House of Representatives. Of course, strictly speaking, it is none of my business, and I have not the least desire to intervene in the matter, but I have a letter written in admirable spirit from Mrs.

Helen H. Gardener, in which she says that she has been told that you had said that you would report out a proposal for such a committee if I should approve. On the chance that I may be of some slight service in this matter, which seems to me of very considerable consequence, I am writing this line to say that I would heartily approve. I think it would be a very wise act of public policy, and also an act of fairness to the best women who are engaged in the cause of woman suffrage."

To Professor Henry B. Fine of Princeton, who wrote of a young American surgeon, M. C. Grow, just back from two years' service in the medical corps of the Russian army, who was convinced that Theodore Roosevelt should be added to the Commission to Russia, because he was "the best known and most admired American private citizen" in Russia:

"I wish I could see Doctor Grow, but it is really impossible. My days are so full now as to come near to driving me to distraction and I could not in any circumstances consider the suggestion of sending Mr. Roosevelt anywhere to represent the administration.

"I am none the less obliged to you for your letter and hope that you will not regard this as a discouragement for writing me anything it comes into your head to write."

Tuesday, May 15th.

The regular Tuesday cabinet meeting was omitted, the President receiving Samuel Gompers and the labor committee of the Council of National Defense Advisory Commission. The committee had recently been meeting with English and Canadian representatives of labor, and with a number of wealthy men of the United States (John D. Rockefeller, Jr., Daniel Guggenheim, Theodore Marburg and others) to discuss the coöperation of capital and labor. The President made a short address. ". . . . We are trying to fight in a cause which means the lifting of the standards of life, and we can fight in that cause best by voluntary co-operation. . . ."[1]

---

[1] For entire address, see *Public Papers*, Vol. V, pp. 36–37.

Also that afternoon the President conferred with: Senator Pomerene of Ohio; former Senator Kern of Indiana. At four o'clock he and Mrs. Wilson attended the wedding of Secretary McAdoos' daughter and M. de Mohrenschildt, at St. John's Church, and were present afterward at a reception at the McAdoos' home. In the evening the President conferred with Secretary Houston and the Senate and House Committees on Agriculture. He emphasized the imperative necessity for prompt action on food control legislation, discussing "the food situation in the United States, in the allied countries, and in neutral countries which the United States must at least help to feed," and stating emphatically "that it would be difficult to express in parliamentary language what should be done with anyone who would speculate in food products in a situation like the present."[1]

General Pétain was appointed Commander-in-Chief of the French armies operating on the French front.

Wednesday, May 16th.

The President spent a number of hours in his study before luncheon. In the afternoon he conferred with: Senator Newlands of Nevada and Representatives Adamson of Georgia and Esch of Wisconsin, in regard to the pending preferential shipment bill; George Creel; Secretaries Baker and Daniels. A short drive with Mrs. Wilson was followed by a quiet family dinner.

The Senate in closed session, led by Henry Cabot Lodge, criticized the administration for lack of an energetic war policy. "I am exceedingly glad that you fearlessly told the truth about the Administration . . ." wrote Theodore Roosevelt to Lodge the following day. "The one real arch offender is Wilson. If our people were really awake he would be impeached tomorrow . . ."[2]

Lord Robert Cecil, speaking as Acting Foreign Secretary (in the absence of Balfour), laid before the Parliament examples of the shocking treatment given by Germany and Turkey to the natives of their colonies; and said he would

[1]New York *Times*, May 16, 1917. The President wrote to Representative Lever on the 16th: ". . . . I felt that the conference of last evening did a great deal of good in clearing up the situation and I hope you felt the same way."

[2]*Selections from the Correspondence of Theodore Roosevelt and Henry Cabot Lodge*, Vol. II, p. 525.

"regard with horror" the idea of returning such colonies to Germany at the end of the war.[1]

To Secretary Daniels, a handwritten note:

". . . I hope Creel will remind the newspaper men of their agreement *not* to publish news of the movements of our naval vessels."

To J. K. M. Norton of Alexandria, Virginia:

". . . I have found by experience that the only place I can get things done is the White House. We are so safely (almost annoyingly) guarded here nowadays that we, as a matter of fact, have a great deal of seclusion and privacy, and the house is by no means as hot as some of its neighbors here, so that I feel that real effectiveness demands that I should stay where I am. . . ."

Thursday, May 17th.

After a round of golf with Mrs. Wilson, the President spent some time in his study before luncheon. During the afternoon he conferred with: Professor Taussig, chairman of the Tariff Commission, who discussed the proposed investigation, by the commission, of economic factors during and after the war; Senator Smith of South Carolina; Representative Riordan of New York and Judge Levy, the latter concerned with the serious situation of the Jews in Palestine; Secretary Wilson and the British labor commissioners; and John M. Parker, who called to urge the President to allow Roosevelt to raise a division with Leonard Wood as commanding general. In the course of a fifteen-minute interview Parker assured the President that "in all the civilized world there is no greater autocrat or more arbitrary ruler than Woodrow Wilson." ". . . . I have spent four days in Washington," he said, "associating with men of nearly every political faith, and deeply regret to state that you have alienated the friendship of those of your own party who would like to be of real service, and have practically brought to your side none of those who have opposed you. . . .

". . . I feel I have the right to criticize, because you are my hired man, just as you are the hired man of the people. . . ."

---

[1]*Current History,* July, 1917, pp. 46–48.

The President was angry, but kept himself in hand.

"It is extremely easy to criticize," he replied. "You make your first reference to General Wood. He has made a splendid officer of the United States army, and a fine record wherever he has been placed, but I call your attention to the fact that Earl Kitchener, regarded as the ablest and most brilliant of all the British generals, instead of being sent to the front, was kept in his own country where his services were invaluable in the direction of efficiency, preparedness, and thorough mobilization; much more important to England in that capacity than he possibly could have been in general command on the front line."

Parker, ignoring this comparison, argued that "surely in a great international crisis personal differences might be put aside." To this the President replied simply that he endorsed the attitude of the Secretary of War, and under no circumstances intended to permit Wood to go abroad in command of troops.

Parker then took up the question of Roosevelt. "I beg you, as head of the Democratic party, at this crisis not to play politics!"

"Sir," replied the President, "I am not playing politics. Nothing could be more advantageous to me than to follow the course you suggest. I have made up my mind in regard to these matters very thoroughly. General Wood is needed here. Colonel Roosevelt is an admirable man and a patriotic citizen, but he is not a military leader. . . . As for politics, it is not I but the Republicans who have been playing politics and consciously embarrassing the Administration. I do not propose to have politics in any manner, shape, or form influence me in my judgment."[1]

This astonishing interview took place at 3:45. At 4 o'clock came the last appointment of the day, with Burleson. Unfortunately no record exists of what the President said to him.

Honduras severed relations with Germany.

A credit of $100,000,000 was established by the United States in behalf of the Russian government.[2]

---

[1]From a complete account of this interview, as written by Mr. Parker himself within twenty-four hours. Hagedorn, *Leonard Wood*, Vol. II, pp. 219–222.

[2]*Foreign Relations*, 1918, *Russia*, Vol. III, pp. 9–10.

To Dr. William L. McEwan, who had presented a resolution in regard to a day of prayer, adopted by the Presbytery of Pittsburgh:

". . . . I am not clear, and shall not be until I have thought the matter over a little further, whether it would be wise at this juncture and on the particular date suggested to set a day of prayer. My feeling is that when such a day is set the object for which our prayers should be offered should be a very definite one indeed, and it is in the confidence that such objects will presently present themselves that I feel like waiting. I am sure the weight of such considerations will be obvious to the members of the Presbytery."

Friday, May 18th.

The President worked in his study until time for luncheon. After the cabinet meeting he received: 75 Spanish-American War veterans; Representative Sabath of Illinois; Samuel Gompers and William English Walling; the Secretary of War. In the evening the President conferred with three Republican senators—Lodge, Gallinger and Knox. All three refused to discuss the interview but Senator Lodge wrote in his diary: ". . . . President has at last discovered that without the Republicans he would not and could not get his legislation. . . . We were there nearly two hours. He was most polite and talked well, as he always does so far as expression goes. We discussed revenue, food control and censorship chiefly. The two latter were his objects, but we chatted cheerfully and of course made no promises. We told him perfectly pleasantly some truths which he ought to have heard from those who surround him . . ." This bitterest of the President's enemies went on to say: ". . . . I watched and studied his face tonight as I have often done before—a curious mixture of acuteness, intelligence and extreme underlying timidity—a shifty, furtive, sinister expression can always be detected by a good observer. . . .

"His war message, to which he was driven by events, was a fine one, but he has not changed his spots. The man is just what he has been all along, thinking of the country only in terms of Wilson . . ."[1]

---

[1] *The Senate and the League of Nations*, pp. 79-80.

At 10 o'clock the President, having signed the draft bill, issued a proclamation designating June 5th as Registration Day.[1]

A. J. Balfour sent the President, as he had promised, texts of "the various Agreements" (secret treaties) between Great Britain and her allies, explaining in his covering letter that it had been necessary to send to England for them since he had no copies with him. He doubted whether they would "add much to the knowledge which you already possess." Enclosed also was a memorandum giving the main points of a statement on foreign policy which Balfour had made to the Imperial War Council, the proceedings of which, he pointed out, were of course "absolutely secret."

Enclosures in Balfour's letter were as follows:

1. Balfour's statement to the Imperial War Council, which is full of extremely interesting and important facts and intimations with regard to certain of the secret treaties, including the assertion that the practical destruction of the Turkish Empire was one of the objects desired; and that Great Britain had agreements to hand over to Italy, Rumania and Serbia parts of Austria-Hungary.

2. Three acts embodying the agreement known as the "Treaty of London."

3. Four prints, each of which is headed: "Printed for the War Cabinet, April 1917":

a. The "Treaty of London," April 26, 1915.

b. The "Sykes-Picot Agreement" of May 1916, with preliminary Sazonov-Paleologue notes and later supplementary exchanges—many of them in French.

c. Exchange of notes in March and April 1915 embodying consent of France and England to Russia's annexation of Constantinople, with England's demand for the neutral zone of Persia.

---

[1]Baker had written on May 1st, enclosing a draft proclamation, and saying: "I am exceedingly anxious to have the registration and selection by draft . . . conducted under such circumstances as to create a strong patriotic feeling and relieve as far as possible the prejudice which remains to some extent in the popular mind against the draft by reason of Civil War memories. With this end in view, I am using a vast number of agencies throughout the country to make the day of registration a festival and patriotic occasion. . . ." Palmer, *Newton D. Baker*, Vol. I, p. 209. The President replied on the 3rd that he fully approved. For the dramatic story of the preparations made for the registration, confidentially, while the bill was still before Congress, see *ibid.*, pp. 212 *et seq.*

d. Treaty of Bucharest with Rumania, August 4–17, 1916, in French.

Certain omissions in this collection of secret treaties sent to the President by Mr. Balfour are noteworthy:

1. There is no mention of the Grey-Cambon letters on the division of Togoland and the Cameroons.[1]

2. The two agreements with Japan regarding the German Pacific Islands and Shantung are not mentioned.[2]

Certain other omissions are, perhaps, understandable:

1. The Franco-Russian understanding of February–March, 1917, on Germany's western and eastern frontiers was not mentioned: but England may not have been completely informed.

2. The recent negotiations at St. Jean de Maurienne, supplementing the treaty with Italy, were not mentioned: but they might be regarded as not yet having reached a conclusion.[3]

Secretary Baker announced that the expeditionary force of approximately one division of regular troops, under Major General John J. Pershing, had been ordered to proceed to France at as early a date as practicable.

The Root Mission left for Russia.[4]

Nicaragua severed relations with Germany.

To George Creel:

". . . . I dare say that I shall attempt some statement to correct the misapprehension apparently existing in Russia, but it is the opinion of the Secretary of State, and I dare say he is right, that I should communicate the statement direct to our Ambassador in Petrograd and let him make it public there. I will, of course, furnish you with a copy with the suggestion that it be withheld from publication

---

[1]See the author's *Woodrow Wilson and World Settlement*, Vol. I, p. 268.

[2]These tremendous omissions from Balfour's report both in the collection of treaties enclosed and in his own "statement . . . to the Imperial War Council" are significant because they concern the disposal of Germany's overseas possessions of which Great Britain was to get the lion's share.

[3]The President did not answer this letter in writing, nor refer to it in writing at any time, so far as the author has been able to discover, nor did he, apparently, give the treaties themselves any study.

[4]For Secretary Lansing's telegram of May 22nd to Ambassador Francis, explaining the purpose of the Commission, see *Foreign Relations*, 1918, *Russia*, Vol. I, pp. 110–111.

until the date of its probable arrival in Petrograd, or until after it has been acknowledged by Mr. Francis."[1]

To Representative J. Thomas Heflin:

"I am sorry that any misunderstanding should have arisen as to the meaning of what I said at the Red Cross the other day.[2] I thought the meaning was obvious. I meant merely that we were not making war against Germany because of any special and peculiar grievance of our own but because her actions had become intolerable to us as to the rest of free mankind and, therefore, we had found it necessary to make common cause against her. Of course, our own people have suffered grievously at her hands. It would certainly be a most extraordinary interpretation of my meaning to read it otherwise."

Saturday, May 19th.

An old friend, Miss Florence Hoyt, was a guest at luncheon. The President had that morning sent his telegram to Theodore Roosevelt, regretting that he could not permit him to raise a division. The President talked freely about it at the luncheon table. ". . . . He explained," wrote Miss Hoyt later, "that in the modern fashion of war we were wholly ignorant, and that

---

[1] The suggestion that the President send a message to Russia had come from a number of sources. On the 17th, for example, Lansing sent over a telegram from Ambassador Francis to that effect, writing in his covering letter: ". . . . It would seem that certain phrases uttered by you are being used by the radical socialists (probably under German influence) to force the Provisional Government to declare a policy which will remove the chief incentive to Russian offensive operations, namely, control of the Dardanelles and possession of Constantinople. . . .

"It is an insidious and ingenious plan to win over the Russian people to the idea of a separate peace . . .

"Cannot some interpretation of the language, which is being used, be given which will remove the idea . . .

"Of course the only way in which that can be done is by a message from you to Francis for the Russian Government and for publication in Russia. . . . It may cost this country millions of men if this movement for a separate peace cannot be checked. . . ."

In this same letter Lansing enclosed a telegram from William English Walling which read: "Immediate renunciation of no annexations no indemnities program by President may save Russia. Nothing else will."

[2] The misunderstood sentence was: "We have gone in with no special grievance of our own, because we have always said that we were the friends and servants of mankind." *Public Papers,* Vol. V, p. 33.

it was dangerous to send over someone likely to try to show
Europe how it should manage its affairs. . . ."[1] Colonel and
Mrs. E. T. Brown arrived to spend the week end with the
Wilsons. Mrs. Brown, in a personal letter written from the
White House, reported that the President looked "strong and
ruddy, and the embodiment of calm and cheerfulness—the kind
that you can *tie* to."

President Wilson published a statement in regard to the
proposed Food Administration, and his intention to put
Hoover at its head.[2]

A coalition government was formed in Russia, and a declaration published renouncing a separate peace and giving the
platform of the new government.[3]

A lull, caused by bad weather and the necessity for the recuperation of the armies, was reported on the battle front
of Arras and the Aisne.

Telegram to Theodore Roosevelt, who on the 18th had wired for
permission to raise two divisions for service at the front:

"I very much regret that I cannot comply with the
request made in your telegram of yesterday. The reasons
I have stated in a public statement made this morning
and I need not assure you that my conclusions were based
entirely upon imperative considerations of public policy
not upon personal or private choice."[4]

---

[1]Miss Florence S. Hoyt to the author.

[2]*Public Papers,* Vol. V, pp. 42–44.

[3]*Foreign Relations,* 1918, *Russia,* Vol. I, pp. 79–81.

[4]For the President's statement, given to the press on the evening of the 18th and
published in the morning papers of the 19th, see *Public Papers,* Vol. V, pp. 40–41.
Newton D. Baker told the author (1928) that he himself made the decision in the case
of Roosevelt. He believed it would have been a tragic mistake to entrust the lives of
American soldiers to a man as utterly unqualified as Roosevelt. Furthermore, it would
have led to no end of embarrassments to have an ex-President in the capacity of a
subordinate commander.

A New York *Times* editorial of the 20th said in part: "With all deference to Mr.
Roosevelt, who in his most stirring mood is still a commanding figure in the national
foreground, it must be said that the President has disposed of his proposal to form an
expeditionary military force, apart from the general army scheme of the Government,
in the most reasonable way. Our military operations must be kept in charge of military
men. . . ."

To Vance C. McCormick:

"I hope that you and Morris won't worry about the leakage with regard to the appointment to Japan.[1] I, of course, knew that neither of you was responsible for it. Goodness knows how these things happen!

"I have just received your letter of yesterday enclosing letters from the State of Washington recommending Mr. Ole Hanson for appointment. I am sorry to say that Senator Poindexter has served notice on me that the appointment of Hanson would be highly objectionable to him, and you know what happens in such circumstances through the so-called 'courtesy' of the Senate. This is a great life we are living here!"

To Senator G. M. Hitchcock:

"I really did desire to conform to your suggestion about authorizing the volunteer divisions [for Roosevelt], but for reasons which I tried very carefully and frankly to state in this morning's papers, it did not seem possible for me to do so. I hope with all my heart that those reasons seemed to you, as they do to me, conclusive."

Sunday, May 20th.

President and Mrs. Wilson and Colonel Brown went to the Central Presbyterian Church in the morning. In the early afternoon the President and Mrs. Wilson with a family party were taken to the Navy Yard, where they boarded the presidential yacht, *Mayflower*, for a trip down the river, returning in the evening.

> Theodore Roosevelt made public a statement announcing the disbandment of the divisions he had enrolled and advising the men to serve the country as best they could in other ways.[2]
> Colonel House to the President reporting upon recent talks with Sir Eric Drummond: ". . . . I have been trying to pin

[1] Roland S. Morris became ambassador to Japan on August 1st.
[2] New York *Times*, May 21, 1917.

Balfour and him down to what they would consider the minimum terms upon which the Allies would consent to go into a peace conference. I am satisfied they would be willing to begin parleys on the basis of complete evacuation of Belgium and France. He at first suggested a like restoration of Russian territory. I showed him this would involve a delineation of the new Poland, which all agree must be created, and that if we began to discuss boundaries before a conference was called, the discussion would be interminable. . . .

"I convinced Drummond that the most effective thing we could do at present was to aid the German Liberals in their fight against the present German Government.

"The idea is for you to say, at a proper time and occasion, that the Allies are ready at any moment to treat with the German people, but they are not ready to treat with a military autocracy . . ."[1]

Monday, May 21st.

The President followed his usual morning routine—golf, and several hours of work in his study before luncheon.

Mrs. Brown wrote: ". . . at luncheon . . . there were only the President and Edith and I at table. They are using the small dining room now, for breakfast and luncheon (of course it would easily seat forty or fifty people, but it looks small compared to the huge one) and as often happens—just because there were so few of us—the talk was even more free and therefore more interesting even than usual. The President is so convinced that he is just like any and every other human being—and often one could think so—and then, suddenly some subject or phrase brings out his greatness . . . You see it and hear it for a few moments . . . and then he is again just a charming, humorous, considerate gentleman, being host to a group of people whom he considers . . . carefully and . . . individually . . ."

Afternoon appointments: the French ambassador and M. Tardieu; Vice-President Marshall; Representatives Borland of Missouri and Doremus of Michigan; Senator Ransdell of Louisiana and William Denman of the Shipping Board; J. A. McIlhenny, president of the Civil Service Commission.

---

[1] An editorial note in the *Intimate Papers* states that the President answered by telephone "in a tone of general approval." (P. 58.)

When the last caller had gone the President and Mrs. Wilson went for a drive. About half past five Mrs. Wilson returned; the President went on to call upon Mr. Balfour.[1]

> The Supreme Court ordered the re-argument of the antitrust suits against the United States Steel Corporation, the International Harvester Company, the Lehigh Valley and Reading railroads and affiliated coal companies.[2]

To Secretary Baker, who wrote of Paderewski's desire to organize a unit of Poles in the army of the United States:

"This is a most interesting proposition but I think your own reflections upon it are very wise and that it would be a mistake, at any rate at this stage of our own preparations, to organize a force of the sort proposed. I agree with you that there are many advantages in this plan and many striking and impressive things about it, but this is not the stage at which to act upon the suggestion. We must keep this in store for later action."

To Secretary Redfield, who had sent the President a letter from the superintendent of the Coast and Geodetic Survey embodying the results of a study of the problem of fencing in the North Sea. Redfield offered to send to England officers of the Survey, "whose duties have for years made them thoroughly familiar with this class of work," and he added that he had so notified the British authorities and the Navy Department:

"I sincerely value your letter . . . about the fencing in of the North Sea and am very glad that you have handed the suggestion on to the active authorities in this all-important matter."

---

[1]While no record exists of this interview, it is practically certain that the subject had to do with the secret treaties.

[2]When the United States entered the war a number of cases were pending, some of them in the Supreme Court. Gregory asked the President what he wanted done. "He [Wilson] remarked that if we attempted at that moment to vindicate the law, we would disorganize industry. We both agreed that we should let up on these people so that they would have no excuse for not contributing to their full capacities in the prosecution of the war. I went to see Chief Justice White and he was delighted. He thought that our course was proper and patriotic, and we let the cases go to sleep until the war was over." T. W. Gregory to the author.

To Representative E. W. Pou:

". . . . Your interpretation of my message I supposed would be the interpretation everybody would give it. I meant just what you say, that our grievance, 'while entirely sufficient, was the same as that of other neutral nations,' perhaps aggravated by the fact that Germany had made us special promises which she had grossly ignored.

"I would be very much obliged to you for any steps you might take to correct this damaging and erroneous and, I must believe, insincere interpretation of my address to the Red Cross."

Tuesday, May 22nd.

After his early-morning golf with Mrs. Wilson and Colonel Brown, the President worked in his study until time for luncheon. The cabinet met as usual at 2:30, otherwise there were no official appointments.

President Wilson's message to the Provisional government of Russia was sent through the Department of State. ". . . . The position of America in this war is so clearly avowed that no man can be excused for mistaking it. She seeks no material profit or aggrandizement of any kind. She is fighting for no advantage or selfish object of her own but for the liberation of peoples everywhere from the aggressions of autocratic force. . . ."[1]

To Representative E. Y. Webb, chairman of the Judiciary Committee of the House:

"I have been very much surprised to find several of the public prints stating that the administration had abandoned the position which it so distinctly took, and still holds, that authority to exercise censorship over the press to the extent that that censorship is embodied in the recent action of the House of Representatives is absolutely necessary to the public safety. It, of course, has not been

---

[1]For entire message see *Foreign Relations,* 1917, Supp. 2, Vol. I, pp. 71–73. It was informally presented on May 25th, formally on May 29th.

abandoned, because the reasons still exist why such authority is necessary for the protection of the Nation.

"I have every confidence that the great majority of the
newspapers of the country will observe a patriotic reticence about everything whose publication could be of
injury, but in every country there are some persons in a
position to do mischief in this field who cannot be relied
upon and whose interests or desires will lead to actions on
their part highly dangerous to the Nation in the midst
of a war. I want to say again that it seems to me imperative that powers of this sort should be granted."[1]

To Representative J. Thomas Heflin of Alabama:

"It is incomprehensible to me how any frank or honest
person could doubt or question my position with regard
to the war and its objects. I have again and again stated
the very serious and long-continued wrongs which the
Imperial German Government has perpetrated against
the rights, the commerce, and the citizens of the United
States. The list is long and overwhelming. No nation that
respected itself or the rights of humanity could have
borne those wrongs any longer.

"Our objects in going into the war have been stated
with equal clearness. The whole of the conception which I
take to be the conception of our fellow countrymen with
regard to the outcome of the war and the terms of its
settlement I set forth with the utmost explicitness in an
address to the Senate of the United States on the 22d of
January last. Again, in my message to Congress on the
2d of April last those objects were stated in unmistakable
terms. I can conceive no purpose in seeking to becloud
this matter except the purpose of weakening the hands of
the Government and making the part which the United
States is to play in this great struggle for human liberty
an inefficient and hesitating part. We have entered the

---

[1] *Public Papers*, Vol. V, p. 46.

war for our own reasons and with our own objects clearly
stated, and shall forget neither the reasons nor the objects.
There is no hate in our hearts for the German people, but
there is a resolve which cannot be shaken even by misrepresentation to overcome the pretensions of the autocratic Government which acts upon purposes to which the
German people have never consented."[1]

Wednesday, May 23rd.

At 9 o'clock the President received the Senate conferees on
the Espionage bill—Overman, Fletcher and Nelson—urging
"the imperative necessity that a censorship be established to
prevent information of the movement of American ships and
other war moves being conveyed to the enemy." He mentioned
the American expeditions that were to start for Europe, and
said it was vital that no hint of such activity get to Germany.
He had confidence, he said, that the majority of the newspapers
of the country would observe a "patriotic reticence," but what
he wanted was a "mild form of censorship that would impose
more than a moral obligation upon any newspapers that might
tend to print news by which the enemy might profit."[2] At
12:30, Ambassador Naón of the Argentine Republic called to
discuss the conference of American nations which Argentina
was proposing.[3] Afternoon conferences: Senator Simmons of
North Carolina, who presented 133 delegates to the American
Cotton Association; Representative Byrnes of South Carolina;
Dr. Irving Fisher of Yale and a committee; Senator McKellar
and Representative Fisher, both of Tennessee.

It was announced that the American government had denied
passports to American delegates to the Stockholm conference of Socialists, and issued a warning that any American
taking part in the negotiations would be legally liable to
severe punishment.[4]

The Italian Commission reached Washington, headed by
Prince Udine.

---

[1]*Public Papers,* Vol. V, pp. 47–48.

[2]New York *Times,* May 24, 1917.

[3]See this volume, p. 89.

[4]New York *Times,* May 24, 1917; also *Foreign Relations,* 1917, Supp. 2, Vol. I, p. 739.
The President's unfavorable attitude toward the proposed Stockholm conference was

To Frank I. Cobb of the New York *World*, who wrote on May 22nd endorsing a plan which, he said, George Harvey had formulated for the solution of the censorship problem. He added: ". . . . Incidentally let me congratulate you on the magnificent way in which you have planned your war policies, and the sure judgment you have shown.":

". . . . You may be sure I am willing to consider any reasonable solution of the censorship question. With ninety-nine out of every hundred papers the question would not arise, but, as I am sure you know better than I do, there are some papers and some news agencies which we simply cannot trust and I felt it absolutely essential for the safety of the country that I should have some power in the premises.

"I am greatly obliged to you for the kind last paragraph of your letter. I think you know how I value your friendship and approval."

To R. W. Woolley, director of publicity for the First Liberty Loan, who had urged the President to make a public appeal for the loan:

"I am not quite convinced by your letter . . . If you think there is no doubt that the first $2,000,000,000 will be taken, and even over-subscribed, by the bankers and that the only difficulty is a lack of widespread interest on the part of the people, it seems to me that I should reserve my fire for later issues which are undoubtedly bound to come. Besides, I have never known anything to have better publicity than this loan has had, and I do not see just what I could say except to issue an appeal in somewhat weak generalities."

shown in his letter of May 11th to Lansing, this volume, p. 65. On the 19th Lansing wrote particularly of the case of Morris Hillquit, who wished a passport to attend the conference. ". . . . I do not see how it can result in good and it may do much harm . . . .

"If we refuse, it may make them martyrs. If we do issue them, we may encourage a dangerous pro-German movement and permit agitators near Russia who are frankly hostile to the Commission to Russia and will seek every means to discredit it and weaken their influence with the socialistic and labor element. . . ." At the top of Lansing's letter is a notation in the President's handwriting: "Ans. orally. W. W."

Thursday, May 24th.

The President received the members of the Italian Mission at noon. Afternoon appointments: Representative Small of North Carolina; Senators Reed of Missouri, and Fletcher and Trammell of Florida; Herbert Hoover; George Creel; Vance C. McCormick; Senator Husting of Wisconsin; and finally, General Pershing, who was presented by Secretary Baker. This was Pershing's first and only meeting with the President before leaving for France. After some discussion of the shipping question, the President turned to Pershing. "General," he said, "we are giving you some very difficult tasks these days." Pershing replied that that was what he was "trained to expect." The President then spoke of the recent Mexican expedition, and inquired about Pershing's acquaintance with France; but said nothing on the subject of the part the American army should play in the war. When Pershing, upon leaving, expressed appreciation of his appointment, the President replied: "General, you were chosen entirely upon your record and I have every confidence that you will succeed."[1] At tea time the President and Mrs. Wilson received Mr. Balfour. A dinner was given at the White House in the evening, in honor of the Italian Mission. "Covers for 66."

Friday, May 25th.

The President's only official appointment, aside from the cabinet meeting, was with William Denman of the Shipping Board, whom he saw at 4:30 in the afternoon. Evening at the National Theater, with Miss Bones, his niece Mrs. Cothran (who, with her little daughter, was a house guest) and Colonel Brown. The President left the theater before the other members of the party, returning to the White House on foot.

Red Cross Week, ending June 25th, was established by proclamation of the President.

The British Mission left American soil, crossing into Canada.

Frank L. Polk wrote Ambassador Page in London: ". . . . He [Balfour] and the President got on tremendously. . . .

---

[1] *My Experiences in the World War*, Vol. I, p. 37. Pershing wrote of the interview, later: ". . . . His manner was cordial and simple and I was impressed with his poise and his air of determination. . . ."

"The difficult problem of course was the blacklist and bunkering agreement, but I think we are by that. . . ."[1]

General Goethals, speaking at the annual dinner of the American Iron and Steel Institute in New York, said that the original wooden ship program was hopeless. His remarks—the birds were "still nesting in the trees from which the great wooden fleet was to be made," etc.— stirred up a considerable pother in the press. In response to his appeal, the steel men pledged all needed material for steel ships.

76 persons (two thirds of them women or children) were killed in an air raid upon Folkestone, England; 174 were injured.

To Secretary Lansing, regarding an inquiry from Ambassador Page, in Rome, as to whether the President would be willing to receive the honorary degree of Doctor of Laws from the University of Bologna:

"... I ... see no impropriety in it and would certainly feel highly honored."

To Jackson S. Elliott, director of the Washington bureau of the Associated Press, who had commended the work of George Creel—"his intelligent cooperation with press correspondents in the face of lukewarm support, even outspoken opposition, from most of the departments.":

"I am warmly obliged to you for your letter . . . I knew that the newspaper men had only to come in contact with Mr. Creel to learn his real quality. He seems to me thoroughly fine and I am sure that he will more and more command the confidence of thoughtful men like yourself who look to his real character and purpose."

To David Lawrence, who had written of the misunderstanding and distrust which had grown up among newspaper men in regard to the censorship situation, and suggested that the President invite the Washington correspondents to the White House, and give them "such information as you must have which prompts you to ask for some kind of a censorship law."

---

[1] *The Life and Letters of Walter H. Page*, Vol. II, p. 264. Sir Eric Drummond wrote House in July that Balfour had "formed a very great personal regard and admiration for the President." *Intimate Papers*, Vol. III, p. 60.

"Thank you for your letter . . . I fear that it would not be wise for me to pursue the course you suggest, just at present, at any rate, because it might look as if I were trying to straighten it out when there is really nothing to straighten out; or, it might look as if I were trying to correct mistakes which Creel is thought to have made when I do not in my heart believe that he has made any.

"I cannot help believing that continued intercourse with Creel such as the newspaper correspondents will have will more and more convince them of his unusual qualities not only of sense but of trustworthiness. I depend upon their perceptions and their candor to find those qualities out, and I have very little doubt as to the result."

To Robert Bridges, poet laureate of England, who had sent the President a handwritten copy of his poem, "To the United States of America.":

"It was certainly most gracious of you to send me the verses . . . and I particularly thank you for the gracious note which accompanies them. It is very delightful to exchange such greetings of genuine sympathy and correspondence of thought, and I beg to be permitted to send you my warmest personal greetings and good wishes."

To Cleveland H. Dodge:

MY DEAR CLEVE:

I am deeply distressed to hear that you are laid up, and beg that you will take care of yourself. I don't think you know how indispensable you are to all of us.

It was generous of you to write, notwithstanding your weakness, and I thank you with all my heart for your letter.

All unite with me in affectionate and sympathetic messages.

Affectionately yours,
WOODROW WILSON

Saturday, May 26th.

After an early golf game, the President spent some hours in his study before luncheon. In the afternoon he took a long drive with Mrs. Wilson and her brother; and went with his niece to Keith's Theater in the evening.

Rear-Admiral Sims became Vice-Admiral, and commander of the United States destroyers operating from British bases.[1]

Secretary Baker signed and the President approved a letter of instructions to General Pershing which said in part: ". . . you are directed to cooperate with the forces of the other countries employed against . . . [the] enemy; but in so doing, the underlying idea must be kept in view that the forces of the United States are a separate and distinct component of the combined forces, the identity of which must be preserved. This fundamental rule is subject to such minor exceptions in particular circumstances as your judgment may approve. . . ."[2]

Sunday, May 27th.

The President and Mrs. Wilson did not go to church, remaining in the private part of the White House all the morning. In the afternoon they took a trip down the river on the *Sylph*, accompanied by Mrs. Wilson's mother, brother and sister.

An open letter from Clemenceau was made public, appealing to President Wilson to reconsider his refusal of Roosevelt's offer.[3]

William Denman put out a statement in defense of the wooden ship program, which was generally taken as a rebuke to Goethals for his remarks on the 25th.

---

[1]*Naval Investigation Hearings*, 1920, Vol. II, p. 1995.

[2]Pershing himself, with the help of Harbord, his Chief of Staff, had likewise prepared instructions, which were signed by General Bliss as Acting Chief of Staff the same day. These latter instructions were, of course, nullified by those signed by Baker and approved by the President. The substance of the paragraph quoted above does not appear in the instructions which Pershing wrote. Account of this controversial incident has been written after consulting documents in the Wilson files and the following books: Pershing, *My Experiences in the World War*, Vol. I, pp. 37-40; Palmer, *Newton D. Baker*, Vol. I, pp. 170-173; March, *The Nation at War*, pp. 243-250.

[3]New York *Times*, May 28, 1917.

Monday, May 28th.

The President spent the morning in his study. Afternoon appointments: M. de Lagercrantz, Axel R. Nordvall and the minister from Sweden; Senator James of Kentucky; Senator Owen of Oklahoma;[1] Representative Rainey of Illinois. Late in the afternoon he attended a reception in honor of the Italian Mission, and at 6 o'clock Henry Morgenthau called. In the evening the President conferred with Secretaries Baker, Daniels and McAdoo, Herbert Hoover and B. M. Baruch, probably in regard to the problem of price fixing for raw materials.

> General Pershing sailed for Europe. Secretary Baker told him before he left that he would give him only two orders, "one to go to France and the other to come home"; in the meantime, Pershing's authority in France would be supreme. He added: ". . . . If you make good, the people will forgive almost any mistake. If you do not make good, they will probably hang us both on the first lamp-post they can find."[2]

To Secretary Lansing, who had sent over the Argentine government's explanation of its attempt to initiate a congress of American nations "with the purpose of trying to come to an understanding between them on the occasion of the present war."[3] ". . . . This proposed conference of American Nations," Lansing commented, "is creating a very bad impression in this country as its purpose is not understood. Mr. Naón appreciates this and is greatly concerned about it. . . .

"I think that the matter is of sufficient importance for you to see Mr. Naón as soon as possible . . ."

The President did see Naón on the 23rd,[4] and on the 28th wrote to Lansing on his own typewriter:

"I have fully informed you orally of what I said to Ambassador Naón, but return his letter for your files.

"The despatches show a very poor chance for Argentina to pull anything off!"

---

[1] See this volume, p. 95.

[2] Palmer, *Newton D. Baker*, Vol. I, p. 180.

[3] *Foreign Relations*, 1917, Supp. 1, pp. 282–283.

[4] This volume, p. 83. On the 25th American diplomatic representatives in Central

To Secretary Lansing, enclosing letters from the ambassadors to Italy and France. T. N. Page's letter, dated April 25th, told of the "unexpected conference last week of the representatives of the British, French, and Italian Governments at St. Jean de Maurienne."[1] He reported that he had made inquiries of Sonnino, but had received an evasive answer—the conference had "discussed many matters rather than settled them." The President's letter was written on his own typewriter:

"All letters coming from the other side nowadays necessarily lag far behind events, but there may be items in the two letters attached which you would like to store up in your memory."

To Secretary McAdoo, enclosing a telegram from Thomas A. Edison, reporting that 200 of his clerks and workmen, organized by a German-American, had subscribed $30,000 to the Liberty Loan and pledged themselves to raise a total of $300,000 among their fellow workmen in the Edison laboratories. Edison suggested that workmen in other factories have active campaigns among themselves for subscriptions:

MY DEAR MAC:

Here is a telegram from Mr. Edison which I am sure will interest you. It seems to be likely that you will wish to act on his suggestion in some way.

Affectionately yours,
WOODROW WILSON

Tuesday, May 29th.

President H. A. Garfield of Williams College was a guest at luncheon; afterward the President saw Gilbert F. Close, a friend and helper of the Princeton days who later became one of his secretaries at the Peace Conference. The cabinet met at 2:30, one of the subjects under discussion being the labor situation in Texas—Mexican laborers were going over the border to Mexico

and South America (with certain exceptions) were notified for their "own information and discreet use should occasion arise" that the Department of State, after careful consideration, did not "consider that such a conference would serve any useful purpose at this time." *Foreign Relations*, 1917, Supp. 1, p. 289.

[1] Which resulted in one of the secret treaties. This volume, p. 25.

to escape registration for the draft.[1] Afternoon appointments: Vance C. McCormick; George Creel; Senator Nelson of Minnesota; Representative Adamson of Georgia.

> In a letter to President Wilson, the Executive Committee of the (British) Union of Democratic Control called attention to the fact that the "declared aims of the Russian Provisional Government ... accurately embody the real ideals of the democracies of the World," and urged the President to take action "with the object of securing a general declaration by all the belligerent States renouncing aggressive aims." The letter was signed by Norman Angell, Charles Roden Buxton, J. A. Hobson, F. W. Jowett, J. Ramsay MacDonald, Arthur Ponsonby, Philip Snowden, Charles Trevelyan, Irene Cooper Willis, E. D. Morel, F. W. Pethick Lawrence, H. M. Swanwick; it was sent through Colonel House, who did not forward it to the President for some time, recording in his diary that he did not "altogether agree with the purpose."[2]
>
> The Italian drive continued successfully, 23,000 Austrian prisoners having been taken since its commencement.

To his secretary, Tumulty, who had passed on to the President an inquiry from Samuel G. Blythe of the *Saturday Evening Post* as to the "biggest and most helpful thing" the *Post* could do not only for the country but for the President:

"The biggest thing the Saturday Evening Post could do at the present juncture would be to plan and publish a series of articles pointing out very clearly,

"First, the objects of the war, drawing from my addresses to Congress;

"Second, the tasks involved (this will, of course, require perhaps several articles);

"Third, the financial necessities and the ways in which they must be met (this should be based upon consultations with the Secretary of the Treasury);

"Fourth, the reasons for believing that this struggle may yet be a very long and anxious one;

---

[1] See this volume, pp. 93–94.

[2] *Intimate Papers,* Vol. III, p. 139.

"Fifth, the Government's programme in respect of food, transportation, shipping, etc., etc.

"The circulation of the Post is so extensive that it could do an immense service in this matter, and I am sure that Creel would be willing to lend his assistance very enthusiastically."

Wednesday, May 30th.

After an early luncheon the President and Mrs. Wilson left for Arlington Cemetery, to attend the Decoration Day exercises. The gathering was held in the amphitheatre behind the historic Lee Mansion; Federal and Confederate veterans as well as men in khaki were prominent in the audience. The President made a short address: ". . . we are saying to all mankind, 'We did not set this Government up in order that we might have a selfish and separate liberty, for we are now ready to come to your assistance and fight out upon the field of the world the cause of human liberty. . . .'"[1] At 3:30 the President received Charles D. Lanier, of the *Review of Reviews*, who presented a plan for raising war revenue by taxing the excess business profits resulting from the war itself.

Thursday, May 31st.

Afternoon appointments: Representative Sinnott of Oregon; Representative Foster of Illinois; Representative Carlin of Virginia; General Goethals; Senators McKellar and Shields of Tennessee and the Tennessee delegation from the House; John Bates Clark of Columbia University; Representative Aswell of Louisiana. The President went to the Belasco Theater in the evening with a family party.

The Austrian Parliament convened, the Emperor stating in his opening speech that the Central Powers had "already expressed readiness for peace in unequivocal terms and emphasized present willingness to make peace with any nation that will give up intention [to] threaten [the] honour and existence of these powers."[2]

[1]*Public Papers*, Vol. V, pp. 52–53.

[2]Minister Stovall in Switzerland to Lansing, June 1, 1917. *Foreign Relations*, 1917, Supp. 2, Vol. I, p. 82.

The Lafayette Escadrille, composed largely of Americans, fought fifteen air battles during the last two weeks of May. 442 German and 271 British and French airplanes were reported to have been shot down during the month, on the Western Front.

To Secretary Baker:

"Thank you for your careful report about the promotions to Major General and Brigadier General which must be made at once.

"I do not feel that I am in a position to correct your judgment in any respect with regard to these promotions, and I am perfectly willing to trust your judgment. It happens that, with perhaps one exception, all the men mentioned are personally unknown to me. . . ."

To Secretary McAdoo, enclosing $10,000:

MY DEAR MAC:

May I not send to you personally my subscription to the Liberty Loan, which I make with great satisfaction and with the wish that it might be a great deal larger?

Affectionately yours,

WOODROW WILSON[1]

To Governor James E. Ferguson of Texas, who had telegraphed about the labor conditions in his state:

"Your telegram . . . of course, made a deep impression on me. I brought it up for discussion in the Cabinet.[2] Our opinion was that it would be very dangerous to attempt what you suggest with regard to a proclamation exempting all Mexicans, whether naturalized citizens of the United States or not, from the military selective draft, because, of course, it would not be right to make such a

---

[1]After this country went into the war, the President was interested in no financial investments but Liberty and Farm Loan bonds. R. S. Weeks, who handled many of the President's financial affairs, to the author.

[2]This volume, p. 91.

determination on a matter of that kind for Texas alone. It would have to be widened, sooner or later at any rate, to other sections of the country. I feel, therefore, that I am estopped and that we must do our best through other means to reassure the farm laborers of Southern Texas and remove wrong impressions from their minds.

"I have conferred with the Secretary of Labor and know that he is doing his active best to assist in the matter.

"I appreciate the quandary and wish that I could have taken such action as you suggested."

Friday, June 1st.

After his morning golf, the President remained in his study until noon. Colonel House's daughter and her husband, Mr. and Mrs. Gordon Auchincloss, were luncheon guests. In the afternoon the President received Representatives Norton and Young and a delegation of five. The cabinet met at 2:30, McAdoo making a number of suggestions regarding credits and supplies for Italy. Later the same day he wrote the President, ". . . I was assured that the power in question would be obliged to quit the war unless its needs for coal could be supplied without delay. That it could not hold out longer than 60 days." He suggested immediate consultation with the British and French governments "and that they be requested to submit their views as quickly as possible in accordance with the suggestions I made at the Cabinet meeting today." Late-afternoon appointments: Representative Kettner of California; Senator Newlands of Nevada, in regard to the enlargement of the Interstate Commerce Commission.

Admiral Sims reported to the Navy Department: ". . . the operations of our forces in these waters have proved not only very satisfactory, but also of marked value to the Allies in overcoming the submarine menace. The equipment and construction of our ships have proved adequate and sufficient and the personnel has shown an unusually high degree of enthusiasm and ability to cope with the situation presented."[1]

---

[1] Sims, *The Victory at Sea*, pp. 76–77.

The Italian offensive having abated, the Austro-Hungarian troops early in June began a series of heavy counter-attacks.

To Secretary Lansing, who had sent the President a copy of the Russian statement of May 19th:[1]

"I have read the attached paper with the profoundest interest. I hope with all my heart that the new forces in Russia may be guided by the principles and objects it sets forth!"

To Secretary Baker:

"Senator Owen of Oklahoma came in to see me the other day very much excited at having heard that several mobilization and training camps were going to be established in Texas while none was to be established in Oklahoma, which he feels offers advantages quite equal to those offered in Texas in respect of location, water supply, climate, and everything else. I promised to bring the matter to your attention, and assured him that such sites were being selected upon a purely practical and business basis, but that I was sure you would like to have your attention called to any sites more advantageous than those that were being chosen."

To Colonel House, who wrote on May 31st that the British ambassador, Sir Cecil Spring Rice, had been to see him, "very much perturbed" over a message which Mr. Balfour had just received from his government. The British War Cabinet thought it desirable "to have some system of generally supervising and coordinating work of representatives of various British Departments in United States who are employed there on matters connected with shipping, food supply, munitions, and War Office and Admiralty business," and proposed therefore to send Lord Northcliffe on such a mission.

In his covering letter to the President, House said:

". . . . Spring-Rice also showed me Balfour's reply, which was a very earnest argument against sending any such repre-

---

[1]This volume, p. 77.

sentative here at this time. He also added that if it was intended to send Northcliffe or anyone else your consent should
first be obtained, for 'you and you alone were the Government
of the United States.'

"I told Spring-Rice that I thought you would agree with
Balfour that it would be best not to send anyone at present.
Will you not confirm this if it reflects your views? . . . ."[1]

The President's reply was telegraphed:

"Action mentioned in your letter of yesterday would be
most unwise and still more unwise the choice of the person
named."

To Colonel House, who had written: ". . . . The pacifists in this
country—in England and in Russia are demanding a statement
of terms by the Allies which shall declare against indemnities
or territorial encroachments. They believe, and are being told,
that Germany is willing for peace on these terms.

"It seems to me important that the truth be brought out,
so that everyone, both in and out of Germany, may know
what the issue is. I hope you will think it advisable to take
some early occasion to do this. Unless you lead and direct the
liberal Allied thought, it will not be done. . . .":

MY DEAR HOUSE,

Your letter of May thirtieth chimes exactly with my
own thoughts, and I wish that you would follow it up with
advice on these points:

I would like to say in substance just what you say in
your letter, that the present military masters of Germany
"have no intention of making peace upon any other basis
than that of conquest," that they already hold Middle
Europe from Bruges to Constantinople, that Belgium,
Poland, Austria-Hungary, European Turkey, and a portion of the Balkan states are completely in their power,
and that they intend that they shall remain so, meaning

---

[1]From unpublished material in the Wilson files. The paraphrased message from the
British government to A. J. Balfour is published, almost entire, in *Intimate Papers,*
Vol. III, pp. 84–85, as a "memorandum which Wiseman gave to House on May 31."

to take a gambler's chance, stand pat if they win, yield a parliamentary government if they lose;

But when shall I say it (on Flag Day?),

And how shall I say it without seeming directly to contradict Cecil and Ribot[1] if I am to add, as I feel that I must, the terms (in general phrase, as in the address to the Senate) upon which we in this country think that a settlement should be made when we win?

I would be immensely grateful to you if you would write me fully in reply to these questions. You are closer in touch with what is being said and thought on the other side of the water than we are here and could form a much safer and surer judgment than I could on how the necessary things ought to be said.[2]

I am grateful to you all the time, for that matter, and every thing you do makes me more so.

I am both glad and sorry that you have got off to the Massachusetts shore,—glad for your sake, sorry for ours, who would wish to be much nearer to you.

All unite in affectionate messages. We are going to have the pleasure of having Mr. and Mrs. Auchincloss in for lunch to-day. We have just discovered that they are in town.

Affectionately Yours,

WOODROW WILSON

---

[1] For Cecil's statement, see this volume, p. 70. For Ribot's words before the French Chamber of Deputies on May 22nd, see New York *Times*, May 23, 1917.

[2] House replied on June 5th: ". . . . If you would send me in advance a copy of the address, I think I would know if there was a word or line which might offend sensibilities . . . ." (This the President did not do. See this volume, p. 114.) House added: ". . . . For your information only let me say that Balfour has given Wiseman his confidence to an unusual degree, and they have arranged a private code . . ." House's biographer quotes Sir William Wiseman as saying: ". . . Colonel House arranged, with the President's approval, that Balfour should cable in a special British Government code direct to me in New York, and that I should make it my chief duty to attend to these cables and bring them immediately to Colonel House, who could telephone them over a private wire to the State Department or to President Wilson. In this way Balfour, speaking for the British Government, could get an answer from President Wilson, if necessary, within a few hours. . . ." *Intimate Papers*, Vol. III, p. 65.

To Frank I. Cobb of the New York World:

"Thank you for the copy of the translation of my address in German which the World was so patriotic as to have made in Paris and scattered over the German trenches by the French aviators. I shall preserve it as a memento of a very remarkable thing."[1]

To his secretary, Tumulty, who had called attention to a request for a statement from the President encouraging undergraduates to continue their educations because of the nation's pressing need of trained leadership:

"It is literally impossible for me to run the country. Of course, there is no reason why the colleges should interrupt their sessions or depart from their usual course, and I cannot believe that this will not be evident before autumn, but you can assure the writer of this letter of this on my behalf."[2]

Saturday, June 2nd.

The President received William Denman of the Shipping Board at noon. Miss Florence Hoyt, an old friend, was a guest. In the afternoon the President and Mrs. Wilson, with a small family party, drove to Annapolis.

Sunday, June 3rd.

The President and Mrs. Wilson went to the Central Presbyterian Church in the morning. Frank I. Cobb was a luncheon guest. In the afternoon President and Mrs. Wilson attended the annual Confederate Memorial Services at Arlington.

Fierce fighting was reported on the battle fronts of Arras and Aisne.

A provisional government was formed in China under a Dictator, Hsu Shih-Chang, 11 provinces being in revolt.

---

[1]The speech was that of April 2, 1917. The parts which had not been published in the German press were printed in red.

[2]However, the President did send telegrams to the presidents of Indiana and De Pauw Universities on June 4th, saying that he saw "no necessity whatever for suspending the sessions of the colleges and think that such a suspension would be very much against the public interest."

Monday, June 4th.

The President's niece, Miss Alice Wilson of Baltimore, arrived for a visit at the White House. Afternoon appointments: Dr. van Dyke; Representative Aswell of Louisiana; Franklin D. Roosevelt, Assistant Secretary of the Navy, probably in regard to a plan to bar submarines from the North Sea. At four o'clock the President went to the Capitol, where he called on Senator Martin, Democratic floor leader, probably as to the amendment to the military appropriation bill upon which the Senate and House conferees were deadlocked. In the evening George Creel called; also Senator Owen, who had had copies of a resolution setting forth an American peace program laid before the President and Secretary Lansing. The President dissuaded Owen, probably intimating his own intention of dealing with the subject in an address.

Secretary Lansing instructed Minister Reinsch in China to express to the Foreign Office "the most profound regret" over the dissension in China, and "the most sincere desire" that tranquillity and political coördination might be reëstablished. ". . . . The entry of China into war with Germany, or the continuance of the *status quo* of her relations with that Government, are matters of secondary consideration. The principal necessity for China is to resume and continue her political entity and to proceed along the road of national development on which she has made such marked progress. . . ."[1]

To Secretary Daniels:

"The other day you wrote me a note about an undertaking of the Scripps' newspapers which they have put in the hands of Mr. H. P. Burton.

"Can you tell me who this Mr. Burton is?

"A man of that name was recently sent over here by Lord Northcliffe, and I want to have as little to do with him as possible, because I don't believe in Lord North-

---

[1] For entire message, see *Foreign Relations*, 1917, pp. 48–49. On the same day Lansing telegraphed American diplomatic representatives in France, Great Britain and Japan, suggesting that they send identic representations. All three refused, Japan being especially irritated. See this volume, pp. 107, 114.

cliffe any more than I do in Mr. Hearst and I wonder if this Mr. H. P. Burton is the man."[1]

To Governor M. G. Brumbaugh of Pennsylvania, who had asked the President's advice as to the modification of labor laws for the period of the war:

". . . . I think it would be most unfortunate for any of the states to relax the laws by which safeguards have been thrown about labor. I feel that there is no necessity for such action, and that it would lead to a slackening of the energy of the nation rather than to an increase of it, besides being very unfair to the laboring people themselves."

To J. A. Berst of the Pathé Company, a letter written at the suggestion of Secretary Redfield, who informed the President on June 1st that the matter had been up before the Council of National Defense:

"Several times in attending Keith's Theater here I have seen portions of the film entitled 'Patria,' which has been exhibited there and I think in a great many other theaters in the country. May I not say to you that the character of the story disturbed me very much? It is extremely unfair to the Japanese and I fear that it is calculated to stir up a great deal of hostility which will be far from beneficial to the country, indeed will, particularly in the present circumstances, be extremely hurtful. I take the liberty, therefore, of asking whether the Pathó Company would not be willing to withdraw it if it is still being exhibited."[2]

Tuesday, June 5th.

The President remained in his study until noon, when he and Mrs. Wilson attended a Reunion of Confederate Veterans, the

---

[1]Daniels replied that the two Burtons were in no way connected.

[2]Considerable correspondence followed. It was revealed that the picture had already been changed, to eliminate the offensive parts.

President making a short address. ". . . you have come through war, you know how you have been chastened by it, and there comes a time when it is good for a Nation to know that it must sacrifice if need be everything that it has to vindicate the principles which it professes. . . . We have been allowed to become strong in the Providence of God that our strength might be used to prove, not our selfishness, but our greatness . . ."[1] Aside from the cabinet meeting, there were no afternoon engagements.

Registration Day. Between nine and ten million men registered for the draft. Patriotic meetings were held in many places and little opposition was shown.

The French Chamber of Deputies adopted a resolution saying among other things that the return of Alsace-Lorraine was expected, "together with liberation of invaded territories and just reparation for damage. . . .

". . . durable guarantees for peace and independence for peoples great and small, in a league of nations such as has already been foreshadowed. . . ."[2]

In the course of the debate, Ribot repudiated with virtuous indignation charges of secret diplomacy. "Secret diplomacy has been mentioned: there can be no secret diplomacy! The fullest publicity should be and shall be given here!"[3]

Wednesday, June 6th.

Afternoon appointments: Manuel L. Quezon, resident commissioner, and three others, from the Philippine Islands; Senator Underwood of Alabama; Senator Chamberlain of Oregon; Senator Walsh of Montana; Senators Smith of South Carolina and Sheppard of Texas; Senator King of Utah. In the evening the President resumed his conferences, seeing Senators Warren of Wyoming and Page of Vermont. These interviews had to do with the grave situation which would result unless ample power were given by Congress to regulate the food supply of the country, the President expressing his

---

[1] *Public Papers*, Vol. V, pp. 54–57 for entire speech.

[2] *Current History*, July, 1917, p. 50.

[3] This is interesting in view of the fact that Ribot was at that moment in the midst of the secret Prince Sixte negotiations, which had been going on for some months. See *War Memoirs of David Lloyd George*, Vol. IV, p. 259.

strong conviction that the Lever bill should be brought out of conference at once and acted upon.

> Announcement was made (it appeared in the New York *Times* of the 7th) that Lord Northcliffe, at the request of the British War Cabinet, had accepted the position of head of the British War Mission in the United States, in succession to Balfour. Lansing telegraphed Ambassador Page in London: "Department is informed on authority not in any way connected with British Embassy that British Government is contemplating sending Lord Northcliffe on special mission to this country. Department feels that nothing can be gained by sending another commission or a commissioner. Impression made by Mr. Balfour was so favorable it would seem better to let matters stand as they are rather than send any one at this time. Discreetly investigate and report as soon as possible."[1]

To Bishop W. F. McDowell, who had written that the Maryland Bible Society planned to present a Bible to every soldier and sailor from Maryland and wished a message from the President for use with it:

> "The enclosed[2] is a very inadequate thing, but it is the best I can do in response to your request . . . amidst the tremendous pressure of things upon my attention, and I hope it may be of some little use."

Thursday, June 7th.

The President and Mrs. Wilson spent two hours in the morning reviewing the Confederate veterans, as they marched up

---

[1] *Foreign Relations*, 1917, Supp. 2, Vol. I, pp. 85–86. House wrote the President the next day: "I am sorry that Northcliffe is coming. I thought Balfour's cable had headed him off. . . .

"Wiseman tells me that Page approved his coming and thought he would be acceptable to you. . . .

"It is to be remembered that Northcliffe comes apparently with your approval and of course expects to be cordially received. I am afraid his visit may stir up the anti-British feeling here that at present is lying dormant."

[2] The enclosure was as follows: "This book speaks both the voice of God and the voice of humanity, for there is told in it the most convincing story of human experience that has ever been written, take it all in all, and those who heed that story will know that strength and happiness and success are all summed up in the exhortation, 'Fear God and keep His commandments.'"

whole nation must be a team in which each man shall play the part for which

he is best fitted. To this end, Congress has provided that ~~this~~ the nation be shall

organized for war by selection and that each man be classified shall ~~so serving~~ for services

in the

place ~~where~~ to which it shall best serve the general good to call him.

The significance of this ~~could~~ can not be overstated. It is a new thing

in our history and a landmark in our progress. It is a new manner of accepting and intelligent,

our duty to give ourselves with thoughtful devotion ~~thoughtful and devoted self-giving~~ to the common purpose of us all. It

is in no sense a conscription of the unwilling; it is, rather, a selection from a

nation which has volunteered in mass. It is no ~~less than~~ more a choosing of

those who shall march with the colors than it is a selection of those who

shall serve an equally necessary and devoted purpose in the industries that be-hind the battle line.

The day here named is the time upon which all shall present themselves

for assignment to their tasks. ~~In this sense it is~~ It is for that reason destined to be remembered

as one of the most conspicuous moments in our history. It is nothing less

than the day upon which the manhood of ~~this~~ the country shall step forward in

one solid rank in defense of the ideals to which this nation is consecrated.

It is important to those ideals no less than to the pride of this generation

in its devotion to them, manifesting that there be no gaps in ~~this~~ the ranks

PRESIDENT WILSON CALLS AN ARMY INTO BEING

Page of the original copy of President Wilson's statement designating June 5, 1917, as Registration Day. Secretary Baker drafted the statement, which the President then corrected in his own handwriting.

Pennsylvania Avenue in a heavy rain. The President stood, hat in hand, acknowledging greetings, some of the veterans even insisting on shaking his hand as the parade went by. Afternoon appointments: former Representative William S. Bennet of New York, who called to discuss the matter of the five ships formerly owned by the Hamburg-American line, the sale of which had been held up; Senator Husting of Wisconsin; E. J. Hale, minister to Costa Rica; Mr. Barrett, president of the Farmers' Union, and a committee; Senators Ransdell of Louisiana and Kendrick of Wyoming. In the evening Senator Wadsworth of New York called.

> Ambassador Page telegraphed from London: "Northcliffe is sent on a purely commercial errand to supervise the purchasing agents of the British Government in the United States. He has no diplomatic errand or standing nor is he a 'commissioner or commissioner general' nor do his duties have any reference to what Mr. Balfour did.
>
> "He knows the United States better than any Englishman except Bryce and he will have no official relations with our Government different from the British commercial agents now there."[1]
>
> Explosions from the battlefields in France could be heard as far away as London—a series of mines were set off by the British, rocking the ground for miles! In the terrific blow that followed, British troops smashed the salient south of Ypres, winning Messines Ridge and other fortified positions which had been held by the Germans for two and a half years.

Friday, June 8th.

The President received Dr. Henry van Dyke at 2 o'clock, and at 2:30 the cabinet met. Evening at Keith's Theater.

> In a message to the British Embassy Balfour said it was considered inadvisable to deny British Socialists permission to attend the Stockholm conference. ". . . . We greatly regret that it was impossible for us to consult Mr. Lansing before reversing our previous decision, but this was inevitable as conditions in Russia have changed so rapidly. . . ."[2]

---

[1]*Foreign Relations*, 1917, Supp. 2, Vol. I, p. 86.

[2]Message left at the State Department. *Ibid.*, pp. 741–742.

General Pershing landed at Liverpool and proceeded at once to London, where, on the 9th, he was received by the King.[1]

J. P. Morgan & Company subscribed $50,000,000 to the Liberty Loan.

To John Skelton Williams, who had recommended Thomas B. Love for the Interstate Commerce Commission:

". . . . My own personal knowledge of Mr. Love would commend him to me very strongly, but I am afraid I have not the face to take another man from Texas. A man's locality ought not to disqualify him, but there is an imperative political consideration in these matters which, after all, has some reasonable foundation."

Saturday, June 9th.

The President spent the morning in his study. In the afternoon he and Mrs. Wilson went to the station to meet his daughter, Miss Margaret Wilson, who was returning from a concert tour; and in the evening they went again, to meet Mr. and Mrs. Sayre. There were no official engagements during the day.

Canadian troops penetrated the German lines on a two-mile front south of Lens.

To William Phillips, Assistant Secretary of State:

"I take it for granted you have discussed with the Secretary of State Mr. H. P. Davison's suggestion of a Red Cross Unit of six or eight persons to be sent immediately to Russia, particularly as he mentions transportation as one of the subjects to be dealt with. There is danger of our having a great mixture and complexity of agents in Russia, and I would want to be very sure just what the errand of the commission was to be and just what it will attempt. Will you not let me know what the joint judgment of the Secretary of State and yourself is?"

---

[1]Pershing, *My Experiences in the World War*, Vol. I, pp. 44, *et seq.*

To Senator J. H. Lewis:

"I have your letter . . . about the kind desire of certain gentlemen representing the large commercial bodies of Chicago to have me make an address in Chicago upon the general issues of the war.

"I feel that for me to go away from Washington upon such an errand at this time would be a blunder. I do not myself believe that the country needs very much enlightenment or stimulation. I believe that it is thoroughly awake and quietly dead in earnest, and I should dislike to play into the hands of those who are trying to muddy the waters by lending color to what they are already saying, namely, that we have to beat the waters to get what we want in the way of a response from the country. Such an impression is most unjust to the country, of course, and I think that anything that it may be necessary for me to say from time to time will best be said from Washington. . . ."

Sunday, June 10th.

Neither the President nor Mrs. Wilson went to church in the morning. In the afternoon they took a trip to Mount Vernon, accompanied by Miss Margaret Wilson, Miss Bones and Mr. and Mrs. Sayre.

President Wilson's message to Russia[1] was published in the morning papers. Editorial comment in the United States was generally favorable. ". . . . The wayfaring man, though a fool, can understand this simple, direct statement of the issues and aims of the war from the American standpoint. . . ."[2]

Monday, June 11th.

The President spent the morning in his study. Afternoon appointments: the minister from Colombia, who presented his credentials; Senator Chamberlain of Oregon, in regard to a

[1]This volume, p. 81.
[2]St. Louis *Post-Dispatch*, June 11, 1917.

pardon case; Henry Morgenthau; Herbert Hoover, with whom the President discussed the necessity for early legislation for food control, the organization of commodity controls and voluntary conservation;[1] Senator Overman of North Carolina; Samuel Gompers and a committee representing organized labor, whose purpose was to make a concerted drive upon Congress for the adoption of food legislation. They urged the President to address a joint session of Congress on the subject. Gompers reported afterward that they had found the President "in hearty accord."

> General Smuts sent a message, through the American ambassador at London, to Howard E. Coffin, chairman of the Aircraft Board: "The decision of this war lies in the air and complete victory can only be won by ten or more thousand airplanes with which enemy aircraft can be annihilated. This achievement would be worthy of America, is a contribution which she alone is capable of making, and would enable her to dictate peace. . . ."[2]

> The Japanese ambassador in Washington called upon Secretary Lansing in regard to the communication to the Chinese government of June 4th,[3] which had much displeased the Japanese, since the United States was thought to be interfering in the domestic affairs of China. Lansing said frankly that "the United States had as much right as Japan had to express its opinion to the Chinese Government."[4]

Tuesday, June 12th.

At the cabinet meeting the possible discontinuance of half holidays during the war was discussed, among other matters. The President wrote Samuel Gompers on the 13th that the members of the cabinet "were unanimously of the opinion that they should, as you suggest, go on as usual. I quite agree with you that no interruption of privileges of this sort should occur unless it is absolutely and manifestly necessary."

---

[1] The President wrote to Hoover on June 13th: ". . . . After you left, I wondered why when you spoke of Doctor Hadley of Yale I had not thought of President Garfield of Williams, a man of fine capacity and of the finest principle and spirit."

[2] *Foreign Relations*, 1917, Supp. 2, Vol. I, p. 92.

[3] This volume, p. 99.

[4] *War Memoirs of Robert Lansing*, p. 288.

Colonel House wrote: ". . . . Northcliffe was not received by any of the staff of the British Embassy and he was angry beyond words. . . .

"The British Government have given him the widest possible powers and it would therefore seem necessary to give him proper consideration.

"At my suggestion, Wiseman is advising him not to talk through the press and not to attempt to force his opinions upon our people. . . ."[1]

The United States railroad commission reached Petrograd.

King Constantine of Greece abdicated, under pressure from England, France and Russia, and was succeeded by his second son, Alexander, who was not under suspicion of pro-German sympathies.[2]

Weekly reports showed that the submarine situation was again becoming serious.

To Representative L. P. Padgett, chairman of the House Committee on Naval Affairs:

"I understand that the House will today be considering the proposition for the establishment of a naval base, and I take the liberty of availing myself of this opportunity to ask you to say to the House how essential it seems to me that a naval base and training station should be established, and established at the earliest possible day, at Hampton Roads.

"I have considered this matter from a great many points of view and am more and more impressed with the immediate necessity for such a training station. If it cannot be had, and had promptly, the most serious embarrassments will ensue. I sincerely hope that it will be the wish of the House to take the necessary steps for its establishment."[3]

---

[1] Sir William's purpose, House thought, was to keep Northcliffe "away from the Wall Street influence," and bring him in close touch with administrative circles.

[2] *Foreign Relations*, 1917, Supp. 2, Vol. I, p. 92.

[3] The President also wrote a letter on the same subject to Champ Clark, Speaker of the House.

GENERAL PERSHING ARRIVING IN FRANCE

Wednesday, June 13th.

The President's afternoon appointments: Senator Calder of New York; Representative Garrett of Tennessee; W. L. Saunders, chairman of the Naval Consulting Board, who had, earlier in the day, submitted the report, approved by Goethals, of a Special Committee in regard to the protection of merchant vessels from attacks by submarines. The President directed that it be laid before P. A. S. Franklin and the other members of the Shipping Control Committee in New York.[1] At 11 o'clock in the evening the President touched a button opening the Rose Festival at Portland, Oregon.

> Major R. C. Bolling, of the Aircraft Production Board, was about this time ordered to England, France and Italy "to arrange with the proper representatives of the Allied air services a joint program for construction of airplanes and engines and all other industrial aspects of the aeronautical situation."[2]
>
> The Root Mission arrived in Petrograd.
>
> General Pershing and his staff crossed the channel to France.
>
> Air raids on England continued. 97 people were killed and 437 injured in London on the 13th.

To Representative J. Thomas Heflin of Alabama, written at the suggestion of Mrs. Helen H. Gardener:

"May I without taking too great a liberty suggest to you that it would be a very wise thing, both politically and from other points of view, if you and the others in Congress who feel like you would consent to the constitution of a special committee of the House on woman suffrage? I perhaps am more in the storm center of this question than you are, and I think I can give this as my mature counsel; and I am sure that you will understand why I do it and forgive me if I have taken too great a liberty."

---

[1] Saunders telegraphed the next day: "On my return to New York this morning I conveyed your message to Mr. Franklin and his associates, at a special meeting . . . They have before them the Goethals Rousseau report on ship protection. They have expressed earnest interest in the matter . . ."

[2] Lansing to W. H. Page. *Foreign Relations*, 1917, Supp. 2, Vol. I, p. 94.

To Albert Kelsey, who had written that the First Presbyterian Church of Staunton, Virginia, was being restored, and asked whether the President would care to place a small memorial in the church to the memory of his father:

". . . . I should be very glad to place some memorial to my father in the church which you are restoring in Staunton. Perhaps you would do me the kindness to tell me the probable cost of a modest bronze tablet to his memory. I would be very glad indeed to supply the inscription if you think there is an appropriate place in which to place it."

Thursday, June 14th.

At three o'clock the President and Mrs. Wilson left for the Monument Grounds, where the President was scheduled to speak at the Flag Day exercises. A tremendous crowd had assembled for the ceremonies, but a severe rain and hail storm sent them to shelter, only about a thousand remaining to hear the address. He wrote Colonel House the next day: ". . . . I delivered the speech in a downpour of rain to a patient audience standing in the wet under dripping umbrellas. . . ." The address was a statement of why we were in the war—one of the most impassioned the President had so far made:

". . . . The war was begun by the military masters of Germany, who proved to be also the masters of Austria-Hungary. . . .

"Their plan was to throw a broad belt of German military power and political control across the very center of Europe and beyond the Mediterranean into the heart of Asia . . .

"If they fail, their people will thrust them aside . . . if they fail Germany is saved and the world will be at peace. If they succeed, America will fall within the menace. . . .

"For us there is but one choice. We have made it. Woe be to the man or group of men that seeks to stand in our way. . . ."[1]

The first American troops sailed for Europe.[2]
Senator Reed made a violent attack on the Lever food bill in the Senate, calling it "vicious and unconstitutional."

[1]*Public Papers*, Vol. V, pp. 60–67 for entire address.
[2]Daniels, *Our Navy at War*, p. 71.

The Committee on Public Information stated publicly that while 99 per cent of the papers in the country were observing the voluntary censorship scrupulously, one per cent were not doing so. A new appeal was made for the suppression of information regarding train and troop movements.[1]

To James L. Davidson, secretary of the Alabama Coal Operators' Association, who had telegraphed that organizers of the United Mine Workers of America were agitating among the open-shop coal miners of Alabama, asserting that their activities were approved by the government and Congress, and, by implication, the President. The President had turned this message over to Secretary Wilson, who replied on June 9th:

". . . . The desire of workers to organize will undoubtedly manifest itself more strongly during the period of industrial activity growing out of the war than at other times. It would be folly, in my judgment, to undertake to repress it. It would be screwing down the safety valve to the point where an explosion would be almost certain. . . .":

"I have read with a great deal of interest and solicitude your telegram relative to the activities of the representatives of the United Mine Workers of America in attempting to organize the coal miners of Alabama. In the absence of more definite information than is contained in your communication as to the exact language used by these men, I do not feel justified in commenting on their attitude. Of course, however, it should be definitely understood that the administration is not engaged in directing or suggesting the organization of either capital or labor, except in so far as may be necessary to coordinate their energies for the promotion of the public welfare.

"It is very generally acknowledged that our laws and the long established policy of our Government recognize the right of workingmen to organize unions if they so desire, just as we recognize the right of capital to organize co-partnerships and corporations. In so organizing each

[1]New York *Times*, June 15, 1917.

is exercising a natural and legal right. When, negotiating with each other in the exercise of these rights, they come to a disagreement concerning the terms of employment, which threatens to cause a stoppage of work, the rest of the public is interested in an adjustment of their differences, because the conflict may interfere with the supplies needed for the sustenance of the people, or the safety of our institutions.

"Congress has consequently created mediation agencies which may be utilized to bring about a mutually satisfactory adjustment of disputes of this character, and I am sure the Department of Labor, which is entrusted with the administration of this work, would be glad to use its good offices in endeavoring to find a common ground acceptable to both sides if any situation develops which is likely to interfere with the production of coal. May I not venture to express the hope, however, that the operators and miners in Alabama may be actuated by a common purpose in the present emergency and both exhibit that fine spirit of cooperation which is so essential for the common defense to the end that the greatest measure of production shall be secured without the need of calling upon the mediation agencies of the Government?"

To his secretary, Tumulty, who reported to the President that Senator Newlands had called that morning in regard to a conference which he and Senators Cummins, Robinson and Kellogg had had with Senators Smith of Georgia, Reed and Hardwick in the hope of adjusting differences on the Priorities bill. The opponents of the bill had suggested substituting the Interstate Commerce Commission rather than the President as the authorized power for dealing with priorities. All had agreed but Newlands, who wanted to know the President's point of view:

"I don't like to handle this matter directly, but I would be very much obliged if you would get Senator Newlands on the telephone and tell him that I consider any suggestions that come from the Senators whose names I have underscored on this memorandum[1] as distinctly hostile, and I should be very much chagrined and disappointed if their suggestions were acted upon, because I believe them to be intended to prevent the very things that are now absolutely necessary. I believe that the granting of the power suggested direct to the Executive is the only wise and feasible thing that can be done in the existing circumstances.

"Please, at the same time, explain to the Senator that my not seeing him this morning was due to the fact that I was so engaged that it was not possible to reach me in time to make the engagement.

"(I think on the whole I had better not be mixed up in these negotiations.)"[2]

Friday, June 15th.

Morning appointments: Senator Martin of Virginia, Senator Gore of Oklahoma, both in regard to the Food bill. After luncheon Frederic C. Penfield, ambassador to Austria-Hungary, called; and at 2:30 the cabinet met. Late-afternoon appointments: Representative Kelly of Pennsylvania; Representative Kahn of California; Senators Hollis of New Hampshire and Kenyon of Iowa, who called upon their own initiative to express their hope that the food legislation would be expedited; George Creel. Sometime during the day the President signed the War Budget bill[3] and the Espionage bill, which had finally passed without the censorship provision to which the press had objected.

The Liberty Loan campaign closed with an oversubscription of more than a billion dollars.[4]

---

[1] The underscored names were Smith of Georgia, Reed and Hardwick.

[2] Next day the Senate passed the bill without the amendment to which the President objected.

[3] Frederick Palmer, commenting upon the passage of the bill, writes: "On June 15, after the War Department had carried on its gigantic operations for ten weeks on thirty millions of dollars, the Appropriation Bill was passed. Baker and his associates . . . were out of danger of jail for spending money without authority. . . ." *Newton D. Baker*, Vol. I, p. 247.

[4] McAdoo, *Crowded Years*, p. 391.

France, Great Britain and Russia announced the raising of the Greek blockade and the purpose of the Entente Powers to safeguard the freedom of Greece.

The Japanese ambassador again called on Secretary Lansing, and read aloud a communication which, he said, was "not to be considered a document." It began: "That Japan has special and close relations, political as well as economic, with China, is well and has long been understood by the American Government. In a note dated March 13, 1915, addressed to Viscount Chinda, my predecessor, by Mr. Bryan, the then Secretary of State, he recognized this state of affairs and declared that the activity of Americans in China had never been political[1]. . . . with regard to the recent important representations made by the American Government to the Chinese Government relative to the political situation in China without previously consulting Japan, the Japanese Government does not entertain the slightest doubt as to the fair and unselfish motives of the United States Government. . . ."

However, the note continued, a "feeling of uneasiness" had been set up in the minds of some of the Japanese people. ". . . . In such circumstance, the Japanese Government believes that if the United States Government sees its way by some appropriate means to confirming the statement made by Mr. Bryan and clearly reasserting its friendly attitude toward Japan in respect of Chinese problems, it would leave a good impression on the minds of the Japanese public . . ." Lansing sent the President a copy of this message on June 30th.[2]

To Colonel House:

". . . . I hope you liked yesterday's speech. I was very much delayed in getting at the composition of it and so did not have a chance to let you see it beforehand. I do not think it contains anything to which our Associates in the war (so I will call them) could object. . . ."[3]

---

[1]For Bryan's statement, see *Foreign Relations*, 1915, pp. 105-111.

[2]*Ibid.*, 1917, p. 259. See also this volume, p. 144.

[3]House had written the day before—a letter which the President had evidently not

Secretary Tumulty to J. D. Moriarity, a letter in regard to the exemption boards. The wording strongly suggests that it was dictated by the President:

". . . . These boards when constituted by the President will be given a great power over the lives and fortunes of these young men who apply for exemption. The exercise of this responsibility is so tremendous that the Government should seek out and select for these positions, regardless of politics, men to whose conduct there will attach not the slightest taint of suspicion of personal interest of any kind. The duty these men will be called upon to perform is so exalted in its character that the injection of politics into their selection would be resented in the most emphatic manner by the people of the country. The impression ought not for a moment to gain root that any political influence even of the smallest kind has played a part in the selection of the members of these important boards. It would be a scandal of the deepest kind if any member of this Administration or their friends could have it to say that his influence in any way had played a part in the selection of the members of these boards. The people of this country are willing to make great sacrifices in blood and treasure for the vindication of the cause which has irresistibly swept America into this war, but they will turn away from and despise those in authority who use their power for selfish ends. . . ."

---

received: "I can hardly express the pleasure your speech of to-day has given me. It has stirred me more than anything you have ever done.

"For two years or more I have wanted some one high up in the Allied governments to arraign Germany as she deserved. You have done it, and done it so well that she will be centuries freeing herself from the indictment you have made. . . ."

And he wrote again on the 15th, telling of the enthusiastic reception of the address, and adding:

". . . . While, of course, you will not want to make another speech of this kind soon, yet when it is necessary, what do you think of challenging Germany to state her peace terms in the open as the other nations have? She should be driven into a corner and made to express her willingness to accept such a peace as the United States, Russia and even England have indicated a willingness to accept, or put herself in the position of continuing the war for the purpose of conquest."

Saturday, June 16th.

The President had a short conference with Secretary Baker at 12 o'clock, and at 12:30 he received Lord Northcliffe,[1] who was accompanied by Assistant Secretary Phillips.

The Senate Committee on Agriculture reported, without recommendation, a bill identical with the Lever food bill, the action being taken in accordance with the President's expressed desire.

To E. P. V. Ritter of the Merchants' and Manufacturers' Exchange in New York:

"In reply to your letter . . . allow me to say that I not only see no reason why commercial conventions should be omitted during the war, but should regret to see any instrumentality neglected which has proved serviceable in stimulating business and facilitating its processes. This is not only not a time to allow any slowing up of business, but is a time when every sensible process of stimulation should be used."

To B. M. Baruch of the Council of National Defense, enclosing a letter from F. N. Hoffstot, president of the Pressed Steel Car Company, discussing the steel situation in the country, and the need for a Priority Board:

"Would you be generous enough to suggest to me what sort of an answer should be returned to the enclosed?"[2]

Sunday, June 17th.

The President and Mrs. Wilson went to the Central Presbyterian Church in the morning. In the afternoon they took a trip down the river on the *Mayflower*, returning to the White House about 10 o'clock in the evening.

---

[1]Colonel House wrote on the 19th: ". . . you charmed Northcliffe in your few minutes talk with him the other day. I have heard from many directions of his enthusiastic praise of you. You seem to have been a revelation to him.

"I am glad you treated him so kindly for he has shown a desire to work in harmony with everyone."

[2]Baruch, upon whom the President, as the war advanced, leaned heavily for advice, replied on the 19th saying that he thought Hoffstot's letter "very much to the point."

Secretary Baker, in a public statement, said: "The War
Department is behind the aircraft plans with every ounce
of energy and enthusiasm at its command. The aircraft
program seems by all means the most effective way in
which to exert America's force at once in telling fashion. . . ."[1]

A Belgian Commission arrived in Washington.

Controversy in the Shipping Board was reported in the press.

Elihu Root telegraphed from Russia, reporting the prevalence
of German propaganda there, and the lack of military
discipline; and asking funds for a campaign to strengthen
the army morale.[2]

Haiti severed relations with Germany.

The week ending June 17th showed the third largest total of
ships sunk since the beginning of the submarine warfare.

A mass meeting in London passed resolutions demanding
immediate reprisals on Germany for recent air raids over
London.

Monday, June 18th.

The President worked in his study until 12:30, when he
received Senator Simmons of North Carolina. At 2 o'clock the
President received the Belgian Commission and made a short
address. ". . . there is not one among us who does not to-day
welcome the opportunity of expressing to you our heartfelt
sympathy and friendship, and our solemn determination that
on the inevitable day of victory Belgium shall be restored to the
place she has so richly won among the self-respecting and
respected nations of the earth."[3] Other afternoon appointments: John Franklin Fort of the Federal Trade Commission;
William Denman of the Shipping Board; members of the
Federal Trade Commission; Senator Johnson of South Dakota.
In the evening President and Mrs. Wilson gave a dinner in
honor of the Belgian Commission. "Covers for 71."

Minister Egan telegraphed from Denmark, quoting the text
of the German "reply to President Wilson's note to Russia

[1]*Official Bulletin*, June 18, 1917. House wrote the President, the same day, saying
that the United States should "overwhelm the enemy by superiority in the air."
". . . . If you will give the word, and will stand for an appropriation of one billion
dollars, the thing is done. . . ."

[2]*Foreign Relations*, 1918, *Russia*, Vol. I, pp. 120–122.

[3]*Public Papers*, Vol. V, p. 68.

printed in the *Norddeutsche Allgemeine Zeitung*, June 16."
The President was charged with a change of front on the
question of war aims, and it was asked "Whence . . .
came so suddenly" his knowledge of Germany's years of
intrigue.[1] ". . . . Most especially however we would like
to recommend to President Wilson that he . . . look into
the agreements of his allies in which the members of the
Entente Cordiale assure to each other their respective war
winnings. . . ."[2]

To Secretary Redfield:

"The suggestion has been made to me that by keeping
open the vocational training schools of the country during
the summer, it will be possible to train a large number of
young men under military age either to fill the places in
our industries of men who may enlist or be withdrawn for
the military services or to carry on special occupations
called for by the war, such, for example, as inspectors of
material and apparatus. At the same time, it would be
possible to give to many men intensive training of such
kind as would enhance their productiveness in industry.

"It is pointed out to me that a large number of educational plants, which would otherwise be idle for about
three months, may thus be made immediately productive
to the country and helpful to our young men.

"The suggestion is a patriotic one and I appreciate that
it will involve sacrifices of time on the part of both teachers
and students. The plan promises, however, so much of

[1] A reference to his Flag Day address. The President had said, in May, 1916:
". . . . With its [the war's] causes and its objects we are not concerned. The obscure
fountains from which its stupendous flood has burst forth we are not interested to
search for or explore. . . ." *Public Papers*, Vol. IV, p. 184. And in October: ". . . . Have
you ever heard what started the present war? If you have, I wish you would publish
it, because nobody else has, so far as I can gather. Nothing in particular started it,
but everything in general. . . ." *Ibid.*, p. 381.

[2] The "reply" continued: "He will find that . . . France, and with France, England,
has promised Constantinople to Russia and as a return Russia has promised to France
not only Alsace-Lorraine but the left bank of the Rhine as well. He will further find
that the Entente Cordiale has formulated a complete plan for the division of Asia
Minor, the detailed settlement of which . . . is still causing difficulties. . . ." See, for
entire message, *Foreign Relations*, 1917, Supp. 2, Vol. I, pp. 104–106.

helpfulness to the country under present conditions that I shall be glad if it can be carried into effect."

To Secretary Daniels,[1] enclosing a telegram from Gavin McNab in regard to the oil situation in California:

"I know, not only from the enclosed telegram but from other sources, how serious the situation which this telegram refers to has become, and I would very much like your advice as to the means of relieving the situation, if there be any, and relieving the state without going too far in opening the door to those who have been trying to get a foothold in the oil fields in a way we cannot approve or sanction."

To Secretary McAdoo:

MY DEAR MAC:

If a fellow wants a particular form of bond (say, for example, I want ten $1,000 bonds in the coupon form), to whom should he express his preference, or is he permitted to express it?

Affectionately yours,

WOODROW WILSON[2]

To Representative William P. Borland of Missouri, who had asked for a word from the President, in view of the fact that "a special effort has been made in the central West to forestall by attack and misrepresentation the benefits of any adequate method of food control.":

"You are quite right about the Food Administration measure. In my opinion, it is one of the most important and most imperatively necessary of the measures which have been proposed in connection with the war.

"A certain disservice has been done the measure by speaking of it as the Food Control Bill. The object of the

---

[1] Same letter also to Attorney General Gregory and Secretary Lane.

[2] McAdoo replied that he would see that the President's wishes were carried out.

measure is not to control the food of the country but to release it from the control of speculators and other persons who will seek to make inordinate profits out of it, and to protect the people against the extortions which would result. It seems to me that those who oppose the measure ought very seriously to consider whether they are not playing into the hands of such persons and whether they are not making themselves responsible, should they succeed, for the extraordinary and oppressive price of food in the United States. Foodstuffs will, of course, inevitably be high, but it is possible by perfectly legitimate means to keep them from being unreasonably and oppressively high.

"I hope and believe that the Congress will see the measure in this light, and that it will come to an early passage. For time is of the essence. The legislation should be secured by the first of July to make the country safe against the dangers it is meant to guard against."

Tuesday, June 19th.

The President remained in his study until noon. Before the cabinet meeting he received a committee of the Presbyterian General Assembly. Late-afternoon appointments: the Prince of Udine, head of the Italian Commission; George Creel.

> Secretary Baker and Samuel Gompers signed an agreement for the creation of an "adjustment commission of three persons, appointed by the Secretary of War; one to represent the Army, one the public, and one labor; the last to be nominated by Samuel Gompers."[1]

The Russian Mission arrived in Washington.

---

[1]See Palmer, *Newton D. Baker*, Vol. I, p. 262. On the 18th Baker had written to the President: "Mr. Justice Brandeis has spent two evenings talking with me about the general labor situation throughout the country and feels very strongly that, as our munitions contracting business, both on our own account and that of the Allies, increases in volume, very special arrangements will have to be made to prevent the labor conditions from being lost sight of in the agitation for hurried quantity production.

"Justice Brandeis, as you may know, has determined to remain in Washington over the summer so as to be available for any help he can give to any of us who are dealing with labor problems. . . ."

To Secretary Daniels, who had written on the 18th discussing the high price of steel and suggesting that the price the government should pay ought to be fixed by the Federal Trade Commission. At his suggestion, he added, the commission was already working out a price for coal and oil, and he thought it would be necessary to pursue the same course with "all the larger items which must be bought by the Government, or some other course having relation to the cost of production.":

"Thank you very much for your letter about the steel prices. I hardly know how to spell the word!"

Wednesday, June 20th.

After an early-morning horseback ride with Mrs. Wilson and Dr. Grayson, the President worked in his study until 12:30, when he received the Russian Commission, headed by Boris A. Bakhmeteff, and presented by Secretary Lansing.[1] Afternoon appointments: Senator Atlee Pomerene of Ohio, who discussed federal control of the coal industry; Senator John Sharp Williams of Mississippi; Raymond B. Stevens of the Shipping Board; Senator Shafroth of Colorado. In the late afternoon the President and Mrs. Wilson took a short drive, as was their daily custom at this time.

> Ambassador Page telegraphed from London a report for the President and the Secretary of State headed "Personal. Very confidential," as to the crisis created by the submarine menace. ". . . . It is the most serious situation that has confronted the Allies since the battle of the Marne."[2]
> Admiral Sims telegraphed Secretary Daniels: "The immediate dispatch to this area of all possible destroyers and anti-

---

[1]When the members of the commission reached the White House gates they were confronted by a large suffrage banner:

"President Wilson and Envoy Root are deceiving Russia. They say 'We are a democracy. Help us win the war so that democracies may survive.'

"We women of America tell you that America is not a democracy. Twenty million women are denied the right to vote. President Wilson is the chief opponent of their national enfranchisement.

"Help us make this nation really free. Tell our government that it must liberate its people before it can claim free Russia as an ally."

Bystanders at once tore down the banner. I. H. Irwin, *The Story of the Woman's Party*, p. 208.

[2]*Foreign Relations*, 1917, Supp. 2, Vol. I, pp. 106–107.

submarine craft of any description is mandatory if the submarine issue is to be effectively met. . . ."[1]
Howard Coffin, chairman of the Aircraft Production Board, announced that automobile, sewing-machine and typewriter plants, as well as machine shops, would be pressed into service to turn out airplane engines.
Italian troops resumed the offensive in the Trentino.

To R. Langton Douglas of the National Gallery of Ireland, in response to a cablegram requesting the President to sit for a portrait by Sargent, to be owned by the National Gallery:

"My delay in replying to the generous suggestion of the Board of Governors . . . has been due entirely to my doubt as to whether I could at this particular time afford Mr. Sargent sufficient opportunity to paint my portrait.

"The suggestion of the Board of Governors . . . has gratified me very deeply. I would be very proud indeed to have a portrait of myself by so eminent an artist as Mr. Sargent placed in the National Gallery of Ireland, and I am sincerely desirous of affording Mr. Sargent an opportunity to make the portrait. I am sorry to say I shall have to delay the decision in order to see whether after the adjournment of the present session of the Congress I may not command sufficient leisure to make the necessary arrangements for sittings.

"With warm appreciation and many apologies for my delay in replying . . ."

Thursday, June 21st.

William J. Bryan, former Secretary of State, called upon the President at noon. Afternoon engagements: Senator Hollis of New Hampshire; the Railroad Brotherhood chiefs; Senators Newlands and Pittman of Nevada; William Denman of the Shipping Board; Senator Kendrick of Wyoming. President and Mrs. Wilson gave a dinner in the evening in honor of the Russian Mission. "Covers for 66 . . . arrangements same as for dinners to other missions."

---

[1]*Naval Investigation Hearings,* 1920, Vol. I, p. 46. This was only one of a number of extremely urgent messages sent by Admiral Sims during this period.

Ambassador Page telegraphed from London that the Prime Minister had that morning discussed with him "the desirability of trying to induce Austria and especially Bulgaria to make separate peace," coming to the conclusion that "under present conditions any effort would be premature in this matter."[1]

Baron Sonnino, Italian Minister of War, said before the Italian Chamber of Deputies: ". . . . The objective for which all our politics are striving and by which all our warfare is being guided is peace, not conquests or imperialism . . . And for a durable peace it is necessary for Italy to have assurance of frontiers according to nationality, a condition which is indispensable to its effective independence. . . ."[2]

To Secretary Baker, who had written that the Aircraft Production Board of the Council of National Defense had been working in association with General Squier of the army, Admiral Taylor of the navy, and the air personnel of both departments. ". . . they have reached the conclusion that perhaps America's most speedy and effective contribution to the Allied cause from a military point of view will be the complete and unquestioned supremacy of the air. . . .

"The General Staff has had the advantage of constant consultation with the English and French air experts who accompanied their respective missions and remained to work out the details of their proposed work. Before presenting the matter to the two Houses of Congress, I beg leave to submit the matter to you for your approval, which I recommend be given."

". . . I am entirely willing to back up such a programme as you suggest. I hope that you will present it in the strongest possible way to the proper committees of the Congress."

Friday, June 22nd.

After his morning horseback ride the President worked in his study until 12:30 when he received the ambassador from Brazil. After the regular cabinet meeting, General Goethals called for

[1]*Foreign Relations*, 1917, Supp. 2, Vol. I, p. 108.

[2]*Current History*, August, 1917, p. 263.

a long conference. Nothing was given out about the interview, but New York *Times* headlines the following day read: "WILSON UPHOLDS GOETHALS IN ROW OVER STEEL SHIPS."[1]

The President established an Exports Council.[2]

Ambassador Page wrote the President a long letter, by hand, suggesting that the United States might well be represented at the war conferences which the Allies held from time to time, if for nothing else, to get a clear insight into the controversies and difficulties under the surface—"the special ambitions for territory of practically every continental Ally, which of course conflict, the commitments of England herself to some of them, made to get them or to keep them in the war."[3]

Admiral Sims telegraphed that the British Admiralty had now adopted the convoy system "and will put it into effect as fast as ships can be obtained for high-sea convoy against raiders and destroyers for escort duty in submarine zone. . . ."[4]

To Mrs. Francis B. Sayre, who had just moved from Williamstown to Nantucket to spend the summer, while her husband was abroad as a Y.M.C.A. worker with the American troops:

"MY DARLING DAUGHTER:

"Thank you with all my heart for your letter from Siasconset. It eased my heart not a little, and along with it came a letter from Frank in New York which spoke of the arrangements he has been making for the summer, which look as if they were satisfactory as far as one can

---

[1] Differences between Goethals and Denman in regard to the shipbuilding program were becoming serious. On the 15th Goethals had urged the President to put the task in the hands of one man. A few days later he had approached the President again, through Lincoln Colcord, Dr. Mezes and Colonel House. House wrote: ". . . . Denman and Goethals are both positive characters and I am afraid are too much alike to ever work in harmony. Is it not possible to divide their authority so as to avoid conflict?" And on the 21st Denman discussed the whole controversy in a letter to the President.

[2] *Foreign Relations,* 1917, Supp. 2, Vol. II, pp. 883–884. This was superseded, on August 21st, by an Exports Administrative Board, and an Exports Council. See this volume, p. 228.

[3] From original copy in Mr. Wilson's files. Published in *The Life and Letters of Walter H. Page,* Vol. III, pp. 381–385.

[4] *Naval Investigation Hearings,* 1920, Vol. II, p. 2162.

judge from this distance. At any rate, I am quite willing to trust his choice.

"It is delightful to think of you and the little ones successfully transplanted to that quiet place. My heart longs to come up and be with you all, but apparently that is something I must not allow myself to hope for even.

"Do let us know, my dear girlie, from time to time how you are all faring, because our hearts will wait anxiously for news. We are all well, over head and ears in work of course but keeping our heads above water by hard swimming. Edith and I have resumed horseback riding and I am sure it is going to do both of us a great deal of good.

"I dare say you heard of the fracas raised by the representatives of the Woman's Party here at the gates of the White House. They certainly seem bent upon making their cause as obnoxious as possible.

"It was indeed a delight to see you and Frank, and the only trouble of it was that it was too short. Nell was quite broken-hearted that she was not here to see you. Mac is overworking himself as usual and the dear girl is very anxious, but I am depending on Mac's extraordinary powers of recovery. He seems tough in spite of his high-strung nerves.

"All unite in sending you and the little ones and Frank messages full to overflowing with love.

"Lovingly yours,"

Saturday, June 23rd.

At noon the President went to the office of the Federal Trade Commission for a conference as to the fixing of prices, particularly coal. The commission members favored determining upon a "uniform average price by means of a government pool." There were no luncheon guests, and no official engagements for the rest of the day. President and Mrs. Wilson drove for two hours in the afternoon, going later to a garden party given by Secretary and Mrs. Lansing in honor of the Belgian Mission, in the grounds of the Pan-American Building.

After a bitter debate, the Food bill passed the House of Representatives, 365–5, with a drastic amendment prohibiting, with certain exceptions, further use of food materials in the manufacture of intoxicating liquors during the war and authorizing the President to commandeer existing stocks of distilled spirits.

Sunday, June 24th.

After attending service at the First Presbyterian Church, the President and Mrs. Wilson were driven to the Navy Yard, where they boarded the *Sylph* for a trip down the river. Dr. E. P. Davis of Philadelphia, one of the President's old friends, accompanied them.

Secretary Daniels telegraphed Admiral Sims that all anti-submarine craft which could be spared from the home waters would be sent; that the question of supplying additional naval forces of types other than anti-submarine craft would be considered; that the construction of the type of destroyer recommended by Admiral Sims would be pushed.[1]

Monday, June 25th.

During the afternoon the President conferred with: Dr. M. A. Matthews; Secretary Lane and ex-President Taft, on Red Cross business; Senator Lewis of Illinois; Secretary McAdoo. President and Mrs. Wilson received Mr. and Mrs. Doheny of California in the late afternoon. Evening at Keith's.

The President made public a statement in explanation of the creation of an Exports Council. ". . . . The whole object will be to direct exports in such a way that they will go first and by preference where they are most needed and most immediately needed, and temporarily to withhold them, if necessary, where they can best be spared. . . ."[2]

To Secretary McAdoo, who had suggested W. C. Adamson of Georgia for the Interstate Commerce Commission:

[1] A general answer to a number of Admiral Sims's letters and cablegrams, the message covered several subjects. See *Naval Investigation Hearings,* 1920, Vol. I, pp. 48–49. (Date of sending unknown; received June 24th.)

[2] See this volume, p. 124; also *Public Papers,* Vol. V, pp. 69–70.

"Thank you for your letter about Judge Adamson. My only doubt about appointing him . . . is his age. He is sixty-three years old, and I have been fighting off all appointments of men over sixty. The appointment is for seven years, as you know, and the Judge would be seventy when his first term ended."[1]

To Secretary McAdoo, who had asked the President's approval of his plan to call a conference of the leading life insurance companies for discussion of the question of insuring the lives of the officers and men of the army and navy. ". . . . If, as a result of that conference, a satisfactory plan is not devised . . . we can consider seriously enlarging the present War Risk Insurance Bureau to perform this service. . . .":

"Thank you for your letter . . . I am glad that you think there is a possibility of a satisfactory solution of the question of insurance for the men in the Army and Navy and that you are taking it up with a prospect of finding one."[2]

To Senator Key Pittman, who had written that he had never been invited to any of the official entertainments at the White House other than the regular public receptions, and that it was becoming noticeable to his constituents:

"Of course, I understand your letter . . . and I hope I may say equally of course I know that you understand that any omission such as you refer to was due to anything but my own choice as to dinner companions and those whom I would prefer to honor. You may be sure that the suggestion of your letter is well lodged and jumps with my inclination."

To his secretary, Tumulty, who had presented Representative La Guardia's request for the President's opinion on a resolution

---

[1] On the 29th the President wrote to Representative T. W. Sims. ". . . I am . . . thoroughly convinced myself of Judge Adamson's high character and ability. I am struggling with a very complicated problem in the matter of appointments to the Interstate Commerce Commission . . ."

[2] The conference met on July 2nd. For Secretary McAdoo's report to the President on the 3rd, see Synon, *McAdoo,* pp. 299–302.

he had introduced in the House, calling upon the President to designate a day for contributions for the relief of the Russians:

"I would be very much obliged to you if you would write to Mr. La Guardia and say that the embarrassment is this: The cases he names[1] are the cases of nations that have been conquered or overrun and are not in charge of their own affairs. The case of the Russian people constitutes a very different matter and I doubt if what he suggests could be done without serious risk of offending the sensibilities of a great free people who are surely ready and willing to take care of their own."

Tuesday, June 26th.

Before the cabinet meeting the President received a commission from Panama. Further afternoon appointments: Senators Ransdell and Broussard of Louisiana "and others"; Lincoln Steffens; John Franklin Fort and Joseph E. Davies, of the Federal Trade Commission. Late in the evening President and Mrs. Wilson appeared at the reception to the Russian Mission, in the Pan-American Building, where the President evidently had a talk with Sir William Wiseman.[2]

The police patrol of the White House was increased because of suffragette disturbances; arrests were made, but the women were subsequently released on bail.

Whistles of harbor craft mingled with cheers from thousands lining the shore greeted the first American troop transport as it steamed into the harbor of St. Nazaire.

To Secretary Baker, who had written of a cablegram from Governor General Harrison of the Philippines, offering the President one infantry division. This offer, Baker thought, was "indicative of the fine spirit of the Filipino people which has

---

[1]La Guardia had said that the text of his resolution followed that of the Lithuanian, Polish, Armenian and Jewish Day resolutions.

[2]Colonel House wrote the President the next day: "I am glad you were so gracious to Sir William last night. You have made him very happy. It is important that he should be able to say that he has met you because he goes to England in about two weeks. . . ."

been shown in many ways since the entry of the United States into the present war.":

"I feel as you do that the offer of troops from the Philippines is a very significant and admirable thing, and I am glad you are laying the matter before the Senate Committee on Military Affairs so that the law may permit our accepting the services of these troops."

Wednesday, June 27th.

At noon the President walked over to the Commerce Building to see Secretary Redfield. Vance McCormick and J. A. Wilson of Pennsylvania were guests at luncheon. Afternoon appointments: Samuel Gompers; a committee of the Southern Baptist Convention; Senator Owen of Oklahoma; Representative Phelan of Massachusetts.

The President called on members of the Sunday schools of the country for contributions to the Red Cross.

Secretary Lansing to Elihu Root: ".... The President, while extending his congratulations to the commission on the skillful manner in which they are performing a difficult task, suggests that it is not advisable for members of the commission to speak of the terms of peace or of settlement which will be insisted on by the United States. The President is himself reserving all such utterances until very different circumstances arise, and hopes that you will pursue the same policy. ..."[1]

Chargé Wheeler in Tokyo telegraphed Secretary Lansing, that the Japanese Premier and Minister for Foreign Affairs, on June 26th, in reply to a question in the Diet "whether any pledge had been secured looking to retention by Japan of Tsingtao and the islands taken from Germany," had stated "that the Japanese Government had taken properly effective measures to protect Japan's rights and interests in Shantung and the Southern Islands . . ." He concluded: "Am very confident that upon restoration of peace the Allied powers will not object to such arrangements as

---

[1] *Foreign Relations*, 1918, *Russia*, Vol. I, p. 127.

Japan will deem necessary in order to ensure peace in the Orient."[1]

Ambassador Page telegraphed from London: ". . . . Sims sends me . . . the most alarming reports of the submarine situation which are confirmed by the Admiralty here. He says that the war will be won or lost in this submarine zone within a few months. Time is the essence of the problem and anti-submarine craft which cannot be assembled in the submarine zone almost immediately may come too late. . . ."[2]

To Louis Seibold of the New York *World*, a letter written at Tumulty's suggestion:

MY DEAR SEIBOLD,

I have been beyond measure distressed to hear that someone told you that I had said that I regarded you as a reactionary and that you no longer had my confidence. Of course, that is absolutely false. My feeling towards you has never changed in the least or my confidence in your character and your principles. I have from time to time been distressed when you have seemed in your articles to be opposed to measures I thought essential for the defense and safety of the country, but I am not the sort to change my opinion of a man I know because he opposed me, and the only reason I did not arrange for the appointment you asked for was a reason which you will readily understand. The fact is I am so desperately pressed that unless an appointment is absolutely necessary I postpone it from day to day in the vain hope of finding a free interval. You know, besides, how awkward it is for me to arrange one such interview, no matter what my feeling for the man involved may be, without creating the expectation that I will see other newspaper men of unusual importance when they are in Washington.

Please, my dear Seibold, believe things only that are

[1] *Foreign Relations,* 1917, Supp. 1, p. 452.
[2] *Ibid.,* 1917, Supp. 2, Vol. I, pp. 111–112.

credible, and whenever you hear anything such as I have alluded to please let me know immediately.

With the warmest cordiality,

Your sincere friend,

WOODROW WILSON

To Representative James A. Frear, a Republican member of the House Committee on Rivers and Harbors, who had written that the River and Harbor bill might fail if it was "pressed for passage in its present form." Within the week the President had received a letter from Representative J. H. Small, chairman of the committee, giving the status of the bill in the House, the necessity for its passage, and the unfortunate character of the opposition to it:

". . . . I regard the passage of some bill for river and harbor improvement at this time as of paramount importance. In my judgment it is imperatively necessary.

"By reason of the World War now raging and other causes, the traffic of our railroads is very much congested. Leading railroad officials admit that the railways of the United States, taxed as they are to their uttermost capacity, are unable to carry the commerce of our country. . . .

"In Germany, France, Austria-Hungary, Italy and to some extent in Great Britain, the freight congestion is relieved largely by inland waterway transportation. . . . There is this further to be said: Before long our railways must carry large bodies of our own troops with their equipment toward the seaboard which will still further aggravate the congestion of freight which now exists here. It seems to me that we should take every necessary step possible to supplement railway freight carriage by inland waterway transportation.

"As you know, under the Constitution I have no authority to veto separate items in any bill, appropriation bills or others. As I have not this authority, you can readily understand that the indication by the Executive of disapproval of any item contained in any bill would be extra-Constitutional and to say the least improper. Of course, I am anxious that every wasteful or extravagant item, if there are any such, should be eliminated from the pending bill before its passage and, should it pass, before action is taken thereon by me, I will take counsel of the Secretary of War and the Chief of Engineers of the Army as to its details. In this connection I trust I may be pardoned for saying that I would be very much pleased if the provision creating the Waterways Commission should be retained in the bill. I regard this as of the utmost importance. If created, to this Commission should be referred all projects for the improvement of inland waterways and other instrumentalities in order that waste may in the future be avoided and that there may exist a coordinated scientific system of waterway improvement and that means may be devised to relieve the growing freight congestion which now exists to plague us. The conditions which now obtain in this regard in my opinion will not end with the war. Our commerce in the recent past grew with astonishing rapidity and I believe that in the future it will grow and expand by leaps and bounds. . . ."[1]

To his secretary, Tumulty, who had called the President's attention to the suggestion of Allan L. Benson, who had been the Socialist candidate for President in 1916, that he, Benson, cable Philip Scheidemann, German Socialist, that as soon as the German people had elected peace commissioners, the American Socialist party would do its utmost to create sentiment looking toward peace negotiations:

"I am very much obliged to Mr. Benson for having made this inquiry and wish you would convey to him with my sincere compliments my opinion that it is not wise to take any further steps in this direction at present. I am

---

[1]Representative Frear reported to the President on the 30th that on the very morning when the President wrote his letter (the 27th) the House had passed the River and Harbor bill "with the strongest protest ever recorded in the House, counting pairs."

afraid it would complicate and embitter the situation rather than clarify it."

Thursday, June 28th.

Samuel Gompers called at the White House before luncheon. In the early afternoon the President attended the ceremony unveiling a statue of Robert Emmet at the National Museum. He returned in time to receive Senator Phelan of California at 3:40; and a little later Prince Udine and four members of the Italian Mission.

A conference of coal operators in Washington adopted a resolution authorizing a committee of operators to confer with a government committee (Secretary Lane, for the Council of National Defense, John Franklin Fort, for the Federal Trade Commission, and F. S. Peabody, for the Committee on Coal Production of the Council of National Defense) as to means of stimulating production and assuring adequate distribution; and to fix a price for coal; a temporary maximum price for bituminous coal was set to apply until the necessary studies could be made.

This action caused a great disturbance in administration circles and the temporary price was repudiated by Baker on June 30th.[1]

Ambassador Page telegraphed from London, a message marked "Greatest Urgency," and "Wholly confidential for the President and the Secretary of State and Secretary of the Treasury"[2]: "Mr. Balfour asked me to a conference at 7 o'clock with him, the Chancellor of the Exchequer and their financial advisers. It was disclosed that financial disaster to all the European Allies is imminent unless the United States Government advances to the British enough money to pay for British purchases in the United States as they fall due.

"Bonar Law reports that only half enough has been advanced for June and that the British agents in the United States now have enough money to keep the exchange up for only one day more. If exchange with England fall, exchange with all European Allies also will im-

---

[1] This volume, pp. 136–138.
[2] See *The Life and Letters of Walter H. Page*, Vol. III, p. 393.

mediately fall and there will be a general collapse. Balfour understood that in addition to our other loans and our loans to France and Italy, we would advance to England enough to pay for all purchases by the British Government made in the United States. He authorizes me to say that they are now on the brink of a precipice and unless immediate help be given financial collapse will follow. He is sending an explanatory telegram to Spring Rice.

"I am convinced that these men are not overstating their case. Unless we come to their rescue we are all in danger of disaster. Great Britain will have to abandon the gold standard."[1]

To Secretary McAdoo:

MY DEAR MAC:

It was mighty kind of you to send us the salmon, and you may be sure it will taste especially good to us because it comes from you.

We all miss you, and our loving thoughts constantly go out to the little family at the Springs.

Affectionately yours,
WOODROW WILSON

To William A. Brady, a letter drafted by George Creel and signed by the President with practically no changes, asking him to organize the motion picture industry in coöperation with the Committee on Public Information:

---

[1]*Foreign Relations,* 1917, Supp. 2, Vol. I, pp. 532–533. Colonel House wrote the President on the 29th: "Things began to break yesterday afternoon in British quarters. . . .

"Northcliffe received a message from Lloyd-George to come here and advise with me before moving further. He was ready to take the ten o'clock train this morning when I received, through Sir William, the cable from Balfour which I sent you by Lansing [in much the same vein as Page's cable, above. See *Intimate Papers,* Vol. III, p. 101]. I therefore advised Northcliffe to go to Washington immediately rather than come here, which he has done. . . . [Northcliffe saw the President on the 30th. This volume, p. 138.]

"What they [the British] need is $35,000,000. on Monday; $100,000,000. on Thursday and $185,000,000. a month for two months beginning ten days from next Thursday.

"This is a staggering amount and indicates the load Great Britain has been carrying for her allies. . . ." Printed in part, *ibid.,* pp. 102–103.

On the 29th Ambassador Page sent the President a long, handwritten letter telling of the financial panic of the British; and again stressing the critical submarine situation.

"It is in my mind not only to bring the motion picture industry into the fullest and most effective contact with the nation's needs, but to give some measure of official recognition to an increasingly important factor in the development of our national life. The film has come to rank as a very high medium for the dissemination of public intelligence, and since it speaks a universal language it lends itself importantly to the presentation of America's plans and purposes. . . ."

To his secretary, Tumulty, who had presented Herbert Hoover's request for some kind of proclamation from the President making July 1st "Conservation Sunday.":

"My judgment is that this would not be wise. I think that such proclamations tend to advertise an anxiety on our part which it would be easy to misinterpret on the other side of the water. It would, after all, be only a repetition of what I have already said, and for that very reason would seem to me to be open to the misconstruction I have suggested."

Friday, June 29th.

The President received Senator Gerry of Rhode Island at 9:30. At 11 o'clock Senator Martin of Virginia called; according to a news report, Senators Lewis of Illinois and Phelan of California were also at the White House during the morning to discuss the prohibition clause of the Food bill.[1] Representative Hulbert of New York called at 2:15; at 2:30 the cabinet met. The general subject of exports was up for discussion, and the President probably spoke of the desire of the Shipping Board for "coordinate recognition in the formation of the Council on Export Control." Later in the afternoon the President received Rabbi Stephen S. Wise, who outlined plans for an American Jewish Congress. Rabbi Wise was authorized, after the interview, to give out a statement as to the President's interest in the proposal, though he added that a temporary postponement might be necessary "because of the urgency at this time of the public business." In the evening the President

---

[1] New York *Times*, June 30, 1917.

talked with Joseph E. Davies of the Federal Trade Commission, by telephone, in regard to the action of the coal operators the previous day in fixing the price of bituminous coal.

> Greece severed diplomatic relations with the Central Powers.
> Lloyd George, speaking in Glasgow: ". . . . In my judgment the war will come to an end when the allied armies have reached the aims which they set out to attain when they accepted the challenge thrown down by Germany. . . ." The independence of Belgium must be restored, he said. Indemnity would be necessary. Neither Mesopotamia nor Armenia would ever be returned to Turkey. As to the German colonies, that matter would have to be settled by the peace conference. ". . . . When we come to settle who must be the future trustees of those uncivilized lands we must take into account the sentiments of the peoples themselves . . .
>
> "Peace must be framed on so equitable a basis that the nations would not wish to disturb it. . . .
>
> "No one wishes to dictate to the German people the form of government under which they should choose to live. But it is right that we should say that we will enter into negotiations with a free Government of Germany with a different attitude of mind and a different temper and different spirit and with less suspicion and more confidence than we should with a Government whom we feel today to be dominated by the aggressive and arrogant spirit of Prussian militarism. . . ."[1]

To Secretary Baker:

"I am very much distressed about what has been done with regard to agreeing upon a price for coal. The price said to have been agreed upon is clearly too high and I do not think that the government departments would be justified in paying it. It happens to be the particular price upon which charges are at this very time being based by the Department of Justice against the coal dealers.

"I am myself personally embarrassed because I had just had conferences with the Federal Trade Commission

---

[1] *Current History*, August, 1917, pp. 261–263.

which made me hopeful that I might be instrumental in bringing about an understanding which would be in every way more fair and reasonable.

"I would very much value your counsel upon this matter, and I would appreciate it very much if you and your colleagues of the Council of National Defense would keep me in touch with plans of this sort, because unconsciously we are working at cross purposes."[1]

To Reverend James Cannon, Jr., chairman of the Legislative Committee of the Anti-Saloon League of America, a letter written at the suggestion of Senator Martin:

".... I regard the immediate passage of the [Food] bill as of vital consequence to the safety and defense of the nation. Time is of the essence; and yet it has become evident that heated and protracted debate will delay the passage of the bill indefinitely if the provisions affecting the manufacture of beer and wines are retained and insisted upon. In these circumstances I have not hesitated to say to members of the Senate who have been kind enough to consult me that it would undoubtedly be in the public interest in this very critical matter if the friends of those provisions should consent to their elimination from the present measure. Feeling that your Committee is actuated by the same patriotic motives which inspire me, I am confident that these considerations will seem to you, as they seem to me, to be imperative."[2]

---

[1] In the evening John Franklin Fort of the Federal Trade Commission, the Attorney General and the Secretary of Labor met in Secretary Baker's office, at Baker's request, to go over the whole coal matter. Governor Fort, reporting this meeting to the President in a letter the next day, revealed the fact that he had made an effort to guide the conference of operators in the right channels. ".... We recognized when we were fixing these prices that they were high, but the motive was to increase production and throw a large amount of coal on the market as rapidly as possible, and then the matter of supply and demand will reduce the maximum tentative price (in our opinion) very much below the maximum tentative price which we named....

"I think it would be a grievous mistake for any suggestion to be made from any official source, pending the ascertainment of the actual costs of the coal and the fixing of a permanent price, disparaging or criticizing the action already taken...."

[2] Dr. Cannon replied on the 30th expressing a desire to coöperate in winning the war,

Saturday, June 30th.

At noon the Attorney General and Secretary Baker arrived for a conference with the President on the bituminous coal price fixed by the coal operators' conference on the 28th. Gregory was especially perturbed, for, he said, the price fixed during the conference and approved by Secretary Lane as a member of the Council of National Defense, was actually higher than the coal price which had previously been fixed in secret, and for which he then had pending indictments against many of the coal operators! The President said, with some indignation, that he planned to repudiate, publicly, the price fixed. Baker, realizing that such a move would probably force the resignation of Secretary Lane, suggested that he himself, as head of the Council of National Defense, repudiate the price. The President agreed, and Baker wrote out then and there the statement which he planned to publish. The President approved it, and it was given to the press the same day.

At 2 o'clock in the afternoon Lord Northcliffe called in regard to England's desperate need for money; later the President and Mrs. Wilson went to a baseball game for the benefit of the Red Cross.

The President authorized the taking over by the United States of enemy ships within its jurisdiction.[1]

A. J. Balfour telegraphed the President (at the request of Ambassador Page and Admiral Sims) urging that more small ships be sent immediately for war against the submarines.[2]

Instructions governing maritime warfare for the United States navy were issued, marking a sharp distinction between ourselves and the Allies in the matter of naval policy in a number of particulars—definition of contraband, diversion of neutral shipping to ports, detention there for investigation, etc.[3]

---

and the President expressed his appreciation, on July 3rd, of the League's attitude—"a very admirable proof of their patriotic motives."

[1] *Foreign Relations*, 1917, Supp. 2, Vol. II, pp. 1257–1259.

[2] *The Life and Letters of Walter H. Page*, Vol. II, pp. 285–286.

[3] See Savage, *Policy of the United States Toward Maritime Commerce in War*, Vol. II, pp. 615 *et seq*. For the President's approval of the sections dealing with contraband, see this volume, p. 32, Wilson to Lansing.

CHAPTER II

"SURELY WE ARE LIVING IN A MAD WORLD"

(July, August, September, 1917)

Wilson repudiates idea of congressional committee on conduct of the war—"a millstone around my neck"; rejects the Pope's peace proposal: "We cannot take the word of the present rulers of Germany."

Drafts Hoover and Garfield to head the food and coal organizations; appoints a War Industries Board.

Suffragettes bedevil the White House.

Labor troubles spread on the west coast, in Arizona, in New York.

Sunday, July 1st.

PRESIDENT and Mrs. Wilson spent the day on the *Mayflower*.

The British Embassy sent the State Department, at Balfour's instruction, an earnest appeal for financial aid. ". . . there is danger that the ability of His Majesty's Government to effect payments in America from to-day onwards will be in jeopardy. . . ."[1] They also sent a memorandum saying that shipping was being sunk around the British Isles faster than new ships could be turned out; immediate help was needed from the United States in the form of small fighting craft.[2]

The long-hoped-for Russian advance began, Kerensky himself leading his troops.

---

[1] *Foreign Relations*, 1917, Supp. 2, Vol. I, pp. 533–535. It was requested, among other things, that "assistance may be given to cover the amount of our overdraft with New York bankers amounting to about $400,000,000." The message was referred to McAdoo.

[2] *Ibid.*, p. 115.

Monday, July 2nd.

The President walked over to the State, War and Navy Building at noon, and upon his return found Secretary Daniels waiting to see him. Dr. and Mrs. Grayson and Dudley Field Malone of New York were luncheon guests. Afternoon appointments: Senator King of Utah and Representative Smith of Idaho, to present the governors of their respective states; Representative Littlepage of West Virginia; Secretary Lane and Senator Myers of Montana; Miss Jeannette Rankin, representative from Montana; Senator Smith of South Carolina; Herbert Hoover. In the evening Secretary Baker called. It was announced from the White House that the President did not intend to take a summer vacation.

Race riots broke out in East St. Louis in the early morning; by eight that night the district was under military law.

To Secretary Daniels, "Confidential":

". . . . As you and I agreed the other day, the British Admiralty had done absolutely nothing constructive in the use of their navy and I think it is time we were making and insisting upon plans of our own, even if we render some of the more conservative of our own naval advisers uncomfortable. What do you think?"

To John Franklin Fort of the Federal Trade Commission, replying to a letter of June 30th:[1]

"You may be sure that I am not in the least inclined to criticize the part you played in the conferences which led to a tentative agreement about the price of coal, but I do think that it was unfortunate that the conference attempted to deal with the matter of prices at all, simply because it is open to so much misconstruction when men, like the operators in this instance, seem to take the initiative in determining what price they shall themselves receive and then arrive at a conclusion which exactly coincides with the agreement which certain operators are

---

[1] This volume, p. 137.

now under indictment by the Government for making 'in restraint of trade.' I think that if the conference could have been confined to the objects stated in the first part of one of the resolutions I read, namely, to the means which would most tend to increase production and facilitate distribution of the product, it would have been wholly admirable. Whenever such conferences go beyond that and deal with matters of price, they open themselves to public misconstruction.

"I feel confident that as a result of the costs to be ascertained by the Federal Trade Commission some government agency can itself arrive at a conclusion with regard to price and a liberal profit which will seem to the country satisfactory and conclusive."

To Vance C. McCormick, who had asked the President's advice as to whether or not he could increase his usefulness by serving on the Administrative Committee of the Exports Council, as he had been requested to do:

"I am heartily glad that you are inclined to accept the duties which the Secretary of State suggested to you the other day. I am particularly desirous to have in that place somebody whom I thoroughly know and whom I can thoroughly trust, and when I was discussing it with the Secretary of State I did not feel, and neither did he, that it would be necessary for you to resign the chairmanship of the National Committee. I should be very much distressed to accept any such conclusion as that. The position is only semi-official and seems to me entirely compatible with the inter-election activities of a National Chairman. Your constant presence in Washington, moreover, will make the other things which you have been doing, and which have been so useful, perhaps easier to do than before.

"I hope very much that you will accept and that you will find it possible to take this view of the situation."

To Representative Halvor Steenerson of Minnesota, who wrote that the Socialists in his region had been spreading stories that the farmers would not be exempt from draft upon any consideration and that Chinese would be imported to take their places on the farms:

". . . I am very happy to assure you that adequate provision is made for the exemption of agricultural labor when cases arise justifying it and that the dependency exemptions of the law will be found as applicable to agricultural people as to any other workers.

"I realize, of course, how much mischief stories of this sort can breed, but the publication of the regulations will compose those who have been misled by misrepresentations of the situation."

To Governor George W. Hunt of Arizona, a telegram:

"I have been very much concerned to hear of the possible serious misunderstanding between the miners and the operators in the copper mines and I would deem it a very great public service on your part if you would be generous enough to do what you could to act as mediator and conciliator. I know how confidently I can appeal to your public spirit."

To Jaime C. De Veyra and Teodoro R. Yangko, resident commissioners from the Philippine Islands, who had urged the President to appoint Filipinos to two positions recently created in the Supreme Court of the Islands:

". . . . My present inclination is to give one of the appointments to the Court to an American and one to a native of the Islands,[1] but that will depend upon whether I am able to find an American otherwise qualified for the post who is able to speak Spanish and who is really conversant by long contact with the affairs and interests of the people of the Islands.

[1]This was Gregory's recommendation.

"Whichever course I pursue, I am sure that I have already given sufficient proof of my sincere desire to have the affairs of the Islands pass more and more into the hands of their own people, and that what I do will not be considered inconsistent with that purpose."

Tuesday, July 3rd.

The President omitted his morning golf, remaining in his study until time for luncheon. Afternoon appointments: John McCalmont Wilson; Senators Husting of Wisconsin and Walsh of Montana; the members of the Florida delegation; Commissioner Brent of the Shipping Board; the British ambassador, probably accompanied by Sir Richard Crawford, commercial adviser of the British Embassy, to discuss Great Britain's financial situation. Sir Cecil later reported to Mr. Balfour that the President "treated us with great kindness." ". . . . He impressed on us the importance of making absolutely full and frank explanations to Mr. McAdoo in whose hands lay the administration of finance. . . . I told him how conscious we were of the immense importance of the rôle which would now have to be played by the President of the United States. He admitted the fact, which he regretted. He said he had not wished it. . . ."[1] At 4:30 George Creel called. The President took a short drive with Mrs. Wilson before dinner; in the evening he conferred with William Denman of the Shipping Board.

Secretary Daniels gave out, through the Committee on Public Information, a statement telling of the safe arrival of the American troop transports and describing in dramatic terms how submarine attacks had been repulsed. This statement was branded as an exaggeration a few days later, both Creel and Daniels being bitterly attacked.[2]

---

[1] *The Letters and Friendships of Sir Cecil Spring Rice*, Vol. II, p. 406.

[2] *Official Bulletin*, July 5, 1917; New York *Times*, July 7, 1917. Creel writes that the statement was based upon Admiral Gleaves's report, and that as he and Daniels were preparing the information for publication it was checked from the Gleaves telegram by naval experts. Creel, *How We Advertised America*, pp. 28 *et seq.* Since an Associated Press cable was at the base of the attack on Daniels, the account of Melville E. Stone, in his book, *Fifty Years a Journalist*, furnishes an interesting sidelight upon this tempest in a teapot. Pp. 326–328. It should, of course, be read in connection with the verbatim report of Admiral Gleaves made at the time of the incident. (Published in the New York *Times*, August 2, 1917.)

To Secretary Lansing, who had sent the President a copy of the communication which the Japanese ambassador read to him on June 15th,[1] with draft of a reply:

"As I have just indicated to you, over the telephone, I entirely approve of this. I hope that you will re-read the latter portion of it, however, with a view to making the idea of Japan's *political* influence over China a little more prominent as the thing we have *not* assented to in the sense she evidently has in mind."[2]

To Secretary Daniels, "Personal and Confidential," enclosing a letter of June 28th from E. Lester Jones of the Department of Commerce in regard to the building of nets as protection against submarines:

"I would be very much obliged if you would read the enclosed. I am afraid from the evidence that lies on the surface that professional jealousy has operated to side-track this important matter, or at least check the serious consideration of it."

To Secretary Daniels, enclosing a draft, written on his own typewriter, of a message for Admiral Sims (see facsimile, pp. 146–147):

"If you approve of the enclosed will you not have it forwarded at once through the State Department. Of course if you do not approve I will gladly heed your advice.

"Perhaps it would be well to add, for yourself, the experience of the convoy of Pershing's troops in keeping the submarines off."[3]

---

[1]This volume, p. 114.

[2]For the message to the Japanese ambassador, as finally delivered, dated July 6, 1917, see *Foreign Relations*, 1917, pp. 260–262.

[3]Daniels replied the same day that he thought the message should go; but he suggested certain changes, since the English had "recently adopted the policy of convoying merchant ships with cruisers from their side." These changes were made. For the message as sent on July 4th, see *Foreign Relations*, 1917, Supp. 2, Vol. I, pp. 117–118.

AMERICAN SOLDIERS IN THE TRENCHES. ONE OF THE FIRST
PHOTOGRAPHS TO ARRIVE IN AMERICA

GENERAL PERSHING INSPECTING THE FRENCH FRONT LINE
ACCOMPANIED BY GENERAL FRANCHET D'ESPEREY

To his secretary, Tumulty, referring to a heated telegram from William English Walling about the "unchecked savagery" of the recent race riots at East St. Louis:

"Please say to Mr. Walling that we are making a rigid investigation of this case and he may rest assured everything within the power of the Federal Government will be done to check these outrages."

To his secretary, Tumulty, regarding a telegram from S. V. Costello, who asked leniency for his client, Henry Rule, arrested for exclaiming "Hypocrite!" when the President's picture was shown at a local theater:

"Please express this hope for me, if that is *all* the man did."

Wednesday, July 4th.

The President and Mrs. Wilson spent the day on the *May flower.*

All France joined in celebrating the Fourth of July, American troops in Paris receiving a veritable ovation—"*Vivent les Américains! Vive Pershing! Vivent les Etats Unis!*" London also observed the day, the American flag flying over the Houses of Parliament.

To his secretary, Tumulty, referring to a request from Richard M. Bolden for an interview for himself and a committee, to present an appeal for the colored people:

"Please say to this gentleman that I am obliged to avoid interviews at the present time if it is possible to do so consistently with the public business; that he cannot feel more distressed than I do at the terrible things [race riots at E. St. Louis] which have recently been happening; and that no suggestion from any quarter is necessary to increase my interest or my purpose to do whatever it is possible to do."

Thursday, July 5th.

The President spent the morning in his study. Afternoon appointments: a delegation of state fairs executives; Dr. R. J.

FOR ADMIRAL SIMS, Confidential from the President:
From the beginning of the war I have been surprised by nothing so much as the failure of the
British Admiralty to use Great Britain's great
naval superiority in any effective way. In the
presence of the present submarine emergency they
are helpless to the point of panic. Every plan
we suggest they reject for some reason of prudence
In my view this is not a time for prudence but
for boldness even at the risk of great losses. In
most of your despatches you have very properly
advised us of the sort of aid and cooperation desired from us by the Admiralty. The trouble is
that their plans and methods do not seem to us
effective. I would be very much obliged to you
if you would report to me, confidentially of
course, exactly what the Admiralty have been doing and what they have accomplished and add to
the report your own comments and suggestions
based upon independent study of the whole situation without regard to the judgments already arrived at on that side of the water. [In particular I am not at all satisfied with the conclusions of the Admiralty with regard to the convoying of groups of merchantmen. I do not see how
the necessary military supplies and supplies of
food and fuel oil are to be delivered at British
ports in any other way than under convoy. There
will presently not be ships enough or tankers

enough and our shipbuilding plans may not begin
to yield important results in less than eighteen
months. I beg that you will keep these instructions absolutely to yourself and that you will
give me such advice as you would give if you were
handling an independent navy of your own.

Woodrow Wilson.

FOR MORE VIGOROUS NAVAL WARFARE

The President urges bold naval action. His draft of a confidential
message to Admiral Sims, written on his own typewriter and corrected
in his own shorthand, sent, with certain omissions suggested by
Secretary Daniels, on July 4, 1917.

G. McKnight and a committee from the Reformed Presbyterian Church; Civil Service Commissioners Galloway and Craven, in regard to unsatisfactory conditions in the commission; the new Russian ambassador, who called to present his credentials. He made a short address, to which the President responded with a warm welcome and an expression of his satisfaction that Russia and America were now "actuated by the same lofty motives";[1] the Tennessee delegation; Senator James D. Phelan, who presented T. P. O'Connor and Richard Hazleton, leaders of the Irish Parliamentary party; Representative Alexander of Missouri.

To Louis Seibold, who had written a fine, friendly reply to the President's letter of June 27th,[2] expressing his admiration and his personal affection:

"Your letter . . . has touched me very deeply and I cannot deny myself the pleasure of sending you at least a line of very grateful acknowledgment. Such letters keep me in heart and make the labor worth while, even amidst the darkness which seems sometimes to gather about the path. Please always believe that your generous confidence is heartily and even affectionately reciprocated."

To Senator William Hughes of New Jersey:
MY DEAR BILLY:

I cannot tell you how glad I am that you are on your feet again. I felt the greatest and most affectionate anxiety about you and it takes a weight off my mind that you are finally getting entirely well. Do take care of yourself and let me know from time to time, if you have an opportunity, how you are faring!

With the warmest good wishes,

Faithfully yours,
WOODROW WILSON

---

[1]For entire address see *Public Papers*, Vol. V, pp. 71–72.
[2]This volume, p. 130.

Friday, July 6th.

Before the cabinet meeting the President conferred with Abram I. Elkus; afterward, with Representative Kahn of California. He accepted, in behalf of the Red Cross, the services of a sanitary corps of over a thousand men, making a brief speech of appreciation. Secretary Baker called. Evening at the National Theater.

During the day Mrs. Wilson's red, white and blue food pledge card was placed in one of the White House windows.

General Pershing telegraphed that plans "should contemplate sending over one million men by next May."[1]

The Russian government, Ambassador Page reported from London, had proposed "an early conference to set forth in concrete terms conditions on which they will make peace." Balfour personally disapproved, fearing "embarrassing controversies about conflicting aims and wishes among the Allies themselves."[2]

To Secretary Redfield, enclosing a clipping from the New York *Journal of Commerce* in which Redfield was quoted as saying that requisition of all United States ships by the government was under consideration:

"I do not believe that you knew of or authorized the enclosed, did you? I know how thoroughly you agreed with me the other day about statements of general policy issuing from any but one source, and statements about a policy of wholesale commandeering from any apparently authoritative source at this moment have the same stimulating effect on ocean freight rates as the reports of heavy sinkings have on the price of war insurance. A mounting freight market is immediately reflected in the market price of ships. The Government is about to become a buyer of a vast tonnage of ships on the stocks and, whether wisely or not, the courts do look at the market in determining what the Government must pay. Our obvious interest is to keep the market down and not

[1] Palmer, *Newton D. Baker*, Vol. I, p. 249.
[2] *Foreign Relations*, 1917, Supp. 2, Vol. I, pp. 119–120.

stimulate it. I have meant to exercise these powers myself with the utmost prudence and in a way that will be most beneficial to all concerned, and I hope that you will again make efforts to see that statements of no kind regarding the general policy of the Government proceed from your department. Knowing as I do that you concur in the wisdom of this, I do not hesitate to make this request very urgently."

To Senator Kenneth McKellar, written as the result of a telegram from Julius Rosenwald of the Council of National Defense, and after consultation with Secretary Burleson:

"May I not take the liberty of asking you if you would not be willing to withdraw the amendment you have proposed to the pending food legislation prohibiting members of the advisory committees of the Council of National Defense from selling to the Government? My reason for making bold to make this request is that the passage and enforcement of such a law would practically break up the instrumentalities we have laboriously created for mobilizing the industries of the country at this crisis.

"As a matter of fact, as the actions of the Council are now guided and determined, no one of these gentlemen sells to the Government in any way which gives him control of the terms upon which he shall sell, and we are rapidly throwing such complete safeguards about the whole question of price that it is already impossible for these advisers to obtain an excessive price, if they were disposed to demand it. Among them are the chief business men of the country, upon whose assistance and advice we are dependent and who are giving that assistance and advice in an admirable spirit of patriotism and disinterestedness.

"It is because I can assure you of these circumstances and can say that it would be nothing less than a calamity to have these means of cooperation withdrawn from us that I am taking what would otherwise be a very great liberty. I am sure that you know me well enough to know that I would not do anything of this sort except upon grave cause.

"I am writing this letter rather than seeking an immediate interview because of the rush of business and because I know that the amendment will probably come up for very early consideration."

Saturday, July 7th.

At 12:30 the President received Secretary Houston and Herbert Hoover, who discussed the "very serious crisis . . . with respect to wheat and corn" and urged the need of an immediate embargo, followed if possible by the early passage of the Food bill.

> Admiral Sims to Secretary Daniels: ". . . . Briefly stated, I consider that at the present moment we are losing the war. This is due to the success of the enemy submarine campaign . . ."[1]
>
> Frank L. Polk telegraphed a message for S. R. Bertron of the Root Commission that the President "approves in principle of educational publicity campaign and authorizes expense $30,000 already incurred. The question of further outlay and a comprehensive plan is receiving . . . careful attention . . ."[2]

To Secretary Redfield, who wrote, in answer to the President's letter of the 6th, that he did not authorize the statement in question:

". . . I felt quite confident that the statement . . . had not been issued by your authority.

"Of course, I realize the necessity in the course of the correspondence of the department of answering questions

---

[1] *Naval Investigation Hearings*, 1920, Vol. I, p. 61.

[2] *Foreign Relations*, 1918, *Russia*, Vol. I, p. 129. For the message of July 2nd, to which this was an answer, see *ibid.*, p. 128.

the answers to which will disclose either partially or wholly the policy of the administration with regard to large matters, and I do not wish to interfere with that at all, but evidently somebody in the Bureau of Foreign and Domestic Commerce has a taste for publicity and is apt to create the greatest embarrassments for the administration by, either directly or indirectly, getting into print with the announcement of 'policies,' and I think that it is imperative to avoid this.

"The letters going out from the several bureaux of the department could easily be marked 'for information but not for publication,' and I would be deeply obliged to you if you would say to Doctor Pratt, the head of the Bureau of Foreign and Domestic Commerce that I shall depend upon him to serve me in this matter so far as his bureau is concerned.

"Of course it is going to be hard to work out all these things, but not impossible, and I am sure we will all co-operate in the same spirit."

Sunday, July 8th.

The President and Mrs. Wilson attended the ancient church connected with the Washington tradition at Pohick, Virginia.

Colonel House sent the President copy of a telegram just received from Balfour, who reported that the British War Cabinet had considered the matter of a naval agreement between the two countries "to allow of extended building of destroyers and light-craft instead of capital ships already authorized by the United States programme." After some discussion of possibilities, Balfour suggested actual terms: that the governments of the United States, Great Britain, France, Italy, Russia and Japan engage to assist each other "against any maritime attack for a period of four years after conclusion of the present war." If the President approved, Balfour was prepared to "take any steps he may desire" toward bringing the plan to fruition; if not, he would "endeavor to find some acceptable alternative."

House commented in his covering letter: ". . . . No one knows of these negotiations excepting Lansing and Polk . . ."[1]

Monday, July 9th.

Afternoon appointments: Senator Owen of Oklahoma and A. C. Bedford, chairman of the oil committee of the Council of National Defense, who was planning a conference of independent oil producers in Washington; the French ambassador, who had asked to see the President about "certain matters relating to the blockade"; Senator Jones of New Mexico; Civil Service Commissioners Galloway and Craven. At 4:15 the President walked over to Secretary Baker's office for a conference. He spent the evening in his study.

The President issued a proclamation in regard to the control of certain exports by license;[2] and a supplementary statement explaining the purpose of such restriction.[3]

McAdoo, replying to the British message of July 1st in regard to the financial situation,[4] expressed the "gravest concern." He pointed out that full information as to the financial needs of Great Britain had not been given him; and stated that no "positive undertakings" existed on the part of the government of the United States with regard to such needs. He had "authorized the advance of the desired $100,000,000; and . . . is now giving consideration to the matter of making further loan . . ." He was also "taking the whole subject of the $400,000,000 overdraft under consideration." "It is true," he wrote, "that the Secretary of the Treasury stated to Mr. Balfour that this item might be included in a statement to be laid before the Secretary of the Treasury of the amounts which the British Government desired to borrow from the United States Government. . . . But no commitment was made by the Secretary of the Treasury concerning any item, whatever its nature, which was suggested for inclusion in the

---

[1] *Intimate Papers*, Vol. III, pp. 68–69.

[2] *Foreign Relations*, 1917, Supp. 2, Vol. II, pp. 903–905. The neutral nations were much disturbed; and several missions were subsequently sent to Washington—from Norway, Sweden, Switzerland, Holland—to discuss the matter.

[3] *Public Papers*, Vol. V, p. 73.

[4] See this vol., p. 139.

statement then being prepared by the British Government for submission to him."[1]

To Representative W. C. Adamson, who had suggested that speculation be curtailed by limiting the per cent of profit which each dealer might realize:

"I realise the point and validity of your contention in your letter of yesterday that the trouble in the food prices is in the margin of profit, but how are we going to reach it by legislation? I dare say you suggested a practicable method to Senator Chamberlain, but you do not in your letter to me, and I should be very much interested if you have one in mind."

To John B. Cohen, congratulating him on assuming the editorship of the Atlanta *Journal:*

". . . . I am heartily glad to know that you have been entrusted with the responsibility of the editorship of the Journal. Under your guidance I am sure that it will support the things that are right and in the public interest. I am all the more interested to have such backing in Georgia because I have not the pleasure of the support of the two Senators from Georgia."

Tuesday, July 10th.

The cabinet met at 2:30, Secretary Redfield remaining afterward for a conference with the President. Senator Johnson of South Dakota called at 4:30, and Breckinridge Long, Assistant Secretary of State, at 5 o'clock.

German troops launched a strong attack against the British north of Nieuport. British losses were tremendous—"a tragic tale."[2]

To Thomas D. Jones, old friend of the Princeton days:

"I hope you will not regard it as an imposition if I ask you to have the writer of the enclosed letter looked up and

[1] *Foreign Relations,* 1917, Supp. 2, Vol. I, pp. 539–543. Communicated to the British ambassador at Washington July 13th.

[2] Philip Gibbs, in *Current History,* August, 1917, pp. 242–243.

satisfy yourself whether there is anything in his mind or plans to which we ought to give careful examination. His proposition looks like a renewal of the nonsense of perpetual motion, but somehow I never like to take chances on finding something unexpected.

"I think of you very often and wish constantly that we might be associated here in the perplexing work that is pressing upon us.

"In haste, with warmest regard to you all . . ."

Wednesday, July 11th.

Secretary Baker was a luncheon guest at the White House. Afternoon appointments: Representative Howard of Georgia; Senators Wadsworth and Calder of New York; David J. Lewis, former representative from Maryland, who discussed his plan for "adapting the federal Constitution of the United States to the purposes of international organization." In a memorandum written later Lewis set down the substance of the President's words as he remembered them: "We must first win the war. When we shall have won the war the great opportunity and duty will be presented. I quite agree with your general purposes, but I fear that no accomplishment so great as our own Constitution can be hoped for. A most happy combination of historical conditions alone made that achievement possible. What I do hope to accomplish is to establish a structure containing the tendencies which will lead irresistibly to the great end we in common with all other rightly constituted persons desire. But there are going to be difficulties even with this modest programme. I have in mind the ridiculous importance which some persons assign to the official who will be charged with such conspicuous work—but, friends and enemies both will admit that my 'jaw' has proved adequate in past struggles!"

Senator Robinson of Arkansas arrived at 4 o'clock, and at 4:30, Secretary McAdoo.

The President appealed to the country against profiteering—
". . . . Patriotism and profits ought never in the present circumstances to be mentioned together. . . ."[1]

---

[1] *Public Papers*, Vol. V, pp. 74–78.

Admiral Sims replied to the President's message of July 4th: The war, he maintained, would be "decided by the success or failure of submarine campaign"; and he set down the steps which he believed should be taken.[1]

To Secretary Daniels, a letter marked "Strictly Confidential," enclosing Denman's comment on the necessity of constructing trawlers for use on this side of the Atlantic, since the Germans were said to be building submarines with a cruising radius of 15,000 miles:

"Here is a letter from Denman which I am sure you will read with as much interest as I read it. I wonder if there is any possibility of taking the prudent course which he suggests?"

To William Denman:

"The other day the War and Navy Departments submitted to me a list of vessels which they deemed suitable for the transportation of troops and represented to me in a way that was entirely convincing to my judgment that these ships ought to be permanently at their disposal to constitute the shuttles of a ferry, and that in view of the uses to which they would be put it was essential, as I believe it is, that they should be manned and officered by Navy crews and officers.

"You will remember that when I transferred to the Shipping Board the whole list of the ships owned by the German trans-Atlantic companies I did so on the understanding that that transfer was not to stand in the way of subsequent transfers to the Navy Department which seemed to me necessary, and therefore I am taking the liberty today of making the assignment.

"The Navy Department is perfectly willing, under my

---

[1] *Foreign Relations*, 1917, Supp. 2, Vol. I, pp. 124–126, for text. Polk sent a copy to the President on the 13th; and on the 14th Secretary Daniels also sent a copy, with a covering letter giving his own comments: ". . . . We are doing all that he suggests except his idea of sending the dreadnaughts. There is no reason he advances that would justify placing our last and main reliance in jeopardy. . . ."

direction and at your suggestion, to arrange that these ships shall bring back cargoes from the belligerent countries if such cargoes should be ready at the time of their return voyage, and I am convinced that they could bring cargoes from no other countries, because the law officers of the Government are unanimous in their judgment, so far as I have learned, that the question could be raised as to the ownership of these vessels if they were to touch at neutral ports and that many influences would be at work which would render it very likely that we should not see them again, at any rate until after very emphatic and prolonged diplomatic correspondence, if they should touch at such ports."

To Representative W. C. Adamson, who had suggested that provisions be placed in the Food bill limiting the profit which the first purchaser from the producer might realize, and preventing the holding of commodities for speculative purposes:

". . . I am going to take the liberty of clarifying my own judgment a little further by consulting Mr. Herbert Hoover about the practicability of enforcing provisions such as you suggest, for I have learned to have great confidence in his practical judgment in these matters."

To King Ferdinand of Rumania, telegram:
"I have received your sad message. The pain and suffering of the people of Roumania and the persecutions they are undergoing, excite the pity and indignation of the civilized world."

To Senator Hoke Smith of Georgia, with whose obstructionist tactics the President was thoroughly disgusted:

MY DEAR SIR:
I received from you several days ago a letter in which you stated that you would not be willing to vote for the confirmation of the nomination of Judge W. E. Thomas

of Valdosta, Georgia, as Judge of the United States District Court for the vacant Judgeship of the United States District Court in Georgia. You did not state any reasons or any objections to Judge Thomas, and I write in order to omit no courtesy and to inform you that I am today sending in the nomination of Judge Thomas for action by the Senate.

Very truly yours,
WOODROW WILSON[1]

Thursday, July 12th.

During the afternoon the President received: Abram I. Elkus, ambassador to Turkey; William J. Harris of the Federal Trade Commission; Senators Martin of Virginia and Simmons of North Carolina, to discuss the legislative tangle over the pending Food bill;[2] Secretary Burleson.

Strikes and threats of strikes: more than a thousand men went out at the Remington Arms Company in Bridgeport, Connecticut.

A message from Secretary McAdoo to Balfour was transmitted through the Department of State:

". . . . At no time, directly or indirectly, has the Secretary of the Treasury, or any one connected with the Treasury Department, promised to pay the Morgan overdraft. . . .

"The United States must of necessity reserve to itself independence of decision and freedom of action with respect to financial matters. Their financial policy will be dictated by a desire to cooperate to the fullest extent possible with the several powers making war in common against Germany, but America's cooperation cannot mean that America can assume the entire burden of financing the war. . . ."[3]

---

[1] Two days later the President sent on to the Attorney General a letter from Hoke Smith, objecting to the appointment of Judge Thomas. The President's covering letter was short and to the point: "What do you think of the enclosed? Please do not reply in writing because I know it would involve profanity!"

[2] See Wilson to Senator Martin, July 13, this volume, pp. 163–164.

[3] *Foreign Relations*, 1917, Supp. 2, Vol. I, pp. 543–545, for entire message; for Page's telegram of July 5th to which this refers, see *ibid.*, pp. 535–536.

Representatives of the big steel interests in conference with
government officials at Washington agreed that the entire
output of their plants should be at the disposal of the
government—this in line with the President's statement
of the 11th. The price was to be fixed by the Federal Trade
Commission.

To T. W. Gregory:

"You may remember that the other day I spoke jest-
ingly at the Cabinet about my perplexity concerning the
varying counsels among the several departments having
secret service with regard to a correlation of those services.
Underneath the jest, of course, lay a very serious difficulty
and I am writing now to ask if you would be generous
enough to cooperate with the Secretary of the Treasury
and Mr. Polk in working out for me a plan for the cooperation of these services into which we can all enter
with spirit and effect. I am genuinely in need of counsel
in this matter and am sure that you three can compound
a plan which will be worth acting upon."[1]

To Senator Duncan U. Fletcher of Florida, who had written of
his anxiety lest Jacksonville might not be chosen as a camp
site:

"I wonder if you know how very difficult the matter
of choosing camp sites has been for the Secretary of War
and how sincerely he has tried to make the choices im-
partially and with a view to nothing but the interests of
the Army. I will, of course, take pleasure in calling his
attention to the matter of the Jacksonville site, but I
know from my conversations with him that it is not neces-

---

[1] An example of the overlapping and confusion which occurred as a result of the
added energy infused into the various departments by the war. When irritation grew
up, McAdoo, with his insatiable appetite for work, and his desire for a finger in every
pie, was often found to be at the center of the trouble. He had in this case been especially
assiduous in writing the President about the difficulties between his department and
that of the Attorney General. The President was always tactful in dealing with such
interdepartmental difficulties.

sary to do so in order to increase his very sober and serious interest and his desire to do the very best thing possible."[1]

To Edward B. McLean of the Washington *Post:*

"The Mexican Ambassador has called my attention to an article recently appearing in the Washington Post under the name of 'Ryley Grannon' to which he has made a protest to the Secretary of State. This is one of a series of articles of misrepresentation and distortion of fact which have recently appeared in the Post under this name.

"I do not believe that you would permit the Post to be used for the embarrassment of the nation, especially now that it is engaged in war, but I am bound in frankness to say that the character of these articles has made me feel that the Post, consciously or unconsciously, is conducting a propaganda for the embarrassment of the nation in its relations with the Allies and in the conduct of its own war against the German Government. I am loath to believe that these misrepresentations have been made by your direction.

"I have no desire to suggest any limitation on criticism of the Government, but in view of our friendly talk at the White House shortly after you assumed control of the Post, I do feel free to call your personal attention to this series of misrepresentations by the unknown writer who calls himself Ryley Grannon."

To Governor Thomas E. Campbell of Arizona, who reported that some twelve hundred members of the I.W.W. had been deported from Bisbee, Arizona; and asked federal aid to maintain peace and insure the continuance of important mining industries. The President's reply was telegraphed:

"Secretary of War has instructed General Parker to send officers to Arizona at once to report to him conditions

---

[1]On the same day the President sent Fletcher's letter to Secretary Baker who replied: ". . . . I have written a very frank personal letter to Senator Fletcher on the subject. His constituents are unbelievably annoying to the Senator and unjust to him, and I

there with a view to cooperating in maintenance of order. Meantime may I not respectfully urge the great danger of citizens taking the law in their own hands as you report their having done. I look upon such action with grave apprehension. A very serious responsibility is assumed when such precedents are set."

Friday, July 13th.

The President's only morning engagement was with Secretary Burleson. After the cabinet meeting he received Representative Littlepage of West Virginia. Sir William Wiseman was a dinner guest, after which he and the President had a long conference which Wiseman recorded that night:

"Wilson produced a memorandum from House regarding the proposed modification of the United States shipbuilding programme.[1] Wilson said that he was not familiar with this proposition, and was therefore discussing it somewhat in the dark. In his own words—he was 'thinking aloud to me.' His observations were approximately as follows:

"That in his opinion the war had proved that capital ships were not of much value; that with this in view he did not consider the question of the United States delaying the building of capital ships as very important from a strategic point of view. He explained, however, that when Congress voted money for the naval programme, a specific estimate had to be made of the exact number of the different classes of ships upon which the money had to be spent. It would therefore be unlawful for him to change that programme and alter the number of ships to be built. The only way in which this could be done would be by laying the whole facts before Congress.

"When asked for a suggested solution [of the problem of defense against the submarine], he stated that he had always been opposed to allowing merchantmen to cross the Atlantic without convoy; that he was strongly in favor of forcing merchantmen to cross in fleets adequately protected by light naval craft. That he believed some such arrangement was now being put in force; that when the merchantmen reached some

am afraid his own feelings have been a good deal disturbed at the decision which I have been obliged to make . . ."

[1] This volume, July 8th, p. 152.

point near the British coast, lanes should be formed, strongly guarded by destroyers, through which the merchantmen could pass, and, again, when they were quite close to shore they should radiate to the various ports. He suggested that if some such scheme could be devised as an American scheme it would undoubtedly require a larger number of destroyers than the United States at present have, but that he could go to Congress with this scheme and ask for an appropriation specifically for this purpose. . . .

"With regard to Balfour's suggestion covering the naval shipbuilding difficulty by some species of defensive alliance:— Wilson stated that in his opinion the Allies had entered during the stress of war into various undertakings among each other which they would find it very difficult if not impossible to carry out when the war was over; and he was not in favor of adding to that difficulty.[1] Moreover he pointed out that while the U.S. was now ready to take her place as a world-power, the strong feeling throughout the country was to play a 'lone hand' and not to commit herself to any alliance with any foreign power. With regard to Japan, Wilson said that in his opinion a successful attack on the Pacific coast was absurd owing to the long distance from the Japanese base and the difficulty they would have in obtaining any suitable base on the Pacific coast. The possibility of their attacking the Philippines or some outlying possession was, he thought, quite another matter, and presented a possibility which could not be overlooked."[2]

In reporting his talk with the President to Northcliffe and Colonel House, Wiseman said: "Wilson urged strongly . . . that more information, both as to actual financial needs and general policy of the Allies, must be given to the United States Government. He pointed out that there was much confusion and some competition in the demands of the various Allies. Specifically, so far as the British are concerned, he pointed out that there was no one who could speak with sufficient financial authority to discuss the whole situation, both financial and political, with the Secretary of the Treasury. All these things should be remedied as soon as possible.

"He was thoroughly in favor of the scheme proposed by McAdoo for a council in Paris. This council, composed of

[1] A reference to certain of the secret treaties.
[2] *Intimate Papers*, Vol. III, pp. 70–72.

representatives of the Allies, should determine what was needed in the way of supplies and money from America. It should also determine the urgency of each requisition and give proper priority. I suggested that such a council should be composed of the military and naval commanders, or their representatives, and that the United States should be represented on it. Wilson did not seem to have any objection, but thought it was unnecessary for the United States to be represented on it until they had their own portion of the front to look after and a large force in Europe."[1]

The invitation of the French government to send a delegate to an Inter-Allied Conference on the Balkan situation was declined by the Department of State.[2]

Sharp aërial fighting on the French front was reported—the worst since the beginning of the war.

To Senator Thomas S. Martin:

"After you and Senator Simmons left me yesterday I applied myself to a very careful study of the bill you left with me,—the bill which, as I understand, is to be introduced as a proposed substitute for the pending Food Administration Bill. Upon examining the bill I was amazed and distressed to find that in practically every important particular it emasculates the original measure, except as regards the provision concerning the use of foodstuffs in liquors. I feel that it would be fatal to pass it or to substitute any part of it except that which I have mentioned for the bill upon the consideration of which the Senate has been engaged. I cannot help believing that it was the intention of whoever framed this bill to rob the proposed legislation of practically all its effective features.

"I would not be so unqualified in these statements if I had not scrutinized the bill with the utmost particularity. I have been amazed to find how carefully, and sometimes how subtly, the effective features of the proposed legis-

---

[1] *Intimate Papers*, Vol. III, p. 108.
[2] *Foreign Relations*, 1917, Supp. 2, Vol. I, p. 118.

lation have been eliminated and the whole character of the bill as an administrative measure weakened and rendered unworkable.

"I, therefore, hope, my dear Senator, most sincerely that so much of the original bill as concerned Food Administration will be passed by the Senate as finally reported by the committee. Undoubtedly that legislation in its main features is what is expected and I may even say demanded by the country.

"May I not also express the earnest hope that the passage of this legislation may be accomplished within the shortest possible time? The delay which has already occurred, and which has arisen out of the opposition of those who are for the most part opposed to the legislation altogether, has caused incalculable injury to the country, and every day of delay adds to the injury and to the embarrassment. The Senate could render no greater public service than by curtailing the process of consideration as much as possible and pressing the bill to a very early passage.

"If it were necessary, I could go into the details of the bill section by section which justify my opinion of it, but I feel confident that you yourself will be convinced of the justice of my judgment if you will give the substitute a more detailed examination than you said you had been able to give when I saw you yesterday."

To Senator Kenneth D. McKellar, who had written that in view of the reorganization of the Advisory Commission of the Council of National Defense, the members of the committees of that commission need not fear the proposed provision of the Food bill:[1]

". . . . I am sorry to say that I cannot construe the language of the provision about which we have been having such an interesting correspondence as you interpret

---

[1] This volume, pp. 150–151.

it. It is to the effect that nobody connected with the Government or any of its instrumentalities, though even in an advisory capacity, may *procure* a contract. That would make it impossible for us to advise with any of the real producers of the country, for they are the only ones with whom we can possibly make contracts, and it would be impossible to discriminate between their procuring and receiving them if they were in conference with us about the supplies.

"I think you will understand how imperatively necessary it is that we should be in constant conference with the committees of the producers in order to ascertain what the supply is, where we can get it, in what quantities and qualities, and when and how fast."

To Amos Pinchot, who had been one of the protestors against the closing of mails to *The Masses* and other papers:

"The letter of yesterday signed by yourself, Mr. Eastman, and Mr. Reed has just been laid before me and you may be sure has been read with a great deal of interest and sympathy. I am going to take the matter you present about the paper called The Masses up with the Postmaster General to see just how the case may best and most justly be handled.

"You will understand, I am sure, why I would hesitate to make a public statement such as you suggest. It would undoubtedly be taken advantage of by those with whom neither you nor I have been in sympathy at all."[1]

---

[1] On the 17th the President sent Amos Pinchot a letter from Secretary Burleson justifying the refusal of the Post Office Department to transmit the August issue of *The Masses* through the mails. Burleson was uncompromising in his attitude. In the case of *The Masses*, the President told him he knew some of the editors, and added: "Now Burleson, these are well-intentioned people. Let them blow off steam!"

"I am willing to let them blow off steam," replied Burleson, "providing they don't violate the Espionage Act. If you don't want the Espionage Act enforced, I can resign. Congress has passed the law and has said that I am to enforce it. We are going into war, and these men are discouraging enlistments."

The President laughed and said, "Well, go ahead and do your duty." (Burleson to the author, 1927.)

Saturday, July 14th.

After a morning in his study, the President went with Mrs. Wilson to St. John's Church, to attend the wedding of Miss Elisabeth Harding, daughter of the governor of the Federal Reserve Board. In the afternoon they went for a long drive, taking a picnic luncheon, and returning about nine o'clock in the evening.

> Georg Michaelis succeeded Von Bethmann-Hollweg as Chancellor of Germany.
>
> Sixteen woman suffragists were arrested for causing unlawful assembly before the White House. The President was not told beforehand that the arrests were to be made.[1]

Sunday, July 15th.

President and Mrs. Wilson took a trip down the river in the *Sylph*, accompanied by Miss Bones, Secretary Baker and J. R. Bolling.

Monday, July 16th.

About noon the President went to Secretary Houston's office for a conference. Afternoon appointments: M. Tardieu, French high commissioner; the Executive Committee of the National Association of Commissioners of Agriculture, the French ambassador and M. Daniel Blumenthal, former mayor of Colmer, Alsace; Senator Husting of Wisconsin; Henry P. Fletcher, ambassador to Mexico.

> Senator Reed launched a bitter attack in the Senate on Herbert Hoover, calling him the "arch gambler of this day."

To Representative W. C. Adamson:

"You know I never like to advise whether a bill should be introduced or not, because I am as far as possible from assuming that my judgments in such matters are the best judgments, but I feel with regard to the matter I took the liberty of referring to Mr. Hoover the other day that it is safe to be bound by his judgment if he thinks that the

[1]Louis Brownlow, one of the commissioners of the District of Columbia, to the author.

provisions of the pending food bill as they will probably come out of conference constitute a sufficient safeguard against the speculators. You may be sure that, [in] whatever is necessary to safeguard the public against those harpies, I shall be glad to cooperate with you."

To Representative W. C. Adamson:

"Alas, there is nothing that I can do about the matter of the military camp. It has been necessary to disappoint a great many communities in this important matter and we have been bound as a matter of duty not to regard these disappointments but to make the choices entirely from the point of view of military advantage and convenience in the tasks we have immediately before us. I beg that if the unwarranted blame put upon you should come to a head in any way you will give me the privilege of writing to those concerned in order that I may assume the full responsibility and exonerate you, for surely you have done all that it was right that you should do."

To E. B. McLean of the Washington *Post*, who had replied to the President's letter of the 12th that he would redouble his efforts to avoid publication of any objectionable matter:

"Thank you for your generous letter . . . It was characteristic of you. May I not say that it has given me the greatest sense of encouragement and support to feel conscious that I could resort to you with the greatest frankness at any time for such assistance and clarification of the public mind as might seem possible and necessary; and your letter gives me the greatest gratification."

Tuesday, July 17th.

After a horseback ride with Mrs. Wilson and Dr. Grayson, the President worked in his study until noon. Before the cabinet meeting he received Senator Fletcher of Florida; Secretary Redfield remained after the meeting probably for a conference on the policy to be followed regarding exports to Norway.

The President gave instructions that permits for all shipments to Norway be granted at once. At 4:30 H. A. Garfield called.

> Suffragists who were arrested on the 14th, being fined $25 each or sixty days in the workhouse at Occoquan, all elected to undergo the sixty days. Dudley Field Malone acted as counsel for the women; soon after the imposition of the sentence his resignation as Collector of the Port of New York was rumored.[1]

> Secretary McAdoo sent the President a draft of a letter which he thought should be written to all governments borrowing money from the United States. It pointed out that loans made "should not be construed as an approval or disapproval by the United States Government of any particular national objectives which your Government may have in view, or which in the future may be claimed by it as having been gained by successful military operations. . . ."[2]

> A Bolshevist uprising was staged in Petrograd, under the direction of Lenin. Though put down within 36 hours, the increasing strength of the movement was evident.[3]

To Secretary Baker, addressed to him in his capacity as chairman of the Council of National Defense:

"I have, as you know, been giving a great deal of thought to the plan of reorganization submitted to me some time ago by the Council of National Defense.

"The more I think of it the more it seems to me that the organization can be still more simplified greatly to its advantage. My suggestion,—a suggestion which I hope you will be kind enough to lay before the Council,—is that the three persons to whom will be entrusted the direction of purchases of raw materials, the purchases of finished products, and the arrangement of priorities of purchase and of shipment shall themselves be members of the War Industries Board, together with Mr. Frayne and representatives of the War and Navy Departments,

---

[1] New York *Times*, July 18, 1917. He did not actually resign until September.

[2] For entire text of letter and enclosure see *Hearings*, Senate Munitions Investigation, 74–2, Pt. 29, pp. 8999 and 9000.

[3] *Foreign Relations*, 1918, *Russia*, Vol. I, pp. 164–169.

under the chairmanship of Mr. Scott; that the War Industries Board serve as a clearing house for the determination of the immediate needs of the Government and the sequence of those needs; and that the three officials I have named, those charged, namely, with the purchase of raw materials, with the purchase of finished products, and with the determination of priorities, shall in association with Mr. Hoover in the matter of the purchase of foodstuffs be the executive agency through which all purchases are arranged for. It seems to me that in this way we shall get rid of what might be in danger of being a complicated piece of machinery without in any way interfering with the independence and energy of the three active officials mentioned.

"There would then be a free field for these three officials to use the various committees now associated with the Council of National Defense for the fullest information and for any kind of assistance which they can properly render, and it would be within their choice, of course, to employ assistants or lieutenants as systematically as seemed necessary.

"I would be obliged if I might have an early opinion from the Council on this suggestion."

To G. W. Norris, executive officer of the Federal Farm Loan Bureau:

"I will be very much obliged to you if you would tell me whether the Farm Loan bonds are available for purchase now and, if so, where. I would like to make a modest investment."

To Allen B. Pond, who wrote about the "patriotic plans of the War Committee of the Union League Club of Chicago" for "making the purposes and circumstances of the war clearer":

"... I am happy to believe that the impression that the country is not generally aware of the objects of the war

is an erroneous one. In some parts of the country there is
very subtle and pervasive agitation against the Government and every possible means should be taken to expose
and neutralize that. There are certain agencies at work,
for example, in the general region with which the Union
League Club would naturally be most in touch which are
very determined, very hostile, and very sinister, and I
believe that a great deal could be accomplished by the
Club if it turned its energies towards meeting those influences directly and running them from cover to their
destruction. Men like Mr. Nieman of the Milwaukee
Journal have been very active and very successful in
unearthing these influences and exposing them, and if
the Club were willing to counsel and cooperate with him
in any way, I think some very noteworthy results might
be achieved, greatly to the benefit of the country."

To William Kent, who had asked the President to receive Victor
Berger, whom he considered a "strong sane and honest representative" of the Socialists:

"I so much respect your judgment that when I find
myself differing from you, I question my own conclusion,
but I must say to you very frankly that I have no confidence whatever in Victor Berger. His recent actions and
utterances have convinced me that he is not to be trusted
as in any sense a friend of the Government and I do not
think that it would be wise or serve any useful purpose
for me to see him personally.

"Not all the Socialists of the country by a great deal
are of his sort or follow his counsel. Indeed, I have seen
very many evidences of late that the bulk of the Socialists
in this country have genuine American feeling and in no
sense represent the revolutionary temper such as Mr.
Berger has shown."

Wednesday, July 18th.

At 12:45 the President received Mr. Sato of the Japanese Embassy. Afternoon appointments: Commissioner Brownlow of the District of Columbia, in regard to the treatment of suffragettes. The President was "highly indignant" over the arrests, saying that the women should never have been indulged in their desire for martyrdom; and he asked that no further arrests be made without notifying him;[1] Senator Owen and Representative Ferris of Oklahoma; a committee of the Maryland Council of Defense; Joseph F. Guffey of Pennsylvania; Samuel Gompers, who presented Edmundo E. Martinez, Mexican consul at Chicago. Martinez brought messages from Carranza on a number of points, including the removal of the embargo on arms to the Mexican government. The President listened courteously and replied that he would take all these matters under consideration; he also said that if any injustice had been done Carranza, he would see that it was righted. The last caller of the day was George Creel. Evening at Keith's Theater.

> Secretary McAdoo proposed the establishment of an Inter-Allied Council on war purchases and finance, and an American purchasing commission. Transmitted to the Allied representatives in Washington July 19th.[2]

To Senator John Sharp Williams, who had sent over a letter from George Sylvester Viereck in regard to the *American Weekly's* campaign for the Britten resolution in the House[3] and a copy of his own reply, in which he excoriated the *American Weekly,* Viereck himself and all his works, and the Britten resolution:

"Thank you from the bottom of my heart for the copy of your letter to Viereck. I have warmed my hands at it. It glows and burns in a way to make me glad."

---

[1] Louis Brownlow to the author.

[2] *Foreign Relations,* 1917, Supp. 2, Vol. I, pp. 546–548. Approved by the President. A reply was made jointly on the 26th by the French, British, Italian and Russian ambassadors, expressing hesitation about lodging so much power in a commission over which they would have insufficient control; and suggesting further discussion. *Ibid.,* pp. 555–558.

[3] Which would exempt German-Americans from military service in Europe.

To John S. Sargent, who wrote that he had been appointed to paint a portrait for the National Gallery of Ireland, if the President would consent to sit for it:

". . . . Apparently it is vain to hope for time for sittings while the Congress is in session and, unfortunately, with the extraordinarily dilatory practices possible in the Senate no man would be rash enough to predict how long the present session will last. I do not see how it can very well continue beyond the first of September, and I had in a general way formed the expectation that I might during that month have a chance to give myself the pleasure of seeing you. I should consider it a privilege to do so . . ."

To Senator B. R. Tillman, who had deplored the "row" between Denman and Goethals, saying it seemed to him Denman had the right of it, and calling attention to the fact that Goethals was very difficult to get on with. "For God's sake take him down a button hole or two." The President's reply was marked "Personal":

"Thank you for your letter . . . It was delightfully outspoken, just the kind I like, and you may be sure that I substantially agree with its conclusions and am trying to work along that line. The General is a most difficult person to deal with."[1]

Thursday, July 19th.

The President's afternoon appointments: James B. Waller; Mrs. Antoinette Funk; Secretary McAdoo.

President Wilson unconditionally pardoned all militant suffragists serving sentences at the workhouse. The women at first refused to accept the pardon, but were finally prevailed upon to do so.

Senator Weeks of Massachusetts, Republican, offered a joint resolution to create a congressional committee on the conduct of the war.

---

[1]The President was a good deal harassed and irritated by the "row" in the Shipping Board. Only such letters regarding it are here published as will indicate his own course.

The German Reichstag adopted a resolution declaring for a peace of mutual agreements and enduring reconciliation of peoples. ". . . . With such a peace compulsory acquisitions of territory and political, economical or financial violence are irreconcilable. . . . The Reichstag will promote actively the creation of international juridical organizations. . . ." But the resolution continued: ". . . . So long however as the enemy governments do not accept such a peace, so long [as] they threaten Germany and her allies with conquest and violence, the German people will stand together as one man . . . and fight until her right and that of her allies to life and development is secured. . . ."[1]

Chancellor Michaelis, speaking after the adoption of the resolution, said: ". . . . We look without serious concern upon the optimistic sentiment in the Entente countries caused by America's intervention. It is easy to reckon how much tonnage is necessary to transport an army from America to Europe, how much tonnage is required to feed such an army. . . . After our previous success we shall be able to master this situation also through our fleet, particularly the submarines. . . .

"The Germans wish to conclude peace as combatants who have successfully accomplished their purpose and proved themselves invincible. . . .

"Peace must offer the foundation of a lasting reconciliation of nations. . . .

"These aims may be attained within the limits of your resolution as I interpret it. We cannot again offer peace. We have loyally stretched out our hands once. . . ."[2]

To General G. W. Goethals of the Emergency Fleet Corporation:
"I am writing you a letter because if I were to ask for a personal interview in the midst of the present elaborate misunderstanding which the newspapers have created it would of course be said that I had sent for you for purposes of discipline, and of course I have no such thought in mind. I merely want to put before you very candidly my

[1]Translation telegraphed from Switzerland by Minister Stovall, July 20th. *Foreign Relations*, 1917, Supp. 2, Vol. I, pp. 139–140.

[2]*Current History*, August, 1917, p. 197.

conclusions with the hope that you will acquiesce in them.

"It is clear that the ship-building programme is subject to the authority and approval of the Emergency Fleet Corporation, both with regard to the programme itself and with regard to the terms of the contracts under which that programme is carried out, and I have no doubt that it is as clear to you as it is to me that the right way to get action harmoniously and at once is to put yourself in the hands of the directors of the Corporation entirely with regard to these matters.

"On the other hand, it is equally clear that it is desirable and that the directors of the Corporation desire to concentrate executive authority in respect of the carrying out of the contracts and the execution of the programme in the hands of a single agent.

"It is of my personal knowledge that this is the desire and purpose of the directors of the Corporation. Anything that may have happened that might be given a different interpretation has, I am sure, been due only to a misunderstanding and, I dare say, to your very natural desire to push the programme forward with the utmost possible rapidity.

"The terms and the conditions of the contract being agreed upon, the way is cleared and I am hoping and expecting that a complete understanding may immediately be arrived at with regard to these matters.

"It was not possible in your judgment to procure wooden ships driven by powerful machinery that would be seaworthy in the trans-Atlantic commerce where high speed is desired in order to secure greater possibilities of immunity from submarine attack; but that we should build wooden ships in considerable numbers for that part of our sea-going trade which will not in all probability be exposed to submarine attack is my very clear judgment, as I believe it is also the judgment of the directors of the Emergency Fleet Corporation. The directors may deem it advisable to carry out the programme for the building of wooden ships in some other way than that which was at first contemplated, as of course they are free to do.

"I take the liberty of suggesting that no further resort be had to the public prints, either directly or indirectly. There is nothing insoluble in the present situation unless it is allowed to grow into a public controversy."

To William Denman of the Shipping Board, a letter marked "Confidential," enclosing a copy of his letter to General Goethals:

"For the same reason that I have stated in the first lines of the enclosed letter to General Goethals, I am not seeking a personal interview of you, because I do not want to lend any further weight to the public impression that there is a row of some sort on. We must work this thing out and work it out along the lines suggested in my letter to General Goethals . . . It follows exactly the lines of several of our conversations and I am sure that the directors of the corporation will do everything in their power to put things upon a clear road.

". . . I think it is imperatively necessary that we ignore public impressions of a controversy at present and also for the time being pay little regard to settling the question as to who was right or who was wrong. To keep counsel and do business it seems to me is the only way to clarify the situation."

To J. C. Hawkins of the Federal Farm Loan Board:
". . . . The amount I wished to put into the Farm Loan Bonds is $6,000. If the bonds are not to be ready for a month yet, I could and would put $8,000 into them. . . ."[1]

[1]On August 9th the President wrote that he would like to put $10,000 into Farm Loan Bonds, "if it is not asking for more than my share."

Friday, July 20th.

Before the cabinet meeting the President received Miss Rankin and a delegation from the Consumers' League of New York; and afterward he conferred with Senators Underwood and Bankhead and Representative Gray of Alabama. In the late afternoon, he and Mrs. Wilson boarded the *Mayflower* for a week-end trip down the river.

> In one of the rooms of the Senate Office Building in Washington, a drawing by lot began at 9:30 in the morning to establish the order in which the nine and a half million men who had registered should be called for examination. Secretary Baker, blindfolded, drew the first capsule from a large glass jar—Number 258—and seven more capsules were drawn by officials, while the cameras clicked. The "regular tellers," students from various universities, then took over, and the drawing continued until 2:15 on the morning of July 21st, the capsules in the jar being stirred from time to time with a long wooden spoon.
>
> Ambassador Jusserand reported that the French democracy was "particularly impressed with the desire manifested by Mr. Wilson that a society of nations be constituted"; M. Ribot had supported such a proposition in the Chamber of Deputies; he now intended to convene a commission to examine the question. The French government desired any suggestions which President Wilson might have to offer.[1]
>
> Ambassador Page telegraphed from London a reply to McAdoo's message of the 12th in the form of a long statement by the British Chancellor of the Exchequer: ".... our resources available for payments in America are exhausted. Unless the United States Government can meet in full our expenses in America, including exchange, the whole financial fabric of the alliance will collapse. This conclusion will be a matter not of months but of days. . . ."[2]
>
> Balfour the same day telegraphed Colonel House asking

---

[1] Quoting a message from the French Minister of Foreign Affairs, *Foreign Relations*, 1917, Supp. 2, Vol. I, pp. 140–141. An answer was sent on August 3rd, the President himself writing part of it. See this volume, p. 203.

[2] *Foreign Relations*, 1917, Supp. 2, Vol. I, pp. 549–554. For McAdoo's reply, sent through the State Department on August 14th, in which he still insisted on the wisdom of his proposals of the 18th (this volume, p. 171), see *ibid.*, pp. 561–564.

him to see that the statement received the "personal attention of the President," and adding: ". . . . I am sure nothing short of full aid which we ask will avoid a catastrophe."[1]

An advance of $85,000,000 to the British government brought the total amount up to $770,000,000.[2]

Polk to Ambassador Page in London, in reply to the suggestion that Admiral Sims and General Pershing be permitted to attend the Allied War Conference in Paris on the 25th as visitors: ". . . . For your confidential information the President [is] unwilling to be represented by conference of all powers engaged in the war, as we are not at war with Austria, Bulgaria or Turkey. Attendance at the conference also might give the impression to this country that this Government was discussing not only the conduct of the campaign, but the ultimate purposes having to do with peace terms."[3]

Kerensky became Prime Minister. A number of Russian regiments threw down their arms and left the trenches when German troops pierced the Russian lines on a wide front.

To W. B. Colver of the Federal Trade Commission:

"Thank you for your letter of yesterday. As a matter of fact, I had not sent word that I thought that iron ore (steel, copper, leather and other basic things) might properly be left out of the Food Bill, but the facts are these:

"These articles were not included in the House bill. They were added in the Senate, and have now been eliminated there because their inclusion would have brought on a long fight and perhaps endangered or indefinitely delayed the passage of the Act itself. Under other laws I feel convinced that power enough has been granted the administration to deal with these articles with some effectiveness, and I am certainly going to use every ounce of power I have. . . ."

---

[1] *Intimate Papers*, Vol. III, p. 106.
[2] *Foreign Relations*, 1917, Supp. 2, Vol. I, p. 548.
[3] *Ibid.*, pp. 131, 138.

To his secretary, Tumulty, regarding the problem of publicity in connection with suffragettes picketing the White House. T. W. Noyes, editor of the Washington *Evening Star*, favored having a bare statement of fact, but no publicity in any paper. Arthur Brisbane of the Washington *Times* was ready to agree if the President approved; however, he feared that a "conspiracy of silence" would drive the women to violent action in order to compel attention:

"My own opinion is that a compromise course ought to be adopted. There is a great deal in what Mr. Brisbane says about entire silence on the part of the newspapers possibly provoking the less sane of these women to violent action. My own suggestion would be that nothing that they do should be featured with headlines or put on the front page but that a bare, colorless chronicle of what they do should be all that was printed. That constitutes part of the news but it need not be made interesting reading."

To his secretary, Tumulty, who had presented a letter from O. G. Villard alleging that fourteen interned Germans at Ellis Island were taken through the streets of New York, chained together; and that many people had been illegally punished in New York for exercising their constitutional rights to criticize existing laws:

"I would like very much to have a verification of the story about the men being taken through the streets of New York chained. I would need a very specific proof of that, and I would like to know who did it.

"Mitchel's administration has done many unwise and unjustifiable things but that ought to be corrected by local opinion, not by federal intervention and I understand that to be what Mr. Villard is chiefly referring to in the latter part of his letter.

"He is entirely mistaken about certain papers having been 'suppressed.' Nothing of the kind occurred. Certain copies of certain newspapers were excluded from the mails because they contained matter explicitly forbidden by law."[1]

Saturday, July 21st.

The President and Mrs. Wilson spent the day on the *Mayflower*.

Oscar T. Crosby, Assistant Secretary of the Treasury, to Secretary McAdoo: ". . . the magnitude of our loans to foreign governments is such as to justify on the part of the United States Government a more searching inquiry than it has yet made into the general conduct of the European war. . . .

"It is quite within my duty to report to you that the Serbian Minister urges, on behalf of his country, that the United States should inform itself of the political determinations that have been made between the Allied Governments since the beginning of the war. The strong desire of the Belgian representatives for an independent financial relationship with the United States in preference to a satisfaction of their needs through English and French channels suggests the same uneasiness on the part of small nations in Europe as to the results to be gained from the war, even on the supposition of a marked success for the arms of the Allies, unless the power of the United States should be felt in the political field as well as on the field of battle. . . ."[2]

Admiral Sims reported that "the success of the convoys so far brought in shows that the system will defeat the submarine campaign if applied generally and in time."[3]

Lloyd George, speaking in Queen's Hall, London, commented on the address of the German Chancellor on the 19th. ". . . . I read that speech, as it was my duty to read it once, twice, thrice, to seek anything in it which would give hope for an end of this bloodshed, and I see a sham independence for Belgium, a sham democracy for Germany, a sham peace for Europe . . ."[4]

---

[1]Villard wrote Tumulty on the 26th that the prisoners had been handcuffed to officers; but that he had no direct proof that they had been chained together.

[2]*Hearings*, Senate Munitions Investigation, 74-2, Pt. 29, pp. 9224–9226.

[3]Sims, *The Victory at Sea*, p. 116.

[4]*Current History*, September, 1917, pp. 464–465.

To Colonel House, in regard to House's scheme for the New York *World* to send a challenge to the *Berliner Tageblatt,* proposing the presentation in each paper of the respective views of the Allies and the Central Powers. House had written to Cobb of the *World:*

". . . . The two papers would at once become a world forum . . .

"Northcliffe . . . thinks it conceivable that such a discussion might lead to peace. . . .

"The German Government would probably decline to permit such a discussion, but the refusal would hurt their cause and help that of the Allies. Before making any move the President should approve . . .":[1]

MY DEAR HOUSE:

Frankly, I see some very grave possibilities of danger in your plan for an interchange of views about peace between THE WORLD and the TAGE-Blatt, particularly if Northcliffe and Tardieu are to be made counsellors in the matter. England and France *have not the same views with regard to peace that we have* by any means. When the war is over we can force them to our way of thinking, because by that time they will, among other things, be financially in our hands; but we cannot force them now, and any attempt to speak for them or to speak our common mind would bring on disagreements which would inevitably come to the surface in public and rob the whole thing of its effect. I saw this all too plainly in a conversation with Viviani.[2] If there is to be an interchange of views at all, it ought to be between us and the liberals in Germany, with no one else brought in.

Even at that, how is the State Department, or any other official agency of the Government going to ask that the TAGEBLATT be allowed to print what the WORLD says without any interference by the censor without its

---

[1] Copy sent to the President. Cobb was much interested. *Intimate Papers,* Vol. III, pp. 142–144.

[2] See this volume, p. 43.

appearing that what is proposed is really an interchange of views between the German liberals and this Government? I do not think it possible to keep the hand of the Administration concealed.

It seems to me that these are very real difficulties and disclose some deep dangers. Our real peace terms,—those upon which we shall undoubtedly insist,—are not now acceptable to either France or Italy (leaving Great Britain for the moment out of consideration).

I have delayed writing you about this deeply important matter until I could think it out; and I must say that I have not been able to think myself on to safe ground regarding it. You may have entirely satisfactory replies to make to my objections; but I cannot think of them myself. Will you not write me again. I have thought about it enough now, I think, to promise a prompt reply.

I am writing on the MAYFLOWER, on which Mrs. Wilson and I are seeking a day or two of relief from the madness of Washington. A point is reached now and again when I *must* escape it for a little.

With affectionate messages from us all,

Your grateful Friend,
WOODROW WILSON[1]

To his daughter, Mrs. Francis B. Sayre, written on his own typewriter:

MY PRECIOUS DAUGHTER,

I cannot put into words the thoughts, the loving, wistful thoughts, I have had of you and of the dear little ones since Frank went away; and they have been with me at all sorts of times, amidst all sorts of business and all sorts of public anxieties. Edith and I are on the MAYFLOWER

---

[1]On August 9th House sent on Frank Cobb's proposed "challenge" (see *Intimate Papers*, Vol. III, p. 148) saying: ". . . . Surely, there could be no objection to putting it in this mild form. Will you not advise me what answer to make?" So far as the author can discover, the President made no answer to this letter, nor did he refer to the subject again, in writing. He may have telephoned his decision, as he frequently did.

to-day to get away from the madness (it is scarcely less) of Washington for a day or two, not to stop work (that *cannot* stop nowadays), for I had to bring Swem and my papers along, but to escape *people* and their intolerable excitements and demands. This is, therefore, the first time in weeks that I have had any chance at all to turn to my private thoughts and to the dear little girl whom I so dearly love in Nantucket and try to say some of the things that are in my heart.

I know that Helen has written to you and I have tried to keep track of you as best I could; but that is not the real thing,—that does not satisfy my heart. I hope that the visit that Margaret was planning to pay you may come off soon. Helen has gone up to Canada . . . She will probably be gone for an indefinite stay. She needs something of the kind. She has been going to lunches and dinners almost every day for months past and must have used up all the strength her nerves contained. Edith and she have been working hard (Edith is working now) on Red Cross supplies and warm things for the sailors. They have made pajamas enough, it seems to me, for a whole hospital! We try to take things light-heartedly and with cool minds, but it is not always possible, and I fear that I notice little signs of its telling on Edith. As for myself, I am surprisingly well, by all the tests that the doctor can apply, though *very* tired all the time. I am very thankful. I do not see how any but a well man could safely be trusted to decide anything in the present circumstances. . . .

My heart goes out to you, my darling Jessie, with unbounded love and solicitude! Please, when you have time, write me how things are going with you, what you hear from Frank, if a real message has had time to get through yet, and all the things, big or little, that you know I want to hear; and I do not know of anything I do *not* want to know about you in your new home.

Edith joins me in warmest love to you all and I send you, for myself, all the love that a father's heart can give to a dear daughter whom he admires as much as he loves.

Your devoted
FATHER[1]

Sunday, July 22nd.

The President and Mrs. Wilson spent the day on the *Mayflower*.

Mutiny was reported to be spreading in the Russian army. Siam declared war against Germany and Austria.

Monday, July 23rd.

The President and Mrs. Wilson returned to Washington early in the morning. Afternoon appointments: Manuel Quezon, resident commissioner from the Philippine Islands; the minister from Switzerland, to present letters of recall; Representative Park of Georgia. At four o'clock the President walked over to the State Department, to confer with Acting Secretary Polk; and from there went to the War Department, where he saw Baker and also Daniels.

At the request of Cambon, Ambassador Sharp telegraphed five questions which M. Ribot had formulated "as likely to be discussed, though unofficially, and exclusive of those relative to the Balkans" in the conference to be opened in Paris on July 25th. The opinion of the United States government was desired. Three points dealt with the rumored desire of Austria for a separate peace, the exact military help which might be expected from the United States, and the method of allotment of sums lent by the

---

[1]Mrs. Sayre replied on August 25th:

"DEAREST FATHER,

"Your beautiful long letter made me so happy! I have been feeding on it ever since. It was so wonderful of you to take the time in all these appallingly busy days to write me. . . .

"Darling Father, how I admire and love you, how wonderful and God-sustained you seem in all these intricate affairs to be, how undeviatingly *right*. I am so proud of you and I love you so dearly, dearly.

"Give my most affectionate love to dear Edith. I wish I could send you both some of this pure air to rest and refresh you!"

United States. The other two concerned certain of the secret treaties: "The Russian Government has proposed to submit to a future conference the examination of the Allied objects of the war. . . ." "The questions concerning Asia Minor have been at several times the objects of agreements between the Allies. . . ."[1]

To Secretary Daniels, enclosing for the Scripture Gift Mission a short message to go with every gift Bible sent to soldiers and sailors of the American army and navy:

"The Bible is the word of life. I beg that you will read it and find this out for yourselves—read, not little snatches here and there, but long passages that will really be the road to the heart of it. You will find it full of real men and women not only, but also of the things you have wondered about and been troubled about all your life, as men have been always; and the more you read the more it will become plain to you what things are worth while and what are not, what things make men happy—loyalty, right dealings, speaking the truth, readiness to give everything for what they think their duty, and, most of all, the wish that they may have the real approval of the Christ, who gave everything for them—and the things that are guaranteed to make men unhappy—selfishness, cowardice, greed, and everything that is low and mean. When you have read the Bible you will know that it is the Word of God, because you will have found it the key to your own heart, your own happiness, and your own duty."[2]

---

[1] See *Foreign Relations*, 1917, Supp. 2, Vol. I, pp. 144–146. These questions were never answered in full; nor was an acknowledgment sent until after the conference had adjourned. This volume, July 31st, p. 200. The President himself wrote out replies to the five questions; but these important and interesting replies were never used. This volume, August 3, p. 204.

[2] *Public Papers*, Vol. V, p. 89. Six months later Dr. William I. Haven of the American Bible Society wrote the President: ". . . in the midst of your innumerable cares and burdens, you may be interested to know how effective your words have been that you have spoken or written for the Bible. . . ." He went on to quote Dr. B. M. Tipple of the Methodist Episcopal Mission in Rome, who said: "President Wilson's words have made a deep impression on the millions in the Latin world in Southern Europe . . . [his] word for the Bible has literally entered not only millions of homes but was scattered

To Louis Wiley:

". . . . The matter of censorship is growing daily more difficult and more important, because there are certain hostile and disloyal elements in the press of the country which are taking advantage of the present situation and are doing the most dangerous and hurtful things."

To Representative A. F. Lever, who had sent the President a copy of the Food bill as it passed the Senate:

". . . . Section 23[1] is not only entirely foreign to the subject matter of the Food Administration Bill in which it is incorporated but would, if enacted into law, render my task of conducting the war practically impossible. I cannot believe that those who proposed this section scrutinized it with care or analyzed the effects which its operation would necessarily have. The constant supervision of executive action which it contemplates would amount to nothing less than an assumption on the part of the legislative body of the executive work of the administration.

"There is a very ominous precedent in our history which shows how such a supervision would operate. I refer to the committee on the conduct of the war constituted by the Congress during the administration of Mr. Lincoln. It was the cause of constant and distressing harassment and rendered Mr. Lincoln's task all but impossible.

"I am not, I beg you to believe, in any way questioning what might be the motives or the purpose of the members of such a committee: I am ready to assume that they would wish to cooperate in the most patriotic spirit, but cooperation of that kind is not practicable in the circum-

---

through the trenches, from the North Sea to the Adriatic, and from the Baltic to the Dardanelles." The President was much cheered by Dr. Haven's letter. ". . . . I had no idea that my very few and simple words about the Bible had had such an effect, and I rejoice that it is so. It was certainly a very delightful act of friendship on your part to tell me."

[1] Which provided for a "Joint Committee on Expenditures in the Conduct of the War."

stances. The responsibility rests upon the administration. There are abundant existing means of investigation and of the effective enforcement of that responsibility. I sincerely hope that upon the reconsideration of this matter both Houses of Congress will see that my objections rest upon indisputable grounds and that I could only interpret the final adoption of Section 23 as arising from a lack of confidence in myself."[1]

To Mrs. Henry F. Osborn, thanking her for sending an article by Frank Perry Olds on "The Disloyalty of the German-American Press":

". . . . I know only too well the foundations for his statements and you may be sure that the matter has been giving me a great deal of deep concern."

To his brother, J. R. Wilson:
DEAREST JOE:

I am ashamed to have overlooked your birthday and thank you with all my heart for your generosity in writing to me. Being ten years ahead of you, I can't feel impressed by your fifty years, but still I shall always try to treat you with moderate respect! I certainly congratulate you on being well in the midst of so much and such hard work. It does my heart good to hear you say that you are.

Can't you, instead of working to get rid of the loneliness, drop over and see us some time if only for an evening and night? Edith and I are all alone. Helen is in Canada with Marion Erskine and her children; Margaret is in Connecticut with her singing teacher; and Nell is seventy miles away at Blue Ridge Summit; so that we have a house

---

[1]Published in the New York *Times*, July 24, 1917. On the same day the President wrote a letter of protest to Senator Robert L. Owen; and in a postscript to a letter of the 24th to Senator B. R. Tillman, he said: ". . . . I am sure you will cooperate with my other friends in preventing my conducting of the war from being put under an espionage committee." These letters represented a part of the struggle, as old as the American system, between the President and Congress for control of essential executive functions of government, especially in times of crisis.

empty except for the painters and can always find joy in putting you up for the night.

Edith joins me in most affectionate messages, and I am as always

Your affectionate brother,
WOODROW WILSON

Tuesday, July 24th.

After the cabinet meeting in the afternoon, the President received: Senator Jones of New Mexico; David Lawrence.

The President signed the Aviation bill, which carried an appropriation of $640,000,000, and Howard Coffin stated that the Aircraft Production Board was prepared to go ahead at once. ". . . . Most gratifying progress on the preliminary organization has been made during the last few weeks. If it progresses in the future at the stride that has been developed there need be no fear as to America's position in the aircraft field by next Summer. . . ."[1]

A statement in regard to resignations from the Shipping Board was given to the press; Edward N. Hurley of Chicago was announced to replace Denman; Rear-Admiral W. L. Capps to replace Goethals, and Bainbridge Colby to replace John B. White.[2]

To Major General George W. Goethals who had submitted his resignation on the 20th:

"Your letter . . . does you great honor. It is conceived in a fine spirit of public duty, such as I have learned to expect of you. This is, as you say, a case where the service of the public is the only thing to be considered. Personal feelings and personal preferences must be resolutely put aside and we must do the thing that is most serviceable.

"It is with that thought in mind that I feel constrained to say that I think that you have interpreted your duty rightly.

[1] *Current History*, September, 1917, p. 514.
[2] New York *Times*, July 25, 1917.

"No impartial determination of the questions at issue can now set the shipbuilding programme promptly and effectively on its way to completion and success. It is best that we take the self-forgetting course you suggest and begin again with a fresh sheet of paper,—begin, not the shipbuilding, but the further administration of the programme. The shipbuilding is, happily, in large part begun and can now readily be pushed to completion, if the air be cleared of the debates that have unfortunately darkened it.

"With deep appreciation, therefore, of your generous attitude and with genuine admiration of what you have been able in a short time to accomplish, I accept your resignation, and feel that in doing so I am acting upon your own best judgment as well as my own. I hope that you will feel the same undoubting confidence that I feel that the people of the country, for whom you have rendered great services, will judge you justly and generously in this as in other things, and that all personal misunderstandings and misjudgments that may have been created will pass in a short time entirely away."

To William Denman:

"I hope and believe that I am interpreting your own best judgment as well as my own when I say that our duty concerning the debates and misunderstandings that have arisen in connection with the shipbuilding programme ought to be settled without regard to our personal preferences or our personal feelings altogether and with the single purpose of doing what will best serve the public interest. No decision we can now arrive at could eliminate the elements of controversy that have crept into almost every question connected with the programme; and I am convinced that the only wise course is to begin afresh,—not upon the programme, for that is already in large part in process of execution, but upon the further execution of it.

"I have found both you and General Goethals ready to serve the public at a personal sacrifice. Realizing that the only manner in which the way can be completely cleared for harmonious and effective action is to carry our shipbuilding plans forward from this point through new agencies, General Goethals has put his resignation in my hands; and I have adopted it in the same spirit in which it was tendered,—not as deciding between two men whom I respect and admire, but in order to make invidious decisions unnecessary and let the work be developed without further discussion of what is past. I am taking the liberty of writing to tell you this in the confidence that you will be glad to take the same disinterested and self-forgetting course that General Goethals has taken. When you have done as he has done I am sure that you may count with the utmost confidence upon the ultimate verdict of the people of the country with regard to your magnanimous and unselfish view of public duty and upon winning in the retrospect the same admiration and confidence that I have learned to feel for you.

"With much regard and very great appreciation of the large services you have rendered . . ."

To William Denman, who wrote that he was under fire in the Hearst papers in California for alleged personal interest in contracts for timber, and asked for an interview:

"I am surprised and indignant to learn of the absurd charges that are being made against you in some of the California papers, and I hope sincerely that if there is any way in which I can be of service to you in exposing their gross injustice you will let me know and I shall be very glad indeed to do anything that I can to express my entire confidence in your ability not only, but in your integrity."

To William Denman:

"You have asked for a personal interview and I want to make a suggestion to you about it. I have learned to have a sincere and warm admiration for your ability and I hope that you have felt my genuine friendship, for it has been very real, and therefore I can say this to you frankly, that I do not think it would be wise for us to have a personal interview at present. It would certainly be misconstrued in ways which I think a moment's reflection will easily reveal to you. It would be taken to mean either that we were still discussing the situation or that there was some difference between us that needed to be straightened out.

"I want to serve your interest in every way that I can, and frankness I am sure is one of the ways. There was, as I take it for granted you also think, no other solution for the *impasse* we had arrived at but that which I suggested, and I have confidence that in the end all the merits involved will be clearly revealed."

To Dr. Charles W. Eliot, who urged the immediate enactment of the Canadian law for the investigation of industrial disputes:

". . . . Unhappily, what you suggest about the labor difficulties is practically impossible. I have dealt with this matter so much now that I have a somewhat intimate knowledge of the feeling of Congress and of the possibilities of legislation along those lines, and I am sorry to say that it would be impossible at this session at any rate to obtain any legislation whatever.

"You do not overstate the dangers and ominous signs of the times and we are watching the whole thing with anxiety. I dare say that if it develops, a time may come when some sort of legislative action dealing with the matter will be obviously necessary."[1]

---

[1]On the same day Secretary Wilson sent over a report on the serious labor situation in the Northwest. The state of Washington was in a particularly bad way—a strike in the lumbering industry, strikes in the street car systems of two cities, and danger of a strike among the longshoremen.

To John D. Ryan, asking him to accept membership in the newly created Red Cross War Council:

". . . . The close cooperation between the American National Red Cross and the military branch of the Government has already suggested new avenues of helpfulness in the immediate business of our organization for war, but the present crisis is larger than that and there are unlimited opportunities of broad humanitarian service in view for the American National Red Cross. Battlefield relief will be effected through Red Cross agencies operating under the supervision of the War Department, but civilian relief will present a field of increasing opportunity in which the Red Cross organization is especially adapted to serve, and I am hopeful that our people will realize that there is probably no other agency with which they can associate themselves which can respond so effectively and universally to allay suffering and relieve distress."

To Daniel Moreau Barringer, a Princeton classmate, who had recommended his cousin for appointment to the Food Control Board:

"I have your letter . . . but if I can help it 'there ain't going to be no Food Control *Board*.' I think that it will come out in conference. It makes the bill practically unworkable.

"I was glad, however, to have a chance to hear from you."

Wednesday, July 25th.

The President's afternoon appointments: Senator John Sharp Williams of Mississippi; Winston Churchill; Gavin McNab; Representative Littlepage of West Virginia; Secretary McAdoo.

An Inter-Allied Conference, at which the United States had declined to be represented, was held in Paris, July 25–26.[1]

---

[1]For Ambassador Sharp's reports both before and after the conference, see *Foreign Relations*, 1917, Supp. 2, Vol. I, pp. 144–151; 154. It was at this time that M. Ribot

To Rear-Admiral W. L. Capps:

"I fear that you have learned rather too informally of the new and exceedingly important duty to which I have taken the liberty to assign you, and if that has caused you any inconvenience I beg to apologize.

"I am sure that you will realize the necessity that existed for prompt and definite action, leaving no elements of conjecture in the settlement, and I want you to know that my selection of yourself for the task which it has been necessary that General Goethals should lay down was based upon a very great confidence in your character and ability. I beg that you will accept the assignment as an evidence of my friendship and trust.

"I have no doubt that General Goethals will be very glad to confer with you about every phase of the business that will need your attention, and I have this to suggest: I am told that General Goethals has brought into association with him some very energetic and capable men and it may be that you will find it to your advantage to retain them at your own side in this undertaking into which you have been so suddenly thrust."[1]

To Major General G. W. Goethals:

"Our crisis is past and I do not believe that anybody concerned need feel apprehensive of the general verdict of opinion when the matter comes to be summed up in retrospect. The whole thing, I dare say, was inevitable, and I have sincerely admired the manly and soldierly qualities you have shown.

"I am sure that no suggestion from me is needed that you get into touch with Rear Admiral Capps and put him in your place as completely as is possible in the circumstances."

---

showed Sonnino all the correspondence in the Prince Sixte negotiations, thus breaking the confidence of Emperor Karl of Austria. *War Memoirs of David Lloyd George,* Vol. IV, p. 259.

[1]Letters in the same tenor went to Bainbridge Colby and E. N. Hurley.

To William Denman, who, in tendering his formal resignation on the 24th, had also sent a personal letter to the President— ". . . . What becomes of the tiny reputation of one man is a matter of insignificance in a World's struggle"—and a copy of his letter to his successor, Mr. Hurley, offering to help in every possible way:

"May I not say that you have acted admirably and in perfect accord with the high estimate I had formed of you?"

To Theodore Brent of the Shipping Board, who had placed his resignation in the President's hands, to be used if desired:

"I have your letter of yesterday. It is an additional evidence of the spirit you have always shown and I thank you for it most sincerely.

"I beg you to believe that in the action I have taken I was not trying to play arbiter on the merits of any question that has been in debate. I merely felt, as I said to Mr. Denman and General Goethals, that no settlement of the controversy would be a clarification of the situation, and they have responded to that suggestion as generously and in as handsome a spirit as could have been shown by anybody.

"At the same time, I believe that I read between the lines of your letter a feeling on your part that you would be happier if released from further service in the Board, and I do not feel at liberty to ask you to remain feeling as intimately identified with the controversy, now happily passed, as you evidently do. I, therefore, accept your resignation without desiring it, and in doing so I want to express my deep appreciation of the conscientious and highly useful service you have rendered the Government and the country."

To Thomas D. Jones, who wrote that he had seen — — ———, in accordance with the President's request of the 10th, and found that his invention was, as the President had suspected, "a renewal of the nonsense of perpetual motion.":

"It was generous of you to see Mr. —— and test his ideas. I hope you derived some amusement from it at least.

"I am afraid I have grown soft-hearted and credulous in these latter days, credulous in respect to the scientific possibility of almost any marvel and soft-hearted because of the many evidences of simple-hearted purpose this war has revealed to me."

To Senator William E. Borah:

"It was very generous of you to put Brailsford's book, 'A League of Nations,' at my disposal. I shall try to look it over promptly and send the copy back to you."

To Henry C. Hall, chairman of the Interstate Commerce Commission:

"Circumstances have arisen which lead me to ask the Interstate Commerce Commission through you to ascertain the capacity of the factories that are now manufacturing railway cars and railway locomotives, and also whether those factories are working and producing at full capacity.

"The supply of rolling stock and motive power to the railways both of the United States and of the countries associated with us in the war has become of such capital importance that I feel justified in asking the Commission to undertake this inquiry."

Thursday, July 26th.

Afternoon appointments: Senator Tillman of South Carolina; Thomas Royden and James Arthur Salter, received at the request of the State Department; Senator Pomerene of Ohio; Senator Newlands of Nevada, in regard to the valuation of property in the District of Columbia; Senator Phelan of California.

J. Ramsay MacDonald, Socialist and Labor Member of the House of Commons, moved that the German Reichstag resolution of the 19th expressed the principles for which Great Britain had stood throughout; and called upon the Allied governments to "restate their peace terms." MacDonald's resolution declared further that "the Allies should accept the Russian proposal that the forthcoming allied conference on war aims shall comprise representatives of the peoples and not solely spokesmen of the Governments."[1]

Senator Borah, speaking in the Senate: ". . . . I am not so sure but that the time has come when the American people should have presented to them more definitely and specifically the terms and conditions upon which we are fighting the war and the terms and conditions upon which we would cease to fight it. . . ."[2]

To T. W. Gregory:

"The Trading with the Enemy Bill is now in the hands of the Senate Committee and Senator Ransdell is anxious to report it out. My advice having been sought in the matter, I have advised the Committee that all of those provisions of the bill which relate to banks and strictly financial business be placed for administration in the hands of the Secretary of the Treasury.

"I did this in order to avoid duplication. The machinery already exists in the Treasury for undertaking this administration, and it would be necessary in any case that that machinery should be used, which would mean a good deal of lost motion unless the responsibility also was placed with the Treasury Department.

"I hope that you will feel as I do, that the reasons for this were conclusive."[3]

Friday, July 27th.

Secretary and Mrs. McAdoo were guests at luncheon. Before the cabinet meeting the President received Representative

---

[1]Defeated, 148-9. *Current History*, September, 1917, pp. 465-466.

[2]*Ibid.*, p. 461.

[3]A similar letter went to Secretary Redfield.

Keating of Colorado and a committee of five. At 4:30 Champ Clark, Speaker of the House, called; at five o'clock, George Creel.

> German aircraft raided Paris on the nights of the 27th and 28th, with but small damage—the first Paris raids in a year and a half.

To Thomas D. Jones:

"I am afraid you will think me very persistent in asking you to render this, that and the other service of capital importance to the Government, but the fact is that I trust and believe in you so entirely that I am, I must confess, covetous of the privilege of having you at hand here to take counsel with.

"Mr. Hurley, as you know, whom I have just asked to serve as Chairman of the Shipping Board, was serving as the representative of the Department of Commerce in the [War Trade] Board to which is assigned the very important duty of working out the practical application and operation of the restrictions we are putting on exports, and his transfer leaves a vacancy on that board which I am particularly anxious to have you fill if you feel that you have the freedom and the strength to devote yourself to what I am afraid are rather arduous duties but duties which I dare not entrust to anybody who will not take a look around the horizon in performing them. The Secretary of Commerce has asked me if I would not write to you.

"I know that you will make the frankest and most candid response. That is one of the reasons I feel at liberty to make such a request."[1]

To his secretary, Tumulty, who had called attention to a letter from L. W. Nieman as to the efforts being made against the draft in Wisconsin. Nieman felt that if something were not done at once, there would be serious trouble for which the President would be held responsible:

---

[1] Jones accepted, and the President telegraphed on August 2nd: "Delighted and grateful that you are coming . . ."

"I wish you would discuss this with the Attorney General. Mr. Nieman seems to think that there is something we can do, whereas there is nothing we can do in addition to what we are doing. Anybody is entitled to make a campaign against the draft law provided they don't stand in the way of the administration of it by any overt acts or improper influences."

Saturday, July 28th.

Since it was Saturday, the President permitted himself more time than usual for golf. His brother, Joseph R. Wilson, was a guest at luncheon. After a conference with Secretary Baker at four o'clock, he took a long drive with Mrs. Wilson.

Acting Secretary Polk wrote the President that at a meeting of the Exports Council the day before, the Advisory Board had recommended that no license be issued for the exportation of foodstuffs to Denmark, the recommendation being backed by a memorandum from Hoover. Upon the letter is a pencilled note in Mr. Polk's handwriting: "President thinks Mr. Hoover goes too far. Said he had stood up for rights of neutrals in past and was not prepared to forbid them to trade with Germany."

Secretary Daniels to Admiral Sims: "The paramount duty of the destroyers in European waters is principally the proper protection of transports with American troops . . . bear in mind that everything is secondary to having a sufficient number to insure protection . . ."[1]

The establishment of a War Industries Board was announced, with the President's approval, as a part of the reorganization of the Council of National Defense. It was to be composed of seven members, with Frank A. Scott at its head.[2]

To Secretary Lane:

"I have been thinking a great deal recently about the chance we shall have in filling the place made vacant by

---

[1]Daniels, *Our Navy at War*, p. 76.

[2]Other members: Lieut. Colonel Palmer E. Pierce; Rear-Admiral Frank F. Fletcher; B. M. Baruch; Robert S. Brookings; Robert S. Lovett; Hugh Frayne. See Clarkson, *Industrial America in the World War*, p. 37.

Mr. Sweeney's[1] death to go out of the beaten track and select somebody from some part of the country which has hitherto been unrepresented but which is showing an inclination to take sides with us and the things we believe in."

To Representative L. C. Dyer of Missouri:

". . . . The Attorney General and I have been giving a great deal of thought to the situation [race riots] in East St. Louis, and the United States District Attorney there as well as special agents of the Department of Justice have been at work gathering information to enable us to determine whether any federal statute has been violated. Up to this time I am bound in candor to say that no facts have been presented to us which would justify federal action, though it is conceivable that a condition which would justify it may develop.

"I am informed that the Attorney General of the State of Illinois has gone to East St. Louis to add his efforts to those of the officials of the county and city in pressing prosecutions under the state laws. The representatives of the Department of Justice are so far as possible lending aid to the state authorities in their efforts to restore tranquility and guard against further outbreaks.

"I need not tell you how much anxiety the whole matter has given me. It is a very serious thing for the whole nation that anything of the sort that happened in East St. Louis should be possible."

Sunday, July 29th.

The President and Mrs. Wilson went to the Central Presbyterian Church in the morning; and in the afternoon took a long drive.

The German Chancellor, speaking to a group of newspaper men, offered what he considered proof of Allied greed for

---

[1]Bo Sweeney, Assistant Secretary of the Interior.

conquest, making a number of references to alleged secret treaties.[1]

Czernin, Austro-Hungarian Foreign Minister, gave out a statement at Vienna: ".... As we have fought in conjunction with our faithful allies, so we shall make peace in conjunction with them, now or later, and we shall fight in conjunction with them to the last extremity unless the enemy shows a willingness to understand our viewpoint. ..."[2]

Monday, July 30th.

The President received Secretary Burleson and Representative Lever at 11:30. The joint conference on the Food bill had adjourned in order to permit Lever, sponsor of the House bill, to ask the President to assist in straightening out the deadlock as to the method of food control; and the question of a joint committee to supervise war expenditures. The President declared himself unalterably opposed to any divided authority. Lever, returning to the conference, reported the President's views; and during the day the Senate conferees yielded on the first point, permitting adoption of one-man control. At 11:50 the President received Senator Chamberlain. Afternoon appointments: Secretary Wilson; Secretary Daniels; E. N. Hurley; Senator Martin of Virginia. In the evening Senator Warren called, at the President's request, to discuss the Food bill deadlock. As a result of the interview Warren accepted the President's views. After he had gone the President telephoned to Lever, asking him to stand pat and saying that he thought things would work out all right in a few days.[3]

London houses were shaken by the terrific cannonading in Flanders, one hundred and twenty miles away.

In the course of a debate in the House of Commons on Lord Robert Cecil's recent statement that "the dismemberment of Austria was not one of Great Britain's war aims," Mr. Balfour said it would not be wise for the Government to declare the details of its policy at this juncture.[4]

---

[1] *Current History*, September, 1917, pp. 467–468. Ribot denied the charges the following day. *Ibid.*, pp. 470–471.

[2] *Ibid.*, pp. 468–469.

[3] A. S. Lever to the author.

[4] *Current History*, September, 1917, p. 469.

André Tardieu, French high commissioner to the United States, made public statistics showing the excellent condition of the French army after three years of war—a reply to American press reports that French morale was low.[1]

To Pleasant A. Stovall, Minister to Switzerland, and a boyhood friend:

". . . . I read all your dispatches and so feel that I am in a way keeping in touch with you, and you may be sure that my thoughts often turn to you. You are in the midst of a whispering gallery and it must be intensely interesting, though very puzzling what to believe."

Tuesday, July 31st.

The President had a morning conference with Representatives Adamson of Georgia, Sims of Tennessee, and Kitchin of North Carolina. Before the cabinet meeting in the afternoon, Senator Newlands of Nevada called.

Acting Secretary Polk telegraphed Ambassador Sharp in Paris, in partial reply to his message of July 23rd: "Question No. 3 refers to agreements between Allies concerning Asia Minor. Department has no information regarding these agreements and would be glad to be informed of their nature in order that it may be in a position to answer the inquiry."[2]

The bombardment in Flanders culminated in a gigantic infantry attack, both British and French troops taking part. ". . . . The fighting on the Western Front," wrote Ludendorff later, "became more severe and costly than any the German army had yet experienced. . . ."[3]

Wednesday, August 1st.

At nine o'clock the President received Representatives Adamson and Sims of the Interstate and Foreign Commerce Committee of the House. Afternoon appointments: William Kent and Clarence Darrow;[4] Kent E. Keller of Illinois; the

---

[1] *Current History,* September, 1917, pp. 481–482.

[2] *Foreign Relations,* 1917, Supp. 2, Vol. I, p. 151.

[3] *Ludendorff's Own Story,* Vol. II, p. 87.

[4] Mr. Kent wrote the President later that he, the President, had gained Darrow's "entire confidence and backing."

minister from Norway, who presented Dr. Fridtjof Nansen, head of a Norwegian special mission to discuss embargo matters. The President and Mrs. Wilson took a long drive late in the afternoon; and a number of Mrs. Wilson's relatives were guests at dinner, going afterward to Keith's Theater.

From this time on, through January, 1918, Allied merchant shipping losses averaged 390,000 tons a month.[1]

The Senate passed a resolution for the submission to the states of a prohibition amendment; it was made inoperative unless ratified by three fourths of the states before July 1, 1923.

Stubborn fighting in Flanders while the rain poured down; infantry slipped and stumbled; tanks lumbered forward through mud up to the hubs.

To Representative L. C. Dyer of Missouri, who had deplored the campaign of slanderous attacks on citizens of German birth and ancestry, especially in St. Louis:

"Your letters . . . have struck a responsive chord in my mind. I have been made aware from various sources of the unfortunate position in which a very large number of our loyal fellow-citizens are placed because of their German origin or affiliations.

"I am sure that they need no further assurance from me of my confidence in the entire integrity and loyalty of the great body of our fellow-citizens of German blood. You know that not once but many times in my public addresses I have expressed this confidence. I do not like to make another occasion to express it simply because it would seem to indicate on my part a doubt as to whether the country had believed my previous assurances to be sincere. May I not very respectfully suggest that it would be easy to make use of the passages I have referred to from my former addresses to do something, I hope not a little, to offset the evil influences that are at work?"

---

[1] *Naval Investigation Hearings*, 1920, Vol. I, p. 36.

To Michael J. Slattery of Philadelphia, explaining why he could not accept an invitation:

". . . I have found it literally impossible to promise to do anything away from Washington, and I am sorry to say that the members of the Cabinet are tied by the leg as I am. Every time I am out of the city for a few hours I come back to find things piled high which ought to have been promptly attended to. . . ."

To his secretary, Tumulty, who reported a steady demand for a statement from the White House regarding the East St. Louis race riots—a delegation of twenty Negroes had called that morning with a petition:

"I wish very much that you would think this over and tell me just what form and occasion you think such a statement ought to take. I want to make it if it can be made naturally and with the likelihood that it will be effective."

Thursday, August 2nd.

The President spent the morning in his study, omitting his usual golf. Afternoon appointments: Former Governor John K. Tener of Pennsylvania, and a delegation of Elks who offered $1,000,000 for the establishment of base hospitals in France; Frank J. Sprague, of the Naval Consulting Board; Royal Meeker, Commissioner of Labor Statistics; Secretary McAdoo; George Creel; Secretary Baker.

Ambassador Sharp reported a talk with M. Cambon (pursuant to the Department's telegram of inquiry, July 31st) during which he had learned a good deal about the secret treaties having to do with Asia Minor.[1]

To Representative Edward J. King:

". . . . I believe that the matter of the Committee on War Expenditures is slowly working itself out and I am very happy to feel that I can count upon the support of

---

[1]*Foreign Relations,* 1917, Supp. 2, Vol. I, pp. 155–156. The copy in Mr. Wilson's files is marked "For the President." It may well have been after reading this dispatch that the President wrote out in shorthand his answers to Cambon's questions of the 23rd of July, which were never used. This volume, p. 204.

the House in resisting the effort to put this millstone around my neck, as you very properly characterize it."

Friday, August 3rd.

Before cabinet meeting the President received Representative Sherley of Kentucky; afterward Senator Robinson of Arkansas. In the late afternoon he and Mrs. Wilson boarded the *Mayflower* for a week-end trip.

Acting Secretary Polk to Jusserand, in reply to his message of July 20th—the following paragraph being written by the President:

". . . . Noting the intention of Mr. Ribot to assemble at some early date a commission to consider the feasibility, the form, and the objects of a society of nations, the President, in response to Mr. Ribot's gracious wish for an expression of his opinion, expresses the fear that such a commission, if constituted at this time, would be premature and unnecessarily introduce new subjects of discussion and perhaps of difference of view[1] among the nations associated against Germany. The President's own idea has been that such a society of nations would of necessity be an evolution rather than a creation by formal convention. It has been his hope and expectation that the war would result in certain definite covenants and guarantees entered into by the free nations of the world for the purpose of safeguarding their own security and the general peace of the world and that in the very process of carrying these covenants into execution from time to time a machinery and practice of cooperation would naturally spring up which would in the end produce something which would in effect be a regularly constituted and employed concert of nations. To begin with a discussion of how such a concert or society should be constituted, under the presidency of which nation, with what common force and under what common command, etc., etc., would be likely to produce jealousies and difficulties which need not be faced now."[2]

---

[1]This phrase appears to have been added, presumably by the President, after his first shorthand draft.

[2]From the President's shorthand draft. Printed in *Foreign Relations*, 1917, Supp. 2, Vol. I, p. 153.

The President's shorthand notes continue with the following passage which, for some reason not revealed by the documents, was never used:

"With regard to the questions propounded in your 2321, July 23,[1] the President requests you to thank M. Cambon for his kindness in submitting the questions it contains and begs that you will convey the following replies:

"1) If the Russian government should propose a conference for the common formulation of the objects of the war against Germany the President does not see how the suggestions could wisely be rejected. The democratic feeling of the world is demanding more and more audibly an insistent statement from the nations associated against Germany, which will show that the object of the war is not aggrandizement but the freedom of the peoples to secure independence ———— and free themselves against aggression whether by physical force or successful economic arrangement. The President hopes that the issue can be met squarely and candidly.

"2) The President believes that if the eastern people could be satisfied on these points the movement in Austria for peace would be irresistible. The acceptance or rejection of any particular ———— that Austria may make and of any particular overtures she may make would necessarily depend upon their free and apparent purpose.

"3) With regard to the agreement concerning Asia Minor the President feels that it would be exceedingly difficult now to conclude peace on any terms which would mean arrangements in Asia Minor for the benefit of particular nations rather than merely for the benefit and protection of the peoples of that part of the world. The sentiment of the world is now aggressively democratic, and will have to be met half way.

"4) The military ———— to be ———— with regard to the United States.

"5) It is the hope of the President that the Government of France and the Governments of our Allies will find it possible to arrange for such a common agency as was recently proposed by the Secretary of the Treasury of the United States for determining the limit of several loans of

[1] This volume, pp. 183–184.

sums to be lent to them by the Government of the United States."[1]

The Russian ambassador transmitted assurances from his Minister of Foreign Affairs that Russia would continue the war in spite of all difficulties.[2]

To Senator R. L. Owen, who had written to explain why he favored a congressional committee on expenditures in the conduct of the war:

"I thank you sincerely for your full and detailed reply to my letter about the Joint Committee of Congress. My own feeling is this, that the creation of such a committee would produce very much such a situation as I have just tried to cure and I think succeeded in curing in the case of the shipbuilding contracts. In such a case there would be, on the one hand, the Executive entrusted with the expenditures of moneys and the making of contracts and, on the other hand, a body, a committee, which would have no authority in the matter and the function only of criticism and publicity, a function not dissimilar to that which the Shipping Board recently performed with regard to the contracts entered into for the ships. Differences of judgment are always possible in such cases and would almost certainly arise, and there would be no immediate means of settling any difference of opinion. Resort would be to Congress and the result, if there were any result, legislative action with regard to executive matters. I cannot help but believing [sic] that this would simply be an arrangement that would produce discussion and not efficiency.

"It is not as if there were not already existing means by which Congress can keep itself apprised of the expenditures of the Government, and I want to assure you that

---

[1] The President's notes have been transcribed as well as possible, since they are important in showing his developing thought on the plan for a League of Nations, and since they deal in part with certain secret treaties.

[2] *Foreign Relations*, 1918, *Russia*, Vol. I, pp. 172–173.

in connection with every spending agency of the Government we are at present interested in nothing so much as in providing instrumentalities which will prevent excessive prices and unreasonable contracts. I have very much at heart the economical and efficient expenditure of the vast sums of money which must be spent for the conduct of this war and I feel that the whole thing should be managed with the daily care of a responsible administrative agency.

"May I not say how glad I am always to exchange opinions upon matters of such consequence and to express my own with the greatest candor as well as with the greatest respect? I have realized throughout that your own personal desire in this case was certainly not to be obstructive in any way but rather to be helpful."

Saturday, August 4th.

The President and Mrs. Wilson spent the day on the *Mayflower*.

Officers of the United Mine Workers of America telegraphed the President asking him to "assist in bringing about conference" with coal operators of Alabama. Unless this could be done, a strike would begin on August 20th. Secretary Wilson, whom the President consulted, replied that he had determined upon two mediators to send to Alabama.

Liberia declared war against Germany.

Sunday, August 5th.

The President and Mrs. Wilson spent the day on the *Mayflower*.

Monday, August 6th.

President and Mrs. Wilson returned to the White House. After a round of golf, and a period of work in his study, the President received Secretary Wilson and Judge J. Harry Covington, who was to be sent to California for consultation with Governor Stephens on the labor situation.[1] Afternoon appointments: Senator James H. Lewis; members of the War Industries Board; Justice Frederick L. Siddons and a committee of the Commercial Law League of America; Representative Garrett of Texas; Frank L. Polk.

> The British ambassador sent over a memorandum drawn up by the British War Cabinet for the President's personal information. "It gives all available facts & figures as to the submarine situation and points out that the part which your government can play in dealing with the menace is absolutely vital to the successful prosecution of the war."
> The first American man-of-war for escort duty arrived at Gibraltar.[2]

Tuesday, August 7th.

The President worked in his study until eleven o'clock, when he walked over to the office of the Federal Trade Commission to ascertain the progress being made in the cost determining work which was being conducted at his request. Evening at Keith's Theater with Dr. and Mrs. Grayson.

To Senator Marcus A. Smith of Arizona, who complained that his recommendations with regard to Boards of Exemption Appeals in his own state had been ignored by Secretary Baker:

"I have your letter . . . I hope that you realize the limitations under which the Secretary of War and all the rest of us are acting in the matter of the enlisting boards. We felt inevitably bound to accept the nominations of the Governors and let the responsibility of the states rest upon them unless definite objections to particular persons named by them should be suggested to us which would make it improper to act upon their nominations.

"And with regard to such appointments as you suggest . . . I beg that you will also realize the limitations to which I feel obliged to restrict myself. Every time I per-

---

[1] In his letter to Governor Stephens, introducing Justice Covington, the President said: ". . . he has my entire confidence and . . . I am glad to call him my personal friend."

[2] *Naval Investigation Hearings,* 1920, Vol. II, p. 2165.

sonally intervene in regard to Army appointments (I have not yet intervened in any case) confusion is sure to arise and the appointment to assume the aspect of an act of personal favoritism. I have put the stern command upon myself to let the appointments alone as severely and entirely as possible.

"I am sure, my dear Senator, with your close observation of public affairs you will see the force of all this and exonerate me from any lack of interest in the suggestions of a friend whom I value so much as I do yourself."

Wednesday, August 8th.

The President's afternoon appointments: Representative Adamson of Georgia and Judge William T. Newman; Elihu Root and the Commission to Russia.[1] Secretary Baker called during the evening.

The Senate passed the conference report on the Food bill, 66 to 7, with a provision for one-man control.

To Samuel Gompers, enclosing a telegram just received from the Arizona State Federation of Labor. The convention of the Federation desired to know if the President intended to "act in restoring law and order in Cochise County, Arizona, and return to their homes the deported men of Bisbee. Are we to assume that Phelps Dodge interests are superior to the principles of democracy. . . .":

"I don't like to trouble you with any larger correspondence than you have, but I would very much like your

---

[1] For the report of the commission and a supplementary report proposing an educational campaign to strengthen the morale of the civil population and the army (sent by Dr. Mott on August 21st in response to a request made by the President) see *Foreign Relations, 1918, Russia,* Vol. I, pp. 131–146 and 147–153. The report was already outdated and misleading, since affairs in Russia were moving too fast for such methods. With the cables and with an eyewitness knowledge of many of the kaleidoscopic events since March, 1917, our regular diplomatic representatives could not send reports complete and numerous enough to keep the Department at Washington up to date. What could have been expected of a group of men, no matter how intelligent and conscientious their efforts, who had spent only a few weeks in the midst of a constantly changing situation?

See *War Memoirs of Robert Lansing,* pp. 337–338. Lansing could not, he said, rely on the views of the commission "without doing violence to" his own better judgment.

advice as to how I should answer the enclosed. I am loath to believe that genuine representatives of the Federation of Labor would send me a message containing so unjust and offensive an intimation."[1]

Telegram to ex-President William Howard Taft, who had fallen ill in Kansas, while on a speaking tour in support of the government's conduct of the war:

"Have been very much distressed to learn of your illness. Hope that it is not serious and that you are rapidly coming to feel like yourself again. Cordially and sincerely."[2]

To Senator G. E. Chamberlain, who had criticized Senator Gore in the Senate for his obstructionist tactics while the country was at war:[3]

"I cannot write you upon another subject without giving myself the pleasure of saying how thoroughly justified I think you were in your remarks of the day before yesterday in the Senate and how sincerely glad I am that you made them. It is time that we put an end in the most emphatic way to the sort of tactics that have been indulged in."

Thursday, August 9th.

Mrs. McAdoo, the President's daughter, had luncheon at the White House. Afternoon appointments: Professor Harry Fielding Reid of Baltimore; Vance McCormick; Senator Smith and Representative Lever of South Carolina; Senator Newlands, who discussed the conservation of water power. Secretary and Mrs. McAdoo took dinner at the White House, and all went to the Belasco Theater in the evening.

---

[1] Gompers wrote on the 10th: ". . . . I quite agree with you that the tone and the intimation in the telegram you received are harsh, and particularly so when those who know you know your high sense of justice and consuming purpose to protect the rights and the needs of our people. . . ." He went on to show, however, how natural it was for men who had been so greatly wronged to express themselves too strongly.

[2] Taft replied by wire the same day: "Thank you for your kind telegram and inquiry. I am better and hope to be out in a few days."

[3] August 6th. *Cong. Rec.*, 65-1, Vol. 55, pp. 5833-5835.

To John Franklin Fort of the Federal Trade Commission, who had suggested that the President call into conference a dozen or so of the leading bituminous coal operators and put up to them the matter of the price of coal, since the Food bill, with its coal provision, was soon to become operative. He felt that such a plan would result in coöperation of every operator in the United States:

"Thank you warmly for your letter of yesterday. It makes a deep impression on me and I will consider its suggestion about the matter of handling the coal prices and the coal production very seriously.

"I am very happy to know that you are going to let me have the facts now in your possession so soon."

To Clarence S. Darrow:

"I agree with Mr. Kent that you could probably do a great deal of good by speaking on the East Side of New York and, as we agreed in our recent conversation, that is a place where wise work is very urgently needed.

"You may be sure I will try to work out with the Postmaster General some course with regard to the circulation of the Socialistic papers that will be in conformity with law and good sense."

Friday, August 10th.

Before the cabinet meeting Senator Bankhead called, to present Dr. Trotter of Alabama. Herbert Hoover saw the President at 4:30, bringing with him, among other memoranda, one on the creation of a board to determine a fair price for 1917 wheat. After his interview Hoover issued a public warning to those who had been gambling with the food supply.[1] In the late afternoon the President and Mrs. Wilson, with Mr. and Mrs. J. B. Bolling, boarded the *Mayflower* for a week-end trip.

The President signed the Food bill; and formally appointed Herbert Hoover Food Administrator.

The great Flanders battle was renewed, General Haig's forces capturing most of the German positions in the sector east and southeast of Ypres.

---

[1] New York *Times*, August 11, 1917.

To A. H. Buckmaster, who had identified himself as an ordinary citizen who had "nothing to get." ". . . Before you broke off relations with Germany I cursed the day I voted for you for I thought you were selling the honor of the country to avoid what seemed to me to be our duty. . . . I am making & shall continue to make all the amends in my power. . . . I meet many men & you would be pleased to know how general the approval of your work is. . . .":

"Your frank letter . . . has given me a great deal of pleasure. I can only thank you very heartily and express the hope that many others have seen the difficulties through which I struggled and the considerations which necessarily controlled my decisions. It is very delightful to receive such assurances."

Saturday, August 11th.

The *Mayflower*, on which the President was supposed to be spending one of his usual week-end vacations, in reality sailed to a point near Yorktown, where the dreadnaughts of the Atlantic Fleet were awaiting him. Without the usual salute of guns he boarded the *Pennsylvania* and there, in strictest confidence, spoke to the assembled officers like "a football coach . . . to his team between the halves":[1]

"I have not come here with malice prepense to make a speech," the President said, "but I have come here to have a look at you and to say some things that perhaps may be intimately said and, even though the company is large, said in confidence. . . .

"Nobody ever before conducted a war like this and therefore nobody can pretend to be a professional in a war like this. . . .

"We are hunting hornets all over the farm and letting the nest alone. . . . I am willing for my part, and I know you are willing because I know the stuff you are made of . . . to sacrifice half the navy Great Britain and we together have to crush that nest, because if we crush it, the war is won. . . .

"We have got to throw tradition to the wind. As I have said, gentlemen, I take it for granted that nothing that I say here will be repeated and therefore I am going to say this: Every

---

[1] Lawrence, *The True Story of Woodrow Wilson*, p. 221.

time we have suggested anything to the British Admiralty the reply has come back that virtually amounted to this, that it had never been done that way, and I felt like saying, 'Well, nothing was ever done so systematically as nothing is being done now. . . .' Do not stop to think about what is prudent for a moment. Do the thing that is audacious to the utmost point of risk and daring, because that is exactly the thing that the other side does not understand, and you will win by the audacity of method when you cannot win by circumspection and prudence. . . .

". . . I have come down here to say also that I depend on you, depend on you for brains as well as training and courage and discipline . . . . do not let anybody ever put one thought of discouragement into your minds. I do not know what is the matter with the newspapers of the United States! I suppose they have to vary the tune from time to time just to relieve their minds, but every now and then a wave of the most absurd discouragement and pessimism goes through the country and we hear nothing except of the unusual advantages and equipment and sagacity and preparation and all the other wonderful things of the German Army and Navy. My comment is always the very familiar comment, 'Rats!'. . . .

"If you ever want me again for anything in particular—because I am a busy man and cannot come for anything that is not particular—send for me and I will come."[1]

Polk wrote Secretary McAdoo in regard to his proposed letter to all governments borrowing money[2]: "I have discussed the attached draft letter with the Secretary and he feels very strongly it would be a mistake to send anything to our associates in this war at this time. He quite sees your point, but feels if we say anything we may raise awkward questions of policy and it would be better not to have anything on record or have any discussion on the subject at this time. . . ."[3]

---

[1]*Public Papers*, Vol. V, pp. 82–88. The address, being confidential, was not published until long afterward.

[2]This volume, p. 168.

[3]*Hearings*, Senate Munitions Investigation, 74–2, Pt. 29, p. 9000. On the 14th McAdoo replied with further arguments: ". . . . If we fail to do this we may be confronted at the peace conference, if we have to raise an objection to the demands of some of the Allied Powers, with the claim that as we furnished money for the purpose

Senator La Follette introduced a resolution for a public restatement of the Allied peace terms.

Secretary Lansing announced that American delegates to the Stockholm conference would not be granted passports; the British and French governments took similar action.

Sunday, August 12th.

President and Mrs. Wilson spent the day on the *Mayflower*.

Hoover announced with the approval of the President that the price for 1917 wheat would be fixed by a commission under H. A. Garfield; as a preliminary step the Food Administration would take control of all grain elevators and mills with a daily capacity of over 100 barrels of flour.

Ambassador Joseph E. Willard reported a personal interview with the King of Spain on August 9th: ". . . His Majesty stated that within the next few months Germany would offer peace terms . . .

"It may be that His Majesty is to be the medium through which these terms will be offered. . . ."[1]

Monday, August 13th.

President and Mrs. Wilson returned to the White House in time for breakfast. At 2:30 the President received Baron Moncheur of Belgium, who discussed the fundamental demands upon which Belgium would insist at the time of peace negotiations.

Professor Benjamin F. Battin called during the afternoon, and also Representative Clark of Florida. At four o'clock President and Mrs. Wilson went to Fort Myer to attend the concluding exercises of the Officers Training Camp.

Colonel House sent the President a number of telegrams from Sir William Wiseman: Mr. Balfour had just received a peace appeal from the Pope[2] and desired to know the

---

of enabling the powers to prosecute the war to a successful conclusion, we tacitly consented to or acquiesced in the national objectives they had in view. My own conviction is that such a statement by this Government will not prejudice its interests in any way, while a failure to make such statement might eventually prove decidedly prejudicial." *Ibid.*, p. 9001.

[1] *Foreign Relations*, 1917, Supp. 2, Vol. I, p. 158, for entire message, which included a brief statement of the expected terms.

[2] This appears to have been the first intimation the President had of the Pope's appeal.

President's views, privately; the British government understood the powerful position of the United States. They trusted the President and would give him all information willingly; Lloyd George was considering visiting the United States.

The terrific artillery duel in Flanders showed no signs of diminishing.

To Senator John Sharp Williams, who had urged that troops should not be sent to Russia:

"I entirely agree with your argument about sending troops to Russia. There are very many reasons why it would be unwise even if it were practicable.

"It is always a great pleasure to get your suggestion and I always feel safe when I agree with it. I know that I have the support of your own judgment."

To Senator Henry F. Hollis:

". . . . Nothing has given me more concern than the matter of priority of shipments on the railroads to which you refer and you may be sure I will not be slack in the matter, but I do not think it would be well to appoint a member of the Interstate Commerce Commission to attend to the matter because the Interstate Commerce Commission is already overburdened with duties and I would only be subtracting an indispensable member where I could not replace him. I shall try, however, to find some effective man."

Tuesday, August 14th.

The President conferred with George Creel just before cabinet meeting. Late in the afternoon Senator Pomerene of Ohio called. After a short conference with Secretary Daniels at a quarter of eight, the President and Mrs. Wilson went to the Belasco Theater.

Ambassador Walter H. Page to the President, a handwritten letter, emphasizing the critical condition of the Allies, and their "pitiful" failure to work together.

China declared war on Germany and Austria-Hungary.

Former Emperor Nicholas of Russia and his family were removed from the palace at Tsarskoe Selo to "an unnamed place."[1]

To Secretary Lansing, who had sent the President a copy of an address issued by the Stevens railroad commission in Russia, and called attention to the fact that Stevens was "assuming an authority and giving the Commission a diplomatic character which neither possesses." Stevens had, said Lansing, given certain *pledges* on behalf of the United States. ". . . . The pledge having been given I think that it would be unwise to repudiate it as the Russian people and Russian Government might misconstrue any repudiation . . . At the same time it would seem advisable I think for Stevens to be told . . . that he has no authority to carry on negotiations or enter into agreements for the United States.":

"Mr. Root had called my attention already to the extraordinary action of Mr. Stevens . . .

"Will you not be kind enough to have the following cable sent to Mr. Stevens:

"'The President appreciates very highly what Mr. Stevens and his associates are doing in Russia but thinks it wise to remind Mr. Stevens that it is important that the impression should not be created that he and his associates represent or speak for the Government of the United States. As the President explained to the Commission before they started, they were sent abroad merely to put themselves at the service of the Russian Government. Any assurances conveyed to the Russian people, therefore, as if authoritatively by the Commission would be a very grave mistake. The President does not wish in this way to discredit assurances already given but merely to convey a very friendly caution for the future.' "[2]

---

[1]According to a report in the New York *Times*, August 16, 1917.

[2]Sent on August 15th. See *Foreign Relations*, 1918, *Russia*, Vol. III, pp. 196–197.

To Senator J. W. Weeks:

"I have your letter . . . and, while I sympathize to a very great extent with your point about the drafting of aliens, I cannot believe that you mean exactly what you say with regard to our treaty obligations,—'whatever may be our treaties with foreign countries on this subject, it is absolutely essential in my judgment that some action should be taken which will include the alien population of the draft age in the draft.' I assume, of course, that you mean that some diplomatic action should be taken to clear the way. That matter is already interesting the Department of State and I have no doubt will be pressed as fast as the circumstances permit.

"Your point with regard to the drafting of men with families is undoubtedly well taken and I have reason to believe that it is very much in the mind at any rate of most of the drafting boards. I shall take pleasure in calling the attention of the War Department again to it."

To Hamilton Vreeland, Jr.:

"I am genuinely obliged to you for your thoughtful kindness in sending me a copy of your Hugo Grotius. He is a man in whom I have long been interested and whose works I have in some degree studied, and I hope I shall be able to appreciate what you have written about him with the more intelligence on that account."

Wednesday, August 15th.

The President remained in his study until 11 o'clock, when he walked over to the State, War and Navy Building and to the Department of Justice. Afternoon appointments: a committee of the chairmen of the New England coal committees; William Kent of the Tariff Commission; Senators Husting of Wisconsin, and Kellogg and Nelson of Minnesota; Vance McCormick.

Ambassador Page forwarded from London, by telegram, the Pope's appeal for peace.[1]

It was announced that the Food Administration, by authority of the President, had formed a $50,000,000 grain corporation, all the stock held by the Federal government: Herbert Hoover, chairman; Julius Barnes, president.[2]

A commission from Switzerland arrived to discuss the embargo problem.

A tremendous demonstration took place in London, when United States troops marched through the streets escorted by the famous bands of the Guards—English, Scotch and Irish. They were reviewed by Ambassador Page and Admiral Sims, and afterward by the King, at Buckingham Palace. The Cabinet adjourned as the parade approached and hurried in a body to the War Office, where they watched from the windows.[3]

Canadian troops smashed forward over a front of nearly three miles north and northwest of Lens, capturing the famous Hill 70, which had been considered impregnable.

Thursday, August 16th.

The President's afternoon engagements: Oliver P. Newman, commissioner of the District of Columbia; Representative Anthony of Kansas; Senator Fletcher of Florida and Representative Small of North Carolina; Senator King of Utah; Franklin D. Roosevelt, Assistant Secretary of the Navy; Secretary Daniels, Admirals Benson and Mayo and Captain Jackson; Judge Robert S. Lovett, within a few days appointed a member of the War Industries Board to superintend the priority of shipments; Attorney General Gregory.

Colonel House sent the President copy of a letter from Lord Bryce, who wrote that those who were "complaining and carping a year ago and would hardly listen" when the President's position was explained were now "extolling his cautious wisdom in awaiting the right moment" for entering the war.

---

[1] *Foreign Relations*, 1917, Supp. 2, Vol. I, pp. 161–164. See the President's notes headed "Papal Plan," facsimile on pp. 221–223, this volume.

[2] *Official Bulletin*, August 16, 1917.

[3] *Current History*, September, 1917, pp. 388–389.

The transfer of General Wood to Camp Funston in Kansas was announced as part of a series of army orders reorganizing the National Guard and Regular and National armies.

To Colonel House, who expressed the hope in his letter of the 15th, after discussing the situation of the countries at war with Germany, that the President would "answer the Pope's proposal in some such way as to leave the door open, and to throw the onus on Prussia." ". . . . This, I think, can be done if you will say that the peace terms of America are well known, but that it is useless to discuss the question until those of the Prussian militarists are also known, and further that it is hardly fair to ask the people of the allied countries to discuss terms with a military autocracy—an autocracy that does not represent the opinion of the people for whom they speak. If the people of the Central Powers had a voice in the settlement, it is probable an overwhelming majority would be found willing to make a peace acceptable to the other peoples of the world—a peace founded upon international amity and justice. . . ."[1]:

MY DEAR HOUSE,

I do not know that I shall make any reply at all to the Pope's proposals, but I am glad to let Mr. Balfour know what it would be were I to make one,—as it is possible I may be led by circumstances to do.

Appreciation should, of course, be expressed of the humane purpose of the Pope and a general sympathy with his desire to see the end of this terrible war come on terms honourable to all concerned; but these objections should be stated:

(1) That no intimation is conveyed that the terms suggested meet the views of any of the belligerents and that to discuss them would be a blind adventure;

(2) That such terms constitute no settlement but only a return to the *status quo ante* and would leave affairs in the same attitude that furnished a pretext for the war; and

[1]Printed in part in *Intimate Papers*, Vol. III, pp. 153–154.

(3) That the absolute disregard alike of all formal obligations of treaty and all accepted principles of international law which the autocratic regime still dominant in Germany has shown in the whole action of this war has made it impossible for other governments to accept its assurances on anything, least of all on the terms upon which peace will be maintained. The present German Imperial Government is morally bankrupt; no one will accept or credit its pledges; and the world will be upon quicksand in regard to all international covenants which include Germany until it can believe that it is dealing with a responsible government.

I see no other possible answer.

I am rushing this through my type-writer (and through my mind, too, for that matter,) on a desperately busy day, and may not have expressed my conclusions happily, but I am in no uncertainty as to their substance.

All unite in affectionate messages. I devour and profit by all your letters, and am

Your devoted and grateful friend,
WOODROW WILSON[1]

To Secretary Baker:

".... I do not feel that the power to determine prices can be *lodged* with the War Industries Board but I do feel that they ought to play a very important function of advice in the matter and I mean to associate myself as closely as I can with them and to be guided by them as much as possible in this important matter."

---

[1]House cabled the substance of this letter to Balfour, who replied, in a telegram of the 22nd which House forwarded to the President on the same day: "I am in fullest sympathy with the President's line of thought as expressed in your telegram . . .

"First thought of the Russian Government is that a reasonable reply on behalf of the Allies should be sent. First thought of the French Government is that no answer is at present necessary. For my own part, I greatly dread idea of any joint endeavor of composing elaborate document dealing with complex problems necessarily looked at from somewhat different angles by each belligerent...." Published in *Intimate Papers*, Vol. III, pp. 155–156.

To Herbert Hoover, who had written of the patriotic spirit of the principal grain dealers and elevator men in cheerfully supporting the Food Administration plan for control of wheat and rye, even though it would put some of them out of business until after the war and would minimize the business of all of them:

"It certainly was a very unusual and stimulating exhibition of patriotism given by the grain dealers and elevator men with whom you consulted the other day and I hope that you will have an opportunity of conveying to them an expression of my admiration and appreciation. I am sure the whole country will feel as I do about it."

To Theodore Wright:

"It causes me genuine grief to be obliged to say . . . that I dare not intervene by way of special exemptions in the matter of the army draft. Perhaps you will realize that I am particularly anxious never to seem to do so on personal grounds as if seeking special favors for my friends. It is a time of hardship in many directions. It bears very sharply upon more than one of my own personal friends, and yet I feel bound in conscience to refrain from interfering with the operation of the law.

"I am sure you will understand and forgive."

Friday, August 17th.

Before the cabinet meeting a number of people called on the President to pay their respects. Late afternoon appointments: Samuel Gompers and a committee; a group of senators, to discuss the Pope's peace note—Martin, John Sharp Williams, Pomerene, Swanson, Lodge, Knox and Brandegee.

Lodge, reporting the interview in his diary, quoted the President: ". . . . The great difficulty is that there is no one with whom to negotiate. You cannot negotiate with a Government like that of Germany, which frankly says that no treaty, no agreement, is binding and which so acts. This is what we ought to say, and yet if we do, the reply is that we are undertaking to say what the Government of the Germans shall be, and one of the principles for which we are fighting is that every people has the right to settle its own form of government. There again the Pope does not touch the objects for which we are fighting. . . ."

Later, replying to Knox's question as to whether we had "any agreement or understanding with our Allies," the President said: ". . . . None whatever. I told Mr. Balfour to whom alone I spoke about it that I thought it best and wisest that there should be no understandings, formal or informal; but of course he knew that we should never go back on them, and that binds us in honor. . . ."

Senator Williams thought the Pope should be told "with every diplomatic politeness . . . that it was none of his business." Knox wanted to say "that there could be no peace, no real peace, until we and our Allies were able to dictate it." [Everybody agreed, writes Lodge, "but the President was of opinion that this could not be said at this time."]

Toward the end of the conference Lodge advised the President to say that no peace could ever be discussed which rested on the *status quo ante bellum*; he added that Senate peace

PAPAL   PLAN.

Status quo ante bellum

PLUS

Condonation, disarmament, general arbitration.

Freedom of the seas

French territorial claims

Italian territorial claims

Balkan questions

Reconstitution of Poland

} Conciliatory adjust-
  ment, taking into con-
  sideration aspirations
  of populations.

Appreciation of motives which prompted the appeal.

It may be taken for granted that he is equally

The appeal itself expresses this solicitude. solicitous that the foundations should be laid for permanent peace and that the peace proposed should not be a mere temporary cessation of arms

Can be discussed only in view of causes and objects (These to be carefully stated).

The objects may be summed up in one: to deliver the free countries of the world from the menace of a vast military establishment controlled by an irresponsible government which acknowledges no obligation or restriction either of treaty or of international practice and long established principle, - which in this terrible war has brushed aside every consideration of humanity even. It is none of our business how the German people got under the control of such a government or were kept under the domination of its power and its purposes, but it is our business to see to it that the history of the world is no longer left to their handling.

To deal with such a power by way of peace would involve a) a recuperation of its power and renewal of its policy, b) a permanent hostile combination against the German people, whereas, in different circumstances the other na-

tions of the world would wish to deprive them
of nothing that the rest of the peoples of the
world enjoyed, and c) an abandonment of Russia to intrigue, interference, and counter
revolution through the subtle and malign influences which such a power is now known in-
dustriously to build up.

Responsible statesmen now everywhere, I believe,
that no peace can rest securely upon vindictive action towards any people or upon political or economic discriminations meant to benefit some and cripple or embarrass others.
It can rest only upon the equal rights of peoples, great and small, upon freedom and security and an equal participation by all in
the economic opportunities of the world,— the
German people with the rest, if the German
people will accept equality and not seek domination.

WILSON ANSWERS THE POPE

The President's working memorandum for his reply to the Pope,
sent August 27, 1917. These notes, written by the President on his
own typewriter, indicate his method of clarifying his own thinking on
important international issues.

resolutions should be laid on the table and killed. The President agreed.[1]

At 5:30 Senator Hollis called; at six o'clock, Herbert Hoover; and Lansing came in for a conference in the evening.

3400 mechanics employed on government work in shipyards in and around New York went on strike.

Ramsay MacDonald sent William H. Buckler "for the benefit of Colonel House and the President" a statement regarding the effect in Great Britain of America's entry in the war. ". . . . Amongst political sections miscalled 'pacifist,' President Wilson's recent pronouncements have been regarded with disappointment, and they are interpreted here by all sections as marking a complete reversal of his old views regarding the war and its settlement, and also regarding the whole European problem. . . .

"They are amazed at the attitude taken by your government regarding the Stockholm Conference, as they expected that America with its republican and democratic traditions would have stood for the rights of the peoples, and would have facilitated the clearing up of the issues and the removal of misunderstandings by direct democratic contact and exchange of opinions. A pronouncement to that effect by America would have had a tremendous influence for good on this side. . . ."[2]

To Attorney General Gregory, enclosing a letter from the Union Against Militarism—a "Memorandum on Invasion of Constitutional Rights":

"Will you not be kind enough to have the enclosed carefully examined by somebody to see whether the allegations contained in these papers are successfully made

---

[1]Lodge makes a characteristic comment on all this: ". . . . I wanted him to declare in the presence of others that he meant to go through with the war to a complete victory. He so declared and such I believe is his intention now. Whether he will steadily adhere to it no man can tell; but he is at least committed. He is a man of words not of action, but in this interview he gave way to phrases less than I ever saw on the other occasions when I have met him. He went off once, something about 'heart-breaking sorrow,' but otherwise talked simply and well. He had been adrift and troubled about the Pope's note. I think in that we helped him with our various suggestions and stiffened him. He appeared better than at the other times when I have seen him." Lodge, *The Senate and the League of Nations*, pp. 80–83.

[2]Nevins, *Henry White*, pp. 344–345.

out? The people who sign the letter which is on top of the other documents are people whom I personally esteem, but I am not always sure that they know what they are talking about."

To Robert S. Lovett, chairman of the executive committee of the Union Pacific railroad system:

"In accordance with our conversation of yesterday, I am writing you this to request and authorize you to undertake the direction in my name of industrial shipments . . .

"May I not express my appreciation of the public spirit with which you have consented to undertake this difficult and delicate work [Priorities Commissioner], and may I not say that I hope you will feel at liberty to consult me at any time concerning the questions that arise? I shall deem it a duty as well as a pleasure to be accessible for counsel in the matter."

To Professor Philip H. Fogel, who wrote that he had been dismissed from Princeton by "the Hibben regime":

"I am genuinely distressed to hear of the severance of your relations with Princeton and I wish sincerely that there were something here to which I could assign you, but the truth of the matter is that I dare not make assignments myself. I am trusting the men whom I put in charge of each thing to secure their own assistance and develop their own administrative machinery. The most I can do is to let them know that upon application to me there are men whom I can suggest, and I will be glad to do this in your case."[1]

Saturday, August 18th.

After a round of golf with Mrs. Wilson, the President walked over to the offices of the Food Administration for a conference

---

[1]Attached to the letter was the following note: "The President asks if there is not some way of letting this be generally known, that there are men whom he could suggest if he were applied to."

with Hoover; and called upon the Attorney General. Vance
McCormick came in at 2 o'clock; at 2:45 the President went
out again, this time to see Judge Robert S. Lovett at the Mun-
sey Building.

> Six militant suffragists who had been arrested in front of the
> White House refused to pay fines and were sentenced to a
> month in the Occoquan Workhouse.
> Secretary Lansing telegraphed American diplomatic repre-
> sentatives in Allied countries: "Please ascertain as
> promptly as possible the views of the Government to
> which you are accredited in regard to the Pope's recent
> peace communication. The above information is desired
> by the President. Cable reply, which will be treated as
> strictly confidential."[1]
> British airplanes dropped 28,000 pounds of explosives on
> enemy establishments.
> A new Italian offensive began during the night for the posses-
> sion of San Gabriele peak—"the battle of the Julian
> Alps."[2]

Sunday, August 19th.

The President and Mrs. Wilson went to St. John's Episcopal
Church, in the morning; and in the afternoon took a long drive.

Monday, August 20th.

H. A. Garfield called to see the President at noon. Afternoon
appointments: Miss Helen Todd, who was planning a speaking
tour to enlighten the women of the country as to America's
purpose in the war; Senators Shields and McKellar, and
Representatives Hull and Byrns of Tennessee; Captain Berry of
the *Mayflower;* Secretary Daniels, Thomas A. Edison, who had
been conducting experiments in the interest of the war, and
Dr. M. R. Hutchison. At 4:30 the President walked over to
the office of the Federal Trade Commission where he discussed
problems of coal and transportation, returning in time to receive

---

[1] *Foreign Relations*, 1917, Supp. 2, Vol. I, p. 165. For replies, see *ibid.*, pp. 165 *et seq.*
All were to some extent unfavorable to the Pope's proposal; and those of Great Britain,
France, Belgium and Italy revealed a desire to know what the President thought before
making a definite answer.

[2] *Current History*, October, 1917, p. 38.

Judge Lovett at six.[1] Ten minutes later he went on foot to Secretary Baker's office.

The Shipbuilding Labor Adjustment Board was created, V. Everit Macy being named by President Wilson and A. J. Berres by Samuel Gompers.[2]

Secretary Lansing wrote McAdoo further in regard to his proposed message to the Allied governments. He had, he said, "gone over the matter very carefully again," and he was more firmly convinced than ever that such a communication would be a grave mistake. ". . . . The same argument which is urged in regard to loans might be advanced in regard to the employment of the embargo, the cooperation [of] our naval vessels about the British Islands, the presence of our military forces in France, and similar active aid of this Government. It seems to me that it is much wiser to avoid statements of this sort, which might be misconstrued. On the other hand, I am not at all afraid that any of the powers will attempt to construe our silence into acquiescence in the national objectives of the various countries. But, even if it should be considered out of abundant caution [sic] to make our position plain, I think that it would be unwise to do so until there is some evidence that such a claim may be made. There is no evidence of the sort now."[3]

French troops broke through the German lines north of Verdun on an 11-mile front.

Tuesday, August 21st.

The President omitted his morning golf, remaining in his study until 12:30, when he received Vance McCormick. Afternoon appointments: Senator Poindexter of Washington; former Governor Longino of Mississippi; the Attorney General. The cabinet meeting was canceled, and the President spent the evening in his study.[4]

---

[1] Soon after his conference with the President, Lovett directed 46 railroads to give precedence to shipments of bituminous coal from the Northwest. New York *Times*, August 1, 1917.

[2] Macy was made chairman, and the board came to be known as the Macy Board. Hurley, *The Bridge to France*, p. 187.

[3] *Hearings*, Senate Munitions Investigation, 74-2, Pt. 29, p. 9004.

[4] Many long hours were spent by the President alone in his study laboriously studying the difficult problems which arose daily. He welcomed the facts supplied by the experts

The President established by executive order an Exports Administrative Board and an Exports Council, to supersede the Exports Council of June 22nd.

Soft coal prices were announced, the President himself writing out a statement.

Ambassador Page telegraphed from London, quoting a private letter from Balfour: the British government relied on the justice and good will of the United States in the matter of taking ownership of British ships building in American yards. They would not press the point, but they would feel "much gratified" if the United States would refrain from taking the proposed step.[1]

The German Chancellor, speaking before the Main Committee of the Reichstag: ". . . . I repudiate the suggestion that the Pope's proposal was inspired by the Central Powers. . . ."[2]

To Secretary Baker, who had transmitted a recommendation by Governor General Harrison that vacancies on the Supreme Court of the Philippines be filled by Filipinos. Baker himself favored the appointment of a Filipino and an American:

"In the matter of the enclosed memorandum, my heart pulls one way (namely, in the direction of Governor Harrison's recommendation) and my head in the other, in the direction of your own judgment. I suppose I must follow my head in this case, and I would be very much obliged to you if you would confer with the Attorney General as to the best selections that can be made."

To Secretary Redfield:

"I think I shall always feel uneasy when I act contrary to your judgment; but the conviction has grown upon me that we began wrong in our arrangements for the ad-

in the governmental departments: but he was unwilling to commit himself to decisions until he thoroughly understood every detail of the problems involved.

[1]*Foreign Relations,* 1917, Supp. 2, Vol. I, pp. 622–623. Lord Northcliffe wrote House on the 25th: "Our people are evidently very agitated about this most delicate and difficult question of the British ships now building here. . . ." Tardieu also protested, for the French.

[2]*Current History,* October, 1917, p. 86.

ministration of the control of exports,—as I explained to you the other day,—and I believe that the only solution is to entrust the whole action and detail of administration in that matter to one instrumentality, the instrumentality already created, namely, the Exports Board.

"I am accordingly signing an Executive Order to that effect; but I shall not publish it. The Exports Board, like the Exports Council, is my own executive agency, and this administrative readjustment concerns only the action of this agency.

"May I not say again how sincerely and deeply I appreciate your own generous and loyal attitude towards my decisions in such matters?"

To S. I. Woodbridge:

". . . . You may be sure we are watching developments in China, so well as we can from this distance, with the greatest solicitude. I hope with all my heart that in the providence of God some permanent and beneficent result may be worked out."[1]

To President Alexander Meiklejohn of Amherst College:

". . . . In these days of strain almost the only voices that reach me are those calling for some kind of difficult action, and to hear in the midst of these the voice of a generous friend is a great solace."

Wednesday, August 22nd.

After a round of golf with Dr. Grayson the President worked in his study until luncheon. In the early afternoon he received a committee from the Philadelphia Navy Yard; and Walter Wellman. At 3:15 he went to the office of the Federal Trade Commission for the second time in a week, remaining there in conference about three hours.

[1] From time to time Lansing sent over memoranda on the progress of affairs in China —the July *coup d'état* to restore the boy emperor to the throne, the civil war which followed.

To E. N. Hurley:

"I do not know anything about Mr. Winchell, the Director of Traffic of the Union Pacific, and I must admit that I am a little shy of seasoned railroad men because I would wish to be surrounded by men who had got out of the ruts and taken a little look around the horizon, but I am perfectly willing to trust to your judgment because I know that you wish men of the same sort that I do."

Thursday, August 23rd.

The President worked in his study until Samuel Gompers came in at 12:30. In the early afternoon he received Viscount Ishii and other members of the Japanese Commission who had arrived in Washington the day before. The President declared that the United States was chiefly interested in having the principles of the Open Door and equal opportunity sincerely followed in China; that he regretted the spheres of influence which had been formed by the Powers, since such a policy threatened the Open Door.[1] Late afternoon appointments: H. A. Garfield; Secretary Lansing; Secretary Baker; George Creel. A dinner was given at the White House in the evening, in honor of the Japanese Mission. "Covers for 72."

The President appointed H. A. Garfield Fuel Administrator; and fixed the price of anthracite coal at the mines.

Ambassador Francis was notified that a further credit of $100,000,000 had been established in favor of the Russian government. ". . . . It is of course understood that these credits are available only during the time Russia is engaged in war against Germany. . . ."[2]

The German Chancellor, speaking before the Reichstag about this time, referred again to Entente secret treaties. ". . . . With such far-reaching enemy war aims it may be understood why Mr. Balfour lately stated that he did not consider it advisable to make a detailed statement on the war policy of the Government. . . ."[3]

[1]From a free translation by Miss Taki Fugita of portions of the memoirs of Viscount Kikujiru Ishii which deal with this period, pp. 136-138. For the President's formal address of welcome, see *Public Papers*, Vol. V, p. 92.

[2]*Foreign Relations*, 1918, *Russia*, Vol. III, pp. 22-23.

[3]Given out on August 23rd. *Current History*, October, 1917, p. 89.

To Colonel House, who had written on the 19th that the Russian ambassador was "very much disturbed over the Pope's peace overture and how you will reply to it." ". . . . He believes if it is treated lightly and not in a spirit of liberalism, it will immediately split Russia . . .

"He hopes you may be willing to say that the United States will treat with the German people at any time they are in a position to name their own representatives. . . .":

"MY DEAR HOUSE,

"Here is a first draft of a reply to the Pope. Please tell me exactly what you think of it.

"I am sure that it should be as brief as possible. I centre it, therefore, on one point: that we cannot take the word of the present rulers of Germany for anything.

"I have tried to indicate the attitude of this country on the points most discussed in the socialistic and other camps. I have not thought it wise to say more or to be more specific because it might provoke dissenting voices from France or Italy if I should,—if I should say, for example, that their territorial claims did not interest us.

"I shall await your comments with the deepest interest, because the many useful suggestions you have made were in my mind all the while as I wrote.

"My own feeling is that we should speak at the earliest possible moment now, and I hope with all my heart that the British and other associated governments will adopt Sir William Wiseman's suggestion and say ditto to us.

"I think of you every day with the greatest affection. I am doing now daily just about twice as much as I can do, and the pace is telling, but I hope that when our organizations (for example our coal organization, at the head of which I am going to put Harry Garfield) are in working order I shall be able to get to sea for a day or two of real freedom and rest. Faith I need it!

"All join in affectionate messages."[1]

---

[1]The enclosed draft is not in the Wilson files. Dr. Seymour writes: "With the ex-

To Senator G. E. Chamberlain, who had enclosed a letter from Senator Fernald of Maine, with the comment: ". . . . It is along the line of my suggestion to you that it would be well if you could say something to the country on the subject of the war, its aims and purposes, in order to stir up a little more enthusiasm.":

"I feel the force of the suggestion conveyed in your letter accompanying the enclosed which I return, and I hope that some proper opportunity will open up for me to say something. In the meantime, and better still, it seems to me that speeches just such as Mr. Fernald seems to have been making are the things that will do the most good, and I am praying that Congress may soon adjourn, not for reasons existing in Washington, but in order that its members may get to their constituents and create just the atmosphere which it is so necessary to create by co-operative effort just now."

To Frank W. McAllister:
"I am sorry to learn from your telegram of yesterday that you regard the prices of coal fixed for the mines of Missouri and Southern Illinois as exorbitant. I beg that you will note that the prices fixed are only provisional and that just so soon as the powers conferred upon me by Congress can be exercised through a regularly constituted agency there will be every opportunity to present objections like your own and to reconsider the prices."

To former Senator Blair Lee:
"I am sorry I cannot agree with the principles suggested in your letter of yesterday. You will realize, of course, that practically none of these officers trained at the various camps had had any previous connections with

---

ception of a half-dozen slight verbal alterations and two short interpolations, the draft note sent for House's inspection was the same as that finally published." *Intimate Papers*, Vol. III, p. 163.

House replied on the 24th: "You have again written a declaration of human liberty. . . . England and France will not like some of it . . ." *Ibid.*, Vol. III, p. 164.

the military forces of their states (though there may have been a few exceptions) and the principle followed in their assignment to the several training camps was the very sound one that men themselves trained together and familiar with one another should be kept together in exercising their duties as training officers. Much more homogeneity is obtained that way than by scattering these men among the states from which they come, where they have very few of them had any military connections whatever.

"I do not think any precedents have been made in this matter which will embarrass future action, because we are creating a National Army, not now solving the question of how the future forces of the republic shall be constituted in time of peace."

Friday, August 24th.
Before the cabinet meeting the President received: Lieutenant Colonel T. Bentley Mott, who had been a member of the Root Commission to Russia; and President Guy Potter Benton of the University of Vermont. Late afternoon appointments: E. N. Hurley of the Shipping Board; Vance McCormick.

Colonel House telegraphed Balfour suggesting that the Allies accept the President's reply to the Pope as their own.[1]

Secretary McAdoo announced the creation of a commission with headquarters at Washington, through which all purchases made by Great Britain, France and Russia in the United States should proceed; members, B. M. Baruch, Robert S. Lovett, Robert S. Brookings, all three being also members of the War Industries Board.[2]

Terrific fighting, as the Italian drive along the Isonzo continued.

To Secretary Lansing, who had written of the desire of the British Parliamentary Commercial Committee to have a

[1]*Intimate Papers,* Vol. III, pp. 166–167.

[2]*Official Bulletin,* August 25, 1917. Similar agreements with the Italian, Belgian and Serbian governments were signed within a few days. See *Foreign Relations,* 1917, Supp. 2, Vol. I, pp. 565–568.

similar committee formed in the United States. The President's letter is marked "Personal and Confidential":

"My judgment about the enclosed is very clear. I do not think that it would be wise to submit this matter to the Houses of Congress. I think that the appointment of such a committee on the part of Congress would complicate matters in a rather serious way, and I wonder that the other parliamentary bodies have done what is here recited."

To Herbert Hoover, who had sent over a copy of a letter circulated by Senator Reed of Missouri in an attempt to undermine the efforts of the Food Administration:

"Thank you for letting me see Senator Reed's letter. Of course, it is perfectly outrageous, but I think that Senator Reed and those who are like him have already tarred themselves so distinctly with the same brush that their influence will be negligible if they will only be kind enough to attach their names always to what they write."

To the president of the Russian National Council Assembly at Moscow, a telegram sent through the Department of State:

"I venture to take the liberty to send to the members of the great council now meeting in Moscow the cordial greetings of their friends the people of the United States, to express their confidence in the ultimate triumph of ideals of democracy and self-government against all enemies within and without, and to give their renewed assurance of every material and moral assistance they can extend to the Government of Russia in the promotion of the common cause in which the two nations are unselfishly united."[1]

---

[1] *Foreign Relations*, 1918, *Russia*, Vol. I, p. 177. This was read at a session of August 27th and was received with "enthusiastic cheers."

To his secretary, Tumulty, who had submitted a request from the Aeolian Company that the President permit a phonograph record to be made of his Flag Day speech:

"The reasoning of this memorandum would be very convincing if, as a matter of fact, I had ever succeeded in getting the 'emotional power' into my voice when speaking into a phonograph. As a matter of fact, I sound like a machine and I should hate to have the address so read given any perpetuity. . . ."

Saturday, August 25th.

The President spent three hours at his golf in the morning; in the afternoon he and Mrs. Wilson went for a long drive, taking a picnic supper with them.

To his secretary, Tumulty, who had called attention to a letter and enclosure from Senator Joseph T. Robinson dealing with the dissatisfaction in Arkansas over America's entrance into the war—it was considered in many quarters a rich man's war —and suggesting a nationwide campaign for enlightening the rural people:

"Please thank Senator Robinson for letting me see the attached letter, and tell him that there is no subject which interests me more than this. I am going to consider very seriously the feasibility of acting upon the suggestion . . ."

Sunday, August 26th.

The President and Mrs. Wilson went to the Central Presbyterian Church in the morning, and took a long drive in the afternoon.

Colonel House telegraphed Lord Robert Cecil,[1] advising that Lord Reading "or some one like him, who has both a financial and political outlook" be sent to the United States and given "entire authority over financial questions, Northcliffe to retain charge of all commercial affairs." ". . . . What is really needed is some one who can dominate

---

[1] Balfour was on a vacation.

and compose the situation and who would have the entire confidence of the President. . . ."[1]

The New York *World* contained an editorial by Frank I. Cobb, "Freedom of Speech in War":

". . . . What is needed is not stern suppression of all seditious and disloyal utterance . . . but a counter-campaign in the name of patriotism and human freedom. How can any government consistently prosecute a soap-box orator for uttering sentiments that are expressed daily in the halls of Congress and circulated at public expense in the *Congressional Record?* . . . ."

The Russian National Council Assembly met in Moscow; Kerensky, opening the session, said: ". . . our authority is supported by the boundless confidence of the people and by millions of soldiers, who are defending us against the German invasion. . . ."[2]

General Pétain's forces delivered a smashing blow to the German line in the Verdun sector, penetrating for a mile on a three-mile front.

Monday, August 27th.

The President's afternoon engagements: Dr. Hans Sulzer, new minister from Switzerland, to present his credentials; Representative Ben Johnson of Kentucky; Senators Chamberlain and McNary of Oregon; H. A. Garfield; Vance McCormick. Evening at the National Theater.

The President's reply to the Pope's peace proposal was sent, through the Department of State.

". . . . We cannot take the word of the present rulers of Germany . . . We must await some new evidence of the purposes of the great peoples of the Central Empires. God grant it may be given soon . . ."[3]

---

[1]*Intimate Papers*, Vol. III, p. 120. Cecil and Northcliffe had asked for House's opinion on the sending of Reading. *Ibid.*, pp. 118–119.

[2]*Current History*, October, 1917, p. 63. In early November Kerensky fell from power.

[3]For entire message see *Public Papers*, Vol. V, pp. 93–96.

The note received enthusiastic approval in the United States. ". . . . The President has not closed the door to peace. He has shown how easily the German people may fling it wide open. His answer expresses the will of the American people." (Extract from the Baltimore *Sun*, reprinted in the New York *Times*, August, 1917.) The Springfield *Republican*, in an editorial which Secretary Tumulty marked for the President's special attention, said: ". . . . Perhaps the deepest significance of the note lies in its

The President issued a proclamation in regard to exports in time of war; and a statement to accompany it. "The purpose . . . is not export prohibition, but merely export control. . . ."[1]

Colonel House read a telegram from Cecil over the telephone, in code, to Gordon Auchincloss.[2] Auchincloss took the numbers down by hand and sent the sheet to the White House immediately, noting at the bottom that he felt it best not to have it typed. The message, as decoded and written out in pencil by Mrs. Wilson, was:

"Following from Lord Robert Cecil who is acting for Balfour:

"'I am grateful information contained in your telegram August twenty-fifth.[3] My view is that it would be very desirable for British and other Allied Governments to accept. Is however one of such importance that I shall have to consult the Cabinet and also our allies. I assume the President's reply follows the lines already sketched out. But I should be very grateful if it were possible to send me a summary of it if the President sees no objection.'

"In order to get cordial cooperation it would seem advisable to give your reply to the governments in advance. It would be particularly desirable in case of Russia."

To Oliver P. Newman, who had tendered his resignation as commissioner of the District of Columbia to accept a commission in the Officers Reserve Corps:

"Of course, I accept your resignation to take effect as you desired, August twenty-fifth, but I cannot do so without telling you how deeply I appreciate the terms of your letter. It is hard to break off official association with a man whom I have so entirely trusted and so sincerely admired as I have you. Please do not feel that I for a moment doubted that your motives for entering the military

---

appeal to the peoples of the Central Empires to assert themselves. . . . " For reaction in Europe, see this volume, p. 247.

[1]*Public Papers,* Vol. V, p. 97.

[2]Assistant to the Counselor of the State Department and House's son-in-law.

[3]Sent August 24th. This volume, p. 233.

THE WHITE HOUSE.
WASHINGTON.

My precious Little Girl,

This is just a love message for your
birthday. I wonder if the letter I wrote you
from the MAYFLOWER just after dear Frank left
for France reached you all right? My heart
was very full of thoughts of your loneliness
then and has been full of you ever since. I
have not seen Nell since she was with you. I
am very eager to get driect news of you and
the darling little ones.

We are all well, and Edith joins me in
messages of warmest love. I am beginning to
feel the strain, of course, and have to admit
that I am very tired, and envy each one of my
colleagues that gets off for a week's or ten
days rest. They seem to me the most fortunate
of men! This does not mean, however, that
there is the least thing the matter with me.
The strain is, of course, more on my mind than
on my body, - comes rather from the things that
I have to decide than from the things that I
have to do, - the things that I have to decide
and the things that I have to see that others

238

do as they should be done. I take exercise every day and sleep like a top whenever I get the chance; I should only like to get more chances!

Take care of yourself, my darling girlie, and when you get a moment sit down and tell me what Frank's plans are about coming back, and what the plans are for the autumn and winter. I am going to keep Garfield down here probably the greater part of the winter. I have put him in charge of the fuel supply of the country, as Hoover is in charge of the food supply. He is talking of leasing a small apartment and bringing Mrs. Garfield down when the cool weather permits. Will all of this interfere with what you and Frank had planned to do, I wonder?

Helen has been out with Marion Erskine, you know, on Georgian Bay, but she is in Chicago on her way back now and may be here again any time, I imagine, though we have had no definite news.

With a heart full of love, and Many, Many Happy Returns,

Your devoted

Father

AN INTIMATE PERSONAL LETTER

During the summer of 1917, while the President was straining every nerve to advance war preparation, he wrote numerous intimate and warm-hearted letters to his daughters and to certain of his old friends. This is a facsimile of such a letter to his daughter Jessie (Mrs. Francis B. Sayre), written August 27, 1917.

service were of the highest character. I never did, and I shall follow your career in the Army with the deepest and sincerest interest and solicitude. May God keep you!"

To Representative Jouett Shouse of Kansas, who had urged the President to issue a proclamation exempting from the operation of the draft all men actually engaged in farming who were so engaged on March 1, 1917:

"I . . . realize the very grave importance of the matter you broach. I cannot see my way, however, to making so wide and sweeping a class exemption as you suggest. The matter of leaving the farmers on the farms has been given the most careful and sympathetic attention by the War Department, and I have before me a letter from the Secretary of War from which I quote the following sentence:

"'General Crowder had foreseen the practical need of enabling men in agricultural work to remain at their tasks until the close of the harvest season, and has ingeniously arranged the details of calling to the colors so that the men on the farms will practically all fall within the last group and will, therefore, not have to report for military service until on or about October first.'

"I feel that a class exemption would lead to many difficulties and to many heartburnings, much as I should personally like to see all the genuine farmers left at their indispensable labors."

To Senator T. J. Walsh:
"I have just heard with the greatest distress of the illness of your wife. Apparently my necessary absorption nowadays in the business of the hour keeps even news of this tragical sort away from me.

"May I not express to you my very deep sympathy? My heart goes out to you, my dear Senator, in this day of your trial and distress, and I hope that you will not think it an intrusion on my part for me to tell you so."

To B. M. Baruch of the War Industries Board:

"Here is a report on the cost of the production of copper which I have just received this morning from the Federal Trade Commission. I wish that you and your colleagues of the Purchasing Commission would be kind enough to look the memorandum and the attached tables over preliminary to conferring with me about the prices to be put upon copper. I shall wish to move very considerately in this big matter and hope that this memorandum will be serviceable to you and your colleagues in determining what advice you give me."

Tuesday, August 28th.

Secretary and Mrs. McAdoo were luncheon guests. At the regular cabinet meeting the members heard for the first time the President's reply to the Pope.[1] Late-afternoon appointments: Daniel C. Roper and his five boys; Senator Owen of Oklahoma; Senator Henry L. Myers and the governor of Montana; Mrs. John W. Kern. About half-past five the President walked over to the War Department, returning in time for the usual short drive with Mrs. Wilson before dinner; in the evening they attended a reception for the Japanese Mission, at the Pan-American Building.

To Rufus M. Jones of Haverford College (Quaker), a letter based in part upon a letter from Secretary Baker to the President:[2]

" . . . . The varieties of conscientious objection developed in the application of the selective conscription law have been so numerous as to make it necessary to delay the establishment of a policy until we can be sure that we have both satisfied the requirements of the law and gone just as far as we can justly go in the recognition of the rights of individual conscience in such a matter. When the total number of persons interposing conscientious objection to

---

[1] *Intimate Papers*, Vol. III, p. 165.

[2] For part of Baker's letter, and for a discussion of the problem of the treatment of conscientious objectors, see Palmer, *Newton D. Baker*, Vol. I, pp. 340 *et seq.*

military service has been ascertained, I hope to be able to work out with the Secretary of War a plan which will give the nation the benefit of the service of these men without injustice to the great company of young men who are free to accept their country's call to military duty.

"In the meantime, I am sure you will permit me to express my deep appreciation of the reconstruction work proposed, and my happiness that it is being carried out in association with the Red Cross which is already doing a great work in France to express the heart of America."

Wednesday, August 29th.

The President's afternoon appointments: Raemakers, the cartoonist;[1] the minister from the Netherlands; Justice Brandeis; Representative Park of Georgia and Judge Chambers,[2] Senators Curtis of Kansas, McCumber of North Dakota, Sterling of South Dakota, and Kellogg and Nelson of Minnesota; Secretary Baker. Mrs. McAdoo and John Randolph Bolling were dinner guests and went with the President and Mrs. Wilson to Keith's Theater in the evening.

To Secretary Baker, enclosing telegrams from the governors of certain Western states, who urged that no publicity be given in the investigation of I.W.W. activities:

"There is a point worth considering in the enclosed telegrams. I did not have in mind the other day when I

[1] Raemakers led the field in the portrayal of German "atrocities." Arthur Brisbane had requested the appointment, and in his note of assent the President said he had greatly admired the cartoonist's work.

[2] During the interview the President asked Judge Chambers to draft a telegram to the general manager and council of the Georgia, Florida & Alabama Railroad Company, union employees of which had struck early in August. Chambers did so, sending his draft to the President within a short time, and the President signed and dispatched it the same day: "With regard to the controversy between your company and its recent employees I beg to inform you that the United States Board of Mediation and Conciliation and William L. Chambers, United States Commissioner of Mediation and Conciliation, are my personal representatives and to request that their offer of mediation as made by Judge Chambers be accepted. In the present circumstances of the country I have the right to expect that this request be fully complied with and the most cordial cooperation be accorded Judge Chambers."

recommended the appointment of such a committee by the Council of National Defense any investigation which would have the I.W.W.'s as a special object of inquiry, but rather a commission to take under review the circumstances which were causing unrest and dissatisfaction on the part of organized labor. I agree with the Governors whose telegrams I am sending that the I.W.W.'s would welcome and profit by the publicity and advertisement of an investigation which put them at the center of the stage, but I take it for granted that that can be avoided."

To Secretary Baker:
"Thank you warmly for remembering to send me Conrad's 'Typhoon.' I shall look forward with the greatest pleasure to reading it, and I thank you for your kindness."

To Senator John F. Shafroth, "Personal":
"I have your letter about Senator Du Bois. The trouble is that there is no vacancy on the Boundary Commission, and I cannot create one without doing one or other of two things, namely, either securing the resignation of the Republican member, who is really doing the best work of all our commissioners, or else bringing very great mortification to one or other of the Democratic members, who I must say are not proving of any particular value so far as I can make out. It is a very embarrassing quandary to me and so I have not permitted myself to consider the matter further since Senator Kern's death."

To E. N. Hurley:
". . . . Our ship owners are not cooperating with us as they should in the adoption of measures of safety and protection and I think their failure to cooperate ought to receive some very public form of rebuke. What are your own feeling and judgment about it?"

Thursday, August 30th.

At eleven o'clock the President received Senators Dillingham and Page of Vermont; at 11:30, Herbert Hoover.[1] Afternoon appointments: Elihu Root, John R. Mott, and Cyrus McCormick, members of the Russian Commission, who discussed their plans for an educational campaign in Russia, the President giving "sympathetic consideration."[2] M. Franklin-Bouillon,[3] Ambassador Jusserand, to present M. Martin Gaston de Leval; the Swiss minister to present the Swiss Commission; Secretary Wilson, who discussed with the President the disturbed labor situation in the Northwest and Southwest; Senator Owen of Oklahoma; H. A. Garfield. In the evening Professor Taussig called.

The President made public a statement announcing the price of wheat.[4]

Secretary Daniels broke ground for the first government-owned armor-plate and projectile plant, at Charleston, West Virginia.

25,000 National Guardsmen paraded in New York City, to the cheers of millions, who lined the streets and hung from the windows of office buildings.

To Attorney General Gregory, calling attention to the fact that the Georgia, Florida & Alabama Railroad Company might not accept mediation, in spite of his telegram of the day before:

". . . . In that case, it is my purpose, unless your department sees serious obstacles, to proceed to take charge of the road and operate it inasmuch as there are supplies on its line which are necessary to be governed. This is a drastic remedy but it might be wholesome by way of example in other quarters if I were to adopt it, and I

---

[1]See the President's letter of this day to John Burke.

[2]John R. Mott to the President, August 30, 1917.

[3]On September 7th Secretary Lansing telegraphed to Ambassador Page in England: ". . . . Mr. Franklin-Bouillon of the French Chamber of Deputies is in Washington in the interests of participation by the American Congress in the Inter-Allied Parliamentary Union. He has been advised that, after very careful consideration, the project of American participation at this time does not meet with the favor of this Government." *Foreign Relations*, 1917, Supp. 2, Vol. I, p. 194.

[4]*Public Papers*, Vol. V, pp. 99–100.

NEWTON D. BAKER
SECRETARY OF WAR

JOSEPHUS DANIELS
SECRETARY OF THE NAVY

should like to know what the law in the matter may be interpreted to be."

To Thomas L. Chadbourne, Jr., who had asked for a message for use during New York City's celebration for drafted men:

"Please say to the men on September fourth how entirely my heart is with them and how my thoughts will follow them across the sea with confidence and also with genuine envy, for I should like to be with them on the fields and in the trenches where the real and final battle for the independence of the United States is to be fought, alongside the other peoples of the world struggling like ourselves to make an end of those things which have threatened the integrity of their territory, the lives of their people, and the very character and independence of their governments. Bid them Godspeed for me from a very full heart."

To Senator John Sharp Williams, who had written: ". . . I think one of the best state papers ever offered to the world was your answer to the Pope. . . .":

". . . . I am greatly delighted that you thought so well of my answer to the Pope. There seemed to me to be no other answer and, therefore, this one was comparatively easy to write."

To John Burke, Treasurer of the United States, who had been fearful that the price of wheat would be fixed at a rate entirely inadequate for the farmers of North Dakota. If that happened, he thought, it would hurt the administration "beyond repair" with the farmers:

"The subject matter of your letter of yesterday was already very much on my mind and has given me a great deal of trouble. I have just this moment come from an interview with Mr. Hoover about it.

"It is a very perplexing thing to know what to do. In the first place, of course, you understand that the Government is not "fixing the price": it is merely determining the price it will offer for wheat in the purchases it must make for itself and on behalf of other governments, and there is nothing in the law that obliges the farmer to sell at that price if he can get a better. In the second place, I take it to be impracticable to fix one price for one part of the country and another for another part, and that the best that we can do if we pay the regard we are in duty bound to pay to the consumer is to fix a price as nearly fair to all as possible. The difficulty in my mind is that in the regions you refer to there have been short crops both this year and the last, and it would be almost impossible to provide compensation for the losses thereby entailed without making the price oppressive to the country at large.

"I set these matters forth merely that you may know how difficult I am finding it to come to a just conclusion and yet how anxious I am to do so."

Friday, August 31st.

The President received George Creel at 11:30, and at 12 o'clock, Secretary McAdoo. The cabinet met, as usual, at 2:30. The room was cool in spite of the Washington heat; during the summer the members, to a man, wore white. A long table in the center of the room was clear except for pens and a memorandum pad in front of the President, and such books as he needed for consultation. A picture of Abraham Lincoln hung on the wall, and there were war maps upon which the changes of battle fronts were marked, day by day.

As each member came in the President shook hands with him. When the group was assembled and all were seated, he would call on the department heads in turn—on Tuesday, say, beginning with Lansing and going back and forth down the table; on Friday, beginning with W. B. Wilson, Secretary of Labor. No minutes were kept; no votes taken; no outsider entered.

During the latter part of the afternoon the President talked with: Vance C. McCormick; Major Moton, principal of Tuskegee Institute; Melville Clark who called, at the request of

Charles M. Lincoln of the New York *World*, to present a plan for scattering printed propaganda over enemy countries by means of miniature balloons. In the early evening the President and Mrs. Wilson, accompanied by Mrs. Wilson's mother and sister, boarded the *Mayflower* for a trip down the river.

> The British and French governments, wrote Colville Barclay of the British Embassy to Secretary Lansing, having obtained the concurrence of the Russian and Italian governments, had decided to accept Secretary McAdoo's proposal for an Inter-Allied [economic] Council in London. He had been instructed also to press once more the desirability of having the United States government represented on such a council. ". . . . It is understood that the French Government have even made such representation a condition of their own agreement to Mr. McAdoo's proposal. . . ."[1]
>
> The first British official expression in regard to the President's reply to the Pope was made in a statement by Lord Robert Cecil: "The President's note is a magnificent occurrence. It thrilled us all over here, and the opinions which I heard expressed by representatives of allied countries were equally warm and appreciative. . . ."[2]

To Samuel Gompers:

". . . . I myself have had sympathy with the fears of the workers of the United States; for the tendency of war is toward reaction, and too often military necessities have been made an excuse for the destruction of laboriously-

[1] *Foreign Relations*, 1917, Supp. 2, Vol. I, pp. 568–569.

[2] *Current History*, October, 1917, p. 89. Ambassador Page wrote Colonel House from London that the reply had been "the best contribution we have made to the war." *The Life and Letters of Walter H. Page*, Vol. II, p. 321. Reception of the note in other Entente countries was likewise cordial. The Paris *Temps* commented: "The sentiment which inspires the entire note, just as it inspires the entire French policy, is the conviction that we cannot treat with the German Government at present. . . .

"The calmness with which Mr. Wilson contemplates future peace corresponds with the energy with which he will continue to conduct the war. . . . More than ever we have faith in his untiring firmness." *Current History*, October, 1917, p. 84. "President Wilson once more has interpreted the voice of millions . . ." said the *Giornale d'Italia. Ibid.*, p. 85.

In Germany, comment, except for the Socialists, was bitter. "Every word of President Wilson's note is grotesque nonsense," said the Cologne *Gazette*. ". . . . Mr. Wilson hopes for disunity in Germany, and therefore offers the German people peace at the cost of the German Government's fall. This trick is too transparent. . . ." *Ibid.*, also *Foreign Relations*, 1917, Supp. 2, Vol. I, pp. 183–186 and 196–197.

erected industrial and social standards. These fears, happily, have proved to be baseless. With quickened sympathies and appreciation, with a new sense of the invasive and insidious dangers of oppression, our people have not only held every inch of ground that has been won by years of struggle, but have added to the gains of the Twentieth Century along every line of human betterment. Questions of wages and hours of labor and industrial readjustment have found a solution which gives to the toiler a new dignity and a new sense of social and economic security. I beg you to feel that my support has not been lacking and that the Government has not failed at any point in granting every just request advanced by you and your associates in the name of the American worker.

"No one who is not blind can fail to see that the battle line of democracy for America stretches today from the fields of Flanders to every house and workshop where toiling, upward striving men and women are counting the treasures of right and justice and liberty which are being threatened by our present enemies.

"It has not been a matter of surprise to me that the leaders in certain groups have sought to ignore our griev-ances against the men who have equally misled the Ger-man people. Their insistence that a nation whose rights have been grossly violated, whose citizens have been foully murdered under their own flag, whose neighbors have been invited to join in making conquest of its terri-tory, whose patience in pressing the claims of justice and humanity has been met with the most shameful policy of truculence and treachery; their insistence that a nation so outraged does not know its own mind, that it has no comprehensible reason for defending itself, or for joining with all its might in maintaining a free future for itself and its ideals, is of a piece with their deafness to the oft-repeated statement of our national purposes.

"Is it, perhaps, that these forces of antagonism have not yet learned to know the voice of that America we love and serve? It may well be that those among us who stand ready to forward the plans of aggression bred in secret do not understand the language of democracy when it proclaims the purposes of war in terms of a peace for the peoples that shall be untroubled by those to whom men are but the pawns in their struggle for power and gain. But true Americans, those who toil here for home and the hope of better things, whose lifted eyes have caught the vision of a liberated world, have said that of the policy of blood and iron there shall be an end and that equal justice which is the heart of democracy shall rule in its stead.

"May not those who toil and those who have made common cause of the larger hope for the masses of mankind take renewed heart as they think on these days when America has taken its stand for the rights of humanity and the fellowship of social and international justice?"

Saturday, September 1st.

The President and Mrs. Wilson spent the day on the *Mayflower*.

To Herbert Hoover, who wrote that since McAdoo did not think it possible to have the Treasury Department audit the accounting of the Grain Corporation, he proposed to engage a firm of public accountants to make a monthly audit. ". . . . My one desire is to surround this operation with all of the safeguards of which we are capable.":

"I am very much obliged to you for your letter . . . about the methods you are adopting with regard to accounting for the funds to be spent by the Food Administration Grain Corporation. I feel confident that I can rely upon you to take measures which will satisfy you to the severest critic."

To Cleveland H. Dodge:

MY DEAR CLEVE:

You always think of me at the right time and always send me the sort of message my heart is waiting for. Whenever I write anything like the reply to the Pope my first and greatest desire is to know what men whose judgment I trust think of it, because I never entirely trust my own instinct and conclusion. A letter like yours, therefore, brings me not only the message of friendship which my heart desires, but also the reassurance which my mind craves, and I thank you for it out of a full heart.

It cheers me to hear that your loved ones are safe. I think of them very often and am grateful to God that at least some element of prudence towards America has been planted in the heart of the Turk.

Always

Affectionately yours,

WOODROW WILSON

To Frank I. Cobb, who had telegraphed about a Washington dispatch to the effect that the State Department had evidence of Germany's plan to make war against the United States after crushing France and Great Britain. If such evidence could be published, Cobb thought, it would have a great effect on public sentiment in the country. The President's reply is marked "Personal":

"Unfortunately, there are no documents in the State Department which could be said to establish the thing mentioned in your telegraphic message to me . . . After receiving your telegram, I conferred with the Secretary of State and found that the statements he had made were based, and I think very reasonably based, upon documents and evidences no one of which plainly declare[s] the fact. In short, it was a conclusion, and no conclusion, however well founded in inference, can be established by evidence. I wish it could be."

To Senator F. M. Simmons:

"Information has come to me through the public prints and otherwise that a fresh attempt is to be made, this time in connection with the revenue measure, to saddle me with a legislative committee with the professed purpose of assisting me to control the vast expenditures of the Government, and I am writing to ask if I may not have your active cooperation in preventing such a burden being put upon me, for an additional authority put alongside of me in this already tremendous task of directing the administrative activities of the Government is just the thing which would create confusion and make my task twice as complex as it is. The burden of responsibility is already all but too great to carry, and to have the responsibility shared would embarrass me without lightening it.

"I am very anxious that my friends in the Senate should understand how serious this is. I am writing to you not because I for a moment doubt your attitude in the matter but in order that, if you care to do so, you may cite my feeling about it."[1]

To Senator John Sharp Williams:

"I know what your attitude is towards the proposal to constitute a Congressional Committee to assist in some way in controlling the expenditure of the vast sums of money which Congress has appropriated and is about to appropriate, and I feel sure that you will do your utmost to prevent the creation of any such body, but I am very anxious that my friends in the Senate should all know how

[1]Similar letters went on the same day to Senators Thomas S. Martin and Ollie M. James. Simmons replied that the matter would have his "hearty and unqualified support in every possible effective way"; Martin replied that he was in "thorough accord" with the President's views; and James wrote that he would do all he could against the creation of such a committee. The New York *Times* of the 2nd contained an editorial called "Hobbling the President" in the course of which it was said: ". . . . Under whatever pretext undertaken and by whatever name called, the proposed committee would be merely a clog on a duty and responsibility that belong constitutionally to the Executive. It would be guided, consciously or unconsciously, by partisan motives on the part of the Republicans. . . ."

serious the matter is. It would constitute a very great added difficulty and burden so far as I am concerned in the administration of the war. The great impediment to an effective control on my part as things stand is that there are so many consultative bodies and so many instrumentalities upon which I must keep my eye at the same time. Fortunately, the instrumentalities which now exist are under my authority. To have another authority put over them or any body which might be conceived of as exercising an independent authority would be fatal to the unity of the administration and to the very kind of control which the proponents of such a committee have in mind. I have taken the liberty of writing this to you in order that I might have your cooperation, which I know you will generously give, in preventing what would undoubtedly be a practical blunder of the gravest sort."[1]

To Dr. John Fox:

"I am glad to have an opportunity to endorse the effort of the American Bible Society to procure a fund of $400,000 to cover the expenses of supplying the men in the National Army with Bibles. This is an object which I am sure all Christian people will wish to see accomplished. I hope that it may be, for the sake of the men who are going to the front. They will need the support of the only book from which they can get it."[2]

To Representative W. C. Adamson, written at the request of Secretary McAdoo:

"May I not express to you and through you to the Committee on Interstate and Foreign Commerce of the House my sincere gratification at the favorable report the Committee has just made on the bill granting family

---

[1]Senator Williams replied that he agreed perfectly with the President's position.

[2]This letter was altered, with the President's permission, to include both the army and navy.

allowances, indemnities and life insurance for the officers and enlisted men of the Army and Navy; and the hope that the proposed measure may receive the prompt approval of the Congress?

"There are so many arguments for the bill that I do not know which to put forward as the most imperative. No doubt you have assembled them in your own mind in their most effective order. But what principally appeals to me about the bill is that it takes into consideration the whole obligation of the soldier not only, but the whole obligation of the Government—the obligations of justice and humanity both to the soldier and to his family. It is one of the most admirable pieces of legislation that has been proposed in connection with the war and I cannot too earnestly urge its adoption.

"I observe with regret that the limit of life insurance available to the officers and men in the service has been reduced from $10,000 to $5,000. I earnestly hope that the $10,000 limit may be restored."

Sunday, September 2nd.

The President and Mrs. Wilson spent the day on the *Mayflower.*

To Colonel House, who had written of the "spontaneous and enthusiastic" reception of the President's reply to the Pope by the American people. ". . . . Even the Providence Journal, that is so pro-ally that it forgets to be American, joins the generous chorus. . . .":

MY DEAR HOUSE,

I am delighted that you thought the reply to the Pope what it should be and that it has, on the whole, been so well received. I did not dare to submit it to our Associates across the sea more than twenty-four hours before I made it public. I felt morally certain that they would wish changes which I could not make. I was confirmed in that view when Jusserand the next day went up in the air because it seemed to exclude economic punishment of Germany after the war. It will work out as well this way as any. The differences of opinion will be less embarrassing now than they would have been if I had invited them beforehand.

I am beginning to think that we ought to go systematically to work to ascertain as fully and precisely as possible just what the several parties to this war on our side of it will be inclined to insist upon as part of the final peace arrangements, in order that we may formulate our own position either for or against them and begin to gather the influences we wish to employ,—or, at least, ascertain what influences we can use: in brief, prepare our case with a full knowledge of the position of all the litigants. What would you think of quietly gathering about you a group of men to assist you to do this? I could, of course, pay all the bills out of the money now at my command. Under your guidance these assistants could collate all the definite material available and you could make up the memorandum by which we should be guided.

Have you had a talk with Frankfurter? If you have not, I wish you would have. He knows what some of the other governments are doing to get their cases ready and their pipes laid, and he might be able to give you a lead as to doing what I am here suggesting.

I am writing from the MAYFLOWER at Hampton Roads. Next week I shall try to get away for a longer time. Do not be alarmed about my health. I need rest, and am growing daily more conscious that I do; but I am fit and all right.

All join in affectionate messages.

Affectionately Yours,
WOODROW WILSON

Monday, September 3rd, Labor Day.

The President and Mrs. Wilson returned to the White House at eight o'clock in the morning. After golf at the Kirkside Club the President spent some hours in his study and in the afternoon took a long drive with Mrs. Wilson.

William Phillips, Assistant Secretary of State, sent the President "four telegrams of intense interest" from Ambassador Page in London, adding that two more of the same character were in process of being deciphered. The enclosures dealt with the famous Luxburg messages between German diplomatic officers and the Berlin Foreign Office, relating chiefly to the Argentine and implicating the Swedish government. One, dated July 9, 1917, and sent by Count Luxburg, German chargé at Buenos Aires, through the Swedish Legation there to the German Foreign Office, read in part: ". . . . As regards Argentine steamers, I recommend either compelling them to turn back, sinking them without leaving any traces ["Spurlos versenkt"], or letting them through. They are all quite small." Page telegraphed on August 31st that he was sending the cipher originals by "a trustworthy messenger personally known to you."[1] ". . . the British Government hope that you will immediately publish these telegrams, asking that their origin be kept secret as in the case of the Z[immermann] telegram."

Lord Robert Cecil sent Colonel House a memorandum which he had prepared for the British government in 1916 "dealing with a particular proposal for diminishing the likelihood of war"; and suggested it might be well if in both England and America "some Commission of learned and distinguished men were entrusted with the duty of examining all these [prevention of war] schemes, in order to see what was possible and useful."[2]

It was officially announced that Riga had surrendered to the Germans. The news produced a profound crisis in Russia, and a wave of unrest spread through the country. In Germany the announcement was received with great enthusi-

---

[1] Sir William Wiseman.

[2] *Intimate Papers*, Vol. IV, pp. 6–7.

asm. Church bells were rung, cities bedecked with flags, thanksgiving services held.[1]

Tuesday, September 4th.

In the early afternoon the President received Judge Chambers of the Board of Mediation and Conciliation. The cabinet meeting was omitted, but Secretary Lansing came in at 2:30 for a conference about exemption of "declarants" from the draft. At a quarter of four the President left for the Peace Monument, to march with the District of Columbia quota of the National Army. He led the parade on foot, carrying a small silk flag, as did the other marchers, while cabinet members walked at the heads of the contingents from their respective departments. Burleson, it was observed, had his ubiquitous umbrella hooked over his left arm! Many members of Congress and representatives of most of the Allied Powers were also in line. The President "stepped out with a long quick stride that made the mounted police ahead of him urge their horses into a faster pace, and brought beads of sweat to the brows of short-legged men behind."[2] At the White House the President left the line and took his place on the reviewing stand.

> Colonel House to the President: ". . . . I shall be delighted to undertake the work and will go about it at once. . . .
> "Lord Robert Cecil cables as follows:
> "'We are being pressed here for a declaration of sympathy with the Zionist movement, and I should be very grateful if you felt able to ascertain unofficially if the President favors such a declaration. . . .'"[3]
> An Inter-Allied Naval Conference met in London September 4th and 5th, taking up among other subjects the project for a mine barrage in the North Sea.[4]
> The first moonlight raid on London. Eleven people were killed; 62 hurt.

---

[1]*Current History*, October, 1917, pp. 68–69.

[2]New York *Times*, September 5, 1917.

[3]On September 7th House wrote: ". . . . Have you made up your mind regarding what answer you will make to Cecil concerning the Zionist Movement? It seems to me that there are many dangers lurking in it, and if I were the British I would be chary about going too definitely into that question."

[4]See Daniels, *Our Navy at War*, p. 132.

To Secretary Lansing, who wrote of the desire of some of the leading editors of the country to coöperate more fully with the government; and suggested that a few trustworthy newspaper men, "fairly representative of the press," be organized into an Advisory Council on Publicity to consult with and advise George Creel:

"I have myself received intimations of the feeling on the part of the men at the head of the news-gathering associations and of some of the leading editors of the country, to which you refer in your letter . . . It is based upon a complex of misunderstandings (many of which are now being removed) and of jealousies which I can expound to you some time, but the net result of my impressions is that it would be safest not to call them into systematic conference. They are a difficult lot to live with. They do not agree among themselves."

To William Phillips, who had reported that M. Tardieu, French high commissioner, desired to see the President in regard to the shipping situation. The President had referred the matter to Hurley, who replied that the whole question of tonnage was being studied, but no decision could be made on the disposition of French and other foreign ships until complete data on United States requirements was available:

"Of course, if Mr. Tardieu insists upon a personal interview with me about the matter of the ships, I shall appoint a time, but I wish very much that Mr. Tardieu might be given politely to understand that I have several times conferred with the Chairman of the Shipping Board about this matter and am convinced that as much progress is being made in determination of our policy as it is possible in the present circumstances to make. I am sure that the desire of the Shipping Board is as genuine as mine to help France in every possible way, but we must not do the thing by bits, we must do it as part of a well-considered policy which takes into consideration the whole difficult question. I do not see anything to be gained by a conference with Mr. Tardieu because I know what he has to say and I have a full memorandum from the Shipping Board as to their point, and I could only return again after such a conference to the Board and repeat the circle."

To Representative John J. Fitzgerald:
"I understand that the latest plan of the Republicans is to tack on the espionage committee as a rider to the Deficiency Bill. If they do, of course I cannot sign it, and yet that would lead to the most undesirable delay in the repassage of the measure, and I am writing this line to ask for your active cooperation to prevent any such tactics from succeeding. You have already told me how you feel in this matter and I know I have the acquiescence of your judgment in my opinion, but I thought I would give myself the pleasure of telling you how I am counting on you to outmaneuver these gentlemen who are doing their best to get their hand on the steering apparatus of the Government."[1]

To Arthur Brisbane, who had sent over a copy of his editorial for the Washington *Times* of August 30th in praise of the President's reply to the Pope:

"I am certainly your debtor for the very generous editorial . . . It is very delightful to have you approve so unqualifiedly a document which I may say to you personally I wrote almost as a matter of course, because the whole body of issues in this great struggle has assumed in my mind a great simplicity, and there seemed to me to be no other way of stating it."

To R. G. Rhett, president of the United States Chamber of Commerce:

"I need not tell you how sincerely I appreciate the desire and the intelligent efforts of the Chamber to render

[1]Fitzgerald replied that he would do everything in his power to prevent the establishment of such a committee.

useful patriotic service in connection with the present war, or that the matter with which your letter . . . deals has been very much in my thoughts.

"It has been so much in my thoughts that I have come to some very definite conclusions about it. The work of the Committee on Public Information in the matter of propaganda is being very simply done through existing means and is quietly and rapidly spreading through one channel and another, and my conviction is that it would be a public mistake to create an instrumentality exclusively for the purpose of propaganda. I think the objects of such a body would be misunderstood, and the misunderstanding would be taken advantage of by those who are trying to make mischief. It would be said that the Government was finding itself in desperate need of assistance in order to clear up the thing which they pretend to consider obscure, namely, the objects of the United States in entering the war. Definite propaganda of this sort is generally futile in this country, while the very simple means of explanation and discussion which the Committee on Public Information is using is familiar to everybody and has nothing unusual about it.

"It may be that my judgment in this matter is not the right one, but it has been very maturely arrived at, and I am sure that your colleagues will understand that in stating it so definitely I am not intending to convey the least intimation of anything but very genuine appreciation of the proposal and offer the Chamber has so generously made."

To the general manager and the general counsel of the Georgia, Florida & Alabama Railroad Company, a telegram:

"Absence from Washington delayed my seeing your telegram of August thirty-first. I am at a loss to understand why you request two weeks longer to decide the question of mediation which has been before you since February. Your recent action in disregard of federal jurisdiction in matters of interstate commerce has created an impression which I take it for granted you will wish to remove very promptly and I renew my request that you do so now."

To Dr. W. L. McEwan, who, in behalf of the National Service Commission of the Presbyterian Church, had requested the designation of a day of prayer:

"I entirely sympathize, as I need hardly tell you, with the objects stated in your two letters . . . which have just been laid before me, but my judgment differs with yours as to whether the time has come which affords an evident opportunity for appointing a national day of prayer. My idea has been that when some definite period comes, like the actual entrance of our men into the fighting, the whole nation will feel the impulse which we can act upon with the greatest effect.

"I have no choice but to write in haste, but you will know, I am sure, that I am writing with no less earnestness or deliberation on that account."

To Mrs. Marguerite Cunliffe-Owen, "Personal":
"After discussing your interesting letter . . . with the War Department, I find that when regiments are consolidated the senior chaplain is retained, whether Catholic or Protestant. The effect of this is, of course, to place some chaplains on the inactive list and in some instances to deprive a regiment of either a Catholic or a Protestant chaplain, as the case may be. It is deemed that no hardship is created, however, as more than one regiment is involved in practically every camp and the men of the several regiments are given access to clergymen of their own persuasion by a system effected by their commanding officers. I have not had brought to my personal attention

the request of any Catholic priest to go as a volunteer chaplain under such circumstances as those described in your letter, but I have had such an application on behalf of a Protestant chaplain, whose request had to be declined on the ground that if one volunteer chaplain was allowed others must be accepted also and the result would be a very large number of unauthorized clergymen in each camp. I think you cannot realize the confusion that this would create or the demands that it would excite on the part of organizations and denominations of every kind.

"I may say that by reason of a recent reorganization of the allotment of chaplains the number of Catholic priests has been greatly increased and I have every reason to believe that the Catholic body is satisfied that it has no grounds for complaint."

To the soldiers of the National Army:

"You are undertaking a great duty. The heart of the whole country is with you. Everything that you do will be watched with the deepest interest and with the deepest solicitude not only by those who are near and dear to you, but by the whole Nation besides. For this great war draws us all closer together, makes us all comrades and brothers, as all true Americans felt themselves to be when we first made good our national independence. The eyes of all the world will be upon you, because you are in some special sense the soldiers of freedom.

"Let it be your pride, therefore, to show all men everywhere not only what good soldiers you are, but also what good men you are, keeping yourselves fit and straight in everything, and pure and clean through and through. Let us set for ourselves a standard so high that it will be a glory to live up to it, and then let us live up to it and add a new laurel to the crown of America. My affectionate confidence goes with you in every battle and every test. God keep and guide you!"

Wednesday, September 5th.

The President's afternoon appointments: Henry P. Davison and John D. Ryan, of the Red Cross; Dr. C. S. Macfarland, general secretary of the Federal Council of the Churches of Christ in America; Roy W. Howard, president of the United Press; Matthew Hale and Mr. Livermore, who told the President of the "existence among certain liberals of a feeling that the administration has shown a tendency to interfere with free speech, free assembly, and free press." Hale wrote the President, two days later: ". . . . Your position as outlined to me is so clear and so convincing that I do hope from the bottom of my heart that you will make an opportunity between now and our liberal conference the first of October to take the people of the country into your confidence and to outline in more detail your general position in regard to these fundamental principles upon which we are all really agreed. . . .

"Of course I appreciate the strength of what you said, that you 'could not just bat balls up into the air.' I do agree with you fully that you have got to have a proper occasion for making this kind of a statement . . ."

At five o'clock Secretary Burleson called; at 5:30, Secretary Baker. Evening at Keith's.

A conference of international Socialists finally convened, September 5–7, at Stockholm; and issued a manifesto, the text of which did not reach the United States for several months.[1]

Thursday, September 6th.

Afternoon appointments: a delegation of 75 representatives of the livestock industry; Senator Ransdell and the Louisiana delegation; Senator Ashurst of Arizona; Justice J. H. Covington, who was just back from a trip through the West, where he had been observing labor conditions; members of the War Industries Board; George Creel.

Secretary Lansing and Viscount Ishii, special ambassador from Japan, began a series of thirteen conferences, which continued until November 2nd, the President following the

---

[1] *Current History*, October, 1917, p. 95. For the manifesto, see *ibid.*, February, 1918, pp. 209–210. The concluding paragraph read: "Long live the international mass struggle against the war! Long live the Socialist peace!"

negotiations carefully and giving his full consent to every step. The conversations all concerned the same subject: agreement upon the principles to be observed with regard to China. The first, Lansing describes in some detail in his *Memoirs*, pointing out in summary "some things which should be particularly noted":

"The assertion that Japan intended to return Kiaochow to China, but that she would retain the German islands in the Pacific north of the equator, a fact of which I had been advised in 1916 by Sir Cecil Spring-Rice, when the United States was neutral and without voice in the matter.[1] The desire of the Viscount to couple with a redeclaration of the Open Door Policy a reference to Japan's 'special interests,' and my doubt of the wisdom of doing so because of the danger that any such declaration might be interpreted 'as a peculiar political interest,' though it was in fact not political but the result of geographical position and based on natural causes."

A statement was finally agreed upon and signed at the thirteenth conference.[2]

The American Alliance for Labor and Democracy—representing leading labor associations of the country, and presided over by Samuel Gompers—met at Minneapolis and adopted resolutions setting forth and approving the war aims of the United States, as stated by President Wilson.[3]

Minister Stovall reported from Switzerland that Austria had "recently been sending to Switzerland a quantity of unofficial agents to work at peace propaganda."[4]

Ambassador Francis telegraphed from Russia: "Nervousness increasing. Rumors of Bolshevik demonstration . . ."[5]

---

[1] In the course of hearings before the Senate Committee on Foreign Relations in 1919, Senator Borah asked, referring to this first Lansing-Ishii conference: "Did he [Ishii] make any other statement indicating to you at all that Japan had any agreement with Great Britain in regard to the German possessions?" Lansing replied: "None at all, sir. After that statement, that it was the intention of Japan to return Kiaochow to China, the subject was never again mentioned during the conversation." *Treaty of Peace With Germany, Hearings*, 66–1, p. 218.

[2] See, in this connection, *War Memoirs of Robert Lansing*, pp. 290 *et seq.* The 10th and 13th conferences (October 27th, November 2nd) are of especial interest and are therefore treated in this volume, pp. 329–330, 336.

[3] *Current History*, October, 1917, p. 90.

[4] *Foreign Relations*, 1917, Supp. 2, Vol. I, p. 195.

[5] *Ibid.*, 1918, *Russia*, Vol. I, p. 181.

To J. W. Harriman, president of the Harriman National Bank in New York:

"I value your letters . . . but must admit that I am at a loss to see what I can do in the circumstances. The Government is not doing anything which anyone is justified in regarding as inimical to business or calculated to upset it so long as it is conducted along reasonable lines and within reasonable limits of profit, and I believe that the reassurance needed will come with the development of policy and events. I do not know any new statement of policy which would effect the purpose. I would be very much interested to receive a suggestion from you on that subject.

"I need not tell you that I am desirous of doing anything that can be wisely done along the line you suggest, but my judgment halts."

Friday, September 7th.

The President returned from his morning golf in time to receive Senator John Sharp Williams. In the early afternoon he conferred with: Senator Thompson of Kansas; the actor, Joseph Cawthorn. Appointments after the cabinet meeting: Judge Martin J. Wade of Iowa; Herbert Hoover and H. A. Garfield. The President remained in his study until 10:30, when he and Mrs. Wilson, accompanied by Mrs. Wilson's mother and sister, left for New York.

> Secretary Lansing telegraphed Ambassador Stimson in Argentina, quoting "for your information and use in event of official inquiry, but not to be given to the press by you," three of the Luxburg telegrams containing matter extremely offensive to Argentina.[1]

To Herbert Hoover:

"I have been very much interested in your letter . . . about the hog supply in the United States. I was discussing

[1] This volume, p. 255, also *Foreign Relations*, 1917, Supp. 1, pp. 322–323. On the same day the Argentine ambassador called to see Secretary Lansing and received copies of the Luxburg telegrams, which he immediately sent to his government. *War Memoirs of Robert Lansing*, p. 328. The telegrams were made public by the Department of State on the 8th and appeared in the papers of the 9th.

the matter this afternoon with the Secretary of Agriculture, since it so directly affects the matter of production, and found his observations and suggestions so interesting that I am going to take the liberty of asking you if you will not avail yourself of an early opportunity to see him and match your views with his in this important matter."

Saturday, September 8th.

The President and Mrs. Wilson arrived in New York at 6:22 in the morning. After breakfast in their private car with Mrs. and Miss Bolling, they motored to the waterfront, where a launch was waiting to take them to the *Mayflower*. The ship sailed at nine o'clock, heading for Gloucester via the Cape Cod Canal. They remained at New London from six to eleven in the evening, while Miss Margaret Wilson, Mrs. Sayre and Mrs. Edward Elliott went aboard for dinner.

The State Department sent over to the White House a decree, signed by the King of Italy, approving the conferring upon the President of the United States, by the Royal University of Bologna, of the degree of Doctor of Laws, "honoris causa."

French troops launched a new offensive on the right bank of the Meuse.

Sunday, September 9th.

The *Mayflower* reached Gloucester Harbor early in the afternoon, and Colonel and Mrs. House were on hand to meet the boat. They went aboard for a short time, then took the President and Mrs. Wilson for a two-hour drive along the shore. Colonel House reported in his diary: ". . . . We stopped first at our cottage and then went over to Mrs. T. Jefferson Coolidge's house to look at her prints, china, etc., which have been inherited from Thomas Jefferson.

"We dined on the *Mayflower*. Before dinner the President and I had an intimate talk of perhaps an hour and again for an hour and a half after dinner. . . .

"He is sending a commission to England recommended at the

suggestion of Arthur Pollen and others . . . We discussed the question of capital ships. . . ."[1]

"After I had made an argument in favor of capital ships, he refused to discuss the question further, declaring that no matter whether I was right or he was right, it was impracticable to make an arrangement with Great Britain at this time looking to our securing some of her capital battleships after the war in consideration of our abandoning our shipbuilding programme of capital ships in order to build submarine destroyers. He thought the only thing that could be binding on Great Britain would be a treaty, and a treaty must necessarily go to the Senate for confirmation. He did not believe this country was prepared for a treaty of that sort with Great Britain. . . ."[2]

". . . . During the afternoon we were discussing Lincoln. We agreed that Washington would continue in history the greater man. . . ."[3]

Monday, September 10th.

The President and Mrs. Wilson again went ashore to meet Colonel and Mrs. House. The President played nine holes at the Essex County Country Club with Hugh Wallace and Randolph Tucker, Colonel House's son-in-law, after which they all lunched at the Colonel's home in Magnolia. ". . . . During lunch," wrote House, "the President spoke of his nervousness when speaking in public. I had thought that he was entirely free from it, and yet he said if he had to walk across a crowded stage, with an audience in front of him, he always wondered whether he would drop before he reached the speakers' stand. . . ."[4] After luncheon the President met a group of newspaper correspondents and was photographed with Colonel House. The party then took another long drive along the North Shore. ". . . . While driving," wrote House, "he described himself as 'a democrat like Jefferson, with aristocratic tastes.' Intellectually, he said, he was entirely democratic, which in his opinion was unfortunate, for the reason that his mind led him where his taste rebelled." House commented, also, that once or

[1] *Intimate Papers*, Vol. III, pp. 175–176.
[2] *Ibid.*, p. 73.
[3] *Ibid.*, pp. 176–177.
[4] *Ibid.*, p. 177.

twice during the day he "threw the President off his line of thought by interpolations, and he found it difficult to return to his subject." "You see I am getting tired. This is the way it indicates itself."[1]

Colonel and Mrs. House dined aboard the *Mayflower* in the evening.

Secretary Baker announced that colored troops of the army would be trained in separate organizations.

Tuesday, September 11th.

The *Mayflower* passed through the Cape Cod Canal, while crowds of people gathered on the banks to cheer, and school children at Bournedale and Sagamore waved little flags and sang.

Wednesday, September 12th.

The *Mayflower* anchored off Old Lyme, Connecticut, while the President and Mrs. Wilson went ashore for a call upon Miss Florence Griswold, at whose house the Wilsons had spent many weeks in former years,[2] and had luncheon with Professor and Mrs. Vreeland, old Princeton friends.

Secretary Baker announced the perfection of the Liberty Motor—the "best . . . produced by any country."

Bonar Law, at a dinner given in London in honor of Representative Medill McCormick, said: ". . . I, as Chancellor of the Exchequer, am ready to say now what I should have been very sorry to admit six months ago, that without the aid of the United States the financial position of the Allies would have been in a very disastrous situation today. . . . But, though we rely upon the United States, that does not mean that we are ceasing our own efforts. . . ."[3]

To Frank I. Cobb, who had passed on Victor Ridder's scheme for sending certain influential German-Americans to Copenhagen, to get in touch with men like Scheidemann and Harden, show the German people that Germany was beaten, and set

[1]*Intimate Papers*, Vol. III, p. 177.
[2]See *Woodrow Wilson, Life and Letters*, Vol. III, *Governor*.
[3]*Current History*, November, 1917, p. 192.

forth what the United States was doing. The President's letter is marked "*Personal*":

"I am very much obliged to you for your letter . . . and beg that you will pardon my delay in replying to it. I have sneaked off from Washington and am trying to get a little rest, and am glad to say that I am succeeding.

"I would suggest that, if possible, you go into the suggestion of Mr. Victor Ridder's a little further and ascertain what particular German-Americans in New York they have it in thought to send abroad on the errand you refer to. I feel pretty sure that in any case it would be unwise even to wink at such an errand, but I would feel the more certain of my judgment if I knew the men and their affiliations. It is very generous of you to offer to make this inquiry for me. It would be serviceable in many directions."

To Dudley Field Malone, who had resigned as Collector of the Port of New York so that he might return to the practice of law and give all his leisure time "to fight as hard for the political freedom of women as I have always fought for your liberal leadership."[1]:

MY DEAR MR. COLLECTOR:

Your letter . . . reached me just before I left home and I have, I am sorry to say, been unable to reply to it sooner.

I must frankly say that I cannot regard your reasons for resigning your position as Collector of Customs as convincing, but it is so evidently your wish to be relieved from the duties of the office that I do not feel at liberty to withhold my acceptance of your resignation. Indeed, I judge from your letter that any discussion of the reasons would not be acceptable to you and that it is your desire to be free of the restraints of public office. I, therefore, accept your resignation, to take effect as you have wished.

---

[1]Malone's letter had been published in the New York *Times* of September 8th.

I need not say that our long association in public affairs makes me regret the action you have taken most sincerely.

Very truly yours,

WOODROW WILSON

Thursday, September 13th.

President and Mrs. Wilson and Mrs. Sayre visited Nantucket. The entire population of the village, including the school children, who had been given a special holiday, welcomed them at the landing; Justice John H. Clarke was the first to greet the President. Later they drove across the island—behind a pair of horses, automobiles being barred—to Siasconset, where the Sayres were spending the summer.

Contracts for the first three government shipbuilding yards at Hog Island, Pennsylvania, were let by the Emergency Fleet Corporation.

To Reverend William J. Hampton:

"I am sure that you will not have misunderstood my long delay in replying to your letter . . . It has been due to an extraordinary pressure of public business not only, but also to a feeling that I really did not know how to write an adequate answer. It is very hard for me to speak of what my mother was without colouring the whole estimate with the deep love that fills my heart whenever I think of her. But while others cannot have seen her as I did, I am sure that every one who knew her at all, must have felt also the charm of her unusual grace and refinement, and have been aware of the clear-eyed, perceiving mind that lay behind her frank, gray eyes. They were not always gray. They were of that strange, changeable colour, which so often goes with strong character and varied ability. She was one of the most remarkable persons I have ever known. She was so reserved, that only those of her own household can have known how lovable she was, though every friend knew how loyal and steadfast she was. I seem to feel still the touch of her hand, and the sweet steadying influence of her wonderful character. I thank God to have had such a mother!"[1]

Friday, September 14th.

The President and Mrs. Wilson spent the day on the *Mayflower*.

Saturday, September 15th.

The *Mayflower* anchored in the North River in the morning, while Mrs. Wilson went into New York for some shopping. The President joined her in the afternoon for a drive around the city and to call on Mr. and Mrs. Cleveland H. Dodge; and in the evening they went to the Belasco Theater—*Polly With a Past.* As people began to recognize the President, there was great excitement, and within a few seconds the entire audience was on its feet cheering enthusiastically.

> The President issued a proclamation to school children in behalf of the Junior Red Cross.[2]
>
> German submarines were reported operating off the New England coast.
>
> General Pershing telegraphed Secretary Baker: "There is considerable talk of possibilities of peace this winter . . . Failure to stop German armies and revolt among Russian troops have had depressing effect upon Allies. President French Cabinet believed to be strongly in favor of continuation of war, but French people in state of mind to accept any favorable proposition. . . . Recent British attacks beginning with latter part of July have been very costly and British morale not as high as two months ago."[3]

Sunday, September 16th.

After a call on Dr. and Mrs. Grayson at the St. Regis Hotel, President and Mrs. Wilson attended morning services at the Fifth Avenue Presbyterian Church. Colonel House came aboard the *Mayflower* for dinner, as did Mrs. Wilson's mother and

---

[1] Hampton, *Our Presidents and Their Mothers*, pp. 236–237. The shorthand notes for this letter remain among the Wilson papers.

[2] *Public Papers*, Vol. V, pp. 102–103.

[3] Pershing, *My Experiences in the World War*, Vol. I, p. 173.

sister. The Colonel reported in his diary: ". . . . We had a talk before lunch. I told him of Lloyd George's desire that a representative from the United States be sent to the Interallied Conference. . . .

"The President thought he could not go much further toward meeting Lloyd George's wishes than to express a feeling that something different should be done in the conduct of the war than had been done, and to say that the American people would not be willing to continue an indefinite trench warfare. He thought it would be inadvisable to commit himself further. . . ."[1]

The party arrived in Washington in the early evening, after the first real vacation the President had had in many months.

A walkout in more than 100 shipbuilding plants was reported from San Francisco.

Monday, September 17th.

The President received Representative Fitzgerald of New York at 9:30, and spent the rest of the morning in his study. His cousin, J. A. Wilson, was a luncheon guest. Afternoon appointments: Secretary Baker; Secretary Lansing; Samuel Gompers, who probably discussed labor conditions in the West; Secretary McAdoo; H. A. Garfield and Herbert Hoover. In the evening E. N. Hurley called.

". . . . Many times lately the Canadians have filled the City of Lens with gas that kills and soaks down heavily into the dugouts and tunnels and stifles the men in their sleep before they have time to stretch out their hands for gas masks . . ."[2]

To Frank P. Glass:

"I know you will overlook my neglect in replying to your letters about water power legislation, important as they are. As a matter of fact, nothing was needed to increase my interest in water power legislation, but all legislation of that sort has been interrupted and embarrassed by cross currents and interests which it would take me a long time to state to you but which have been very

---

[1] *Intimate Papers*, Vol. III, p. 188.

[2] Philip Gibbs, *Current History*, October, 1917, p. 48.

distressingly evident throughout the last two sessions of Congress. I shall try my best to work the thing out at the earliest possible time along some line that would be serviceable.

"Thank you with all my heart for your personal words about my vacation. I did indeed need it and I think it has done me a lot of good."

To his secretary, Tumulty, who had called attention to the message of a Catholic churchman from Wisconsin, as to Gompers' alleged statement that the President had agreed to appoint on war commissions and boards at least one representative agreeable to American labor and especially to American Federation officers. "Prominent ecclesiastics say Gompers lies. . . . Worth attention as matter is creating feeling in ticklish pro-German neighborhood.":

"I don't like the tone of this inquiry. I cannot believe, in the first place, that he is correctly quoting Gompers, to whom I gave no definite assurances but to whom I did say, I believe, that I thought it fair and wise that there should be representatives of labor on all boards dealing with industrial questions in the present crisis. To get into a debate as between Mr. Gompers and the representatives of the Roman Catholic Church, however, would be most indiscreet and unwise, and we particularly cannot just now do anything to discredit Mr. Gompers who is doing such valiant service."

Tuesday, September 18th.

After the cabinet meeting the President received the Georgia delegation; and at five o'clock, Samuel Gompers. The evening he spent in his study.

Samuel Gompers sent a message, through the State Department, urging the Russian people to be "patient and forbearing in the effort now being made to give to Russia a definite permanent democratic government."[1]

---

[1]See, for entire message, *Foreign Relations,* 1918, *Russia,* Vol. I, p. 194.

Ambassador Page telegraphed confidentially from Rome: "Informed by Minister for Foreign Affairs he has reliable information Germany increasing and making disposition of submarines to attack unexpectedly American transport flotilla when bringing over our army."

Entrainment of conscripts for their cantonments began—the "largest troop movement ever undertaken in this country."[1] Secretary Baker wrote the President a few days later: ". . . . When it is remembered that this great movement has taken place without suspending ordinary passenger and freight traffic on the roads, and without inconveniencing them noticeably, it really makes a remarkable story. . . ."

To Max Eastman, who, while congratulating the President on his reply to the Pope, deplored what he considered the violation of the rights of free speech and assemblage and the freedom of the press:

"I thank you very warmly for your generous appreciation of my reply to the Pope, and I wish that I could agree with those parts of your letter which concern the other matters we were discussing when you were down here. I think that a time of war must be regarded as wholly exceptional and that it is legitimate to regard things which would in ordinary circumstances be innocent as very dangerous to the public welfare, but the line is manifestly exceedingly hard to draw and I cannot say that I have any confidence that I know how to draw it. I can only say that a line must be drawn and that we are trying, it may be clumsily but genuinely, to draw it without fear or favor or prejudice."

To J. W. Harriman of the Harriman National Bank, New York, a letter marked "Personal":

". . . . I feel confident that the tremors and uneasiness of the business world will presently pass and I think what

[1] *Literary Digest*, September 29, 1917, p. 68.

we do down here will steady it more than anything I can say. I have tried to make it clear in what I have said about profits and the business processes of the Government that we intended to do full justice, but I also meant to make it clear that we did not think that large profits were justifiable in the circumstances. I think this is a time when everybody must make the utmost sacrifice for the common objects we have in view in this great struggle, and I am sure that is your own feeling and judgment also. If the endeavor to restrict profits within some reasonable limit unsteadies the business world, I am afraid I can give it no assurance which will steady it again.

"But you may be sure, nevertheless, that whenever I have an occasion to say anything I will seek to keep your advice in mind and find some means of reassurance, for there certainly is no justification for discouragement or pessimism of any kind or degree. . . ."

Wednesday, September 19th.

Just before luncheon the President received Colonel Harts and Major Ridley, and in the afternoon: Justice Covington; the War Industries Board; Cyrus H. McCormick; Senator Swanson of Virginia; Henry Morgenthau, who reported on his recent trip abroad, bringing the President word of the "universal desire of our European associates, that he should exert the intellectual and moral leadership of the common cause." The President was deeply impressed. ". . . . He seemed for the moment almost overpowered at the thought of the stupendous responsibility that it thrust upon him . . . . he seemed perplexed, he seemed almost to despair. 'They want me to lead them!' he exclaimed. 'But where shall I lead them to? . . . .'"[1]

The President signed a membership card of the Pocket Testament League, thereby making it, as the card read, "the rule of my life to read at least one chapter in the Bible each day," a rule which he himself had followed all his life.

[1]Morgenthau, *All in a Life-Time*, p. 277.

Secretary Baker sent over a list of conscientious objectors reported at cantonments—in seven out of the ten camps reported on, there were none—and commented: "I don't want the inclosed to be too encouraging, because, of course, it represents only our experience with the first five percent of the men called under the draft, but it does not seem from this first survey as though our problem was going to be unmanageably large, or so large that a very generous and considerate mode of treatment would be out of the question. . . ."

To Colonel House:

"Lansing is not only content that you should undertake the preparation of data for the peace conference but volunteered the opinion that you were the very one to do it, and I promised him I would send you the enclosed memorandum, which he had drawn up. Of course we shall have to define the studies of our assistants with as much precision as possible or they would all be as thorough and exhaustive (and therefore as useless) as Frankfurter would be if he went to the depths he proposed."[1]

To Secretary Baker:

"Here is another snag. The gentlemen who sign this memorandum as conscientious objectors belong to a church which keeps the seventh day as the Sabbath and therefore they don't want to work on Saturday. Could it be arranged to have them work on Sunday?"[2]

---

[1]Dr. Mezes, president of the College of the City of New York, and Colonel House's son-in-law, was named director of the "Inquiry" thus established; and Walter Lippmann of the *New Republic*, secretary. ". . . . Headquarters were in New York, where the American Geographical Society offered its offices, library, and map-making facilities, as well as the invaluable services of its Director, Dr. Isaiah Bowman . . . . the President at various times approached the Inquiry for data and advice on current policy, even before its collections were complete . . ." *Intimate Papers*, Vol. III, p. 170. For an account of the early stages of the organization, see Shotwell, *At the Paris Peace Conference*, pp. 3 *et seq.*

[2]Secretary Baker replied that he would keep the point of view in mind when it came to arranging non-combatant service for conscientious objectors. ". . . . I am beginning to feel that nothing short of a comprehensive knowledge of Professor James's book on 'Varieties of Religious Experience' will ever qualify a man to be a helpful Secretary of War."

To William J. Bryan, who had asked that a certain young man be pardoned the day before his sentence expired:

"I have your letter . . . written from the Lafayette while I was away taking a much-needed breathing spell and I need not tell you that my heart prompts me to do what you ask for young ———, but when I consider the effects such action as you suggest would have on other cases that I have been recently dealing with, difficulties stand up very formidably in front of me. I believe that it will be necessary to wait a while in the usual way before issuing a pardon. Such pardons come in due course as a matter of routine almost if the released prisoner's behavior is good, as I am sure it will be in this case, and no serious detriment I hope will ensue to the young man. If I were to issue a pardon immediately upon his release from prison, I could hardly find any good reason to give why I had not issued a pardon to begin with.

"I was very sorry to miss you. I did not know that you were coming to Washington last week. We have all warmly admired your generous and patriotic course."

To Senator William Hughes of New Jersey:
MY DEAR BILLY:

It was mighty good to see your handwriting. I am sorry, very sorry, that you feel that your recovery is slow, but just so you take care to make it sure it will come out all right in the end and we will all be so delighted to see you back again. We have missed you very much.

I have the warmest feeling for ex-Senator Johnson and you may be sure will consider his name very seriously in connection with the Maine vacancy on the bench.

With warmest regards from us all,

Faithfully yours,
WOODROW WILSON

Thursday, September 20th.

In the morning the President received Representatives Humphreys and Collier and Senator John Sharp Williams of Mississippi. Afternoon appointments: Lord Reading, who presented a letter from Lloyd George;[1] Colonel William Libbey of New Jersey; Misha Applebaum and a committee, to present a humanitarian medal; Senator Chamberlain of Oregon and a committee of wheat growers; Representative Lazaro of Louisiana; Senator James of Kentucky; Representative Cannon of Illinois.

The President's commission to investigate labor conditions in the West was announced.

British troops in the early morning advanced a mile on an eight-mile front in Flanders, taking 2,000 prisoners. ". . . . All through the night the British heavy guns were slogging . . . Before dawn a high wind was raging at thirty miles an hour across Flanders . . .

"The troops had lain out all night in the rain . . ."[2]

To Henry Ford:

"I have just learned of your characteristic generosity in turning over to the use of the Quartermaster's Department

[1] Lloyd George set down his views, unofficially, as to the cause of the comparative failure of the Allies during the past year—chiefly the Russian collapse and lack of unity as to military operations. He felt that attack should be directed upon the front of Germany's allies, since that was the weakest part of their line, "not only militarily but politically." He urged that the United States should be present at conferences of the Allies, since decisions made there would vitally affect the American army in France. ". . . . But another reason weighs still more strongly with me. I believe that we are suffering to-day from the grooves and traditions which have grown up during the war, and from the inevitable national prejudices and aspirations which, consciously or unconsciously, influence the judgment of all the nations of Europe. I believe that the presence at the deliberations of the Allies of independent minds, bringing fresh views, unbiassed by previous methods and previous opinions, might be of immense value in helping us to free ourselves from the ruts of the past . . ." He concluded:
". . . may I say how much we all here have appreciated the speeches you have made about the war. If you will permit me to say so I believe that your statements have been not the least important of the contributions which America is making to the cause of human freedom. . . . They have recalled to many the ideals with which they entered upon the war, and which it is easy to forget amid the horrors of the battlefield and the overtime and fatigue in the munition shops. They have given to the bruised and battered peoples of Europe fresh courage to endure and fresh hope that with all their sufferings they are helping to bring into being a world in which freedom and democracy will be secure, and in which free nations will live together in unity and peace." Published in full in *War Memoirs of David Lloyd George*, Vol. IV, pp. 518–524.

[2] Philip Gibbs, in *Current History*, November, 1917, p. 208.

10 DOWNING STREET
WHITEHALL, S.W.

3rd. Sept. 1917.

Dear Mr President

      I am taking advantage of the visit of
Lord Reading to Washington to lay in front of you certain
views about the conduct of the war which I have formed
in the light of my experience during the last three years.
We are approaching a very difficult period in which it
will be necessary to take far reaching decisions which
will be of the utmost importance as regards our future
campaign - decisions which will be of vital moment to all
the armies in the field. In arriving at these decisions
I think it is essential that the heads of the British
and the United States Governments should fully understand
one another's views. I avail myself of this method of
communication because I do not wish my remarks to have
an official character. I am only anxious that you should,
as far as that is possible without direct conversation,

278

have appreciated the speeches you have made about the
war. If you will permit me to say so I believe that
your statements have been not the least important of
the contributions which America is making to the cause
of human freedom. They have not only been a profound
and masterly exposition of the Allied case. They have
recalled to many the ideals with which they entered
upon the war, and which it is easy to forget amid the
horrors of the battlefield and the overtime and fatigue
in the munition shops. They have given to the bruised
and battered peoples of Europe fresh courage to endure
and fresh hope that with all their sufferings they are
helping to bring into being a world in which freedom
and democracy will be secure, and in which free nations
will live together in unity and peace.

Ever sincerely

D Lloyd George

LLOYD GEORGE WRITES A PERSONAL LETTER TO WILSON

First and last pages of an important "Private and Personal" letter
from Lloyd George to the President, September 3, 1917, delivered by
Lord Reading at Washington, September 20th. Further extracts
quoted on p. 277.

(By permission of Little, Brown and Company, publishers of *The War Memoirs of
David Lloyd George*)

your splendid plant in Boston. May I not send you my personal thanks and admiring appreciation?"

Friday, September 21st.

Before cabinet meeting the President received the new minister from Greece, Georges Roussos, who presented his credentials.[1] Late-afternoon appointments: the Prime Minister of New South Wales; Representative Eagle of Texas. President and Mrs. Wilson and a small family party spent the evening at Keith's Theater.

Saturday, September 22nd.

The President spent the latter part of the morning at work in his study, and had lunch served in his room. At three in the afternoon members of the War Industries Board called for a conference, probably in regard to steel price fixing.[2] At five o'clock Dr. Sterling Ruffin called to attend Mrs. Wilson, who was ill with grippe; and in the evening, Senator Saulsbury of Delaware saw the President.

To Secretary Baker:

"I dare say you are right about not insisting upon the immediate retirement of General Duvall, but I must admit I am sorry about it because I know that his attacks on the present administration have been very frequent and very violent and very unfair. Perhaps we can find an early opportunity to let him resume his 'innocuous desuetude.'"

Sunday, September 23rd.

The President went alone to the Central Presbyterian Church and in the afternoon went for a drive with his cousin, Mrs. Wilson being ill in bed. Dr. Ruffin called during the day.

Telegram to Boyle, Stack and O'Connell, labor leaders in West Coast labor troubles, sent as the result of a conference between

[1] *Official Bulletin,* September 25, 1917, for the President's reply.

[2] The New York *Times* reported that the heads of practically all the big steel industries involved in price-fixing negotiations had appeared before the board that morning. September 23, 1917.

Hurley, Gompers and Macy and merely signed by the President:

"Mr. Hurley has just informed me that a unanimous agreement has been reached in the San Francisco situation to refer the entire subject matter to the ship building and labor adjustment board. The sole remaining issue is the temporary wage at which the men will agree to return. This point probably will be cleared up today. This is most gratifying as it assures a prompt and satisfactory settlement. Mr. Hurley has also informed me that he has asked the wage adjustment board to make findings in the Seattle and Portland situations as well and with equal promptness. I need not say that this happy solution of the labor trouble on the Pacific Coast would be most gratifying to me as it is a further evidence of the patriotism of labor. In view of it I would ask that no cessation of work occur at Portland or Seattle. The wage board begins functioning at once and will announce its findings with expedition. I count confidently upon the patriotic cooperation of the workmen and their leaders. The men can count upon just and prompt action. . . ."

Monday, September 24th.

At 12:30 the President received Roland S. Morris, recently appointed ambassador to Japan, who was about to leave for his post. The President said: "Don't write me too many letters!"[1] The head usher's diary again reported "Lunch & dinner served in room." During the afternoon the President received: General Hugh L. Scott; the Commission from the Netherlands; Speaker Clark and a committee; Representative Austin of Tennessee; Representative Rucker of Missouri; George Creel; Judge Adamson and a committee representing farmers' organizations, who presented the serious situation due to lack of farm labor.

---

[1]Roland S. Morris to the author.

To Colonel House:

" . . . . I was mighty sorry to head you off from coming down to-day; but Mrs. Wilson is really suffering a great deal, with a severe attack of grippe and every minute I can spare from the work of the day I ought to spend making it easier for her. I am hoping each day that she will be much better, and then I can have a free mind for the many things we must talk over, you and I."

To T. W. Gregory, in regard to Colonel House's conviction that the Mooney case ought to be investigated:

"The enclosed letter from House explains itself and I am sending it along with the enclosed editorials in order to ask you if you will not be kind enough to have the investigation suggested by House made with as much thoroughness as possible. We cannot leave any stone unturned to prevent or soften labor troubles."

Tuesday, September 25th.

At 12:30 the President received a sub-committee from the Senate and House committees on foreign affairs. He saw the Guatemalan Special Mission after luncheon. Later in the afternoon Rev. John M. Wells, moderator of the General Assembly of the Presbyterian Church, called, with a conference committee of the Southern Presbyterian Church; and at 5 o'clock Mrs. Vira B. Whitehouse. The President's brother, Joseph R. Wilson, was a guest at dinner.

To Secretary Lansing, who had reported on his interviews of the 6th and 22nd with Viscount Ishii and had enclosed a draft of a note relative to the "Open Door" policy which he proposed, if the President approved, to submit to Ishii at their next conference. The President's note was written by hand:

"Thank you for letting me have these. I spent half an hour with Viscount Ishii. I did most of the talking (to let him see my *full* thought) and he seemed to agree throughout in *principle*."[1]

[1] The President had seen Viscount Ishii on August 23rd (this vol., p. 230) and saw

Viscount Ishii "and suite"—in his account of the interview, Ishii reported that the President was even more friendly than he had been in August;[1] Dr. John R. Mott, probably in regard to the educational campaign in Russia.

A "round-up of enemy aliens" began in New York and neighboring New Jersey cities.

A British Admiralty report for the past week showed the smallest U-boat toll since February.

To his daughter, Miss Margaret Wilson:
"MY DEAREST DAUGHTER:

"I hate to dictate a note to you but I want to hasten to assure you before I can get the time to write one myself that I have very cheerfully consented to the dedication to me of Mr. Macmillon's and Mr. MacKaye's national hymn. How I would love to hear you sing it!

"Poor Edith has been suffering terribly for a week now with a grippe which seems to go uncommonly hard with her, but her general condition is improving and I hope that the awful headaches will presently relax their grip and be done. The rest of us are well and we all unite in messages and dearest love . . ."

Thursday, September 27th.
At 12:30 the President received Secretary McAdoo and the members of the Second Liberty Loan Committee. Afternoon appointments: about 70 members of the Woman's Liberty Loan Conference, to pay their respects; the British ambassador, to present the new military attaché of the Embassy; Senators Ransdell of Louisiana and Fletcher of Florida, and Representative Small of North Carolina; a committee representing the churches of the country, in regard to an increase in the number of chaplaincies in the army; Secretary Wilson and the commission which was about to begin investigation of Western labor conditions; Senator Phelan of California.

The new Liberty Loan was announced for $3,000,000,000 and as much more as the public wished to take.

[1] Viscount Ishii's *Memoirs*, p. 144, as translated by Miss Taki Fugita.

To Secretary Baker, enclosing a number of telegrams and letters about the reorganization of the National Guard in Missouri:

"I have no doubt that you feel as I do that a great deal of the esprit de corps of the National Guard units will depend upon keeping men from the same state together and, therefore, I take the liberty of sending you the two enclosures. In the case of the Missouri troops, the regiment which it is planned to divide is the one 'historic' regiment in the state and a special degree of sentiment seems to attach to it."

Friday, September 28th.

Omitting his golf because of the weather, the President spent the morning in his study. He received J. T. Newton, Commissioner of Patents, before cabinet meeting; and in the late afternoon went out alone in the car for an hour or so. Dr. Ruffin called three times during the day, to attend Mrs. Wilson.

The German Chancellor, addressing the Reichstag Committee, declined to specify German war aims; and concluded with the statement that the President's attempt to sow discord between the German people and the German government was hopeless.[1]

To Representative T. L. Blanton, one of whose constituents was concerned with the sale of two ships to French interests. The President had turned Blanton's letter over to Hurley of the Shipping Board; his reply to Blanton was based largely on Hurley's advice:

"I have your letter . . . Upon receiving it, I immediately consulted with the Shipping Board. I find that they have felt constrained to deny, except in isolated and altogether exceptional circumstances, all applications for the sale of American ships to foreign interests.

"Among the purposes for which the Shipping Board was created was the development of a merchant marine to provide for our foreign trade and also for the transport of war materials for our Army. The world-wide scarcity

[1] *Foreign Relations*, 1917, Supp. 2, Vol. I, p. 215.

of tonnage is such that unless a prohibition were interposed against the sale of American ships the competition of foreign buyers might strip the United States of its merchant tonnage. To guard against this danger Congress inserted in the Shipping Act a provision forbidding all such transfers except in cases where the Shipping Board might give its consent. The Shipping Board has construed this prohibition, I think, very properly as being intended to be absolute and the permission given the Shipping Board to waive the prohibition as intended to provide only against unusual hardship or to meet quite unexpected conditions.

"In these circumstances I do not see how the Shipping Board could do otherwise than express its disapproval of such sales as the one you refer to on the part of the Seaboard & Gulf Steamship Company."

To his secretary, Tumulty, in regard to a request from the Committee on Labor of the Council of National Defense that an appropriation of $100,000,000 be recommended to Congress to provide houses for war workers in government emergency plants:

"I know absolutely nothing about this matter, but it is clear to me that it ought to be handled through the Council of National Defense. I would not dare recommend this enormous expenditure, $100,000,000, without knowing very much more about this matter than I do and I think I ought to have the advice of someone who knows before taking any action at all."

Saturday, September 29th.

The President had no official appointments during the day. Luncheon was served in his room. In the late afternoon he went out alone in the car; and in the evening, to the Belasco Theater with Mrs. Wilson's brother.

The President's reply to the Pope, reported the American chargé in Switzerland, had had "a great effect" in Germany. ". . . unrest among the working classes is causing the German Government very great anxiety . . . At a very recent meeting called by the Kaiser at which Hindenburg and the leaders among the naval and Government officers were present the German Emperor informed his guests that if it was the desire of the Army, Navy, and the people of Germany that he abdicate he would do so. All present pledged their loyalty, offered their general support of his dynasty."[1]

To H. B. Brougham, who had sent the President a copy of the editorial comment in the Philadelphia *Public Ledger* of the 28th upon the Inquiry and had suggested a public statement by the President:

"It was through the very inconsiderate talk of some people who ought to have known better that any public mention was made of my request to Colonel House to prepare all the materials that we would need in discussing any and all questions that might come up in the eventual peace conference which is sure to come at some time or other, and I am afraid the impression has got about that we are contemplating an early conference, as of course, we are not. I must frankly say that I feel that the best and most patriotic course just now is to say nothing about it at all.

"Of course, I do not mean to reflect in the least on your own kind efforts at interpretation. I merely mean that all discussion of peace at this time, so long as the German Government remains so stubbornly insincere and impossible, is unwise."

Sunday, September 30th.

Instead of going to church in the morning the President walked over to see Secretary McAdoo, who was about to leave on a Western trip. He and Mrs. Wilson's brother took a drive in the afternoon; and Mrs. McAdoo, Miss Bones and Mrs. Grayson had dinner at the White House.

---

[1]*Foreign Relations*, 1917, Supp. 2, Vol. I, pp. 216–217.

CHAPTER III

INSISTS UPON A "UNIFIED CONDUCT OF THE WAR"

(October, November, December, 1917)

The President sends Colonel House to the Allied War Conference—"Take the whip hand. We not only accede to the plan for a unified conduct of the war but insist upon it"; demands a Supreme War Council; guides "Inquiry" in preparing information for use at a future peace conference—"what we . . . are seeking is a basis which will be fair to all."

Takes over the railroads of the country; asks Congress for war with Austria-Hungary and is greeted by a roar of enthusiasm.

The Bolsheviks seize power, but Wilson has "not lost faith in the Russian outcome."

Italy falters—disaster at Caporetto.

American troops get into the trenches.

Monday, October 1st.

THE President received Matthew Hale before luncheon. Afternoon appointments: the members of the Supreme Court; Representative Jeannette Rankin; Senator Lewis; Senator Smith of Arizona and Representative Stedman of North Carolina; Governor Gardner of Missouri.

Conservative London newspapers were reported clamoring for reprisals, as a result of the greatest air attack on London since the beginning of the war.

French airplanes dropped half a ton of projectiles on Stuttgart—one of a series of reprisals.

To Mitchell Kennerley:

"May I not thank you for your courtesy in sending me the little volume, 'Woodrow Wilson and the World's Peace,' by George D. Herron? I have read it with the deepest appreciation of Mr. Herron's singular insight into all the elements of a complicated situation and into my own motives and purposes."

Tuesday, October 2nd.

The President played golf with the Attorney General, returning for a couple of hours of work in his study before luncheon. He received Representative Dupré of Louisiana at 2:15. Secretary Redfield remained for a conference after the cabinet meeting; and at 4:30 Representative Adamson called.

The Austro-Hungarian Foreign Minister, Count Czernin, delivered an address on the peace terms of his country— "obligatory international arbitration and general disarmament on land"; "freedom on the high seas and naval disarmament"; a "new international basis of right"; "free economic activity of all and absolute avoidance of future economic war."[1]

To Secretary Baker, who had written of spending considerable time at Camp Meade with the 27 conscientious objectors (out of 18,000 enlisted men) already there. ". . . . Of course, it is too soon to speculate on the problem because we do not yet know how large the number will turn out to be . . . but if it gets no worse . . . I am pretty sure that no harm will come in allowing these people to stay at the camps, separated from the life of the camp but close enough gradually to come to understand. The effect of that I think quite certainly would be that a substantial number of them would withdraw their objection and make fairly good soldiers.":

". . . . I am greatly interested by what you tell me of the conscientious objectors and believe with you that the matter will in part solve itself by the experiences of these men in camp."

To Matthew Hale, who had received the Democratic nomination for lieutenant governor of Massachusetts. The President's letter was marked "Personal":

"I am not at all satisfied that I can give it the best formulation but my idea would be that in order to offset

---

[1] See James Brown Scott, *Official Statements of War Aims and Peace Proposals*, pp. 152–156. Hereafter called *War Aims and Peace Proposals*.

Governor McCall's effort to make capital of his being a 'war Governor' a plank something like the following would be advisable:

"'The greatest task of its history is at present before the nation and the greatest necessity of its life for the effective display of its unity and patriotism. We, therefore, recognize it as our duty to give the fullest and most ungrudging support to the present national administration in the prosecution of this war and of the policies associated with it, and in order to do that we believe it the duty of every voter to associate himself upon every public occasion that offers with the forces that have indisputably supported the administration from the first. Only in this way can it be made clear on both sides of the water what the purpose and spirit of America is. We cannot make that purpose clear by supporting those who are known on both sides of the water to have been the earnest antagonists and severe critics of the administration at a time when the lines of action seemed to lie too near the question of allegiance or lack of allegiance to America as against all the world.'

"I hope you will think this comes somewhere near it."

Wednesday, October 3rd.

Mrs. Wilson had luncheon and dinner downstairs for the first time since her illness. Afternoon appointments: Senator Newlands of Nevada; the New York and New Jersey Port and Harbor Development Commission; Representative Lever of South Carolina; Vance C. McCormick, who left with the President a draft executive order creating a War Trade Board; George Creel.

The President signed the War Revenue bill with no provision for a supervising committee.
Secretary Lansing wrote the President regarding the French ambassador's report that an Inter-Allied Conference was to be held in Paris soon to "consider what means might

be adopted to aid Russia and prevent further disintegration." The French were most anxious that the United States be represented. Lansing himself felt that something might be gained by having an "observer" at least. ". . . the situation in Russia is certainly critical and everything should be done that can be done to give stability to the Government there . . ."

In reply to the demand for reprisals Lloyd George promised to "bomb Germany with compound interest."[1]

Thursday, October 4th.

The President's afternoon appointments: Cyrus H. McCormick; Representative Madden of Illinois; Representative Eagan of New Jersey; Senator Walsh of Montana; William A. Brady.

Secretary Baker authorized the statement that work had been begun on more than 20,000 airplanes.

3,000 prisoners, "haggard and white-faced men," were taken by the British in a new drive in Flanders. ". . . the most terrible bombardment I had ever seen . . ." wrote Philip Gibbs. "The whole of Passchendaele crest was like a series of volcanoes belching up pillars of earth and fire. . . ."[2]

To Secretary Burleson, in regard to a series of articles by Samuel Hopkins Adams in the New York *Tribune:*

"Thank you for letting me see the enclosed. I have looked over them very carefully. It makes up a tremendous case, of course, against Mr. Hearst, but there is nothing new about that and I am sorry to say there is nothing brought out in these articles which would seem to me to prove that Mr. Hearst had overstepped the bounds of law, outrageous as he has been."

To Representative J. J. Fitzgerald, who had asked the President's endorsement of his bill to center control of all appropriations in a single committee during the existing emergency:

". . . . The proposed action has my hearty approval. Indeed, I feel that there is no other means by which we can

[1] *Current History*, November, 1917, p. 268.
[2] *Ibid.*, p. 214.

prevent very serious confusion and perhaps serious mistakes in the matter of appropriations during this very critical period where coordination is above all things else imperatively necessary."

Friday, October 5th.

Secretary Redfield remained after the cabinet meeting for a conference; and at 4:30 Vance McCormick called. The President's brother-in-law, Dr. Stockton Axson, arrived for a visit.

> Colonel House sent over to the President a message just received from Balfour announcing receipt from the Spanish government of information that a Spanish diplomatic representative had "officially reported German Government would be glad to make a communication to us relative to peace." It was not thought either possible or wise to refuse to listen; though no discussion would be undertaken without consultation with Great Britain's co-belligerents. It was proposed to answer in this sense.
>
> Owing to conditions in Russia no decision had been reached, Balfour continued, as to whether to inform the other principal Allies of the matter before sending a reply— he had so far spoken of it only to the French ambassador in London—but he wished President Wilson to know exactly how matters stood.
>
> With the President's consent, House telegraphed approval of the proposed British reply.[1]

To Richard H. Edmonds, editor of the *Manufacturers Record,* who had written that there was still need in the country for

---

[1] For Lloyd George's account of the peace move initiated by Von Kuhlmann, German Foreign Minister, see *War Memoirs of David Lloyd George,* Vol. IV, pp. 299 *et seq.* This was one of the early guns fired in the "peace offensive" of the Central Powers. During the winter of 1917–1918 secret conversations about a possible peace, initiated by Germans, Austrians, Bulgarians, became so numerous and so complicated that they form a subject for separate study in themselves and are not here included except where the President's hand is directly discernible from the documents. Professor George D. Herron, for some years a resident of Switzerland, was much involved, his reports going not only to the State Department and the President, but also, separately, to the British War Office and the British Foreign Office.

See M. P. Briggs, *George D. Herron and the European Settlement;* and *Foreign Relations,* 1917, Supp. 2, Vol. I; 1918, Supp. 1, Vol. I. Confidential discussions carried on with the British and French are described in *War Memoirs of David Lloyd George,* Vols. IV and V.

education as to the reasons for the war. He hoped the President could make a public statement or speech stating the facts:

"The suggestion contained in your letter of yesterday has been conveyed to me from a good many quarters and I dare say that an opportunity may arise when it will be well for me to make some such utterance as you outline.

"At the same time, I get widely variant accounts of the matter from different parts of the country, or rather it would be more correct to say that from most parts of the country I get the report that the people do very distinctly comprehend what the war is about and are very thoughtfully back of the administration.

"All I can say now is that I am watching the situation with the greatest interest and shall be ready to speak at the right time, if I know the right time when it comes."

To David Lawrence, who had written on the 3rd: "The morning papers today represent you as being very much annoyed over the publication of certain reports about Colonel House.[1] I have been informed . . . that you particularly disliked my article of yesterday . . .

"There has been some criticism in the editorial press concerning the placing in the hands of one man such an important work as that of gathering data for the Peace conference, and my purpose was to show that men of prominence, of all political parties, and every variety of view, would certainly be *consulted*, and a true consensus of opinion thus obtained. I made this suggestion entirely on my own authority, and without committing you, Col. House, or the Government to any special intention. . . .

"I cannot believe what I have heard, that you deprecate editorial discussion of these very important matters, and I am confident either that you were told only about the headlines over the article in question, and did not have time to read it, or that you could not have had in mind the article I wrote."

---

[1]The New York *Times* of September 29th had carried on the front page a story about the Inquiry. Headlines read: "AMERICA TO SPEAK IN HER OWN VOICE AT PEACE TABLE."

Personal.

5 October, 1917

MY DEAR LAWRENCE:

My whole feeling is this: I think you newspaper men can have no conception of what fire you are playing with when you discuss peace now at all, in any phase or connection. The Germans have in effect realized their programme of Hamburg to Bagdad, could afford to negotiate as to all the territorial fringes, and, if they could bring about a discussion of peace now, would insist upon discussing it upon terms which would leave them in possession of all that they ever expected to get. It is, therefore, very indiscreet in my judgment and altogether against the national interest to discuss peace from any point of view if the administration is brought in in any way. It is perfectly evident to everyone that what Colonel House is attempting to do neither brings peace nearer nor sets it further off, and it is my stern and serious judgment that the whole matter ought to be let alone.

Sincerely yours,

WOODROW WILSON[1]

Saturday, October 6th.

The President went to the Capitol for the closing of Congress in the afternoon, and signed a number of bills: Soldiers' and Sailors' Insurance bill; Trading with the Enemy bill; Urgent Deficiency bill. Mrs. McAdoo was a dinner guest and went with the family to the National Theater in the evening.

Adjournment of the 65th Congress; the President publicly commended its work—a "remarkable session."[2]

---

[1]Lawrence wrote the next day, thanking the President and saying he was forwarding his letter, in confidence, "so that the editorial writers may have the benefit of your point of view." The newspapers of the country were, of course, operating under what was known as "voluntary censorship." Lawrence himself says of this correspondence: ". . . . On a subject as delicate as the one described, obviously the President was the only man who really knew what was or was not important to the prosecution of the war and hence he had every reason to raise the question . . ." (David Lawrence to the author.)

[2]*Public Papers*, Vol. V, p. 104.

Secretary Lansing telegraphed to American diplomatic representatives in Spain, Denmark, the Netherlands, Norway, Sweden and Switzerland and to Ambassador Page in London, explaining the embargo policy of the United States. ". . . . Department does not wish the peoples and the governments of neutral countries to gain the impression that this Government is dictating to England and France an embargo policy hostile to neutral countries. As a matter of fact, England has been urging us to adopt even a stricter control than we have been willing to sanction. This Government is quite prepared to assume full responsibility for such restrictive measures as it may be called upon to enforce. These will in every case be dictated by necessity with all possible regard for justice and for the feelings of neutrals. . . ."[1]

Peru severed diplomatic relations with Germany.

Sunday, October 7th.

President and Mrs. Wilson and Dr. Axson went to the Central Presbyterian Church in the morning and took a long drive in the afternoon.

Uruguay severed relations with Germany.

Monday, October 8th.

At 12:30 the President received Representative Sherley of Kentucky. Afternoon appointments: Representative Littlepage of West Virginia; Representative Collier of Mississippi; Senator Fletcher and Representative Drane of Florida; H. A. Garfield; George Creel and a committee from the newly organized League for National Unity, to whom the President made a short address endorsing the purposes of the league. The war, he said, should end only when Germany was beaten and her rule of autocracy superseded by the ideals of democracy. ". . . . Talk of early peace before Germany is defeated is one of the evidences of misdirected thought . . . and should not cloud the vision . . .

". . . it should not be forgotten that German success would mean not only prevention of the spread of democracy, but

---

[1] *Foreign Relations,* 1917, Supp. 2, Vol. II, pp. 960–961.

possibly the suppression of that already existing."[1] In the late afternoon Senator Lee S. Overman called; and Herbert Hoover.

To Colonel House:
MY DEAR HOUSE:

At last Mrs. Wilson, while not well I am sorry to say, has thrown off the poison of the grippe which got so deep a hold on her, and my mind is free to take up the important matters we ought to confer about. Any time you name this week would be convenient, if you will come down, and I hope that it may be soon.

With affectionate messages from us all,

Faithfully yours,
WOODROW WILSON

To Franklin D. Roosevelt, who had reported the loss of the first United States vessel in European waters. The sinking was due to weather conditions, not to the enemy; and all on board were saved:

"Thank you for your letter of yesterday about the REHOBOTH. I am heartily glad that no lives were lost."

Tuesday, October 9th.

The President received Senator Williams of Mississippi at eleven o'clock; and at 12:30 Senator Simmons of North Carolina. Before the cabinet meeting, Mr. Goltra called. Late-afternoon appointments: Senator Pomerene, chairman of the Senate committee investigating the charges against La Follette; O. T. Crosby, Assistant Secretary of the Treasury; Vance McCormick. Sometime during the day the President discussed the proposed delay of the Food Pledge Campaign with Hoover.[2] Dr. Axson, who had been a guest for several days, left; and

---

[1]Report of the substance of the President's remarks in the New York *Times*, October 9, 1917. No exact copy exists, so far as the author has discovered.

[2]The next day the President signed a letter to Hoover—drafted by Hoover himself—asking that the Food Conservation Pledge Campaign be put off; and expressing appreciation of the importance of the work being done by Hoover's organization.

Colonel House arrived. After dinner he and the President "went into executive session until ten o'clock." (Mrs. Wilson was also present.) ". . . . We threshed out the question of my going abroad to represent the United States at the Allied War Council . . . . Wiseman has pointed out the danger of transferring the center of gravity from this country to Europe. He believes this is inevitable if I go abroad to remain as long as the President has in mind, and take with me a military, naval, and economic staff.

"This shook the President because he has no intention of loosening his hold on the situation. . . .

". . . the President authorized me to see both Baker and Daniels and tell them of our plans and ask them to suggest suitable military and naval officers to accompany me. The President thought General Bliss, Chief of Staff, would be the proper man to represent the Army, in which Baker later readily acquiesced. . . ."[1]

The German Foreign Minister, speaking in the Reichstag on German peace terms: ". . . . There is but one answer to the question, 'Can Germany in any form make any concessions with regard to Alsace-Lorraine?' The answer is—'No, never!' . . . .

". . . there is (with the exception of the French demand for the conquest of Alsace-Lorraine) no absolute impediment to peace; no question which could not be solved by negotiations and settlements . . ."[2]

Chancellor Michaelis, on the same day: ". . . . So long as our enemies confront us with demands which appear unacceptable to every single German . . . so long shall we with folded arms refuse the hand of peace. . . ."[3]

Secretary Daniels made public the navy construction program—787 vessels of all types, some of which had been completed within the past few weeks and were already in service.

Mutiny in the German navy at Wilhelmshaven.

---

[1] *Intimate Papers*, Vol. III, p. 203.

[2] *War Aims and Peace Proposals*, pp. 157–161. On the 11th Lloyd George said, speaking of von Kuhlmann's words: "I can think of no statement more calculated to prolong this terrible war . . ." *Ibid.*, p. 161.

[3] *Ibid.*, pp. 156–157.

To Secretary Lansing, a letter written at the suggestion of George Creel:

"Is not this a very opportune time to negotiate with the Japanese Government with a view to improving the existing cable and radio communication between this country and Asia, and perhaps adding additional facilities?

"Any permanent improvement of news service across the Pacific depends, of course, on the establishment of ample facilities and reasonable rates. The Japanese Government owns, I believe, the telegraph lines and wireless stations within its own borders and one leg at least of the trans-Pacific cable. It seems to me exceedingly desirable that special arrangements should be made for ample news communication between the two continents and I would be obliged if you would discuss the matter with the Japanese Ambassador. . . ."

To Cardinal Gibbons, who had just been made honorary chairman of the newly created League for National Unity, and who had written the President expressing sympathy for the heavy burdens of office, saying that he was trying to make his people see that they must give unswerving loyalty to the administration:

"May I not express my very deep and sincere appreciation of your letter . . . It has brought me cheer and reassurance, and I want you to know how much I appreciate your own action in consenting to preside over the important and influential group of men and women who have so generously undertaken to support the administration in its efforts to make the whole character and purpose of this war and of the Government of the United States in the prosecution of it clear to the whole people."

To Mrs. Mary B. Perkins, who wanted her eighteen-year-old son, who had enlisted when the first call came for men, released to continue his education. The President's letter is based upon one from Secretary Baker:

"I am sure I need not tell you with what genuine sympathy I read your letter . . . for I felt very keenly the force of everything that you urged, but I beg you to realize that the lad could be excused only by an act of arbitrary power which would be a discrimination between him and other young men which it would be very difficult for me to justify. I do not believe that it would be really for his permanent interest to release him. His spirit rose to a great adventure and I think that all that goes to the making of a man is involved in his being permitted to see it through. The education he will receive from doing a man's part in the world and following through a brave resolution will, I cannot help believing, more than compensate for any loss of formal instruction involved in his separation from school at this time, and I hope with all my heart that he may return to resume his education with a newer and fuller comprehension of all that it means."

To his secretary, Tumulty, referring to a request that the President make a Liberty Loan address at Carnegie Hall.

"I must not do this unless it is absolutely necessary. My own feeling is that there are several more campaigns of this sort to come and that I ought to reserve myself for a later effort in case the subsequent loans should prove more sluggish than this one."

Wednesday, October 10th.

The President's afternoon appointments: Senator Thompson of Kansas and a committee; Representative Park of Georgia. The President spent some time in his study in the afternoon, as well as the usual morning hours.

The President issued a proclamation authorizing the Food Administration, after November 1st, to control the manufacture, storage, importation and distribution of certain essential foodstuffs.

To W. P. G. Harding of the Federal Reserve Board, who had submitted a draft letter from the board to non-member banks, urging membership for patriotic reasons:

"I am returning the enclosed to make this suggestion: Would it not be possible to redraft this letter so that it might come from me rather than from the Governor of the Federal Reserve Board though drawn along the same lines? It occurs to me that this would be a better way to give it my backing than to add a statement as if I were merely supporting the Board itself in this suggestion and request.

"What do you think? Do you think well of the suggestion?"[1]

To his secretary, Tumulty, asking him to send the following letter to Elisha M. Friedman, who had suggested the creation of a committee on reconstruction:

"The President has requested me to acknowledge your letter . . . and to say that he has read it with interest, but he thinks it much too early to contemplate the creation of a committee on reconstruction after the war shall be over. He does not believe it possible to foresee the conditions which will then exist and therefore deems it impracticable to formulate plans with regard to dealing with post-war conditions."

Thursday, October 11th.

Senator Robinson of Arkansas called at 12:30. Afternoon appointments: Thomas L. Chadbourne; Senator Underwood and Representative Oliver of Alabama; Speaker Clark; Monsignor Thomas, whose invitation to attend the Pan-American Mass on Thanksgiving Day the President accepted; members of the War Industries Board.

H. H. Asquith, speaking on war aims at Liverpool: ". . . the worst thing that could happen for the world would be a

---

[1] The President made public, through the Federal Reserve Board on October 13th, a statement urging membership in the system. New York *Times*, October 16, 1917.

patched up peace . . . . an arrangement, or set of arrangements, of such a character that they contain within themselves the germs of future trouble . . ."[1]

To Secretary Burleson, enclosing an editorial from the Springfield *Republican* of October 9th,[2] which said: "Increasing uneasiness is to be observed among supporters of the war who hold
liberal democratic views concerning the freedom of the press
and the unhampered exercise of constitutional rights in legitimate agitation and propaganda because of the postal censorship
on the mailable publications of the country. . . .":

"I am sure you will agree with me that we must act with
the utmost caution and liberality in all our censorship, and
in connection with it I want you to read the enclosed very
thoughtful editorial from the Springfield Republican
which is always moderate and always reflects the opinion
of the very sort of people whose judgment we would like
to have approve what we do."

To Secretary Redfield, who had called attention to a suggestion
that men who were rejected for the American army because of
minor disabilities be sent to France for agricultural work, but
added that he supposed it could not be done. The President's
letter is marked "*Confidential*":

"The matter to which you call my attention . . . has
given me a great deal of thought and a great deal of
concern, but I am afraid that the suggestion . . . could not
wisely be complied with.

"It would take a great deal of explaining to our American farmers and others; but more than that, there lies
very near the surface in France, I have been told, a very
considerable revolutionary feeling and this feeling may
easily, it is thought, be stirred by any indication that men
or women from other countries are going to take the place
of French men and French women in the industrial life of

---

[1] *War Aims and Peace Proposals*, pp. 162–167.
[2] No enclosure in the files; but the editorial was almost certainly that of the 9th.

that country. They have no objection, of course, to auxiliary forces of the Army working on the railways behind the lines and doing the things that are obviously connected with the operations and the supply of the armies, but they are intensely jealous of the intrusion of outsiders in the general industrial work of the country."

To John Singer Sargent:
MY DEAR MR. SARGENT:

Congress has adjourned and my mind turns to the suggestion I made that probably after the adjournment it would be possible for me to sit for the portrait which the Governors of the National Gallery of Ireland so generously desire.

I would be very glad to know your own engagements and whether it would be convenient for you to come down next week or the week after.

I would also like to know, if it is possible for you to answer such a question, how much time it would probably be necessary for me to set aside for the purpose.

With the pleasantest anticipations of knowing you,

Cordially and sincerely yours,

WOODROW WILSON

To J. W. Harriman, "Personal":

"Your letter . . . presents a very serious picture of affairs. I must frankly say that I cannot believe that the situation looks so dark in most parts of the country, but, of course, I have no pride of opinion in the matter and it is one in which I would not venture to speak with confidence, since no one can thread the complexities of the situation without a very much wider observation and a very much fuller knowledge than I can pretend to.

"You will understand that I may very often find it necessary to sign a bill like the tax bill, for example, in which there are items in which my judgment would not at all have concurred but the major features and parts of which seem to me necessary and legitimate. It is not possible for me to veto individual items and I must judge a bill by the large.

"I do not see just what sort of statement I could make at present which would convey the reassurance you so much desire, but you may be sure that whatever uncertainties now distress the business world will be removed one by one at the earliest possible moment."

To S. R. Bertron, who was disturbed because he thought the price of soft coal too low; and who urged that the Interstate Commerce Commission, as a war measure, permit the railroads to increase their rates:

"Of course, I did not mean to imply in my earlier letter that you were not speaking upon sufficient information. I merely meant to tell you the fact that I did not get such views of the depression in business circles from anywhere but New York, with the possible exception of certain banking circles in Boston. I meant to convey to you that cheering information.

"I realize the importance of the matters that you call my attention to and they have caused me a great deal of concern, as well as having absorbed a great deal of my thought and attention. You may be sure I am glad to have them set forth by those who, like yourself, are in direct contact with business matters, and you may also be sure that I want to do everything in my power to help."

To John Skelton Williams, Comptroller of the Currency, who on October 9th had sent over a statement which he was giving to the press in regard to the second Liberty Loan, the national banks, and the country's financial condition in general, saying in his covering letter: ". . . . It is deeply significant to realize that the resources of all the banks in the country—National and State and Trust Companies—have increased during the four and a half years of your Administration nearly fifty per cent, or approximately twelve billion dollars. . . .

"As I heard Mr. Balfour say to Secretary McAdoo a few months ago, 'This country has now become the sole remaining reservoir of credit on earth'. . . .":

"This is a very striking statement which you send me . . . and I am warmly obliged to you for sending it to me."

Friday, October 12th.

The President conferred with Lord Reading at noon. Colonel House, who was present, wrote in his diary afterward: "Reading knew what the President intended to propose [that House should represent the United States in the Allied War Council], and the President knew what Reading expected. He seemed pleased with the President's reception. . . ."[1] Early-afternoon appointments: F. D. Underwood; Representative Talbott of Maryland: and after the cabinet meeting, Alva A. Smith of Colorado.

The President established a War Trade Board; a Board of Censorship; and an Alien Property Custodian.[2]

The President proclaimed October 24th Liberty Day. ". . . . The people responded nobly to the call of the First Liberty Loan . . . Let the response to the Second Loan be even greater and let the amount be so large that it will serve as an assurance of unequaled support to hearten the men who are to face the fire of battle for us. . . ."[3]

Ambassador Page telegraphed from London, quoting a secret document just received from the British Foreign Office about a German plot to get Mexico into war with the United States, to destroy Mexican oil wells, and to encourage sabotage in the United States.

Rain in Flanders. ". . . . Every shell hole was brimful of brown or greenish water. . . ."[4]

[1]*Intimate Papers*, Vol. III, p. 203.

[2]The War Trade Board was to consist of six members, Vance C. McCormick, chairman and Thomas L. Chadbourne, counselor. The Board of Censorship was to consist of representatives of the War and Navy Departments, the Post Office Department, the War Trade Board and George Creel. A. Mitchell Palmer became Alien Property Custodian.

[3]*Public Papers*, Vol. V, pp. 105–106.

[4]Philip Gibbs, in *Current History*, November, 1917, p. 218.

Saturday, October 13th.

The President spent the morning in his study. After a short conference with the Attorney General in the early afternoon, he and Mrs. Wilson went to the Washington Barracks to watch a drill. Colonel and Mrs. Brown and their daughter arrived for a visit.[1]

To Colonel House:

"I find in my pocket the memorandum you gave me about the Zionist movement. I am afraid I did not say to you that I concurred in the formula suggested from the other side. I do, and would be obliged if you would let them know it."

To Raymond B. Fosdick:

"The other day an anxious committee of gentlemen representing the picture film service, a committee which I myself had authorized to cooperate with us in any way that is possible, came to see me in a good deal of distress, because they felt that you had turned down their offers to cooperate in the entertainment of the camps. I did not understand just what the trouble was, but their feelings were evidently hurt in some way, and since they are very good and, I believe, sincere friends of ours and desirous of helping generously, I thought I would write and ask you what was the matter and if there was anything I could help straighten out."

[1] In a personal letter of this period, Mrs. Brown described the White House routine: ". . . there are no guests—no gaieties or ceremonies of any kind. Even the usual tourist groups who drift through the lower part of the house are forbidden just now—on the pretext that the house is undergoing some repairs . . .

"But the real reason . . . is the danger to the President who proceeds about his daily business with the calm cheeriness of a man who never had heard of war—politics—or assassinations in his life. But the Secret Service men and watchmen are on duty day and night . . ."

After April 6, 1917, the White House grounds were closed and guarded; soldiers with loaded guns and bayonets took their places about fifty paces apart on the sidewalks surrounding the White House grounds. No loitering whatever was permitted after sundown. Whenever the President walked or drove outside the grounds, the police guard about him was doubled. As his car swung out of the White House gate, two motor-cycle policemen would pick it up, following within five feet. In an automobile twenty to thirty feet in the rear rode half a dozen secret service men. "A War-Time Day with the President," in the *Literary Digest*, September 8, 1917.

To Mrs. Carrie Chapman Catt:

"May I not express to you my very deep interest in the campaign in New York for the adoption of woman suffrage, and may I not say that I hope that no voter will be influenced in his decision with regard to this great matter by anything the so-called pickets may have done here in Washington? However justly they may have laid themselves open to serious criticism, their action represents, I am sure, so small a fraction of the women of the country who are urging the adoption of woman suffrage that it would be most unfair and argue a very narrow view to allow their actions to prejudice the cause itself. I am very anxious to see the great State of New York set a great example in this matter."

To his secretary, Tumulty, referring to an invitation to attend Thanksgiving Day service at the Metropolitan Memorial Methodist Episcopal Church:

"I told Monsignor Thomas the other day that I would hope to attend the Pan-American Mass on Thanksgiving Day. Now I am wondering whether I ought not to alternate between that and a Protestant service such as this to which the memorandum is attached. I am inclined to think that I ought and if you agree with me, I wonder if you would be willing to explain the matter to Monsignor Thomas. I ought to have thought of it when I had my interview with him."[1]

Sunday, October 14th.

The President and Mrs. Wilson spent a quiet morning, with no church; in the afternoon they took a long drive, accompanied by Colonel and Mrs. Brown.

---

[1] The suggestion was made that the President attend both services; and he wrote again to Tumulty: "I am sorry to trouble you again about this thing, but really the feeling between Protestants and Catholics, greatly as I deplore it and much as I despise it, is so sensitive and 'queer' that I don't think it feasible to try and do both these things, and I hope that Monsignor Thomas will see the propriety of my at least alternating. I have never yet been to a Protestant service on Thanksgiving Day."

To Colonel House, enclosing a telegram from Ambassador Page in London to Lansing regarding "imperative demands which the Foreign Office suggests should be made of neutrals." ". . . . The British Government are confident that complete demands can now be made without risk of driving any border neutral into the war on the side of Germany. . . . An Allied victory is now so certain that none of these states if it wished would dare join the enemy. . . ."[1] The President's letter was written on his own typewriter:

"You will read this with interest. Is this the latest English view with reference to the neutrals & the war?"[2]

Monday, October 15th.

After early golf with Colonel Brown, the President worked in his study until luncheon. Afternoon appointments: Senator Hitchcock of Nebraska; George Foster Peabody; Governor Dorsey of Georgia; Senator Myers of Montana; Senator King of Utah. In the evening the President and Mrs. Wilson went, with a family party, to the National Theater, where they saw a play called *Under Pressure.* The party was in celebration of Mrs. Wilson's birthday, but the play proved to be impossible— "*so* bad both in manner and matter that we would gladly have departed en-masse before the second act was finished—but bethought ourselves that for the rest of the season the whole country would be invited in large capitals to 'Come and see the Play the President wouldn't stand For!' . . . So we stuck it out . . ."[3]

To Secretary Baker:

"The authorities of the Federal Reserve Bank in New York (and many others, for that matter) have been urging me to attend a meeting at Carnegie Hall on the eighteenth of this month, at which they expect to make their chief

---

[1] *Foreign Relations,* 1917, Supp. 2, Vol. II, pp. 970–971.

[2] House replied on the 17th: "If Page's telegram concerning the embargo of the European neutrals is a fair reflection of the opinion of the British Government, it is a direct contradiction of what they have told us privately. Wiseman is sending a cable outlining the matter and requesting a definite statement as to what they really think desirable. . . ."

[3] Mrs. E. T. Brown in a personal letter.

effort to commend the Liberty Loan to lukewarm and panicky New York.

"I am taking the liberty of sending you one of Mr. Strong's letters. He is Governor of the Federal Reserve Bank in New York. I have consulted not only my own judgment but a good many people whose knowledge of the situation is better than mine and my conclusion is that it would not be best for me to go, but I do think that it might be wise for some prominent member of the administration to be present to represent it and to speak. Would you feel that you could go?

"I sincerely beg that you will give me the frankest answer and if you think that it is too much of a burden or something which would too seriously interfere with your own work, I want you to say so frankly with the assurance that I would understand and approve your declining; but if you can go, it would be a very great advantage and help. I, therefore, lay the matter frankly before you."

To W. P. G. Harding, who wrote that the country banks were not taking the interest they should in the Liberty Loans:

"Do you think it would be well for me in addition to my recent letter to the banks about joining the Federal Reserve System[1] to issue such a statement or appeal as you speak of in your letter of October thirteenth? As a matter of fact, I had no such statement in mind, but I would be very glad to have your advice about the matter, and am very much obliged to you for sending me a copy of the resolutions of the American Bankers Association."

To Senator Francis G. Newlands, explaining why he could not grant an interview:

". . . I must really, my dear Senator, deny myself all interviews for some time to come. I have been waiting for

[1]This volume, p. 300, footnote.

the adjournment of Congress to do some consecutive work it is imperatively necessary for me to do, and if I don't do it, very serious inconvenience may ensue to the Government . . .''

To Samuel G. Blythe:
"Just a line to say how much and how sincerely I appreciate the generous praise and appreciation you give me in your article in the current Saturday Evening Post."

Tuesday, October 16th.
Before cabinet meeting the Russian ambassador called to present Admiral Koltchak, formerly Commander-in-Chief of Russia's Black Sea fleet, who was in the United States at the invitation of the Navy Department. Late-afternoon appointments: George Creel; E. N. Hurley. ". . . Tuesday evening," wrote Mrs. Brown, "when we sat quietly in the lovely big rose damask oval room upstairs and listened till train time to the most wonderful President talking of all sorts of things in his own beautiful humorous broad-minded gentle way—he claimed not yet to have recovered from the frightful effects of it [the bad play they had seen the night before]. He said it had made him cross and unreasonable all day—and caused him to lose his game of golf with Edward in the morning, and speak harshly to his friends at Cabinet meeting—and put his typewriter out of commission when he needed it most, just before dinner!"[1]

Acting Secretary Polk notified Allied representatives in Washington that a delegate would be sent by the United States to the Inter-Ally Council [on War Purchases and Finance], "in a consultative capacity." ". . . the Secretary of the Treasury hopes that the European Governments will proceed to formulate a memorandum of the constitution and the function of the Inter-Ally Council on the lines indicated in his letter of July 18 and the replies thereto."[2]

---

[1] In a personal letter.
[2] *Foreign Relations*, 1917, Supp. 2, Vol. I, pp. 572–573. For McAdoo's letter see this volume, p. 171.

To Mrs. Hope H. Barroll:

"I need not tell you what my impulse was when I read your letter, but I beg that you will forgive me if I differ from you in judgment entirely about what it is wise to do in the case of your son. Nothing but credit, of course, accrues to him for having volunteered and I for one do not believe that the only place where such a man can serve with credit and distinction is as an officer. This war is going to be rich with possibilities of distinction for the enlisted man, as for the officer, and I believe that the finest thing that well-bred young men can do is to share the conditions of the ranks and prove that this is in real truth a democracy for which we are fighting.

"If this view of the matter distresses you, I am sorry, but it is a conviction which I hold very deeply and I cannot help feeling that your son himself would subscribe to it."

Wednesday, October 17th.

The President had no official engagements during the day. His first sitting for the portrait by Sargent began at 2:30 in the afternoon.

Secretary Lansing sent to Ambassador Page in London, and to diplomatic officials in Spain, Denmark, the Netherlands, Norway, Sweden and Switzerland, a statement as to United States policy regarding exports to neutrals. ". . . . The policy of this Government is in no way inspired by a desire to hamper or interfere with the normal life of neutrals. On the contrary we are willing to help these neutrals even at a sacrifice to ourselves in allowing export to them of commodities we can ill afford to spare, but in return for this friendly service we must demand some guarantee that these supplies will not be turned against us to kill our sons and prolong the war. . . ."[1]

The transport *Antilles*, returning from Brest to the United States, was torpedoed, with a loss of 67 lives—the first transport lost in the United States service.

[1]*Foreign Relations*, 1917, Supp. 2, Vol. II, pp. 974–976.

To Vance C. McCormick, enclosing a letter from Thomas Nelson Page, telling of Italy's need of grain for bread—"even a moderate quantity sent at once would do much to relieve the situation which is a psychological one as well as a practical one." The President's letter is marked "Confidential":

"Here is a letter . . . which I am sure you will read with interest. I know from independent sources that the situation in Italy with regard to the attitude of the people in general is a very critical one and I hope that you may be able to bring the various agencies together which can and will supply these pressing needs in Italy, at any rate in some considerable part. . . ."[1]

To Raymond B. Fosdick, who had explained his difficulties in reconciling the rivalries and professional jealousies of the various motion picture interests:

". . . . I had, as you may suppose, surmised most of the explanation you give, but this occurs to me: Mr. Klaw[2] is naturally not very enthusiastic about motion pictures, and the motion picture men either take for granted or imagine his hostility. I think that the interests of our men so overcrow every other consideration that it would be worth while to make another attempt to arrive at an arrangement which would soothe the feelings and allay the jealousy of Mr. Brady and his committee, and also secure for us the cooperation of the motion picture people who are at present excluded or think that they are.

"I know from experience how much patience and tolerance it takes to do these things, but I believe you have the tact to accomplish this, and I think that Mr. Klaw ought to be willing to make very considerable concessions inasmuch as he must understand, of course, that

[1]McCormick replied on the 19th that he had taken up with Hoover, Crosby and Hurley the problem of helping Italy.

[2]Marc Klaw, who was in charge of the military entertainment service of the Commission on Training Camp Activities.

he is not acting in his own interest anyway but in the interest of the country."

To Henry Morgenthau, who had suggested the organization of regiments to plow the fields in France. The President's letter is marked "Personal":

"Thank you for your letter . . . The suggestion it contains has come to me from one or two other friends. The difficulty is this: I have received very direct intimations that the people of France would feel very much disturbed by the introduction of foreign labor in their fields or anywhere else and that to introduce it there would contribute to the somewhat disturbed feeling which underlies the surface because of the long continuance and dreadful strain of the war. I am afraid that the formation of regiments for the purpose would hardly be feasible, but I am going to take the liberty, nevertheless, of sending your letter to the Secretary of War for his consideration. . . ."

To his secretary, Tumulty, referring to a request for a letter or statement from the President to be used by the Army Liberty Loan Association:

"I doubt if Baker would ask this if he were at home. My own taste decidedly dissents from an appeal by the Commander-in-Chief to the men of the Army to give their money. I think it would probably have a bad effect rather than a good one, and I hope you will make my excuses to Mr. Ingraham."

Thursday, October 18th.

The President received Governor Beeckman of Rhode Island at two o'clock; at 2:30 he sat again for Sargent. Sam Macmillan was a dinner guest, and in the evening John Skelton Williams called.

To Secretary Burleson, referring to a hearing on the case of the Milwaukee Leader, which was ordered suppressed[1]:

[1] The courts sustained the suppression of the paper.

"I am afraid you will be shocked, but I must say that I do not find this hearing very convincing. Some of the things quoted probably cross the line and I have very little doubt that they were all intended to have sinister results, but I must frankly say that I do not think that most of what is quoted ought to be regarded as unmailable. I have read the hearing with some feeling of misgiving as to the impression that was created upon the representatives of the paper which had been summoned, not because I doubt for a moment the purposes or the intelligence or the careful and conscientious methods of the public officials concerned, but because there is a wide margin of judgment here and I think that doubt ought always to be resolved in favor of the utmost freedom of speech.

"It does not appear from the hearing what was done. Was the paper, as they so earnestly urged, given another chance?"

To Grenville S. MacFarland, who had objected to Burleson's attitude toward alleged "seditious" newspapers:

"Immediately upon receiving your letter . . . I conferred with the Attorney General who replied . . . in a letter of which I take the liberty of sending you a copy in order that at any rate part of the impression you have had may be removed.

"For I think you have misinterpreted the spirit and purpose of the Postmaster General. I have been keeping in close touch with him and I think that he is as anxious as I am to see that freedom of criticism is permitted up to the limit of putting insuperable obstacles in the way of the Government in the prosecution of the war."

Friday, October 19th.

Before luncheon, the President received Vance McCormick; and Harry S. Morrison. In the early afternoon the Japanese ambassador called, to present a commercial commission from

Japan; after the cabinet meeting the President talked with Secretary Daniels and Admiral Mayo, who was recently back from Europe; and Senator Chamberlain of Oregon.

The President signed a proclamation making October 28th a Day of Prayer.

To T. W. Gregory, referring to A. E. Kern's protest against the refusal of the mails to his paper, the *Nachrichten*, of Portland, Oregon:

". . . . The treatment of foreign language publications is giving me a great deal of anxiety these days and I would appreciate it very much if you would have this case looked into to see if there is any just basis for the complaint made."

To George Creel, who had sent over a dispatch from the London *Times* suggesting that Ambassador Page was to resign:

"Regarding the enclosed, it is evidently entirely off the Times' own bat. I did not even know that Mr. Page was ill until last evening. I sincerely regret his illness, and his resignation has not recently been suggested."

To Edward W. Sheldon, a classmate at Princeton:

"It was a very generous thought that prompted you to write your letter of October seventeenth and I thank you for it out of a very full heart. I think you must know how I value your friendship and approval, and such a letter coming from you has brought me deep cheer and encouragement.

"I am happy to say that those who have reported to you that I am physically well and fit have spoken the truth. I really never was better in my life, though how it happens I cannot explain. I think it must in part be the stimulation of great duties and the absolute necessity to spend my energies equably throughout the twenty-four hours.

"I hope, my dear fellow, that you are keeping well, and

it is delightful to think of such a friend in the midst of the financial affairs which mean so much in their right guidance to the prosperity and success of the country."

To Winthrop M. Daniels, enclosing a suggestion that the Interstate Commerce Commission announce publicly that rates ought to be increased to allow the carriers to make headway against the recent larger costs:[1]

"I would not send you the enclosed if I did not think it of the utmost importance. It is a memorandum to me from Mr. John Skelton Williams, the Comptroller of the Currency.

"I would have preferred to see you personally and talk this matter over, but I know how the newspapers start reports of some kind of 'influence' being attempted to which the Commission ought not to yield and therefore I am sending this by the hand of a special messenger.

"I can add my testimony to that of Mr. Williams that if the Commission could see its way to making some such statement as he suggests by, let us say, Monday morning, it would have an immensely beneficial influence on the progress of the Loan.

"I must admit to having a very profound contempt toward a business world which needs reassurance of this sort, but as you know it does need it and we cannot afford to let any legitimate means go unused which may make this loan an impressive success.

"I know that you will understand and sympathize and will feel that I am justified in urging this very seriously."

Saturday, October 20th.

There were no official engagements during the day. The President spent the morning in his study, sat for Sargent during

[1] O. T. Crosby, Acting Secretary of the Treasury, made a suggestion similar to that of Williams, and the President wrote him the next day: ". . . . I have had very much in mind the matter you refer to in connection with the Interstate Commerce Commission and have been doing what I could to convey the impression."

the early part of the afternoon, and later took a short drive with Mrs. Wilson and his daughter Margaret. Evening at Keith's Theater.

The President purchased $13,500 worth of Liberty Bonds.

Appeals from the President to mayors of 28 cities, in behalf of the Second Liberty Loan, were sealed in bombs and dropped by aeroplanes.

To Secretary Baker, who had suggested that the President, if he planned to speak at the American Federation of Labor convention, "warn labor not to make an inelastic ultimatum but to leave their accredited representatives free to work out with the Government those just rearrangements which are necessary by reason of war conditions.":

"Thank you for your letter . . . with its suggestion about the approaching convention of the American Federation of Labor. It is a very wise suggestion and I shall keep it in mind."

To Winthrop M. Daniels, who had written in reply to the President's letter of the 19th that it was not possible for the Interstate Commerce Commission to go as far as the Comptroller of the Currency wished, but that he had suggested to his colleagues that they make such statement as they could, to help along the Liberty Loan:

"Thank you very much for your note of yesterday. I am sincerely glad to have new and fuller light thrown on the situation of the railroads. I took it for granted that things were being exaggerated in order to 'work' us to some extent, and yet I believe the situation justifies a statement on the part of the Commission and I think the statement you suggest will probably be of the greatest value."

Sunday, October 21st.

The President and Mrs. Wilson went to St. John's Episcopal Church in the morning. In the afternoon they took a long drive.

Monday, October 22nd.

Toward noon the President received former Governor Ralston of Indiana, and a delegation from Indianapolis; Senator Bankhead and Representative Dent of Alabama; John R. Rathom of the Providence *Journal*. J. A. Wilson and John Singer Sargent were luncheon guests. The President saw Matthew Hale and a committee at two o'clock and then sat for Mr. Sargent for an hour and a half. L. W. Nieman of the Milwaukee *Journal* called at four o'clock and, later, H. A. Garfield.

American soldiers of the First Division went into the trenches —"a notably quiet sector which had seen no violent action for three years"[1]—for the culminating phase of their training. They were warmly greeted by the French. "Every American was shaken by the hand, some were hugged, and even kissed on both cheeks."[2]

Lloyd George writes: ". . . . In the autumn of 1917 . . . [American] reinforcement was arriving with what seemed to be disconcerting and perplexing slowness. Both the French and ourselves were apprehensive lest, if it were not speeded up, it should arrive too late to save the Allied Front from collapse in face of the formidable German attack. The reservoir of French man power had almost run dry and ours was approaching exhaustion . . ."[3]

British and French troops struck again in Flanders. Writing years later, Ludendorff described this new phase of the battle: ". . . . Enormous masses of ammunition . . . were hurled upon the bodies of men . . . scattered about in mud-filled shell-holes. . . . It was mere unspeakable suffering. And through this world of mud the attackers dragged themselves, slowly but steadily, and in dense masses. Caught in the advanced zone of our hail of fire they often collapsed, and the lonely man in the shell-hole breathed again. Then the mass came on again. Rifle and machine gun jammed with the mud. Man fought against man . . .

"What the German soldier experienced, achieved, and

---

[1]Palmer, *Newton D. Baker*, Vol. I, p. 382.
[2]*Current History*, December, 1917, p. 388.
[3]*War Memoirs of David Lloyd George*, Vol. V, p. 397.

suffered in the Flanders battle will be his everlasting monument of bronze . . .”[1]

To Herbert Croly of the *New Republic*, who had written that a number of men of moderate opinions and high intelligence considered that the suppression of the Socialist press was raising “an issue of importance scarcely inferior to that of the war itself.” Croly asserted that the government should negotiate with the Socialist press and “persuade them to keep their agitation within certain limits without at the same time forcing them to abandon the kind of agitation which they consider essential to their convictions.” He added: “. . . . There is no public object in which I more profoundly believe than the object for which you are waging this war, but just because of the attitude of the government in respect to the censorship, and because the war propaganda is being conducted in such a way that militarists like Mr. Roosevelt are allowed to appropriate it, I have the utmost difficulty in writing about it from week to week without making an appearance of opposing what our government is trying to do. I deeply regret being forced into such a position . . .”:

“I thank you sincerely for your thoughtful and important letter . . .

“I can assure you that the matter of the censorship has given me as much concern as it has you and after frequent conferences with the Post-master General I have become convinced that not only have his statements been misunderstood but that he is inclined to be most conservative in the exercise of these great and dangerous powers and that in the one or two instances to which my attention has been called he has sought to act in a very just and conciliatory manner. I hope and believe that as the processes of censorship work out and the results become visible a great part of your apprehension and my own will be relieved.”

To his secretary, Tumulty, referring to a letter from Upton Sinclair, who objected to Burleson’s treatment of Socialist and

---

[1] *Ludendorff’s Own Story*, Vol. II, p. 105.

other papers. Sinclair suggested that offending publications be offered the choice of being barred from the mails or of opening their columns to an official answer to objectionable passages to be prepared by a Bureau of Information:

"Will you not be kind enough to write Mr. Sinclair a letter saying how much I appreciate the frankness and sincerity and also the generous personal kindness of his letter, and adding this, that I feel convinced that as case follows case in dealings of the Post Office Department with this matter his impression will be very much altered as to the way in which they are being handled? I certainly sympathize with his own principles in this delicate business as stated in his letter.

"Please tell him that his suggestion interests me very much and I shall certainly consider the feasibility of acting upon it."[1]

To Mrs. Hugh C. Wallace:

"I beg you to believe that I am denying myself a personal pleasure and acting against all my inclinations when I say that it will really be impossible for me to attend your son's wedding. I have attended one church wedding outside of my family circle, but I have so far attended no wedding at a private house and the one church wedding I attended has, I am afraid, got me into trouble because of the many public officials who first and last very kindly expect me to display the same interest in the marriages which occur in their families.

"I hate like poison to consider these matters of precedent and convenience, but if you realized how extraordinary the pressure upon me is in matters big and little, I think you would appreciate this self-protective instinct on my part.

---

[1] The President passed the suggestion on to Burleson on the 30th, asking what he thought of it.

"I know in any case that you are generous enough to understand and excuse."

Tuesday, October 23rd.

At 12:30 the President received George Creel, with Mr. Hutchins of the National Bank of Commerce and Edgar Sisson, whom he was planning to send to Russia in connection with the work of the Committee on Public Information:

".... We were all standing, and at the beginning of the talk the President walked back and forth, three or four paces, treading deliberately. Finally, he stood still, continuing to speak in short, conversational sentences. The gist of his talk was the necessity of making understandable to a newborn democracy the fellow feeling of our own older state, our friendliness, our unselfishness toward Russia, and our desire of helpfulness. The war aspects, he seemed confident, would take care of themselves if a bond were forged between the Russian and the American people. Of details of what I was to do he said nothing. Principles with him were the essential. Operation he delegated. . . .

"The President's physical state that afternoon was of the best. The arduous months of war had not worn him down. His face, indeed, was setting in sterner lines than of old, but became singularly kind when he smiled. . . ."[1]

The cabinet meeting was omitted, afternoon appointments being, in addition to a sitting for Sargent: the Commissioner of Pensions; B. M. Baruch; D. W. Griffith, recently returned from France, where he had been taking pictures in the trenches; Herbert Hoover. In the evening Mrs. Wilson went, without the President, to the Monument Grounds to attend the lighting of the first of hundreds of bonfires planned for that evening in every part of the country in celebration of the Liberty Loan. Colonel House, who was still a guest, spent most of the day conferring with the various men who were to accompany him to Europe.[2]

The French delivered a smashing blow northeast of Soissons, taking more than 8,000 prisoners.

---

[1]Sisson, *One Hundred Red Days*, pp. 8–9.

[2]House wrote in his diary: "The President decided this morning that it would be well for me to take over representatives of the Army, Navy, Munitions, Food, Finances, Shipping, and Embargo. . . ." *Intimate Papers*, Vol. III, p. 204.

To Winthrop M. Daniels, referring again to Daniels' letter of the 19th:

"I think it would be of the very greatest service to the country if a statement such as you suggest in your letter . . . namely, 'to show exactly how the gross and net revenues to date for the current year compare with 1916; affirm that the showing of earnings completely negatives the pessimism that is so prevalent; and reiterate that in constant touch as we are with revenues and expenditures we shall not suffer inadequate revenue to impair the efficiency or the reasonable earning power of the carriers,' should be made by the Commission and made at once. The announcement this morning of a hastened hearing of the Eastern cases is very valuable. I wonder if the Commission would be willing to add the other?"

To his secretary, Tumulty, enclosing a letter of protest against the treatment of imprisoned suffragettes:

"I do not think that this lady is in the condition of mind to discuss this matter, but I would be very much obliged if you would take this letter to Louis Brownlow and find out whether he really knows the conditions at Occoquan, letting him see how very important I deem it to see that there is certainly no sufficient foundation for such statements . . ."

To his secretary, Tumulty, referring to a request from the managing editor of the New York *Evening Sun* for the President's opinion as to whether a game of football between West Point and Annapolis for the benefit of the Red Cross was desirable:

"It seems to me to be infernal cheek for this man to ask me this question. I am not in favor of any such game as that proposed or of any public game between Army and Navy teams this season; and a newspaper is certainly not the place for me to express any such official judgment."

Wednesday, October 24th.
Liberty Loan Day.

The President worked in his study until quarter past twelve, when he received Governor Holcomb and Homer Cummings of Connecticut; Pleasant A. Stovall, a boyhood friend, who was now minister to Switzerland; Dr. Glazebrook was the only afternoon caller. Colonel House left, after a last talk with the President which he reported in his diary: "He outlined a 'letter of marque' for me to use with the Governments of Great Britain, France, and Italy. Neither of us knew how it should be addressed, whether to the sovereigns or prime ministers. It was decided to consult the State Department to-day, which I have done. Lansing thinks, since the invitation came to participate in the War Council through the French Ambassador, Dean of Diplomatic Corps, that the acceptance should go through the same channel. Therefore the President wrote a letter to the Secretary of State, asking him to inform the French Ambassador that he was pleased to accept the invitation of the Allied Governments to participate in the War Council and that he had commissioned me to represent him. He decided that I should also keep the letter he wrote last night addressed to the Prime Ministers, even though that was not the proper procedure. . . ."[1]

German and Austrian forces struck a great blow at Caporetto —the beginning of a disastrous defeat for Italy. 250,000 prisoners were taken within the week. Italian morale collapsed, the Italian Cabinet fell.[2]

To Secretary Lansing, a letter marked "Confidential":
"Thank you for sending me Mr. Phillips' memorandum about the question put by Mr. de Laboulaye.

"I think that it would be a mistake for the British and French Governments to address the Japanese Government with the request that Japan should send troops to the West Front next spring and summer, but, of course,

---

[1] *Intimate Papers,* pp. 205, 206. See this volume, p. 325, for the method of accrediting House which was finally used.

[2] For description of German propaganda which contributed to the disaster, see Irwin, *Propaganda and the War,* pp. 167–170.

To T. W. Gregory, enclosing a sheet called *The People's Counselor:*

"I would very much like you seriously to consider whether publications like the enclosed do not form a sufficient basis for a trial for treason. There are many instances of this sort and one conviction would probably scotch a great many snakes. So far as I can see, an indictment could easily be founded upon such utterances as this."[1]

To Walter Lowrie, who had written from Italy: "Today in this little alpine village the local deputy of parliament gathered the people in the square to hear from him a patriotic speech. He had much to say about the noble and encouraging example of America and about the clear words of President Wilson. The enclosed translation of your Decoration Day speech was then distributed to his electors. . . .":

"It was certainly very thoughtful of you to send me your letter . . . with its enclosure. It has interested me not only, but cheered me very much. Such incidents as you relate encourage me to believe that influences which I thought might be weak may possibly turn out to be very strong in the direction of an ideal attitude throughout the war and something like an ideal solution after it. I pray with all my heart that this may be so.

"I wish I had time for a real letter. I have only time for this line of greeting and gratitude."

Wednesday, September 26th.

Secretary Baker called for a conference with the President just before luncheon. Afternoon appointments: the minister from Sweden; Representative Dickinson of Missouri; Senator Newlands of Nevada; Senator Smith of South Carolina;

him again on September 26th. It is possible that the date on this note is wrong and that it was written after the interview of the 26th.

[1]Gregory replied that the matter in the paper did not constitute treason as defined by court decisions; but that it fell within the provisions of the Espionage Act and he had therefore transmitted it to the United States Attorney at Chicago for investigation and action.

I do not wish to press the objection and think it would be unwise to raise one."

To George Creel, who had sent over suggested letters to Colonel William B. Thompson[1] and Edgar G. Sisson, and a request for the allotment of one million dollars to the Committee on Public Information, to be used in Russia for the purchase of motion-picture equipment, cable service, etc.:

"I am glad to sign the letters you have suggested and am hurrying them over to you."[2]

To J. Edwin Webster, a Princeton classmate, who had invited the President and Mrs. Wilson to his home in Belair, Maryland, for a week-end visit:

MY DEAR DAN'L:

Your invitation attracts me mightily and I thank you for it with all my heart, but, my dear fellow, it is literally

---

[1] Head of the Red Cross Mission to Russia.

[2] The letter to Sisson read: "Mr. Creel informs me that you are leaving for Russia at once. In our conversation of yesterday I tried to make clear my views as to the nature and extent of any manifestation of our interest in the Russian struggle, and I know that you will be guided by them in everything that you say or do.

"We want nothing for ourselves and this very unselfishness carries with it an obligation of open dealing. Wherever the fundamental principles of Russian freedom are at stake, we stand ready to render such aid as lies in our power, but I want this helpfulness based upon request and not upon offer. Guard particularly against any effect of officious intrusion or meddling, and try to express the distinterested friendship that is our sole impulse.

"It is a distinct service that you are privileged to render your country and the whole democratic movement, and I know that this will serve at once as reward and inspiration."

That to Colonel Thompson:

"I had heard already of your helpful interest in Russia's fight for freedom, but not until my talk with Mr. Hutchins today did I fully appreciate the extent of your generosity and the finely practical expression of your sympathy.

"It is a great thing at a great time that you have been privileged to do, and I hold it all the more effective in that it is the effort of an individual concerned only with the success of the human struggle. The experience of Europe has made national disinterestedness almost incredible to its peoples, and even the United States, with its demonstrable lack of selfish purpose, cannot go too carefully in the business of helping Russia to help itself.

"Mr. Hutchins informs me that you are to remain in Russia as long as you see an opportunity for usefulness. I trust that this is indeed the case, for there is need of some one there to represent unofficially the fraternal interest of America. I am convinced that your whole-heartedness admirably fits you for this important duty, and I hope that you will accept it as another call upon your patriotism."

impossible for me to give myself such pleasures and the attempt never works out right because I have to be accompanied by a whole retinue of Secret Service men and "sich," and the attempt to be quiet and secluded always ridiculously breaks down. I am hoping some day to be a free man and then I can enjoy my friends as my heart longs to do.

With warmest regards to you both,

Affectionately yours,

WOODROW WILSON

Thursday, October 25th.

Mr. Wilmer Bolling and Dr. Rudolf Teusler, were guests at luncheon. In the early afternoon the President received a committee from the New York State Woman Suffrage Party, headed by Mrs. Norman de R. Whitehouse, and made a short address. ". . . . I think the whole country has appreciated the way in which the women have risen to this great occasion. . . .

"I . . . am very glad to add my voice to those which are urging the people of the great State of New York to set a great example by voting for woman suffrage. . . ."[1] The President sat for Sargent until Judge Lovett called at four o'clock to submit a priority order as to the transportation of coal.

> Secretary Burleson's letter to publishers regarding the Espionage and Trading with the Enemy Acts as they affected the postal service was made public. The loyal press, he said, need not fear—no one connected with the government sought through these laws to avoid criticism or attack— but no prohibited matter would be permitted to circulate.[2]

To Secretary Lansing, who had written: "I have been thinking over further the matter of credentials for Colonel House and I have come to the conclusion that a simpler way than giving him a certified copy of the letter addressed to the French Ambassador here would be for you to give him a formal designation. I therefore enclose a letter which I would suggest be given

[1] *Public Papers,* Vol. V, pp. 108–110. Suffrage carried in the New York November election.

[2] New York *Times,* October 26, 1917.

him. In view of the regard for formality which prevails among European governments it might be well for me to countersign your letter and place upon it the seal of the Department. . . .":

"I am very glad to comply with your suggestion about this letter to House and I would be obliged if you would be kind enough to countersign it and see that it is promptly forwarded to him. I believe he leaves New York on Sunday."[1]

To Secretary Houston, who had written of the Allied governments' plan for a nitrate commission in London, to be called the "Nitrate of Soda Executive," and financed by the American government:

"I feel that you and Polk and Baruch are very much better qualified to judge than I am where the management of the distribution of nitrate should center, and I shall have no objection to the establishment of a board for that purpose in London if you three are convinced that that is the only feasible arrangement at present.

"In case of the establishment of such a board, I think the proposals contained in your letter are quite sensible, except that I do not think that the American Government should finance the operations of the Nitrate of Soda Executive. On the contrary, I think that each government should finance its own operations in respect of nitrate and pay its own share of the general cost of the Executive."

To Major Henry L. Higginson:
". . . I want to assure you that I have had the interests of the railways very much in my mind, particularly of late, and that I hope from what I have learned that the members of the Interstate Commerce Commission are also sincerely concerned that the railroads should suffer no impairment of efficiency and should be enabled in any

---

[1]On October 25th House acknowledged the receipt from the President of $2500 in cash for personal expenses on his trip abroad.

way that is within the Commission's power to do their business with efficiency and success."

To George W. Anderson, new member of the Interstate Commerce Commission:

"I know how much the friends of liberal government are depending on you in the Massachusetts constitutional convention. I take the liberty, therefore, of asking whether you think you could consistently with your new duties (or, rather, before getting fully into harness) and without injustice to the Commission as a whole return for a while to the sessions of the convention while, at any rate, the most critical matters are pending?

"I ask this only because my own interest in what I have learned of the convention is so great and because I thought you would not mind my indicating to you my feeling that perhaps the convention was for a brief time more important than the duties of the Commission."

Friday, October 26th.

Vance McCormick called at 12:30; and before the cabinet meeting in the afternoon, Assistant Secretary Crosby. Late-afternoon appointments: Senator Owen of Oklahoma; Dr. Frank Billings, just back from Russia, where he had headed the American Red Cross Special Commission; Victor Murdock and William Allen White; Bainbridge Colby. Mrs. Edward Elliott[1] arrived as a house guest sometime during the day.

> Ambassador Francis telegraphed Secretary Lansing urging that the Allied conference be postponed or abandoned. ". . . . Russia is sick but can be more effectively treated at home than abroad. Paris conference looked upon here as a peace meeting and if should not so develop, which God forbid, may increase peace sentiment in Russia . . .
>
> "Government is doing its best to restore army discipline and any conference looking to peace renders such task more difficult. If ten million or more soldiers should be demobil-

---

[1] A sister of the first Mrs. Wilson.

ized under present prevailing Bolsheviki sentiment, God
pity Russia. . . ."[1]

Brazil declared war on Germany.

To William Phillips, referring to George Grey Barnard's
much-criticized statue of Abraham Lincoln which was to be
set up in London as a gift by Charles P. Taft. Robert Todd
Lincoln had objected strenuously to the presentation of this
particular statue of his father; and protests had come from
many others.

"I have shared to some extent the feeling which you
express about the statue of Lincoln, but within the last
forty-eight hours I have come to think that perhaps our
alarm was not justified. Mr. Barnard says that the photographs of his statue are a libelous travesty of the real
statue and shows letters from some of the finest sculptors
of the country praising the statue in unqualified terms,
and I know of several who have suspended judgment until
they may see the bronze itself. I think that perhaps we
ought to go slowly in forming a final judgment."

To Judge W. L. Chambers of the Board of Mediation and Conciliation, who had reported his efforts among the executives of
the labor unions engaged in train operation; and suggested
that the President write a letter of endorsement:

"May I not express my very deep and serious interest
in your efforts to bring the railroad executives and the
brotherhoods engaged in train operation to an agreement
that there shall be no interruption in their relations on
either side until ample opportunity shall have been afforded the United States Board of Mediation and Conciliation to bring about if possible an amicable agreement,
and that in the event of a failure to bring about such an
agreement any controversy that may have arisen will be
submitted to arbitration in accordance with the provisions
of the Newlands law. I take it for granted that your efforts

[1] *Foreign Relations*, 1917, Supp. 2, Vol. I, pp. 284–285.

will succeed, because it is inconceivable to me that patriotic men should now for a moment contemplate the interruption of the transportation which is so absolutely necessary to the safety of the nation and to its success in arms, as well as to its whole industrial life; but I wanted, nevertheless, to express my deep personal interest in the matter and to wish you Godspeed. The last thing I should wish to contemplate would be the possibility of being obliged to take any unusual measures to operate the railways, and I have so much confidence that the men you are dealing with will appreciate the patriotic motives underlying your efforts that I shall look forward with assurance to your success."

Saturday, October 27th.

From 2:30 until four the President sat for Sargent. In the late afternoon he and Mrs. Wilson went to the Episcopal Cathedral of St. Peter and St. Paul for the wedding of Senator Owen's daughter.

> The second Liberty Loan was pronounced by Secretary McAdoo an "overwhelming success," the total being 54 per cent over the amount asked.
>
> Colonel House sent the President, in "view of our conversation concerning your coming message to Congress," a memorandum written by Dr. Mezes, giving the ideas of Secretary Houston and F. W. Taussig as to economic policies which ought to be adopted at the Peace Conference. In his covering letter House said: ". . . . I feel very strongly that something should be done at the Peace Conference to end, as far as practicable, trade restrictions. . . .[1]
>
> "If you write such a message as we talked of, I hope you will think it well to say that the worst thing that could happen to Germany would be a peace made by a government that was not representative. That such a peace would inevitably lead to economic warfare afterwards—a warfare

---

[1] From the earliest years the President of course had believed in freer trade relations between nations.

in which by force of circumstances this Government would be compelled to take part.

"I shall think of you and dear Mrs. Wilson constantly while I am away, and I shall put forth the best there is in me to do the things you have intrusted to me. I am sure you know how happy you have made me by giving me this great opportunity to serve.

"Will you not remember that one of the highest duties imposed upon you is to care for yourself, for I do not put it too strongly when I say you are the one hope left to this torn and distracted world. Without your leadership God alone knows how long we will wander in the wilderness.

"Yours with devotion and affection . . ."

The tenth Lansing-Ishii conference was held, Lansing writing to the President afterward, in a letter marked *PERSONAL AND CONFIDENTIAL*:

". . . . As you know I submitted to him last Monday a memorandum relative to the important clause which had been stricken out of the note to be sent him. He submitted the matter to his Government and has received a proposed protocol instead of the memorandum suggested by me. I enclose a copy for your consideration. It is my view that this practically covers the ground and of course avoids the idea of suspicion as to Japan's purpose which might have been drawn from the memorandum submitted by us.

"This protocol would be signed by the Viscount and myself and retained confidentially, but he informs me that his Government does not feel it would have to be kept as secret as a memorandum such as we proposed.

"I would be obliged if you could indicate your wishes as soon as possible as Viscount Ishii is very anxious to set out on his homeward journey."

The enclosed secret protocol was as follows:

"In the course of the conversations between the Japanese Special Ambassador and the Secretary of State of the United States which have led to the exchange of notes between them dated this day, declaring the policy of the two Governments with regard to China, the question of embodying the following clause in such declaration came up for discussion: 'they (the Governments of Japan and the United States) will not take advantage of the present conditions to seek special rights or privileges in China which would abridge the rights of the subjects or citizens of other friendly states.'

"Upon careful examination of the question, it was agreed that the clause above quoted being superfluous in the relations of the two Governments and liable to create erroneous impression in the minds of the public, should be eliminated from the declaration.

"It was, however, well understood that the principle enunciated in the clause which was thus suppressed was in perfect accord with the policy actually pursued by the two Governments in China."[1]

The American ambassador at Rome, reporting the serious character of the German-Austrian offensive on the Isonzo front, suggested that "it would be a great advantage and important reenforcement here if we declared war to exist with Austria."[2]

To George Creel, who wrote that the publishers of *Vorwärts* were boasting of their influence in Washington:

"Please don't pay any attention to such boasts as you quote from the Vorwarts. This is a thorny business we are handling in the matter of these disloyal newspapers, but I am keeping in close touch with the Postmaster General and I believe the thing is being worked out with some degree of equity and success."

Sunday, October 28th.

The President, Mrs. Wilson and Mrs. Elliott went to the Central Presbyterian Church in the morning.

The President appealed to the American people for economy in the use of food.[3]

---

[1]The President's reply does not appear in his files; it may have been made by word of mouth. It was evidently in the affirmative, for at his next conference with Ishii, October 29th, Lansing agreed to the protocol, with "a few verbal changes." *War Memoirs of Robert Lansing*, p. 301.

[2]*Foreign Relations*, 1917, Supp. 2, Vol. I, p. 282.

[3]Drafted by Hoover. See *Official Bulletin*, October 29, 1917.

The American War Mission, Colonel House at its head, left for Halifax under the closest secrecy.[1]

To Colonel House:
"DEAR HOUSE,

"I think it will be well for you to take this memorandum with you. It is very specific and I think speaks the full truth about the shipping situation. It also shows how seriously we are taking it and trying to solve it. It will serve as an answer to the message you sent me a week or so ago.

———

"I hate to say good-bye. It is an immense comfort to me to have you at hand here for counsel and for friendship. But it is right that you should go. God bless and keep you both! My thoughts will follow you all the weeks through,— and I hope that it will be only weeks that will separate us.

"Mrs. Wilson joins in all affectionate messages.

"Affectionately Yours,"[2]

Monday, October 29th.

The President received Secretary McAdoo at noon. In the early afternoon he sat for Sargent; and at four o'clock A. Mitchell Palmer, recently appointed Alien Property Custodian, called.

The President issued an appeal in behalf of Armenian and Syrian relief. (See facsimile, p. 332.)

Ambassador Page telegraphed from Rome: ". . . . Press generally asserts that not only Italy's but the Allies' cause is at stake. I believe this to be true . . .

"England and France reported rushing artillery to Italy's support."[3]

———

[1] The mission included: Colonel E. M. House, with his son-in-law, Gordon Auchincloss, as secretary; Admiral W. S. Benson; General Tasker H. Bliss; Oscar T. Crosby, Assistant Secretary of the Treasury; Vance C. McCormick of the War Trade Board; Bainbridge Colby of the Shipping Board; A. E. Taylor of the Food Administration; and T. N. Perkins of the War Industries Board.

[2] The President forgot to sign this letter. No enclosure came with the copy of the letter supplied to the author by Colonel House.

[3] *Foreign Relations,* 1917, Supp. 2, Vol. I, p. 283.

AN APPEAL TO THE AMERICAN PEOPLE

One year ago in compliance with resolutions passed by the Senate by the House of Representatives, I appointed days upon which the peopl of the United States might make such contributions as they felt dispose for the aid of the stricken Armenian and Syrian peoples.

American consuls and other American residents recently returned f Western Asia, assure me that many thousands of lives were saved from starvation by the gifts of the American people last winter. They al bring full assurance of effective distribution of relief and report th the suffering and death from exposure and starvation will inevitably be very much greater this winter than last unless the survivors can be helped by further contributions from America.

Reports indicate that of orphans alone there are more than 400,00 besides women and other dependent children. The situation is so dis- tressing as to make a special appeal to the sympathies of all.

Responding to an urgent request from the American Committee for Armenian and Syrian Relief, I am glad to call again upon the people of the United States to make such further contributions as they feel disposed in their sympathy and generosity to make for the aid of these suffering peoples. Contributions may made through the American Red Cross, Washington, D. C., or direct to the treasurer of the American Committee for Armenian and Syrian Relief, Cleveland H. Dodge, One Madison Avenue, New York.

To Secretary Baker, enclosing a letter from A. H. Frazier, First Secretary of the American Embassy in Paris, to Colonel House:

"House has sent me the enclosed which I think is of rather serious significance. It seems that General Pershing, having known Marshal Joffre before going to France, has quite naturally been consulting him a great deal and General Petain very little. Petain has been hurt by this, and it would doubtless be very well to have a hint dropped to General Pershing.

"In House's letter which accompanied this he says, 'I shall give Bliss a hint of the trouble and let him try to straighten it out.' Perhaps that is the best way."

To T. W. Gregory:

"I dare say we should only be assisting Mr. Hillquit by apparently making him a martyr if the Government should pay any attention to his recent outrageous utterances about the Liberty Loan, but so many people have been disturbed by what he has said that I take the liberty of sending you the enclosed letter and of asking what you have been thinking about the matter."

To Secretary Redfield, who felt that New York would be in for four bad Tammany years if Mayor Mitchel were not reëlected; and who hoped, therefore, that the President would publicly favor Mitchel. The President's letter is marked "Personal":

". . . . I am sorry to say that I cannot take any part in the mayoralty campaign in New York. To tell you the truth, I have lost confidence in Mayor Mitchel of late, for reasons which I hope I may have an opportunity of

THE PRESIDENT'S INTEREST IN THE ARMENIANS AND SYRIANS

(*On opposite page.*) Draft of an appeal to the American people on behalf of Armenian and Syrian relief, corrected in the President's handwriting, with two notes showing the method of work: the first, to Tumulty, dictated by the President to one of his secretaries, Charles L. Swem; the second written by hand.

explaining to you soon. I dare say that from the point of view of those who, like myself, cannot admire him it is Hobson's choice in this respect, and I realize how serious the issues involved are."[1]

Tuesday, October 30th.

The President worked in his study until noon, and from twelve to one sat for Mr. Sargent. After the cabinet meeting Secretary Redfield remained behind, probably to discuss the New York political situation.

> The American War Mission sailed from Halifax on two armored cruisers, convoyed by a destroyer.
> The United States placed $230,000,000 to the credit of Italy.

To Franklin D. Roosevelt, who had sent over "in view of our several talks during the summer" a copy of his memorandum of "Proposed measures to close English Channel and North Sea against submarines by mine barrage." Urging the necessity of more haste and efficiency, Roosevelt concluded: ". . . . I dislike exaggeration, but it is really true that the elimination of all submarines from the waters between the United States and Europe must of necessity be a vital factor in winning the war.":

"Thank you for your letter of yesterday. I am interesting myself in the matter."

Wednesday, October 31st.

At 12:30 the President received the Mexican ambassador, who presented General Obregon. After the usual sitting for Sargent, President and Mrs. Wilson went to the American University Camouflage Camp to watch a demonstration; and in the late afternoon Samuel Gompers called, with a Committee on Housing.

> Secretary McAdoo wrote, from Virginia: ". . . . You would be gratified with the genuine affection that is manifested by the people everywhere towards you. It isn't merely admiration for what you have done for the country, but a genuine

---

[1]Hylan (Tammany) won the New York election.

affection for you personally, which I think counts for more than anything else. . . ."

Thursday, November 1st.

The President received Professor William E. Rappard at noon. Afternoon appointments: the Swiss Commission; a sitting for Sargent; Lord Reading; Senator Wadsworth of New York.

To Secretary Lansing, enclosing a memorandum of statements made by William Bayard Hale, who alleged that he had been subjected to persecution by men claiming to be secret service agents. The President's letter is marked "Personal":

"I am sure that you will be interested in this memorandum from the Executive Clerk in my office, Rudolph Forster. If the statements Mr. Hale made to Mr. Forster are indeed true, it is a very serious case of misbehavior on the part of somebody, but I particularly wanted you to note Mr. Hale's offer to submit to investigation of any kind."[1]

To A. Mitchell Palmer, Alien Property Custodian, enclosing a letter from Lansing suggesting that it be made clear that the property of allies of the enemy would not be taken over unless it was being used in the interest of the enemy country:

"There is a great deal of force in what the Secretary of State urges in the enclosed letter. There is very serious danger to American property in Turkey in case there should be any mistaken action on our part with regard to Turkish property in the United States, and I would be very much obliged to you for a suggestion apropos of the Secretary of State's representations in the enclosed letter."

To Judge Robert S. Lovett:

"You will remember, I believe, my speaking to you the other day about the monument to the first Mrs. Wilson

[1] The President sent a copy of the memorandum to the Attorney General on the same day; and when investigation revealed that the agent accused was one of the secret service men of the Treasury Department, he took the matter up with McAdoo.

which is to be erected at Rome, Georgia, and your kind
suggestion that you would have the shipment followed up
and facilitated if I would let you know the particulars.
I am, therefore, taking the liberty of sending you the
enclosed letter from the artist, Mr. Herbert Adams, of
New York.

"I am deeply indebted to you for your generous courtesy in offering to take a personal interest in this."

Friday, November 2nd.

The President received George Creel in the early afternoon.
During the cabinet meeting, or later in a private talk with
Secretary Redfield, the President discussed the propaganda
being circulated against the Liberty Motor. At 4:30 he conferred with Thomas D. Jones of the War Trade Board.

> The thirteenth and last Lansing-Ishii conference was held,
> during which Lansing handed Ishii a letter giving his own
> understanding of the agreement reached in their recent
> conversations as to the "desires and intentions shared" by
> the two governments in China; and Ishii confirmed the
> understanding.[1]
>
> Secretary Lansing telegraphed Ambassador Francis in Russia
> that the Allied Conference at Paris was "to discuss vigor-
> ous and successful prosecution of the war and not to discuss
> peace terms or war settlements. You may so state to
> officials if they labor under any misapprehension and
> publicly if necessary."[2]
>
> Balfour conveyed to Lord Rothschild the following state-
> ment, approved by the British Cabinet: "His Majesty's
> Government view with favour the establishment in Pales-
> tine of a national home for the Jewish people, and will use

---

[1] For the published agreement, see *Foreign Relations*, 1917, pp. 264–265. See also
War Memoirs of Robert Lansing, pp. 301–302. No mention was made of the secret
protocol, nor does Viscount Ishii mention it in his *Memoirs*. Lansing, while he discusses
the protocol, says that since it was confidential it "cannot be published, although its
undertakings came to an end with the close of the war." (p. 301.) The whole episode
constitutes a singular inversion of the usual secret diplomacy: instead of a bargain
between predatory interests, it was an idealistic self-denying ordinance which had to
be kept dark because one party feared opposition among its own people.

[2] *Foreign Relations*, 1917, Supp. 2, Vol. I, p. 286.

their best endeavours to facilitate the achievement of this object, it being clearly understood that nothing shall be done which may prejudice the civil and religious rights of existing non-Jewish communities in Palestine or the rights and political status enjoyed by Jews in any other country."[1]

To Richard H. Edmonds, "Personal," a letter based in part upon one from Herbert Hoover:

". . . . We were all aware of the facts to which you call my attention, but it is nevertheless true that with the necessary saving and conservation we have abundant foodstuffs to do the great task which has now fallen upon us.

"I beg that you will realize what the effect would be of giving a general impression to the country that there was a shortage of food. It would undoubtedly create a panic, a state of mind which would be most hostile to the performance of our present duties to the rest of the world, and the panic would be unjustified, because with the proper care and conservation we undoubtedly have enough, though by no means a wide margin."

Saturday, November 3rd.

Sargent completed his portrait. After the last sitting, the President and Mrs. Wilson went out in the car for two hours, returning in time for a conference with George Creel before dinner.

Count Georg F. von Hertling became Chancellor of Germany, succeeding Michaelis.

"While it is yet too early from the fragmentary comment which has reached us from Berlin, to interpret the full significance of the change in the chancellorship," wrote

---

[1]*Op. cit.*, p. 317. When Lansing, on December 15th, instructed Ambassador Page to "investigate discreetly" the reasons for this statement, Page replied that the French and British governments had an understanding that Palestine should be internationalized. Balfour's statement merely indicated British determination that Jews should be on the same footing as other nationalities. Lord Robert Cecil, "speaking informally and only for himself," hoped that the United States would be the protecting power for Palestine. *Ibid.*, pp. 473, 483.

J. C. Grew of the State Department on the 5th, "one point stands out with startling clearness: autocracy has met its first signal defeat . . ."

Three Americans were killed in a German raid; and the first American prisoners taken.

To Secretary Baker, who had reported that no alien enemies were now employed in any arsenal in the United States:

"I am very much gratified by the report conveyed by your letter of yesterday as to the employment of alien enemies. It reassures me very much.

"It leaves, however, the big problem of the employment of alien enemies in factories supplying the war-making departments. As to that I wish very much that I had some notion of what ought to be done."

To Abram I. Elkus, Ambassador to Turkey:

"I appreciate the seriousness of the question of Turkish property in the United States being taken over by the Alien Property Custodian, and I have already had a conference with the Custodian, Mr. A. Mitchell Palmer, about the matter which I think will safeguard it efficiently, but I am none the less obliged to you for the letter and the caution which it conveys.

"As a matter of fact, no confiscation of any kind is in contemplation. The Alien Property Custodian will act just as a trust company would in keeping the funds intact and administering them without loss, the only restriction being that the proceeds shall not go to an enemy."

Sunday, November 4th.

The President and Mrs. Wilson went to the Central Presbyterian Church in the morning, and after church to the Bureau of Standards, where the President conferred with Secretary Redfield.

The American minister in China telegraphed Secretary Lansing: "Japanese Minister has shown me the text of your note to Baron Ishii in which the American Government recognizes the special interest of Japan in China. While I understand that the reasons which prompted this momentous decision are confidential, I have the honor to ask whether at the time of publication of this note you desire me to present to the Chinese officials any explanation of this action which so profoundly affects their interests and which at first sight appears a reversal of American policy in China." The following day, Reinsch telegraphed again: ". . . . The Foreign Office is making inquiry here. This Legation is in a highly embarrassing position . . ."[1]

Monday, November 5th.

Afternoon appointments: Luther D. Wishard, a Princeton classmate, and Duncan M. Stewart, recently returned from France—joint bearers of a medal from the Committee of Verdun to the President. Stewart told of being asked by an old French woman whether there were really American soldiers in France. Assured that there were, she continued, "And will they fight?" They would indeed, replied Stewart. The tears rolled down the woman's cheeks. "*Oh, monsieur,*" she cried, "*nous prions pour Monsieur Wilson!*" The President seemed much touched by this incident. "Don't you see," he said, "what a great responsibility rests upon me when the French people think of me like that?"[2]

In the later afternoon, five members of the War Industries Board called to discuss "some price-fixing matters"; and at 4 o'clock, Chief Justice Hernandez of Porto Rico.

Secretary Lansing sent the President a copy of a secret memorandum from the British Embassy: "An agent has been sent to Switzerland, according to confidential information received by the British Minister at Berne, for the purpose of letting Great Britain know 'officieusement' that if she is prepared to enter into 'officieuses' conversations on the subject of peace, the Austrian Government would

---

[1] The Lansing-Ishii agreement had been communicated by the Japanese government to their minister in China and by him to Reinsch and the Chinese Foreign Office in spite of the fact that it was not to be given to the public until the 6th. Moreover, an objectionable interpretation was placed upon the words "special interest." *War Memoirs of Robert Lansing*, pp. 302–303.

[2] D. M. Stewart to the President, May 7, 1918, recalling the incident.

pledge their honour that the matter would be kept secret. Count Czernin would be ready to make an immediate declaration that, in spite of the recent Austrian success against Italy, the integrity of Italian territory as it existed before the war will be guaranteed.

"The British Minister at Berne has been instructed to advise his informant that he is convinced that peace can only be discussed by his Majesty's Government with their Allies but that if the Austrian Government have a definite proposal to make, he will forward it. The French, Italian and Russian representatives at Berne will be informed by the British Minister of what has passed."[1]

Secretary Lansing telegraphed the American ambassador in Japan, quoting the Lansing-Ishii agreement and the statement which would be given out on the 6th. He also sent the agreement to Reinsch in China, adding a statement to be repeated to the Chinese Foreign Office: this exchange of expressions (said the statement) not only contained a reaffirmation of the Open Door policy, but introduced "a principle of non interference with the sovereignty and territorial integrity of China, which, generally applied, is essential to perpetual international peace, as has been so clearly declared by President Wilson."[2]

To Mrs. W. M. Irvine, whose husband was headmaster of Mercersburg Academy:

"I am very glad to answer your letter and thank you most warmly for all its generous friendship.

"I have no hesitation in saying Doctor Irvine has made the right decision. It is clearly his duty to keep the school going at its highest capacity if he can, and I think that it is the duty of the teachers associated with him to stick to their tasks unless they are manifestly indispensable to the direct work of the war itself. I think it would be a very great detriment to the country to have our higher schools and the colleges interrupted and unnecessarily depleted, particularly at this time.

---

[1] *Foreign Relations*, 1917, Supp. 2, Vol. I, p. 289.
[2] *Ibid.*, 1917, pp. 266–268.

AMERICAN TROOPS GOING OVER THE TOP IN ONE OF THEIR EARLY BATTLES

"May I not congratulate you both on the decision you have made and on the work you are doing?"

Tuesday, November 6th.

The President went to Princeton to vote, dictating the letters of the day to his stenographer while on the train.

Secretary Lansing notified Allied diplomatic representatives in Washington that Oscar T. Crosby had been designated as United States representative to the Inter-Ally Council and that there was no objection to his accepting the presidency.[1]

The Lansing-Ishii agreement was given to the press by the Department of State. New York *Times* headlines of the 7th read: "INDEPENDENCE OF CHINA GUARANTEED."

The Italians were reported to have abandoned their entire line along the Tagliamento.

The Provisional government of Russia, alarmed by increasing activity among the Bolsheviks, called out military cadets to guard the Winter Palace, where the government was installed. In the evening Lenin sent a letter to the Bolshevik Central Committee demanding action—paraphrasing the words of Peter the Great, he wrote: "To delay in setting forth means to die." This done, he made his way in disguise to the Smolny Institute, to direct the revolutionary movement. Troops commanded by the Bolsheviks occupied the chief governmental buildings, railway stations and main telegraph office during the night.[2]

Wednesday, November 7th.

Afternoon appointments: Joseph E. Davies of the Federal Trade Commission; Secretary Baker. Dr. Stockton Axson arrived for a visit.

The President issued his Thanksgiving Proclamation. " . . . even amidst the darkness that has gathered about us

---

[1] *Foreign Relations*, 1917, Supp. 2, Vol. I, p. 576. Done at McAdoo's request and with the President's approval.

[2] George Vernadsky, *Lenin, Red Dictator*, p. 174.

we can see the great blessings God has bestowed upon
us . . .

"We have been given the opportunity to serve mankind . . . A new vigor of common counsel and common
action has been revealed in us. . . ."[1]

The American War Mission, headed by Colonel House,
arrived in London. When the news reached the United
States a statement was made public giving the personnel
and emphasizing the fact that the conference at which
they were to represent the United States was essentially a
war conference.[2]

British, French and Italian representatives assembled at
Rapallo agreed upon the organization of a Supreme War
Council.[3]

In the early morning Kerensky escaped from Petrograd,
sending word to Ambassador Francis as he went that he
"expected [the] whole affair to be liquidated within five
days." At ten o'clock Lenin proclaimed to the citizens of
Russia that the Provisional government had been overthrown.[4]

To Secretary Lansing, written on the President's own typewriter:

"I hope that the proper reassurances have gone, or will
go at once, to Reinsch. There has not only been no change

[1] *Public Papers*, Vol. V, pp. 111–112.

[2] *Foreign Relations*, 1917, Supp. 2, Vol. I, pp. 295–296. Negotiations of the mission
are not here included for lack of space, except where the documents show that the
President touched them directly.

[3] See *War Memoirs of David Lloyd George*, Vol. IV, pp. 550–551.

[4] *Foreign Relations*, 1918, *Russia*, Vol. I, pp. 224–225; Vernadsky, *Lenin, Red Dictator*,
p. 175. The news first reached Washington through diplomatic channels in the form
of a telegram from Minister Morris in Sweden, which arrived at 11:50 on the night of
November 9th. Dispatches from Ambassador Francis began coming on the 10th, but
considerable intervals of silence followed. Morris, who saw many refugees as they came
out of Russia and who had other methods of inquiry, filled in the gaps so far as he could,
but at best the information received by Lansing and the President was scattering and
incomplete for many months.

From November 7th until March 16th, affairs in Russia developed in two directions:
first, the progress of government under the Bolsheviks; second, the initiation and
progress of peace negotiations. One bore upon the other. The position taken by the
Allied and Associated Powers, it was realized, would have an important effect upon
Russia's relations with Germany. How prevent the harassed Russians from falling
into the hands of the Central Powers—and still refrain from any recognition of the
only government which seemed to be functioning at all in Petrograd!

of policy but there has been a distinct gain for China, of course, and I hope that you will be kind enough to send Reinsch such a message as will serve him to put the whole thing in the right light at Peking and throughout China."[1]

To Secretary Lansing, referring to Ambassador Stimson's report that he had been invited by the Allied ministers in Argentina to a conference on the means of obtaining internment of any submarines which might arrive. Lansing had telegraphed Stimson the day before that it was "considered inadvisable" for him to attend the conference.[2] The President's letter was written on his own typewriter:

"Surely the Ministers of the Allies are going too far in trying this sort of thing on the impossible gentleman who is President of Argentina. The position they are purposing to take is the one the Allies tried to force on us when we were neutral, and they must realize that they are putting us in a very awkward position. If Stimson does not join with them, he will seem, on our behalf, to put our sanction on the admission of the boats to Argentine harbours, which we desire as little as they do; and yet he cannot take part with them in any such representations. I suppose it is too late to head the whole thing off?

"This is of a piece with the stupid performance in Sweden!"

To Secretary Baker:
"You probably know Mrs. Pickett. The Pickett men have been prominent in the wars of the country ever since Washington's time, when I believe one of them was on General Washington's staff, and it is a matter of the keenest grief to Mrs. Pickett that her son, George Pickett, Junior, though able to qualify in every other respect, has discovered for the first time that he is color blind and that

---

[1]Lansing on the same day sent over a copy of the statement which had gone to Minister Reinsch on the 5th.

[2]*Foreign Relations*, 1917, Supp. 2, Vol. II, p. 1297.

his color blindness excludes him from the service. Do you think it would be right and proper to accept him and put him into some branch of the work in which color blindness counts least? The case somehow appeals to a very real sentiment in me."

To Secretary Daniels, who had sent over a memorandum prepared by Admiral Taylor:

"Thank you for letting me see the enclosed report. Some very dirty work is being done about the Liberty Motor, and I understand that the active man in it is one ————, who is frequently if not permanently here in Washington. He ought to be smoked out."

Thursday, November 8th.

The President lunched alone while Mrs. Wilson entertained the ladies of the cabinet. The only official appointment of the day was at 2:30, when George Creel and Otto Kahn called. Evening at Keith's.

> Mr. Balfour expressed to Colonel House his great pleasure at the coming of the American Commission, declaring that it "meant much, not alone to Great Britain but to the Entente cause, on account of the débâcle in both Russia and Italy."[1] Colonel House gave out a statement, emphasizing the desire of the United States to coöperate.[2]
>
> Henry Ford announced that for the duration of the war his plant would be devoted entirely to the production of war necessities.
>
> Austro-German forces were reported in close pursuit of the Italian armies, the territory already occupied being estimated at 2,000 miles. Total number of prisoners taken, 250,000.

To Secretary Daniels:

"I saw in a letter the other day the suggestion that the Navy and Army football teams be allowed to play in New

[1]*Intimate Papers*, Vol. III, p. 226.
[2]*Foreign Relations*, 1917, Supp. 2, Vol. I, pp. 339–340.

York an exhibition game for the benefit of some one of the war funds. I take it for granted that your judgment is mine in such a matter, that the Army and Navy ought not to be used for that or any similar purpose, but my own judgment goes further. It seems to me that the Army and Navy game ought to be omitted altogether this season. It is largely a social event and would go very much against my own grain, I know. Indeed, I should not feel disposed to attend it.

"I need not say that I heartily approve of athletics for both academies, and hope that they will play all they please on their own grounds, but I think it would make a bad impression if they did more than that this year."[1]

To John Jay Chapman:

"I have just had the pleasure of reading twice aloud in my little family circle your Ode on the Sailing of our Troops for France which you were generous and gracious enough to dedicate to me, and I want to express to you my sincere admiration of the poem, an admiration which all my little circle share, and also my feeling that you have caught in a singular degree the spirit of America at her best and of the mission which it is now her duty to perform."

To John S. Sargent, who wrote the President that he had now seen the much criticized Barnard statue of Lincoln, and was "much more favorably impressed with it" than he had been with the photographs. He had also had a talk with Barnard about certain proposed changes:

"Thank you for your kindness in writing us about Mr. Barnard's statue of Lincoln, now that you have seen it. I am very much interested in what you say of it and delighted that the artist is inclined to take your very interesting suggestions about modifying the posture of it. I am

[1]The same letter went to Secretary Baker. Daniels replied on the 10th that he and Baker agreed and had notified the teams.

reassured, also that you should think that with the suggested changes made the statue will probably be worthy of the very unusual distinction which is to be conferred upon it.

"It was a great pleasure to know you personally and Mrs. Wilson joins with me in kindest regards."

To his secretary, Tumulty, who had reported a request from G. S. MacFarland that the President see William Randolph Hearst. MacFarland had asked that his suggestion be kept confidential if the President did not wish to see Hearst:

"It is out of the question for me to see Mr. Hearst on any business of any kind and I would be very much obliged to you if you would convey that intimation to Mr. MacFarland so that this suggestion might be as if it had never been made."

Friday, November 9th.

Before cabinet meeting the President received Governor McCall of Massachusetts; the executive committee of the Gridiron Club. In the late afternoon Dr. Anna Howard Shaw and Mrs. Carrie Chapman Catt, president of the National American Woman Suffrage Association, called with a group of representatives of the suffrage movement from Ohio and Indiana.

Colonel House sent the President an "extraordinary memorandum" written by Buckler of the American Embassy in London, reporting a conversation on November 2nd with Lord Milner.[1] The paper contained hints of the secret treaties—". . . . With regard to the Balkans in general he [Milner] failed to see how the promises which England had made to individual States could possibly be redeemed in full. . . ."—and a very confidential message to be given to Colonel House: ". . . . 'Our diplomacy,' he [Milner] said, 'has been in my opinion and still is deplorably weak in its attitude towards our enemies. For the past ten months we

---

[1]Milner had not yet endorsed the paper. "If this memorandum should get out," House cautioned, "it would be the undoing of Milner, therefore I hope you will keep it for your own information."

have been receiving all kinds of intimation, more or less definite, as to German offers of negotiation. Not only have we taken absolutely no steps to test the sincerity or the extent of these offers, but if anyone however remotely connected with this country is seen so much as talking to anyone however remotely connected with Germany, there is at once an absurd outcry of "peace trap" and an insinuation that we are about to betray this or that ally. I hope that America will not imitate our timidity. How *are* we ever to know what our enemies will offer, unless we keep our ears open? We ought to listen to every "peace whisper"—of course on the distinct understanding that all offers must be considered by the Entente as a whole. . . .'"

Saturday, November 10th.

The President and Dr. Grayson played golf until about eleven o'clock. The only official appointment for the day was in the afternoon, with George Creel.

The President made public a foreword to the new selective service regulations. ". . . . The time has come for a more perfect organization of our man-power. The selective principle must be carried to its logical conclusion. . . ."[1]

41 suffragette pickets were arrested in front of the White House, but were later released on bail. Other arrests were made from time to time during this period, but attracted little notice.

Secretary Lansing telegraphed American ambassadors in London, Paris and Rome: "The Department is advised that the French Government have informed the British Government that they are not prepared to invite the smaller Allies to take part in the coming Inter-Allied Conference and that the British Government have replied that they are inclined to the view that the conference proper should be confined to the larger powers with the smaller powers invited to attend when subjects affecting them are discussed, and furthermore the British Government are of the view that all the Allies should be invited to be represented at a final session of the conference and given an opportunity to state their views.

[1] *Public Papers*, Vol. V, pp. 113–115.

"Inform the Minister for Foreign Affairs that this Gov ernment shares the opinion of the British Government and believes that an unfortunate situation would be created which might affect the issue of the war if smaller powers were given cause of complaint that they were not permitted to discuss war measures affecting their welfare with their larger Allies."[1]

Secretary Lansing authorized Ambassador Sharp to extend formal recognition to the Polish National Committee in Paris as an official Polish organization.[2]

Passchendaele Ridge, chief objective of the British in their Flanders offensive, passed entirely into their hands.

To Frank P. Glass, referring to the government's suits against paper manufacturers:

"Thank you for your letter. . . . I must very frankly say that I do not entirely sympathize with your point of view. It would be very much more serious for the Government to forego a criminal prosecution on the ground that an understanding could be reached that the men under indict-ment would not hereafter do criminal things. That way lies scandal, though I admit that the other way is filled with practical difficulties and disadvantages.

"I will take pleasure in sending your letter to Gregory, and I know from my dealings with him how perfectly rational and sensible he is inclined to be, though always stiff to do his duty. I am not at all afraid of any erring [airing?] of the difference between the Federal Trade Commission and the Department of Justice. This is one of the interesting cases where it would probably appear that both were right, each from his own point of view."[3]

---

[1]*Foreign Relations*, 1917, Supp. 2, Vol. I, p. 301. Ambassador Sharp telegraphed on the 16th: "Foreign Office replies that the smaller powers have been invited to assist at the military session of the Inter-Allied Conference of Paris and that they have re-served for decision at that time what will be the working procedure to be followed subsequently." *Ibid.*, p. 308.

[2]*Ibid.*, p. 778.

[3]On the same day the President wrote to T. W. Gregory: "I would be very much obliged if you would read this letter from my friend and college-mate, Frank P. Glass. I have written to him that I was sure that you would take any course which could be

To Charles Edward Russell, who had suggested a campaign to show the Russian people that the success of their revolution depended upon the continuance of the war:

"I deeply appreciate your letter. It runs along the lines of my own thought, only you speak from knowledge and I have thought by inference, and you may be sure that I will do my best to act along the lines it suggests, though all sorts of work in Russia now is rendered extremely difficult because no one channel connects with any other, apparently."[1]

Sunday, November 11th.

The President, Mrs. Wilson, Mrs. Elliott and Dr. Axson went to the Central Presbyterian Church in the morning. After a drive in the late afternoon, President and Mrs. Wilson left for Buffalo, with a considerable party—Dr. Grayson and Tumulty, stenographers, secret service men.

Colonel House wrote the President: ". . . . I saw the King this morning. He sent his compliments to you and wanted you to know how much he appreciated what you had done for the allied cause. . . ."

Aided by Allied reinforcements, Italian resistance on the Piave front began to stiffen.

News reached Washington that the All-Russian Congress of Soviets had adopted a resolution calling upon all belligerents to commence negotiations for an immediate peace, without annexations or forcible conquests, and without indemnities; all negotiations were to be entirely open; and the secret treaties of the former Russian government were to be published and declared null and void. A three months' armistice was to be sought immediately.[2]

conscientiously justified, and I am sending his letter to you because I know that you are just as inclined to find a legitimate way out in this complicated business as the rest of us are."

[1]The President sent Russell's letter on to George Creel, saying: "Here is a very important letter which I wish you would read and inwardly digest. It seems to me to hit very near the heart of the subject it is concerned with."

[2]*Foreign Relations,* 1918, *Russia,* Vol. I, pp. 242–243.

Monday, November 12th.

President and Mrs. Wilson arrived in Buffalo at nine o'clock in the morning and were driven to the Broadway Auditorium, where the President was to address the American Federation of Labor Convention. He began with a stern indictment: ". . . . The war was started by Germany. Her authorities deny that they started it, but I am willing to let the statement I have just made await the verdict of history. . . ." And he continued:

". . . . While we are fighting for freedom we must see, among other things, that labor is free . . .

"Nobody has a right to stop the processes of labor until all the methods of conciliation and settlement have been exhausted . . . I am not talking to you alone. . . . Everybody on both sides has now got to transact business, and a settlement is never impossible when both sides want to do the square and right thing. . . ."

One paragraph was eloquent of his dismay over the news from Russia:

". . . it is amazing to me that any group of persons should be so ill-informed as to suppose, as some groups in Russia apparently suppose, that any reforms planned in the interest of the people can live in the presence of a Germany powerful enough to undermine or overthrow them by intrigue or force. Any body of free men that compounds with the present German Government is compounding for its own destruction. . . ."[1]

The address was delivered at ten o'clock; the presidential party left soon afterward, reaching the White House at eleven that night.

Ambassador Sharp wrote the President from Paris that he found no singleness of purpose among the Allies. Hints of the secret treaties appear in his letter, with direct reference to the Treaty of London.

---

[1] *Public Papers*, Vol. V, pp. 116–124. The effects of the address were immediate, more than one strike being called off.

Senator J. H. Lewis telegraphed: ". . . . I must inform you of the great service your Buffalo speech has done in Illinois on every side. I am informed by acknowledged authority that no less than six disturbances of business and industries were expected and prepared for to arise this week. The employers have made the necessary sacrifice and the employees the needed concessions . . ."

W. J. Bryan wrote Tumulty that he planned to have the speech printed in full in the December *Commoner*.

The Chinese minister in Washington handed Secretary Lansing a memorandum stating that the Chinese government would not allow itself to be bound by any agreement entered into by other nations. The Lansing-Ishii agreement was then discussed, Lansing maintaining that it left China better off than before.[1]

"Before the Russian revolution took place," telegraphed the American special agent at Cairo, "the Allies came to a mutual understanding concerning the dismemberment of the Ottoman Empire and the partition of its various parts. . . ." Details follow, with a discussion of Mark Sykes and M. Picot and their part in the affair.[2]

Lloyd George in an address in Paris deplored the lack of unity among the Allies. ". . . You have only to summarize events to realise how many of the failures from which we have suffered are attributable to this one fundamental defect . . ."[3]

To Secretary Baker, who had sent over a memorandum by Sir Stevenson Kent, British coal-mine and ship owner, who had been making a trip through the Middle West to address chambers of commerce and trade unions. The memorandum dealt with labor difficulties in the United States, the bad feeling between capital and labor, etc., and had a number of suggestions to make for improving conditions. Baker, in his covering letter, said:

". . . . It was because of this situation that I felt especially concerned to have you make the Buffalo trip, if possible . . . . what you . . . say would undoubtedly be accepted on both sides as the war duty of the country, and I confess I am more concerned to have industry and capital know what you think they ought to do with regard to labor than to have labor understand its duty. In my own dealing with the industrial problems here, I have found labor more willing to keep step than capital.":

"I have read with a great deal of interest the paper by Sir Stephenson Kent . . . and it gives me matter for grave thought. I would like very much to know your own

[1]*Foreign Relations,* 1917, pp. 270, 273.
[2]*Ibid.,* Supp. 2, Vol. I, pp. 490–492.
[3]*War Memoirs of David Lloyd George,* Vol. IV, pp. 554–555.

opinion as to the wisdom and feasibility of what he suggests, and I should particularly like to know whether you know of any one man who would enjoy the confidence alike of labor and capital and who could organize this matter of adjustment very much as the Food and Fuel Administrations are organizing their efforts throughout the country."

To Dr. S. E. Mezes, who had sent over a preliminary outline of the subjects to be dealt with by the Inquiry, which included five general headings: suppressed, oppressed and backward peoples; international business; international law; analysis of serious proposals for an organization to insure peace; restoration.
The President's reply is marked "Personal":

"Thank you for the preliminary and brief outline of the subjects to be dealt with in the inquiry. It seems to me to suggest most of the chief topics that will have to be studied, though it occurs to me that there is one omission, though it may be only apparent.

"It seems to me that it will be necessary to study the just claims of the larger states, like Russia and Austria, and Germany herself, to an assured access to the sea and the main routes of commerce not only, but to a reasonable access to the raw materials of the world which they themselves do not produce.

"Of course, what we ourselves are seeking is a basis which will be fair to all and which will nowhere plant the seeds of such jealousy and discontent and restraint of development as would certainly breed fresh wars."

To J. W. Harriman, who suggested the formation of a War Finance Board, headed by McAdoo:

". . . . It has been in my mind for some time to attempt some such thing . . . and if I can devise the right way and get the right materials, I may yet be able to do it.

"It is very difficult to effect guidance in such complicated matters, and I am afraid that the Congress is particularly jealous of such instrumentalities."

To Dr. Albert Shaw, who had written his approval of the Barnard statue of Lincoln:

"Thank you for your long letter about the Barnard statue of Lincoln. I have myself suspended judgment about it entirely and have not allowed myself to be drawn into the controversy at all. I was very much interested to receive a letter from Mr. Sargent after he left here the other day saying that he had seen the statue itself and felt confident that if certain alterations which he suggested to Mr. Barnard could be successfully carried out, as Mr. Barnard seemed to think they could, the statue would be worthy of any distinction.

"My only fear has been that Mr. Barnard has been intent upon being too absolutely realistic and that the mystical spirit of our great President would not be adequately indicated.

"I value your judgment in the matter very highly."[1]

To Judge Nash B. Broyles:

"It certainly seems a work of supererogation to deny such extraordinarily silly rumors as that to which your letter . . . refers. Of course, there is not one iota of truth in it, and nothing but malice can have suggested it. No disloyalty of any kind has touched the inner counsels of the administration or come anywhere near the seats of authority.

"It seems particularly incredible that the rumor you speak of should have been for a moment credited, when Mr. Tumulty may be seen by anybody who cares to see him at the Executive Office on any day.

---

[1] After months of controversy a statue by Saint-Gaudens was erected in London and Barnard's statue was set up in Manchester.

"With warm appreciation of your expression of support and approval."

Telegram to John Donlin, president of the Building Trades Department of the American Federation of Labor convention, who had wired the President of a resolution passed by the presidents of the Building Trades to stop the strikes on the construction of shipbuilding plants. 12,000 men were ordered back to work "pending investigation and adjustment.":

"Your telegram of yesterday has cheered me very much and I hope that you will convey my sincere thanks and appreciation to those associated with you in the patriotic action of which you give me information. You may be sure that there will be all possible cooperation at this end."

Tuesday, November 13th.

The President played golf in the morning with Dr. Grayson, spent two hours in his study, and, before luncheon, walked over to George Creel's office. A. Mitchell Palmer called in the early afternoon. The cabinet met as usual at 2:30, taking up among other subjects the question of regulations governing the departure of aliens from the United States during the war. Later the President joined Mrs. Wilson and a party at the National Theater, to hear the Philadelphia Symphony Orchestra.

A monument by Herbert Adams was erected, with simple ceremonies, over the grave of Ellen Axson Wilson at Myrtle Hill Cemetery, Rome, Georgia.

Colonel House telegraphed the President: ". . . . The Italian situation is desperate. . . .

"France, England, and Italy have agreed to form a Supreme War Council and believe that it is imperative that we should be represented in it because of the moral effect that it will have here. . . .

"I would advise not having a representative on the civil end . . . but would strongly urge having General Bliss on the military end . . .

"Your beautiful speech came at the right time and has been enthusiastically received. . . ."[1]

[1]From the President's shorthand notes made upon decoding House's message.

General Pershing reported to Secretary Baker upon conditions in France and future plans, adding: ". . . permit me to congratulate you and the country in that we have you as Secretary. You are doing a great work and doing it well. . . ."[1]

The French Cabinet resigned, following a debate over the power and scope of the proposed War Council; within forty-eight hours M. Georges Clemenceau had completed the formation of a new Cabinet.

London newspapers criticized Lloyd George's "brutally frank" Paris address.

To Representative Frank Clark of Florida, a letter marked, in the President's handwriting, "Personal and Confidential. W.W.":

". . . . I have not lost faith in the Russian outcome by any means. Russia, like France in a past century, will no doubt have to go through deep waters but she will come out upon firm land on the other side and her great people, for they are a great people, will in my opinion take their proper place in the world."

Wednesday, November 14th.

At a quarter of nine in the morning the President and Mrs. Wilson went to the Navy Yard to inspect the submarine destroyer, *Manley*. Afternoon appointments: E. W. Scudder; Senator Owen of Oklahoma; State Senator Kent E. Keller of Illinois; Secretary Baker.

An editorial in the London *Morning Post:* "No one will dare to impugn President Wilson's essential pacifism; but just because of it, he sends Colonel House to Europe, not to negotiate peace, but to determine how the war is to be won. Our Pacifists are fertile in resource for explaining away many stubborn facts; but it is beyond their ingenuity to explain away President Wilson. . . . He has given not only to his own countrymen but to all the Allies just the forthright, unflinching lead that they needed—a lead that he

---

[1] Pershing, *My Experiences in the World War*, Vol. I, pp. 227–231.

renews unfailingly when it is most needed. As we have said before, President Wilson is a good man to go tiger-shooting with."

To his brother, Joseph R. Wilson, who had passed on a report by one of the agents of his company that people in the Southern "sticks" had little understanding of the reasons for the war, and no enthusiasm for it:

"I do not quite know what your agent in Mississippi means by the people in the Southern 'sticks,' but I take leave to doubt whether he is wholly right in the report he makes to you. We are by no means idle about the matter of keeping the people of the country informed as to all matters concerning the war and its causes and purposes and the necessities which it involves, and a recent letter from Senator Williams, who has made an extended tour of Mississippi, leaves upon me quite a different impression from that which Mr. Williams expresses. But in any case we are on the job!"

Thursday, November 15th.

The President conferred with Secretary Daniels at 12:15. Joseph R. Wilson and Secretary and Mrs. McAdoo were luncheon guests. Afternoon appointments: a committee from the American Jewish Relief Association, who presented plans for aiding the Jews in Poland and Lithuania;[1] Dr. S. E. Mezes; Herbert Hoover, who discussed the crop situation in the country; Thomas D. Jones. After the conference Jones sent the following telegram, through the Department of State, to Vance McCormick: "The President sent for me this afternoon to ascertain the exact situation of Norwegian negotiations in preparation for appointment which he has made for Doctor Nansen. . . . He . . . directed me to cable you that he is entirely unwilling to go any farther than the principle of action already settled namely that we will supply or attempt to supply nothing to Norway except what we can be shown the people actually

---

[1]The committee included, among others: Abram I. Elkus, Cyrus Adler, Henry Morgenthau, Oscar S. Straus, Julius Rosenwald, Julian W. Mack, Jacob H. Schiff, Louis Marshall, Alexander Kahn, Otto A. Rosalsky, Felix W. Warburg.

lack and we cannot undertake to supply them with any food elements of which they deprive themselves by exportation. He is not willing to take part in insisting that there be no export from Norway to Germany as he regards that as inconsistent with the principle upon which the United States has always insisted and the rights which she has always demanded for herself. In view of above he further directs me to say that in his judgment we cannot in good faith hold up the Danish agreement awaiting any other negotiations."

Colonel House telegraphed the President: ". . . . We are finding it difficult to bring these people down to a satisfactory working basis, but we will succeed in doing so shortly. The Prime Minister has just called and he promises to use all his influence in this direction. . . . The entire situation is critical . . ."[1]

Secretary Lansing to Ambassador Page in Rome: "Your Nos. 1205 and 1206 regarding the Italian situation[2] have had the President's earnest consideration. Your reports go to Colonel House for use in the conference of co-belligerents.

"The heart of the American nation is in keen sympathy with the Italian people. Our people have confidence in their Italian brethren. We realize that the Italians possess in a remarkable degree the strength to achieve, the will to dare, and the patient skill to aid their strength and will to win. Our representatives in the present conference are keenly alive to Italy's needs and are inspired with the determination to leave no effort unessayed whereby America may advance our common cause against the common enemy of free mankind."[3]

General Pershing to Secretary Baker: ". . . . Viewed at its best, the situation is, of course, grave, and (this) should be fully realized. America must stand firmly behind the Allies, as any sign of weakness may cause the collapse of Allied resistance. The contingency must also be faced of Great

---

[1]From Mrs. Wilson's handwritten transcription of House's code telegram. Published in part in *Intimate Papers*, Vol. III, pp. 239–240.

[2]Sent November 10th, stressing the immediate need of "a strong propaganda . . . to counteract effect of the propaganda urging immediate peace proposals," and the earnest hope of the Italian government that America would declare war on Austria and send troops to Italy. *Foreign Relations*, 1917, Supp. 2, Vol. I, pp. 301–302.

[3]*Ibid.*, pp. 305–306.

IMMEDIATE BUSINESS.

Further investigate possibility of getting food
    to Poland (on behalf of the Jewish Relief
    Committee)

Find means of forcing Britain et al to get wheat
    from Australia until the Argentine crops
    are ready and then get~~ting~~ it from Argentina,
    reserving our supply till the last (See mem.
    from Hoover as to our wheat supply).

To House: Take the whip hand. We not only accede
    to the plan for a unified conduct of the war
    but insist upon it. It is not practicable
    for us to be represented in the same way as
    the other governments on the civil side, but
    we will be on the military.

          Bring into the conference as of the ut-
    most importance, the food source question, as
    ~~to~~ to which Taylor is fully informed, and
    insist upon shipping being sent to Australia
    and afterwards to Argentine.

          The position I have taken with regard
    to Norway and Sweden in message sent by T.
    D. Jones to McCormick.

QUERY.

Is the Mediterranean impracticable?

"TAKE THE WHIP HAND!"

Intimate memorandum written by the President on his own type-writer, probably November 15, 1917. It formulates his instructions regarding the unified conduct of the war.

Britain and ourselves being left to carry on the war without material aid from any other power. I have pointed out the dark side of the picture, but in war we must prepare to meet the worst. . . .

" . . . . It is . . . urged that—

"1. The most intense energy should be put into developing America's fighting forces for active service during the coming summer. Winning the war is vital to our future, and if humanly possible it ought to be done in 1918. There is no telling what might happen if we defer our utmost exertion until 1919.

"2. All available sources of supply of artillery and ammunition should be investigated and developed, having in mind Japan's resources in this regard. . . .

"3. Finally, every possible ton of shipping should be secured . . . with the least delay for use in carrying our armies to France. . . ."[1]

To Secretary McAdoo:

"I appreciate the importance of the report which Doctor Rupert Blue, Surgeon General of the Public Health Service, has made concerning the matter of health and sanitary conditions in the war industries, and also of the recommendations which he makes, but we must be careful not to get wires crossed here, as they have been in many other matters. I am going to refer your letter and the report to the Chairman of the Council of National Defense, which I know has had these very matters in mind

---

[1] Pershing, *My Experiences in the World War*, Vol. I, pp. 237-238.

and without whose cooperation I think it would be a mistake to call such a conference as you suggest. I expect prompt attention to this matter, because I know the interest of the Council in it."[1]

To King Albert of Belgium,[2] a telegram:

"I take pleasure in extending to Your Majesty greetings of friendship and good will on this your fete day.

"For the people of the United States, I take this occasion to renew expressions of deep sympathy for the sufferings which Belgium has endured under the willful, cruel, and barbaric force of a disappointed Prussian autocracy.

"The people of the United States were never more in earnest than in their determination to prosecute to a successful conclusion this war against that power and to secure for the future, obedience to the laws of nations and respect for the rights of humanity."

Friday, November 16th.

In the morning the President and Mrs. Wilson went to the funeral of John W. Foster, Secretary Lansing's father-in-law, and himself Secretary of State under President Harrison. At two o'clock the President received a delegation of directors of the war-savings campaign and made a short address: ". . . if this country can learn something about saving out of the war, it will be worth . . . the literal cost of it in money and resources. I suppose we have several times over wasted more than we are now about to spend . . ."[3] Appointments after the cabinet meeting: Representative Carlin of Virginia; Herbert Adams.

---

[1]On the same day the President sent McAdoo's letter to Secretary Baker, saying: ". . . . I would be very much obliged if you would suggest to me the best methods of cooperation.

"Probably, since we already have an organized Public Health Service, it would be wise to employ it in the active investigation and correction of sanitary conditions, but I want to draw the various counsellings in this matter and actions in it together."

[2]Most of the many messages to rulers of Europe are here omitted, since they are formal and lack interest.

[3]*Official Bulletin,* November 17, 1917.

Roland S. Morris, new ambassador to Japan, reported to Secretary Lansing his arrival in Tokyo; and discussed the attitude of the Japanese press and public toward the Lansing-Ishii agreement: "... I have observed two tendencies in the comments of those Japanese with whom I have had the privilege of talking during the past week: One is to interpret very broadly the definition of 'special interests,' and if possible to disconnect it from any geographical considerations. The second is to express a rather exaggerated delight at what is termed in official Government circles 'Viscount Ishii's great diplomatic victory'. . . ."[1]

Colonel House wrote in his diary of a talk with Reading, Lloyd George and Wiseman: ". . . I find it will be useless to try to get either the French or British to designate [peace] terms. Great Britain cannot meet the new Russian terms of 'no indemnities and no aggression' and neither can France. Great Britain at once would come in sharp conflict with her colonies and they might cease fighting, and France would have to relinquish her dream of Alsace and Lorraine. . . ."[2]

To Colonel House, a telegram, written on the President's own typewriter:

"Please take the position that we not only accede to the plan for a single war council but insist on it, but think it does not go far enough. We can no more take part in the war successfully without such a council than we can lend money without the board Crosby went over to join. The war council will, I assume, eventually take the place of such conferences as you went over to take part in and I hope that you will consider remaining to take part in at any rate the first deliberations and formulations of plans. Baker and I are agreed that Bliss should be our military member. I am happy the conference is to be postponed until the recalcitrant parliaments have settled to their senses. Please insist in the conference on the imperative

---

[1] *Foreign Relations*, 1917, pp. 271–272.
[2] *Intimate Papers*, Vol. III, p. 233.

necessity of getting wheat first from Australia then from the Argentine and last from us. Taylor has the facts and they are of the gravest significance. McCormick will show you despatch from Jones.[1] I felt obliged on principle to take the position therein stated. It is based not only on principle but on the facts and advice contained in the confidential memorandum brought over by Reading and is all the more dictated by good sense in view of the present critical situation."

To the Northwest Loyalty Meetings at St. Paul, a telegram:

". . . . It is to the Great Northwest that the Nation looks, as once before in critical days, for that steadiness of purpose and firmness of determination which shall see this struggle through to a decision that shall make the masters of Germany rue the day they unmasked their purpose and challenged our Republic."[2]

To his secretary, Tumulty, who called attention to a letter from Mrs. Norman de R. Whitehouse, in regard to the alleged ill treatment of the suffragists detained in the workhouse:

"I think our present reply to Mrs. Whitehouse ought to be to the effect that no real harshness of method is being used, these ladies submitting to the artificial feeding without resistance; that the conditions under which they are made to work are being thoroughly investigated for the second or third time, and that any abuses that may exist will certainly be corrected but that none has as yet been disclosed, there being an extraordinary amount of lying about the thing; and that these ladies cannot in any sense be regarded as political prisoners. We have no political prisoners and could have none under the law. They offended against an ordinance of the District and are undergoing the punishment appropriate in the circumstances."

[1] This vol., pp. 356–357.
[2] For entire message, see *Public Papers*, Vol. V, p. 127.

Saturday, November 17th.

There were no official appointments during the day. Golf in the morning; a long drive in the afternoon.

Minister Vopicka telegraphed from Rumania, quoting a note which the British and French ministers were, at the request of the King of Rumania, sending to their governments, and which he himself had been requested to telegraph to the United States government—an inquiry as to the attitude of these Powers toward Rumania, in case of a separate peace between Russia and the Central Powers, or of a "general *débandade*" on the Russian front. ". . . . If, notwithstanding the defection of Russia and the failure of Italy, France and Great Britain confirmed their engagements regarding Roumania and declared their firm intention of insuring their execution on the final victory, the King would try with a portion of his troops to force a passage through Russia. . . ."[1]

Sunday, November 18th.

President and Mrs. Wilson attended a service at All Saints Church in the morning. Dr. E. P. Davis of Philadelphia, a classmate of the President, and Mr. and Mrs. Thomas D. Jones, were luncheon guests.

Colonel House received the President's telegram of the 16th, and in the evening gave out the following statement:

"Colonel House . . . has received a cable from the President stating emphatically that the Government of the United States considers that unity of plan and control between all the Allies and the United States is essential in order to achieve a just and permanent peace. The President emphasizes the fact that this unity must be accomplished if the great resources of the United States are to be used to the best advantage, and he requests Colonel House to confer with the heads of the Allied Governments with a view of achieving the closest possible cooperation.

"President Wilson has asked Colonel House to attend the first meeting of the Supreme War Council with General Bliss, Chief of Staff of the United States Army, as the

[1] *Foreign Relations*, 1917, Supp. 2, Vol. I, p. 309. The copy in the Wilson files is marked, "For the President." See this volume, p. 376, for reply.

military adviser. It is hoped that the meeting will take place in Paris before the end of this month."[1]

To his secretary, Tumulty, enclosing a telegram from the president of the Florida Federation of Women's Clubs, asking whether the rendering of music from German composers was considered unpatriotic:

"Please reply yourself to this and say that I do not regard the use of any good music as unpatriotic."

Monday, November 19th.

Sometime during the morning Secretary Tumulty sent the President a London dispatch clipped from a newspaper—House's statement of the 18th. With the clipping was a note: "The newspaper men are asking about the attached and are anxious to get a copy of the message. What can I tell them?" The President immediately returned a memorandum: "Please tell the men that this must certainly have been built up merely upon my general attitude as known to everybody, and please beg that they will discount it and make no comment upon it. If they did, I would have to be constantly commenting upon similar reports." Tumulty had this read to the correspondents word for word; and that afternoon the International News Service reported that the President, through Tumulty, had denied sending a telegram to Colonel House—a denial which plunged House into trouble the next day. Afternoon appointments: Secretary Redfield; members of the Aircraft Board; members of the Japanese Financial Commission.

The British House of Commons debated the Rapallo agreement and Lloyd George's demand for greater unity of control—a bitter attack upon the Prime Minister—and Lloyd George defended himself.[2] The London *Times* commented editorially: "The latest, and incomparably the most important, development of the Allied Council scheme is the statement issued last night by Colonel House on behalf of President Wilson. It is as guarded in tone as it is comprehensive in scope. Manifestly it is not intended to serve any controversy over detail in this country. But it

---

[1]*Foreign Relations*, 1917, Supp. 2, Vol. I, pp. 339–340.

[2]See *War Memoirs of David Lloyd George*, Vol. IV, pp. 559 *et seq.*, for description of the debate.

does emphasize unmistakably the central principle for which Mr. Lloyd George is standing at this moment—that 'unity of plan and control' which received partial recognition at Rapallo. . . ."[1]

To Colonel House, who had telegraphed on the 18th: "McCormick and Lord Robert Cecil appreciate how delicate the situation is and nothing is contemplated which will bring about a crisis in Norway and Denmark. They believe Nansen and the Norwegian Secretary of State for Foreign Affairs are pro-German and do not represent the sentiment of either the Government or the people. McCormick believes if you will allow him to go ahead as planned a speedy agreement can be secured. He proposes not to press the matter beyond the safety line. . . ." The President's telegram was written out on his own typewriter and coded, as usual, with the help of Mrs. Wilson:

"Am distressed to differ with McCormick but inasmuch as we are fighting a war of principle I do not feel that I can consent to demand of Norway what we would not in similar circumstances allow any government to demand of us, namely the cessation of ex[p]orts of her own products to any place she can send them. I am convinced that our only legitimate position is that we will not supply the deficiencies which she thus creates for herself if the exports are to our enemies."[2]

Tuesday, November 20th.

Aside from the regular cabinet meeting at 2:30, there were only two official appointments during the day: with Dr. Nansen, and with Thomas D. Jones. Both concerned the negotiations with Norway.

---

[1] Report of the House Commission, *Foreign Relations*, 1917, Supp. 2, Vol. I, p. 340. House commented: ". . . . I took care to have the true scope of my statement explained to Geoffrey Dawson, the editor of the *Times.* . . ." *Ibid.*

[2] From the President's original copy, written on his own typewriter.

The next day Thomas D. Jones telegraphed McCormick: "The President showed me his message to you through House of the 19th. I pointed out to him that it would probably convey to you the meaning that he is opposed to any restriction or limitation of exports by Northern neutrals to Germany of their own products as distinguished from products received from us. He directs me to cable you that this was not his meaning; that by cessation of exports he meant complete cessation and not limitation." *Foreign Relations*, 1917, Supp. 2, Vol. II, pp. 986–987.

Daniel Willard's appointment to succeed Frank A. Scott as chairman of the War Industries Board was made public.

The London *Daily Mail* announced, in the morning, that President Wilson had denied telegraphing Colonel House that the United States considered a united plan and control essential. At noon Bonar Law's secretary called upon House to ask what the Chancellor might say in the House of Commons that afternoon, when a question was to be put. House explained; and when the question came up in the House, Bonar Law replied: "President Wilson has directed Colonel House to take part not only in the Inter-Allied Conference, but also in the Supreme War Council, and General Bliss is to be his special military adviser. . . . We had the information quite officially."[1]

Colonel House telegraphed the President, in the morning: "A very difficult and dangerous situation has been rife here since the Prime Minister made his Paris speech announcing the formation of a Supreme War Council. . . . The announcement along with his implied criticism of the military authorities precipitated a political crisis that threatened to overturn his Ministry.

"In the very critical condition of affairs elsewhere in the Allied States this might have proved the gravest disaster of the war. The Prime Minister was constantly urging me to say something to help the situation. This I refused to do until I had heard from you. The statement I gave out purposely refrained from approving the Prime Minister's plan, but merely stated the necessity for military unity and your instructions for Bliss and me to attend its first meeting following the Paris Interallied Conference.

"The situation had become completely composed, but Tumulty's denial has started everything afresh, and the Government is to be questioned in the House of Commons this afternoon.

"I am refraining from and am asking the Press to refrain from any further statements. If this is done the incident will be closed."[2]

The American Mission met at 10 Downing Street with the

---

[1] Report of the House Commission, *Foreign Relations*, 1917, Supp. 2, Vol. I, pp. 340–341.

[2] *Intimate Papers*, Vol. III, pp. 224–225.

British War Cabinet and the heads of departments. House was not present, being represented by Admiral W. S. Benson.[1]

Secretary Lansing sent the President a memorandum prepared by Solicitor Woolsey of the State Department, on our grounds of complaint against Austria, himself commenting: ". . . . We have not a very strong case against Austria so far as hostile acts are concerned. It seems to me that it comes down very largely to a matter of national safety in having at large and free to act a very considerable body of Austrian subjects in this country."

The press of this country was filled with reports and rumors about Russia: the Bolsheviki were about to withdraw from the war; no supplies would go from this country to Russia until the situation cleared up; General Kaledine, of the Cossacks, was "the man of the hour."[2]

British forces under the command of General Sir Julian Byng launched an attack on a 32-mile front, penetrating the Hindenburg line to a depth of five miles. Wholly unexpected, this sudden movement, led as it was by large numbers of British tanks, was one of the most sensational and dramatic episodes of the year's fighting.[3] After the initial onrush, however, the gains could not be maintained, and the whole operation proved a costly one for the British.

To Breckinridge Long, who had sent the President a memorandum suggesting the formation of an advisory committee of newspaper men to deal with the censorship and allied subjects. "The suggestion is for a constructive purpose, and is not a criticism of anyone." The President's reply is marked "Personal":

"You need not have hesitated to send me the memorandum . . . It concerns a matter which has caused me a

---

[1]For the *procès-verbal* of the meeting, see Report of the House Commission. *Foreign Relations*, 1917, Supp. 2, Vol. I, pp. 366–384.

[2]New York *Times*, November 21, 1917.

[3]Philip Gibbs, in *Current History*, January, 1918, pp. 31–32. Hindenburg writes: ". . . . The English attack at Cambrai for the first time revealed the possibilities of a great surprise attack with tanks. . . . The physical effects . . . were far less destructive than the moral effect . . ." *Out of My Life*, p. 291.

great deal of thought and which I recognize as of capital importance.

"Unfortunately, personally, I believe the proper co-operation of the newspapers to be impossible because of the small but powerful lawless elements among them who observe no rules, regard no understandings as binding, and act always as they please.

"The Committee on Public Information, of which Mr. George Creel is Chairman, was created by me for the very purposes you outline, and if it had met with the cooperation of the newspaper men instead of their petty jealousy, it would have answered its purpose at once. Moreover, it has been very difficult to get one or two of the executive departments, notably the Department of State, to act through Mr. Creel's committee in the matter of publicity, and the embarrassments of lack of coordination and single management have been very serious indeed.

"Such headings and colorings of the news as you quote from the Washington Post apparently nobody can control. It would be easy every day to pick out from the Washington Post glaring breaches of patriotic procedure, but I think in the long run they take care of themselves.

"Your memorandum will cause me to review the whole situation in my own thoughts and to see whether anything additional can be accomplished."[1]

---

[1]The President sent Long's letter with his own answer on to Creel, who replied on the 28th: ".... I have put the question of an advisory committee up to every prominent newspaper man in the country, not because I thought it was possible, but because I wanted *them* to admit the impossibility. The press is the only profession in the world without an organization of any kind. There is no one body to speak for it, to make bargains for it, or to enforce discipline of any kind. It is torn to pieces by every rivalry —political and commercial. An advisory committee with any authority would have to be made up of the editors of *every metropolitan daily*, and when these were gathered together, the only certainty as to their actions would be with regard to lack of unity....

"As a matter of fact, I have been surprised and gratified at the results I have been able to achieve. The volunteer censorship is being observed with few violations. Our matter goes into the papers by thousands of columns, and aside from the personal attacks of a few New York papers, like the World, feeling has grown very friendly. It is the best we can do, and it's really very good...."

To Herbert Hoover, who had written of the temperance agitation for further restricting the manufacture and sale of alcoholic beverages:

"Thank you for your memorandum . . .

"I am fully in sympathy with your suggestion that the percentage of alcohol in beer should be reduced to three per cent., and I think probably it would be wise to reduce the amount of grains used by each brewer, but I am inclined to think that fifty per cent. reduction is too severe, at any rate for a beginning, because I take it for granted that such a reduction would by reducing the supply greatly increase the price of beer and so be very unfair to the classes who are using it and who can use it with very little detriment when the percentage of alcohol is made so small.

"This other question arises in my mind: Is the thirty per cent. of the grain value really being saved for cattle feed systematically and universally, and if not, are there not some regulations by which we should make sure that the full saving was effected and made available in the right way?"

Wednesday, November 21st.

The President and Mrs. Wilson went to the funeral of Warren Young, long a member of the Executive Office staff. Afternoon appointments: Mrs. George B. Bass; George Creel. In the late evening the President and Mrs. Wilson went to a Charity Ball for the benefit of the Eye, Ear and Throat Hospital.

Colonel House wrote the President: "The announcement which we made on Sunday and which brought forth Tumulty's denial was not written by me and was badly put out from here. However, I approved it hurriedly. It was written as a paraphrase of your message and was given out in order to meet Lloyd George's insistent demand. Only the last paragraph should have been used as that would have told the story. I shall not let it happen again.

"I had every newspaper and every Government official

in London on my back yesterday because of it, and it prevented me from attending the conference at 10 Downing Street. However, the incident is now happily closed.

"Lloyd George and Reading dined with us last night, and I had a satisfactory conference with the Prime Minister. It is the first time I have been able to pin him down to something concrete. I am afraid to write details but I have careful memoranda[1] to go over with you when I return. . . .

"I had George delineate pretty carefully last night England's war aims, and he and I and Balfour sit again this afternoon to discuss the same situation.[2] It will be impossible for me to go into a discussion of this in a letter, for there are certain phases of it explanatory of England's position which would not be safe to write. . . ."

Reports from Palestine indicated that the British troops were within five miles of Jerusalem and rapidly closing in.

Thursday, November 22nd.

From 2:30 until four o'clock in the afternoon the President conferred with executives of the railroad brotherhoods whom he himself had summoned. Afterward the men put out a statement giving their case for higher wages, but saying also that in a national emergency they would be "more than willing to discuss and consider any solution of the difficulty which presented itself, doing so in the spirit of patriotic cooperation." The President likewise authorized a statement: "In addition to the statement given out by the heads of the railway brotherhoods, the President authorized the representatives of the press to say that he had got from the interview exactly the impression con-

---

[1]House wrote in his diary: ". . . . I pinned George down to British war aims. What Great Britain desires are the African colonies, both East and West; an independent Arabia, under the suzerainty of Great Britain; Palestine to be given to the Zionists under British or, if desired by us, under American control; an independent Armenia and the internationalization of the Straits. . . ." *Intimate Papers*, Vol. III, p. 235.

[2]For diary account, see *Intimate Papers*, Vol. III, pp. 236–237.

". . . . We . . . went into the question of war aims. Maps were brought and Mr. Balfour started in with his ideas of territorial division. . . . I thought what we agreed upon to-day might be utterly impossible to-morrow, and it seemed worse than useless to discuss territorial aims at this time. . . .

"What I thought was necessary and pertinent at this time was the announcement of general war aims and the formation of an international association for the prevention of future wars."

veyed by the statement of the heads of the brotherhoods, namely, that the men whom they represented were not inclined to contend for anything which they did not deem necessary to their own maintenance and the maintenance of their families, and that they would be willing in case any critical situation of controversy should arise to consider any proposed solution in a spirit of accommodation and of patriotic purpose."[1]

The members of the House Mission crossed the channel and went directly to Paris.

Ambassador Francis telegraphed Trotsky's proposal for an armistice on all fronts and the opening of peace negotiations. Later the same day he reported that the Allied representatives in Petrograd had met that afternoon and "agreement was unanimous and emphatic that no notice should be taken of note."[2]

To Jacob H. Schiff:

"I understand that a campaign for funds for Jewish War Relief as well as for Jewish welfare work among American soldiers and sailors is shortly to be initiated in New York, under your leadership.

"From statements which I have previously made, you know how sincere my belief is that the American public, irrespective of race or creed, should respond liberally to the call for help from stricken Europe, and I feel confident that the needs of the Jewish people in the war zones will find a ready response from their co-religionists in this country.

"No less important, in my opinion, is the work of the Jewish Welfare Board. . . . The spirit with which our soldiers leave America, and their efficiency on the battle fronts of Europe, will be vitally affected by the character of the environment of our military training camps, and by the moral stimulus which they have received while there. . . ."

[1] New York *Times*, November 23, 1917.
[2] *Foreign Relations*, 1918, *Russia*, Vol. I, pp. 244–246.

To Douglas Fairbanks:

"George Creel was kind enough to hand me yesterday a copy of your 'Laugh and Live' which you were thoughtful enough to send me, and I want to send you this line of sincere appreciation. If laughter can keep me alive, I am apt to live, because I fortunately come of a race that had laughter implanted in them. . . ."

To his secretary, Tumulty, who had called attention to a letter from Gutzon Borglum alleging that the program of the aeronautic board was invented by automobile production interests:

"Gutzon Borglum is a sincere fellow and this letter disturbs me. Is there not somebody you can consult about how to reply to it? Perhaps you might have a few words with Baker about it."

Friday, November 23rd.

In the early afternoon the President received Senator Pomerene of Ohio; and after the cabinet meeting, Mr. Goltra. Miss Marjorie Brown of Atlanta arrived for a visit, and in the late afternoon the President joined Mrs. Wilson and their guest at the National Theater, for a concert by the Russian Orchestra. Thomas D. Jones and Paul Fuller of the Bureau of War Trade Intelligence called before dinner.

Colonel House wrote the President: "I foresee trouble in the workings of the Supreme War Council. There is a tremendous opposition in England to Lloyd George's appointment of General Wilson. . . .

"Some of the French want a 'Generalissimo' but they want him to be a Frenchman. This, too, would meet with so much opposition in England that it is not to be thought of. Any government that proposed it would be overthrown.

"I have had long conferences with Bliss and Pershing on the subject and I think they see the danger as I do. I am trying to suggest something else which will give unity of control by uniting all involved rather than creating dissension.

"I have just had a conference alone with Clemenceau. Without my saying a word upon the subject he practically repeated the opinion that I have expressed to you above concerning the Supreme War Council. . . .

"He has nothing in mind and says that he dares not formulate a plan because it might be looked upon with suspicion. He wants us to take the initiative and he promises that we can count upon him to back to a finish any reasonable suggestion that we make. . . ."[1]

Secretary Baker wrote the President of having seen at one of the New York piers a few days before, "Christmas on a larger scale than I had ever seen it"—300,000 wooden boxes containing Christmas gifts for American soldiers in France. ". . . . Each box was being opened, its contents examined, matches and perishables taken out . . . One box contained dressed birds; many of them contained fruit . . . Many packages were in frail boxes, and for these new and stronger boxes were being made. . . ."

Secretary Baker sent over a telegram from General Judson, military attaché at Petrograd, who spoke of the possibility that Russia might go out of the war and suggested that there ought to be an effort "to state practical terms [of] peace which neither side could refuse without appearance of unfairness to simple but honest minds."

To Secretary McAdoo:

". . . . I have your letter of yesterday about the request of an additional credit on the part of the Italian Government of $40,000,000 and the practice which the Italian Government has been indulging in of buying in this country otherwise than through the Purchasing Commission. Your letter to the Italian Ambassador was quite justified, and I hope that you will see the imperative necessity of keeping very strictly to the agreements upon which our loans are based in regard to the method of purchase."

Saturday, November 24th.

The President, Mrs. Wilson and Dr. Axson spent the greater part of the morning on the golf course. In the early afternoon they went to Fort Myer to watch the drill.

---

[1]Published in part in *Intimate Papers*, Vol. III, pp. 251–253.

Colonel House telegraphed, in reply to Lansing's request for advice on the Russian situation: ". . . . In Great Britain the Russian situation is considered at the moment hopeless. There is no responsible government within sight. I would advise making no more advances at present or permitting any further contracts for purchases. . . ." Later in the day he telegraphed again saying that Clemenceau endorsed his opinion.[1]

Ambassador Francis telegraphed extracts from an address in which Trotsky paid his respects to Russia's former allies and associates, the hated capitalistic Powers, in no uncertain terms, saying among other things: "The United States intervened in war after three years had elapsed under the influence of sober calculation of American stock exchange. . . ."[2]

The American Federation of Labor, in convention at Buffalo, unanimously adopted a resolution expressing appreciation of the President's address, and pledging "undivided support in carrying the war to a successful conclusion, in supporting him in his efforts to apply the principles of democracy to the solution of the problems which arise in industry, and in conducting the war so that it shall be a war of the people, continued in defense of the fundamental institutions for human liberty . . ."[3]

To J. R. Kenley, president of the Atlantic Coast Line Railroad, a telegram:

"I am much gratified to learn of the patriotic disposition of both sides to the dispute between the Atlantic Coast Line Railway and its clerks, as shown by their near approach to a settlement. May I not urge, in the interest of the country at this war time, and as a further means of strengthening the confidence of the wage earners of the United States in the good will of employers, that you yield

---

[1] *Foreign Relations*, 1918, *Russia*, Vol. III, p. 28.

[2] *Ibid.*, Vol. I, p. 246.

[3] *Report of the Proceedings of the 37th Annual Convention of the American Federation of Labor*, p. 462. When Gompers forwarded a copy to the President, he was deeply appreciative: ". . . . I hope that you will have some early opportunity of conveying to the members of that convention the very deep gratification which those resolutions have given me. They have done not a little to keep my heart strong."

the difference now remaining between you and your organized clerks by immediately reinstating all who wish to return to their former places in your service."

Sunday, November 25th.

President and Mrs. Wilson and Dr. Axson went to the Central Presbyterian Church in the morning; and the President spent the afternoon in his study.

> Colonel House telegraphed: ". . . . I am refusing to be drawn into any of their [the Allies'] controversies, particularly those concerning war aims of a territorial nature. We must, I think, hold to the broad principles you have laid down and not get mixed in the small and selfish ones."[1]
>
> Certain of the secret treaties recently published in Russia were reported in the New York *Times*. The same issue carried a scathing editorial on this "act of dishonor," but did not discuss the treaties themselves!
>
> Elections for the Constituent Assembly—the "authority to which all Russia has been looking since revolution began"—finally opened.[2]

Monday, November 26th.

The President and Mrs. Wilson attended exercises at Fort Myer in the afternoon, inspecting the successful candidates at the Officers Training Camp. Late-afternoon appointments: Walter E. Hope of the Fuel Administration; Secretary Daniels.

Tuesday, November 27th.

The Belgian minister, with General Le Clerque, called in the early afternoon. Appointments after the cabinet meeting: W. E. Gonzales, minister to Cuba, probably in regard to the Cuban sugar situation; H. A. Garfield.

> Secretary Lansing sent a circular telegram to American diplomatic representatives in the countries at war with Germany, asking for names of men "from whom will probably be selected the representatives of the Govern-

---

[1]Published in *Foreign Relations*, 1917, Supp. 2, Vol. I, pp. 317–318.
[2]*Ibid.*, 1918, *Russia*, Vol. I, p. 267.

ment at the conference which will negotiate terms of peace" with a biographical sketch of each man, his political affiliations, his views on international questions and other facts showing his probable attitude toward subjects which might arise at the conference, or influence his course. ". . . . You will understand that this information is desired for distant future and has nothing whatever to do with present situation."[1]

To Secretary Lansing, who had sent over a draft of a telegram to Minister Vopicka in Rumania, in reply to his of the 17th[2]— "a clear-cut statement of our determination to support Rumania after the war to the best of our ability." The President's reply was marked "Personal and Confidential":

"I have taken the liberty of changing a couple of words in the enclosed telegram, but entirely approve it."[3]

To Herbert Hoover, who had recommended, as one of the guiding principles of the Food Administration, "that any profit in excess of the normal pre-war average profit of that business and place where free, competitive conditions existed is deemed to be unjust, unreasonable, unfair profit"; and suggested that the President sign "an instruction" to that effect:

". . . I am acting, and acting willingly, upon your judgment, because I cannot pretend to the knowledge of the case which you have. I should have assumed that possibly it would be fair to allow a somewhat increased margin above the pre-war margin, because these dealers, like all the rest of us, have to adjust themselves to an enhanced cost of living so far as their own personal support is concerned, but I have no doubt you have taken that into consideration along with the other matters affecting your judgment."

To Harry Steele Morrison, whom the President had helped when he was in trouble, and who was now doing good work

---

[1] *Foreign Relations*, 1917, Supp. 2, Vol. I, p. 321.

[2] See this volume, p. 363.

[3] For the message as sent see *Foreign Relations*, 1917, Supp. 2, Vol. I, p. 325.

under J. Lionberger Davis, in the office of the Alien Property Custodian:[1]

"Your letter . . . shows that you are standing steadfast in your new determination and I want to express my warm gratification and wish for you a truly happy Thanksgiving. I am sure it will be a happy one in view of the new light that has come to you."

To the Reverend Doctor John Fox:

". . . I take pleasure in writing to say that the setting apart of a universal Bible Week and Bible Sunday and the designation of Sunday, December ninth, as the day upon which the work shall receive its emphasis meet with my very cordial approval. I hope that it will be possible for you to work the plan out and to carry it to a very successful consummation, for I have the deepest sympathy with the work which it will represent."

To M. Clemmons:

"May I not have the pleasure, in replying to your letter of the twenty-fifth, of calling your attention to the following passages:

"'We are such stuff as dreams are made on . . .'
—The Tempest
(Act 4; Scene 1; 154th line)
"'What stuff wilt have a kirtle of?'
—Henry IV
(Part 2; Act 2; Scene 4)
"'Do not squander time; for that is the stuff which life is made of.'
—Franklin
(Way to Wealth; 1st paragraph)

"And may I not add that that rule that a sentence shall not end with a preposition is a mere piece of rhetorical affectation?"

[1] J. Lionberger Davis to the author. Morrison later committed suicide.

To Major Wallace Winchell:

"I am very much interested to hear of the campaign the Salvation Army has undertaken for money to sustain its activities, and want to take the opportunity to express my admiration for the work that it has done and my sincere hope that it may be fully sustained."

Telegram to J. R. Kenley, president of the Atlantic Coast Line Railroad, who had replied to the President's wire of the 24th that while he would yield if the President insisted, still he would like a chance to present the matter in person before making the decision. The President's telegram was sent upon the advice of Louis F. Post, Assistant Secretary of Labor, to whom the correspondence had been referred:

"Replying to your telegram . . . I appreciate the patriotic spirit of it, all the more because I understand just the embarrassments which would be involved in complying with the request I made of you by telegram on the twenty-fourth? It would give me a great deal of pleasure to see you but I venture to suggest that that is not necessary because my request was based rather upon national considerations than upon the special circumstances connected with the present difference between the Atlantic Coast Line and its employees. I beg you to believe that I made the request, and now renew it, only because of my familiarity with the general labor situation in the country and my conviction that a compliance with my request by the Atlantic Coast Line will distinctly contribute to the conditions upon which we must depend for the full energy and continued quiet of the country. May I not again express my warm appreciation of your attitude?"

Wednesday, November 28th.

The President spent the morning in his study. Afternoon appointments: Senators Martin and Swanson of Virginia; Cyrus E. White; Senator Pomerene of Ohio; Thomas D. Jones.

The President issued two proclamations—one prohibiting certain imports except under license, the other further restricting exports.[1]

Colonel House telegraphed: "There have been cabled over and published here statements made by American papers to the effect that Russia should be treated as an enemy. It is exceedingly important that such criticisms should be suppressed. It will throw Russia into the lap of Germany if the Allies and ourselves express such views at this time."[2]

A letter from Lord Lansdowne to the London *Daily Telegraph*[3] declared that the war had lasted too long, and suggested that the British state certain principles (no annihilation of Germany; an "international pact . . . for the settlement of international disputes," etc.) in order to forward the cause of an honorable peace. Ambassador Page reported on the 30th that public opinion in government circles was "surprised and shocked," though "pacifists and semi-pacifists and a war-weary minority" and a few papers "like the London *Daily News* which is almost Socialist and the *Manchester Guardian*" approved it.[4]

To Secretary Lansing, in regard to a telegram of the 23rd from the American ambassador in London in which he said: "I learn from an authoritative source that certain of the Prime Minister's political advisers are anxious that he should persuade Turkey to conclude a separate peace and think that the recent military successes in Palestine make the present moment propitious for an attempt to buy offhand Turks. I understand that there is considerable opposition in naval and military circles to this idea for the following reasons: First, they consider that the Turkish Government are far too deeply in the hands of Germany to be able to make a separate peace. Secondly, the Palestine operations have not yet reached their fullest develop-

---

[1] *Foreign Relations*, 1917, Supp. 2, Vol. II, pp. 989–992.

[2] *Ibid.*, 1918, *Russia*, Vol. I, p. 271.

[3] It appeared in the issue of November 29, 1917. Dickinson, *Documents and Statements Relating to Peace Proposals and War Aims*, pp. 84–89.

[4] *Foreign Relations*, 1917, Supp. 2, Vol. I, pp. 327–328. H. A. Garfield wrote to the President on the 30th: "Lord Lansdowne's letter published in the Washington Post of this morning is the most noteworthy and noblest utterance that has come out of England. It seems to me to run with your purpose and I can well believe brings you both encouragement and relief. Lloyd George and, one might well add, Roosevelt are dangerous leaders in the present emergency."

ment. Thirdly, they believe that other powers such as France, Italy, and Greece have ideas of their own as to future of Asiatic Turkey which might be difficult to put into effect if the Turks made peace now and the consent of these powers to such a peace might be difficult to obtain. . . ."[1] The President's letter was written on his own typewriter:

"I wish that you would be kind enough to intimate to Page (if, as I take for granted, it is your own opinion as well as mine) that we regard this as chimerical and of questionable advantage, even if it could be accomplished.

"Arrangements must be made at the conference which closes the war with regard to Constantinople which could hardly be made if Turkey were first made peace with. Indeed, I suppose that peace could be made only on terms which would preclude any radical changes of control over Constantinople and the straits.

"The only advantage to be gained would be to prevent the bargains of the Allies with regard to Asia Minor from being carried out."[2]

To Secretary Lansing, to other cabinet members, and to Hoover and Garfield:

"I would be very much obliged to you if I might have a memorandum from you as to any legislation which you think it imperative should be considered at this session of Congress.

"I assume that the Congress will prefer to confine itself entirely to matters directly connected with the prosecution of the war, and in my judgment that is the policy which it should pursue. My request, therefore, concerns only such matters as you think should be provided for at once and cannot be postponed."[3]

[1] *Foreign Relations*, 1917, Supp. 2, Vol. I, p. 317.

[2] Sent November 30th. *Foreign Relations*, 1917, Supp. 2, Vol. I, p. 326.

[3] Replies came in promptly, and the President, in his address, discussed a number of the subjects suggested—needed authority for the extension of price fixing; water power legislation; promotion of the Webb bill permitting coöperation in export trade. See *Public Papers*, Vol. V, pp. 136–137.

Thursday, November 29th.
Thanksgiving Day.

President and Mrs. Wilson attended a Thanksgiving service at the Metropolitan Memorial Methodist Episcopal Church. The President spent the afternoon in his study; and a family party came in for Thanksgiving dinner in the evening.[1]

Ambassador Francis telegraphed Trotsky's announcement that military operations on the Russian front had been brought to a standstill, and that preliminary negotiations for peace would begin on December 2nd. "... The Council of the Commissaries of the People, as formerly, so also now, considers necessary the simultaneous conducting of the negotiations by all the Allies with a view to attaining a speedy armistice on all fronts and to secure a universal democratic peace.

"The Allied Governments and their diplomatic representatives in Russia will be good enough to reply whether they wish to take part ..."[2]

The Inter-Allied Conference held its opening session in the Salon de l'Horloge of the French Ministry for Foreign Affairs on the Quai d'Orsay—the same room in which, fourteen months later, the plenary sessions of the Peace Conference were to be held. Colonel House wrote in his diary: "... After Clemenceau had read a short address of a few lines, the French Minister for Foreign Affairs made exactly the speech we agreed upon yesterday, and the Conference immediately adjourned and the different sections went into executive session.[3] It was dramatic and unusual. ... I feel sure there has never been a conference of such importance with so little said and which was so promptly closed. ..."[4]

---

[1]The turkey was as usual a gift from South Trimble, Clerk of the House of Representatives.

[2]*Foreign Relations,* 1918, *Russia,* Vol. I, p. 253. On December 1st Lansing instructed Francis to make no reply to this, or to Trotsky's message sent on the 27th, or to the Lenin-Trotsky Manifesto of the 28th. *Ibid.,* pp. 254, 250, 252–253.

[3]For the five committees of the conference, see Report of the American Mission, *Ibid.,* 1917, Supp. 2, Vol. I, p. 349.

[4]*Intimate Papers,* Vol. III, p. 267. For various reports of this meeting, see: Report of the American Mission, *Foreign Relations,* 1917, Supp. 2, Vol. I, pp. 349 *et seq.;* Pershing, *My Experiences in the World War,* Vol. I, pp. 248–249. Minutes of the sessions of this and following meetings were kept by Sir Maurice Hankey, but they do not

Friday, November 30th.

The President spent the morning in his study. Appointments after the cabinet meeting: Representative Adamson of Georgia and Judge Sullivan; George Creel; Secretary McAdoo. Evening at Keith's.

> Colonel House telegraphed to the President: "Yesterday afternoon at a conference of the Prime Ministers and Foreign Secretaries of England, France, and Italy in which I sat, England was authorized to instruct her representatives in Switzerland to ascertain what terms Austria had to offer for a separate peace, which she has indicated a desire to make. . . .
>
> "This action was taken because of the probability of Russia soon making a separate peace."[1]
>
> In another message the same day House said: "I intend to offer this resolution for approval of the Inter-Allied Conference:
>
> "'The Allies and the United States declare that they are not waging war for the purpose of aggression or indemnity. The sacrifices they are making are in order that militarism shall not continue to cast its shadow over the world and that nations shall have the right to lead their lives in the way that seems to them best for the development of their general welfare.'
>
> "If you have any objections, please answer immediately. It is of vast importance that this be done, the British have agreed to vote for it."[2]
>
> Lansing to the American minister in Sweden: "Department informed secret treaties are being published by Bolsheviki government in Petrograd but their publication here held up by Allies' censor. Please telegraph substance of all treaties so far published."[3]

---

appear in *Foreign Relations*, because permission to publish from the other governments taking part was not forthcoming. *Ibid.*, 1917, Supp. 2, Vol. I, Preface.

[1] No copy of this message appears in the Wilson files. For the portion here quoted, see *Intimate Papers*, Vol. III, p. 277. For House's diary account of the conference, see *ibid.*, pp. 276–277. General Smuts was subsequently sent to Switzerland to meet Count Mensdorff. Negotiations lasted into the spring of 1918 but nothing conclusive was accomplished. *War Memoirs of David Lloyd George*, Vol. V, p. 19 *et seq.*

[2] *Foreign Relations*, 1917, Supp. 2, Vol. I, p. 328.

[3] *Ibid.*, p. 327.

The New York *Times*, in a dispatch of the 30th, reported that the Lansdowne letter had become the center of a raging sea of controversy in England. Bonar Law, Chancellor of the Exchequer, publicly repudiated it, declaring its publication at that time "a national misfortune."

German troops made two simultaneous counter-attacks upon the British positions before Cambrai, the British suffering a series of reverses which were later subjected to inquiry in Parliament.

To George Creel, who had sent over a letter from William English Walling to the editor of the New York *Globe and Commercial Advertiser*, accusing the *New Republic* of "high-brow Hearstism." In his covering letter to the President, Creel said that the *New Republic* attacked him, Creel, from time to time because he failed to "arouse interest of public opinion in the constructive problems of settlement." ". . . . I do not feel," remarked Creel, "that it is wise to do this, nor my province.":

"Thank you for your note . . . and the enclosed article. . . . Walling seems to me to have a great deal of sense, and certainly your attitude towards what Lippmann and others have suggested to you is entirely correct."

To Huston Thompson:
"I am sometimes startled to find how many things that I am deeply interested in my absorption in public work cuts me off from. I learned only last evening that you had actually been operated on for appendicitis and were out again. I was delighted to be told that you were looking unusually fit and well and had said that you felt greatly improved and strengthened. It was very delightful to get this news, and yet it caused me a pang to think that you had been in the hospital and I had not sent you any word of my sympathy and interest."[1]

---

[1] Thompson, in his letter of thanks, said: "This sort of kindness towards others as well as me reveals your kinship with your great predecessor, Lincoln, as much as does your patience and wisdom.

"I only wish the world knew how often you have helped the other fellow to 'carry on.' It is my earnest desire that men will some day learn of this 'sweetness and light' which you dispense so generously and yet so secretly. . . ."

To Robert Bridges, a Princeton classmate and a dear friend, who had sent the President advance sheets of an article to appear in the January number of *Scribner's Magazine*, called "The American College and The Great War." He suggested also that Charles Talcott, another classmate, would be happy to have some war work in Washington; and he added: ". . . . I am glad to hear from those who have seen you that your health and energy and poise were never better. . . .":

"Thank you for the article by Lincoln Kelly. I shall read it with the greatest interest because, although, as you say, the days of college work now seem a long way behind me, I haven't lost any of my interest or any of my consciousness of the vital way in which the college affects the life of the country.

"It was a great pleasure to hear from you, and you may be sure that I will keep Talcott in mind. Indeed, I have thought of him a number of times in the same connection. The trouble is that, to the great credit of the country be it said, the material is abundant: men of all sorts and capacities have volunteered and I have not been able to guide the choices in most cases but have been obliged to leave that to those to whom I have deputed sections of the great work.

"Please let me know if you are ever in Washington. It would be a great delight to see you."

To J. R. Kenley, president of the Atlantic Coast Line Railroad, who replied to the President's message of the 27th that he was directing that the striking clerks who wished to return be reëmployed as rapidly as practicable:

"I am sure I need not tell you how sincerely I appreciated your telegram . . . The spirit in which you have acted gives me the greatest reassurance and makes me feel how sincerely the forces of the country are uniting for common action.

"You may be sure that I would not have asked what

I did if I had not known the necessity for it in view of the labor situation throughout the country, and that you were willing to take my word with regard to this is a matter of peculiar gratification to me."

To Governor W. P. Hobby of Texas:
"Upon the receipt of the telegram . . . in which you joined other gentlemen in calling my attention to the distressing situation existing as to the cattle industry in some 150 of the 250 counties of Texas, I at once, of course, got into consultation with such of my colleagues as were prepared to advise me in the matter.

"I learn from the Secretary of Agriculture that that department has taken the deepest and most serious interest in this problem and that it is doing everything possible to put all the instrumentalities at the command of the Government at the disposal of those who are trying to solve this question, and that the Food Administrator is also interested in it in a very practical way.

"Unhappily, there is no appropriation available from which the pecuniary aid you suggest could be extended, and the extension of such aid would be a matter which I should feel in duty bound to bring to the attention of Congress before taking any action. Moreover, I believe that in view of economic situations existing elsewhere in the country the Congress would feel that it could not enter upon such enterprises without involving the national treasury in the most serious way.

"All I can do, therefore, I am sorry to say, is to assure you that every sort of aid within our power will be extended. We appreciate the seriousness of the problem and are disposed to help."

To his secretary, Tumulty, enclosing a confidential report from the Office of Naval Intelligence on the labor situation in England and labor's fight against Lloyd George. Henderson, it was thought, would, if he should be the next Prime Minister, be in favor of peace. He was said to have "considerable admiration" for Samuel Gompers; and it was suggested the Allied cause would benefit if Gompers were to go to England for a conference with him:

"Would you not be kind enough to show the enclosed to Mr. Gompers in strict confidence and consult him as to whether he knows of any means by which he could help to steer Mr. Henderson?"

Saturday, December 1st.

The President spent the morning in his study; and by afternoon had a copy of his message to Congress ready for the Public Printer.

In reply to House's message of November 28th[1] Lansing telegraphed: ". . . . I made a verbal statement to the press this morning deprecating such sensational stories and urged that they be counteracted. I said we realized Russia was going through a very difficult time and has suffered severely as a result of German intrigue; that every effort is being made to assist the Russian people in working out the salvation of the country . . .

"Will you not issue such statement along these lines [as] you deem advisable and add that there is no truth in the report that officials of this Government have voiced sentiments hostile to Russia?"[2]

The Supreme War Council held its initial session at Versailles, France, Great Britain, Italy and the United States being represented.[3]

Trotsky ordered the removal of all diplomats who were not in sympathy with the Soviet regime.[4]

---

[1]This volume, p. 379.

[2]*Foreign Relations*, 1918, *Russia*, Vol. I, pp. 276–277.

[3]Frederick Palmer calls this the second session, the one at Rapallo being the first. *Bliss, Peacemaker*, p. 199. For Dr. Seymour's comments on the meeting, for House's diary account—"all talk and no concerted action"—and for the text of resolutions passed, see *Intimate Papers*, Vol. III, pp. 271–273, 287 *et seq. War Memoirs of David Lloyd George*, Vol. V, pp. 216 *et seq.*

[4]*Foreign Relations*, 1918, *Russia*, Vol. I, p. 257.

To Colonel House, telegram:

"The resolution you suggest[1] is entirely in line with my thought and has my approval. You will realize how unfortunate it would be for the conference to discuss peace terms in a spirit antagonistic to my January address to the Senate. Our people and Congress will not fight for any selfish aim on the part of any belligerent, with the possible exception of Alsace Lorraine, least of all for divisions of territory such as have been contemplated in Asia Minor. I think it will be obvious to all that it would be a fatal mistake to cool the ardour of America. Answering your cable after conferring with Clemenceau[2] I favour the most effective war council obtainable whether directed by one man or not."

Sunday, December 2nd.

The President and Mrs. Wilson spent the day quietly at home, with an old friend of the President's, Mrs. Burd Grubb, as a guest at luncheon.

Colonel House telegraphed the President and Lansing of long discussions on Russia. ". . . . It was decided finally that each Power should send its own answer[3] . . . the substance of each answer to be that the Allies were willing to reconsider their war aims in conjunction with Russia and as soon as she had a stable government with whom they could act. . . ."[4]

General Pershing, in a telegram to Secretary Baker and the Chief of Staff, reported the emergency caused by the "apparent total collapse of Russia and the recent success of the Central Powers in Italy," and urged that America "move swiftly."[5]

---

[1]This volume, November 30th, p. 382.

[2]House had telegraphed after a conference with Clemenceau and Pétain. ". . . . Pétain believes that whatever Supreme War Council is created should have a president or executive officer to execute its decisions. This is sure to meet with English opposition. What is your opinion of it? . . . ." *Foreign Relations*, 1917, Supp. 2, Vol. I, p. 318.

[3]To Trotsky. See this volume, November 29th, p. 381.

[4]*Intimate Papers*, Vol. III, pp. 284–285.

[5]Pershing, *My Experiences in the World War*, Vol. I, pp. 249–250.

Lloyd George sent a memorandum to Colonel House, through Reading, asking whether it would be possible for America to provide "a company of infantry to replace a British company in such a number of British battalions as America could bring over men . . . . they could later on be recalled and posted to the American divisions."

In his covering note to Reading, Lloyd George said: ". . . . We shall be hard pressed to hold our own and keep Italy standing during 1918. Our man-power is pretty well exhausted. . . . France is done. . . ."

House consulted General Pershing, who replied that Lloyd George's plan would not do at all.[1]

Fierce hand-to-hand fighting was reported, as German troops made a desperate attempt to retake ground lost the week before to the west and south of Cambrai.

Monday, December 3rd.

Afternoon appointments: Manuel de Freyre y Santander, the new minister from Peru, to present his credentials; Senator Robinson and Governor Brough of Arkansas; Representative Fitzgerald of New York; Representative Lunn of New York; Representative Dill of Washington and a committee of six members of Congress, with General Biddle, who presented the shell of the first shot fired in France by the American army.

Colonel House to the President reporting a conference with Balfour, after which Balfour prepared a dispatch to be sent, if his government agreed, to the British ambassador at Petrograd: the action of the Bolshevik government in opening armistice negotiations was protested, but the Allies would not, it was said, attempt to hold "the present provisional government at Petrograd" back by treaty. ". . . . They base their claims on deeper principles . . ." Great Britain and Russia, broadly speaking, wished the same kind of peace, but it was felt that when "arms have failed rhetoric is not likely to succeed."[2]

George Creel telegraphed Edgar Sisson in Petrograd: "Drive ahead full speed regardless expense. Coordinate all American agencies in Petrograd and Moscow and start aggressive

[1]Pershing, *My Experiences in the World War*, Vol. I, pp. 255–256.
[2]*Foreign Relations*, 1918, *Russia*, Vol. I, pp. 256–257.

campaign. Use press billboards placards and every possible medium to answer lies against América. Make plain our high motives and absolute devotion to democratic ideals. Den that supplies are going to be stopped and state America's eagerness to help. Have Breshkovskaya and others issue statements and translate pamphlets. Engage speakers and halls. Urge Red Cross and Y.M.C.A. to fullest effort. Cable if send motion pictures and give necessary details. Sending thousand words daily from Sayville via Eiffel Tower to Bullard Moscow. . . ."

The Inter-Allied Conference held its second and final plenary session "like the first purely formal in character and devoted to the brief reports of the expert committees."[1] An official summary of its accomplishments was made public on the 5th: agreement upon coördination of sea transport facilities; discussion of man power; formation of inter-allied committees to carry out the decisions of the conference, etc.

The second session of the 65th Congress opened at noon.

To Colonel House, who had telegraphed on the 1st: "I hope you will not think it necessary to make any statement concerning foreign affairs until I can see you. This seems to me very important. I should be in Washington by December 17th."[2]:

"Sorry impossible to omit foreign affairs from address to Congress. Reticence on my part at this juncture would be misunderstood and resented and do much harm."

Tuesday, December 4th.

The President played a round of golf with Mrs. Wilson in the morning, returning in time to receive Judge Lovett at eleven o'clock. At quarter past twelve he left for the Capitol to address the Congress.

". . . . Let there be no misunderstanding," he said. "Our

---

[1]*Intimate Papers*, Vol. III, p. 291.

[2]A memorandum on House's copy of his telegram of the 2nd reads: "I sent this cable to the President because I had in mind his making a statement giving our war aims. I tried to get this done at Paris, but failed. The next best thing was for the President to do it." *Ibid.*, Vol. III, p. 286.

present and immediate task is to win the war, and nothing shall turn us aside from it until it is accomplished. . . ." When this end was achieved, we would "be free to base peace on generosity and justice, to the exclusion of all selfish claims to advantage even on the part of the victors." Of Germany's chief ally, he said: ". . . we do not wish in any way to impair or to re-arrange the Austro-Hungarian Empire. . . ." But the present status of our relations with her constituted a "very embarrassing obstacle" and he therefore recommended a declaration of war. ". . . . The same logic would lead also to a declaration of war against Turkey and Bulgaria. . . . But they are mere tools and do not yet stand in the direct path of our necessary action. . . ."[1]

The President's call for a declaration of war with Austria-Hungary was received with great enthusiasm.[2] ". . . Congress was more responsive than I had ever seen it," wrote Colonel Brown.[3] "Time after time the Senate, House & Galleries rose as one man & cheered to the utmost—The only Senator who kept his seat & did not applaud was La Follette—I have been told this was also true of Hardwick, but I did not see him . . ." The New York *Times* reporter gave a colorful account, commenting upon the President's unusual vigor of appearance—and upon his remarkable new necktie! When the call for a declaration of war upon Austria-Hungary was reached, "a cheer that came from a dozen places at once broke the silence that had been intensified by the sense of disappointment over the feeling he had created that the day of reckoning with the Vienna Government, and particularly with those Austrian subjects in America who were playing Germany's game of intrigue and incendiarism under the very nose of the United States, was not at hand." The cheer became a great shout, and the audience rose to its feet in its enthusiasm. Women in the galleries waved their handkerchiefs, the "yip-yip-yip" of the Rebel yell punctuated the even roar of the steady cheering, and the President was forced to suspend his address for a time. ". . . . He stepped aside while the cheering lasted, and waited

---

[1]*Public Papers*, Vol. V, pp. 128–130.

[2]Indeed the difficulty was to restrain Congress from declaring war also on Turkey and Bulgaria. On the 6th Secretary Lansing sent the Senate Committee on Foreign Relations, at the request of Senator Stone, a confidential memorandum as to the inadvisability of taking such action at that time. *Foreign Relations*, 1917, Supp. 2, Vol. I, pp. 448–454.

[3]In a personal letter of the time.

without show of any elation or other feeling for an opportunity to resume the reading. . . ."[1]

The President's brother, Joseph R. Wilson, came over from Baltimore with his wife and daughter to hear the address. They remained at the White House for luncheon, as did Colonel Brown. After the cabinet meeting (probably) Secretary Lansing submitted to the President a draft declaration of the policy of the United States with regard to Russia, which expressed the "disappointment and amazement" with which America had watched the "rise of class despotism in Petrograd" and the Bolshevik efforts toward a separate peace. The President felt that it was not opportune to make such a public declaration at the time. ". . . . He nevertheless approved in principle . . ."[2]

> At 12:30 noon the Committee on Public Information began sending the President's address to "every principal point in Europe, Scandinavia, South America, Orient and Mexico."[3]

Wednesday, December 5th.

Afternoon appointments: the French ambassador, to present a medal; Dr. Albert Shaw, editor of the *American Review of Reviews*, and a friend of the President's student days at Johns Hopkins; Chief Justice Covington of the Supreme Court of the District of Columbia; Senator Pittman of Nevada.

> The first black list of the United States against enemy firms and corporations was issued by the War Trade Board.[4]
> Ambassador Francis telegraphed translations of the secret treaties as they had appeared in the organ of the Soviets.[5]

---

[1]New York *Times*, December 5, 1917. The address was well received in this country; "illuminating and inspiring," said the New York *Times*. In the Allied countries, also, there was approval. ". . . except the President's speech which brought us into the war," Walter Page telegraphed from London, "it is regarded as his most important utterance. . . ." *Foreign Relations*, 1917, Supp. 2, Vol. I, pp. 454–455. T. N. Page wrote from Rome: ". . . . No other message of yours, not even that of April 2nd, and certainly nothing else that I can recall, made such an impression. It went straight to the heart of the Italian people and it has had an extraordinary inspiriting effect . . ." German reaction was extremely critical. *Ibid.*, pp. 467–469.

[2]*War Memoirs of Robert Lansing*, pp. 343–345.

[3]George Creel to the President, December 4, 1917.

[4]*Official Bulletin*, December 5, 1917.

[5]*Foreign Relations*, 1917, Supp. 2, Vol. I, pp. 493–507.

To Representative John J. Fitzgerald:

"I write to beg that you will lay before the Appropriations Committee my very earnest request that the balance now remaining of the appropriation of $100,000,-000 for national security and defense be continued at my disposal until the end of the present fiscal year, June 30, 1918.

"The fund has proved indispensable. It was impossible to foresee what the undeveloped necessities of war expenditure would be, and this fund has been available where it would have been fatal if means had been lacking. It would be not only a very serious inconvenience but it might almost amount to a fatal miscarriage of many important war activities if the fund were not available any longer than the thirty-first of December, its present limitation.

"I have expended the fund upon a large variety of objects, of which I am ready at a proper time, of course, to render a full account to Congress, all of them objects which contributed not a little to the success of the vast undertakings we are now engaged in, and yet could not conveniently have been provided for by the regular process of appropriation.

"I will, of course, be glad to give you, Mr. Chairman, any particulars you desire me to give. I am writing now merely to present to you the very great urgency and importance of this matter."

To Cleveland H. Dodge, who had expressed the hope that the United States would not have to declare war on Turkey and Bulgaria, since such a move would have a serious effect upon missionary activities in those countries:

MY DEAR CLEVE:

Just a line to say that I sympathize with every word of your letter . . . about war with Turkey and am trying to hold the Congress back from following its inclination to include all the allies of Germany in a declaration of a state of war. I hope with all my heart that I can succeed.

In a tearing haste, but with the warmest affection,

Faithfully yours,

WOODROW WILSON

To Miss Flora L. Robinson:

"It is not at all necessary for you to recall yourself to my recollection. I remember with the greatest pleasure meeting you, and my daughter Jessie and I have often since spoken of you and I have through her kept track in some degree of your own work.

"I entirely agree with you with regard to the missionary work. I think it would be a real misfortune, a misfortune of lasting consequence, if the missionary programme for the world should be interrupted. There are many calls for money, of course, and I can quite understand that it may become more difficult than ever to obtain money for missionary enterprises. It may be, too, that the extension of those enterprises is for the present impracticable, but that the work already undertaken should be continued and should be continued as nearly as possible at its full force seems to me of capital necessity, and I for one hope that there may be no slackening or recession of any sort.

"I wish that I had time to write you as fully as this great subject demands, but I have put my whole thought into these few sentences and I hope that you will feel at liberty to use this expression of opinion in any way that you think best."

To Gutzon Borglum, a letter written at Secretary Baker's suggestion:

" . . . . Of course, what you say disturbs me not a little and I write to ask you if you will not do me the great favor of indicating as specifically as possible the weaknesses you see in our present organization in the matter of aeronautics. I would also appreciate it very warmly if you would tell me what men of practical gifts not now connected with the service of the Government you think could be serviceable to us in working towards a successful result."

Telegram to the Association of National Advertisers, in conference in New York:

"Mr. Creel . . . has told me of the generous mobilization of the advertising forces of the nation in support of the effort of the government to inform public opinion properly and adequately. America asks nothing for itself that it does not ask for the rest of the world. Our devotion to great principles is not stained by any selfishness. This purity of purpose commends absolute openness in every approach to our people and the peoples of the world. The great advertising bodies constitute a medium peculiarly fitted to make frank presentation of America's meaning and purpose in an hour when full understanding is so essential to success. I accept your services with gratitude and deepest appreciation."

Thursday, December 6th.

Afternoon appointments: Representative Candler of Mississippi; Interstate Commerce Commissioners Hall, Clark and Meyer, to discuss, probably, the commission's recommendations with regard to the railroads. In a report to Congress, which the President had just received, they had set out two alternatives: unite the railway systems of the country into one aggregate force under their own operation; or provide for their operation as a unit by the President. Secretary McAdoo arrived for a conference at 4 o'clock.

Secretary McAdoo to the President, urging him to assume control and operation of the railroads of the country for the period of the war, any necessary additional legislation to be secured later.[1]

---

[1] Printed in part in Synon's *McAdoo*, pp. 309–311.

Trotsky's announcement that peace negotiations had been postponed, in order that the Allies might have time to define their attitude, was reported by Ambassador Francis.[1]

A munitions ship, taking fire in the harbor of Halifax, Nova Scotia, set up a series of fearful explosions. Bitter suffering resulted, and great loss of life. Help was rushed from this country on special trains; and President Wilson sent a telegram of sympathy from the people of the United States to the people of Canada.

A powerful Austro-German assault was launched against Italian troops on a ten-mile front.

To Secretary Baker, enclosing a telegram from the Democratic state chairman of Indiana and one of his colleagues, who claimed that the Republicans were making use of the draft organization for political purposes:

"The subject matter of the enclosed has given me a great deal of concern. It is becoming more and more evident that throughout the country the draft organization, the public defense organization and the Fuel and Food Administrations are being made use of for political purposes. I dare say that you have thought as much about this as I have and I wonder if any course of action has suggested itself to your mind which it would be permissible and wise for us to take?"[2]

---

[1] *Foreign Relations*, 1918, *Russia*, Vol. I, p. 258.

[2] Baker replied. ".... I am afraid the Governors in some of the States have used the Federal machinery which it has been necessary to create among them for political ends, and yet I imagine we have had a hard choice in the matter between erecting an entirely independent machine which would likely have been partisan our way, because our friends and acquaintances lie chiefly in our own party, or to rely upon the Governors of the several States and thus have here and there the political complexion of the Governor reflected into his choice.

"Under all the circumstances the latter plan, which we did adopt, seems to have worked without much cause for criticism. . . .

"I am keeping in mind your wish that we shall make no obvious partisan distinctions in our war activities, and equally that we shall not allow them to be made against us; but in dealing with so political a people as ours I fear it is impossible to prevent at all times the manifestations of partisanship on the one side, or the suspicion of it on the other."

To William Phillips:

".... I prepared my address to Congress without consultation with anyone and went up to the Capitol with a very serious doubt in my mind as to the effect it would have on the international situation. I knew that I was bound in conscience to say what I did and I did not hesitate to say it, but I have been greatly relieved by what appears to have been its reception on both sides of the water, because even the truth spoken out of season is sometimes harmful."

To Lincoln Colcord, staff correspondent of the Philadelphia *Public Ledger,* who urged that a second mission be sent to Russia—one with a sympathetic understanding of the situation which, he thought, the Root Mission never had. He predicted at Petrograd within a short time a strong coalition government, fully representative of Russia, and with the Bolsheviks in the majority. If such a government were not recognized, America and the Allies must thereafter "stand frankly on a basis of imperialistic war aims." The President's reply was marked "Personal":

". . . I have your letter . . . which I have read with a great deal of interest and upon which I have thought a good deal since reading it. I do not believe that at present, at any rate, I could send such a mission to Russia as you suggest. For one thing, I do not know where I would find the men suited to the purpose, but your interpretation of what is going on over there corresponds with so much that has come to me in one way or another, directly and indirectly, that I have been very much impressed by it and thank you for it very warmly."

To George Foster Peabody, who had congratulated the President upon his address of the 4th, but deplored his criticisms of the pacifists in his Buffalo speech of November 12th. The President's letter is marked "Personal":

"I am grateful to you for your letter . . . and I am none the less grateful because of the feeling you express that

I have been doing injustice to some very rare souls. I dare say it must seem so, and nobody regrets more than I do that the generalization to which I was obliged to confine myself sweeps within it those who do not deserve the condemnation which my words imply. I feel, however, my dear Mr. Peabody, that I could not have discriminated without offering a refuge of excuses and protestations to men who do not deserve consideration. I have not known in this instance how to do definite and particular justice."

Friday, December 7th.

Colonel Brown wrote to his wife: "I have played golf almost every morning this week with the President—we leave the House promptly at 8:30, arrive at the Course in ab't twenty minutes, play twelve holes, and back in the Car at 10:15 or 10:20, the difference being attributed to my loss of balls—I don't think the President ever lost a ball in his life. He doesn't play what 'we Golfers,' call a long game, but his direction is simply remarkable—He is almost invariably straight down the course . . .

"Tomorrow morning (being Saturday) we will play eighteen holes . . .

"Mrs. W. has gone out with us every morning this week, but has not played golf—She takes part of her morning mail, the paper & her knitting and waits for us in the car. This week, is the first time I have noticed we have secret service men stationed at different parts of the course. . . ."

The railroad situation was discussed at the cabinet meeting. Late-afternoon appointments: A. Mitchell Palmer, Alien Property Custodian; George Creel; Thomas D. Jones; Representative Shouse of Kansas and the presidents of the Farmers' Coöperative Unions of Kansas, Oklahoma, Missouri and Nebraska. At three minutes past five, the President signed the resolution for war against Austria-Hungary, which had passed both Houses of Congress in the afternoon. Dr. Axson, whose acceptance of the national secretaryship of the American Red Cross was announced during the day, arrived for a short visit.

The House Mission sailed for home.

Count Czernin, Austrian Foreign Minister, said in the course of an address: ".... We are fighting for the defense of Germany just as Germany is fighting for our defense.... If ... there should still be people on the side of the Entente living under the impression that they might succeed in separating us from our allies, I say that they are bad politicians . . ."[1]

"It is very easy to speak of transporting an army of millions from America to Europe, but whether such plans can be realized remains to be proved. The military authorities consider it out of the question. . . ."[2]

To David B. Jones, a friend and strong supporter of the Princeton days:

"I was genuinely disappointed not to see you while you were here. If I had known sooner that you were coming, I would have kept a place open on my day's calendar. Please let me know next time.

"I hope that you found your brother[3] stronger. I must admit I have been a bit anxious about him and a bit conscience-stricken to have put such heavy work upon him."

Saturday, December 8th.

The President omitted his golf because of snow and spent the morning in his study. At 2:15 he conferred with Representative Sherley of Kentucky; later he and Mrs. Wilson walked over to the Corcoran Art Gallery, which he had long enjoyed. In the evening the President, Colonel Brown and Dr. Grayson went to the Gridiron dinner, where the President spoke; but since addresses on such occasions are "off the record," no copy exists.[4]

---

[1] Lansing, in his *Memoirs* (p. 255), makes the flat statement that the possibility of a renewal of "secret and informal attempts at a separate peace . . . was the reason for delaying a declaration of war against Austria-Hungary for eight months . . ."

[2] *War Aims and Peace Proposals*, pp. 204–205.

[3] Thomas D. Jones, whom the President had appointed to the War Trade Board in August.

[4] A verbatim report of all such presidential talks which are likely, since they are informal and unpremeditated, to be highly interpretative, ought to be made and kept for the future use of the historian. The writer himself remembers hearing several such "off-record" talks or addresses which were followed by garbled and sensational reports

Reorganization plans for the Council of National Defense were announced. Coöperative committees of industry, formation of which had been authorized by the council in a crisis, would now be dissolved, with appreciation for the fine work done: the industries themselves were now asked to form committees which would "render immediately available valuable sources of information upon which the Government can draw . . ."[1]

To Frank I. Cobb:

". . . thank you very warmly . . . for your generous words about the address. I hope with all my heart that it may have some effect in the enemy countries on the other side of the water."

To Louis F. Post, Assistant Secretary of Labor, a letter which was read to Post over the telephone:

"I have read with close attention the memorandum you were kind enough to prepare for me on December fifth with regard to the Minneapolis–St. Paul situation [street railway strike] and I find that my mind is left in very serious doubt as to what our proper course in the case would be. I see very clearly the case as the Governor of the State puts it, and I am not sure that he is not right in fearing that out intervention and insistence upon a re-arbitration of the whole matter would make matters worse rather than better and lead to an extension of the area of trouble and contention. I would be very glad to know what your latest judgment in the matter is."

To Representative John J. Fitzgerald, chairman of the House Committee on Appropriations, who, in reply to the President's letter of the 5th, had asked for a "detailed statement of the expenditures to date" from the President's Fund:

"I enclose such a statement as you requested of my expenditures under the appropriation for 'National Se-

which cannot be denied by the biographer because there is no dependable or authorita tive record.

[1] *Official Bulletin,* December 8, 1917.

curity and Defense.' I have made one of the larger items very inexplicit, for reasons which I am sure the Committee will understand. I mean the one for 'Secret and Confidential Service.'

"You will observe that the bulk of this expense has been in connection with the exercise of the functions which Congress has allotted to me. I do not see that it would be possible,—indeed, my brief experience shows me that it will be impossible,—to make definite estimates for the cost of exercising these functions, and they would not only be embarrassed but absolutely cut off and my powers nullified if the appropriation were not continued."

To his secretary, Tumulty, who had called attention to a letter from William J. Bryan saying that Carl Ackerman, in his book, *Germany, the New Republic,* implied that Bryan's resignation as Secretary of State was due to the Dumba incident and that it was demanded by the President. Bryan intended to ask for a retraction; but he wished the matter submitted to the President first:

"I am perfectly willing that Mr. Bryan should say as from me that Ackerman's statements, or, rather, his implications, are entirely false. Of course, I did not request or desire Mr. Bryan's resignation, and his resignation had no connection whatever with the so-called Dumba incident."

To his secretary, Tumulty, who had called attention to a letter from Edward McLean saying he had heard there was to be an official criticism of the Washington *Post* by members of the cabinet or some bureau head. Tumulty suggested that he himself let McLean know "in a diplomatic way" what the administration's criticism was:

"I think you could very properly do what you suggest. I would like Mr. McLean to know our real feeling. I think you could tell him that what he states in the first sentence of the letter that he has heard is absolutely new to me.

I have heard nothing of it, and certainly nothing of that sort ought to happen."

Sunday, December 9th.

The railroad situation had become acute, and the President was probably occupied with some phase of it during most of the day, even omitting church in the morning. Presidents of the Eastern railroads were holding meetings in New York to prepare their case for the President and Congress; and Fairfax Harrison during the day wrote Senator Newlands, chairman of the Committee on Interstate Commerce, that the railroad system had not broken down.[1]

There had been some pressure upon the President to make McAdoo Director General if the railroads were taken over, but the recent talk of a "prince-imperial" in the administration may have reached his ears; at any rate, he was not at first in favor of the appointment. Tumulty urged him to summon Justice Brandeis to discuss the situation, knowing that Brandeis favored McAdoo, but this the President would not do. At five o'clock, however, he went himself on foot to Stoneleigh Court, where the Justice lived, appearing at the door quite unannounced. "I could not request you to come to me," he said, "and I have therefore come to you, to ask your advice." They conferred for an hour or so, Brandeis advising that McAdoo be appointed Director General of railroads, provided he would resign from the Secretaryship of the Treasury. He felt that the new task would be so great that no man should attempt both offices.[2]

Monday, December 10th.

Afternoon appointments: a committee of the National Party; a committee of the Society of Friends, who presented a memorial; Senator Newlands, who probably brought with him Harrison's letter of the previous day in regard to the situation of the railroads.[3] When questioned after the conference, Newlands was reticent, but he did admit that the President would

---

[1] New York *Times*, December 10 and 11, 1917.

[2] Justice Brandeis to the author; also R. W. Woolley (then a member of the Interstate Commerce Commission) to the author. After seeing the President, Brandeis gave the same advice to McAdoo.

[3] Given to the press during the day.

address Congress very soon;[1] former Justice Charles E. Hughes; the Attorney General. The President had asked Gregory, when the railroad situation became acute, whether he had power to take over the roads. Gregory had had the matter thoroughly looked up; and it may have been at this time that he gave the President his opinion. The law, he said, gave the President power to demand priority in shipments and to use the railroads if necessary, but not to take full control.

"What do you think I ought to do?" asked the President.

Gregory said that it was a question of policy as well as of law.

"Do you think the successful prosecution of the war depends upon taking over the railroads?"

"Yes, I do," said Gregory.

"Then I think I should do it and go to Congress for the legislation."[2]

At five o'clock the President walked over to Secretary Baker's office; and Secretary McAdoo came in at 5:30 for a conference on the railroads.

Panama declared war on Austria-Hungary.

The British under General Allenby occupied Jerusalem. So came to an end nearly thirteen centuries (with two brief interludes) of Mohammedan domination of the city. Jews and Christians all over the world rejoiced.

To Senator John Sharp Williams:

"I hope my address to Congress the other day justified in your mind my telegram to you. I did not like to have you absent when so important a matter as the declaration of a state of war with Austria-Hungary was under consideration. . . ."

To George Creel, who sent the President a circular which had been criticized because of its use of the words "Our Allies." ". . . . It is a term," Creel wrote, "that I have avoided myself. The people who are protesting are undoubtedly pro-German, and I would like to have your view before I answer any of the numerous letters.":

---

[1]New York *Times*, December 11, 1917.

[2]T. W. Gregory to the author.

"I have your memorandum . . . about the circular using the words, 'Our Allies.' I have written Mr. Hoover a line about it, but don't think you need answer the letters you speak of, but if you do, just say no significance is to be attached to the words, they are merely used for short."

To Herbert Hoover, "Personal":

"I have noticed on one or two of the posters of the Food Administration the words, 'Our Allies.' I would be very much obliged if you would issue instructions that 'Our Associates in the War' is to be substituted. I have been very careful about this myself because we have no allies and I think I am right in believing that the people of the country are very jealous of any intimation that there are formal alliances.

"You will understand, of course, that I am implying no criticism. I am only thinking it important that we should all use the same language."

To Dr. Albert Shaw, who had written of his ideas as to the conduct of the war, and his approval of the stand taken by the President. ". . . . This latest Congress message of yours has won great approval, not only from newspapers but from men of independent mind and judgment who think for themselves and who have sometimes been opposed to you. I have spoken with a good many such men, and they are now completely in accord with what you say. . . .":

"You may be sure I greatly enjoyed our talk the other day. It is a long time since we had one.

"I am sincerely glad to have your views, for you may be sure they carry a great deal of weight with me, and no excuse was needed for the length of your letter. It was not too long. . . ."

To John S. Sargent, who wrote that the National Gallery of Dublin had consented to have the President's portrait exhibited for one month each in the Corcoran Gallery, the Metropolitan Museum, and the Pennsylvania Academy:

"Thank you for sending me a copy of the cablegram from the Dublin people. I am glad that they have consented . . ."

To Representative W. C. Adamson, who urged that the work on the Muscle Shoals Dam be begun right away, since such a course would go far toward improving the feeling of the farmers:

". . . . The Secretary of War tells me that there has been a good deal of trouble in connection with the Muscle Shoals Dam, in getting the property at reasonable prices. At one time I feared that we might have to abandon the project rather than be seriously imposed upon by the land owners of the adjacent country. I have not heard from him recently and hope sincerely that that obstacle may be overcome. It would be too bad to lose the chance because of local greed and unfairness. . . ."

To Henry C. Frick:

". . . . I have had the feeling recently that the sentiment of the country is more and more uniting for a great demonstration of the power of the nation as well as of its high purpose, and I value your letter as an additional evidence of the fact."

To his secretary, Tumulty, referring to the suggestion of Louis F. Post, Assistant Secretary of Labor, that in view of the serious street car strike situation in St. Paul and Minneapolis, the advice of John Lind of the Public Safety Commission of Minnesota be secured, and certain other steps taken to deal with the matter without the appearance of federal coercion:

"Please get Gov. Lind and Mr. Kerwin (separately or together) into immediate conference with the Sec'y of War."[1]

---

[1] John Lind was found to be in Washington and Secretaries Baker and Post immediately had a talk with him, reporting to the President afterward that they agreed with

To his secretary, Tumulty, who had called attention to a request for an appointment for Father O'Callaghan and a delegation of Irishmen, to discuss the Irish question:

"I think this is a most inopportune time for any delegation to visit me on the so-called Irish question, and I beg that you will express this judgment to Father O'Callaghan."

Tuesday, December 11th.

The railroad situation was discussed by the cabinet; after the meeting newspaper men sent the President a request for information on specific points. He replied through his secretary that he could not answer the questions at present, but that he had the matter under most careful scrutiny and consideration. He added that if he should conclude that a change from the present method of control was necessary he would feel obliged to say the first word to Congress.[1] Late-afternoon appointments: a committee of the American Union of Rumanian Jews; Representative Dallinger of Massachusetts; Representative Small of North Carolina. At eight o'clock in the evening Secretary Lansing called to discuss the Russian situation. It was after this conference, probably, that he telegraphed Page and Sharp for information as to the policy which Great Britain and France proposed to follow toward Russia. Page replied that the British government would "not recognize the Lenin so-called Government, certainly not until it can show some sort of authority from the people." Sharp replied that the French government would "ignore" the Russian government "as now constituted."[2]

The President proclaimed a state of war between the United States and Austria-Hungary.

Secretary Baker wrote the President: "I have your note returning to me the confidential copy of General Bliss' tele-

---

Lind and the governor of Minnesota that the Federal government should not interfere. The President wrote to Senator Nelson of Minnesota a few days later: ". . . . I do not know any situation which has puzzled me more; I mean about which it has been harder to decide how to help and how not to help."

[1] New York *Times*, December 12, 1917.

[2] *Foreign Relations, 1918, Russia,* Vol. I, pp. 297, 299, 322.

gram of December 4th.[1] You ask 'is such a program possible'; it can only be made possible by sacrificing other things, which up to now we have believed to be of equal, if not of greater, importance.

"As General Bliss will be home now in a few days, perhaps the relative importance of these things can be determined and a conclusion reached as to just where our strength can best be exerted."

Two inquiries were initiated in the Senate: one by the Military Affairs Committee under Senator Chamberlain of Oregon, to investigate the alleged failure of the War Department to adequately equip men in army cantonments; and one by the Committee on Manufactures under Senator Reed of Missouri, to investigate the fuel and sugar shortages. Both Chamberlain and Reed disclaimed any hostile attitude, saying that the committees merely wanted to get at the facts and apply corrective measures if faults were found.

A coal famine was reported threatening because of the lack of cars for distribution.

To W. P. G. Harding, governor of the Federal Reserve Board:

"May I not acknowledge the receipt of your letter . . . enclosing the resolutions of the Federal Reserve Board in favor of the establishment of a War Emergency Finance Corporation? I have several times discussed a similar suggestion with the Secretary of the Treasury and with others who are as deeply interested as the rest of us in the proper financial arrangements for the conduct of the war, and have been awaiting the recommendation of the Secretary himself with regard to the matter. I am sure that it will soon be forthcoming, and I shall be very glad indeed to give the whole matter my most careful consideration."

---

[1] Bliss telegraphed that "an arrangement had been made about artillery and munitions, in order to facilitate the arrival of twenty-four American divisions in France not later than the end of June, 1918," the British and Americans to furnish the tonnage. Neither the telegram from Bliss nor the President's note are in the Wilson files. See, for quotation from Bliss's message, Palmer, *Bliss, Peacemaker*, p. 201.

Wednesday, December 12th.—

At 2:30 the President received the Railroad War Board—Fairfax Harrison, Howard Elliott, Hale Holden, Julius Kruttschnitt and Samuel Rea—for an hour's conference. Immediately afterward the board conferred with more than a score of railway presidents and other executives representing most of the great railway systems of the country.[1] Other afternoon appointments: George Creel; Representative Sims of Tennessee, new chairman of the Committee on Interstate and Foreign Commerce, with whom the President discussed the railroad situation; ex-President Taft, who explained the purpose of a proposed speaking mission to Great Britain. The President was strongly opposed to the whole idea, showing considerable feeling on the subject. ". . . . He was opposed to putting the United States in a position of seeming in any way to be involved with British policy. There were divergencies of purpose, he said, and there were features of the British policy in this war of which he heartily disapproved. . . ." He cited the Treaty of London as an instance of British self-interest. When Taft explained that the idea of a speaking mission had originated with Ambassador Page, in London, it "did not improve the President's temper." "Page is really an Englishman and I have to discount whatever he says about the situation in Great Britain."[2] At five o'clock the President received representatives of the railway brotherhoods; and at 5:30, Hoover and Garfield.

The investigation by the Senate Military Affairs Committee opened, General Crozier being the first to testify.

German troops endeavored to smash the Ypres salient by a surprise attack, but penetrated only 300 yards into British lines.

To his secretary, Tumulty, enclosing a letter from Gutzon Borglum, who complained of deficiencies in the aeronautic board and program, and suggested a reorganization:

"I have forgotten who is directly in charge of the aviation programme, but I would be obliged if you would find out and see that this letter is placed in his hands. The

---

[1] New York *Times,* December 12, 1917.

[2] *The Life and Letters of Walter H. Page,* Vol. II, pp. 346–348.

statements in it are so serious, though I must say so vague, that I don't see how I can absolutely pass them over; although I take little stock in them."

Thursday, December 13th.

Mr. and Mrs. Charles R. Crane and Colonel Brown were luncheon guests. Afternoon appointments: the heads of fraternal organizations, accompanied by Secretary McAdoo; Representative Jacoway and nine suffragettes from Arkansas; G. S. MacFarland; William Kent in regard to the Shields Water Power bill; Governor Dorsey of Georgia; Representative Fitzgerald of New York; Senator Martin of Virginia. In the late afternoon the President joined Mrs. Wilson for a concert in the New National Theater. Evening at Keith's.

> An Inter-Allied Council on War Purchases and Finance was organized, Oscar T. Crosby of the American (House) Mission having stayed in London to represent the United States as its president.[1]
>
> The *Manchester Guardian* published texts of the secret treaties as released by the Bolsheviks.
>
> American casualties were beginning to be known, although the numbers were as yet very small.

Friday, December 14th.

At two o'clock the President received Secretary McAdoo and the heads of twelve fraternal organizations. After the cabinet meeting, he talked with Baker, Houston and Lane about a proposed bill for water power development. Both Houston and William Kent telephoned the White House during the day to say that the Shields Water Power bill was before the Senate and would probably be brought to a vote on that or the next day. Kent suggested that "steps should be taken at once to forestall action" in accordance with his talk with the President. Late afternoon appointments: Judge Ben B. Lindsey; F. W. Taussig of the Tariff Commission.

> Secretary McAdoo wrote the President, confidentially, that security markets in New York were very much demoralized and confidence badly impaired, one reason being un-

---

[1]For Crosby's report, see *Foreign Relations*, 1917, Supp. 2, Vol. I, pp. 589–590.

certainty concerning the railroad situation. He thought action should be taken immediately; and suggested that the President or someone in the administration make a statement to allay apprehension and check panic tendencies.

Claus A. Spreckels of the Federal Sugar Refining Company declared before the Senate Committee on Agriculture that the sugar shortage in the country was "created" by the Food Administration.

Investigation into the Navy Department's conduct of the war was ordered by the House Committee on Naval Affairs.

Secretary Daniels announced the formation of an Inter-Allied Naval Council, to "insure the closest touch and complete cooperation between the allied fleets": France, England, the United States, Italy and Japan were to be represented.[1]

"Lightless nights" on Sundays and Thursdays were ordered by the Fuel Administration for Broadway and other "white ways" throughout the country.

Lloyd George, speaking in London: "Victory is an essential condition for the security of the free world."[2]

Reports from the Flanders front became more vague, as the news grew worse.

"It was manifest now at the beginning of winter that the English Army was passing through a phase of weariness, a consequence of the substantial and sustained efforts put up throughout the summer; it was at length beginning to experience the gravest difficulty in reconstituting its forces; in mid-December, its infantry showed a deficit of 116,000 men."[3]

News from the Italian front also failed to improve. Thousands of prisoners were taken by the enemy, though little actual advance was made.

To Lawrence C. Woods, an old friend, who had written: ". . . . I am moved to write now as somehow I feel that we are facing

[1]*Official Bulletin*, December 15, 1917.

[2]London *Times*, December 15, 1917. Louis Wiley sent the President a copy of this speech on January 15, 1918.

[3]Quoted, in *War Memoirs of David Lloyd George*, Vol. V, p. 5, from the French Official History of the War.

very critical months with the possibility of all but staggering reverses to our cause, and I want you to feel thru it all that as far as it is given me to judge, you have the American people back of you as no war President of our country ever had them. Living as I do in the stronghold of stand pat Republicanism . . . I know whereof I speak. . . .":

"... I cannot let so exceedingly kind a letter go by without at least an acknowledgment and an expression of my very genuine and profound thanks. It pleases me mightily that you find such a sentiment as you report prevailing in 'standpat' Pittsburgh, and it was certainly most thoughtful of you to send me word of it. I assure you I need all the cheer I can get these anxious days."

Saturday, December 15th.

Secretaries Baker and McAdoo conferred with the President early in the afternoon, and Baker afterward announced the creation of a Military War Council, to be composed of the Secretary of War, the Assistant Secretary of War and five high-ranking officers of the Regular Army. It would devote itself to problems of supply for the American forces in the field and would serve as a connecting link between those forces and the War Department.[1]

Colonel House wrote the President that the members of his mission would land that afternoon and their reports would "go forward along with my own to Washington . . . tonight."[2]

A pessimistic note is discernible in most of the reports. Even House, customarily optimistic, said: ". . . . Unless a change for the better comes the Allies cannot win, and Germany may. For six months or more the ground has been steadily slipping away from the Allies. . . ." But he added that the morale of the people was good both in England and France.

". . . . I have been unable to escape the conviction," wrote Admiral Benson, "that all countries opposed to

[1]New York *Times*, December 16, 1917.
[2]The full report is printed in *Foreign Relations*, 1917, Supp. 2, Vol. I, pp. 334–445.

Germany in this war, except ourselves, are jealous and suspicious of one another. They believe, however, in the sincerity and unselfishness of the United States; and feeling thus, they are not only willing for the United States to take the lead in matters which affect our common cause; but they are really anxious that we should dominate the entire Allied situation, both as regards active belligerent operations against the enemy, and economically. . . ."

General Bliss was even more forthright:

"1. A military crisis is to be apprehended culminating not later than the end of the next spring, in which, without great assistance from the United States, the advantage will probably lie with the Central Powers.

"2. This crisis is largely due to the collapse of Russia as a military factor and to the recent disaster in Italy. But it is also largely due to lack of military coordination, lack of unity of control on the part of the Allied forces in the field. . . .

"National jealousies and suspicions and susceptibilities of national temperament must be put aside in favor of this unified control, even going if necessary (as I believe it is) to the limit of unified *command*. . . .

". . . we must meet the unanimous demand of our allies to send to France the maximum number of troops that we can send as early in the year 1918 as possible. There may be no campaign of 1919 unless we do our best to make the campaign of 1918 the last. . . ."

Bainbridge Colby, representative of the Shipping Board, reported: ". . . sinkings by submarine are not only in excess of present shipbuilding, but in excess of projected building by Great Britain and the United States for the year 1918. . . ." and also: ". . . I question whether coordination by agreement between the Allied nations is a genuine possibility. Inveterate jealousy, traditional mistrust, acute self-interest, domestic politics, irreconcilable slants of racial and national bias—all conspire to baffle attempts at coordination. . . ."

T. N. Perkins of the War Industries Board: ". . . . The situation of the war is extremely critical. . . ."[1]

---

[1]For specific quotations, above, see *Foreign Relations*, 1917, Supp. 2, Vol. I, pp. 356, 357, 385, 386–388, 412, 419, 441.

Secretary Lansing telegraphed American diplomatic representatives in European countries, Japan, China and Siam: "Pending further instructions you should have no official relations with Russian diplomatic officers who recognize or who are appointed by Bolshevik government."[1]

An armistice was signed between Russia and the Central Powers.

To his secretary, Tumulty, enclosing a letter from Howard Huntington, who made serious charges against the Aircraft Production Board—among others, that it was controlled by the automobile industry:

"This letter contains some very explicit statements, and I know the writer. I believe him to be entirely honest, although I have never had much confidence in his ability. I would be very much obliged if you would take this letter yourself to whoever is the head of the aircraft production management and find out just how much is in it."

Sunday, December 16th.

President and Mrs. Wilson spent a quiet morning, with no church. The President conferred with Secretary McAdoo[2] and Messrs. Todd and Leffingwell in the afternoon in regard to the railroad matter. Dr. Axson came in for dinner.

Cuba declared war on Austria-Hungary.

To Colonel House, a telegram:

"Delighted that you are safely back. Will look forward with the greatest pleasure to seeing you tomorrow. Hope you will stay with us."

---

[1] *Foreign Relations,* 1918, *Russia,* Vol. I, p. 317.

[2] McAdoo had written earlier in the day: "We have encountered some insuperable obstacles in the R.R. matter and I see no way to overcome them except by legislation. I don't see how you can address the Congress until a more definite program is decided upon. I am at your call any hour today." Attached to this letter in the Wilson files is a proposed address to Congress on the railroad situation, written on the President's own typewriter and much crossed out and corrected in his shorthand and longhand, and in at least one other handwriting. It differs widely from the address finally delivered.

Monday, December 17th.

William J. Bryan called at noon, probably in regard to the false accusations about which he had written the President. Early afternoon appointments: a committee of physicians; Hoffman Philip, recently appointed minister to Colombia. A State Department memorandum of the interview reports: ". . . . Especially does he [the President] consider a prompt and generous settlement of the Panama question with Colombia advisable owing to the favorable bearing it will doubtless have upon the attitude of the South American States . . . The President remarked that he believes that much of the apparent mistrust of this country, which is evident in South America is due to a persistent misconception of the Monroe Doctrine. The fact that the inviolability of the South American States against European invasion is openly championed by that Doctrine does not prevent the existence of a very general suspicion that such principles probably would not govern the actions of the United States Government in like case. Mr. Philip understands that the President desires to eliminate by treaties such misconception and to definitely confirm the territorial disinterestedness of this Government, etc. The President mentioned the recent activities of the Argentine Government[1] as evincing an endeavor to bring about a coalition of the States in a contrary direction to that desired by us. A generous and amicable settlement of the Panama matter with Colombia would, in the President's opinion, render the reaching of a general understanding much less difficult and would also disarm much of the studied and manufactured opposition to the United States in South America.

"The President further stated that he entirely endorses the latest draft of the treaty as proposed (with the exception that the expression of regret should be mutual [i.e. not by the United States only]). He does not consider such an expression in the light of an excuse, or detrimental to the dignity of the United States. . . .

"The President is of the opinion that a treaty, such as last proposed, would be entirely acceptable to the American people at large, and that the most strenuous opponents to it are con-

---

[1]Early in 1917 Argentina had initiated a movement for a conference of neutral American states, which the United States did not favor. See *Foreign Relations*, 1917, Supp. 1, pp. 232 *et seq.*

fined to a comparatively small class of cultured but more or less badly informed and prejudiced people in the Eastern States. The President agreed that a quiet canvass of the principal opponents of the treaty in the Senate and out of it, might be most useful, and stated that he authorized Mr. Philip to say, to anyone with whom it might have weight, that the President is convinced that the United States representative now being sent to Colombia should go there with definite assurance before-hand of what the Senate will agree to for the purpose of settling our differences with that Government, and that he considers such settlement of high importance to the South American policy of the United States.

"Mr. Philip received the impression from the President's remarks that he deems our treatment of Colombia in the past to have been such as, firstly, to create a wrong impression of this Government's attitude toward our sister republics of the South, and secondly, to cause Colombia loss of prestige, as a sovereign state as well as important financial damage which it would be in the best American spirit to assuage by means of a treaty on the lines of that already drafted."

At 3:30 Secretary Lansing called: at 4:30, Mr. Hoover; and in the late afternoon Colonel House arrived.

". . . I found the President in his study waiting for me," House wrote in his diary. "We had a conference which lasted from five until seven o'clock. . . .

"I gave . . . a report of my activities in London and Paris and he seemed deeply interested. . . . I recommended that he send General Tasker H. Bliss over as soon as he could make ready to act as our Military Adviser in the Supreme War Council. I explained the formation and working of that Council and how inefficient it had been made because of [the] determination to eliminate the British Chief of Staff and the General Commanding in the Field.

"In reply to his query as to how matters could be remedied, I thought it would be necessary to wait until we had a force on the firing line sufficient to give us the right to demand a voice in the conduct of the military end of the war."[1]

Dr. Seymour, carrying on the account of the interview, writes: "The President then took up the advisability of sending an American political representative to sit in the Council with

[1] *Intimate Papers*, Vol. III, p. 306.

the Prime Ministers, and expressed his determination to send over Colonel House within a month or so. He added that he could not send any one else. Quick decisions would be necessary and a representative must be there who would not have to refer every detail back to the President.

"This decision Wilson did not carry out until the following autumn, when he sent House over as his personal representative in the Supreme War Council. On the other hand, arrangements were made for despatching General Bliss immediately, as Military Adviser . . ."[1]

A Red Cross membership campaign began. "Ten million Americans," wrote the President in his appeal, "are invited to join . . . during the week ending with Christmas Eve. . . ."[2]

E. N. Hurley of the Shipping Board wrote the President some "encouraging news" about the shipbuilding program, concluding his letter: ". . . . As the labor situation in our shipyards at the present time seems most favorable, I am hopeful that our goal of 6,000,000 deadweight tons of shipping for 1918 will be reached."

Lloyd George meanwhile was telegraphing House: "We are receiving information from very trustworthy source to the effect that the United States shipbuilding programme for 1918 is not likely to exceed 2,000,000 tons. You will realize from our discussions here and in Paris, which were conducted on basis that United States would produce 6,000,000 tons—afterwards increased to 9,000,000, how serious a view the War Cabinet take of this news. The American shipbuilding programme is absolutely vital to the success in the War. May I urge that immediate steps be taken to ascertain the real situation . . ."[3]

Senator Lewis, Democratic whip, warned the Senate against investigations which might prove more harmful than beneficial to the country.

To H. A. Garfield, who had sent over a letter from M. L. Requa of the Food Administration, whom Garfield proposed to place in charge of oil. Requa urged the necessity for creating a

[1] *Op. cit.,* pp. 306–307.
[2] *Official Bulletin,* December 11, 1917.
[3] *Intimate Papers,* Vol. III, pp. 310–311.

petroleum department "having powers delegated through the President such as I hope the Food Administration will have in the not distant future.":

". . . . I am quite willing to accept your judgment about Mr. Requa.

"I am a little shy about creating a separate oil control. There are enough *separate* things now and the greatest need in every direction is coordination and unification of administration. But I dare say it is true that we need an extension of powers over the fuel oil situation."

To William Jennings Bryan, written at Bryan's request:

"My attention has been called to a book in which the author states by very clear implication that I demanded your resignation as Secretary of State because of language used by you in an interview with Ambassador Dumba soon after the first Lusitania note. You may quote me as saying that I did not ask for your resignation or desire it, as anyone can learn from my note accepting your resignation. And this statement ought also to be sufficient answer to the criticism of you based upon the Dumba interview, for I could not make it if I thought you responsible for the misinterpretation placed upon that interview in Berlin. But knowing at the time all the facts, I did not give the matter serious thought and I may add, in justice to you, that as you promptly corrected the misinterpretation when, within a few days, it was brought to your attention, it could not have affected the diplomatic situation."[1]

To R. S. Lovett of the War Industries Board, who had sent over a memorandum on the taking over of the railroads:

"Thank you for your letter . . . with its enclosure. You may be sure I welcome all the light I can get on the exceedingly difficult question to which your letter refers."[2]

---

[1] Published in the New York *Times*, December 18, 1917.

[2] On the same day the President thanked Senator Newlands for a number of mem-

Tuesday, December 18th.

At eleven o'clock Colonel House arrived for a conference, in the course of which he described his unsuccessful effort to persuade the Allies "to join in formulating a broad declaration of war aims that would unite the world against Germany, and would not only help to a solution of the Russian problem but would knit together the best and most unselfish opinions of the world."

The President thereupon decided that, lacking an inter-Allied manifesto, an address by himself might prove to be the moral turning point of the war, just as the coördination of war boards and policies was likely to be the military turning point. "We did not discuss this matter more than ten or fifteen minutes," continued House in his diary.[1]

The President received Senator Saulsbury of Delaware before the cabinet meeting; afterward he walked over to the Belasco Theater to join Mrs. Wilson, her mother, and Miss Bones, at a concert for the benefit of the Red Cross. In the late afternoon Secretary Baker called for the second time that day.

> Secretary Baker, following his morning conference with the President, Colonel House and Bliss, telegraphed to General Pershing: "Both English and French are pressing upon the President their desire to have your forces amalgamated with theirs by regiments and companies and both express belief in impending heavy drive by Germans somewhere along the line of the Western Front. We do not desire loss of identity of our forces but regard that as secondary to the meeting of any critical situation by the most helpful use possible of the troops at your command. The difficulty of course is to determine where the drive or drives of the enemy will take place; and in advance of some knowledge on that question, any redistribution of your forces would be difficult. The President, however, desires you to have full authority to use the forces at your command as you deem wise in consultation with the French and British commanders in chief. It is suggested for your consideration that

---

oranda on the railroad situation, saying: ".... I am giving the subject matter my most careful and anxious thought." And to Secretary Daniels: ".... I am going through some deep waters in considering the railroad question."

[1] *Intimate Papers*, Vol. III, p. 317. Secretary Baker and General Bliss were also present at the interview.

possibly places might be selected for your forces nearer the junction of the British and French lines which would enable you to throw your strength in whichever direction seemed most necessary. This suggestion is not, however, pressed beyond whatever merit it has in your judgment, the President's sole purpose being to acquaint you with the representations made here and to authorize you to act with entire freedom in making the best disposition and use of your forces possible to accomplish the main purposes in view.

"It is hoped that complete unity and coordination of action can be secured in this matter by your conferences with the French and British commanders. . . ."[1]

Ambassador Francis telegraphed Secretary Lansing: ". . . . Soviet bulletin printing many secret treaties and cables gives to-day under heading 'Secret convention between Russia and Japan having in view joint armed action against America and England in the Far East before 1921' and [a] secret treaty of July 3, 1916, negotiated by Sazonov and Motono which you will recall I have been endeavoring to get since its execution. . . ."[2]

Secretary Baker made public a report by Major General W. C. Gorgas, surgeon general of the army, as a result of his personal inspection of four of the training camps of the country. Many conditions would have to be corrected—overcrowding, insufficient clothing, etc.[3]

Late in the day Senator Frelinghuysen of New Jersey, a member of the Military Affairs Committee, put out a statement declaring that the evidence before the investigating committee revealed "innumerable delays and almost inconceivable blunders" and expressing the hope that President Wilson would retire any officials who were to blame.[4]

The Senate decided upon two more inquiries—one to cover the Shipping Board; the other to cover the railroads.

---

[1]A paraphrase of this telegram was given to the French ambassador by Secretary Lansing on the following day. *Foreign Relations*, 1917, Supp. 2, Vol. I, pp. 475–476.

[2]*Foreign Relations*, 1917, Supp. 2, Vol. I, pp. 709–710.

[3]New York *Times*, December 19, 1917.

[4]*Ibid*. The Kansas City *Star* of the 19th published an editorial headed "Baker Should Go."

The Senate concurred in the joint prohibition resolution which had passed the House the day before, providing for a vote by the states. It was sent immediately to the Secretary of State, whose duty it was to notify the secretaries of the various states. The time limit allowed for ratification was seven years.

To his secretary, Tumulty, enclosing a letter from Senator J. H. Lewis, who wanted to introduce a bill providing for government ownership of railroads, if the President approved; and who had passed on, though without recommending it, the suggestion of Eugene V. Debs's attorney that if the President should send for Debs and ask him to help in the prosecution of the war, Debs would support the government's war efforts against all Socialist obstructors:

"I don't like to answer this in writing. Perhaps you will be kind enough to seek out Senator Lewis and tell him,

"First, that I do not think it would be wise for me to send for Debs. I suspect, as he does, that the leadership of the Socialists is in some way involved, and the rivalry between Debs and Hillquist [Hillquit], and there might be serious embarrassment connected with involving myself in any way;

"Second: My judgment is that it would be very unwise to introduce or press at this time any bill for the national ownership of the railroads. It would inject an element into the situation which need not just now be injected, and would seriously conflict with any solution that I am able to think out as a war solution. The purchase of the railroads during the period of the war would, of course, be a financial impossibility."

Wednesday, December 19th.

The President spent the morning in his study. Afternoon appointments: a committee from the National Geographic Society, to present a certificate of honorary membership; Professor Taussig of the Tariff Commission; E. N. Hurley, Vance C. McCormick and Bainbridge Colby; Secretary McAdoo.

Secretary Baker to the President: "You will be interested to
    know that last week we received, completed, 125 training
    airplanes, and that our weekly production will increase.
    That means that we are now getting more airplanes a week
    than the Army had altogether before we entered the war.
        "Other parts of the airplane program are progressing
    satisfactorily."
The American consul at Tiflis reported an armistice between
    Turks and Russians along the whole Caucasus front.[1]
Secretary Daniels, testifying before the House Sub-Commit-
    tee on Naval Affairs, made it clear that he was proud to
    have the public know what the navy had done.
Lansing sent the President a packet of telegrams to and from
    the American Embassy in Russia, in regard to the activities
    of Edgar G. Sisson, who was there under the Committee
    on Public Information. Sisson appears to have established
    relations with the Bolsheviks—which was forbidden to
    the Embassy. The ambassador entirely disapproved of
    Sisson, though he used him to a certain extent. Soon after
    this, probably, the President discussed the matter with
    Creel, who then telegraphed to Sisson: ". . . . President
    insists that you avoid political entanglements and personal
    matters."[2]

To Breckinridge Long, Third Assistant Secretary of State, who
had written of an organization of newspaper men in Paris "for
the purpose of facilitating the sending of *proper* and accurate
information concerning the military and political situations,"
and suggested the need for the same sort of thing in this country:

"I have read very carefully your letter . . . and need
hardly say that I sympathize with the object you have in
mind in the matter of organizing the newspaper men in
some serviceable way to put the news service upon a
higher plane of intelligence and public duty, and I sincerely hope that something may come of the organization

---

[1] *Foreign Relations*, 1918, *Russia*, Vol. II, pp. 594-595.

[2] Sisson, *One Hundred Red Days*, p. 90. Sisson explains that Creel telegraphed him
later that his message had been sent to "satisfy opposition" and was "not at all . . .
a rebuke." *Ibid.*, p. 94.

which is being formed in Paris. Certainly, its personnel would promise good results; but I do not believe, from experience which I hope some time to have an opportunity of narrating to you, that anything of the same sort would be possible on this side the water. There are too many irregular, irresponsible and unmanageable forces amongst us, and while the members of a particular group would no doubt be honorably bound by their engagements, they could bind nobody else and control nobody else. If there should by any chance come a breathing spell when I can talk this matter over with you, I shall be very glad to do so."

To Charles W. Russell:

"I hope that you will not feel hurt or neglected, as I am led by your letter . . . to believe that you do feel, because you may rest assured that if your patriotic tender of your services to the Government is not taken advantage of it is only because there is no appointment to which you could be advantageously assigned.

"To the great credit of the country be it said, such offers of services come to us from every quarter and it is, of course, our duty to assign those who offer, if we assign them at all, to the places for which they would be most suited. The failure to assign you, therefore, is not at all due to lack of appreciation, but only to a lack of suitable opportunities, and certainly throws no question upon your ability."

To A. W. Tedcastle, a Boston business man and an old friend:

"Of course I wish that the excess profits tax might bear evenly and fairly upon all. It is a thorny business, the solution of which is not, I am sorry to say, perfectly plain, but you may be sure we are thinking a great deal about it and if any action is possible, it will be taken."

Thursday, December 20th.

In the early afternoon the President conferred with Senator Newlands of Nevada and with George Creel.

Lloyd George, speaking in the House of Commons, repeated much of what he had said in Glasgow on June 29th;[1] and also his statement of December 14th, that victory was the essential thing. ". . . . It is not because it satisfies some low vindictive sense in human nature, because you want merely to punish, but it is because we realize that victory is the only thing that will give reality to peace terms. A league of nations in which Germany is represented by that military caste triumphant would be a hollow farce, but the people of Germany must be there, and that is why victory in itself is more important than mere terms. . . ."[2]

Desperate fighting was reported from the Italian front, with untold losses on both sides.

To Dr. A. J. McKelway of the National Child Labor Committee:

"As the labor situation created by the war develops, I am more interested than ever, if that were possible, in throwing all the safeguards possible around the labor of women and children in order that no intolerable or injurious burden may be placed upon them. I am, therefore, very glad indeed that the National Child Labor Committee is diligently continuing its labors and extending its vigilance in this important matter. By doing so it is contributing to efficiency and economy of production, as well as to the preservation of life and health."

To Mrs. Palmer Axson:

MY DEAR MARGARET:

This is a charming letter which I have just read from you about Margaret's[3] visit to Savannah and her concert

---

[1] This volume, p. 136.
[2] *War Aims and Peace Proposals*, pp. 216-220.
[3] The President's oldest daughter.

there, and I thank you warmly for it. It gives me a real glimpse of the dear girl in her success, both as a person and as a singer, and makes my heart very warm.

It is delightful, too, to get a glimpse of the dear ones whom she has been visiting and, I know, enjoying. I wish I had time for a real letter but these few lines carry the most affectionate messages to you all.

Cordially and sincerely yours,
WOODROW WILSON

To Professor George M. Harper of Princeton:
"Thank you for your little note. As a matter of fact, the copy of the Alumni Weekly which contained your too generous article did get through the mill and reach me, and I read the article aloud to Mrs. Wilson with genuine appreciation. Thank you very warmly.

"You are quite right. I take no stock at all in the Alumni Weekly. It has been full of falseness from the first, and so I had not seen a copy of it for a long time. I am very glad I saw this copy."

To Cardinal Gibbons, who had urged, in behalf of the Pope, that the President use his influence toward making Serbian relief possible:

"Your letter . . . concerns a matter which I have thought about a great deal and in which I am sincerely anxious to help. The difficulties in the way are many, largely because we find that we cannot rely upon the promises of the belligerents opposed to us in the matter of the transmission and distribution of relief. But you may be sure that if any way can be found, I shall be glad to find it."

To his secretary, Tumulty, referring to a letter from Arthur Brisbane, who deplored Roosevelt's outbursts and the fact that his words could go freely to the British press but that those of W. R. Hearst could not:

"I very much appreciate this letter of Mr. Brisbane's and hope that you will tell him so. I hope you will tell him at the same time that I really think the best way to treat Mr. Roosevelt is to take no notice of him. That breaks his heart and is the best punishment that can be administered. After all, while what he says is outrageous in every particular, he does, I am afraid, keep within the limits of the law, for he is as careful as he is unscrupulous."

Friday, December 21st.

The President and Dr. Grayson played golf for the first time in many days. Before the cabinet meeting in the afternoon the President received the Serbian War Mission, with Dr. Milenko Vesnitch at its head; after the meeting, Representative Raker of California. The President and Mrs. Wilson gave a dinner in honor of the Serbian Mission.

Frank I. Cobb to Colonel House—a letter which House turned over to the President—discussing the evident plan of the Old Guard Republicans to "make their appeal for Republican support on the ground that the President's appointments are mainly partisan, that the war is incompetently conducted, and that Republicans have been excluded from the conduct of the war." This was a fake issue, he said, but dangerous nevertheless, and it would of course have the support of Roosevelt. He told of an interview he had had that morning with William R. Willcox, chairman of the Republican National Committee, in whose character and integrity he, Cobb, had faith. Willcox was much disturbed over the situation—he had been supporting the administration in the war, and he was being fought by the Old Guard as a result. Willcox had suggested that it would help if the President could draw into the war administration a few more Republicans of the type of Root.

James Bryce wrote to Elihu Root: ".... The feeling that this war will have been fought in vain unless it lead to some permanent machinery for averting wars in future by a league of peace-loving free peoples, has been growing constantly stronger here, and we now feel that the question has become so urgent that steps should be taken to work out in detail a scheme for the purpose which could be presented to the Governments of the Allied Nations, especially of course to those of the United States and Great Britain. These Governments are now too busy to be able to give much thought to the subject—and it may be doubted whether here or in France they contain men thoroughly competent to deal with it. Could you and we do something to prepare a joint scheme by means of an International Committee of skilled men?"[1]

E. N. Hurley, testifying before the Senate committee investigating the shipping situation, said that the Shipping Board's program of creating an adequate merchant marine was moving steadily to a successful completion in spite of great obstacles and past dissensions.[2]

Saturday, December 22nd.

Harry Lauder called to see the President at noon. Luncheon guests: Secretary and Mrs. McAdoo, the Sayres, who arrived with their two children during the morning, and Mrs. Edward Elliott: and the whole party went to hear Harry Lauder in the afternoon. At 5:30 the President had a conference with McAdoo. The head usher's diary records: "Evening with family."

Secretary Daniels telegraphed to Admiral Sims: "At House committee hearing of conduct of Navy, Representative Britten said 'I would like to have copy of complaints which have come from Admiral Sims on the other side.' If you desire to make statement of action of department in reference to sending and supplying force under your command since war began, please send in code." Admiral Benson also telegraphed Sims on the same day: "Effort being made to create impression you have been hampered by failure of Navy Department to meet your request for

---

[1]Fisher, *James Bryce*, Vol. II, p. 178.

[2]Hurley writes that shortly before this and several times afterwards the President went over to his [Hurley's] office, the real purpose of his visits being "to show the country and the committee of the Senate that he really was supporting me." Hurley, *The Bridge to France*, pp. 67–68.

various things, particularly personnel. I feel that a strong positive statement on this subject from you is highly desirable."[1]

Peace negotiations were begun at Brest Litovsk between Russia and the Central Powers.

The Supreme War Council at Paris agreed on a policy with regard to Russia: each government was to "at once get into relations with the Bolsheviki through unofficial agents, each country as seems best to it."

"We should represent to the Bolsheviki that we have no desire to take part in any way in the internal politics of Russia and that any idea that we favour a counter-revolution is a profound mistake. . . .

". . . we should continually repeat our readiness to accept the principles of self-determination and this includes that of no annexation or indemnities. . . ."[2]

Sunday, December 23rd.

President and Mrs. Wilson and Mr. and Mrs. Sayre went to the Central Presbyterian Church in the morning; in the afternoon they visited the Corcoran Art Gallery. Winthrop M. Daniels called at six o'clock; and at 6:30, Colonel House arrived. He brought to Washington and may have given the President at this time part of the material which the Inquiry had been gathering, and which the President wanted to see in connection with the preparation of his January 8th address to Congress.[3]

Admiral Sims telegraphed Secretary Daniels: "I strongly deprecate any effort to create an impression that our naval forces in European waters have been avoidably hampered by failure of the Navy Department to comply with my recommendations for various things, particularly personnel. . . .

". . . I consider it the first duty of those at the front loyally to accept decisions and to make the best of conditions which are at present admittedly unsatisfactory and must so remain until the energetic measures now being

[1]*Naval Investigation Hearings*, 1920, Vol. I, p. 8.
[2]For entire memorandum, see *Foreign Relations*, 1918, *Russia*, Vol. I, pp. 330–331.
[3]The Fourteen Points address.

taken to increase our antisubmarine forces produce the necessary reinforcements."[1]

German troops drove in British advanced posts on a 700-yard front northeast of Ypres.

Monday, December 24th.

Afternoon appointments: Daniel Willard; Senator Kellogg of Minnesota; H. A. Garfield; Representative Hayden of Arizona; the minister from Switzerland; Secretary Baker. While the President was meeting his appointments, Mrs. Wilson and Dr. Grayson drove over to Virginia to distribute presents to the children who were on hand every day to wave to the President when he drove to the golf course. In the early evening President and Mrs. Wilson called on Mrs. Wilson's family at the Powhatan. After dinner everyone went to the oval room to decorate the big Christmas tree.

> Secretary McAdoo sent the President a telegram from Crosby, who discussed the serious lack of coal in Italy because of inadequate shipping arrangements, and suggested the immediate creation of an Inter-Ally Shipping Board, himself to represent the United States for the time being. McAdoo endorsed the suggestion in view of the "great urgency of the matter."[2]

To Secretary McAdoo, referring to a paper by Oscar T. Crosby, the chief conclusion of which was that steps should be taken at once to secure the establishment of an international tribunal which should have at its disposal an international force sufficient to maintain peace:

"If Mr. Crosby were not connected with the Government, of course I would welcome the publication of his article on the maintenance of international peace without

---

[1]*Naval Investigation Hearings,* 1920, Vol. I, p. 8.

[2]The President's reply of the 26th, while it is not in his files, almost certainly disapproved Crosby's suggestion. McAdoo wrote again on January 2nd saying that he had notified Crosby as the President directed: ". . . . I confess, however, that it has been my own view that the Inter-Ally Council must concern itself with matters of this character. . . .

"The impressive fact is this: That the credits we are asked to extend to Great Britain, Italy and France must be predicated upon the ability to ship the supplies, materials, etc., which those credits are to purchase in America. Therefore, unless the shipping situation is considered along with the application for such credits, it is impossible to determine them intelligently. . . ."

competitive armaments, but inasmuch as he is connected with the Government, I think it would be a very great mistake for him to publish it. No member of the Government ought to put forth a specific plan at so critical a time as this. It would inevitably carry the implication that it was more than an individual opinion. I would be very much obliged if you would convey this judgment of mine to Mr. Crosby."

To the Rt. Rev. William F. McDowell:

"With regard to the resolutions of the Board of Temperance, Prohibition and Public Morals of the Methodist Episcopal Church, which I recently acknowledged, the Secretary of War now advises me that he and General Pershing have discussed this subject and that General Pershing has been in conference with the authorities of France on the general subject of police regulations affecting American soldiers in that country and has received a most hearty co-operation at their hands.

"I have asked the Secretary of War to make special inquiry of General Pershing as to whether any representations to the commanding generals from me would aid his efforts in the matter.

"You will be interested to know that the Secretary of War has in France at this time a special agent investigating this entire subject, and hopes soon to be able to have Mr. Fosdick go in person to France to investigate and report. Mr. Fosdick would be particularly valuable in this connection, because of his familiarity with continental police regulations and methods of enforcement, and also because of the constructive work done by his Commission, in our own training camps at home."

Tuesday, December 25th.
Christmas Day.

The entire White House family had breakfast together in the small dining room. Immediately afterward they went to the

GENERAL JOHN J. PERSHING

REAR-ADMIRAL WILLIAM S. SIMS

Oval Room in the basement for the tree, and after that to the library for the opening of the presents. During the morning the President's brother and his family came over from Baltimore. President and Mrs. Wilson, with two or three others, went to Keith's late in the afternoon to attend a special performance for the soldiers. The family dinner was at eight o'clock in the evening.

Secretary Lansing to the President: ". . . . I have the impression that the repeated efforts of the Imperial Government for peace-negotiations are due in considerable measure to pressure by these economic interests in order to prevent as far as possible the commercial isolation which is more and more feared as the war goes on.

"Whether these fears are or are not justified seems to me of less importance than the fact that they exist. If they do, and I think that that can hardly be doubted, ought we not to turn to advantage this mental state of the influential business class in Germany by making their fears as to the *post-bellum* trade conditions more intense. . . .

"One method would seem to be to threaten commercial retaliation or reprisal after the war. Personally I do not believe such a method of imposing penalties could be carried out as it would be against the almost irresistible processes of trade, but the threat might have the desired psychological effect in Germany and prevent the conditions on which the adoption of the method is predicated. . . ."

Count Czernin, Austro-Hungarian Foreign Minister, acted as spokesman of the Central Powers in offering terms for a general peace at the first Brest Litovsk conference. ". . . . Forcible annexation of territory seized during the war does not enter into the intention of the allied [Central] powers. . . .

"It is not the intention of the allies [of Germany] to deprive of political independence those nations which lost it during the war.

"The question of subjection to that or the other country of those nationalities who have not political independence cannot, in the opinion of the powers of the Quadruple Alliance, be solved internationally. . . .

". . . the protection of the rights of minorities constitutes an essential component part of the constitutional rights of peoples to self-determination. The allied [Central] governments also grant validity to this principle everywhere, in so far as it is practically realizable. . . .

"The return of colonial territories forcibly seized during the war constitutes an essential part of German demands, which Germany cannot renounce under any circumstances. Likewise, the Russian demand for immediate evacuation of territories occupied by an adversary conforms to German intentions. Having in view the nature of the colonial territories of Germany, the realization of the right of self-determination, besides the above outlined considerations, in the form proposed by the Russian delegation, is at present practically impossible. . . ."[1]

To his secretary, Tumulty, enclosing a letter from Gutzon Borglum, who urged that the aircraft situation be corrected from within, without publicity; and suggested the selection of three competent men, himself to be one of them, to conduct an investigation:

"What did you find out about these matters that Mr. Borglum is so excited about? I think it important that we should get at the root of this thing and find out if there really is anything lagging or anything the matter. I had a very full report about it not long ago and things seemed going very satisfactorily. If Mr. Borglum has a grievance or has any personal element in it, it is rather important that we should know."

Wednesday, December 26th.

The only official appointment of the day was at five in the afternoon, when Secretary McAdoo and Secretary Baker called for a conference.

The President's proclamation assuming control of the transportation systems of the country and naming W. G. McAdoo as Director General was given out in the evening. It was accompanied by a statement of explanation. ". . . . This is a war of resources no less than of men,

[1]*Current History*, February, 1918, p. 263.

perhaps even more than of men, and it is necessary for the complete mobilization of our resources that the transportation systems of the country should be organized and employed under a single authority and a simplified method of coordination which have not proved possible under private management and control. The committee of railway executives who have been cooperating with the Government in this all-important matter have done the utmost that it was possible for them to do; have done it with patriotic zeal and with great ability; but there were difficulties that they could neither escape nor neutralize. . . .
"A great national necessity dictated the action and I was therefore not at liberty to abstain from it."[1]

About five hours earlier, confidential messages had gone to the heads of the principal railway systems of the country indicating that when possession had been taken a board of five or seven members would be appointed to advise with the Director General. Railroad executives and bankers interviewed by the New York *Times* reporter in the evening were pleased at the whole arrangement; the *Times* of the 27th carried an approving editorial; railroad stocks soared.

Secretary Baker to the President: "I have conveyed to the Secretary of State your suggestion, and he today notified the British, French and Italian Governments of the determination of the United States to participate in the Supreme War Council, and of the designation of General Bliss as our representative. . . ."

H. A. Garfield was the first witness before the Senate committee investigating coal problems. The situation, he said, was grave; he thought the unification of railroads under some plan necessary; and he would like to see both railroads and mines operated by the government.

To Secretary McAdoo, a letter written on the President's own typewriter:

"The proclamation is all right. I will have it copied here and copies made for the press, to be released to-morrow morning, along with a statement from me. If you are thinking of making a statement, too, you had better bring

---

[1] *Public Papers,* Vol. V, pp. 143–149.

it over this afternoon (say about 5.30) so that we can compare the two and have them gee in every particular.

"Meanwhile I will show the proclamation to Baker and make sure that he is in entire accord with us in all respects. . . ."

To B. M. Baruch:

"Thank you for your generous letter. You *are* doing all that is possible for you to do to relieve me, and you may be sure I am very grateful. My very best and warmest good wishes go out to you and yours for the Christmas Season and the New Year."

Thursday, December 27th.

The President received the French ambassador and Admiral Grasset in the early afternoon, and then went, with Mrs. Wilson, to the funeral of Senator Newlands. Late-afternoon appointments: representatives of the railroad brotherhoods; Vance C. McCormick. Mrs. Wilson's nieces, the Misses Maury, arrived for a visit; Colonel and Mrs. House and Mr. and Mrs. Auchincloss were guests at dinner.

By authorization of the President, Hoover's statement of the sugar situation—the gist of what he had planned to say to the Senate investigating committee, had he been called as he expected to be on the 23rd—was given to the press.[1]

Lansing's memorandum of his interview with the Japanese ambassador, Aimaro Sato: ". . . . He first asked in regard to the situation in Russia and I told him that our purpose was to remain quiescent and await developments. He said that that was the view of his Government.

"I then spoke to him about the situation at Vladivostok and told him that the view of this Government was that it would be unwise for either the United States or Japan to send troops to Vladivostok as it would undoubtedly result in the unifying of the Russians under the Bolsheviks against foreign interference. He said to me that that was the exact view of his Government and that they have no intention of sending troops to Vladivostok for the same

---

[1] *Official Bulletin*, December 27, 1917.

reason . . . He said that both Great Britain and France had made the suggestion but that the Japanese Government did not consider it wise . . ."[1]

To Secretary Baker:

"Will you not upon the proper occasion send to General Pershing some such message as the following:

"'The President requests me to send to you and to all the American officers and forces associated with you the most cordial New Year's greetings and to express his unqualified confidence that the American forces under your command may be counted upon to render the name of their country still more glorious, both by feats of arms and by personal conduct characterized by the highest principles of bravery and honor.' "

To Thomas D. Jones, who had presented his resignation from the War Trade Board because of ill health:

MY DEAR FRIEND:

Your letter . . . deeply distresses me. I have found your counsel and aid invaluable in the extremely important work of the War Trade Board and it is not going to be possible to replace you, but I haven't it in my heart to ask anything which would demand of you sacrifice of your health and, therefore, I must yield with a very heavy heart.

I hope it will be possible for you to recuperate rapidly, and my thoughts shall follow you with genuine affection.

With the warmest good wishes for the New Year to you all,

Faithfully yours,
WOODROW WILSON

To Mrs. Howard Gould:

"I wish with all my heart that I could comply with the request contained in your letter of Christmas day, but I

---

[1] *Foreign Relations*, 1918, *Russia*, Vol. II, p. 13.

am sure you will understand why I cannot when I say that our experience has taught us that it is really unconscientious on our part to give passports and letters to any except those who are doing the imperatively necessary war work. This experience on our part is reinforced most emphatically by advice from foreign governments. The difficulty of national housekeeping, so to speak, is constantly increasing over there, and those who do not come for absolutely necessary work are, to speak plainly, not welcome.

"You will see, therefore, that I have no choice, and I am sure that you will justify my decision in your own judgment."

To his secretary, Tumulty, enclosing a petition from a group of naturalized American citizens who were natives of Rumania and who asked that the government of the United States urge upon the government of Rumania the abolishment of restrictions upon Jews in that country:

"I would be obliged if you would make a cordial acknowledgment of this as at my request and say that the petitioners may rest assured not only that I deeply value their loyal sentiments but am sympathetically concerned with their desires in this matter."

Friday, December 28th.
The President's sixty-
first birthday.

Early-afternoon appointments: Judge Hylan; Midshipman Earle H. Kincaid. In the late afternoon the President conferred with the Attorney General; and in the evening with Senators Chamberlain and Hitchcock. They discussed various methods for coördinating and speeding up the military program, and Chamberlain said he had in mind a bill to create a munitions department. At dinner the President had a large birthday cake, with sixty-one candles on it, which Mrs. Josephus Daniels had made for him.

The government of the United States assumed control of the railways of the country at noon.

To Secretary Wilson:

"It was good to see a letter from you written in Washington, because I have been anxious about your health and am delighted that you are back. I hope with all my heart that you are feeling better and will take the rest necessary entirely to restore your health.

"It was kind and thoughtful of you to write me on my birthday and you may be sure I appreciate it as coming from one whom I count a real and invaluable friend."

To Herbert Hoover, who wrote that Judge Lindley was no longer well enough to handle the work of chief counsel for the Food Administration:

"In reply to your request for a suggestion as to a successor to Judge Lindley, I am going to take the liberty of suggesting Mr. Samuel Untermyer of New York. Of course, we now know that the man who is going to fight you until the war is over is Senator Reed of Missouri. Mr. Untermyer is one of the few men who can beat him. I believe it would stop many investigations of the type which Senator Reed is conducting if it could be understood that in the various departments there was some lawyer like Mr. Untermyer who is genuinely to be feared. We have nothing to fear from investigations conceived in the right spirit, and we have every right to defend ourselves against the other sort."

To Governor F. D. Gardner of Missouri, who had submitted a circular being sent out by Senator Reed, from which it appeared that the President had justified Reed's attitude on the Food bill:

"I have your letter . . . and in reply would say that I do not agree and have never agreed with Senator Reed in his views about the food legislation, and believe that his present conclusions are absolutely unjustified."

Saturday, December 29th.

The President spent the morning in his study. Ambassador Jusserand called at two o'clock, probably in order to present a message from President Poincaré of France (see p. 457, this volume); and at three o'clock, Secretary Baker.

Sir Cecil Spring Rice sent the President, in a letter marked "personal and secret," a memorandum of an informal and private conversation he had had that day with the Japanese ambassador. Mr. Sato desired an appointment with the President, since he was soon to leave for Japan and wished to be able to explain the American situation over there. He stressed Japan's unwillingness, on grounds of honor, to depart from any of her engagements unless she was treated as "outside the pale"; he urged that the Western nations treat Japan on a basis of mutual respect, confidence and equality; and he spoke of Japan's great fear of the situation which would be created if Germany should obtain control of Russia.

A coal famine was feared in New York, with the thermometer below zero.

All Belgium and northern France lay under deep snow.

Trotsky made public an address to the peoples and governments of the Allied countries, inviting them to share in peace negotiations. The program proposed by Germany, he said, was "profoundly inconsistent . . . an unprincipled compromise between the pretensions of imperialism and the opposition of the laboring democracy." ". . . . But," he added, "the very fact of the presentation of this program is an enormous step forward. . . ." The Allies were once more urged to state their aims. Finally he pronounced his ultimatum:

". . . if the Allied Governments in blind obstinacy, which characterizes the falling and perishing classes, again refuse to participate in the negotiations, then the working class will be confronted with the iron necessity of tearing the power out of the hands of those who cannot or will not give peace to the nations. . . ."[1]

". . . Irkutsk in flames," reported the United States consul at Harbin. "Bolsheviks murdering and plundering in-

---

[1] *Foreign Relations*, 1918, *Russia*, Vol. I, pp. 405–408.

habitants, ravishing women, corpses [of] murdered children cover streets. French and British exterminated, French consular agent and two French officers murdered, help implored. . . ."[1]

To Secretary Redfield, who had written on the President's birthday: ". . . we may, indeed we ought to tell you on these anniversaries of the faith that is in us, of our trust in God and in you His servant, doing His work, speaking to our people as I verily believe in His spirit. . . .":

"Your letter written on my birthday reached me yesterday and made me feel, I want you to know, very proud to have gained your confidence in such a degree. Even when one does not feel that he deserves the praise he gets, it is peculiarly acceptable when it comes from real friends who are constantly at his elbow to help, and I thank you with all my heart."

To Mrs. Josephus Daniels:
"The cake was perfectly beautiful and as palatable as it was good to look at, and I am deeply and sincerely grateful to you for thinking of me in such a delightful way on my birthday. The sixty-one candles on the cake did not make so forbidding a multitude as I should have feared they would, and our little family circle had a very jolly time blowing them out and celebrating. It was a regular 'blow-out.' "

Sunday, December 30th.
The President and Mrs. Wilson spent a quiet day; no church, and no official engagements.

The cold weather held, with intense suffering because of the coal shortage. The New York *Times* reported a three-hour conference at Secretary McAdoo's home, to plan for the relief of a dangerous situation, and the following day McAdoo ordered that trains carrying coal should have the right of way, even over passenger service.

---

[1]Lansing replied on January 2nd: ". . . . Department anxious to keep close touch developments also all available information welfare Americans Siberia. . . ." *Op. cit.,* Vol. II, pp. 16, 18.

Monday, December 31st.

The President worked in his study until noon, when he walked over to the offices of the Shipping Board for a conference. Afternoon appointments: the Japanese ambassador; Secretary Redfield and Dr. Stratton of the Bureau of Standards, who had worked out a memorandum showing the great need of additional equipment and laboratories for studying problems presented by the war. Their estimated expenses were over a million dollars. The President listened intently to their presentation, and decided on the spot to give them what they needed, appropriating it from his special fund;[1] Senator Pomerene of Ohio; Representative Sherley of Kentucky; the Right Honorable Sir Frederick Smith; Representative Sims of Tennessee.

The Director General of railroads announced the resignation of the Railroad War Board and the appointment of a new Advisory Board.[2]

To Secretary McAdoo, "Personal":

"You know of course what I am going to recommend to Congress with regard to guarantees to the roads. It would be of great service to me if the lawyers who are serving you would have ready for me by the time Congress opens, if possible, a bill embodying the guarantees which I could place in the hands of the Chairmen of the committees concerned."

To Secretary Lane, written after reading a letter from the Attorney General setting out developments in the California oil situation. The President's letter is marked "Personal":

"I have seen a copy of the newly-formulated leasing bill and am distressed to find that it goes practically as far as was proposed the last time in the matter of indulgence of the oil men in the disputed districts. I have gone over this matter so often and with such close attention that I am very clear in my conviction about it, and per-

---

[1] W. C. Redfield to the author.

[2] John Skelton Williams; Hale Holden; Henry Walters; Edward Chambers; Walker D. Hines.

sonally I cannot go an inch further than was embodied in the proposals of Senator Swanson, with which I think you are familiar, and my conclusion affects not only the naval reserve, so-called, but the other areas under discussion. I wish very much that you could exert your influence to get this modification of the proposed concessions adopted, not as your own judgment, for I know it is not, but as my judgment, and one which must necessarily be reckoned with in the final settlement. I am suggesting this to you because I think you may have some more open and tactful approach to the matter than I could have. My intervention at this stage would seem a bit blunt. . . ."[1]

To George Creel:

"The other day you called my attention to the immense amount of government publicity matter being unloaded on the newspapers . . . and I brought the matter up in Cabinet where we discussed it rather fully, and my net conclusion from the discussion is this, that the matter with which the newspapers are burdened goes out, not directly from the departments themselves, but from the Congressmen and Senators who have mailing lists and who send to the newspapers within their constituencies practically everything that the Government publishes, with many duplications of course and without any attempt at winnowing the wheat from the chaff, and I must say I despair of suggesting a solution for that difficulty."

To Mrs. Charles W. Mitchell, whose husband had been a Princeton classmate of the President's:

"I am sure I need not tell you how my heart aches at the news of Charlie's death. He was very near and very dear to me, one of the best and truest friends I ever had, and while I know that the loss to his profession has been

[1]Lane replied that he was heartily in favor of the solution proposed by the President.

very great, what fills my heart just now is my own personal loss and, above that, your own irreparable bereavement. My heart goes out to you in the deepest and truest sympathy. I wish there were some great word of comfort that I could speak to you. The only comfort I have for myself is that the memory of him will always be exceedingly sweet."

To Dr. Hiram Woods, a Princeton classmate:

"Charlie Mitchell's death has grieved me most deeply, as you may imagine, and you may be sure that I would have got over to his funeral if it had been possible for me to do so; but it was impossible, and the fact that I could not be there adds to my grief. Thank you very warmly, my dear fellow, for sending me the sad news. I am writing to Mrs. Mitchell today. The old circle is broken and I am very sad."

To Hale Holden, president of the Chicago, Burlington & Quincy Railroad, who had just been appointed to McAdoo's Advisory Board:

"Your very generous letter . . . has given me a great deal of pleasure . . . I hope and believe that by hearty cooperation, which I do not for a moment doubt, we shall be able to work out something that will be for the real and permanent benefit of the railroads. The difficulties are many and tremendous, but we shall overcome them."

To his aunt, Mrs. James Woodrow of Columbia, South Carolina, wife of the Rev. Dr. James Woodrow, one of the inspirers of the President's boyhood, who had written:

MY DEAR TOMMIE,

Not a letter, but just a line to let you know that I am thinking of you, and that my daily prayer for you is

"As thy days, so shall thy strength be."

With love to you and your dear Wife,

Affectionately,
AUNT FELIE.

MY DEAR AUNT FELIE:

Your little note . . . gave me the greatest pleasure and cheer, and I want to send you in return for myself and from all my little household the warmest and most affectionate greetings of the New Year.

I wish I had time for a real letter but you will know how much this message means, even though it is short.

Affectionately yours,
WOODROW WILSON

To his secretary, Tumulty, referring to resolutions adopted by university presidents and engineering deans, suggesting that the youth of the country ought to be impressed with "the necessity of preparing themselves for engineering duties in the Army and Navy, for the successful prosecution of the war, and for the reconstruction period which must follow the war.":

"I wish you would acknowledge the receipt of this for me and assure those concerned of my very serious interest, and ask them whether there is likely to arise some early occasion, some gathering or something of that sort, when I could make such an utterance as they suggest without seeming just to fire it off into the open air."[1]

---

[1] Suggestions for better educational preparation of the youth of the country always met the President's warm approval, even when his time was most absorbed.

CHAPTER IV

"A RAMPAGING MOOD OF HOSTILE CRITICISM"

(January, February, 1918)

America begins to feel the pinch of war—heatless, meatless, wheatless, sweetless days.

Wilson brands Senator Chamberlain's charges of military inefficiency as "an astonishing and absolutely unjustifiable distortion of the truth"; backs Garfield's bitterly resented coal order— "We must just bow our heads and let the storm beat."

He states his Fourteen Points—"a summing up of all that I have been thinking recently"; replies to the Austrian Emperor's suggestion of a direct exchange of views on peace, asking him to be more explicit.

Secretary Baker meets criticism of the War Department before a Senate Committee. Ollie James reports to the President: "He's eating 'em up!"

New Year's Day.
Tuesday, January 1, 1918.

THE President had no official appointments. In the late afternoon he and Mrs. Wilson went to Keith's, with Mr. and Mrs. Edward Elliott. Fifteen people sat down to a family dinner in the evening, using the small dining room because the State Dining Room, the East Room, and one or two others were cut off to save coal.

The British War Cabinet, reported Sir Robert Cecil, were uneasy about military stores at Vladivostok, fearing that they might be seized by Bolsheviks at any moment and sent to Petrograd for sale to Germany. It was felt therefore that the question of landing a force large enough to guard these stores should be reconsidered. Such a force would have to be mainly Japanese, but it should certainly contain an element of other nationalities. The British force avail-

442

able in that region was small, hence it seemed "of great importance" that the United States send a contingent to co-operate.

The American consul at Vladivostok telegraphed that the consular corps agreed upon the necessity of foreign warships in the harbor to preserve order. He was notified on the 5th by the State Department that the *Brooklyn* had been ordered to Yokohama for further instructions.[1]

Wednesday, January 2nd.

The President spent the day in his study, with three appointments only: Representative Foster of Illinois; Senator Thompson of Kansas; Charles R. Crane.

Hoover appeared before the Senate sub-committee investigating the sugar shortage; according to press reports, the Reed-Hoover feud "came to the surface" a number of times.[2]

Balfour reported to the President through Colonel House upon the "informal conversations" on peace terms which the British had been authorized by the Paris Conference to carry on with the Austrians.

A British and an Austrian representative[3] had met secretly in Switzerland, holding "friendly and unofficial" interviews for two days. The British representative, acting on instructions, refused to discuss a general peace which would include Germany; nor would the Austrian representative, also acting on instructions, hold out hopes of a separate peace with Austria. It was gathered, however, that Austria was anxious for peace and that while she would not abandon Germany, she would be prepared to try to induce her to accept a "reasonable settlement." Nor (it was also gathered) had Austria any desire to be Germany's vassal after the war. The statement that British war aims did not include the destruction of Austria was received by the Austrian representative with "much satisfaction."

---

[1]British and Japanese ships were likewise ordered to Vladivostok. *Foreign Relations,* 1918, *Russia,* Vol. II, pp. 16, 19.

[2]New York *Times,* January 3, 1918.

[3]General Smuts and Count Mensdorff. For a memorandum by Czernin on these negotiations, see *Intimate Papers,* Vol. III, pp. 379–381.

The Allied governments had not yet been told of the conversations, said Balfour in conclusion; and it was thought that as few persons as possible should be informed of them until something "definite and tangible" resulted.

Lansing to the President, a long letter enclosing Trotsky's appeal of December 29th. He was impressed, he wrote the President, with the "adroitness" of the author, "whose presentation of peace terms may well appeal to the average man, who will not perceive the fundamental errors on which they are based."

". . . . If the Bolsheviks intend to suggest that every community . . . can determine its allegiance to this or that political state or to become independent, the present political organization of the world would be shattered . . . It would be international anarchy. . . .

"The document is an appeal to the proletariat of all countries, to the ignorant and mentally deficient, who by their numbers are urged to become masters. Here seems to me to lie a very real danger in view of the present social unrest throughout the world. . . .

"I think in considering this address it might properly be asked by what authority the Bolsheviks assume the right to speak for the Russian people. . . .

"I feel that to make any sort of reply would be contrary to the dignity of the United States and offer opportunity for further insults and threats, although I do not mean that it may not be expedient at some time in the near future to state our peace terms in more detail than has yet been done."

To Secretary Baker, referring to the charge that men were being sent away from camps too soon after suffering from measles:

"Apparently this *is* a serious matter to which my friend, Gavit, managing editor of the New York Evening Post, calls our attention, and I hasten to send his letter to you. You will know how to find out the facts and deal with them. . . ."[1]

---

[1] Gavit wrote later, referring, probably, to this incident: ". . . . So emphatic had been the President's personal explosion of wrath that Surgeon General Gorgas came

Telegram to David Lloyd George, who had sent greetings to the government and people of the United States:

"I am sure that I am expressing the feeling and purpose of the people of the United States as well as my own in sending you and through you to the Government and people of Great Britain a message of good will, and of resolution to continue to put every man and resource of the United States into the imperative task and duty of winning for the world an honorable and stable peace based upon justice and honor, and securing to the peoples of the world, great and small alike, the blessings of security and opportunity and friendly and helpful intercourse. . . ."

To George Creel, referring to a statement of war progress in the United States which Creel desired to have issued from the White House:

"I couldn't get hold of you yesterday afternoon and, therefore, had to arrange for the 'killing' of that statement, because the more I thought about it the more it seemed to me an unnecessary risk to make such a statement while uncertain in my own mind of the effect it would have, not upon our own people, for that would be easily calculable, but upon the international situation, coming in the midst of peace intimations of every kind.

"You can see that it might be construed as a note of defiance and as if calculated in time to operate as a rebuff of all peace offers.

"I would like a little more time, too, to consider the scope and character of the statement, and a short delay, if we should ultimately determine to issue it, will not be of great disadvantage."

---

personally to New York to explain to me how fearfully handicapped his department was by reason of raw incompetent subalterns down the line. . . ." J. P. Gavit, in the *Survey Graphic*, December, 1937.

To Gutzon Borglum, a letter written upon the advice of Secretary Baker:[1]

". . . . Knowing the earnest and loyal purpose with which you have written me, I have conferred with the Secretary of War and, at his request and my own hearty concurrence, I urge you to come at once to Washington, lay the whole matter frankly and fully before the Secretary, and by your own investigation discover the facts in this business. The Secretary of War assures me that he will be delighted to clothe you with full authority to get to the bottom of every situation, and that he will place at your disposal the services of Mr. Stanley King, a member of his own personal staff, if you desire to have his counsel in your inquiries. The Secretary further says that he will bring you into personal contact with General Squier, whom you doubtless already know personally, and will direct that every facility of inquiry be placed at your disposal. When you have thus investigated, if the other experts whom you suggest in your letter of December 25 still seem desirable to be appointed you can say so to the Secretary; and in the event of any difference of judgment between you, which seems to me impossible, I would be most happy to have a report from you personally to me on any phase of the matter which remains in the slightest degree doubtful in your mind."

To Robert Bridges, a Princeton classmate:

MY DEAR BOBBIE:

Thank you for the book, "The United States and Pangermania." I have heard a good deal of Cheradame's articles in the Atlantic Monthly but have never had time

---

[1] In the course of his letter on the Borglum matter, Secretary Baker said he felt that some of Borglum's statements were difficult to accept, but he added: " . . . yet I never feel it safe to rely on any situation so long as there is one upright, responsible doubter, and for this reason I earnestly hope that Mr. Borglum can be asked to come to Washington to see me. . . ."

at the right moment to turn to them. I hope I shall have better luck with this book.

It was a deep distress to me that I could not get over to Charlie Mitchell's funeral. His death has affected me very deeply. My thought, like yours, goes back to the old days of our delightful comradeship, and those memories, thank God, are a permanent possession. Death seems to me in such instances a very unreal thing, but it has this terrible aspect of reality, that it does take the dear fellow away from us for the days to come, and I grieve with all my heart.

It would have been a pleasure to see the rest of the crowd even in such distressing circumstances and to have the benefit of sharing their sympathy would have been a great comfort to me.

With the best wishes for everything that is good in the New Year,

Affectionately yours,
WOODROW WILSON

Thursday, January 3rd.

At 2:30 the President received Sir Cecil Spring Rice, retiring British ambassador, who presented a telegram from Balfour announcing the appointment of Lord Reading as his successor. Reporting the interview to Balfour, Spring Rice said the President had reminded him that during the first year of the war his, the President's "chief preoccupation" was the imminent danger of civil discord. ". . . . Now . . . the country had not been so thoroughly united for years. . . . He went on to say that the problem which an American President had to face was in the main a psychological one. He had to gauge public opinion. He had to take the course which commended itself to the great majority of the American people whose interpreter he was bound to be. No action could be taken or at least usefully taken unless it received the support of the great majority. It was not so much a question of what was the right thing to do from the abstract viewpoint as what was the possible thing to do, from the point of view of the popular condition of mind. It was his duty to divine the moment when the country required action and to take that action which the great majority demanded. It was from this point of view that certain considerations had lately presented themselves to him with great force. He himself with the full consent of the American people and with their express approval had made an appeal to the German people behind the back of the German Government. The Bolsheviki in Russia were now adopting the same policy. They had issued an appeal to all the nations of the world, to the peoples and not to the governments. He was without information at present, or at least without certain information, as to what reception had been given to this appeal. But there was evidence at hand that certainly in Italy and probably also in England and France, the appeal had not been without its effect. In the United States active agitation was proceeding. It was too early yet to say with positive certainty how successful this agitation had been. But it was evident that if the appeal of the Bolsheviki was allowed to remain unanswered, if nothing were done to counteract it, the effect would be great and would increase. The main point of the appeal was this. War should not be waged for purposes of aggression. The war should be brought to an end but not on a basis of conquest. The proper basis was satisfaction of legitimate desires of the separate peoples who had a right to satisfy those desires. They should be allowed to live their own lives according to their own will and under their own laws. In point of logic, of pure logic, this principle which was good in itself would lead to the complete independence of various small nationalities now forming part of various Empires. Pushed to its extreme, the principle would mean the disruption of existing governments, to an undefinable extent. . . .

"The American people were engaged in this war with all their heart. They were convinced that no course was open to them with honour except to engage in the war. But they would not engage in a war in which America was involved except on American principles. They would not fight this war for private ends, either for themselves or for anyone else. Their object was a stable peace and they did not believe that a stable peace could be based upon aggression. The German people had been worked upon by their Government, which had persuaded them that they were fighting not for conquest but for defence and that the object of the Allies was to crush and disrupt the German Empire and place German peoples under foreign rule. A formidable weapon was in the hands of the German Government as long as the German people could be brought to believe that such was the object of the alliance which they had to face. It was also very widely felt here that the Allies now fighting in Europe would find it extremely difficult to agree on any definite programme which did not look on the face of it as if its object, and its main object, was aggression and conquest. . . .

"Thus, speaking in general terms, it seemed to him that the American people were inclined to receive with favour a statement of a moderate and unaggressive character and would welcome such a statement. He had already in general terms indicated the general lines on which he thought American policy should be based. These statements had met with general approval. Each one had been more detailed than the last, and it might become necessary, as the war continued, to define even more clearly those objects for which America was waging war. . . .

"He begged me to remember that our conversation was wholly unofficial and that he was not speaking as President. . . ."[1]

Secretary Baker sent over a copy of General Pershing's reply to his message of December 18th:[2] ". . . . Do not think emergency now exists that would warrant our putting companies or battalions into British or French divisions, and would not do so except in grave crisis. Main objections are first, troops would lose their national identity; second, they probably could not be relieved for service with us without disrupting the allied division coming up especially if engaged in active service; third, the methods of training and instruction in both Allied armies are very different from our own which would produce some confusion at the start and also when troops return for service with us. Attention should be called to prejudices existing between French and British Governments and armies, and the desire of each to have American units assigned to them to the exclusion of similar assignments to the other. Also each army

---

[1] Gwynn *The Letters and Friendships of Sir Cecil Spring Rice*, Vol. II, pp. 422–425. See this interesting report entire.

[2] This volume, pp. 417–418.

regards its own methods as best and they do not hesitate to criticise each other accordingly. We have selected what we consider best in each and added to our own basic system of instruction. . . ."

Baker commented, in his covering letter to the President: ". . . . I am assuming that we ought to rely upon General Pershing to decide this kind of question, as he is on the ground and sees the needs as they arise and, of course, will desire to preserve the integrity of his own forces for independent operations unless the emergency becomes overruling."

Charles R. Crane sent the President a report from the American commercial attaché at Petrograd, who urged that the United States should not desert Russia in the crisis, pointed out the failures of Allied diplomacy in that direction, and indicated that it was up to the Allies to restate their aims.[1]

To Secretary Burleson, a letter written on the President's own typewriter:

DEAR BURLESON,

I send this sketch of a legislative programme over to you for any comments or suggestions you may have to make. Have I omitted anything that is not covered by its general terms?

I would be very much obliged if you would annotate it and send it back to me as soon as you can, for final statement.

Faithfully,
W. W.[2]

---

[1]Advice of this character was coming from a number of directions. The Springfield *Republican*, a paper which the President saw frequently, maintained that terms should be re-stated, "because peace terms are as much a part of strategy as the planning of battles." January 2, 1918.

[2]The enclosed program was as follows:

"(Assuming the Webb Bill and the two constitutional amendments to be out of the way.)

"Necessary measures in direct furtherance of the war: E.g., financial and military measures for the carrying out of the present programme and, if necessary, for its

Friday, January 4th.

The President conferred with Senator Sheppard of Texas at 11 o'clock; at 12:20, accompanied by Dr. Grayson and Tumulty, he left for the Capitol, where he was to address Congress on the railroad matter and recommend legislation.[1] Aside from the cabinet meeting there were no afternoon appointments. In the early evening the President received a group of congressmen, to discuss water power; and about nine o'clock Colonel House arrived, and "went into immediate conference with the President concerning the proposed message to Congress on our war aims."

".... We were in conference until half-past eleven, discussing the general terms to be used, and looking over data and maps which I had brought with me, some of which the Peace Inquiry Bureau had prepared."[2]

> The President designated Secretary Wilson War Labor Administrator.
> Senator Chamberlain introduced a bill to create a department of munitions for the period of the war.

Saturday, January 5th.

The President conferred with Colonel House in the morning, beginning the "final outline of his speech and the arrangement

---

extension. Removal of all statutory obstacles to the most effective business organization of the work of the War and Navy Departments.

"Government control of all necessaries and their production and price.

"Railway legislation.

"Extension of alien enemy legislation to women and enactment of adequate penalties for violation of proclamations in execution of all such legislation.

"Water power legislation.

"General leasing bill, for release of natural resources."

[1]*Public Papers*, Vol. V, pp. 150–154. That afternoon legislation designed to carry out the President's recommendations was introduced in both Houses.

[2]*Intimate Papers*, Vol. III, p. 322. For a brief discussion of the material brought by House, see *ibid.*, pp. 320 *et seq.* Dr. Seymour writes that the President decided to frame his speech with three special purposes in mind: (1) As an answer to the Bolshevik demand for an explanation of objects of the war, which might persuade Russia to stand by the Allies; (2) as an appeal to the German Socialists; (3) as a notice to the Entente that there must be a revision "in a liberal sense of the war aims which had been crystallized in the secret treaties."

In studying the President's preparation for his Fourteen Points address we are unfortunately (as Dr. Seymour points out) dependent upon Colonel House's diary accounts almost entirely. It is a pity here, as at many other points, that the President did not himself keep a record of his interviews or have one kept. No detailed description of his definite points."[1] Secretary and Mrs. McAdoo were luncheon guests, and McAdoo remained with the President afterward, for a conference. Sometime before evening Lloyd George's address came out in the Washington papers. The President, when he first read it, thought the terms given were so nearly akin to those he had worked out that it would be impossible for him to make his contemplated address to Congress; House, however, insisted that the situation had been changed for the better. ". . . . I thought," he wrote afterward in his diary, "that Lloyd George had cleared the air and made it more necessary for the President to act."[2]

The President wrote a message for Balfour on his own typewriter, and it was telegraphed by Colonel House in the morning, *before* Lloyd George's address had come out:

"The President wishes me to let the Prime Minister or you know that he feels he must presently make some specific utterance as a counter to the German peace suggestions, and that he feels that in order to keep the present enthusiastic and confident support of the war quick and effective here, an utterance must be in effect a repetition of his recent address to Congress in even more specific form than before.

"He hopes that no utterance is in contemplation on your side which would be likely to sound a different note or suggest claims inconsistent with what he proclaims the objects of the United States to be.

"The President feels that we have so far been playing into the hands of the German military party and solidifying German opinion against us, and he has information which seems to open a clear way to weakening the hands of that party and clearing the air of all possible misrepresentation and misunderstandings."[3]

Balfour telegraphed Colonel House, for the "information of the President, private and secret": "Negotiations have been going on for some time between the Prime Minister

---

of the conferences during which the President and House studied the findings of the Inquiry is included here, since it is all to be found in Volume III of *Intimate Papers*.

[1] *Intimate Papers*, Vol. III, p. 324. Colonel House's account, pp. 325-329, 334-337, should be consulted.

[2] *Ibid.*, p. 341.

[3] *Ibid.*, p. 339.

and the Trade Unions. . . . Finally the negotiations arrived at a point at which their successful issue depended mainly on the immediate publication by the British Government of a statement setting forth their war aims. This statement has now been made by the Prime Minister. It is the result of consultations with the labour leaders as well as the leaders of the Parliamentary Opposition.[1]

"Under these circumstances there was no time to consult the Allies as to the terms of the statement . . . It will be found . . . to be in accordance with the declarations hitherto made by the President on this subject.

"Should the President himself make a statement of his own views which in view of the appeal made to the peoples of the world by the Bolsheviki might appear a desirable course, the Prime Minister is confident that such a statement would also be in general accordance with the lines of the President's previous speeches, which in England as well as in other countries have been so warmly received by public opinion. Such a further statement would naturally receive an equally warm welcome."[2]

Lloyd George, addressing an audience of trade-union delegates in London, restated Great Britain's war aims:

". . . . We are not fighting a war of aggression against the German people. . . . The destruction or disruption of Germany or the German people has never been a war aim with us from the first day of this war to this day. . . .

"Nor did we enter this war merely to alter or destroy the Imperial Constitution of Germany, much as we consider that military and autocratic Constitution a dangerous anachronism in the twentieth century . . . . after all, that is a question for the German people to decide.

"We are not fighting to destroy Austria-Hungary or to deprive Turkey of its capital or the rich lands of Asia Minor and Thrace which are predominantly Turkish. . . .

"The settlement of the new Europe must be based on such grounds of reason and justice as will give some promise of stability. Therefore, it is that we feel that government

---

[1]Also approved by the Cabinet and the Dominions before delivery. *War Memoirs of David Lloyd George*, Vol. V, p. 39.

[2]Received on the 6th. Published in Baker, *Woodrow Wilson and World Settlement*, Vol. I, p. 40.

with the consent of the governed must be the basis of any territorial settlement in this war. . . ."[1]

Sunday, January 6th.

The President spent a good part of the day working on his forthcoming Fourteen Points address. House reports that the President read the message to him. ". . . . I thought it was a declaration of human liberty and a declaration of the terms which should be written into the peace conference. I felt that it was the most important document that he had ever penned, and remarked that he would either be on the crest of the wave after it had been delivered, or reposing peacefully in the depths.

"The point we were most anxious about was as to how this country would receive our entrance into European affairs to the extent of declaring *territorial* aims. . . .

"He was quite insistent that nothing be put in the message of an argumentative nature . . . because it would merely provoke controversy. . . .

"The other points we were fearful of were Alsace and Lorraine, the freedom of the seas, and the leveling of commercial barriers. However . . . there was not the slightest hesitation on his part in saying them. The President shows an extraordinary courage in such things, and a wisdom in discussing them that places him easily in a rank by himself, as far as my observations go. The more I see of him, the more firmly am I convinced that there is not a statesman in the world who is his equal."[2]

Monday, January 7th.

The President and Colonel House had a short talk after luncheon. The President then called in Secretary Lansing and upon his advice made various verbal alterations in the address.[3] George Creel arrived at 4:30, to bring, as he had promised two days before, "much cheering news" from Petrograd, and to discuss, probably, a memorandum of Colonel Thompson's view on Russia. Thompson laid great stress on the necessity for counteracting German propaganda in Russia, and for contact with the Bolsheviks, though not recognition of them as a

---

[1]Specific terms follow. See *Foreign Relations*, 1918, Supp. 1, Vol. I, pp. 4–12. See also Baker, *Woodrow Wilson and World Settlement*, Vol. I, pp. 40–41, 71.

[2]*Intimate Papers*, Vol. III, pp. 342–343.

[3]*Ibid.*, pp. 329–332, 343.

government. They were not, he said, the "wild-eyed rabble that most of us consider them." At six o'clock the President received the Finance Committee of the Red Cross.

Secretary McAdoo sent over to the President a letter from Secretary Baker, who agreed there should be a War Department representative on the Inter-Ally Council, and said he had instructed Bliss to confer with Crosby, especially with a view to determining what restrictions on War Department expenditures were advisable, considering the restrictions imposed by the shipping problem. McAdoo enclosed to the President, also, a copy of his own telegram to Crosby, passing on the information in Baker's letter.[1]

Mutiny at Kiel, German naval base.

Tuesday, January 8th.

At noon the President delivered his Fourteen Points address to the assembled Houses of Congress:

". . . . Within the last week Mr. Lloyd George has spoken with admirable candor and in admirable spirit for the people and Government of Great Britain. There is no confusion of counsel among the adversaries of the Central Powers, no uncertainty of principle, no vagueness of detail. . . .[2]

"There is . . . a voice calling for these definitions of principle and of purpose which is, it seems to me, more thrilling and more compelling than any of the many moving voices with which the troubled air of the world is filled. It is the voice of the Russian people. . . .[3]

". . . the only possible program, as we see it, is this . . ." [there follow the Fourteen Points][4]

Since no advance notice was given, the audience was neither as numerous nor as distinguished as the subject warranted.

---

[1] For the President's sharp comment on the message to Crosby, see this volume, pp. 459–460.

[2] The President often laid himself open to attack by making rhetorical general statements such as this regarding the unity of the Allies, when he knew better than anyone else how far short in certain aspects that unity really was.

[3] The address was at once telegraphed to Ambassador Francis, with instructions to have it "conveyed unofficially to Trotsky." *Foreign Relations*, 1918, *Russia*, Vol. I, p. 426. It was sent also through the Committee on Public Information and was, by a "successful maneuver," published in full in the Soviet news organ and liberally used in other Russian newspapers. Creel, *How We Advertised America*, pp. 377, 379.

[4] *Public Papers*, Vol. V, pp. 155–162.

Very few, even among the Allied diplomats and the cabinet members, realized what the subject was to be. House was in favor of giving notice to the world that the President was about to state America's war aims, but Wilson objected; if such notice were given, he thought, the newspapers would as always comment and speculate as to what he might say, and such forecasts would be taken in some cases for what he really said.[1] Once the address was published, however, there was no lack of interest.[2]

The cabinet met as usual at 2:30, Secretary Lansing remaining afterward to discuss the Russian situation; later the President received a committee of the National Woman's Trade Union League; and Ambassador Jusserand.

---

[1] *Intimate Papers*, Vol. III, pp. 343–344.

[2] ". . . . Your speech . . . was clear as crystal," wrote Speaker Clark to the President. "Anybody that can't understand it, whether he agree with it or not, is an incorrigible fool." He voiced the opinion of a majority of Congress. In spite of certain Republican fears, the impression made upon Washington was excellent. The press of the country was equally favorable—"one of the great documents in American history." (New York *Tribune*, January 9, 1918.)

European comment was varied, each nation examining the Fourteen Points with its own future in mind. The British, while they appreciated the President's idealism, looked askance at Point II, which spoke with painful frankness of "freedom of . . . the seas." "Our chief criticism . . ." said the London *Times*, "is that . . . it seems not to take into account certain hard realities of the situation. . . ." (Quoted in *Intimate Papers*, Vol. III, p. 346.) British Liberals were on the whole enthusiastic; and many labor organizations considered the President's views "identical with their own." (Pershing to the Chief of Staff, January 17, 1918.) In France the pronouncement as to Alsace-Lorraine was hailed with joy and relief. The Italian government was more skeptical, fearing that certain of the Points would mean a loss of juicy plums guaranteed under the Treaty of London. The people, however, as Ambassador Page wrote the President, were "tremendously impressed and encouraged." Bolshevik Russia remained suspicious; and the Rumanian government was unsatisfied: ". . . if Roumania should now have her occupied territory returned without occupying Transylvania there is no necessity to stay in the war any further . . ." (*Foreign Relations*, 1918, Supp. 1, Vol. I, p. 752.) Nor was Serbia entirely pleased: ". . . 43 millions foreign peoples are left in the Austro-Hungarian Empire which so long as Hapsburg dynasty remains will remain instruments of German militarist policy." (*Ibid.*)

The Foreign Minister of Austria-Hungary was reported to be "practically in entire accord with the views expressed." (*Ibid.*, p. 36.) But from Germany came blasts of indignation. ". . . . Wilson again brings all his demagogic artifices to play to prevent Russia from closing a separate peace with the Central Powers. . . ." ". . . the right thing is to reject the competence of this American busybody. Not one of the problems with which he deals in his fourteen commandments . . . is any concern of America. . . ." (Berlin *Lokal-Anzeiger*, and *Mittags Zeitung*, quoted in the New York *Times*, of January 11 and 12, 1918.) German liberal opinion was more reasonable, but even there, though many of the President's ideas were acceptable, it was alleged that Lloyd George was "making similar statements in an apparently different spirit" and the Germans were "not sure what to believe." (*Foreign Relations*, 1918, Supp. 1, Vol. I, pp. 26–28.)

Heavy snows and severe cold were reducing action on the Italian front to a minimum.

To T. W. Gregory:

"I dare say you have seen various things in the papers about the question of the election of an alien enemy as Mayor of Michigan City, Indiana. Is there no way, do you think, in which we could prevent his occupying the office?"

To President Raymond Poincaré of France, who had sent thanks to President Wilson for his decision "concerning the mode of action of the American army," and had gone into considerable detail as to the best ways of using American regiments with more experienced troops:

". . . I want to assure your Excellency that the question is one to which we have been giving a great deal of careful and anxious thought and with regard to which we are all not only willing but anxious to do the best and most effective thing for the accomplishment of the common purpose to which we are devoting our arms.

"General Bliss, who is kindly conveying this letter to you for me, is, as your Excellency probably knows, to be the representative of the United States in the Supreme War Council, and I have instructed him that this particular question which you have very properly called to my attention ought to be discussed with the greatest fullness and frankness in that Council. The judgment of the Council with regard to it will, I need hardly assure you, be conclusively influential with the Government of the United States. Our only desire is to do the best thing that can be done with our armed forces, and we are willing to commit ourselves to the general counsel of those with whom we have the honor to cooperate in this great enterprise of liberty.

"Meantime, let me assure you that this question seems to us quite as pressing and important as it does to your-

self, and our own desire is to settle it promptly as well
as wisely. . . ."

To Frank J. Hayes, president of the United Mine Workers of
America, explaining why he could not address their International Convention, and asking to have his cordial greeting
conveyed to the delegates:

". . . say to them that I would like to be present to say
something, if I could, which would make them realize how
much the safety of America and the whole honor and
dignity and success of her action in the present crisis of the
world depends upon their fidelity and energy and devotion.
I do not doubt that they will rise to the occasion, but I do
want them to realize how deeply and sincerely interested
the Government is in their welfare and how anxious it is
to be instrumental in doing anything that it is possible
to do to further it."

Wednesday, January 9th.

At twelve o'clock the President received the Governor Gen-
eral of Canada (the Duke of Devonshire), who was accompanied
by the British ambassador and Breckinridge Long, Assistant
Secretary of State. The Duke and Duchess of Devonshire and
Ambassador and Lady Spring Rice were luncheon guests.
Afternoon appointments: Senator Lewis of Illinois; Herbert
Hoover; the Attorney General, Secretary Daniels and Senator
Swanson of Virginia, who discussed oil legislation; Representative Taylor of Colorado and a number of Democratic members
of the House, who remained for an hour's conference on the
subject of woman suffrage. After the interview a statement—
which the President himself wrote out in the presence of the
committee—was handed to newspaper men: "The committee
found that the President had not felt at liberty to volunteer
his advice to members of Congress in this important matter,
but when we sought his advice he very frankly and earnestly
advised us to vote for the amendment as an act of right and
justice to the women of the country and of the world." Evening
at the National Theater.

Ambassador Spring Rice sent a memorandum to the Department of State: ". . . . The British Government feel it essential that in some way or other relations should be kept up between the Allies and the Bolsheviki authorities at Petrograd, and the former Acting British Consul General at Moscow, Mr. Lockhart, is being sent to Petrograd with instructions to keep unofficially in touch with them. The British Government will also, by means of unofficial channels, keep in touch with the newly appointed agent of the Bolsheviki government in London, M. Litvinov. . . .

". . . the present system does not entail the recognition of the Trotsky-Lenin government either by the British Government or the Governments of the Allies."[1]

To Secretary Baker:

"I have a young friend, ———, who is a Captain of the First Company, Coast Artillery, Maryland National Guard, and whose Major has had some sort of inquiry instituted as to his efficiency. I, of course, do not want anything but justice done in his case, but I would be very much obliged if you would see that a careful enough scrutiny of it is made by the reviewing officers to make sure that he is not the subject of any political prejudice, as I fear, on the part of his Major. There are some very deep lines in Maryland politics!"

To Secretary McAdoo:

"I have your note of the seventh[2] sending me the message which you asked the Secretary of State to send to Mr. Crosby about General Bliss's consulting with the Inter-Allied Council.

"I hope, my dear Mac, that hereafter you will let me see these messages before they are sent and not after, because they touch matters of vital policy upon which it is imperative that I should retain control. My particular job is to keep things properly coordinated and if they

---

[1] *Foreign Relations,* 1918, *Russia,* Vol. I, p. 337.

[2] See this volume, p. 455.

are coordinated without my advice, some very serious consequences might ensue. In this case, so far as I can see, nothing is likely to go wrong, except that I must frankly say to you again that I am very much afraid of Mr. Crosby's inclination to go very much outside his bailiwick, an inclination of which I have many evidences."

To Representative Jouett Shouse, who had urged the President to call prominent men from various Southern delegations to the White House and appeal to them to lay aside their personal prejudices and, for the sake of the party, vote for the woman suffrage amendment:

"It is extremely hard to reply to generous letters like yours . . . without seeming to do violence to my real personal sentiments, but the most I have felt at liberty to do (for reasons which I am sure you know) has been to give my advice to members of Congress when they have asked for it. Not as many have asked as I could wish. When they do ask, you know what the advice is.

"Personally, I am not afraid of the strategy of the Republican management. It can be counted upon to be stupid, and it is always stupid to be insincere, as in this instance I am sure it is."[1]

To Champ Clark, Speaker of the House of Representatives:

"I desire to bring to your consideration a matter of grave national importance.

"The course of events of the past year has brought to the attention of both myself and my advisers, as well as to that of all thinking men, the supreme importance of conserving in every possible way the tonnage of the Merchant Marine. Our ultimate success or failure in this great struggle will depend on our ability, first, to transport and

---

[1]The President wrote a similar letter to Mrs. George Bass. Theodore Roosevelt, in a letter to the chairman of the Republican National Committee on January 3rd, had urged that everything possible be done to get Republican congressmen to vote for the suffrage amendment; and had advocated adding to the National Committee a woman member from every suffrage state. New York *Times*, January 4, 1918.

supply our armies in the field and, second, to transport food and vital necessary material of all kinds to the Allies, who have borne the heat and burden of the battle during the past three and one-half years. Our failure in either of these great functions will seriously jeopardize the success of our cause.

"The developments of modern warfare, particularly with respect to the evolution of submarines, mines and torpedoes, together with their absolutely illegal and unscrupulous use by the enemy, have made the problem of adequately protecting our existing merchant tonnage one of the greatest difficulty. I feel I do not exaggerate when I say it is one of the major problems confronting this government today, a matter urgent and immediate.

"A prerequisite to all measures of protection of merchant vessels is that the masters and officers be thoroughly indoctrinated with the necessary and essential precautions to be taken to insure to the maximum degree the safe passage of vessels, passengers and cargoes through dangerous areas. To this end a set of complete, clear Authoritative War Instructions for merchant vessels is a prime necessity.

"Our associate in the war, Great Britain, through the experience gained by three and one-half years of combating the submarine menace, has developed a most excellent and complete set of War Instructions for the guidance of her merchant shipping in dangerous areas.

"These instructions are more properly orders, positive and mandatory. They are backed by the full force of duly enacted law. The law prescribes severe penalties to be visited on any persons who shall be found for any reason to have contributed to the loss of a vessel. Our own War Instructions, which have just been revised and rewritten to include the fruit of recent Allied experience, are excellent in form and substance. They have, however, one fatal defect. They have not the backing of duly enacted law by the Congress of the United States. They are at the most advisory, not positive and mandatory as is absolutely essential they should be. . . .

"I have accordingly caused to be drafted a bill . . . which is designed to correct conditions as set forth above. I recommend it most earnestly to your very serious consideration and attention. The need for such legislation cannot be over-estimated at this time. I recommend that its importance warrants it being presented and passed as a piece of urgent emergency war legislation."[1]

Thursday, January 10th.

At 2:30 the President received and said a few words to a committee who presented him with a small replica of a statue of Robert Emmet. Shane Leslie, one of the committee members, wrote afterward to Tumulty that he was greatly impressed by the President's address, "not so much for its adroitness as for the lofty plane on which it finished." "I am sure I felt that the President will be the best representative Ireland can have at the Peace Conference. . . ." George Creel called at three o'clock; and at 3:30 the French high commissioner, M. Tardieu.[2] ". . . . The President," wrote M. Tardieu later, "to whom I pointed out the difficulties attendant upon . . . [unified military control] replied: 'You will have to come to it, just the same. What does Mr. Clemenceau think?' 'He is thoroughly in favour of it,' I said. 'Whom does he suggest?' asked the President. I answered, 'General Foch.' By his influence on England, Mr. Wilson from that moment never ceased to pave the way for the decision reached in March, 1918."[3]

Late-afternoon appointments: Senator Myers of Montana; Senators Shafroth of Colorado, Smith of Arizona and King of Utah.

---

[1]Clark replied that he agreed and would coöperate.

[2]Tardieu probably presented at this time M. Clemenceau's letter to the President of December 21, 1917, expressing warm appreciation of the "magnificent example" of the United States and saying that the French thought of the American people as "brothers in the highest sense of the word."

[3]Tardieu, *France and America*, p. 235.

Colonel House wrote the President: "I want to congratulate you and felicitate with you over the astounding success of your address to Congress. . . .

"It took tremendous courage, but the reward is great, as indeed it should be."

Secretary Baker, summoned before the Senate investigating committee, began a testimony which continued from four to six hours a day for three days. Questions and cross questions were put about every detail of War Department activity. While admitting certain delays and errors, Baker maintained that the Department had put through a huge undertaking in as efficient a manner as possible. Writing after the hearings, he said: "I don't think that those who criticize the 'delays' of the War Department have any other than a patriotic purpose. Indeed, I share their feelings of deep anxiety to speed our preparation along and bring the full strength of America to bear to end this conflict successfully; and I share, too, their impatience to get rid of all fretting causes of delay. The only difference between them and me, I think, is that, having been busy at the infinite detail of the undertaking for a long time, I have a better realization of the fact that some delays are inherent in the very size and difficulty of the task . . ."[1]

The House adopted the suffrage amendment, 274–136.

The Russian ambassador called upon Breckinridge Long, Third Assistant Secretary of State, to urge that the Allies make all decisions and take all action in the Far East in combination, in order that Japan might not be able to act alone. It was feared, he said, that the Japanese were preparing to occupy Vladivostok and Khabarovsk.[2]

To Charles W. Russell, former ambassador to Persia, who had expressed the hope that the President would support the cause of Persian independence:

". . . . You may be sure that my sympathy goes out to Persia with the greatest heartiness and that I shall be

[1]See Palmer, *Newton D. Baker*, Vol. II, pp. 53–61.

[2]*Foreign Relations*, 1918, *Russia*, Vol. II, pp. 23–24. The next day the State Department telegraphed the American ambassador in Japan to "discreetly ascertain and report what foundation if any for these suspicions." *Ibid.*, p. 24.

glad to do anything that it is possible to do to secure her complete autonomy. Just at present the whole situation in that part of the world is confused, and it is impossible to say whether any immediate steps are possible."

To L. S. Rowe:
"The address I delivered the other day to Congress was a summing up of all that I have been thinking recently, and that it should have met with such a reception as has been accorded it has given me the greatest gratification and encouragement . . ."

Friday, January 11th.
Appointments after the cabinet meeting: M. L. Requa, recently appointed general director of the oil division of the Fuel Administration; Dr. Atwood Smith and a committee of the International Bible Students Association; Representatives Borland of the Committee on Appropriations and Olney, Shallenberger, Lunn and Caldwell of the Committee on Military Affairs, to whom the President indicated his disapproval of the proposed department of munitions.[1]

Hoover called for greater efforts toward food saving, so that more meat and wheat could be sent to the Allies.

Garfield warned that in the face of a coal shortage of 38,000,000 tons it would be impossible during the next sixty days to give any section of the country its normal supply. Sufficient coal would be provided for New York to prevent suffering, and so far as possible all industries would be provided; but the strictest economy would have to be practised. He added, however, that there was no cause for alarm.[2]

The author wrote in his notebook: "I took a long tramp in the afternoon on the lower west side. I saw several long lines of poor people waiting to get baskets of coal. The shortage is now dangerous. They were coming at Vandam and Varick streets with bags, pans and boxes, no one getting more, I should say, than thirty pounds."

[1] New York *Times*, January 12, 1918.
[2] *Ibid.*

To Senator John H. Bankhead:

"I am writing to enlist your help, if I may, in straightening out the coal mining situation in Alabama. I am exceedingly loath to take over the mines and have them operated by the Government, and yet I must frankly say that I see no other alternative if the mine owners should remain unwilling to accept the settlement which Doctor Garfield has so laboriously worked out after conference with all parties and in the sincere desire to be just to each and prejudice the future in no respect. I myself think the proposed settlement the right one; I know it is the only practicable one, and I am sure you would be rendering a very great service to the country in this critical time of the war if you would lend your valuable counsel to obtain the assent of the coal operators."

To Senator G. E. Chamberlain, "Personal":

"When you and Senator Hitchcock were at the White House the other evening we were discussing various suggestions of coordination and means of speeding up the military programme and among other things you told me that you had in mind a bill for the creation of a munitions ministry.

"That, of course, set my mind to work on that particular suggestion, and I feel that I ought to say to you, now that the matter is clear in my mind, that I hope sincerely no such re-coordination will be attempted. For one thing, it would naturally include the Navy as well as the Army and would, so far as the Navy is concerned, bring about, I fear a dislocation of activities which would cause delay where there is none that is avoidable; and in regard to the Army, I think that nothing substantial would be accomplished. Indeed, I believe that delay would inevitably be produced by such a measure.

"I have had in the last few months a great deal of experience in trying to coordinate things, and upon every fresh coordination delay inevitably results and not only delay, but all sorts of cross currents of demoralization which are very serious impediments to the effective conduct of business.

"Rather intimate information from the other side of the water convinces me that the munitions ministries which have been set up there have not fulfilled the expectations of those who advocated them, and the structure of those governments is so utterly different from our own that we could not, if we would, create any such parity of power and influence between the head of such a bureau and the heads of the permanent departments as can be created under such political arrangements as the French and English.

"In short, my dear Senator, my judgment is decidedly that we would not only be disappointed in the results, but that to attempt such a thing would greatly embarrass the processes of coordination and of action upon which I have spent a great deal of thought and pains, and which I believe are more and more rapidly yielding us the results we desire.

"I felt that I ought not to keep you in ignorance of what had been going on in my mind with regard to this important matter."

To Thomas W. Lamont of J. P. Morgan & Co.:

". . . . I need not tell you that my address to Congress the other day came from the deepest sources in me, and I pray with all my heart that it may bear some sort of substantial fruit.

"I was aware of the feelings in England to which you refer, and I felt that it was imperatively necessary to give definition at every point to the situation. The Germans can now never pretend that we have not stated our position and that they do not know where we stand.

"I have been much interested in what I have heard of Colonel Thompson's activities in Russia."

To Rabbi Stephen S. Wise:

"Your friendship always cheers me and your praise always encourages me very much, and I want you to know how deeply I appreciate your judgment of my last address to Congress. I hope from the bottom of my heart that it will clear the air and lead to saner attitudes of mind."

To President John Grier Hibben, who had telegraphed a resolution adopted by the Board of Trustees of Princeton University, expressing appreciation of the President's Fourteen Points address. ". . . . They beg leave also to express their admiration of its lofty eloquence and their sympathy with the patriotism which it inspires, and they are unanimous in their support of the measures to be employed in giving effect to the policy they announce and expound.":

MY DEAR PRESIDENT HIBBEN:

I am in receipt of your telegram . . . conveying the very generous resolution adopted by the Board of Trustees of the University at their session on January tenth. I beg that as the first opportunity presents itself you will convey to the Trustees my warm appreciation of that message and my hope that the address to Congress which it so generously supports may bear some substantial fruit in the year which has just opened.

Sincerely yours,
WOODROW WILSON

To Ignace Jan Paderewski, a telegram:

"I warmly appreciate your message of yesterday and wish to convey to you my warmest thanks not only but also my hope that the year just opening may bring to the people of Poland a real fruition of their hopes."

To S. R. Bertron:

" . . . . I am heartily glad that you think the passages in my recent address about Russia are the sort that will do good in that disturbed and distressed country."[1]

Saturday, January 12th.

The President spent the morning in his study, taking the afternoon for golf. Dr. Axson and Colonel Brown were guests at luncheon. In the late afternoon Vance McCormick called; and Secretary McAdoo. President and Mrs. Wilson went to a Charity Ball in the evening, in behalf of the Children's Hospital.

Sunday, January 13th.

After attending the Episcopal Church in the morning, the President and Mrs. Wilson returned to the White House for luncheon with Dr. E. P. Davis of Philadelphia and Dr. Axson. Daniel Willard called in the late afternoon, to explain his resignation as chairman of the War Industries Board—he wished to be free to give his whole time to the service of the Baltimore & Ohio Railroad, where he felt he was most needed.

Monday, January 14th.

The President walked over to the Shipping Board offices about noon, and also called upon Secretary Baker. Afternoon appointments: Franklin P. Glass, editor of the Birmingham (Alabama) *News;* Senator Calder of New York; Representative Slemp of Virginia; Maurice Francis Egan, United States minister to Denmark; Representative Small of North Carolina. Mrs. Sayre and her children, who had been at the White House during the holiday season, left in the early evening.

Secretary Baker sent the President a confidential telegram from General Pershing, reporting upon a conference with Clemenceau and Pétain: " . . . . Have now a definite understanding with the French satisfactory to them and to me that our divisions now in France shall complete their training as already begun. In the future divisions arriving in

---

[1] On the same day the President telegraphed to S. Slenim:

" . . . . Nothing would afford me deeper ground for gratitude than to be able to help in any way the great Russian people to find their way to solid ground."

zone of French [army?] are to have a period of training
with the French, each regiment in a French division. When
sufficiently experienced by training in a quiet sector with
French, our divisions are to be united under their own
commanders . . ."

The New York *Times* contained one more in a series of
critical editorials upon the testimony of Secretary Baker:
". . . . The atmosphere of self-satisfaction with which authority at Washington surrounds itself does not extend
over the whole country. The people are anxious, growing
more anxious. They are not to be put off with the easy
insolence of observation about omniscience and omnipo-
tence. . . ."

An attempt was made to assassinate Lenin.

To George Creel:

"I have just finished reading the report of the Committee on Public Information which you were kind enough
to bring me last week, and I want to say how much it has
gratified me and how entirely the work being done by the
Committee meets with my approval. I have kept in touch
with that work, piece by piece, as you know, in our several
interviews, but had not realized its magnitude when
assembled in a single statement.

"I feel confident that as the work of the Committee
progresses it will more and more win the public approval
and confidence."[1]

To his old friend, Cleveland H. Dodge:

MY DEAR CLEVE:

Please never refrain from writing me when you feel like
it. Your letters are always a joy to me. They bring such a
breath of reassuring friendship as keeps me in spirits for
many days together, and I can assure you I need all the
tonic I can get during these anxious days.

I have been as much reassured and heartened as I have
been surprised at the reception of my recent address to

---

[1]Published in the *Official Bulletin*, February 4, 1918.

Congress and your own approval of it gives me the keenest pleasure, for I know that you have thought of many
phases of the subject for a long time and are competent
to judge whether I have proposed the wise programme
or not.

Bless you, my dear fellow! May all the best things of the
New Year come to you and yours is the wish of all of us.

Affectionately yours,
WOODROW WILSON

To Miss Lucy M. Smith:
MY DEAR COUSIN LUCY:

Your and Cousin Mary's letters always give us genuine
joy, and it was with real delight that I opened yours . . .
Our friendships seem to mean more to us than ever in these
days of stress and anxiety, and I was so much delighted to
learn from Margaret how well you were looking and that
Cousin Mary, too, was well, though Margaret reported
her as looking tired. Please above all things take care of
yourselves.

I hardly have time to think of my own personal affairs
these days, but there are two friends to whom my thoughts
turn very often with unalloyed joy. May God bless you
both for the year to come is the prayer of us all, and
particularly of

Your friend,
WOODROW WILSON

Tuesday, January 15th.

At 2:15 the President received the first minister from Rumania, Dr. Constantin Angelescu, who presented his credentials
and made a short address. Replying, the President said: ". . .
Rumania and the United States are now drawn closer together
as common sufferers in a common cause, and the action of the
Government of Rumania in sending a diplomatic representative to this country is accepted as an added evidence of fraternal

good will . . ."[1] After cabinet meeting the President conferred with Representative Meeker of Missouri; Vance McCormick and Wilbur Marsh, treasurer of the Democratic National Committee; Representative Montague of Virginia.

> Lansing telegraphed the American ambassador in Russia: ". . . . This Government not disposed as yet to recognize any independent governments until the will of Russian people has been more definitely expressed on this general subject. The public utterances of the President have defined clearly the sympathy of the United States for democracy and self-government."[2]

To his secretary, Tumulty, enclosing a letter from William J. Bryan, who said: ". . . . Acting on the theory that I may be honored with a place on the peace commission, am devoting all my time this winter to study of European politics of the past century. . . .":

"What do you think of this and what possible answer can I make, for, of course, the assumption he is acting on will never be realized?"[3]

Wednesday, January 16th.

Afternoon appointments: H. B. Brougham and Lincoln Colcord of the Philadelphia *Public Ledger;* Judge Gordon of Philadelphia; Representatives Ferris of Oklahoma and Foster of Illinois in regard to oil lands in Wyoming; Secretaries Baker and Daniels, and H. A. Garfield, in regard to the necessity for the coal order of the 17th. Garfield had consulted Baker and Daniels, who thought such an order would "let loose a whirlwind," but did not oppose it. They willingly agreed to go with him to the White House to discuss the matter; and Baker, to keep the whole thing secret, made the appointment directly with the President.

". . . . The President listened to the proposal, asked a few questions, made a few suggestions, and then without hesitation approved the issuance of the order. He appreciated the storm

---

[1]*Public Papers*, Vol. V, pp. 163–164.

[2]*Foreign Relations*, 1918, *Russia*, Vol. II, p. 743.

[3]For the President's reply to Bryan, see this volume, p. 489.

of protest that must inevitably follow, but having satisfied himself of the need of instant action, gave his approval firmly and without flinching. His courage was magnificent. Not until nearly a month had passed was it feasible to explain to the public the reasons which made the order imperative. Meanwhile, as the President is reported to have said, 'there was nothing to do but retire to the cyclone cellar.' . . . ."

After the conference at the White House, and in accordance with the President's wish, Garfield conferred with McAdoo, who also realized the trouble ahead but finally said, "All right. Go ahead, I'm with you."

Work on the order went on until late that night; it was released in time for the morning papers of the 17th.[1]

Late-afternoon appointments: Representative Gray; Senator Robinson of Arkansas.

> Representative William B. Oliver, chairman of the Senate committee which had investigated the naval conduct of the war, issued a report showing "phenominal" progress in warship construction and "efficient and expeditious methods" in various naval bureaus.

To Secretary Burleson, enclosing bills on price fixing and food conservation, sent by Secretary Baker, with the approval of Hoover, Garfield and Willard:

"Enclosed are drafts of two bills the great importance of which you will see at once. I am sending them to you to ask your judgment as to how they should be brought to the attention of the leaders on the Hill. My trouble is that I do not know what committee chairman or chairmen should be consulted. Won't you give me the right tip?"

To Secretary McAdoo:

"I take it for granted that all our Collectors of Customs are under instruction to search every outgoing vessel for possible explosives, etc., but I have just received a letter from California, the writer of which I do not know, in

---

[1]H. A. Garfield to Josephus Daniels, March 3, 1921, and to Newton D. Baker, March 24, 1922, both supplied to the author by Dr. Garfield.

which this definite statement is made, that there is a carefully concerted plot on the part of all the pro-German and anti-American agencies in this country, including those disaffected elements among the Irish-Americans who are thought to be cooperating with such agencies, for a general effort to destroy American and British shipping in every port, in every shipyard, and at sea, and that the date set is the twenty-second of this month (January). His information is that where the vessel is not accessible in our harbors or in our shipyards, the purpose is to destroy it at sea on the date mentioned. I think you will agree with me that no pains should be spared to take extra precautions."[1]

To George Creel, who wrote that the British had sounded him with regard to having James M. Beck make a speaking tour in England, and that Beck was willing to go. Creel enclosed a speech which Beck had made in 1916, which, he thought, "seems to prove that he acted very decently even before the war, while ever since he has been your devoted follower.":

"The address of James M. Beck which you send me certainly shows that he can restrain himself with a certain degree of handsomeness, and I dare say he would do as well as most others for the errand suggested, but personally I strongly disapprove of the English idea of having speakers come from the United States and make anything like a systematic canvass of Great Britain. I think they have made an error in sending speakers over here, and they are making a similar error in desiring our speakers to go over there. It is the idea I am opposed to."

To Roy Howard, president of the United Press Association, who had called attention to the efforts of German propagandists in South America to misinterpret the President's purpose in

---

[1] The same information was sent to the Attorney General and to E. N. Hurley of the Shipping Board. McAdoo replied that extra precautions had been and were being taken.

urging other American republics to help the Allies in their fight for the principles of democracy:

". . . . Certainly I never had anything in mind in regard to cooperation among neutrals which would be particularly advantageous to the United States. My thought was only to unite the opinion of the world so far as I could in protesting against the flagrant violations of right and of international justice which had been committed. At no stage of this distressing war have I ever entertained the slightest idea of making any combination for the special benefit of the United States. My thought has been merely the establishment of international justice and humane dealing and the safeguarding of universal interests.

"With regard to the question whether the war and the participation of the United States in it has served to strengthen the common bond between the democracies of the Western Hemisphere, I will say that I think that it has. I think that thoughtful men in all the democracies of that hemisphere are beginning to see the real purpose and character of the United States. She is offering in every proposal that she makes to give the most sacred pledges on her own part that she will in no case be the aggressor against either the political independence or the territorial integrity of any other state or nation, at the same time that she is proposing and insisting upon similar pledges from all the nations of the world who have its peace at heart and are willing to associate themselves for the maintenance of that peace. The very strength of her appeal in this direction comes from the fact that she is willing to bind herself and give pledges of the utmost solemnity for her own good faith and disinterestedness. If this is understood, there could be no question of fear or suspicion. . . ."[1]

---

[1] On the 29th the President wrote a letter of introduction for Mr. Howard, saying that he felt the "greatest interest" in his errand. ". . . . His purpose is to establish a

To Colville Barclay, counselor of the British Embassy, who had reported the substance of a telegram just received from London: ". . . . The Prime Minister hopes you will have seen the report of Mr. Balfour's speech in Edinburgh on January 10, which gave him a welcome opportunity of recognising to the full and dwelling on the admirable character of your address to Congress on January 8.[1] Mr. Lloyd George desires me to add that he is grateful for your declarations, and is happy to find that the peace policies of the United States and Great Britain as expressed by yourself are so entirely in harmony. . . .":

". . . . It has been a matter of genuine gratification to me to find my own programme of peace so entirely consistent with the programme set forth by Mr. Lloyd George, and the speech of Mr. Balfour to which Sir Cecil Spring-Rice was kind enough to call my attention has afforded me the deepest satisfaction."

Thursday, January 17th.

Afternoon appointments: Senators Stone, Owen, Calder and Borah, and Representatives Flood and Cooper, who presented a plan for dealing with Russia; John R. Mott; Marc Klaw and a committee of theater managers, including George M. Cohan and David Belasco, who discussed the prospective Monday closing of theaters according to the coal order; Governor Yager of Porto Rico; Secretary Baker.

The morning papers carried Garfield's coal order, together with his statement of explanation.[2] The whole nation was shocked. The Senate immediately adopted a resolution requesting that the order be suspended for five days until

---

more extensive and adequate and reliable system of interchanging news between the northern and southern continents . . ." For a brief discussion of Howard's projects see Irwin, *Propaganda and the News*, pp. 191–192.

[1] Which Balfour characterized as a "magnificent pronouncement." New York *Times*, January 12, 1918.

[2] Manufacturing plants, with certain necessary exceptions, were closed from January 18th to 22nd inclusive, and on each following Monday through March 25th; business and professional offices, wholesale and retail stores, theaters and other places of amusement were, with certain exceptions, to close on Mondays until March 25th; the whole order was to be effective in the territory east of the Mississippi. See *Official Bulletin*, January 18, 1918.

it could be investigated. Frank I. Cobb dictated a long message over the telephone for the President—"a terrible calamity." Tumulty protested that the order, even though necessary, would shake the people's confidence in the administration, but the President replied, in a note written on his own typewriter, that the "direct road is the road out of difficulties which never would have been entirely remedied if we had not taken some such action. We must just bow our heads and let the storm beat."[1]

Large sections of the press reacted violently. "We hope," said the New York *Times*, "the President will immediately reconsider and revoke Mr. Garfield's astounding order . . ." And on the 18th: ". . . . The courageous, resourceful, American way to meet a coal shortage is to provide more coal, better distribution through quicker transportation. . . .

"The American people know where the fault lies. They expect the President to find the remedy."

The author of this biography wrote in his notebook: "The morning papers bear the startling news of Garfield's order . . . This is sudden and drastic and certainly not well staged nor prepared for with a proper understanding of public opinion. . . ." And the next day: "Great commotion everywhere . . . Virulent attacks upon Wilson and his administration. . . . The very elements that were loudest in demanding that we get into the war and 'lick Germany' are the elements that howl loudest the first time a real pinch comes. . . .

"Nevertheless, Garfield's action was not well executed. . . ."

To Frank I. Cobb, a telegram:

"You may be sure that I appreciate to the full the seriousness of the fuel order and the weight of the considerations urged in your telephone message. I beg to assure you that I approved the order only because I believed it to be necessary and the only practicable way of clearing up a situation which needed to be cleared up at once in order that we might not continue for an indefinite time to limp along imperfectly in the matter of the trans-

[1]Tumulty, *Woodrow Wilson As I Know Him*, pp. 362–364.

portation of fuel. The working people thrown out of employment ought not to be allowed to suffer. Their employers ought to pay their wages."

To Edward A. Filene of the United States Chamber of Commerce:

"I beg to assure you that it never entered my mind that you and the gentlemen associated with you had any but the very best motives in submitting the referendum about an economic boycott, but I must say to you that I am exceedingly sorry that this was done without first consulting me. No matter which way the vote turns, it will embarrass my handling of international affairs and the policy of the Government.

"I dare say that it is too late now to recall the referendum, but I beg very earnestly that you will assist me in advising the directors of the Chamber of Commerce that it is my earnest hope that they will consult with me in matters of this sort before acting. I am, as you will realize, in some peculiar sense entrusted with directing the foreign relations of the nation."[1]

To Daniel Willard, accepting "with the utmost regret" his resignation as chairman of the War Industries Board:

". . . . I do so only because I am convinced with you that the matter of moving the coal is so critically and immediately important that it is probably your duty to give that your first attention as president of a road which does a very large part of the coal carrying.

"I hope that it will be possible for you to defer the actual severance of your connection with the Board until a new chairman has been selected, but I do not wish to interfere even to that extent with the important duty to which you are turning, if you think it imperative that you should turn to it at once.

---

[1]The President wrote to Secretary Lansing the same day, thanking him for "seeing the officers of the Chamber about this indiscretion."

"I have greatly admired the spirit of your public service and have highly valued that service in every respect. I hope you are turning away from it only for the time being."

Friday, January 18th.

After cabinet meeting the President conferred for an hour and a half with a delegation of leaders of various crafts employed in packing plants. They were headed by James Fitzpatrick, president of the Chicago Federation of Labor, and accompanied by Samuel Gompers and Frank Morrison of the American Federation of Labor. Secretary Baker, as chairman of the Council of National Defense, was also present, and Secretary of Labor Wilson. The delegation urged the government to take control of the packing trade; the President replied that he would move carefully in the matter, first referring it to the Mediation Commission in the hope that some other remedy might be found. As the delegation left the White House, Gompers was questioned and replied that the situation was so acute that some remedy must be found quickly.[1]

The President signed a proclamation urging further effort to conserve food.

"... Mondays and Wednesdays should be observed as wheatless days each week, and one meal each day should be observed as a wheatless meal. ...

"... Tuesday should be observed as meatless day in each week, one meatless meal should be observed in each day; while, in addition, Saturday in each week should further be observed as a day upon which there should be no consumption of pork products.

"A continued economy in the use of sugar will be necessary until later in the year. ..."[2]

Congressional indignation over Garfield's order ran high, and demands for a "new deal" in carrying on the war were heard.[3] The President issued a public statement:

"I was, of course, consulted by Mr. Garfield before the fuel order of yesterday was issued, and fully agreed with

[1]New York *Times*, January 19, 1918.
[2]*Official Bulletin*, January 28, 1918.
[3]New York *Times*, January 19, 1918.

him that it was necessary, much as I regretted the necessity. . . .

"We are upon a war footing, and I am confident that the people of the United States are willing to observe the same sort of discipline that might be involved in the actual conflict itself."[1]

The Senate Committee on Military Affairs introduced, with its unanimous approval, the revised Chamberlain bill providing for a Director of Munitions.

The Constituent Assembly finally convened in Petrograd. As the day approached, street fights had grown more frequent, the atmosphere increasingly tense. About four o'clock something over four hundred delegates assembled, only a third being Bolsheviks. The president of the Petrograd Soviet took the chair with a high hand. All power, he asserted, was with the Workmen-Soldiers-Peasants Deputies (the Bolsheviks). No sooner had he finished than a voice from the audience spoke up: "All power is in the Constituent Assembly."

Here, shot into immediate prominence, was one of the chief issues agitating Russia. The voice was ignored; and further remarks were lost in a lusty singing of the "Internationale."[2]

To H. A. Garfield, referring to a request that theaters be allowed to close Tuesday instead of Monday nights:

"Do you think it would be wise or possible to comply with this suggestion of the theatre men? They are pretty hard hit, of course, and what they want is to take advantage of the holiday Monday crowd."[3]

To J. Lionberger Davis, referring to the suicide of a young man in whom the President had been interested:[4]

"I am heartily glad you think I was of some help to poor Morrison. His death has distressed me very much

---

[1]*Public Papers*, Vol. V, p. 165. Garfield also put out a statement and McAdoo gave an informal interview in support of the order.

[2]*Foreign Relations*, 1918, *Russia*, Vol. I, pp. 351–352.

[3]The request was granted.

[4]See this volume, pp. 376–377.

indeed. I wish I could have done more for him than I did. . . ."

Saturday, January 19th.

The President went over to the War Department offices just before luncheon. In the early afternoon he had a photograph taken (Clinedinst). Evening at the Belasco Theater.

30,000 plants were reported closed by the coal order in New York City alone; a large number of violent protests from manufacturers, trade boards and labor bodies appeared in the press.[1] Garfield, however, announced that the Fuel Administration was receiving fine coöperation and that the situation was improving.

". . . the military establishment of America has fallen down," declared Senator Chamberlain, in an address before the National Security League. "There is no use to be optimistic about a thing that does not exist. It has almost stopped functioning, my friends. Why? Because of inefficiency in every bureau and in every department of the Government of the United States. We are trying to work it out. I speak not as a Democrat, but as an American citizen. . . ." As Chamberlain sat down, Theodore Roosevelt, who was also present, jumped to his feet, applauding loudly.[2]

The Bolshevik government, it was announced, would hold the American ambassador personally responsible for the lives of Emma Goldman, Alexander Berkman, Thomas Mooney and others mistreated in the United States.[3]

Bolsheviks withdrew in a body from the Constituent Assembly; it was dissolved that evening by decree of the Central Executive Committee.[4]

To B. M. Baruch:

"I am glad you understand and approve Garfield's order. I knew that you would. It is extraordinary how some people wince and cry out when they are a little bit hurt. . . ."

[1] New York *Times,* January 20, 1918.

[2] *Ibid.* See the President's challenge of Chamberlain's statement, this volume, p. 485.

[3] Published in the anarchist news organ and telegraphed by Francis to Lansing. *Foreign Relations,* 1918, *Russia,* Vol. I, pp. 353-354.

[4] *Ibid.,* p. 352. Vernadsky, *Lenin, Red Dictator,* p. 195.

To Senator J. S. Frelinghuysen:

"I need not tell you that the subject matter of your letter of yesterday has been constantly in my mind, but I believe that the fuel order was absolutely necessary in the national interest as a war measure and that it would not be wise to modify it in any particular.

"I hope you understand, however, that the local fuel administrators,—I mean the state administrators,—are left a very considerable degree of discretion as to particular instances in which it might seem imperative to grant some sort of relief.

"Personally, I believe that it would be very dangerous for them to exercise this discretion except in the rarest cases, because cases are very hard to discriminate one from another, but in the very nature of things this is the utmost leeway which is practicable in such circumstances. I think the public necessity for this action will be more and more perceived as the days go by."

Sunday, January 20th.

The President and Mrs. Wilson went to the Central Presbyterian Church in the morning. Late in the afternoon the Postmaster General arrived for a conference; and also Senator Simmons. The President and Dr. Axson had a long talk in the evening about the work of the Red Cross in Europe. A week or so later Axson's description of a typical evening in the Wilson family appeared in a published article.[1] They were apt to gather after dinner, he wrote, in the Oval Room—"large, with massive furniture, upholstered in rose color but the real 'living room' of the family, and made cosily livable by a hundred intimate touches, of books and family pictures and friendly oil lamps on the tables and a cheery wood fire crackling on the hearth, and, above all, by the human occupants in the simplicity of a life as domestic as any in America." The President often had to go to his study early in the evening to read and sign papers, or to talk to a cabinet member over a private wire,

---

[1] "An Evening with the President," in the New York *Tribune*, January 27, 1918.

or, rarely, to meet an appointment: but he would rejoin the family as soon as possible and read aloud, or to himself, while Mrs. Wilson and the girls, if they were there, knitted. During these wartime evenings, Dr. Axson said, the women seemed to be always knitting, and sometimes the President himself was pressed into service to hold the yarn between his hands while it was rolled into balls.

President Wilson to the men of the army and navy, urging reverent observance of the Sabbath. ". . . . Such an observance . . . is dictated by the best traditions of our people and by the convictions of all who look to Divine Providence for guidance and protection . . ."[1]

Acting Secretary Polk telegraphed to the American ambassador in Japan: ". . . . The American Government feels very strongly that the common interests of all the powers at war with Germany demand from them an attitude of sympathy with the Russian people in their present unhappy struggle and that any movement looking towards the occupation of Russian territory would at once be construed as one hostile to Russia and would be likely to unite all factions in Russia against us thus aiding the German propaganda in Russia. The American Government trusts the Imperial Japanese Government will share this conviction and hopes that no unfortunate occurrence may make necessary the occupation of Vladivostok by a foreign force. The information received by this Government indicates that the situation there is quiet and is not one to cause alarm. You will say to the Minister for Foreign Affairs that in the opinion of the American Government the presence of more than one Japanese war vessel at Vladivostok at present is likely to be misconstrued and create a feeling of mistrust as to the purposes of the Allied Governments which Japan does not desire any more than the United States."[2]

Strikes were reported spreading in Austria, with increased rioting and anti-war sentiment.

---

[1] *Public Papers*, Vol. V, p. 166.

[2] The message was repeated to our representatives in England and France with instructions to show it to the governments to which they were accredited; and to our minister in China, for his own information only. *Foreign Relations*, 1918, *Russia*, Vol. II, p. 31.

To Secretary Lansing, who had presented a message from the American chargé in Denmark, suggesting that one of the Allied nations might well establish relations with the Bolshevik *de facto* government as "the first practical step towards combating German intrigue in Russia," and that the United States would seem to be the best nation for the task.[1] The President's reply was written on his own typewriter:

"Here is the ever-recurring question, How shall we deal with the Bolsheviki? This particular suggestion seems to me to have something in it worth considering, and I am writing to ask what your own view is."

To Secretary Baker, who recommended a plan for aiding the British with American troops which, he said, had the approval of General Pershing and the United States Staff, as well as of the British and French General Staffs. ". . . the suggestion is that 150 battalions of United States troops be transported by the British, in their own tonnage, and assigned by them three battalions to each of their divisions . . . General Pershing's stipulation is that these troops are to be transported by the British without interfering with or lessening the tonnage aid which they are to give us to carry out our own military program as agreed upon with General Bliss."[2] The President's reply was written on his own typewriter:

"I have one fear about this. It is that, whatever they may promise now, the British will, when it comes to the pinch, in fact cut us off from some part of the tonnage they will promise us for our general programme in order themselves to make sure of these battalions; or will promise us less for the general programme than they would otherwise have given, had their plan for these reenforcements for their own front not been accepted. I believe, therefore, that, while we must acquiesce in this plan for battalions to recruit their own divisions, it would be wise to caution General Bliss a little more explicitly

---

[1] *Foreign Relations*, 1918, *Russia*, Vol. I, pp. 337–338.
[2] Palmer, *Newton D. Baker*, Vol. II, pp. 114–115.

about these risks. He has the general shipping programme in his hands and will understand."

To Senator George E. Chamberlain:
MY DEAR SIR:

You are reported in the New York World of this morning as having said at a luncheon in New York yesterday:

"The military establishment of America has fallen down; there is no use to be optimistic about a thing that does not exist; it almost stopped functioning. Why? Because of inefficiency in every bureau and in every department of the Government of the United States. I speak not as a Democrat but as an American citizen."

I would be very much obliged if you would tell me whether you were correctly quoted. I do not like to comment upon the statements made before learning from you yourself whether you actually made them.

Very truly yours,
WOODROW WILSON[1]

Monday, January 21st.
The first "heatless Monday."

The President received Representative Kitchin of North Carolina at 10:30; and at 11:30, Senator Martin of Virginia. Afternoon appointments: the Italian ambassador; the Belgian minister; the Norwegian minister; Representatives Dent, chairman of the House Committee on Military Affairs, and Kahn, a member of the committee, who came at the President's request to discuss the proposed war cabinet bill; Representatives Lever, Lee, Candler, and McLaughlin of the House Committee on Agriculture; Senators Martin, Swanson, Hoke Smith, Robinson, Williams, Myers, Hollis, Simmons, Fletcher, Pomerene, Beckham. No senator would talk about the conference afterward,

---

[1]Chamberlain replied that the words quoted by the President were substantially those used by him; but he asked the President to read the whole of his speech. The Committee on Military Affairs had been trying to work these matters out, he said, and would be glad to confer with the President at any time. He hoped that "defects in the military code may be cured, and inefficients later weeded out."

but the *Times* reported that they also had been summoned to discuss the war cabinet bill.

The President publicly branded Senator Chamberlain's criticism of the War Department as "an astonishing and absolutely unjustifiable distortion of the truth": ". . . . As a matter of fact, the War Department has performed a task of unparalleled magnitude and difficulty with extraordinary promptness and efficiency. There have been delays and disappointments and partial miscarriages of plans, all of which have been drawn into the foreground and exaggerated by the investigations which have been in progress . . . But, by comparison with what has been accomplished, these things, much as they were to be regretted, were insignificant, and no mistake has been made which has been repeated. . . .

"My association and constant conference with the Secretary of War have taught me to regard him as one of the ablest public officials I have ever known. . . ."[1]

Secretary Baker wrote the President: "I have just read, with infinite gratitude, your generous public expression of confidence in the War Department and in me.

"As I know the impersonal quality of your purpose I know that you will not keep me here a moment longer than is wise and I can well imagine that a time may come when you will find it possible to advance the cause and consolidate the sentiment of the country by making a change either by sending me to other service or to none. As my whole desire is to serve, not in my way but in yours, I shall neither question nor misunderstand what you think best to have me do."

Senator Chamberlain introduced a bill providing for a war cabinet of "three distinguished citizens of demonstrated executive ability" to be appointed by the President and confirmed by the Senate; this cabinet to be given full control of the war under the direction and supervision only of the President.

Senator Stone attacked Republicans in the Senate with extreme bitterness, charging them with infidelity to the "cause of world democracy," and denouncing Theodore

[1] *Public Papers*, Vol. V, pp. 167–168.

Roosevelt as "the most potent agent of the Kaiser." Lodge, Penrose and others replied.

The author of this biography wrote in his diary:

"A battle royal between Congress and the President is developing at Washington. The President, powerful as he has become with the people on account of his idealistic leadership, has not yet gained their confidence as a strong administrator. The attack is especially upon the War Department and Secretary Baker, and is largely traceable to the great business interests of the country which resent governmental control of the railroads and the mines, chafe under taxation, fear the growing power of labor.

"Still, Wilson must now demonstrate as never before, his ability to cope with the administrative problems. He must convince the people. He has many of the strongest newspapers in America, several of which, like the *Times* and the *World*, supported his re-election, now in a rampaging mood of hostile criticism. . . ."

To Samuel Gompers:

"I liked your suggestion about a message to the Russian Constituent Assembly, but apparently the reckless Bolsheviki have already broken it up because they did not control it. It is distressing to see things so repeatedly go to pieces there."

To Dr. Charles W. Eliot:

". . . . You may be sure that I wrote the passages about Russia in my recent address to Congress from the heart. I wish most earnestly that it were possible to find some way to help, but as soon as we have thought out a working plan there is a new dissolution of the few crystals that had formed there. . . ."

To Judge R. S. Lovett, who had presented his resignation from the Priorities Commission:

"I need not tell you how it distresses me to think of your leaving Washington and the duties which you have so acceptably and efficiently performed . . .

". . . I am going to take the liberty of asking you to postpone it for a few days until we can relieve the hysteria which has taken hold for the time being of the United States Senate by coming to calmer counsels and enabling everybody concerned to understand the real facts of the situation.[1]

"With warm regard and real gratitude to you for your generous support and belief in my efforts . . ."

To J. W. Harriman:

"I warmly appreciate your letter of approval of the coal order. It is astonishing how hard it is to get a right thing understood promptly."

To George Foster Peabody:

"Your telegram was immensely appreciated. The storm evidently has passed and the skies begin to clear, but how unnecessary this all was!"

Tuesday, January 22nd.

In the early afternoon the President conferred with Secretary Redfield and the Canadian commissioners. Appointments after the cabinet meeting: Senator Ashhurst of Arizona; Representative Gard of Ohio.

The last day of the factory-closing order. In his final report upon the activities of the Fuel Administration, Garfield said: "In spite of the recurring blizzards the congestion upon our railroads was broken; bunker coal went forward; the ships held in harbor were released, and finally shipments of steel products essential for war manufacture were increased and continued to increase until the old normal levels were reached."

Theodore Roosevelt arrived in Washington. Questioned, he avoided any direct attack upon the President, saying only that he was there to help every man who desired to speed up war work.

General Bliss wrote Secretary Baker in some detail about

---

[1] Lovett replied that he would do as the President suggested.

"many reckless remarks made by General Wood in regard to our military situation." ". . . . The sum and substance of it seems to be that he has done his best to discredit the United States here in Europe. He has told of everything that has not been done and nothing as to the things which have been done. . . . I think that I can already see the evil effect produced on the minds of British officials here. It is going to make it much more difficult for us to negotiate about getting aid in shipping if people here believe that whatever sacrifices they make to give us additional tonnage are only for the purpose of bringing over an unorganized and undisciplined mob. From what I am told as to his sayings in France, I should think that it would add very much to the difficulties of General Pershing's position. . . ."[1]

Consul General Summers reported that a Bolshevik celebration in Moscow over the dissolution of the Constituent Assembly had ended in general fighting. Artillery and machine guns were being placed at strategic points, and the city was in a state of terror. ". . . . Americans all safe and everything has been done to protect them."[2]

Two meatless days a week for England were announced.

To Governor William D. Stephens of California, a letter written at Secretary Wilson's suggestion, and based upon recommendations in the Mediation Commission report on the Mooney case. [See facsimile, pp. 490–491, for notes exchanged as to the wisdom of making the report public.]:

"Will you permit a suggestion from me in these troubled times which perhaps justify what I should feel hardly justifiable in other circumstances?

"The suggestion is this: Would it not be possible to postpone the execution of the sentence of Mooney until he can be tried upon one of the other indictments against him, in order to give full weight and consideration to the

---

[1] Copy supplied to the author by Newton D. Baker. About this time Representative Medill McCormick was giving confidential testimony before the Senate Military Affairs Committee to the effect that Lloyd George had expressed to him the desire that General Wood represent the United States on the Supreme War Council. A portion of the testimony was published in the New York *Times* of January 26, 1918.

[2] *Foreign Relations*, 1918, *Russia*, Vol. I, p. 355.

important changes which I understand to have taken place in the evidence against him?

"I urge this very respectfully indeed but very earnestly, because the case has assumed international importance and I feel free to make the suggestion because I am sure that you are as anxious as anyone can be to have no doubt or occasion of criticism of any sort attach itself to the case."[1]

To William J. Bryan:

"I have time for only a line but I want to acknowledge your letter of the fifteenth and tell you of my sincere interest in reading it. I find nothing more interesting or opening more avenues for reflection than the study of the various national problems on the other side of the water."

To Mrs. George Bass, who had sent the President an account of the suffrage situation, and especially of how Theodore Roosevelt's suggestion that a woman be added to the Republican National Committee from every suffrage state was turned to good account by the Democratic National Committee. She added a word of appreciation for the President's help in the matter of the Federal Suffrage Amendment. ". . . it is willingly conceded that it could not have passed but for you.":

"Thank you for your letter. . . It posts me about things in which, as you know, I am deeply interested, and I am particularly interested in the way you have dished Colonel Roosevelt."

To Dr. E. P. Davis, a Princeton classmate who had sent the President, as he often did, a poem of his own composition:

MY DEAR E. P.:

My heart comes into my throat while I thank you for the lines you have just sent me. I do not deserve any such

---

[1]Governor Stephens replied, giving the status of the case and saying that, if it should come before him, consideration would be given to the President's communication. Two months later, when Senator Poindexter attacked Mooney and the I.W.W. in the Senate, Senator Phelan asked, and received, the President's permission to read this letter aloud to the Senate.

THE WHITE HOUSE,
WASHINGTON.

January 23, 1918

Dear Governor:

   Is it your purpose to give publicity to

the report in the Mooney case?

                            J. P. T.

What does the Secy of Labour
advise. The effect on Mooney
himself must be considered.

                            W. W.

THE WHITE HOUSE,
WASHINGTON.

January 23, 1918.

MEMORANDUM:

Secretary Wilson states that the Commission would be satisfied to have publicity given to the report. He stated that the Commission felt that the effect on Mooney was of less importance than the effect on this country and the effect on our foreign relations. The all-important thing in the mind of the Commission is the effect on the people as a whole in this country and the effect in connection with our foreign relations. The Commission thought that either the beneficial or injurious effect on the individual was of less consequence.

PRESIDENT WILSON'S INTEREST IN THE MOONEY CASE

Note from Secretary Tumulty to the President (whom he always addressed as "Governor") as to whether publicity should be given to the report of the President's Mediation Commission on the Mooney case; the President's reply, written in his own hand; and Tumulty's memorandum, made after consulting Secretary Wilson.

491

praise or confidence, but it touches me most deeply that you feel as you do. God grant I may lead somewhere! It will be better than the present.

Affectionately yours,
WOODROW WILSON

To George S. Johns of the St. Louis Post-Dispatch:
"It is fine to be supported by such editorials as you have just sent me . . . It is reassuring to have such evidences of sanity in the midst of a lot of hysteria."

To his secretary, Tumulty, referring to a request from Emerson Ela, whose firm had been retained to defend the Wisconsin *State Journal* in Senator La Follette's suit for libel. The President's statement of March 4, 1917, about the "little group of willful men," said Ela, would have an important bearing on the case; he wished to have the statement correct and to know whether La Follette was one of the men included, and he also asked whether the President would, if necessary, make a brief deposition for use at the trial:

"Of course, these gentlemen are at liberty to use any statement I have made, but I do not think that it would be proper for me to make any deposition in connection with a trial of this sort. I think the whole country would feel that it was unjustifiable on my part. At the same time, Mr. Ela ought to know that Senator La Follette was one of the men whom I referred to in the statement."

Wednesday, January 23rd.
Afternoon appointments: Colonel Thompson, Major Shepherd, and W. A. Thiel of the Winchester Repeating Arms Company, who presented the President with a rifle; Representative Foster of Illinois; Senator Pomerene of Ohio; Sir William Wiseman; Senator Owen of Oklahoma; Secretary Baker. At 4:30 the President and Mrs. Wilson received the Italian ambassador and Countess Cellere; and later Dr. Vesnitch of the Serbian Mission. Evening at Keith's.

In reply to a message from Lord Rhondda, British Food Controller, Hoover telegraphed: ". . . we will export every grain of wheat that the American people save from their normal consumption. We shall appeal to them for greater endeavor and have already introduced stronger measures and we believe our people will not fail to meet the emergency."[1]

It was reported that Theodore Roosevelt had practically assumed the leadership of the Republican party. At a dinner given in his honor by Nicholas Longworth the night before, the war situation had been discussed, with especial reference to the tactics to be followed by the Republicans in Congress.[2]

Acting Secretary Polk telegraphed to the American minister in Rumania: ". . . . This Government has no knowledge of any understanding between Roumania and her other allies in regard to peace terms,[3] but is, however, committed to safeguard the integrity and freedom of smaller nations."[4]

To Frank L. Polk, who quoted M. Jusserand as saying that item 10 in the President's Fourteen Points address was not clearly understood abroad, and that he himself interpreted it to mean that the United States wished the place of the *peoples* of Austria-Hungary, rather than the place of Austria-Hungary among the nations, "safeguarded and assured":

"I have your letter of yesterday and in reply would say that the French Ambassador has correctly interpreted my peace terms with regard to Austria-Hungary."

To Herbert Hoover, enclosing a letter from Secretary McAdoo, who wrote, with some asperity, that certain demands made by the British upon the United States Treasury were the result of demands upon the British government by the United States Food Administration. Although his disapproval was evident, McAdoo said he would not undertake to pass upon the wisdom

---

[1] *Foreign Relations,* 1918, Supp. 1, Vol. I, pp. 536–537.

[2] New York *Times,* January 24, 1918. Roosevelt left Washington on the 25th.

[3] See Vopicka's telegram of January 12, 1918, this volume, p. 456, footnote.

[4] *Foreign Relations,* 1918, Supp. 1, Vol. I, p. 752.

of this policy; but he felt that it constituted an additional argument for Food Administration representation upon the Inter-Allied Council. The President's letter is marked "Confidential":

"I would be very much obliged if you would give your careful consideration to the enclosed and let me have your confidential advice. The Secretary of the Treasury is, I think, right in the position he takes. The financial problems we are now handling and are facing in the immediate future are of such magnitude that I believe it is absolutely essential that we should avoid every ounce of additional weight that can be avoided. Whether the representation of the Food Administration in the Inter-Allied Council will accomplish just what the Secretary of the Treasury has in mind or not, I am not clear, but that there should be coordination of the most intimate sort in big transactions of this kind will, I am sure be your judgment as it is mine."[1]

To E. N. Hurley of the Shipping Board:
"After all, the International Mercantile Marine Company do not appear to be the actual owners of the ships referred to. They are merely stockholders, are they not, in British corporations, and in those circumstances it is clear that you are right in saying that we have no control over the matter.

"As to whether we shall say to them that we are opposed to their selling their stocks or not, I would like your own advice. It comes to this, does it not, whether we want them to transfer their capital from these English companies to American shipbuilding endeavor? I assume that there is hardly any opportunity for private capital to engage in shipbuilding just at present and that it is hardly desirable that it should do so in view of the big programme of the

---

[1]Hoover, in reply, blamed the railroads for the very critical food situation in the country—a letter which the President passed on to McAdoo.

Shipping Board and the desirability of concentrating the whole shipbuilding industry of the country upon that programme.

"If I am correct in these assumptions, then we do not lose any shipping by the sale of the securities referred to, but only release a certain body of American capital."[1]

To Gutzon Borglum, written after receiving Secretary Baker's report that Borglum had been "seeing a large number of people, exhibiting to some of them, at least, the letter signed by you, and making seemingly irresponsible statements about the Aircraft Board and the aircraft program.":

"I am interested to learn that you are ready to report to me in the matter about which we have corresponded and about which you came to Washington. Mr. Tumulty has conveyed to me your desire to see me.

"Before I see you, may I not take the liberty of making this request, that you put your report in writing for my mature consideration and that you attach to it the material upon which it is based.

"I am sure it is unnecessary to say to you that this whole matter is of such a nature that it must be dealt with with the greatest care and caution, because it would be so easy to aid the enemy by any kind of information, direct or indirect, concerning the processes we are using or the details of the programme we are seeking to carry out. I must regard our relationship in this matter as entirely confidential and express the hope that you will not commit any of the matter to others, not even to stenographers. It has been necessary to deal with these matters with the

---

[1]Hurley replied on the 25th: "Your opinion confirms my own conclusion that we have no reason for opposing the sale which the International Mercantile Marine Company proposes to make of the British shipping securities owned by it. I shall so inform Mr. Franklin.

"Possibly in future negotiations with the British regarding shipping matters, it may be useful to remind them that without protest we allowed them to acquire this large American interest in their ships."

utmost caution even in respect of the knowledge communicated to officers and officials of the Government itself. I beg, therefore, that you will put the whole matter as you have found it in my hands together with the evidence."

To Mrs. Manuel Bittencourt, who had contributed six sons to the service of the United States:

". . . . I know what it must have cost you to send these sons to danger and to sacrifice, but the spirit you have shown in doing so is one of the finest evidences of patriotism and devotion that a mother could possibly give and makes me feel that I must ask the privilege of calling you my friend and of sending you this message of cheer, congratulation and sympathy."

Thursday, January 24th.
Early-afternoon appointments: Dr. Vesnitch of Serbia; Senator McCumber of North Dakota; Senator Poindexter of Washington.

Secretary Baker sent the President copies of a redrafted bill (later known as the Overman bill), asking whether he should himself take it up with the necessary members of Congress. A note in Secretary Burleson's handwriting reads: "Took up matter at the Presdt request."

Dr. Walcott telephoned a message for the President: the Advisory Committee on Aeronautics had been investigating the exact status of the aircraft production program, and "found a condition very encouraging."

Senator Chamberlain in a three-hour speech in the Senate defended himself against the President's accusation that he had distorted the truth, reiterating his charges of gross mismanagement and incompetency.

Amos Pinchot informed Colonel House that the text of the secret treaties, brought to him by "Russian residents of New York," had been given to the New York *Evening Post*, and would begin serial publication the following day. ". . . . I was amazed," wrote Pinchot, "to learn that

Colonel House had not received or read the Secret Treaties, and did not know of their contents . . ."[1]

Chancellor von Hertling, speaking before the Reichstag Committee, replied to the addresses of Lloyd George and President Wilson. He saw no serious will for peace in Lloyd George's speech; but the Fourteen Points of the President he reviewed with care. With some—open covenants, freedom of the seas, removal of economic barriers—he agreed. He found "quite discussable" the limitation of armaments and declared himself sympathetic with the idea of a league of nations. Certain points he felt should be left to Germany's allies, or should be settled later by negotiation. With regard to Russia, he rejected interference, maintaining that the whole matter was one between Russia and the Central Powers.

". . . . Our military situation was never so favorable as at present. Let the Entente bring new proposals. We shall then seriously study them. Lasting peace is impossible unless the integrity of the German Empire is recognized. . . ."[2]

The Austro-Hungarian Minister of Foreign Affairs, Count Czernin, speaking before the Reichsrath Committee on Foreign Affairs: ". . . I do not hesitate to say I find in the last proposals of President Wilson a considerable approach to the Austro-Hungarian point of view . . ." Taking up the Fourteen Points, he agreed to a considerable number of them—open covenants (though he thought this would present difficulties), freedom of the seas, removal of economic barriers, reduction of armaments, an independent Polish state, a league of nations. As to Russia, he said: ". . . we are proving with deeds that we are ready to create a friendly, neighborly relationship. . . ."

". . . Austria-Hungary and the United States of America are the two great Powers among the two groups of enemy states whose interests least conflict . . . an exchange of ideas between these two Powers might be the starting point for conciliatory discussions between all states which have not entered into peace conversations. . . ."[3]

---

[1]Pinchot to W. E. Borah, August 20, 1919.
[2]*Foreign Relations*, 1918, Supp. 1, Vol. I, pp. 38–42.
[3]*Ibid.*, pp. 54–59.

To Secretary Burleson, enclosing a letter from John R. Bland of Baltimore who told of organized Republican efforts to discredit the administration:[1]

"I wish you would read the enclosed. It has some rather interesting information in it and it may be that the National Committee can do some very useful work in exposing this growing organization."

To Champ Clark, Speaker of the House:

"Your letter of yesterday is mighty fine for one's spirits. It is astonishing to me what partisanship and the spirit of criticism is capable of at a time when what we need above all things else is cooperation and helpfulness. I would have expected such an assurance from you as you have sent me, but it is none the less delightful to have it thus generously volunteered."

Friday, January 25th.

The President had a severe cold and remained in his room all day, Mrs. Wilson taking her meals there with him. The cabinet meeting was canceled.

Surgeon General Gorgas testified before the Senate Military Affairs Committee that the National Guard and National Army had been rushed into cantonments which were not yet ready, causing a number of deaths by disease; and that his urgent recommendations for the construction of hospitals coincidentally with the building of cantonments went unheeded, as did his warnings to Secretary Baker against overcrowding.[2]

Secretary Baker requested permission to appear again before the Military Affairs Committee in order to answer Chamberlain's allegations. Permission was granted, and the 28th of January was named as the day for his appearance. Discussing this situation many years later, Baker said that he decided that the time had come to reply to the wholesale charges being flung out. The war work was so

[1]It may have been about this time that seeds were sown in the President's mind which resulted in his much-discussed call for a Democratic Congress in October, 1918.

[2]New York *Times*, January 26, 1918.

far advanced that there seemed now no danger in letting the world know just what had been accomplished. The President agreed.[1]

Secretary Baker's appointment of Edward R. Stettinius, of J. P. Morgan & Co., as Surveyor General of all army purchases was made public.[2] Secretary McAdoo wrote the President by hand on the 27th: ". . . . Confidentially I think the Stettinius appointment very unfortunate. As I have been going over the country I have been impressed with the suspicion of and feeling against the big interests —and J. P. Morgan & Company—particularly as they are believed (and justly, I think) to have made enormous sums through financing and purchasing for the allies prior to our entrance into the war. This is one of the reasons I was so anxious to create the Inter-Ally Purchasing Commission here and to get away from the Morgan connection and influence. . . ." The possible appointment of T. F. Ryan, president of the Amalgamated Copper Company, had also been discussed, and McAdoo objected strenuously to this, on the same general grounds, adding also that such an appointment would be very hard on Baruch. And he continued: ". . . . Recently Mr. Baker made Mr. McRoberts (vice-president of the National City Bank) a Colonel & put him in charge of very important matters. McRoberts is a protege of Armour & Co., I am told, and was put in the National City through their influence. McRoberts & Stettinius are Republicans, and while this alone does not disqualify them, it is not possible to count on their complete loyalty, I fear, when bitter partisan attacks are under way by their party. . . .

"Please don't think I want to interfere in Baker's department. The matter concerns the Treasury as well as the whole Administration. . . ."

Ambassador Page telegraphed from Italy that he had just seen a copy of the Treaty of London; and that Orlando had gone to England to seek its reaffirmation.[3]

---

[1]Newton D. Baker to the author. Mr. Baker bore no grudge on account of the general criticism directed against the Department—"back-seat driving" he called it —believing that it was inevitable.

[2]New York *Times*, January 26, 1918.

[3]*Foreign Relations*, 1918, Supp. 1, Vol. I, pp. 42–43. On the 31st Page reported: "Press declares that Orlando's visit to London entirely satisfactory, Orlando says

To Governor Arthur Capper of Kansas:

"I have your letter . . . in which you call my attention to the labor situation in Kansas and in which you especially request that the skilled farmers in cantonments and training camps be given furloughs at planting and harvest time. I note also your statement that under the present drafting methods, there is no intelligent selection possible between essential, trained and experienced farmers and the unskilled, non-essential men of the farms and small towns.

"As to your latter suggestion, I am inclined to believe from the whole tenor of your letter that you do not refer to the new Selective Service Regulations, under which the present classification of registrants is now progressing since, in very specific terms in those Regulations, it is provided that skilled farm laborers essential to the continued and undiminished operation of our farms shall be deferred in Class II. It is our present hope and belief that we shall be able to raise all the forces in immediate prospect without invading any deferred class and therefore, we can assume, I think, that future drafts will not interfere with your supply of skilled farm labor.

"I have also had very prominently in mind the advisability of furloughing selected men during planting and harvest time and to this end the War Department has asked of Congress authority to grant such furloughs without pay whenever, in the opinion of the Secretary of War, the military situation justifies such a step. Of course, it is impossible to say in advance what the changing conditions of warfare may impose upon us, but I can assure you that, if this authority is granted by Congress, we shall permit these furloughs whenever it is possible to do so.

"I take it that what I have said is precisely responsive

same. . . . I hear on good authority Lloyd George satisfied Orlando, telling him that one does not go into details in public speeches but that England does not repudiate treaties."
Op. cit., p. 60.

to what you have in mind and I hope and believe that the various Selection Boards composed of men of your choice will exercise the authority to defer skilled farm laborers in such a way as to meet the situation you present in the fullest way that it could be met under our present circumstances."

Saturday, January 26th.

The President worked in his study until 11:30, when Secretary Baker called. The only other appointment of the day was a conference in the afternoon with the Postmaster General.

> General Pershing and General Bliss conferred with General Robertson, Robertson arguing for the incorporation of American units into British divisions, and Bliss supporting him under the impression that that plan had been approved by the War Department. Pershing expressed his strong opposition, and Bliss later, after a private conference with Pershing, changed his attitude. On the same day Pershing talked with Joffre, who pointed out the unwisdom of amalgamating American forces with the British.[1]

To Attorney General Gregory:

"I know how difficult it is for you to deal with Senator John Sharp Williams because of the attitude he has taken under a very serious misapprehension, but I quite agree with his judgment that we not only ought to pay no attention to Senator Vardaman's recommendations for office, but that we ought studiously to avoid nominating men whom he picks out. . . ."

To Representative Milton A. Romjue, who had asked the President's opinion on the war cabinet issue and universal military training, so that he might be able to help as much as possible:

"I warmly appreciate your letter . . .

"My attitude with regard to the proposed War Cabinet is that it would add machinery without adding efficiency

---

[1] Pershing, *My Experiences in the World War*, Vol. I, pp. 304–306.

and that to introduce men inexperienced in the great task we have been working at for ten months and make them masters of that great task would be hardly less than childish.

"My opinion with regard to universal military training is exactly that stated by the Secretary of War to the Senate Committee on Military Affairs. It would manifestly interfere with and not advance our present military preparations and activities to add universal military training to our present programme now, and the question whether it should be added after the war is over seems to me to depend entirely upon circumstances which we cannot now forecast. In both these respects I am glad to find my own judgment in accordance with your own."

To Chauncey M. Depew, who had said, in an address before the Pilgrims Society in New York on January 23rd: ". . . President Wilson . . . in an address to Congress, which is one of the ablest and most illuminating state papers in our history, made so clear and emphatic what we are all fighting for, that his utterance has been accepted by the world as the purpose and object of our alliance, of our diplomacies, armies and navies. . . .

"We have the highest respect and the greatest loyalty for our President, and we want to strengthen his hands. . . .":[1]

"May I not express my warm appreciation of the generous speech you delivered last Wednesday evening? It is such speeches that clear the air and contribute much more than the present sort of criticism and cross purpose can to the real advance of the cause of liberty throughout the world."

To Senator Ollie M. James:
"You did a great piece of work in the Senate the other day in handling Senator Chamberlain's unfair attack and I am warmly obliged to you. It was an artistic job. How much stronger the truth always is than the false!"

[1]Depew, *Speeches and Literary Contributions at Fourscore and Four,* pp. 316–317, 319.

To Mr. and Mrs. Charles A. Wimpfheimer, who had just lost a son in the service:

"I . . . want to send you this line of deep and sincere sympathy. I hope that your consciousness that your son died in the service of his country will be, at any rate as the years soften your loss, a matter of deep and abiding consolation and pride to you. I know that you will agree with me in feeling that no cause ever more truly justified such sacrifices."

To John H. Fahey, honorary vice-president of the United States Chamber of Commerce:

"I am glad to get the information which your letter . . . brings me about the attitude of the Chamber of Commerce of the United States. Nobody who is not in direct contact with the problems of organization and cooperation as I am daily can realize how imperfectly and crudely such propositions as are now being widely discussed for radical readjustments meet the difficulties and necessities of the case. The faith that some people put in machinery is child-like and touching, but the machinery does not do the task; particularly is it impossible to do it if new and inexperienced elements are introduced."

Sunday, January 27th.

The President did not leave the house all day. Colonel House was a guest at dinner.

Monday, January 28th.

The President spent the whole morning in his study. There were no official appointments, with the exception of a call from Dr. Garfield in the early afternoon. Colonel House came in again for dinner.

Secretary Baker spoke for five hours before the Senate Committee on Military Affairs.[1] The large hearing room

---

[1]Testimony published in full in *Official Bulletin,* January 29, 1918.

was packed, for Baker had told the newspaper men he intended to make an important statement. Throughout the whole time Senator Ollie James, towering in height and bulk, sat on the front row before the speaker, his hands resting on the top of his cane and his chin on his hands. He listened intently until the noon recess came, then hurried from the room, got into a cab and drove to the White House. Rushing into the President's office, he exclaimed: "Jesus, you ought to see that little Baker. He's eating 'em up!" When the afternoon session began, he was back in his place, ready for the rest of the speech.[1]

Representative Charles P. Caldwell of New York wrote the President, directly after the address: ". . . I cannot let this opportunity pass without congratulating you upon the magnificent presentation of the facts by Secretary Baker. I believe that a great service has been done to the people . . ."[2]

". . . . Outside of your own addresses," wrote Creel to the President, "I consider the Baker statement the most forceful accounting to the people that has yet been made, and took pains to give it one hundred per cent. circulation."

France decreed bread rations.

To Professor Frank Gardner Moore, of Columbia University:

"I am very much complimented that you should be turning anything I have written into Latin. I hope the boys who have to read it in that language will not dislike me, as some of the young readers of Cicero dislike him, but, after all, the responsibility for that rests on you! . . . ."

---

[1] About this time also, while the senatorial critics were still peppering away at the War Department, Baker one day heard Burleson coming down the corridor toward the office. He recognized the tap, tap, tap of Burleson's umbrella on the tile floor. The Postmaster General came in quietly, looked all around and said softly:

"They're after you, Baker."

"Are they, Albert?"

"Yes, but never mind, I'm going to put them after me presently." (A reference, according to Baker, to his intention of taking over the telephones and telegraphs of the country.) Newton D. Baker to the author.

[2] The President, thanking Caldwell, said: ". . . . I think the Secretary entirely deserves the praise you bestow upon him. I have found him in every relationship frank, able and courageous, and I am delighted that he has had this chance to show his quality."

Tuesday, January 29th.

The President conferred with Colonel House sometime during the day, and House wrote in his diary that evening: "The President told X that 'we have tentatively decided to answer the Hertling and Czernin speeches in this way: In reply to Hertling's assertion that differences between Russia and Germany must be settled between the two, and questions between France and Germany should be settled in like manner, we will call attention to the fact that this is the old diplomacy which has brought the world into such difficulties, and if carried to its logical conclusion Germany and the rest of the world cannot object if England and the United States should conclude between themselves treaties by which the balance of the world would be excluded from their raw materials.'

"We discussed the best method of making his views public. . . . Lansing suggested that he give out an interview. . . . The President disagreed with this conclusion. He said he wanted to make a habit of delivering through Congress what he had to say. . . .

"He wondered what excuse he could make for going before Congress again. I suggested that he get a member of the Foreign Relations Committee to write him a letter which would call forth a promise to address Congress on the subject upon which he desired information. He objected to this, as he did not wish Congress to think they could control him in any way or take part in handling foreign affairs. I then suggested that he state that the questions now pending between the nations were of such importance he felt that every move he made, or contemplated making, or whatever thought he had concerning the international situation, should be communicated through Congress."[1]

Afternoon appointments: the Attorney General; Richard Hooker of the Springfield *Republican*; Raymond B. Stevens of the Shipping Board.

Ambassador Page telegraphed the State Department: ". . . . London press of yesterday published a report pur-

---

[1] *Intimate Papers*, Vol. III, p. 367. About this time the President asked Colonel House to supervise the collection of excerpts from the Socialist press and speeches in enemy countries. Dr. Seymour writes: ". . . . The President by utilizing the criticism leveled at the German Government by the Socialists themselves, using their own phrases, could emphasize the sympathy between them and Wilsonian principles and the mutual hostility to German imperialism. . . ." The collection was made by W. C. Bullitt. *Ibid.*, pp. 365–366.

porting to be of Vienna origin suggesting that the President was fully informed of the contents of the recent speech delivered by Count Czernin . . . This caused something like consternation here. The tone of the London press in presenting this information indicates a belief that Austria is suggesting separate peace negotiations with the United States and that she is not unwilling to have it believed that she has secret means of communication with the United States Government.

"Your denial of any foreknowledge of Czernin's speech[1] is noted by London press today without the least appearance of incredulity . . ."[2]

To Secretary Lansing, who had written of Italian disappointment at references in the President's Fourteen Points address to Italy and Austria-Hungary. ". . . . The point which the Italians seem to make is that if their frontiers are to be rectified only on the basis of nationality, they will be as vulnerable to attack from Austria-Hungary as they have been in the past. . . .

"I think that this . . . is not entirely without justification.

"While, as you know, I am strongly inclined to nationality as the basis for territorial limits I believe that it cannot be invariably adopted, but that in certain cases physical boundaries and strategic boundaries must be considered and modify boundaries based on nationality. . . .

"Do you not think that something could be done to restore Italian confidence that a satisfactory settlement of the Adriatic Question will be made at the peace conference? If anything can be done it seems to me it ought [to] be done without delay.":

"This is a very delicate matter; but while you were away from your office I took occasion to say to the Italian

[1]Because of rumors, a positive statement had been made from the White House that President Wilson was not in possession of Czernin's address before its delivery (New York *Times*, January 29, 1918), and two hours before Page's telegram arrived in Washington an official denial had been sent out by telegraph. *Foreign Relations*, 1918, Supp. 1, Vol. I, pp. 51–52. Two months later Czernin said: ". . . I must dispel a misunderstanding. . . . I declared in my last speech to the committee of the Austrian Delegation that Mr. Wilson must already have had my declarations in his possession. Mr. Wilson later corrected this and made it plain that this was a mistake. In order to avoid the semblance of possible misapprehension or distortion, I had drawn up the text beforehand and I thought that that text should have already arrived in Washington at the time I made my speech. . . ." *Ibid.*, p. 190.

[2]*Ibid.*, p. 52.

Ambassador (who, oddly enough, had called to thank me in the name of his Government for what I *had* said) that I had limited my statement about Italian rights as I did because I was taking my programme as a whole, including the league of nations through which mutually defensive pledges were to be given and taken which would render strategic considerations such as those affecting the Adriatic much less important. I told him that, failing a league of nations, my mind would be open upon all such matters to new judgments.

"I am clear that I could not pledge our people to fight for the eastern shore of the Adriatic; but there is nothing in what I have omitted to say to alarm the Italian people, and it ought to be possible for Orlando to make that plain to his own followers."

To Gutzon Borglum:

"It certainly is unfortunate that I should have been confined with a heavy cold just at the time when you had finished your work here and was [sic] ready to report to me. I beg that you will not feel this to be an element of discouragement. I would be very much obliged if you could send me the report that you wished to place in my hands, with the data which you have collected to support it. Uncomfortable as I am with this cold, I can go over it at intervals during the day when my head is clear, and would value an opportunity to examine it."

To Cyrus H. McCormick, who urged universal military training and service. The letter is marked "Personal":

". . . . Of course, I have given a great deal of thought to the question of universal military service and have by no means turned away from it in the sense of rejecting it, but it is clear to me and it is clear to many who have studied our present military problem that it would be unwise, and indeed impracticable, to institute such train-

ing now. We have not the officers with which to undertake
it and we have not the equipment, and the additional
financial strain would be too great: besides which, its
immediate institution would seriously interfere with the
more immediate task we have of preparing and sending an
Army across the seas.

"My feeling is that it is impossible to forecast now what
the condition of the world will be, and therefore our own
military task and duty, when the war is over. When we
do see the conditions which follow the war, I hope and
believe that we shall know what to do, and it may be that
we shall have to undertake some such great plan."

To David Lawrence:

"I beg that you will never allow yourself to be hurt by
anything I do or do not do. We are working under the
sternest conditions that men ever worked under since
civilization began. We can't afford to have personal feelings, and for my part I earnestly and sincerely try to
exclude them.

"You will see, I think, upon reflection how impossible
it would be for me to guide even writers like yourself whom
I know, and how undesirable, because the facts seem to
me to lie patent to everybody and the duty of every man
in the United States just now is to look at the facts and
not at the color which anybody puts upon them, and look
at the facts with a view, not to criticism but to cooperation, to putting everything before the public in a way
which will help the public to help the administration by
straight thinking on the actual facts.

"The plan you have in view seems to me an excellent
one of setting forth just how European conditions, which
have again and again undergone kaleidoscopic change,
necessarily react upon our work and condition it on every
side. Since our entrance into the war, we have had to

AMERICAN TROOPS—THE 166TH INFANTRY IN A WINTRY MARCH TO THE FRENCH FRONT

change our plans half a dozen times upon earnest representation upon the other side as to radically altered conditions. Unfortunately, not all of this can be put into the public prints, because to do so would reveal many difficulties and disappointments on the part of the Allies which it is not necessary or desirable that our enemies should know, but the work of interpretation should rest, it seems to me, upon such statements as the Secretary of War made yesterday.

"As a matter of fact, all the matter gone over in that report was carefully gone over by the House Committee on Military Affairs when considering the Army appropriations, but the whole scene needed to be described in a single statement, and I am glad that you think as I do that the Secretary of War showed his admirable insight, ability and candor in the way in which he did it."

Wednesday, January 30th.
The President spent the morning in his study. Afternoon appointments: Secretary Houston; Secretary Baker.

A Shipping Control Committee was established, P. A. S. Franklin, chairman, to have control of all ships—American, Allied and neutral—entering and leaving American ports.
Secretary Baker announced that American troops had taken over a small section of the Western Front.
The Supreme War Council convened, General Bliss sitting as Military Representative of the United States.[1] " . . . . Gen-

---

[1] General Bliss became an indispensable member of the Council; he was always calm, whereas the others were frequently in turmoil. "It is probably no exaggeration to say that General Bliss had the greatest mind of any soldier of the war. He was a statesman as well as a military man, broad-guaged, far-sighted and astute. He had no greed for the spoils of the war and never 'lost his head'. . . . He commanded the admiration, respect and trust of the President from the beginning to the end . . ." Newton D. Baker to the author.

" . . . . He was one of the most valuable contributions America made to the successful prosecution of the War . . . ." writes Lloyd George. *War Memoirs of David Lloyd George*, Vol. V, p. 401.

When Baker notified Bliss, on May 31, 1918, that the brevet rank of general had been conferred upon him, he added: "The gratifying part of the whole matter was the enthusiasm with which the President accepted the suggestion, because it involved a

eral Foch, General Pétain, and General Haig agreed that
the American army, if taken as an autonomous unit, could
not be counted upon for effective aid during the present
year, and that the only method of rendering them useful
at the earliest possible moment would be by amalgamating
American regiments or battalions in French or British
divisions. . . ."[1]

An agreement was signed by Lloyd George, General Maurice
and General Pershing, with the approval of General Bliss,
which provided for the transportation to Europe by British
shipping of six entire American divisions, under certain
stipulated conditions, the first of which was that the
infantry and auxiliary troops thereof were to be trained
with British divisions by battalions "or under some plan
to be mutually agreed upon."[2] This new arrangement
would, if adopted, make the earlier 150-battalion plan[3]
"so much paper in the files."[4]

The American minister in the Netherlands, upon instructions
from the State Department, reported the point of view of
Kurt Hahn, German liberal leader, as to Hertling's recent
speech. ". . . . He again emphasizes what he pretends to
consider the futility of public statements and says that
if the United States really wishes to know if peace is
possible it should designate some American who enjoys the
confidence of both Governments to converse informally
and secretly with a corresponding German so that each
Government may receive first hand information as to the
bona fides of the other. . . ."[5]

recognition of your work, of which he entertains the highest possible opinion . . . . the
President has a number of times commented to me upon what he called your 'robust
good sense'; and both he and the Secretary of State have a kind of confidence in your
recommendations to us which would be most gratifying to you could I set forth all
the evidences which I have seen."

[1]Report by A. H. Frazier, United States diplomatic liaison officer with the Supreme
War Council. *Foreign Relations*, 1918, Supp. 1, Vol. I, p. 63; also *War Memoirs of
David Lloyd George*, Vol. V, pp. 240 *et seq.*

[2]For Pershing's seven conditions, see *Foreign Relations*, 1918, Supp. 1, Vol. I, pp.
64–65.

[3]See this volume, January 20th, p. 483.

[4]Palmer, *Newton D. Baker*, Vol. II, p. 116. Pershing's telegram to the War Department (January 30th) transmitting this agreement was immediately sent over to the
President by Secretary Baker. Pershing, *My Experiences in the World War*, Vol. I,
pp. 308–310.

[5]*Foreign Relations*, 1918, Supp. 1, Vol. I, p. 60.

The author wrote in his notebook: "Everyone is talking of
Baker's defense of the War Department. He met his
enemies squarely and will certainly win.

"Boston is the hotbed of criticism of the administration . . . they don't like the progressive democracy of
Wilson. They don't like freer trade, they fear honest
taxation, they dread a fair policy toward the workers."
For the first time since July, 1917, Paris was raided by air.
Twenty persons were killed and fifty injured. A German
account declared this to be in reprisal for bombs dropped
"on open German towns outside the region of operations."[1]

To John Palmer Gavit:

". . . . I hope and believe that the country will slowly
get the impression that you are yourself getting, that we
are acting with as much energy and comprehension as
possible in the face of immense difficulties, and I think
that the statement of the Secretary of War made the
other day must convince the country that the successes
have been vastly more noticeable than the failures."

To John J. Cavanagh:

". . . . You are quite right in thinking that what I desire
is peace, though at present the only way to get it is to overcome those who are its inveterate enemies and who are
unwilling to maintain it except in their own interest. . . ."

Thursday, January 31st.
Afternoon appointments: representatives of the Tokyo
Y.M.C.A., whom the President received at the request of
John R. Mott; Robert A. Woods and William T. Cross;
Secretary McAdoo. Evening at the National Theater.

The President sent a message to the Farmers' Conference at
Urbana, Illinois: ". . . the culminating crisis of the struggle
has come and . . . the achievements of this year on the
one side or the other must determine the issue . . . . the

---

[1] *Current History*, March, 1918, p. 386.

forces that fight for freedom . . . depend upon us in an extraordinary and unexpected degree for sustenance, for the supply of the materials by which men are to live and to fight . . .

". . . the Government will help and help in every way that is possible. . . .

"I hope and believe that the farmers of America will willingly and conspicuously stand by . . ."[1]

In reply to an inquiry from the President as to the Treaty of London (one of the secret treaties), A. J. Balfour sent over a private letter, hitherto unknown, dealing with the subject. The Treaty, he said, was evident proof of Allied anxiety to get Italy into the war, and objections to it were obvious enough. Nevertheless England and France were "bound to uphold it in letter and in spirit." While admitting that "great crimes against the principle of nationality" had been committed in the name of strategic necessity, he did not rule out such arguments entirely, maintaining that strong frontiers made for peace. In this case, however, he himself doubted whether Italy would really be strengthened by acquiring all her claims in the Adriatic. At any rate he felt sure she would not prolong the war to get them; she might not, indeed, continue to fight even for "Italia Irredenta." He concluded with a pessimistic word as to the situation in Europe—Russia in dissolution; internal forces threatening Austria, Germany, Italy; France depending on the vigor of an old man; "some faint signs of unrest even in Britain"—and asserted that the war seemed likely to be won by the nations having most endurance and political stability. ". . . . Since America came in I have never doubted the result!" A postscript reiterated his willingness to answer "with complete frankness" any question the President cared to ask.

The Supreme War Council met again, Baron Sonnino of Italy pressing the question of the use of American troops "in such a way that it could not be avoided." General Bliss emphasized the fact that permanent amalgamation of American units with British and French units would not be permitted; but that in an emergency American troops

---

[1]*Public Papers*, Vol. V, pp. 169–174. The New York *Times* reported that stocks soared upon the publication of this message, February 1, 1918.

would undoubtedly be used to prevent disaster. Clemenceau remarked: "That point is now settled."[1]

Senator Owen offered a resolution committing the United States to support of the nation's war aims as stated by President Wilson in his address of January 8th.

Strikes in Germany, engineered by Independent Socialists, reached their peak; the primary cause was thought to be the failure of the German government to obtain peace.[2]

To Colonel House, enclosing a telegram from the American ambassador in Italy: "Secret. I am sensible of growing feeling here among men in control that America is becoming too potent and that we are too democratic and too little in sympathy with European interests but I do not believe the people have this idea at all. Newspapers talk of Latin race league or union with Italy as head to counterbalance the power of the Anglo-Saxon peoples and I hear that some leading men have same idea. I hear that French Ambassador is very critical of President's last message apparently resenting that he should take so firm and directive a position in European affairs. This also is, I hear, somewhat Baron Sonnino's private view. They seem now closer than even formerly. . . .":

"Such symptoms make me uneasy. To my mind they furnish additional arguments why I should presently attempt to show that each item of a general peace is everybody's business. If we have to fight an All-Latin combination, we must fight it. I trust they will have no stomach for such a combination as we could form against them. Is not this the way your mind works on what it [is] to be got from this message of Tom. Page's?

"After all, it may be merely the resentment brought about by the prospect that, without our support, Italy cannot get what she went into the war, on cold-blooded calculation, to get."[3]

---

[1]Palmer, *Bliss, Peacemaker*, pp. 223–224.

[2]Bullitt's memorandum, sent to the President by Colonel House on February 7th.

[3]House replied: ". . . . Unfortunately the reactionaries are in control of almost all the belligerent governments, but they represent the necessities of their peoples rather than their real sentiments. . . ."

To Secretary Baker, written on the President's own typewriter:
"We are having hard luck with our military attaches at Petrograd, are we not. I should think that being sent to Petrograd would drive most men to drink, but anyone who is so driven is the very man who cannot be trusted to do the real job there, am I not right?"

To Secretary Daniels, written on the President's own typewriter:
"I appreciate fully the spirit in which this honour is offered Sims, and I wish he could accept it; but I am afraid it would be a mistake for him to do so. The English persist in thinking of the United States as an English people, but of course they are not and I am afraid that our people would resent and misunderstand what they would interpret as a digestion of Sims into the British official organization. What do you think?
"I would be very much obliged if you would show this note to Lansing and confer with him about this matter."

To Thomas W. Lamont of J. P. Morgan & Company, who wished the President to see Colonel W. B. Thompson. ". . . . Colonel Thompson is actuated I can assure you only by the finest motives of patriotism, neither he nor we having financial interests in Russia. . . .":

". . . . I have heard a great deal about Colonel W. B. Thompson, and everything that I have heard has attracted me. Some day I hope I shall be able to have a deliberate talk with him, but just at present the changes taking place in Russia are so kaleidoscopic that I feel that information and advice are futile until there is something definite to plan with as well as for."

To Professor Charles H. Haskins of Harvard University:
MY DEAR HASKINS:
It was with real pleasure that I received a copy of your book, "Norman Institutions," and I shall hope for some time of leisure when I may really read it comprehendingly,

because it is on a subject on which I have often wished to have more complete and trustworthy information.

It gives me peculiar pleasure, my dear Haskins, to believe that I have been of service to you in your studies. My interest in you and in your career has been very sincere and very great from the first, and it has been a real pleasure to me to see your unusual gifts recognized.

It is delightful to hear that your children and my grandchildren are likely to become chums. I hope that the small people will really get to know each other.

With the best wishes,

> Cordially and sincerely yours,
> WOODROW WILSON

To his secretary, Tumulty, referring to the request of J. H. Odell of the *Outlook* for an interview:

"My trouble about this is that the Outlook is entirely antagonistic, antagonistic in a very ugly way. I don't feel like assisting any of its writers. The journal carries very little weight anyhow now."

Friday, February 1st.

The President conferred, at noon, with a group of senators: Thomas, Owen, Gerry, Phelan, Shields, Underwood, James, Jones of New Mexico, King and Smith of South Carolina. He was reported to have reiterated his objections to a war cabinet and a secretary of munitions; and urged the necessity for avoiding, as far as possible, agitation which might encourage the enemy by giving an impression of discord.[1] Late-afternoon appointments: a committee of the Lord's Day Alliance, headed by H. L. Bowlby; George Creel; Vance C. McCormick; Reverend Robert O. Kirkwood. Evening at the Belasco Theater.

Secretary Lansing telegraphed Ambassador Francis in Russia: "Department appreciates gravity of the political situation and the possible danger of a crisis. Do you recommend any moderation of Department's attitude

---

[1]New York *Times,* February 2, 1918.

towards the Bolsheviki authorities? If so, explicitly state
your views. Department is not disposed to put you and
the members of the Embassy staff in personal danger if it
can be avoided without compromising the position of the
Government."[1]

Secretary Lansing replied to Ambassador Page's telegram as
to the President's alleged possession of Czernin's speech
before delivery:[2]

".... Endeavor to ascertain confidentially whether
British Government entertains any apprehension that this
Government might have communications or even enter
into conversations about peace with one or other of the
Central Empires without the knowledge of the Allies. If
so, you should informally express the distress felt by this
Government that such a thing should be thought possible
by editors and others. ..."[3]

Secretary Lansing advised the British government that the
President had appointed Raymond B. Stevens of the
Shipping Board as United States representative on the
Inter-Allied Shipping Council.[4]

The Supreme War Council adopted a resolution addressed
to the four governments, "stating as an absolutely necessary condition for the safety of the Western front during
the year 1918 that American troops must arrive at the rate
of not less than two complete divisions per month."
Bliss, reporting this to Washington by telegram, said:
".... This rate of movement must begin at once. If it can
be done we will have here 21 divisions by about July.
It is of vital importance that this be done. Can you do
it? ...." And he said in a letter of the same day to Secretary Baker: "I doubt if I could make anyone not present
at the recent meeting of the Supreme War Council realize
the anxiety and fear that pervade the minds of political
and military men here."[5]

[1]*Foreign Relations*, 1918, *Russia*, Vol. I, p. 364.

[2]See this volume, pp. 505–506.

[3]*Foreign Relations*, 1918, Supp. 1, Vol. I, p. 67. Sent also to our ambassadors in
France and Italy. Page replied on the 4th: "Mr. Balfour perfectly understands and
feels no apprehension." *Ibid.*, footnote.

[4]*Ibid.*, p. 501.

[5]Palmer, *Newton D. Baker*, Vol. II, p. 117.

Much of the Western Front lay buried under snow; no major operations took place during February. In the East, General Allenby made further advances beyond Palestine.

To Secretary Baker:
"Here is Mr. Borglum's preliminary report. Is there not someone entirely disconnected from aeronautics and from those who are prominent in carrying out the aeroplane programme whom you can ask to go over this thing with an unbiased mind and give us his naïve impressions of it? There may be something worthy of our consideration, and suggestions worthy to be adopted."

To William Kent, who felt sure that the Federal Trade Commission investigation of the packers, then in process, would prove "far reaching and infinitely beneficial." He warned the President, however, that he could "expect misrepresentation and requests for your interference from all sorts of suspected and unsuspected sources.":

"Thank you for your letter of yesterday about the Packers. I am very much obliged for the tip."

To Senator Robert L. Owen:
"I have your letter . . . in which you suggest that the Attorney General frame a law authorizing the trial by court-martial of all alien enemies detected in conspiracy against the law and order of the United States and that citizens of the United States detected in conspiracies involving treason be made subject to the same method of trial.

"I shall be glad to consult the Attorney General about this, though I must frankly say, my dear Senator, that my present opinion is that it would be a very serious mistake to put our own citizens under court-martial, for I think it would make an impression with regard to the weakness of our ordinary tribunals which would not be justified.

"Just how the law of court-martial would operate in

regard to alien enemies detected in conspiracies I do not yet clearly see, but my discussion with the Attorney General will no doubt clear it up."

To Senator Robert L. Owen:

"I have your letter . . . suggesting that negotiations be entered into with our associates in the war to transfer to America German and Austrian prisoners who are not now employed by the Allies, in order that they may be put to work in America in useful ways.

"This is a subject which has several times engaged our attention in the Cabinet, and it is our present information that there are so few Austrian or German prisoners who would be available for such transportation, that is to say, so few who are not already usefully engaged on the other side, that there would be very small advantage to be derived from their work. I will take pleasure in looking into the matter further and confirming this information if it is true."

Saturday, February 2nd.

Except for a conference with Secretary Baker at noon, there were no official engagements. In the evening the President attended a banquet for ordnance officers at the Army and Navy Club.

General Bliss in his report to the War Department upon the general work of the Supreme War Council at its third session (January 30–February 2) said "in absolute confidence": ". . . . The general plan of campaign for 1918 is to be one of general defense on the western, the Italian, and the Macedonian fronts. The English insisted upon an offensive campaign in Asia Minor with a view to detaching Turkey from alliance with the Central powers [making it clear, however, that no forces for this purpose would be detached from the Western Front] . . . .

". . . the Supreme War Council decided to establish a general inter-allied reserve. . . ."

This report was immediately called to the President's attention.

The Supreme War Council drafted, for simultaneous publication in Paris, London and Rome on February 4th, a statement regarding the work of the conference, the following paragraph of which greatly disturbed President Wilson since it was political in character and would, he feared, be taken as representing the United States, whereas the United States was not politically represented on the Council[1]: "The Supreme War Council gave the most careful consideration to the recent utterances of the German Chancellor and of the Austro-Hungarian Minister for Foreign Affairs but was unable to find in them any real approximation to the moderate conditions laid down by all the Allied Governments. This conviction was only deepened by the impression made by the contrast between the professed idealistic aims with which the Central Powers entered upon the present negotiations at Brest-Litovsk and the now openly disclosed plans of conquest and spoliation. Under the circumstances the Supreme War Council decided that the only immediate task before them lay in the prosecution with the utmost vigor and in the closest and most effective cooperation of the military effort of the Allies until such time as the pressure of that effort shall have brought about in the enemy Governments and peoples a change of temper which would justify the hope of the conclusion of peace on terms which would not involve the abandonment in the face of an aggressive and unrepentant militarism of all the principles of freedom, justice and the respect for the law of nations which the Allies are resolved to vindicate. . . ."[2]

To his secretary, Tumulty, who had called attention to a request that the President express his opinion about the play, Peter Ibbetson, which he had recently seen:

"I am very sorry but I can't do this, because, while I enjoyed the play and thought it very beautiful, there were some things about Mr. Barrymore's acting which did not seem to me an interpretation of the real Peter Ibbetson.

[1] See this volume, p. 549.

[2] *Foreign Relations*, 1918, Supp. 1, Vol. I, pp. 70–71. For Frazier's report to Colonel House on the discussion that led up to this statement, see *Intimate Papers*, Vol. III, pp. 361–362.

The book upon which the play is founded happens to be
one with which I am especially familiar, because it fasci-
nated me, and I could not write about the play without
a criticism which would be entirely useless, now that it has
been on so long and the method of its presentation so
firmly established in the habit and conception of the
players themselves. Personally, I enjoyed it very much."

Sunday, February 3rd.

The President and Mrs. Wilson went to the Central Presby-
terian Church in the morning. Secretary Baker and Sir William
Wiseman were luncheon guests, and afterward, probably, the
President had a talk with Wiseman. Reporting the interview to
Balfour, Wiseman said: ".... The President asked me to send
you a cable explaining his views regarding the disposal of
American troops in France. The following is the substance of
his arguments:

"In the first place the President is confident you will believe
that he is actuated solely by what he considers the best policy
for the common good. The President says American troops will
be put into the line by battalions with the French or British if
it should become absolutely necessary, but he wishes to place
before you frankly the very grave objections he sees to this
course.

"Apart from the serious danger of friction owing to different
methods, it is necessary that an American army should be
created under American leaders and American flag in order
that the people of America shall solidly and cheerfully support
the war. The placing of American troops in small bodies under
foreign leaders would be taken as a proof that the recent criticism of the War Department was justified and that the American military machine had broken down. The American people
would not, he fears, understand the military reasons and the
necessary secrecy would prevent a very full explanation being
given. . . .

"At the same time the President repeats most earnestly that
he will risk any adverse public criticism in order to win the
war and he has told Pershing that he may put American troops
by battalions in the British line or use them in any way which

in his, Pershing's, judgment may be dictated by the necessities of the military situation. . . ."[1]

Colonel House to the President: "I am disturbed at the statement given out by the civil end of the Supreme War Council. It seems to me a monumental blunder. It is the old belligerent tone and will serve the purpose of again welding together the people of the Central Empires back of their governments.

"I would not let this deter me from making the statement to Congress you have in mind. I think it is now more necessary than ever. It is a pity that the Entente will insist upon undoing your work, built up with so much care. Until you began the direction of the Allied diplomacy it was hopelessly bad.
_____

"Sir William has told me of the substance of your conference today. I agree absolutely with your position. . . ."

Monday, February 4th.

Afternoon engagements: Representative Eagle of Texas; Representative Sabath of Illinois; Senator Jones of New Mexico; Secretary Wilson. In the evening the President and Mrs. Wilson went to the New Willard Hotel for the Southern Relief Ball.

Senator Hitchcock of Nebraska, Democrat, opened the fight for the War Cabinet bill with a three-hour speech in which he attacked the administration for failure to coördinate the nation's war activities. The President, he said, did not know the real situation, which was "worse than alarming." Secretary Baker was "out of touch" with War Department details. Senator John Sharp Williams replied, opposing the proposed legislation as a usurpation of the powers of the President; and Reed of Missouri also spoke against the bill, declaring that it would be unconstitutional.

To Secretary Baker, who had sent over a telegram of January 30th from General Bliss in which Bliss recommended that the agreement of that date[2] be adopted. In his covering letter,

_____

[1] *Intimate Papers,* Vol. III, pp. 431–432.
[2] This volume, p. 510.

Baker wrote: "This . . . seems to cover the entire situation. If the arrangement meets with your approval I will so notify General Bliss. . . ." The President's letter was written on his own typewriter:

"How do you think this would do for instructions to General Bliss,—or General Pershing, whichever is the right one to receive them?

"That we consider the objections to the plan just those which he states in the enclosed despatch and that in our judgment those objections are final.

"That we have no objection to the programme which he here suggests by way of substitute (repeating it), but that our judgment is that the British should undertake to transport six complete divisions across the sea, to be disposed of and trained as General Pershing directs, in conference, of course, with the commanding officers of the other forces.

"That we are willing to trust to his judgment upon all points of training and preliminary trying out alike of officers and men, but advise that nothing except sudden and manifest emergency be suffered to interfere with the building up of a great distinct American force at the front, acting under its own flag and its own officers."

To Secretary Daniels, who wrote that while he himself still felt sure of Baruch's fitness for the chairmanship of the War Industries Board, he had been told by Mr. Fahey, former president of the National Chamber of Commerce, that the appointment would not be well received by many business men:

"Thank you for your report of your conversation with Mr. Fahey about the chairmanship of the War Industries Board. I do not feel that we can venture to delay that matter very long, but I wish with you to follow the line of action which will bring the least criticism.

"I think you will find that members of the two Houses are learning very fast to have a very great confidence in

Baruch and, after all, they are our only authoritative critics."[1]

To Herbert Hoover:

"I have your letter . . . in which you speak of the tendency on the part of flour mills, canneries, candy manufacturers, sweet drink manufacturers, and some others whose productive capacity is at present more than sufficient to take care of the country's needs to enter upon a speculative expansion of their production with the result of spreading their production over a much larger body of machinery and thus increasing the cost of production by the decreased proportion of the output, and also increasing the demand for labor, for capital, and for transportation. If such expansion can be discouraged through the Food Administration, it is clear to me that it is in the national interest that it should be discouraged, and I am very glad to confirm your view in the matter."

To Henry P. Davison, chairman of the Red Cross War Council. The letter is marked "Personal":

". . . . Frankly, my delay in replying has been due to the fact that I did not find in the list your letter contained of those whom you are suggesting as new members of the National War Finance Committee of the American Red Cross more than one or two men who seem to me to entertain any sort of liberal views with regard to the political development of the country and the world. I hope you know how entirely and sincerely disinclined I am to bring any political considerations to bear upon such choices, and I can well understand that in a finance committee particularly it may be unnecessary to consider matters of this sort, and I am writing now to say that I have no objection to the appointments, but inasmuch as they are, I believe,

---

[1]There had been some difference of opinion in the cabinet about this appointment, Houston, for one, feeling that it would be most unwise.

made in my name, I must admit a little embarrassment because of the impression that will be made that I am choosing almost no men of my own way of thinking.

"I am sure, my dear Mr. Davison, that you will read this in the spirit in which it is intended, and I beg to assure you that I do not mean to imply any criticism. I have learned to have a great deal of confidence in your judgment."

To Representative Edward T. Taylor of Colorado, who had asked the President to see a number of oil men from the West:

"I am sure you will understand when I say that I dare not undertake to see the oil men as you so earnestly request . . . I say I dare not, because if I did, the result would be that I would have practically to hold hearings on every important piece of legislation. I have sought to avoid this, and I think you will see how imperative it is that I should avoid it.

"This does not mean, however, that I am out of touch with the considerations which the oil men are urging. They have been presented to me not once but very often, by members of the Senate in particular and also by members of the House who were in touch with the whole situation and all its circumstances. I feel, of course, very much impressed with the complexity and the difficulties of the subject, and I shall be very glad to receive any memoranda that anyone interested may wish to lay before me, but I must confine myself, I am afraid, in matters of this sort to consultation with the committees and members of the two Houses."

To Dr. Sidney L. Gulick, secretary of the Commission on Relations with the Orient, of the Federal Council of Churches of Christ in America:

"You were kind to remember my request that if you should publish anything on American-Japanese affairs, I would like to see a copy of it. I am very much obliged to you for sending me your 'Anti-Japanese War Scare Stories.' It is very important indeed that the public opinion of the country should be steadied and informed in this important field."

To his old friend and classmate, Robert Bridges, who wrote: ".... I have gone to see the Sargent portrait of you three times, and like it hugely. I can see you getting ready to tell a story, with the quirk to the right side of your mouth. None of the art critics seem to like it—*but for me it's you*—and the real human you that they could not see if they tried: I'd stand on that! What they want is a stern-looking Covenanter with a jaw like a pike, Damn 'em! ....":

"Bless you, my dear Bobby, for your generous and affectionate letter. It was just what I stood in need of, and my heart responds with the deepest gratitude and affection. . . .

"These are certainly times that try the soul, try indeed everything that is in a man, but I believe that what is fair and right will prevail so long as those who are partisans of what is fair and right do not lose heart or let their lines be broken at all.

"I am heartily glad you like the portrait. Of course, I do not know what judgment to form of it myself, but the family like it and that is a pretty good test.

"With all my heart

"Your affectionate friend,
"WOODROW WILSON"

To Theodore N. Vail:
"May I not express to you personally my appreciation of the endeavors which are being made by the League for National Unity to swing the whole force of the nation behind the constitutional authorities now conducting the war? I think my feeling in this matter is entirely impersonal, but there is obviously but one instrumentality

through which the war can be carried out to a successful issue, and I have a feeling of great personal admiration, therefore, for those who are devoting themselves to the genuine support of the Government."[1]

To his secretary, Tumulty, who had called attention to a request for some expression as to how commercial travelers could help in winning the war:

"It is very clear to me that the commercial travelers of the country can be of the utmost service to the Government and in that way to the whole world by taking pains to acquaint themselves with the real facts of governmental activity and of governmental policy, facts which the Committee on Public Information will, I know, be glad to supply them with in perfectly unpartisan form, and then making themselves agents to see to it that everybody they run across gets straightened out as to what the facts really are and so gets in an attitude of support and cooperation rather than of criticism and pulling-apart.

"For example, if they would make themselves thoroughly familiar with the recent statement of the Secretary of War, they would be equipped to discuss the preparations of the Government as they could be equipped in no other way. They could then read, as they chose, the testimony taken before the Military Affairs Committee of the Senate with a view to getting the mistakes and delays into proper perspective and relation to the work as a whole.

"I almost envy them their opportunity to do work of this sort, because I want the people of the country ready to know and understand. When they do know and understand, I am sure their enthusiasm in supporting the Government will be increased and confirmed."

[1]On the same day the President wrote to Rabbi Stephen S. Wise: ". . . . It is fine to know that you prepared the statement which the League for National Unity has just issued. . . ."

Tuesday, February 5th.

At two o'clock the French ambassador called to present a memorandum from the Prime Ministers of France, Great Britain and Italy in regard to the shortage of bread cereals from North America. ". . . . In the opinion of the Prime Ministers, the dearth of wheat, with the effect it may produce on the morale of the populations (and the important part such a dearth played in the Russian collapse is well known) is at the present time the greatest danger threatening the allied nations of Europe."

Appointments after the cabinet meeting: a committee from the New Freedom Society—American citizens of Hungarian descent; E. N. Hurley of the Shipping Board; Herbert Hoover, from whom the President probably requested information on the cereal situation; Senator Owen of Oklahoma.

Mrs. Wilson and Dr. Anna Howard Shaw joined in an open letter to the women of the Allied countries, urging united effort toward protecting the morals of the soldiers and war workers.[1]

Acting Secretary Polk telegraphed Minister Garrett in the Netherlands, in reply to Garrett's report of January 30th: ". . . . The person mentioned in your despatch [Kurt Hahn] . . . apparently is now speaking not as a representative of a group of German Liberals, but as an informal representative of the German Government. You should make it perfectly clear to him that the Government of the United States under no circumstances will enter into secret negotiations of any sort with representatives of the German Government, that the Government of the United States has no secret purposes or desires, that the aims of the United States will be stated only in public by the President. . . ."[2]

Acting Secretary Polk to A. H. Frazier, liaison officer with the Supreme War Council, referring to the political statement drawn up by the Council: ". . . . Department is most particular that in future it be clearly understood that you attend the meetings of the Council simply for the purpose

---

[1] *Official Bulletin*, February 6, 1918.
[2] *Foreign Relations*, 1918, Supp. 1, Vol. I, pp. 80–81.

of reporting its proceedings, but with no voice in the political discussions. You should make it very clear to the members of the Council that this Government objects to the publication by the Supreme War Council of any statement of a political character which carries with it the inference that the United States Government, on account of your presence and the presence of General Bliss, has been consulted and approves of such statement. You should point out to the members of the Council that statements issued by the Supreme War Council, upon which the United States Government has a military representative, naturally carry the inference that they are issued with the approval of the United States Government. The United States Government objects to the issuance of such statements by the Council as may in any way be considered political unless either (1) the text of the statement is first referred to the President for his approval or (2) it is expressly stated in the statement that it is made upon the authority of France, England and Italy and that it has not been submitted to the Government of the United States."[1]

The author wrote in his notebook on this date: "I attended a dinner at the Harvard Club of a group of authors and artists to discuss methods of helping to stimulate interest in the war. . . . A definition of 'victory' was attempted. . . . Augustus Thomas said this had been well phrased by Henry Watterson, 'To Hell with the Hohenzollerns and the Hapsburgs.' But Mayor Mitchel was not content with as easy a victory or as light a punishment. Reciting certain bloody deeds committed by the Germans on helpless Belgians—the hanging of a living girl child on a butcher's hook in a Belgian town to die there (which I simply do not believe) and other atrocities as brutal, he said the war would not end victoriously until the Germans had been forced to similar sufferings upon their own soil. He wanted reprisals and was savage about it. The applause he received showed that this doctrine of hatred is growing enormously . . ."

Bitterly cold weather in the East—and coal still short!

---

[1] *Foreign Relations*, 1918, Supp. 1, Vol. I, pp. 81-82.

Wednesday, February 6th.

Late afternoon appointments: O. A. Somers, commander-in-chief of the Grand Army of the Republic, with his staff; Pleasant Stovall, minister to Switzerland and a boyhood friend of the President; Senator Thomas of Colorado; Representative Osborne of California. The President went to Keith's in the evening with Mrs. Wilson and a family party; when he returned, news of the sinking of the *Tuscania* was awaiting him.

The *Tuscania*, a British ship carrying 2,179 American troops, was reported torpedoed and sunk off the coast of Ireland. It seemed certain from early reports that the entire body of troops had been lost; for the first time Secretary Baker's assistants saw him "very much shaken." Later messages showed that most of the men had been safely brought ashore.[1]

Secretary Baker wrote the President of General Leonard Wood's intrigues to get to France. Like other division commanders, he explained, Wood had been sent over to see what he should teach his troops; and while there he had tried to undermine Pershing. ". . . . Would it not be wise for you to talk to Lord Reading a bit, so as to prevent the possibility of Mr. Lloyd George embarrassing us by any request for a return of General Wood, via London?"[2]

Senator Overman introduced a bill giving the President power to "coordinate and consolidate" governmental activities as a war measure. The New York *Times* reported that the bill had been handed to Overman by Secretary Burleson, "the recognized intermediary between the White House and Congress." A number of Senate leaders were irritated at the bill—"We might as well abdicate."[3]

To Senator John Sharp Williams:

". . . I do not know that I have ever had a more tiresome struggle with quicksand than I am having in trying to do the right thing in respect of our dealings with Russia. . . ."

---

[1]Palmer, *Newton D. Baker*, Vol. II, p. 85.

Newton D. Baker to the author.

[3]February 7, 1918.

To Senator Joseph T. Robinson, written at Secretary McAdoo's suggestion:

"I have been distressed to hear that you were somewhat in doubt about seeking a reelection to the Senate. I hope with all my heart that there is no foundation for this impression. I should deem your retirement from the Senate a real national loss. My close and confidential association with you has taught me to value your counsel and your support in these trying times in a very unusual degree, and I am writing this as an earnest and friendly protest against any thought you may have had of retiring. This is a time when it is necessary that men who know each other's talents and principles and objects, and who feel themselves united in a common cause, should stand together not only, but keep together. I know that is your own thought and spirit, and it is because I have found your aid and counsel so exceedingly valuable that I am making this appeal to you."

Thursday, February 7th.

Afternoon appointments: the minister from the Netherlands; B. M. Baruch; "Billy" Sunday and Mrs. Sunday; George Creel and Major Frederick Palmer.

To Frank I. Cobb, "Personal":

"Your editorial, 'Vicious and Unconstitutional,' I had seen and it is certainly unanswerable. But, after all, answers do not reach these gentlemen no matter how overwhelming and convincing. Their purpose is not to help but to take the management of the war out of my hands. Senator Chamberlain is in conference much more often with systematic opponents of the administration than with its friends, and is particularly exposed to be used by those Republicans who find it intolerable that this war should be under Democratic direction. They seem apparently to believe that the only real executive ability in the country is possessed by Republicans and that the country is unsafe so long as Republicans do not dominate the guiding counsels of the country. They are a singularly provincial and small-minded coterie, representing not the great body of Republicans in this country, but only certain preconceived notions and small privileged groups."

To Captain Perry Belmont:

"I have your letter of February first proposing a badge or emblem to be worn by all whose interest and activity have been engaged in the public service, and I of course appreciate the force of the arguments you urge in favor of the adoption of such a badge, but I see objections which outweigh the affirmative argument altogether, I am afraid. For one thing, it would not do to take the motto of any single country. For another, I think an international badge is of questionable inspiration. Our own people are acting upon the proper impulse themselves and wearing little national emblems of all sorts, chiefly copies of the flag itself, and, frankly, I think this very much better and very much more stimulating than the adoption of any sort of emblem.

"I am sorry to differ from you about this matter, but it is one which I have had occasion to think about more than once."

Friday, February 8th.

After cabinet meeting the President received a delegation from the Farmers' National Coöperative and Educational Union, and made a short address. ". . . . This is the final tackle between the things that America has always been opposed to and was organized to fight and the things that she stands for . . . . to lose it would set the world back, not a hundred—perhaps several [hundred?]—years in the development of human rights. . . ."[1] Late-afternoon appointments: Governor Cox of Ohio; Dr. Garfield. Colonel House had been summoned to discuss the President's next address to Congress.

[1]*Public Papers*, Vol. V, pp. 175-176.

"We first cleared the decks," he wrote in his diary, "by reading all the despatches bearing on foreign affairs that had come during the day," and also the President's address which he had written out on his own typewriter.

". . . . We did not finish and start to dress until seven minutes of seven. I walked out of my room at seven o'clock, to find that the President had beaten me by a half-minute.

"After dinner we went into executive session and continued until bedtime. I did not interrupt him while he read the draft of the message, but made mental notes of changes I thought necessary. . . . I felt that it was a remarkable document, but knew that much of it would have to be eliminated. . . .

"When he had finished polishing it off, we went to bed with no conversation upon other subjects."[1]

A. J. Balfour sent the President secretly, through Colonel House, the following information received from "a source in touch with Count Czernin" and believed to have been communicated "under instructions":

Public opinion in Austria was becoming impatient at the way in which negotiations with Russia were being prolonged without results. Czernin was understood to favor a separate peace, but wished a pretext for breaking with Germany, such as, perhaps, that his hand had been forced by Austria; the Austrian Emperor, fearing the "red wave," also desired peace. Tension between Austria and Germany was greater than at any time since the beginning of the war. Under these circumstances it was thought that if Austria could be assured of financial help from America in case of a separate peace, her public opinion would force the issue. Special emphasis was placed on America as the desirable intermediary.

This, Balfour commented, was the first authentic suggestion of the sort, and might of course represent a "passing mood," or be an effort to divide the Entente. However, the British were not inclined to let the matter drop; and it was thought that the American government was the one to deal with it.

The Department of State to the British Embassy in reply to

[1] *Intimate Papers*, Vol. III, pp. 368–369 for further description of the conference.

various memoranda on the Siberian situation,[1] saying that the American government believed ". . . any foreign intervention in Russian affairs would, at the present time, be most inopportune. . . .

"Should such intervention unfortunately become necessary in the future, the American Government is disposed at present to believe that any military expedition to Siberia or the occupation of the whole or of a part of the Trans-Siberian Railway should be undertaken by international cooperation and not by any one power acting as the mandatory of the others."[2]

Strikes in Germany and Austria had quieted temporarily, reported the American chargé in Switzerland.[3]

Questionable conditions at the Hog Island shipyard were revealed in testimony before the Senate committee investigating the shipping situation.

To Secretary Daniels:

"Frank Latimer Janeway, now the Assistant Pastor of the Brick Presbyterian Church of New York, is anxious, I learn, to get a commission as chaplain in the Navy. If there is a vacancy available, I hope sincerely he may get it. He was a pupil of mine at Princeton and is one of the finest fellows I have ever known. It is delightful to see such men turn to this service."

To Mrs. Theodore Roosevelt, a telegram, sent upon learning that her husband had undergone an operation and was seriously ill:

"May I not express my warm sympathy and the sincere hope that Mr. Roosevelt's condition is improving?"[4]

---

[1]Among others, one of January 28th, advocating the occupation of the Siberian Railway by Japan as the mandatory of the Allies, in order to assist various autonomous bodies in southeast Russia. This message concluded: ". . . . His Majesty's Government . . . would request an urgent decision as events are moving rapidly in Russia," and Balfour sent a separate message to House, emphasizing the "immediate urgency" of the subject. *Foreign Relations,* 1918, *Russia,* Vol. II, pp. 35–36; *Intimate Papers,* Vol. III, pp. 390–391. When this matter was submitted to the President, his judgment was that there was nothing wise or practicable in this scheme and that the American government should decline to take part in its execution.

[2]*Foreign Relations,* 1918, *Russia,* Vol. II, pp. 41–42.

[3]*Ibid.,* Supp. 1, Vol. I, pp. 105–107.

[4]Mrs. Roosevelt telegraphed in reply: "Many thanks for your kind message."

To Charles Scribner:

". . . . I am heartily glad that you should have such a desire as you express about publishing for me again something in addition to my little volume, 'An Old Master,' but as I look forward to my tasks, even after the end of my term as President, I must admit that I see little opportunity or prospect ahead for writing any essays which I could use for additional volumes. All my life I have had a definite plan in mind with regard to what I wanted to write, which has been set aside and postponed by one task after another, and if this office does not entirely wear me out, I want to turn to that as soon as I can. . . ."

To Charles A. Greathouse, chairman of the Democratic State Central Committee of Indiana:

"When the Democratic Editorial Association of Indiana meets on the twenty-fifth, will you not convey . . . my very cordial greetings? The editors of the country have a great responsibility at present, the responsibility of holding the attention of the country steady to the truth. Extraordinary efforts are being made, I am afraid, to mislead the people with regard to the actual facts of the war administration, and there is a particularly strong effort being made to take the direction of the war out of the hands of the constitutional authorities. The best way to meet such efforts and to neutralize unfair opposition is to bring the actual truth constantly to the attention of the people. The things that are wrong must and will be corrected, but the things that are right must and will be maintained, and the cure for all distempers is in every instance the real facts. These I shall always be rejoiced to have the people of the country know, and I am sure I can count on the loyal editors of the country everywhere and of whatever party to put upon those facts the true and just interpretation.

"A task of unparalleled magnitude and dignity is now imposed upon the United States and I for one have supreme confidence in the wish and power of our people to rise to the great opportunity."

Saturday, February 9th.

The President and Colonel House spent further time on the message to Congress. ". . . . Contrary to his usual custom," reports House, "he had Swem write the address in its entirety after we finished the corrections. . . ." At noon Lansing came in at the President's request and heard the revised message read aloud, making a few suggestions which were adopted. Hoover called later in the afternoon. "I walked to Gregory's again after Hoover left," writes House. "While I was there the President came in and I returned with him to the White House. I was glad I did so, because it gave me the opportunity to express my feeling that his address to Congress still lacked something, and the something I thought it lacked was the focusing of the world's attention on the military party in Germany. I thought he should say that the entire world was now in substantial agreement as to a just peace with the exception of this small group who seemed determined to drive millions of men to their death in order to have their will.

"The President . . . took a pad and pencil and began to frame a new paragraph. . . .

"The President is not enthusiastic about it [the message] but I was certain it would meet with almost universal approval."[1]

Evening at the National Theater, with a short stop at a charity ball for the Children's Episcopal Home.

Hoover to the President, a long letter beginning: "I send the following response to your desire for a memorandum as to our cereal food position for your consideration of the cable from the Premiers of England, Italy and France . . ."[2] Hoover laid great emphasis upon the need for immediate improvement in the country's transportation situation.

---

[1] *Intimate Papers*, Vol. III, pp. 369–370.
[2] This volume, p. 527.

The American ambassador in Russia telegraphed the first of the so-called "Sisson documents," the authenticity of which was later critically questioned. They were taken, Francis reported, from papers which he himself had seen, whose authenticity he did not doubt, and "the originals of which we are endeavoring to procure"; and they indicated that Lenin and Trotsky and other Bolshevik leaders were in German pay and that "disruption of Russia is but one move in plan of Germany to sow disorganization in Entente countries."[1]

The Ukraine and the Central Powers signed a treaty of peace.[2]

Sunday, February 10th.

President and Mrs. Wilson went to the Episcopal Church in the morning and spent the rest of the day quietly, with no appointments and no guests.

The British Labor Mission arrived in New York; a great loyalty meeting was held in the evening, the workers of Great Britain and America pledging, through their spokesmen, united and unswerving effort toward the defeat of Germany. Charles Duncan, M.P., spoke for the British; Secretary Wilson and American Federation of Labor officials for the Americans.

Monday, February 11th.

At 9 o'clock the public printer came in, presumably to bring a completed copy of the President's address. The President, Tumulty and Dr. Grayson left for the Capitol at 12:15. As the text of his address, the President took the recent war-aims speeches of Hertling and Czernin. He said comparatively little of the latter, merely indicating satisfaction at its friendly tone; his main argument was aimed at the "vague and very confusing" address of Hertling. ". . . . The method the German Chancellor proposes is the method of the Congress of Vienna. We cannot and will not return to that. What is at stake now is the peace of the world. . . ."

---

[1] *Foreign Relations*, 1918, *Russia*, Vol. I, pp. 371–378.
[2] For text, *ibid.*, Vol. II, pp. 665–671.

He then set forth the four principles which must lie at the base of any peace to be considered.[1]

The address made, on the whole, a favorable impression. Colonel House, however, who returned with the President to the White House, relates that he, the President, was "only half pleased with his reception and only scantily hopeful of the success of his speech."[2]

Late-afternoon appointments: Andrew Furuseth, leader of the Seamen's Union; Vance C. McCormick, who presented the War Trade Board report, and from whom the President requested the board's budget, promising to send it on to McAdoo with his approval; Representative Sherley of Kentucky; Senators Overman and Nelson of the Judiciary Committee, with whom the President discussed the Overman bill. A day or so later Overman told newspaper men that his bill was being worked over as the result of White House conferences.[3]

In the afternoon Colonel House called upon Lord Reading, new British ambassador, who had recently arrived in Washington. "I would have given a year of my life," said Reading, "to have made the last half of the President's speech." When House reported Reading's reaction, the President was delighted.[4]

In the evening moving pictures of the navy were shown in the East Room, twenty-five guests being present.

[1] *Public Papers*, Vol. V, pp. 177–184. Allied approval of the address was general although there was a feeling, especially among the British and Italians, that less difference existed between the pronouncements of Hertling and Czernin than the President had found. Pichon sent word that the French government endorsed the address in every respect.

German and Austrian comment was varied and, as always, somewhat suspicious. ". . . all Wilson's fine words," said the *Tageblatt*, "cannot make us forget decision of Versailles conference to continue war with utmost vigor until Allies' terms are accepted. . . ." Liberal papers of both countries, however, found the address hopeful, and by the 19th of February the American vice-consul was telegraphing from Zurich—an optimistic report, surely—". . . the recent speech from the President of the United States is received heartily and appreciated by the German Government and the people, and Hertling hopes to continue to interchange expressions, confident that the President's attitude will open a way to peace. The feeling in Germany towards the President is completely revolutionized and he is hailed as a conscientious, honest man doing his best to prevent further bloodshed. His utterances in the interest of peace are a great blow to the ambitions of the Pan-Germans who have been making every effort to lessen its effect. . . ." See *Foreign Relations*, 1918, Supp. 1, Vol. I, pp. 113 *et seq.*

[2] *Intimate Papers*, Vol. III, p. 371.

[3] New York *Times*, February 14, 1918.

[4] *Intimate Papers*, Vol. III, pp. 371–372.

Peace negotiations at Brest Litovsk were terminated. Trotsky refused to sign an "annexationist treaty" but announced that Russia "declares on her part the state of war . . . has ceased." Russian troops were ordered to demobilize on all fronts.[1] ". . . . Russia has fallen," ran an editorial in the New York *Times*, "and for generations to come will take the place of the Balkan States as a chessboard of international chicanery . . ."[2]

To Secretary McAdoo:

"I do not think it would be wise to appoint Crosby a member of the Supreme War Council. I have a very clear conception of the relations of the Inter-Allied Council and the Inter-Allied Shipping Board to the Supreme War Council. That Council can and will at any time call in the chairmen or other representatives of these two bodies for consultation upon the matters which should be concerted through the instrumentality of those who are conducting them. I was having a talk the other day with House about the practice of the Supreme War Council in this matter (he is a member of it, you know) and he confirmed my impression that they freely consulted with anybody, Cabinet officers, members of consultative bodies, or any others, whenever it was necessary to coordinate information and effort, and this is as it should be. If I made Crosby a member of the Supreme War Council, I would have to make Stevens also, who has gone over to represent us in the shipping matters, and this would be inconsistent with any practical development and is, moreover, I am convinced, unnecessary.

"I utter these opinions confidently because I have given the matter a great deal of thought, and I am sure you will understand that I am not dismissing the suggestion hastily."

---

[1] *Foreign Relations*, 1918, *Russia*, Vol. I, pp. 428–429.
[2] February 12, 1918.

To Louis F. Post, who suggested granting a blanket pardon to "such of the persons early convicted under its provisions as were not consciously disloyal in their opposition" to the conscription law. The President's letter is marked "Personal":

"Your suggestion about pardoning the men who at first resisted the conscription interests me very much and appeals to me not a little, but I think perhaps it is unwise to show such clemency until we have got such a grip on the whole conduct of the war as will remove all doubts and counteract all cross currents. I don't feel that I can follow my heart just now."

To Vance C. McCormick:

"Have you and the Shipping Board people made any progress in the matter of the control of imports that we were discussing the other day? I ask this question, not because of any impatience, but just out of a sincere desire to keep in touch and to know whether there is any way in which I can help."

To Judge W. L. Chambers:

"I was touched to the quick when I read your letter of yesterday telling me of your daughter's death, and my heart goes out to you in the warmest and sincerest sympathy. The beautiful spirit in which you take your loss assures me that you know the only Source of comfort, but as your sincere friend I want to add, if I may, such comfort as heartfelt sympathy can bring."

To Edgar B. Davis who wrote that Theodore Roosevelt had said to him: "I will do anything that President Wilson or Secretary of War Baker wants me to do.":

". . . I appreciate your thoughtfulness in repeating to me the remark made to you by Mr. Roosevelt. I am very glad to learn of his rapid improvement and probable entire recovery."

Tuesday, February 12th.

Appointments after the cabinet meeting: Representative Barnhart of Indiana; Herbert Swope; Representative Small of North Carolina; Senator Nugent of Idaho; Senator Thomas of Colorado.

Jusserand invited the American government to join in a declaration which the Allies proposed to make to Rumania, in the hope of preventing a separate peace between Rumania and the Central Powers: ". . . the Allied Powers adhere to all the engagements made with Roumania, in accordance with the terms of the convention concluded at Bucharest in August 1916 . . ."[1]

Strikes in shipyards were reported to be holding up the production of ships; a crisis was feared.

Lloyd George told the House of Commons he found little difference in substance between the addresses of Hertling and Czernin. ". . . an examination of these two speeches proved profoundly disappointing to those who are sincerely anxious to find any real and genuine desire for peace in them. . . ."[2] Balfour spoke in the same vein the following day.

To E. N. Hurley:

"Will you not permit this suggestion? I make it because of a dispatch which has turned up among those sent me by the State Department in which it appears that the Dutch Government is very much embarrassed in coming to the agreements with us which we are pressing upon it by the publication of such announcements as appeared under the Washington date of February ninth, for example, in the New York Times, headed, 'Will free ships for our troops.' The suggestion is this: Such publicity is in itself, of course, legitimate and useful enough, but everything ramifies in every direction now apparently and I hope that it will be possible to direct the publicity matter in

---

[1] *Foreign Relations,* 1918, Supp. 1, Vol. I, p. 756. A reference to one of the secret treaties.

[2] *War Aims and Peace Proposals,* pp. 271–273, 273–277.

such a way as to avoid similar collateral embarrassments. It unfortunately happens that what is good news for our people is sometimes bad news for our State Department, using the word 'bad' in two very different senses. It occurs to me that it would be feasible for your representative on the War Trade Board to confer with the representative of the State Department on that board with regard to such matters.

"I know you will recognize how legitimate and important this suggestion is."[1]

To H. A. Garfield:

"Senator Thomas of Colorado called to see me today very much perturbed over the possibility of a decrease in the price of coal for the Colorado district. He made certain representations which impressed me a good deal, and I would like very much to confer with you in case you have any such action in contemplation for that district. I owe this to Senator Thomas and would like to give you the benefit of what he told me."

To Representative J. W. Alexander:

".... I entirely agree with you that it is highly important that liquor and vice zones should be established in the areas surrounding shipyards ... I wonder if you would be kind enough to confer in this matter with Mr. Dent, the Chairman of the Committee on Military Affairs, whose committee I assume would deal with such amendments. I do not like to have this important matter fall between stools, and would be very glad to confer with Mr. Dent about it if he expresses a wish that I should do so."

To his secretary, Tumulty, referring to a letter from Grenville S. MacFarland, who was concerned over the serious effect which

[1]Hurley replied on the 13th, thanking the President for the "characteristically kind spirit" of his note and saying that he felt his "foot had slipped" but that it would not occur again.

Hog Island revelations were having on the public mind in his part of the country (Boston):

"I would be very much obliged if you would send a kind reply to this letter over your own signature telling Mr. MacFarland how much surprised and disturbed we have been about the Hog Island matter and how determined we all are to go to the bottom of it and expressing from me my appreciation of his thoughtful letter."

Wednesday, February 13th.

Lord Reading arrived at two o'clock, to present his credentials. He was accompanied by a staff of nine, and the usual formal remarks were exchanged. Afterward the President retired to his study for two hours. Late-afternoon callers: the Market Committee of the American Livestock Association; Representative Anderson of Minnesota and a committee of wheat growers; Abram I. Elkus, ambassador to Turkey; Representative Carter Glass of Virginia.

Garfield announced the suspension of heatless Mondays. However, continued economy in the use of coal was urged.

To Secretary Lansing, enclosing a memorandum—the result of a number of conferences between Gompers and W. E. Walling —in which a warning was issued against encouraging the Bolsheviks, since any such policy would be interpreted as an acknowledgment by the "imperialist" governments of partial defeat; and against sanctioning the growing labor-Socialist movement to end the war—the Stockholm conference:

"I wish you would read (it deserves a very careful reading) the enclosed paper by Mr. William English Walling which Mr. Gompers was kind enough to send to me. It seems to me to speak an unusual amount of truth and to furnish a very proper basis of the utmost caution in the conduct of the many troublesome affairs that we are from time to time discussing. . . ."[1]

[1]Lansing replied that he agreed entirely with Walling's views: ". . . . We will soon have to face this proposed socialist meeting at Stockholm and determine upon the

To T. W. Gregory:

"Mr. Hurley, of the Shipping Board, has called my attention to some very serious facts which have recently been developed with regard to contracts made in connection with the shipbuilding programme with the company operating at Hog Island.[1] They are so serious indeed that I do not think that we can let them be taken care of merely by public disclosure and discussion. I would be very much obliged if you would have some trustworthy person in your department get into consultation with Mr. Hurley about the whole matter with a view to instituting criminal process in case the facts justify it."

To Charles Warren, Assistant Attorney General, who had enclosed a paper describing congressional attacks on President Lincoln in 1861–1863:

On January 27, 1863, Senator Saulsbury of Delaware described Lincoln as "a weak and imbecile man; the weakest man that I ever knew in a high place."

". . . I never did see or converse with so weak and imbecile a man . . . If I wanted to paint a despot, a man perfectly regardless of every constitutional right of the people whose sworn servant, not ruler he is, I would paint the hideous form of Abraham Lincoln. . . ."

And a month later Senator Powell of Kentucky stated categorically that Lincoln should be impeached, and added: ". . . . In two years and two days more Abraham Lincoln will go out of office; and I have no doubt the whole country except thieves, public plunderers, office holders and the tools of powers will rejoice when the day shall arrive. . . .":

"It was certainly very kind of you to prepare the statement in which the extreme language used and the bitter-

---

attitude we should take in dealing with it. . . . The meeting of this element of society, imbued with the idea of an international social revolution, might become a very real menace to all existing forms of government, democratic as well as monarchical. And yet, if we prevent Americans from attending there is danger of seemingly confirming the charge that this nation is controlled by a capitalistic class. I see no middle course. No avoidance of a decision. . . ."

[1] Hurley had written on the 12th: ". . . I have been investigating this particular project and am convinced that we will have to take radical action. . . ."

ness of the attacks made on Mr. Lincoln in Congress are shown so strikingly. I have looked it through with the greatest interest and with no little astonishment. I knew that the attacks had been of the extremest sort, but I did not realize how extreme they had been.

"I wonder if I am at liberty to keep this copy which you have sent me, and whether you have it in mind to make any public use of the document? I think interest in it would be very wide, and the publication of it might serve to clear the air a good deal just at this moment when it is thick."

To Matthew Hale:

"Your letter . . . is very delightful to read. How much finer the whole war would be if everybody took the position that you take in the matter of profits derived from the war expenditures of the Government! . . . .

"When it comes to advising you, I find myself a good deal at a loss because I do not know the activities in which you are most interested. I do not know, for example, whether you would feel like devoting the money you speak of to the Red Cross or to some other humane activity, or whether you would wish to put it into something that you might possibly regard as more constructive and directly contributory to the nation's strength. I think you could do nothing finer than give it to the Red Cross."

Thursday, February 14th.

Late-afternoon appointments: the Vice President; Theodore F. Green; George Creel; Vance C. McCormick.

The entire foreign commerce of the United States was, by presidential proclamations, made subject to control by license from February 16th onward.[1]

Secretary Lansing telegraphed the American ambassador in Russia that one million dollars had been made available

---

[1] *Foreign Relations*, 1918, Supp. 1, Vol. II, pp. 958–962.

for the purchase of supplies there which Germany would otherwise appropriate; the same amount had been made available by the French and British.[1] Later in the day another telegram was sent: ".... Department ... desires you gradually to keep in somewhat closer and informal touch with Bolshevik authorities using such channels as will avoid any official recognition. . . ."[2]

Crosby, in a report to Secretary McAdoo, quoted a statement which the Finance Section of the Inter-Allied Council had, on the 8th, recommended for the consideration of the governments represented, setting out the reasons why the obligations of the Russian government could not be repudiated by any authority in Russia. ".... Most important part," Crosby pointed out to McAdoo, "has to do with suggestion that no recognition of new States carved out of original Russian territory should be made without provision for adoption of part of general debt."[3]

Hurley called on striking shipyard carpenters to resume work; Secretary Wilson appealed for skilled shipyard volunteers; and it was announced that the Shipping Board would within a few days commandeer certain inefficiently managed shipyards.[4]

To Senator Joseph I. France, a letter marked "Personal":

"Thank you for the courtesy of your letter . . . I have read the bill . . . with close attention. It amounts, does it not, to a universal draft, industrial as well as military, and constitutes a departure from the policy of the Government, and indeed of the governments of other free states, which is so radical that I take the liberty of saying that I do not think it would be wise even if it were possible.

"The working men of this country are very warmly opposed, and I think quite justifiably opposed, to being drafted and subjected to compulsory labor. The labor difficulties are many and it is not at all clear how some of

---

[1] *Op. cit.*, 1918, *Russia*, Vol. III, pp. 107–109.
[2] *Ibid.*, Vol. I, p. 381.
[3] *Ibid.*, Vol. III, pp. 34–35.
[4] New York *Times*, February 15, 1918.

them are to be overcome, but I believe that it would be a very serious mistake to depart from the methods which are already available. I mean that the men must be sought out and the conditions of labor must be acceptable, and that we must accomplish the results we desire by organized effort rather than by compulsion.

"I speak frankly about this matter, because my conviction with regard to it is very deep-seated, and I beg that you will not regard my expression of this judgment as in any way subtracting from my appreciation of your courtesy in consulting me."

Friday, February 15th.

The British ambassador called in the morning, probably in regard to the death of his predecessor, Sir Cecil Spring Rice. Appointments after the cabinet meeting: Mayor Hylan of New York City and a committee; Representative Garrett of Texas; Senators Dillingham of Vermont and Wolcott of Delaware. Evening at Keith's.

The author of this biography was appointed Special Assistant of the Department of State to go abroad and report upon certain increasingly disturbing conditions in England, France and Italy, concerning which the President and Colonel House felt that they were not being sufficiently informed. Disruptive influences were at work, especially among labor and radical groups, stimulated in some measure by the Bolshevik upheaval in Russia. War weariness was beginning to express itself strongly in all the Allied nations. The author was asked to determine if he could the extent of this unrest, what the demands really were, and whether or not the movements had any effective organization. He was provided with a diplomatic passport and authorized to make confidential reports by code or through the Embassy pouches to Assistant Secretary of State Frank L. Polk, for the information of the President and Colonel House. In order to cover his real mission, it was arranged that he should be the accredited representative of the *New Republic* and the New York *World*. He sailed on February 26th, remaining in Europe to the close of the war and through the Peace Conference.

Secretary Lansing to Chargé Wilson in Switzerland, a telegram headed: "Secret for Wilson alone to decode," and sent, probably, as a result of Balfour's message through House to the President, received February 8th.[1]

"Concerning the possible need of Austria to obtain financial aid after the war under certain conditions I think that it would be wise at this time to convey secretly, unofficially and orally to Lammasch or his agent that, in the event of Austria being deprived of German financial support through acting contrary to the wishes of the German Government in independently arranging a cessation of hostilities and negotiations for peace at the present time, person conveying information has strong impression amounting to conviction that Government of the United States will exert its influence to the end that financial assistance may be obtained in the United States as nearly as possible to the extent that Germany would have furnished it if there had been no breach in their relations.

"As to the most expedient channel to convey this secret and unofficial information to Lammasch I rely wholly upon your discretion, though I think that it would be unwise to employ Herron, whose relationship with Lammasch should in no way be embarrassed by making him the agent of delivery of even the most unofficial message. Herron has acted so wisely and shown such discretion his future usefulness must in no way be endangered. Please act promptly and discreetly in this matter and report fully."[2]

Saturday, February 16th.

President and Mrs. Wilson attended the services for Sir Cecil Spring Rice, at St. Alban's Chapel, in the early afternoon. The only appointment of the day was with Samuel Gompers

---

[1]This volume, p. 532.

[2]*Foreign Relations*, 1918, Supp. 1, Vol. I, p. 119. The chargé reported on the 21st that the message had been given to one York-Steiner, an Austrian for whose fitness Chargé Wilson vouched in the strongest terms, with instructions to deliver it secretly, orally and unofficially to Lammasch; and on the 25th he telegraphed that the message had been delivered. *Ibid.* pp. 129–130.

and a committee, at six o'clock. "Evening, worked in study," records the head usher.

> Lord Robert Cecil wrote Colonel House of the formation of the Phillimore Committee to "enquire, particularly from a juridical and historical point of view, into the various schemes for establishing, by means of a league of nations or other device, some alternative to war as a means of settling international disputes . . ." "I do not know," he added, "whether your staff is also engaged on a similar task, but if they are it has occurred to me that if we could establish coöperation it would be a mutual benefit to us. If you share this view would you be inclined to let me know, for our confidential information, the lines on which you are working and I will undertake to keep you similarly informed?"[1]

To Secretary Lansing, a letter written on the President's own typewriter, in regard to reports of German influence in Portugal and the Azores:

"This looks very serious. I hope that we shall have sufficient information to follow it very carefully and make the most definite protest, should the facts justify it, to the Portuguese government. What do you make of it all. Is it possible, in your judgment, that there may be a plot afoot to supply Germany with a submarine base on the route of American ships to the Mediterranean?"[2]

To Secretary Lansing, who had sent over a copy of Crosby's message of the 14th[3] with the comment that he considered such resolutions valueless, and that in any event he thought it "unwise for Mr. Crosby to act in a matter which is chiefly political rather than financial." The President's letter was written on his own typewriter:

"I was indeed very much disturbed by this message. I will speak to McAdoo about the impropriety of Crosby's taking part in any such action in the future. The Inter-

---

[1] *Intimate Papers*, Vol. IV, pp. 8–9.

[2] Lansing replied that he was having the matter looked into.

[3] This volume, p. 545.

Allied Board was certainly not constituted to give political advice.

———————

"And this leads me to beg that you will communicate with the Governments of Great Britain, France, and Italy to the following effect,—referring to the recent action of the Supreme War Council with regard to conditions of peace and to this action of the Inter-Allied Board with regard to the recognition of the Bolshevik authorities:

"That the President wishes very respectfully but very earnestly to urge that when he suggested the creation of the Inter-Allied Board and gave his active support to the creation of the Supreme War Council it was not at all in his mind that either of these bodies should take any action or express any opinion on political subjects. He would have doubted the wisdom of appointing representatives of this Government on either body had he thought that they would undertake the decision of any questions but the very practical questions of supply and of the concerted conduct of the war which it was understood they should handle. He would appreciate it very much if this matter were very thoroughly reconsidered by the political leaders of the governments addressed and if he might be given an opportunity, should their view in this matter differ from his, to consider once more the conditions and instructions under which representatives of the United States should henceforth act.

"This is, it may be, a bit blunt, but I think it imperative that we should safeguard ourselves in this all-important matter. Perhaps you will think it best to communicate these views through the diplomatic representatives here, so that they may put it in their own language after being given to understand how grave our objection is."[1]

———————

[1] Lansing wrote the British, French and Italian ambassadors on the 18th, using the President's exact wording. *Foreign Relations*, 1918, Supp. 1, Vol. I, p. 125. For Sir

To Secretary Lansing, referring to a memorandum on the Gomez regime in Venezuela which had been sent him from the Department of State:

"I have read this Memorandum with the greatest concern, as I have also the many recent communications from our Minister in Venezuela. This scoundrel ought to be put out. Can you think of any way in which we can do it that would not upset the peace of Latin America more than letting him alone will?"

Sunday, February 17th.

The President and Mrs. Wilson went to the Central Presbyterian Church in the morning and spent the rest of the day quietly, with no official appointments.

To William L. Hutcheson, general president of the United Brotherhood of Carpenters of America, who asked for an appointment with the President to discuss the ship strike crisis:

"I have received your telegram . . . and am very glad to note the expression of your desire as a patriotic citizen to assist in carrying on the work by which we are trying to save America and men everywhere who work and are free. Taking advantage of that assurance, I feel it to be my duty to call your attention to the fact that the strike of the carpenters in the ship yards is in marked and painful contrast to the action of labour in other trades and places. Ships are absolutely necessary for the winning of this war. No one can strike a deadlier blow at the safety of the nation and of its forces on the other side than by interfering with or obstructing the ship-building programme. All the other unions engaged in this indispensable work have agreed to abide by the decisions of the Shipbuilding Wage Adjustment Board. That Board has dealt fairly and liberally with all who have resorted to it. I must

William Wiseman's message to the British Foreign Office, explaining the President's attitude, see *Intimate Papers,* Vol. III, pp. 364–365.

say to you very frankly that it is your duty to leave to it the solution of your present difficulties with your employers and to advise the men whom you represent to return at once to work pending the decision. No body of men have the moral right in the present circumstances of the nation to strike until every method of adjustment has been tried to the limit. If you do not act upon this principle you are undoubtedly giving aid and comfort to the enemy, whatever may be your own conscious purpose. I do not see that anything will be gained by my seeing you personally until you have accepted and acted upon that principle. It is the duty of the government to see that the best possible conditions of labour are maintained, as it is also its duty to see to it that there is no lawless and conscienceless profiteering and that duty the government has accepted and will perform. Will you cooperate or will you obstruct?"[1]

Monday, February 18th.

In the afternoon the President went over to see the Attorney General; and also called at the offices of the Shipping Board. He returned in time to confer with Garfield and later with Senators Pomerene of Ohio and Sheppard of Texas. Evening at the National Theater.

Emperor Karl of Austria informed President Wilson that such harmony existed between the principles enunciated in the address to Congress of February 11th and his own that results might be expected from a conference. The message was sent to the King of Spain, for transmission to the President.[2]

Germany served notice upon Russia that the armistice would terminate at noon that day. In spite of shocked protest the

[1]*Public Papers*, Vol. V, pp. 185–186. Hutcheson made energetic efforts to call off the strike.

[2]This was done, through the Spanish ambassador in Washington, on February 25th. However, the wireless message was meanwhile intercepted by the British, and given to Ambassador Page in London, who transmitted it to the President on the 20th. *Foreign Relations*, 1918, Supp. 1, Vol. I, pp. 126–127.

German advance began promptly as scheduled, and the remnants of the Russian army fled, panic-stricken.[1]

To Senator T. S. Martin, chairman of the Senate Committee on Appropriations, and to Representative A. F. Lever, chairman of the House Committee on Agriculture, enclosing a letter from Hoover regarding agitation for legislation to increase the minimum guarantee for wheat:

" . . . . He [Hoover] makes a very strong case indeed, it seems to me, against the agitation of legislative action to secure higher prices for wheat while the existing crop is unhandled and unsold. There could hardly be a more dangerous field of agitation than this, and I am writing to ask if it would not be possible to check such agitation in some kind and tactful way.

"The food situation in the world is one of the most serious that we have to face, and one of the most difficult to handle. We are handling it with reasonable success, and I should look with peculiar apprehension upon anything that would disturb the present comparatively even course of affairs.

"I am confident in the hope that you will regard this matter as of such critical consequence as to justify my calling it to your attention in this way."

To Charles W. Eliot, who had suggested, with Secretary Lane's approval, that certain subjects be detached from the over-worked Department of the Interior and added to the Department of Labor under a new title, such as the Department of Public Health:

" . . . . The bill now pending in Congress which authorizes the President to redistribute functions in the several departments does in its comprehensive phraseology no doubt permit what you suggest, but I have presented it

---

[1]*Foreign Relations*, 1918, *Russia*, Vol. I, p. 429; Vernadsky, *Lenin, Red Dictator*, p. 206.

to the Congress as a war measure and with the explanation to members of the committees handling the bill that I intended to exercise the powers granted only for the purpose of coordinating in the best and most effective way the activities which bear directly upon the conduct of the war. Even its comprehensive terms do not authorize me to create new departments, and such a redistribution of bureaus as you suggest would almost necessitate that. Clear as it is that the bureaus you mention ought not any longer to embarrass the many-sided administration of the Department of the Interior, there is no other department to which they could with any particular propriety be transferred. After all, the Department of the Interior is the particular department with which a miscellany of bureaus has been left awaiting further distribution by the creation of new departments."

To Miss Lucy M. Smith:
MY DEAR COUSIN LUCY:

It was most cheering and delightful to get your letter, and after Edith and I had read it I felt almost as if I had had a little glimpse of you and Cousin Mary. Stockton [Axson] had just been telling us of his little visit to you and delighting us by telling us how well you both looked and seemed, and so our hearts are gladdened every way.

We are pegging along here, weathering the storms that come from Capitol Hill as well as we can and praying that sober thought and sanity may get and keep the upper hand.

Poor Helen [Bones] is just now confined in a sort of quarantine because of an attack of pink-eye, which, fortunately, is not painful; it has no physical result except making a hermit of her! Margaret [his oldest daughter] has gone again to New York to get ready for some concerts she is going to give at the various cantonments within reach of us here; and Nell [Mrs. McAdoo] is the only member of the family who is laid up for repairs, she having made the mistake of contracting a case of tonsilitis.

This is our bulletin for the present, but this letter goes to you not as a health report, but as a love message from us all.

Affectionately yours,
WOODROW WILSON

To Senator John Sharp Williams:

"Thank you for letting me see the enclosed letter from Mr. Erving Winslow. I was in hopes that men like Mr. Winslow would realize that in discussing the utterances of the German and Austrian Ministers I was acting upon considerations and information which did not lie upon the surface but were derived from the many confidential sources of information which the Government must use. I am, therefore, not in the least afraid that I am walking into a German trap or that I am playing into the hands of the pacifists and pro-Germans. Nobody can be more wary of those groups than I wish to be, and I think it is rather a pity to discountenance, as Mr. Winslow seems to try to do, all processes of diplomacy even in the midst of arms."

To Howard Huntington, who had written on the 15th, mentioning earlier efforts to call the President's attention to "many appalling facts" in the aeronautical administration; and asking again for an appointment:

"I have received your communications, but it is, as you must realize upon reflection, absolutely impossible for me personally to go into such investigations as you propose. I have entire confidence in the men whom I have charged with the oversight of aeronautics. You are entirely mistaken in supposing that Liberty Motors have not yet been produced and that not a single battleplane has been completed, and in the absence of definite testimony as to unjustifiable acts or abuses, it would not, of course, be right for me to form any judgment that would disturb my confidence in the men to whom I have referred."

To Robert S. Brookings:

" . . . . May I not say . . . how much I appreciate the course of action you have imposed upon yourself, of refraining from the almost universal habit of public discussion about things that must necessarily be handled by slow evolution?"

To Senator Ollie M. James, who had spoken in the Senate on the 14th in answer to Chamberlain's charges and in defense of the administration:

"That was a corking good speech you made the other day and I would be indeed insensible if I did not send you a line of very warm and grateful thanks for your generous attitude towards myself. It is delightful to have such whole-hearted champions, friends that really stand up and are counted in every time of crisis, and my heart goes out to you in the warmest and deepest appreciation."

Tuesday, February 19th.

Before the cabinet meeting the President received the new minister from the Netherlands, who presented his credentials. The cabinet met at 2:30, Lansing remaining afterward to report that he had seen Lord Reading and that he was much perturbed over the President's attitude on the Supreme War Council declaration and the resolutions of the Inter-Allied Council. Late-afternoon appointments: a committee of the New York branch of the National Association for the Advancement of Colored People; Representative Littlepage of West Virginia.

William Phillips handed Lansing a memorandum reporting that the French had informed the Bolsheviks that if they resisted the German menace, France would help them with money and material. " . . . . The French Government now inquire whether the United States will give similar instructions . . ." On the margin of the paper in the State Department files at Washington is the following note: "This is out of the question. R L. Submitted to Prest who says the same thing. R L 2/19/18"[1]

General Bliss to the Chief of Staff, for Secretaries Lansing and Baker: ". . . . The permanent military advisers yesterday and today carefully considered the question of Japanese intervention in Siberia by their occupation of the Trans-Siberian railroad in behalf of the allies. . . ." They had adopted a joint note, Bliss continued, the substance of which was that the military advantages of such occupation would outweigh any possible political disadvantage. They recommended occupation by a Japanese force, but specified the creation of a joint allied commission, and the obtaining of suitable guarantees from Japan. Bliss himself felt that the military advantage of such a move would be small, and could be secured simply by the occupation of Vladivostok.

Russia in turmoil. In the early morning hours a telegram was dispatched agreeing to accept the German terms; but the enemy advance continued.[2]

To G. S. MacFarland, who had thanked the President for obtaining the removal of the British mail and cable ban on Hearst's International News Service. The President's letter is marked "Personal":

". . . I must not take credit where it is not my due. I had absolutely nothing to do, as a matter of fact, with the restoration of the cable service you mention and did not know until the day before yesterday that it had been restored. To tell the truth, I do not know that the advice came from anybody connected with the administration."[3]

[1] *Foreign Relations*, 1918, *Russia*, Vol. I, p. 383.

[2] *Ibid.*, p. 429.

[3] The following day the President wrote Lansing of MacFarland's letter, saying: ". . . of course, I had absolutely nothing to do with it. I am, however, anxious to find out how it did happen. Do you know?" When Lansing replied that Treasury officials had been interesting themselves in the matter, the President immediately wrote to McAdoo. See this volume, pp. 562–563.

Wednesday, February 20th.

The President drove out after luncheon with Mrs. Wilson, stopping to talk with the Alien Property Custodian about the desire of the Hamburg-American Line to sell two ships to the government. Late-afternoon appointments: Secretary Baker; Henry P. Davison of the Red Cross; the President's brother, Joseph R. Wilson, to present Major Kilpatrick of the Canadian Overseas Forces, who had been twenty months in a German prison; Representative Clark of Florida; Senator John Sharp Williams; F. B. Noyes, president of the Associated Press.

Ambassador Page in London telegraphed the President a translation of Emperor Karl's letter of the 18th; and pointed out that the message was to be communicated in writing to the King of Spain, "which makes it appear certain that it is sent with the knowledge and approval of the German Government."[1]

Secretary Baker announced that the first American-built battle planes were "en route to the front in France," equipped with Liberty Motors.[2]

An Inter-Allied Labor and Socialist conference met in London, February 20th–24th. Wide divergences of opinion appeared, but a resolution was finally passed providing for an international conference in some neutral country, to be attended by Socialists from belligerent countries; and on the 23rd a "Memorandum on War Aims" was adopted.[3]

"Soviet government demoralized . . ." telegraphed Ambassador Francis. "Germans could control city within forty-eight hours. . . ."[4]

To Secretary McAdoo, enclosing a letter from Hoover about the grain situation in the West:

"The situation stated by Mr. Hoover in the enclosed letter has been presented to me from various quarters. I know that you will wish to know about it and that you will make every possible effort to get cars into the West.

[1]*Foreign Relations,* 1918, Supp. 1, Vol. I, pp. 126–128.
[2]*Official Bulletin,* February 21, 1918.
[3]See *Foreign Relations,* 1918, Supp. 1, Vol. I, pp. 154–167, 168.
[4]*Ibid., Russia,* Vol. I, p. 383.

I know that Mr. Hoover does not exaggerate when he says that the situation is extremely critical, and while I cannot judge the practical aspects of the matter, his contention is that if the empty cars were got out of the East into the West and there distributed throughout the grain regions, they would relieve the situation as much as it can be relieved."[1]

To Secretary McAdoo, who had sent the President a letter from Oscar T. Crosby, with the comment: ". . . I wish to call your attention to the fact that Mr. Crosby has been consulted by Ambassador Page in connection with the Swedish negotiations, by Mr. McCormick and Mr. Sheldon in connection with the Swiss negotiations, and by Mr. Auchincloss in connection with certain Polish matters but has hesitated to intervene in these affairs in the absence of instructions from here. If you approve, I should like to direct Mr. Crosby to give such advice and assistance as may be desired in connection with these or other matters which concern the financial problem.":

"Thank you for letting me see the enclosed letter from Crosby. I have never had any objection to his giving any advice he is asked for concerning financial matters. What I have been made uneasy about was his participation in political matters. For example, just the other day he joined his colleagues of the Inter-Allied Board in advising us not to recognize the Bolshevik Government. That, it seems to me, was a very serious departure from his instructions. The fact is that in my view neither the Supreme War Council nor the board of which Crosby is chairman has any business to formulate political opinions and give political advice. Their doing so has already complicated the European situation very seriously and nullified much of what we have been attempting to do. I have even gone so far as to make representations to this effect to the other governments in an informal way. The utterance of the

---

[1]McAdoo sent back a sharp comment on Hoover's letter. Both men were by this time extremely irritated—and this was only one of a number of similar situations which confronted the President.

Supreme War Council the other day in Versailles has played into the hands of the Germans in a way that is most discouraging."

To James W. Gerard, former ambassador to Germany, who had passed on a suggestion that the President address a message to Austria and Hungary equally:

"Thank you for your letter . . . enclosing the quotation from 'an American citizen born in Hungary.'

"I see and sympathize with his point of view, but he doesn't make his suggestion in a very practical way, because he does not suggest *how* I could address the Hungarians.

"I have been acting on exactly the theory which he states and have been assuming that Austria, and not Hungary, stands in the way of a reasonable settlement."

Thursday, February 21st.

The President conferred with Secretary Burleson in the morning. Late-afternoon appointments: Secretary Baker; Walter Lowrie; E. N. Hurley; Senator Shields of Tennessee; Senators Swanson of Virginia and Hollis of New Hampshire.

The next sixty days, declared Hoover in a public statement, would be the most critical in the food history of the nation; 8,000,000 bushels of grain must be loaded every day if the crisis was to be met. He implied that blame for the congestion rested upon the Railroad Administration.[1]

Secretary Lansing to the American minister in Rumania:

". . . . You are . . . instructed to represent to the King and to the Government of Roumania that this Government is unwilling to unite in a joint declaration as suggested[2] but that acting independently it desires to give assurance that it will, so far as it may, give support to the following propositions . . ." Five propositions follow, reference to the treaty of 1916 being conspicuously absent.[3]

---

[1] *Official Bulletin*, February 23, 1918.
[2] This volume, p. 540.
[3] *Foreign Relations*, 1918, Supp. 1, Vol. I, pp. 758–759.

To Secretary Lansing, referring to an offer from the International Red Cross to use its good offices in obtaining the cessation of the use of poison gas; and to the British suggestion that the Allies and the United States return identic replies, framed in Paris. Lansing enclosed a suggested message to Sharp, authorizing consultation:

"I must say I am afraid of *any* expression of policy framed jointly at Paris. There has been none yet that seemed to me even touched with wisdom. I see that you have sought to suggest and safeguard, but I am afraid that statesmen like our friend L-G. will not care to be guided and will rather rejoice in a somewhat crude and cynical rejoinder to the Red Cross.

"I approve the despatch to Sharp, however, and am quite willing to subscribe to proper reply if they will let us see it beforehand. Sharp can cable it, and the delay will not be serious."[1]

To Herbert Hoover, who wrote that, since the operations of the Grain Division of the Food Administration would undoubtedly come up for assault or investigation by Congress sooner or later, it "might be worth while taking time by the forelock and having an investigation of our own.":

"If Mr. Taussig has the time, I should entirely approve of his investigating the grain division of the Food Administration as you suggest in your letter of yesterday."

Friday, February 22nd.

The cabinet meeting was omitted, the President conferring with Secretary Lansing in the early afternoon; and with Secretary Baker at five o'clock. Evening at Keith's.

Secretary Lansing wrote that the French ambassador was far more excited over the President's attitude toward the Versailles declaration and Inter-Allied Council resolutions than the British ambassador had been. ". . . . He said that you had received him recently and had never mentioned

---

[1]No results were obtained.

the matter to him nor had you done so to Reading, a fact which he considered most unfortunate. He said that he was sure that 'your rebuke' would be very badly received. . . ." The Italian ambassador, however, agreed that the President's attitude was quite correct, and reported that Sonnino fully understood it.

Ambassador Francis telegraphed that the Bolsheviks had decided to resist the Germans, although the army was still disintegrating, stations and trains being crowded with soldiers who wanted to go home. "Five Allied Ambassadors agreed to support resistance if offered . . ."[1]

To Secretary Baker:

"I . . . concur in your judgment that General Pershing's repeated requests that you should visit our expeditionary forces in France should be complied with. I believe that it will add to the morale, not only of our forces there, but of our forces here, to feel that you are personally conversant with all the conditions of their transportation and treatment on the other side, and I believe that it will be serviceable to all of us to have the comprehensive view which you will bring back with you.

"I sincerely hope that your journey will be safe. We shall look for your return with impatience, because your guidance is constantly needed here."

To Secretary Baker, a letter marked "Private":

"I think it would be of the greatest service so far as the spirit of things is concerned if you would visit Italy and get in touch, if even for a very brief time indeed, with the military people there. It would gratify them deeply and would show our interest in the best way in which we can show it for the present."

To Secretary McAdoo:

"I have received several letters of thanks recently for the removal of the British ban on the International News Service (Hearst's). Inasmuch as I had made it a principle

[1] *Foreign Relations*, 1918, *Russia*, Vol. I, p. 386.

to have nothing to do with the dealings of the British Government with any news service, I, of course, had nothing to do with this. When Mr. Balfour was here, and afterwards when other British representatives have said to us that if the State Department would request the removal of the ban, it would be removed, we have invariably replied that we would make no such request. I have, therefore, been inquiring what influence, if any, was exerted from Washington, and I have been told that Treasury officials had something to do with it. I can't believe this, but I wish you would be kind enough to make inquiry and let me know."

To George Creel, who explained the difficulties of getting proper world circulation for the President's addresses; and asked whether he might not have the next address the day before its delivery. "I can guarantee an absolute secrecy.":

"Yes, if I can finish the next address in time, I will certainly see that the experiment is tried of complying with the suggestions of your letter of yesterday. Those suggestions are entirely reasonable. I have realized the difficulties you have contended with. You know, I am sure, the only reason why I have embarrassed you. We will see next time if the thing can be done secretly when so many people are concerned."

To R. E. Byrd:
"You are a brick, and your letter ... is warmly appreciated. It is very surprising to me sometimes how, after having had five years experience of me and my principles, so many Senators, even on our own side, should look askance at necessary proposals of power."

Saturday, February 23rd.
There were no official engagements. The President spent the morning in his study; and in the afternoon took a long drive with Mrs. Wilson.

The President fixed a guaranteed price for 1918 wheat, continuing the rate for the previous year; and issued an explanatory statement: ". . . . This guaranteed price assures the farmer of a reasonable profit even if the war should end within the year . . .

"I know the spirit of our farmers and have not the least doubt as to the loyalty with which they will accept the present decision. . . .

". . . peculiar circumstances governing the handling and consumption of wheat put the farmer at the very center of war service. . . . He sees this and can be relied upon as the soldier can. . . ."[1]

Secretary Lansing wrote the President that he had been thinking over the course to be followed with regard to the intercepted letter from Emperor Karl of Austria: ". . . . It seems to me we might do this: Give the text to our principal cobelligerents and say to them that through the same channel as we received the communication we intend to reply by asking whether the document has been submitted to the German Government and, if so, whether it meets with its approval as no answer could be made until we are advised of German knowledge or ignorance of Austria's action. . . ."

To his secretary, Tumulty, referring to Simeon Strunsky's suggestion that the United States guarantee the people of Russia against the return of autocracy. In his memorandum Strunsky admitted that this was not according to diplomatic precedent, but he felt that the old diplomatic proprieties had given way to a more enlightened procedure. Bolshevism, he thought, was succeeding because the people were afraid that if a movement were instituted to overturn it, the old Czarist regime might come back:

"Mr. Strunsky has entirely misinterpreted the spirit and principles of this Government if he thinks it possible for it to propose to interfere with the form of government in any other government. That would be in violent contradiction of the principles we have always held, earnestly

---

[1]*Public Papers*, Vol. V, pp. 187–190, for entire statement.

as we should wish to lend every moral influence to the support of democratic institutions in Russia and earnestly as we pray that they may survive there and become permanent."

Sunday, February 24th.

The President, Mrs. Wilson, and Colonel House attended service at the Episcopal Cathedral in the morning, and Colonel House returned with them to the White House. "We had time before lunch," he wrote in his diary, "to discuss the Austrian Emperor's note to the President . . . We agreed that it would be well to ask Balfour's opinion of it . . ." They outlined a message for House to send, the President writing it out on his typewriter:

"In view of the intercepted message from the Emperor of Austria to the King of Spain and your recent message to the President through me which I received on the eighth,[1] the President would very much appreciate any comments or suggestions you may be kind enough to make. The actual message has not yet been received from Spain. How far would you think it necessary to go in apprising the Entente Governments of the character of the message from Austria?"[2]

At six o'clock Secretaries Baker and Daniels arrived for a conference.

General Pershing sent Secretary Baker two memoranda, one dealing with officers whom he found "unavailable" as division commanders—General Leonard Wood among them—and the other dealing with Wood alone. Pershing had little to say for Wood, found him generally disloyal, and cited instances.[3]

The Bolshevik Executive Committee telegraphed to Berlin their acceptance of new German peace terms, which proved to be worse than the old![4]

---

[1]This volume, p. 532.

[2]*Intimate Papers*, Vol. III, p. 374. Dr. Seymour writes that House had been warned about the danger of negotiations with Austria by Wickham Steed and André Chéradame. *Ibid.*, pp. 384–385.

[3]Palmer, *Newton D. Baker*, Vol. II, pp. 238–239.

[4]*Foreign Relations*, 1918, *Russia*, Vol. I, pp. 432–435.

Monday, February 25th.

The Spanish ambassador arrived at two o'clock, to present the Austrian Emperor's letter of the 17th. The President, as he told Colonel House afterward, had "difficulty in composing his face and in trying to look surprised."[1] Late-afternoon appointments: George McAneny; Crawford Vaughan; Representatives Harrison and Doremus; George Creel. Colonel House was a guest at dinner and had a long talk with the President about possible Japanese intervention in Siberia.[2]

General Bliss telegraphed that there seemed to be "among military men generally as well as politicians a very strong feeling that some sort of intervention in Siberia will be necessary." This view Bliss did not share, but he warned that strong pressure would probably be put upon the United States. Baker passed Bliss's message on to the President.

The German Chancellor, speaking in the Reichstag, expressed agreement with the four principles enunciated by President Wilson on February 11th, but added that one reservation must be made: ". . . . These four principles must not only be proposed by President of United States but must actually be proposed by all states and nations. . . .

"The world yearns for peace but it does not seem as if this deep longing met with any response in the Entente . . . Therefore our splendid troops shall continue to fight . . . our sturdy people will continue to hold out . . ."[3]

Tuesday, February 26th.

At the cabinet meeting—or possibly afterward, with Secretary Lansing alone—the subject of Japanese intervention in Siberia was discussed. Appointments: Senator Ransdell of Louisiana; Senator Johnson of South Dakota.

Hoover sent the President a copy of his letter of that day to the British ambassador in regard to the March program of Allied shipments—125,000 tons of wheat, 300,000 tons of flour—which he promised to supply if at all possible,

---

[1] *Intimate Papers*, Vol. III, p. 375.

[2] *Ibid.*, pp. 391–392.

[3] *Foreign Relations*, 1918, Supp. 1, Vol. I, pp. 135–138.

even though it would involve some bread shortage in this country. ". . . this shipment," he wrote the President, "amounts to a very considerable diversion from our domestic demands and will sooner or later precipitate us into difficulties with our own supplies. We felt, however, that it was your wish that we should take care of their pressing necessities."

The German advance into Russia continued. Ambassador Francis left Petrograd in the evening, with his staff, the American Red Cross Mission, and a number of missions of other countries. ". . . . Planning to await developments [at] Vologda . . ." he telegraphed.[1]

To Colonel House:

"Would you be generous enough to convey the substance of what follows to Harper & Brothers?

"(1) I would not feel justified now in making any decisions with regard to the literary work that I am to do after the expiration of my term, or the conditions under which I am to do it. My own expectation is that I shall wish to be absolutely free. I none the less appreciate the generous suggestions of Harper & Brothers.

"(2) The only item with regard to the programme for a collected edition of my works which seems to call for comment is that concerning the little book, AN OLD MASTER and OTHER ESSAYS, which the Scribners publish. I had a letter from Mr. Charles Scribner, and indicated to him that I would be very glad to see him comply with the request of Harper & Brothers with regard to it.

"With regard to CONGRESSIONAL GOVERN-MENT and MERE LITERATURE, published by Houghton Mifflin and Company, of Boston: I believe that the sale of MERE LITERATURE has been comparatively small of late, but the sale of CONGRESSIONAL GOVERNMENT has been maintained at a steady,

[1]*Foreign Relations*, 1918, *Russia*, Vol. I, p. 388.

though not high, level ever since the early years of its currency. The publishers of these two volumes were my first publishers, they treated me with unusual generosity as a newcomer into the field when I was a youngster, and I don't like to insist upon anything that they think will be to their disadvantage. I, therefore, do not like to make the request of them suggested by Mr. Hitchcock. I take it for granted that they would be willing to disclose to a representative of Harper & Brothers the full commercial value of the books, but, as I understand it, the objection is on sentimental rather than on commercial grounds."

To Secretary McAdoo:

"I am mighty sorry but I can't let you have Baruch for the Finance Corporation. He has trained now in the War Industries Board until he is thoroughly conversant with the activities of it from top to bottom, and as soon as I can do so without risking new issues on the Hill I am going to appoint him chairman of that board."

Wednesday, February 27th.

The British ambassador called at noon, to present the Right Honorable Sir Robert Borden, Premier of Canada. Reading at this time spoke to the President of two secret messages from Balfour about Japan's desire to occupy Siberia with a military force; and later in the day he sent over copies for the President's information. [See below.] Charles R. Crane was a luncheon guest. Late-afternoon appointments: Edward A. Filene, who discussed the recent referendum of the United States Chamber of Commerce "on a proposal to discriminate against Germany in trade after the war if necessary for self-defense." The preliminary count the previous night showed 1204 in favor and 154 opposed; Madame Paderewska, who urged that a day be set aside for aid to the Polish people; the Alien Property Custodian. Colonel House was a guest at dinner and in the evening went with the President and Mrs. Wilson to the National Theater.

Secretary Lansing to the President:

"I have had, this afternoon, interviews with the British and French Ambassadors in relation to Japan's desire to occupy Siberia with a military force.

"Lord Reading informed me that he had seen you and had given you a copy of a secret telegram which he had received from Mr. Balfour and of which I received a copy this morning and append to this letter.[1]

"The French Ambassador gave me the substance of a telegram which he had received from his Foreign Office containing a summary of a telegram they had received from their Ambassador at Tokio. This latter is to me of especial interest in view of the avowal of Motono to declare publicly the disinterestedness of Japan and also the pledge to carry on military activities as far as the Ural Mountains—that is, to the confines of Asia. This memorandum I also enclose.

"I also would call your attention to the enclosed telegram from Stevens, at Yokohama, which may not have attracted your attention, but bears directly on the present subject. . . ."[2]

Balfour, replying to the President's message, sent through House on the 24th,[3] expressed his "very high appreciation of the President's confidence." He went on to give his views on Emperor Karl's letter to the President; and on the information "from a source in touch with Count Czernin"

---

[1] Balfour's first message, dated February 26th: ". . . . The most important Allied interests in Siberia are: (1) The preservation of the military stores now lying at Vladivostock which were bought with our money, and (2) the denial to the enemy of the vast agricultural resources available to the west of Lake Baikal. . . .

". . . the suggestion which I make on behalf of His Majesty's Government is:

(1) That the United States should join Great Britain, France and Italy in immediately inviting Japan to occupy the Siberian Railway;

(2) That this occupation should be extended, if possible, to Chiliabinsk and, in any case, as far as Omsk;

(3) That a declaration should accompany the occupation, from all the Allies, in which it should be explained that it was only a temporary measure rendered necessary, in the interests of Russian independence, which was left at the mercy of German militarism as a result of the collapse of the Government at Petrograd."

The second message, also sent on the 26th, stated that it had just been learned that "enemy prisoners in Siberia are being organized with a view to cutting the Railway." "This demonstrates the extreme urgency of action by the Japanese. . . ."

[2] Dated February 26th. The German menace was "imminent and increasing," Stevens said, and Japan would soon go in whether the Allies joined or not.

[3] This volume, p. 565.

of which he, Balfour, had informed the President earlier in the month.[1]

For the former he had little to say: such proposals "can hardly be reconciled with public declarations of President on the subject of peace terms."

Of the latter, however, he felt more hopeful, though it, too, was dangerous. ". . . . But some risks must be run and, if President feels strongly that it is really essential not to close door to further discussion, it seems to me that it might be worth while to take some steps to ascertain if the Lammasch conversations really represented the mind of the Emperor and whether he would be prepared to treat them as a basis of discussion. . . . In answer to question which President asks me about taking the Allies into his confidence, I suggest it must largely depend on policy he intends to pursue. . . ." He saw no reason for concealing Emperor Karl's letter from the "great belligerents"; ". . . if, on the other hand, the President means to follow up Lammasch-Herron line I should in his place content myself with telling the Allies very confidentially that I was carrying on informal conversations with Austria and would communicate further with them if occasion arose. . . ."[2]

Balfour, discussing Hertling's address of the 25th in the House of Commons, spoke of German policy and practice in extremely blunt terms, and declared: ". . . . I am convinced—and I beg the House to weigh my words—that to begin negotiations, unless you see your way to carrying them through successfully, would be to commit the greatest crime against the future peace of the world. . . ." The proper time had not yet arrived.[3]

The American ambassador in London reported a "private and wholly unofficial conversation" in the course of which Balfour had pointed out that the treaty of London "which is regrettable, but by which Great Britain and France are in honor bound, cannot be overcome to square with the President's just conditions of peace." "If this fact leaked out in a conversation and [should] be made known by Ger-

---

[1]Received February 8th. This volume, p. 532.
[2]*Intimate Papers*, Vol. III, pp. 375–377.
[3]*War Aims and Peace Proposals*, pp. 285–295.

many, Italy might abandon the war. Balfour thinks that this unfortunate treaty will not give trouble in the end, but any premature discussion or even mention of it might [give] trouble. . . ."[1]

To Hamilton Holt, who wished to publish, side by side, an article of 1864 entitled "A Talk With Abraham Lincoln," in which much light was shed upon how Lincoln acquired his power of expression, and an interview with President Wilson on the same subject:

". . . . I am, of course, deeply complimented that you should wish to put me alongside of Lincoln in any kind of brace, but what you propose is, I beg you to believe, impossible. It is impossible because I couldn't for the life of me tell you how I got my training in writing, except that it was superintended by a very wonderful father, and, besides, the thing I have always made a terrible fist of is talking about myself or analyzing any process of my own development."

To Dr. Charles D. Walcott, secretary of the Smithsonian Institution:

"Thank you for your letter of yesterday about my typewriter. Evidently you have been reading some more of the fiction that constantly appears about my typewriting machine. I have been several times represented as pounding away on a worn-out machine that is an interesting antique, when, as a matter of fact, I have a perfectly able-bodied machine of recent manufacture, with all the appliances and new notions which the manufacturers have seen fit to add to their newer machines, and I am not by any means through with it. It is likely to see many more years of work. I should be very much distressed to put a new one in its place.

"I am none the less obliged to you for your suggestion

[1]*Foreign Relations*, 1918, Supp. 1, Vol. I, pp. 140–141.

about the interest that would attach to this particular machine and feel very much complimented that you should have wished it for the museum."

Thursday, February 28th.

The French ambassador called at 12:30, having urgently requested an interview in order to lay before the President certain secret proposals for peace which the Central Powers were making.[1] Colonel House wrote in his diary: "The President was pleased with his interview . . . He expected rather a stormy time because he intended to tell him of his communication to the Austrians. Jusserand thought he was acting wisely. The Ambassador said that his Government had picked up some information which led them to believe that the two Kaisers . . . had gotten the Apostolic Delegate in Munich to take their peace terms to Rome for the purpose of having the Pope use his good offices toward peace."[2] Afternoon appointments: the minister from the Netherlands; Samuel Blythe and Frank I. Cobb, who presented a plan to bring the writers of the country into service in order to inform the people more completely as to what the government had done and was trying to do. At 5:30 the Spanish ambassador called, and received the President's reply to the letter from Emperor Karl, in which he asked for more specific information as to the Emperor's views.[3] (See facsimile here reproduced.)

> General Pershing telegraphed: "Newspaper clipping from United States received here to effect that United States has thousands of fliers in France and that thousands of American airplanes are flying above the American forces in Europe to-day. As a matter of fact there is not to-day a single American-made plane in Europe. In my opinion the result of such bombastic claims in the American press has had the effect of materially stiffening German production. Some sane statement might be given the press at home to counteract these exaggerations. . . ."[4]

[1] *Foreign Relations,* 1918, Supp. 1, Vol. I, p. 140.
[2] *Intimate Papers,* Vol. III, p. 375.
[3] *Foreign Relations,* 1918, Supp. 1, Vol. I, pp. 183–184.
[4] Pershing, *My Experiences in the World War,* Vol. I, p. 334.

I am ~~~~~~~~~~ gratified that my recent statement of the principles that ought to be observed in formulating terms of peace should ~~receive~~
in so large a measure by accepted by His Majesty the Emperor of Austria and that His Majesty
should ~~~~~~~~~~ *desire* a more particular comparison of
views between the two governments and I would
be very glad if His Majesty felt at liberty to
be more explicit ~~about~~ *concerning* the application of the
four principles I outlined in my address to the Congress of the United States on the eleventh of
February last. My address of the eleventh of
February merely undertook to state, perhaps more
clearly than I had stated them before, the
principles which I had sought *definitely* to apply in my
address to the Congress on the eighth of January preceding. In that previous address I ~~did~~
set forth ~~very~~ *with* definitely *particularity* the way in which I
thought those principles ought to be carried
out in action. *I assume that the* ~~The~~ Emperor ~~therefore already~~ *has my ad-*
dress of the Eighth of January and that he has already
~~has~~ before him the detailed programme ~~so I do~~ *which I think should form the basis for a general peace stated*
~~think it ought to be formulated~~ in as clear
and specific terms as any personal representative of mine could ~~present the~~ *state* it. It would,

REPLY TO THE EMPEROR OF AUSTRIA
First page of an important draft of the President's reply to the
Emperor of Austria regarding peace proposals, written on his own
typewriter and corrected in his handwriting. Presented to the Spanish
ambassador, for secret transmission, February 28, 1918.

To Secretary McAdoo, who had urged that matters of priorities be left with him and his railroad organization:

"I don't agree with you about the paragraph in the War Industries Board reorganization to which you refer in your letter of yesterday, because I think you have mistaken its purpose. I do not wish to disturb the existing methods of conference and cooperation with regard to priorities of shipment, but there are matters 'of delivery' very much larger than mere questions of transportation. The Shipping Board must be brought in and, even more necessarily, the War Trade Board, because they control all movements in and out of the country by their control over both exports and imports, and it is in my judgment absolutely necessary to have a supplementary body of regular constitution which will be available to see to it that all obstacles may be removed from the free movement of articles, not only within the country but out of it and into it."

To William Kent of the Tariff Commission, who had offered to produce quotations disclosing the attitude of the packers toward the administration:

". . . . If I don't ask you to let me see the evidence to which you refer, I mean the evidence of the attitude of the packers, it is only because I don't want to see red. I am sure you will understand."

INDEX

The following index has been made as complete as possible by subject; only page references, therefore, have been supplied for the names listed.

Ackerman, Carl: 400
Adams, Herbert: 336, 354, 360
Adams, Samuel Hopkins: 291
Adamson, Congressman W. C., Ga.: Wilson to, 154, 157, 166, 167, 252, 404. Also 7, 67, 70, 91, 126, 200, 208, 281, 289, 382
Addams, Jane: 52
Adler, Cyrus: 356
Agriculture (see also Army, American): 17, 104, 166, 281, 356, 385, 397, 511–12, 531
Air Force, American: more American planes needed, 107; R. C. Bolling goes abroad on industrial aspects, 109; War Dept. behind plans for, 117; automobile plants, machine shops, to make engines for, 122; conference on, 123; Wilson signs aviation bill, 187; Liberty Motor, 267, 336, 344; work begun on 20,000 planes, 291; Wilson receives Aircraft Board, 364; Borglum charges, investigation, 372, 393–4, 407–8, 430, 446, 495–6, 507, 517; Huntington charges, 412, 554–5; 125 completed training planes, 420; production program encouraging, 496; first American-built battle planes en route to front, 558; Pershing deplores bombastic claims about, 572
Aldunate, Don Santiago, Chilean Ambassador, Washington: 22
Alexander, Congressman J. W., Mo.: Wilson to, 541. Also 60, 148
Alexander, Moses, Governor of Idaho: 140
Alien Enemies: treaty obligations on, 58, 216; alleged bad treatment of, 178; round-up of, 284; Palmer, Alien Property Custodian, 304; property of allies of enemies, 335, 338; no alien enemies in U. S. arsenals; problem of, in munitions factories, 338; departure of, from U. S. during war, 354; office-holding, 457; Wilson disapproves trial of, by court-martial, 517–18
All in a Life-Time, Henry Morgenthau in collaboration with French Strother (Doubleday, Page & Co.): 274
Allenby, Gen. E. H. H.: 402, 517
Allied War Conference: British, French, want U. S. represented at, 277; Wilson appoints Col. House, 297, 304, 320; method of accrediting House, 322, 324; is looked on in Russia as peace meeting, 326; Lansing says will discuss war, 336; personnel of House Mission, 331; sails, 334; reaches London, announced as war mission, 342; Balfour pleased at coming of, 344; small nations invited to military session, 347–8; difficulty

of bringing British to "satisfactory working basis", 357; Mission meets British War Cabinet, heads of departments, 366–7; goes to Paris, 371; opening session, 381; House reports on, to Wilson, 382; final plenary session, 389; Mission sails for home, 397; pessimism in reports of, 410–11; House reports to Wilson, 414–15
American Federation of Labor: see Labor
American Legion Monthly: 22
American Weekly: 171
Anderson, G. W.: Wilson to, 326
Anderson, Congressman Sydney, Minn.: 542
Angelescu, Constantin, Rumanian Minister, Washington: 470
Angell, Norman: 91
Anthony, Congressman D. R., Jr., Kan.: 11, 217
Antilles: 310
Applebaum, Misha: 277
Argentina: 83, 89, 343, 413
Armenia: Wilson appeals for relief for Syria and, 331–2
Army, American (see also War; War Department): National Guard, 20, 31, 285; aid for dependents of men in, 28, 127, 252–3, 294; conscientious objectors, 45, 241, 275, 289; religious activities, 102, 184, 252, 260–1, 284, 482; Wilson sends message to soldiers of, 261; refuses Liberty Loan statement for use in, 312; disapproves wartime benefit games between Navy and, 321, 344
Conscription: Wilson approves, 2; writes Eliot about, 5; confers on, 8, 16, 23, 43; explains, 30–1; proposed Congressional committee to study, 36–7; Wilson insists on, 48–9; objects to compromise, 50–1; signs draft bill, designates Registration Day, 74; on attempts to evade draft, 91, 93; little opposition on Registration Day, 101; Wilson on politics in exemption boards, 115; exemption of agricultural labor, 142, 240, 500–1; drawing begins, 176; legality of campaign against draft, 196–7; Wilson on special exemptions, 220; message to New York City drafted men, 245; exemption of "declarants", 256; entrainment for cantonments, 273; Wilson's foreword for selective service regulations, 347; Wilson on pardons for opponents of, 539
European Service: medical and other aid to French, British, 47–8; Pershing instructed to preserve identity of U. S. forces, 88; troops receive ovation, Paris, 145; Per-

Army, American—*Continued*
shing wants million men by May, 1918, 149;
Ribot asks about number of troops; Wilson's reply never sent, 183–4, 204; Elks
give $1,000,000 for base hospitals in France,
202; troops warmly greeted, London, 217;
proposal to send men to France for agricultural work, 301, 312; Christmas boxes
for men in Europe, 373; Wilson gets shell
of first shot fired; Lloyd George asks U. S.
replacements in British battalions, 388;
plan for 24 divisions by end of June, 1918,
405–6; Bliss urges maximum number
possible by spring, 1918, 411; Baker on
preserving identity, 417–18, 449–50; conservation of morals of men, 428, 527; Wilson's
New Year's greetings to, 433; writes
Poincaré about use of U. S. troops, 457;
understanding with French on, 468–9;
150-battalion plan, 483–4; Robertson urges
incorporation of U. S. troops with British,
501; Foch, Pétain, Haig, agree on desirability of amalgamation with French or
British; U. S. troops take over small section
of Western Front, 509–10; Lloyd George-
Maurice-Pershing plan, 510, 521–2; Bliss
tells Supreme War Council permanent
amalgamation impossible, 512–13; Council
agrees two complete divisions a month required for safety of Western Front, 1918,
516; Wilson sends views on use of U. S.
troops to Balfour, 520–1; Secy. Baker to
visit troops in Europe, 562
    *Roosevelt, Theodore, Proposal to Head
Volunteer Division:* calls on Wilson, 11;
refused, 17; Bridges, Joffre, object to non-
professionals, 48; J. M. Parker urges granting T. R.'s request, 72; Wilson issues statement on refusing, 77; divisions disbanded, 78
    Shipment of: Wilson approves dispatch of
Pershing, small expeditionary force, 62;
announced, 75; Pershing sails, 89; reaches
England, 105; France, 109; first troops sail,
110; arrive, 128; Daniels announces arrival,
describes repulsing of submarines, statement attacked, 143; Michaelis belittles
U. S. intervention because of shipping
difficulties, 173; protection of transports,
197; alleged plot to attack transports, 273;
returning transport *Antilles* sinks, 310;
Pershing urges more tonnage for, 359;
Czernin says transportation of millions
impossible, 398; transport *Tuscania* torpedoed, 529
    Training: Wilson on, 14, 232–3; Com-
mission on camp activities, 52; camp sites,
choice of, 95, 159, 167; separate training for
colored troops, 267; Pershing wants troops
trained, ready for active service, summer,
1918, 357–8; camps, conditions in, 418, 444,
498
Ashurst, Senator H. F., Ariz.: 262, 487
Asquith, H. H.: 300
Aswell, Congressman J. B., La.: 92, 99

At the Paris Peace Conference, James T. Shot-
well (Macmillan Co.): 275
Atlanta *Journal:* 154
"Atrocities": 242, 528
Atlantic Monthly: 446
Auchincloss, Gordon: 94, 97, 237, 331, 432,
559
Auchincloss, Mrs. Gordon: 94, 97, 432
Austin, Congressman R. W., Tenn.: 281
Austria, Emperor Karl of: Wilson to, 572, 573.
Also 192, 442, 532, 551, 558, 564, 565, 566,
569–70, 572
Austria-Hungary (see also Peace, Discussions
of; Russia; War): severs relations with
U. S., 8; Wilson's war address dropped in,
by airplanes, 14; Wilson buys 80,000 tons
of Austrian shipping, 56; treaties affecting
territory of, 74; Page at Rome suggests
U. S. declare war on, 330; grounds of com-
plaint against, 367; Wilson recommends
war on; Congress passes resolution for;
Wilson signs; proclaimed, 390–1, 397, 405;
Czernin says Entente cannot separate
Austria, Germany, 397–8; strikes, rioting,
reported spreading in, 482, 533
Axson, Mrs. Palmer: Wilson to, 422
Axson, Stockton, brother-in-law of Woodrow
Wilson: 5, 8, 292, 295, 296, 341, 349, 373,
375, 397, 412, 468, 481, 553
Azores: German influence in, 548

Baker, E. Carleton: 25
Baker, Newton D., Secretary of War: Wilson
to, 14, 20, 47, 48, 62, 80, 93, 95, 123, 136,
168, 219, 228, 242, 243, 275, 280, 285, 289,
307, 316, 333, 338, 343, 345, 351, 360, 385,
433, 444, 459, 483, 514, 517, 521–2, 562.
Also numerous other references
Baker, Ray Stannard (see also *Public Papers
of Woodrow Wilson, The; Woodrow Wilson
and World Settlement*): 464, 476, 511, 528, 546
Bakhmeteff, Boris A., Russian Ambassador,
Washington, from July 5, 1917: 121, 148,
171, 205, 309, 463
Bakhméteff, George, Russian Ambassador,
Washington, to April 20, 1917: 56
Balfour, A. J. (see also *Retrospect*): 1, 3, 13,
33, 34, 37, 40, 43, 44, 47, 52, 54, 65, 66, 70,
74, 75, 79, 80, 85, 86, 95, 96, 97, 102, 104,
133, 134, 138, 139, 143, 149, 152, 158, 162,
176, 213, 218, 219, 221, 228, 230, 233, 235,
237, 292, 304, 336, 337, 344, 370, 382, 388,
443, 444, 447, 452, 475, 512, 516, 520, 532,
533, 540, 547, 563, 565, 568, 569, 570, 571
Balkans: 163, 177, 191
Bamberger, Simon, Governor of Utah: 140
Bankhead, Senator J. H., Ala.: Wilson to, 465.
Also 46, 176, 210, 317
Barclay, Colville, Counselor of British Em-
bassy, Washington: Wilson to, 475. Also 247
Barnard, George Grey: 327, 345, 353
Barnes, Julius: 217
Barnhart, Congressman H. A., Ind.: 540
Barrett, Charles S.: 104

Barringer, D. M.: Wilson to, 191
Barroll, Mrs. Hope H.: Wilson to, 310
Barrymore, John: 519
Baruch, B. M.: Wilson to, 116, 241, 432, 480. Also 35, 89, 197, 233, 320, 325, 499, 522, 530, 568
Bass, Mrs. George B.: Wilson to, 52, 460, 489. Also 369
Battin, Benjamin F.: 213
Beck, James M.: 473
Beckham, Senator J. C. W., Ky.: 484
Bedford, Alfred C.: 153
Beeckman, R. L., Governor of R. I.: 312
Belasco, David: 475
Belgium: welcomes America to war, 8; minister from, presents credentials, 33; loan to governments of France and, for relief, 61; Commission from, arrives; Wilson receives; White House dinner; garden party for, 117, 125; Moncheur on war aims of, 213; message to King Albert of, 360
Belmont, Captain Perry: Wilson to, 531
Benham, Edith (later Mrs. James M. Helm), secretary to Mrs. Wilson: 8
Bennet, William S.: 104
Benson, Allan L.: 132
Benson, Rear-Admiral W. S.: 217, 331, 367, 410, 425
Benton, Guy Potter: 233
Berger, Victor L.: 170
Berkman, Alexander: 480
Berliner Lokal-Anzeiger, 456; Tageblatt, 180-1, 537
Berres, Albert J.: 227
Berry, Captain, of the Mayflower: 226
Berst, J. A.: Wilson to, 100
Bertron, S. R.: Wilson to, 303, 468. Also 18, 28, 39, 53, 55, 62, 151
Bethmann-Hollweg, T. T. F. A. von, German Chancellor to July 15, 1917: 166
Biddle, Maj. Gen. John: 388, 556
Billings, Frank: 326
Bittencourt, Mrs. Manuel: Wilson to, 496
Black List: 86, 391
Bland, John R.: 498
Blanton, Congressman T. L., Tex.: Wilson to, 285
Bliss, Peacemaker, Frederick Palmer (Dodd, Mead & Co.): 386, 406, 513
Bliss, Gen. Tasker H.: 88, 297, 331, 333, 354, 361, 366, 372, 387, 405-6, 411, 414, 415, 417, 431, 455, 456, 457, 459, 483, 487, 501, 509, 510, 512, 518, 521-2, 528, 556, 566
Blue, Dr. Rupert: 359
Blumenthal, Daniel: 166
Blythe, S. G.: Wilson to, 309. Also 91, 572
Boardman, Mabel T.: 29
Bolden, Richard M.: 145
Bolivia: 17
Bolling, Bertha, sister of Mrs. Wilson: 8, 88, 247, 264, 265, 271
Bolling, John Randolph, brother of Mrs. Wilson (see also Woodrow Wilson's Scrapbooks): 7, 8, 37, 39, 66, 88, 166, 242, 286, 287

Bolling, Maj. R. C.: 109
Bolling, Rolfe E., brother of Mrs. Wilson: 16, 39
Bolling, Mrs. W. H., mother of Mrs. Wilson: 8, 88, 247, 264, 265, 270, 417
Bolling, Wilmer: 324
Bones, Helen W., cousin of Woodrow Wilson: 1, 4, 8, 16, 20, 32, 40, 43, 67, 85, 106, 166, 182, 186, 239, 280, 287, 417, 553
Bonillas, Señor Ygnacio, Mexican Ambassador, Washington: 23, 26, 160, 334
Borah, Senator W. E., Idaho: Wilson to, 194. Also 195, 263, 475, 497
Borden, Sir Robert, Premier of Canada: 568
Borglum, Gutzon: Wilson to, 393, 446, 495, 507. Also 372, 407, 430, 517
Borland, Congressman W. P., Mo.: Wilson to, 119. Also 79, 464
Bowlby, Harry L.: 515
Bowman, Isaiah: 275
Boyle, Charles W.: Wilson to, 280
Brady, W. A.: Wilson to, 134. Also 291, 311
Brailsford, H. N.: 194
Brandegee, Senator F. B., Conn.: 220
Brandeis, Louis D., U. S. Supreme Court: 53, 120, 242, 401
Brazil: 14, 20, 28, 327
Brent, Theodore: Wilson to, 193. Also 143
Breshkovskaya, Catherine: 389
Brest Litovsk, Treaty of: see Russia
Bridge to France, The, Edward N. Hurley (J. B. Lippincott Co.): 22, 227, 425
Bridges, Gen. G. T. M.: 35, 47, 48
Bridges, Robert: Wilson to, 384, 446, 525
Bridges, Robert, Poet Laureate of England: Wilson to, 87
Briggs, Mitchell P.: see George D. Herron and the European Settlement
Brisbane, Arthur: Wilson to, 36, 258. Also 178, 242, 423
Britten, Congressman F. A., Ill.: 171, 425
Brookings, R. S.: Wilson to, 555. Also 197, 233
Brough, Charles H., Governor of Ark.: 388
Brougham, H. B.: Wilson to, 287. Also 471
Broussard, Robert F.: 128
Brown, E. T.: 34, 77, 78, 81, 85, 305, 306, 307, 309, 390, 391, 397, 398, 408, 468
Brown, Mrs. E. T.: 77, 79, 305, 306, 307, 309
Brown, Miss Marjorie: 305, 372
Brownlow, Louis: 166, 171, 321
Broyles, Nash B.: Wilson to, 353
Brumbaugh, M. G., Governor of Pa.: Wilson to, 100
Bryan, William Jennings: Wilson to, 6, 276, 416, 489. Also 21, 114, 122, 350, 400, 413, 471
Bryce, James: 52, 63, 104, 217, 424
Bryn, H. H., Norwegian Minister, Washington: 484
Buchanan, Sir George W., British Ambassador, Petrograd: 388
Buckler, William H., special agent of Department of State, American Embassy, London: 224, 346

Buckmaster, A. H.: Wilson to, 211
Bulgaria (see also Peace, Discussions of): 390, 392–3
Bullard, Arthur: 389
Bullitt, William C.: 513
Burke, John, Treasurer of U. S.: Wilson to, 245. Also 244
Burleson, Albert S., Postmaster General: Wilson to, 291, 301, 312, 450, 472, 498. Also numerous other references
Burnquist, J. A. A., Governor of Minn.: 404–5
Burton, H. P.: 99–100
Burton, Pomeroy: 99–100
Business Conditions in U. S.: commercial conventions during war, 116; appeal against profiteering, 155; government not inimical to business reasonably conducted, 264; large profits unjustifiable in war; no justification for pessimism, 273–4; uncertainties to be removed as soon as possible; extreme pessimism nowhere but New York, banking circles, Boston; excellent financial condition of country, 302–4; New York lukewarm, panicky, 307–8; plan to publish statement disproving pessimism, 321; railroad situation tends demoralize New York security markets, 408–9; bankers pleased that railroads are taken over; railroad stocks soar, 431; battle between Wilson, Congress, traceable to big business interests, 486; country suspicious about big interests, 499; Wilson, Hoover disapprove speculative expansion, 523
Buxton, Charles Roden: 91
Byng, Gen. Sir Julian: 367
Byrd, Richard E.: Wilson to, 563
Byrnes, Congressman J. F., S. C.: 83
Byrns, Congressman J. W., Tenn.: 226

Cadorna, Gen. Luigi: 66
Calder, Senator W. M., N. Y.: 61, 109, 155, 468, 475
Caldwell, Congressman Charles P., N. Y.: 464, 504
Caldwell, John K., U. S. Consul, Vladivostok: 443
Cambon, Jules: 202
Cambon, Paul: 75, 183, 204
Campbell, T. E., Governor of Ariz.: 160
Canada: see Great Britain; War
Candler, Congressman E. S., Miss.: Wilson to, 60. Also 394, 484
Cannon, James Jr.: Wilson to, 137
Cannon, Congressman J. G., Ill.: 277
Caporetto: see War
Capper, Arthur, Governor of Kan.: Wilson to, 500
Capps, Rear-Admiral W. L.: Wilson to, 192. Also 187
Carlin, Congressman C. C., Va.: 92, 360
Carranza, Gen. Venustiano, President of Mexico: 26, 38, 171
Carson, Sir Edward: 13

Catt, Mrs. Carrie Chapman: Wilson to, 59' 306. Also 346
Cavanagh, John J.: Wilson to, 511
Cawthorn, Joseph B.: 264
Cecil, Lord Robert: 70, 97, 199, 235, 236, 237, 247, 255, 256, 337, 365, 442, 548
Censorship (see also Committee on Public Information; Communications; Espionage Act): early evidence of self-imposed, 32; growing resentment against, 57; agreement on, 71; Wilson discusses, with Sens. Lodge, Gallinger, Knox, 73; upholds certain degree of, over press, 81; new appeal, 111; Wilson, Burleson, discuss closing of mails to The Masses, 165; difficulty of problem grows, 185; World editorial on freedom of speech in war, 236; Wilson explains position on, 262; wartime "wholly exceptional" but line hard to draw, 273; sends Burleson editorial on, advising caution, liberality, 301; Board of, established, 304; Milwaukee Leader hearing; courts sustain Burleson, 312–13; Wilson on Burleson's handling of, 313, 318–19; advisory newspaper men's committee suggested, to deal with; Wilson believes impossible, 367–8
Chadbourne, T. L., Jr.: Wilson to, 245. Also 300, 304
Chadbourne, Mrs. T. L., Jr.: 61
Chamber of Commerce, U. S.: offer of, to help with propaganda, 258–9; referendum on economic boycott, 477; on trade discrimination against Germany after war, 568
Chamberlain, Senator G. E., Ore.: Wilson to, 209, 232, 465, 484. Also 22, 101, 106, 154, 199, 236, 277, 314, 406, 434, 442, 451, 480, 485, 496, 498, 502, 530, 555
Chambers, Edward: 438
Chambers, W. L.: Wilson to, 327, 539. Also 242, 256
Chapman, John J.: Wilson to, 345
Cheradame, André: 446, 565
Chicago Tribune: 33
China: Japanese activities in, 25; provisional government formed in, 98; Lansing sends message in regard to; France, Great Britain, Japan refuse similar action, 99; Japan wishes Bryan's March, 1915, statement in regard to, confirmed, 114; U. S. does not approve Japanese political influence over, 144; declares war on Germany, Austria-Hungary, 215; Wilson watches with "solicitude," 229; tells Ishii U. S. chiefly interested in Open Door, equal opportunity in, 230; Lansing-Ishii conferences on "desires and intentions shared" by Japan, U. S. in, 262–3, 336, 338–9, 341; Lansing telegraphs text to American minister in, with statement on favorable aspects for China, 340; Wilson urges reassurances to China, 342; government of, will not be bound by agreements between other nations, 351
Chinda, Viscount: 114

Choate, Joseph H.: 63

Churchill, Winston: 191

Civil Service Commission: 148, 153

Clark, Congressman Champ, Mo.: Wilson to, 460, 498. Also 14, 60, 108, 196, 281, 300, 456, 462

Clark, Edgar E.: 53, 394

Clark, Congressman Frank, Fla.: Wilson to, 355. Also 213, 558

Clark, John Bates: 92

Clark, Melville: 246

Clarke, John H., U. S. Supreme Court: 269

Clarkson, Grosvenor B. (see also *Industrial America in the World War*): 46

Clemenceau, Georges, French Prime Minister from November 16, 1917: 88, 355, 372, 374, 381, 382, 387, 462, 468, 513, 527, 535, 549

Clemmons, M.: Wilson to, 377

Close, Gilbert F.: 90

Coal (see also Labor; Priorities): Italian need of, 94, 427; Wilson confers on Federal control of, 121; on fixing price of, 125; operators, government officials appoint committee on price of; fix temporary price of bituminous, causing trouble, 133, 135–6, 136–7, 138, 140–1; Fort suggests price be left to conference of operators, 210; Wilson receives chairmen, New England Coal Committees, 216; discusses problems of, with Federal Trade Commission, Lovett, 226; fixes price of anthracite at mines; Garfield heads Fuel Administration, 230; prices fixed, only temporary, 232; Senate inquiry into shortage, 406; famine of, threatening, "lightless nights", 409; Garfield favors Govt. operation of railroads, mines, 431; famine of, feared in New York, 436; shortage worse; McAdoo orders right of way for coal trains, 437; no section to have normal supply for 60 days, 464; Wilson confers on Garfield's proposed order; approves, 471–2; order given out, with statement; nation is shocked; Wilson stands firm, 475–6, 478–9, 481, 487; 30,000 New York City plants closed; Garfield announces situation improving, 480; railroad congestion broken, 487; continuing shortage, bitter weather, 528; price of, in Colorado, 541; heatless Mondays suspended, 542

Cobb, Frank I.: Wilson to, 84, 98, 250, 267, 399, 530. Also 180–1, 236, 424, 476, 572

Coffin, Howard E.: 107, 122, 187

Cohan, George M.: 475

Cohen, John B.: Wilson to, 154

Colby, Bainbridge: 18, 187, 192, 326, 331, 411, 419

Colcord, Lincoln: Wilson to, 396. Also 124, 471

Coleman, R. B.: Wilson to, 259

Collier, Congressman J. W., Miss.: 277, 295

Colombia: 106, 413–14

Colver, William B.: Wilson to, 177

Committee on Public Information (see also Russia): created, Creel, head; controversy over functions, 20–21; first issue, *Official Bulletin*, 61; Creel commended, 86; Wilson thinks newspaper men will discover Creel's quality, 86, 87; organization of moving picture industry in co-operation with, 134–5; Daniels announces through, arrival of American troop transports, statement attacked, 143; suggested Council on Publicity to consult with Creel, 257; Wilson approves leaving propaganda to, 259; sends war with Austria-Hungary address to Europe, Scandinavia, South America, Orient, Mexico, 391; Wilson "kills" statement of, on war progress, because of possible international complications, 445; approves work done by, 469; promises next address to, for world circulation, 563

Commoner, The: 350

Communications (see also Censorship): government control of radio, 2; mail service to Germany suspended, 5; censorship over telephones, telegraphs, 7, 40; question of censorship over mails, 47; hope for improvement of cable, radio, between U. S. and Asia, 298; removal of British mail, cable ban on Hearst's International News Service, 556, 562–3

Confederate Veterans: 100–1, 102, 104

Congress (see also Wilson, Woodrow): debates war resolution, 1; Wilson hears Balfour speak in, 52; 1st session 65th, adjourns; Wilson commends work, 294; requests memoranda on legislation for, 380; 2nd session 65th, opens; Wilson cannot omit foreign affairs from address to, 389; Senate inquiries into War Dept. activities; into fuel, sugar shortages, 406; House investigation into Navy Dept.'s conduct of war, 409; J. H. Lewis warns Senate against harmful investigations, 415; Senate inquiries into shipping, railroads, 418; Wilson submits legislative program to Burleson for comment, 450

Committee on Conduct of War, Proposals for: resolutions for; Root says coalition government not needed, 10; Wilson disapproves, 24; Sen. Weeks offers joint resolution to create, 172; Wilson disapproves section of Food bill providing for, 185–6, 202–3, 205–6; protests fresh attempt to "saddle" him with, 251–2; protests Republican plan to add, as rider to Deficiency bill, 258; signs War Revenue bill, with no provision for, 290; confers with members of Congress on proposal for, 484–5, 515; Sen. Chamberlain introduces bill providing for a war cabinet, 485; Wilson objects, 501–2, 515; Hitchcock opens fight for war cabinet bill in Senate, 521; Republican efforts for; Cobb's editorial against, 530–1

Congressional Record: 209, 236

Conrad, Joseph: 243

Conscientious Objectors: see Army, American

Conscription: see Army, American

Constitutional Rights in Wartime: Wilson on, 40–1; Union Against Militarism presents memo. on invasion of; Wilson has allegations looked into, 224–5

Contraband: 31, 138

Convoys: see War

Coolidge, Mrs. T. Jefferson: 265

Cooper, Congressman Henry A., Wis.: 475

Costello, S. V.: 145

Cothran, Mrs. A. H., niece of Woodrow Wilson, 85, 88

Council of National Defense: votes Hoover to head food committee; Willard to help expedite freight movements, 5; labor subcommittee of, issues statement in support of war, 7–8; shipping committee named, 33; Wilson addresses members of State Councils, 46; addresses Gompers, labor committee of Advisory Commission, 69; requests withdrawal of Food bill amendment prohibiting members of advisory committees from selling to government, 150–1, 164–5; reorganization of, 168–9, 399; report of Surgeon General, Public Health Service, to be taken up with, 359

Covington, J. Harry: 206, 262, 274, 391

Cox, James M., Governor of Ohio: 531

Crane, C. R.: 18, 28, 61, 408, 443, 450, 568

Crane, Mrs. C. R.: 60, 408

Crane, Mrs. Richard: 60

Craven, Hermon W.: 148, 153

Cravens, Ben: 64

Crawford, Sir Richard, Commercial Adviser, British Embassy, Washington: 143

Creel, George (see also War, the World, and Wilson, The; How We Advertised America): Wilson to, 75, 314, 323, 330, 349, 383, 402, 439, 445, 469, 473. Also numerous other references

Crisp, Congressman Charles R., Ga.: 24

Croly, Herbert: Wilson to, 318. Also 33

Crosby, Oscar T., Assistant Secretary of the Treasury: 179, 296, 311, 315, 326, 331, 341, 361, 408, 427, 455, 459, 538, 545, 548, 559

Cross, William T.: 511

Crowded Years, William G. McAdoo (Houghton Mifflin Co.): 113

Crowder, General Enoch H.: 240

Crowell, Benedict, Assistant Secretary of War: 410

Crozier, Maj. Gen. William: 407

Cruttwell, C. R. M. F.: see History of the Great War, A

Cuba: 5, 44, 375, 412

Culberson, Senator Charles A., Tex.: Wilson to, 67

Cummings, Homer S.: 322

Cummins, Senator A. B., Iowa: 112

Cunliffe-Owen, Mrs. Marguerite: Wilson to, 260

Current History: see numerous references

Curtis, Senator Charles, Kan.: 242

Czernin, Count Ottokar, Austro-Hungarian Prime Minister, Minister for Foreign Affairs: 199, 289, 340, 397, 429, 443, 456, 497, 505, 506, 516, 519, 532, 536, 537, 540, 554, 569

Da Gama, Domicio, Brazilian Ambassador, Washington: 27, 123

Dahne, William: Wilson to, 22

Dallinger, Congressman F. W., Mass.: 405

Daniels, Josephus, Secretary of the Navy (see also Our Navy at War; Navy and the Nation, The): Wilson to, 71, 99, 119, 140, 144, 156, 184, 344–5, 417, 514, 522, 533. Also numerous other references

Daniels, Mrs. Josephus: Wilson to, 437. Also 434

Daniels, Winthrop M.: Wilson to, 315, 316, 321. Also 426

Darrow, Clarence: Wilson to, 210. Also 200

Davidson, James L.: Wilson to, 111

Davies, Joseph E.: 128, 136, 341

Davis, E. P.: Wilson to, 489. Also 66, 126, 363, 468

Davis, Edgar B.: Wilson to, 539

Davis, J. Lionberger: Wilson to, 479. Also 377

Davison, Henry P.: Wilson to, 523. Also 61, 105, 262, 558

Dawson, Geoffrey: 365

Dearborn Independent: 11

Debs, Eugene V.: 419

De Cartier de Marchienne, E., Belgian Minister, Washington: 33, 375, 484

De Lagercrantz, M.: 89

De Leval, M. G.: 244

De Mohrenschildt, Ferdinand: 70

De Mohrenschildt, Madame Ferdinand (Nona H. McAdoo): 70

Denman, William: Wilson to, 156, 175, 188, 189, 190, 193. Also 2, 14, 24, 33, 34, 35, 45, 53, 55, 79, 85, 88, 98, 117, 122, 124, 143, 172

Denmark: see Trade, Foreign

Dent, Congressman S. H., Jr., Ala.: 8, 23, 317, 484, 541

Depew, Chauncey M. (see also Speeches and Literary Contributions at Fourscore and Four): Wilson to, 502

De Veyra, Jaime C.: Wilson to, 142

Devonport, Lord Hudson E. K.: 35

Devonshire, Duke of, Governor General of Canada; 458

Devonshire, Duchess of: 458

Dickinson, Congressman C. C., Mo.: 283

Dickinson, G. Lowes: see Documents and Statements Relating to Peace Proposals and War Aims

Dill, Congressman Clarence C., Wash.: 388

Dillingham, Senator W. P., Vt.: 244, 546

District of Columbia: 171, 194, 237, 256

Documents and Statements Relating to Peace Proposals and War Aims, December 1916 to November 1918, introduction by G. Lowes Dickinson (Macmillan Co.): 379

Dodd, William E.: see Public Papers of Woodrow Wilson, The

Dodge, Cleveland H.: Wilson to, 87, 250, 332, 392, 469. Also 32, 46, 270
Dodge, Mrs. Cleveland H.: 270
Doheny, Mr. and Mrs. Edward L.: 126
Donlin, John: Wilson to, 354
Doremus, Congressman F. E., Mich.: 22, 79, 566
Dorsey, Hugh M., Governor of Ga.: 307, 408
Douglas, R. Langton: Wilson to, 122
Drane, Congressman H. J., Fla.: 295
Drummond, Sir Eric: 3, 78, 86
DuBois, Fred T.: 243
Dumba, Constantin T., former Austro-Hungarian Ambassador, Washington: 400, 416
Duncan, Charles: 536
Duncan, James: 19, 39, 62
Dupré, Congressman H. G., La.: 289
Dyer, Congressman L. C., Mo.: Wilson to, 198, 201

Eagan, Congressman John J., N. J.: 291
Eagle, Congressman Joe H., Tex.: 280, 521
Eastman, Max: Wilson to, 273. Also 165
Economic After-War Policy: proposed Tariff Commission investigation of economic factors during and after war, 71; Houston, Taussig, on economic policies at peace conference, 328; Lansing suggests threats of retaliation, reprisal against Germany, 429; Wilson disapproves U. S. Chamber of Commerce referendum on economic boycott, 477; U. S. Chamber of Commerce on after-war trade discrimination against Germany, 568
Edison, Thomas A.: 90, 226
Edmonds, Richard H.: Wilson to, 292, 337
Education in Wartime: 98, 118, 340, 441
Egan, Maurice F., U. S. Minister, Denmark: 31, 117, 295, 310, 468
Eight Years with Wilson's Cabinet, David F. Houston (Doubleday, Page & Co.): 17
Ekengren, W. A. F., Swedish Minister, Washington: 89, 283
Ela, Emerson: 492
Eliot, Charles W.: Wilson to, 5, 190, 486, 552
Elkus, Abram I., U. S. Ambassador, Turkey: Wilson to, 338. Also 149, 158, 356, 542
Elliott, Edward: 442
Elliott, Mrs. Edward (Margaret R. Axson): 265, 326, 330, 349, 425, 442
Elliott, Howard: 18, 407
Elliott, Jackson S.: Wilson to, 86
Elston, Congressman J. A., Cal.: 57
Emergency Fleet Corporation: see Ships
Emmet, Robert: 133, 462
England, King George V of: 105, 217, 349
Erskine, Mrs. Marion: 186, 239
Esch, Congressman J. J., Wis.: 70
Espionage Act: New York *Times*, American Newspaper Publishers Assn., protest censorship provision of, 14, 35, 51; Wilson approves, 36; passes House, with modified censorship provision, 51; Wilson considers

amendment limiting embargo powers of executive unwise, 53; insists on mild censorship provision in, 83; signs bill, 113; offenses of *The People's Counselor* and others, within provisions of, 283; Burleson's letter to publishers regarding, 324
Excess Profits Tax: see Finance
Exports: see Trade, Foreign

Fahey, J. H.: Wilson to, 503. Also 522
Fairbanks, Douglas: Wilson to, 372
Federal Reserve Board: 300, 406
Federal Trade Commission: Wilson receives Fort of, 117; Secy. Daniels suggests government steel price be fixed by, 121; Wilson consults Fort, Davies, Colver of, on price fixing, 125, 128, 135-6, 140-1, 177; big steel interests agree to put output at disposal of government, price to be fixed by, 150; Wilson confers with, on cost determining work, 207; discusses coal, transportation problems with, 226, 229; report of, on copper production, 241; Wilson warned to expect trouble in investigation of, into packing industry, 517
Ferguson, J. E., Governor of Tex.: Wilson to, 93
Fernald, Senator Bert M., Me.: 232
Ferris, Congressman Scott, Okla.: 171, 471
Fifty Years a Journalist, Melville E. Stone (Doubleday, Page & Co.): 35, 143
Filene, E. A.: Wilson to, 477. Also 568
Finance (see also Inter-Allied Council on War Purchases and Finance; Liberty Loans): Wilson urges financial legislation for conduct of war; huge bond issue agreed on, 13; signs national security, defense bill, 23; signs bill for issue of $7,000,000,000 Treasury obligations, 34; $200,000,000 loan to Great Britain, 35; Wilson, McAdoo discuss foreign loans, 39; $75,000,000 loan to French, Belgian governments for relief, 61; $100,000,000 credit for Russian government, 72; Wilson discusses revenue with Republican senators, 73; plan for taxing excess war profits, 92; Wilson confers on military appropriation bill, 99; signs War Budget bill, 113; British financial crisis, 133-4; Northcliffe presents England's desperate need for money, 138; Balfour appeals, 139; Spring Rice discusses crisis; Wilson urges full explanations to McAdoo, 143; $30,000 for educational publicity in Russia, 151; McAdoo states no "positive undertakings" on part of U. S. regarding finances, 153-4; notifies Balfour no promise given to pay Morgan overdraft, 158; Wilson requests more information on Allied financial needs, general policy, 162; McAdoo submits proposed letter to borrowing governments, 168; British Chancellor on financial situation; $85,000,000 advanced to British government, 176-7; Crosby says magnitude of loans justifies searching

Finance—*Continued*

inquiry into conduct of war; repeats hints of secret treaties, 179; Ribot inquires about method of allotment of sums loaned; Wilson's answer never sent, 183–4, 204–5; aviation bill appropriates $640,000,000, 187; State Dept. disapproves McAdoo's letter to borrowing governments; McAdoo presents further arguments, 212–13, 227; Food Administration forms $50,000,000 grain corporation, 217; $100,000,000 credit for Russian government available while Russia is in war, 230; British advised to send representative to dominate, compose financial situation, 235–6; British Chancellor of Exchequer on importance of U. S. financial aid, 267; Wilson on $100,000,000 appropriation for war workers' houses, 286; signs War Revenue bill, 290; approves bill to center control of appropriations in single committee during war, 291–2; signs Urgent Deficiency bill, 294; considers War Finance Board, 352–3; Italy's request for additional $40,000,000 credit, failure to buy in U. S. through Purchasing Commission, 373; Col. House advises no more advances to Russia now, 374; Wilson finds fund for national security, defense "indispensable"; furnishes detailed statement of expenditures, 391, 399–400; excess profits tax a "thorny business", 421; finance, shipping closely involved, 427; $1,000,000 to Bureau of Standards, 438; $1,000,000 for purchase of supplies, Russia, 544–5; U. S. inclined to aid Austria if separate peace, 547

Fine, Henry B.: Wilson to, 69

Fisher, H. A. L.: see *James Bryce*

Fisher, Congressman H. F., Tenn.: 17, 83

Fisher, Irving: 83

Fitzgerald, Congressman J. J., N. Y.: Wilson to, 258, 291, 392, 399. Also 24, 60, 271, 388, 408

Fitzpatrick, James: 478

Fletcher, Senator D. U., Fla.: Wilson to, 159. Also 22, 57, 83, 85, 160, 167, 217, 284, 295, 484

Fletcher, Rear-Admiral Frank F.: 197

Fletcher, H. P., U. S. Ambassador, Mexico: 166

Flood, Congressman H. D., Va.: 60, 475

Foch, Marshal Ferdinand: 462, 510

Fogel, Philip H.: Wilson to, 225

Food: Hoover to head committee on, 5; conferences on increased production, 14; methods for increasing supply of, transporting, 34; French, British needs, 38; Col. House advises full control for Hoover, 51; Hoover on need for conservation, distribution of, under government direction, 53; urges separate department, 57; Wilson urges immediate passage of administration bills, 61; emphasizes need for prompt action, 70; confers on control of, 73, 101, 107, 113; Hoover will head Food Administration, 77;

Sen. Reed's attacks on Food Administration, Hoover, 110, 166, 234, 435, 443; Food bill reported, 116; Wilson explains objects, importance of, 119–20; bill passes House, 126; Wilson disapproves "Conservation Sunday"; confers with senators on prohibition clause of bill, 135; Mrs. Wilson's food pledge card, 149; Wilson discusses wheat, corn crisis with Houston, Hoover, 151; trouble in prices of, in margin of profit, 154; proposals for limiting profit of first purchaser, in Food bill, 157; Wilson confers on bill, 158; disapproves substitute for, 163–4; safeguarding public against speculators, 166–7; Wilson disapproves food control *board*, 191; insists on one-man food control, 199; Senate agrees on one-man control, 208; Wilson signs bill; appoints Hoover Administrator; Hoover issues warning to those gambling with supply of; presents memo. on wheat price, 210; price of 1917 wheat to be fixed by a commission; Food Administration will take over grain elevators, mills, 213; $50,000,000 grain corporation, 217; Wilson approves patriotic spirit of grain dealers, elevator men, 220; announces price of wheat, 244; is perplexed over it, 245–6; monthly audits of Grain Corporation, 249; hog supply, 264–5; Wilson receives representatives of livestock industry, 262, 542; receives wheat growers' committee, 277, 542; appreciates work of Hoover's organization, 296; authorizes Food Administration to control manufacture, storage, importation, distribution of certain foodstuffs, 299; appeals for economy in use of, 330; danger of creating impression of shortage, 337; Wilson on wheat supply, 361–2; reduction of grain for brewing, 369; regulation of profits, 376; Senate inquiry into shortage, 406; Spreckels alleges sugar shortage "created" by Food Administration, 409; Hoover on sugar situation, 432; Wilson suggests Untermyer as counsel for Food Administration, 435; Hoover testifies before Senate committee, 443; Hoover calls for greater saving, more meat, wheat to Allies, 464; bill on price fixing, conservation of, 472; Wilson receives delegation for government control of packing industry; urges further efforts to conserve, naming meatless, wheatless days, 478; Hoover promises U. S. will export all wheat America can save, 493; Wilson warned to expect trouble, packing industry investigation, 517; Allied bread cereals shortage; Wilson, Hoover discuss, 527; Hoover alleges transportation difficulties partly responsible, 535; Wilson deplores agitation for higher wheat price legislation, 552; critical Western situation due to lack of grain cars, 558–9; Hoover blames railroad congestion, 560; suggests investigation of grain division from within, 561; Wilson fixes

1918 wheat price; issues explanatory statement, 564; Hoover promises Allies wheat, flour, though U. S. bread shortage involved, 566–7; Wilson on packing industry, 574

Ford, Cornelius: 386, 536

Ford, Henry: Wilson to, 277. Also 344

Foreign Relations of the United States: see numerous references

Forster, Rudolph: 1, 335

Fort, John Franklin: Wilson to, 140, 210. Also 117, 128, 133, 137

Fosdick, Raymond B.: Wilson to, 305, 311. Also 52, 428

Foster, John W.: 360

Foster, Congressman M. D., Ill.: 92, 443, 471, 492

Fourteen Points Address: see Peace, Discussions of

Fox, John: Wilson to, 252, 377

France (see also Army, American; Finance; Peace, Discussions of; Russia; Secret Treaties; Stockholm Conference; Unity of Control; War): Commission to U. S. from, 4, 35, 37, 38, 45; welcomes U. S. into war, 8; wants American flag at front, 46; celebrates July 4th, 145; government of, impressed with Wilson's desire for League of Nations, will convene commission to examine; desires suggestions, 176; Tardieu on excellent condition of army of, 200; disposition of French ships, 257–8; Clemenceau forms new cabinet, 355; Lloyd George says France is "done", 388; Poincaré to Wilson, 436; Wilson replies, 457; bread rations, 504

France and America, André Tardieu (Houghton Mifflin Co.): 462

France, Senator J. I., Md.: Wilson to, 545

Francis, David R., U. S. Ambassador, Russia: 11, 45, 47, 75, 76, 230, 263, 326, 336, 342, 371, 374, 381, 391, 395, 418, 420, 455, 471, 480, 515, 536, 544, 558, 562, 567

Frankfurter, Felix: 254

Franklin, P. A. S.: 109, 495, 509

Franklin-Bouillon, Henri: 244

Frayne, Hugh: 168

Frazier, A. H.: 3, 333, 510, 519, 527

Frear, Congressman J. A., Wis.: Wilson to, 131. Also 132

Frelinghuysen, Senator J. S., N. J.: Wilson to, 481. Also 418

Freyre y Santander, Manuel de, Peruvian Minister, Washington, 385

Frick, Henry C.: Wilson to, 404

Friedman, Elisha M.: 300

Fuel Administration: see Coal

Fugita, Miss Taki, translator of portions of the *Memoirs* of Viscount Kikujiru Ishii: 230, 284

Fuller, Paul: 372

Funk, Mrs. Antoinette: 172

Furuseth, Andrew: 537

Gallinger, Senator J. H., N. H.: 60, 73

Galloway, Charles M.: 148, 153

Gard, Congressman Warren, Ohio: 487

Gardener, Mrs. Helen H.: 68, 109

Gardner, F. D., Governor of Mo.: Wilson to, 435. Also 288

Garfield, H. A.: Wilson to, 15, 415, 479, 541. Also numerous other references

Garfield, Mrs. H. A.: 239

Garner, Congressman J. N., Tex.: Wilson to, 63

Garrett, Congressman D. E., Tex.: 2, 109, 207, 546

Garrett, John W., U. S. Minister to the Netherlands: 295, 310, 510, 527

Gavit, John P.: Wilson to, 511. Also 444–5

George D. Herron and the European Settlement, Mitchell P. Briggs (*Stanford University Publications, University Series, History, Economics and Political Science,* Vol. III, No. 2): 292

Gerard, James W.: Wilson to, 560

German-Americans: loyalty of, 22-3; Wilson on exemption of, from military service in Europe, 171; concerned over German-American press problems, 186; unfortunate position of large number of loyal, 201; Wilson questions wisdom of plan for sending influential, to Copenhagen to spread U. S. propaganda, 267–8

Germany (see also Peace, Discussions of; Russia; War): proclamation of war with, 2; ships of, in American ports taken into custody; policy toward, 2, 11, 31, 41, 56, 104, 138; Wilson on German music, 4, 364; prevention of food from reaching, 31; munition factories of, under martial law, 33; Col. House would treat with people of, not with existing government of, 79; Wilson's war address dropped over trenches of, 98; Wilson on responsibility of military in, for war, 110; House urges challenging, to state peace terms, 115; Wilson accused in, of changing front; Allied secret treaties alleged, 118; Michaelis becomes Chancellor, 166; belittles American intervention, 173; alleges Allied secret treaties, 198–9, 230; effect of Wilson's reply to Pope in, 286–7; mutiny in navy of, 297, 455; Von Hertling becomes Chancellor, 337; Wilson's indictment of, 350; Lansing suggests threats of after-war trade retaliation, 429; Kurt Hahn liberal, urges informal, secret negotiations, 510; strikes in, 513, 533

Dangerous Activities in the Americas: Wilson confers on, 7; malicious destruction in Springfield Arsenal, 44; alleged plan to war on U. S. after crushing France, Great Britain, 250; Luxburg telegrams ("spurlos versenkt"), 255, 264; alleged plot to get Mexico into war with U. S., 304; alleged plot to destroy American and British shipping, 472–3

Germany, Emperor Wilhelm II of: 287, 486, 572

Gerry, Senator P. G., R. I.: 57, 135, 515

Gibbons, James Cardinal: Wilson to, 298, 423
Gibbs, Philip: 47, 154, 271, 277, 291, 304, 367
Gibson, Braxton D.: Wilson to, 53
Gillett, Congressman F. H., Mass.: 60
Giornale d'Italia: 247
Glass, Congressman Carter, Va.: Wilson to, 10. Also 11, 542
Glass, Frank P.: Wilson to, 271, 348. Also 468
Gleaves, Rear-Admiral Albert: 143
Glennon, Rear-Admiral James H.: 62
Globe and Commercial Advertiser: 383
Goethals, Maj. Gen. G. W.: Wilson to, 15, 173, 187, 192. Also 22, 55, 86, 88, 92, 109, 123-4, 172, 175, 189
Goldman, Emma: 480
Goltra, Edward F.: 296, 372
Gomez, Juan Vicente: 550
Gompers, Samuel (see also *Seventy Years of Life and Labor*): Wilson to, 29, 208, 247, 486. Also numerous other references
Gonzales, W. E., U. S. Minister, Cuba: 375
Gore, Senator T. P., Okla.: 113, 209
Gorgas, Maj. Gen. W. C.: 418, 444, 498
Gould, Mrs. Howard: Wilson to, 433
Grain Corporation: see Food
Grant-Smith, Ulysses, U. S. Chargé d'Affaires, Denmark: 483
Grasset, Rear-Admiral: 432
Grayson, Rear-Admiral Cary T.: 4, 23, 35, 37, 38, 44, 64, 66, 121, 140, 167, 207, 229, 270, 347, 349, 354, 398, 424, 427, 451, 536
Grayson, Mrs. Cary T.: 66, 140, 207, 287
Great Britain (see also Army, American; Finance; Peace, Discussions of; Russia; Secret Treaties; Stockholm Conference; Unity of Control; War): welcomes U. S. into war, 8, 24, 31; Wilson's confidential message to Lloyd George urging self-government for Ireland; food situation in, critical, meatless days, 14, 35; Wilson favors discussion with, on protection of Mexican oil wells, 26-7; receives Labor Commissioners of, 57, 71; government of, proposes sending Northcliffe to U. S.; Spring Rice, Balfour, Wilson disapprove, 95-6; pacifists in, 96, 224; secret communication system between Wilson, Balfour, 97; Northcliffe's appointment announced; errand purely commercial; advised by Wiseman, 102, 104, 108; Wilson receives Northcliffe, 116; Sargent's portrait of Wilson for National Gallery, Ireland, 122, 172, 302, 310, 403-4, 525; Wilson criticizes British use of navy, 140; receives leaders of Irish Parliamentary Party, 148; proposed naval agreement between, and U. S., 152, 161, 266; British critics of previous year now praising Wilson, 217; government of, hopes U. S. will not take ownership of British ships building in U. S. yards, 228; Parliamentary Commercial Committee of, wishes similar committee in U. S.; Wilson disapproves, 233-4; Pershing

thinks morale of, lower, 270; Wilson on Barnard statue of Lincoln for England, 327, 345-6, 353; Balfour statement, national home for Jews in Palestine, 336-7; Pershing says U. S. and, may have to carry on war, 357-8; Wilson suggests Gompers might influence Henderson in British labor's fight on Lloyd George, 385-8; British man power "pretty well exhausted", 388; Wilson's call for war with Austria-Hungary considered in, his most important utterance, 391; Wilson refuses to receive a delegation on the Irish question, 405; opposes speaking mission to England, 407, 473; Lloyd George greets U. S.; Wilson replies, 445; Reading to be ambassador from; presents credentials, 447, 542; Wilson receives Canadian Governor General, 458; addresses committee to present replica of Robert Emmet statue, 462; meatless days, 488; Hoover promises U. S. will export all wheat America can save, 493; Labor Mission from, 536; death of Spring Rice, 546, 547; Wilson receives Canadian Premier, 568
    Balfour Commission: Wilson recognizes dangers of, but says will be welcome, 2, 3; commission arrives; received by Wilson; Balfour says no alliance proposed; White House dinner for; reception in honor of, 32-4; methods of conferring with, 35; British needs as presented by, 38; Balfour dines at White House, 43-4; Commission leaves U. S., 85
Greathouse, C. A.: Wilson to, 534
Greece: question of, discussed at St. Jean de Maurienne, 25; King Constantine of, abdicates under pressure from England, France, Russia; Alexander I succeeds, 108; blockade of, raised, purpose of Entente Powers to safeguard freedom of, announced, 114; severs diplomatic relations with Central Powers, 136; Wilson receives new minister from, to present credentials, 280
Green, Theodore F.: 544
Green, Congressman W. R., Iowa: 60
Gregory, T. W., Attorney General: Wilson to, 159, 195, 224, 244, 282, 283, 314, 333, 457, 473, 501, 543. Also numerous other references
Grew, J. C., U. S. Counselor of Embassy, Berlin: 338
Grey, Sir Edward (later Viscount, of Falloden): 75
Griffith, David L. W.: 320
Griswold, Miss Florence: 267
Grotius, Hugo: 216
Grow, M. C.: 69
Grubb, Mrs. Burd: 387
Guatemala: 38, 282
Guchkov, Alexander, I.: 47
Guffey, Joseph F.: 171
Guggenheim, Daniel: 69
Gulick, Sidney L.: Wilson to, 524

Gwynn, Stephen: see *Letters and Friendships of Sir Cecil Spring Rice, The*

Hadley, Arthur T.: 107
Hagedorn, Hermann: see *Leonard Wood*
Hahn, Kurt: 510, 527
Haig, Field Marshal Sir Douglas: 17, 210, 510
Haiti: 117
Hale, E. J., U. S. Minister, Costa Rica: 104
Hale, Matthew: Wilson to, 289, 544. Also 262, 288, 317
Hale, William B.: 335
Halifax Disaster: 395
Hall, H. C.: Wilson to, 194. Also 53, 394
Hampton, William J.: Wilson to, 269
Hankey, Sir Maurice: 381
Hanson, Ole: 78
Harbord, Maj. Gen. James G.: 88
Harden, Maximilian: 63, 267
Harding, Elisabeth: 166
Harding, W. P. G.: Wilson to, 300, 308, 406. Also 46, 166
Hardwick, Senator T. W., Ga.: 112–13, 154, 390
Harper, George M.: Wilson to, 423
Harper, Samuel N.: 18
Harriman, J. W.: Wilson to, 264, 273, 302, 352, 487
Harrington, Emerson C., Governor of Md.: 34
Harris, William J.: 43, 158
Harrison, Fairfax: 401, 407
Harrison, F. B., Governor General, Philippines: 128, 228
Harrison, Congressman Pat, Miss.: 566
Harrison, William H.: 360
Harts, Col. William W.: 274
Harvey, George B. M.: 84
Haskins, Charles H.: Wilson to, 514
Haugen, Congressman G. N., Iowa: 61
Haven, William I.: 184
Hawes, T. S.: Wilson to, 259
Hawkins, J. C.: Wilson to, 175
Hayden, Congressman Carl, Ariz.: 427
Hayes, Frank J.: Wilson to, 458
Hazleton, Richard: 148
Hearings Before the Special Committee Investigating the Munitions Industry, United States Senate, 74th Congress, 2nd session, Part 29 (Government document): 168, 212, 227
Hearst, William R.: 100, 291, 346, 424, 556, 562
Heflin, Congressman J. T., Ala.: Wilson to, 76, 82, 109
Helm, Mrs. James M.: see Benham, Edith
Helvering, Congressman Guy T., Kan.: Wilson to, 30. Also 67
Henderson, Arthur: 385–6
Hendrick, Burton J.: see *Life and Letters of Walter H. Page, The*
Henry White, Allan Nevins (Harper & Bros.): 224
Hernandez, José C.: 339
Herron, George D. (see also *George D. Herron*

and the European Settlement): 288, 292, 547, 570
Hertling, Count Georg F. von, German Chancellor, from November 3, 1917: 337, 497, 505, 510, 519, 536, 537, 540, 554, 566, 570
Hibben, J. G.: Wilson to, 467. Also 225
Higginson, Henry Lee: Wilson to, 325
Hillquit, Morris: 84, 333, 419
Hindenburg, Field Marshal von (see also *Out Of My Life*): 367
Hines, Walker D.: 438
History of the Great War, A, C. R. M. F. Cruttwell (Oxford University Press): 3
Hitchcock, Senator G. M., Neb.: Wilson to, 78. Also 60, 307, 434, 465, 521
Hitchcock, Ripley: 568
Hobby, W. P., Governor of Tex.: 385
Hobson, John A.: 91
Hoffstot, Frank N.: 116
Hog Island: see Ships
Holcomb, M. H., Governor of Conn.: 322
Holden, Hale: Wilson to, 440. Also 407, 438
Hollis, Senator H. F., N. H.: Wilson to, 214. Also 113, 122, 224, 484, 560
Holt, Hamilton: Wilson to, 571
Honduras: 72
Hooker, Richard: 505
Hoover, Herbert: Wilson to, 220, 234, 264, 369, 376, 403, 435, 493–4, 523, 557, 561. Also numerous other references
Hoover, Irwin H.: 1, 33, 425
Hope, Walter E.: 375
Hopkins, John A. H.: 67
House, Col. Edward M. (see also *Intimate Papers of Colonel House, The*): Wilson to, 3, 55, 95, 96, 114, 180, 218, 231, 253, 275, 282, 296, 305, 307, 331, 361, 365, 387, 389, 412, 513, 567. Also numerous other references
House, Mrs. Edward M.: 265, 266, 267, 432
House Mission, 1917: see Allied War Conference; Supreme War Council
Houston, David F., Secretary of Agriculture (see also *Eight Years with Wilson's Cabinet*): Wilson to, 325. Also 2, 17, 51, 61, 70, 151, 166, 265, 328, 385, 408, 509, 523
Hovelaque, Emile: 46
How We Advertised America, George Creel (Harper & Bros.): 21, 61, 143, 455
Howard, Roy W.: Wilson to, 473–4. Also 262
Howard, Congressman W. S., Ga.: 155
Howe, George, nephew of Woodrow Wilson: 8
Hoyt, Florence S.: 8, 76, 98
Hoyt, Mary E.: 8
Hsu, Shih-Chang: 98
Hughes, Charles E.: 16, 402
Hughes, Senator William, N. J.: Wilson to, 148, 276. Also 22
Hulbert, Congressman Murray, N. Y.: 135
Hull, Congressman Cordell, Tenn.: 226
Humphreys, Congressman B. G., Miss.: 277
Hunt, G. W., Governor of Ariz.: Wilson to, 142

Huntington, Howard: Wilson to, 554. Also 412

Hurley, E. N. (see also *Bridge to France, The*): Wilson to, 230, 243, 473, 494–5, 540. Also 187, 192, 193, 196, 199, 233, 257, 271, 281, 285, 309, 311, 415, 419, 425, 527, 541, 543, 545, 560

Husting, Senator Paul O., Wis.: Wilson to, 50. Also 16, 85, 104, 143, 166, 216

Hutcheson, W. L.: Wilson to, 550–1

Hutchins, of National Bank of Commerce: 320, 323

Hutchison, M. R.: 226

Hylan, John F., Mayor, New York: 334, 546

Imports: see Trade, Foreign

Industrial America in the World War, Grosvenor B. Clarkson (Houghton Mifflin Co.): 14, 197

Ingraham, W. M., Assistant Secretary of War: 312

Inquiry: see Peace, Discussions of

Inter-Allied Council on War Purchases and Finance; project for, 64–5; Wilson favors, 162–3; McAdoo proposes Council in Europe, Purchasing Commission in U. S., 171; Purchasing Commission created, headquarters in Washington, 233; Allied governments accept proposal for Council in Europe; urge U. S. government be represented, 247; U. S. representative will be sent, in "consultative capacity", 309; Crosby named, 341; Italy's failure to buy through Purchasing Commission, 373; Council organized; Crosby president, 308; McAdoo, Baker agree there should be War Department representative on; McAdoo instructs Bliss to confer with Crosby, 455; Wilson reproves McAdoo, 459–60; McAdoo urges need for Food Administration representative on, 493–4; Wilson on relation of, to Supreme War Council, 538; Council makes political recommendation as to Russia, 545; Wilson objects to political pronouncements on part of, 548–9; objects to Crosby's participation in political matters, 559–60

Inter-Allied Parliamentary Union: 244

Inter-Allied Reserve: see Supreme War Council

Inter-Allied Shipping Board: see Ships

Interstate Commerce Commission: Wilson discusses enlargement of, 94; asks, to investigate production of railway rolling stock, motive power, 194; opposes turning priority of shipments on railroads over to, since already "overburdened", 214; statement by, that railroad rates should be increased, would help Liberty Loan, 315; Commission cannot go so far, but will make some statement, 316; proposed statement disproving business pessimism, 321; Wilson hopes Commission is concerned with efficiency of railroads, 325–6; receives

members of, to discuss railroad situation, 394

Intimate Papers of Colonel House, The, edited by Charles Seymour (Houghton Mifflin Co.): see numerous references

Ireland: see Great Britain

Irigoyen, Hipolito, President of Argentina: 343

Irvine, W. M.: 340

Irvine, Mrs. W. M.: Wilson to, 340

Irwin, Inez H.: see *Story of the Woman's Party, The*

Irwin, William H. (see also *Propaganda and the News*): 21

Ishii, Viscount Kikujiro (see also *Memoirs*): 230, 262, 263, 282, 284, 329, 336, 339, 341, 351, 361

Italy (see also Finance; Peace, Discussions of; Secret Treaties; Unity of Control; War): welcomes America into war, 8; Commission to U. S. from, 83, 85, 89, 120, 133; need of, for coal, 94, 427; Wilson receives degree from Royal University of Bologna, 265; Wilson's influence in, 283; need of, for grain, 311; U. S. ambassador suggests situation in, would be improved by U. S. declaration of war with Austria, 330; situation of, desperate, 354; message of encouragement to, 357; Wilson's address on war with Austria-Hungary approved in, 391; feeling in, that U. S. is becoming "too potent"; Wilson uneasy about, 513; Baker to visit, 562

Italy, King Victor Emmanuel of: 265

I. W. W.: see Labor

Jackson, Andrew: 49

Jacobus, M. W.: Wilson to, 7

Jacoway, Congressman H. M., Ark.: 408

James Bryce, H. A. L. Fisher (Macmillan Co.): 425

James, Senator Ollie M., Ky.: Wilson to, 502, 555. Also 60, 89, 251, 277, 442, 504, 515

James, William: 275

Janeway, Frank Latimer: 533

Japan (see also Russia; Secret Treaties): Wilson asks report on activities of, in China, 25; message to "made-in-Japan" banquet, 38; Morris named ambassador to, 78; film, "Patria," unfair to, 100; government of, thinks U. S. interfering in domestic affairs of China, 107; wishes Bryan's March, 1915, statement confirmed, 114; U. S. does not approve *political* influence of, over China, 144; does not fear Pacific Coast attack from, 162; Commission to U. S. from, received by Wilson, who says U. S. chiefly interested in Open Door, equal opportunity in China; White House dinner in honor of, 230; reception for, 241; first of 13 Lansing-Ishii conferences, 262–3; Wilson receives Morris, 281; confers with Ishii, 282, 284; suggests negotiating with government of, to improve cable, radio communication with Asia, 298;

receives commercial commission from, 313–14; thinks would be mistake for British, French governments to request Japan send troops to Western Front in spring, summer, 1918, 322–3; tenth Lansing-Ishii conference; Ishii submits secret protocol; Lansing agrees, with "verbal changes", 329–30; last Lansing-Ishii conference; agreement as to desires, intentions shared by U. S., Japan, in China; no mention of secret protocol, 336; American minister in China embarrassed by lack of information about agreement; is informed by Lansing, 338–40; agreement made public, 341; Pershing urges development of artillery, ammunition supply sources, with Japan's resources in mind, 359; press, public of, on Lansing-Ishii agreement, 361; will not depart from engagements unless treated as "outside the pale"; fears German control of Russia, 436

Jefferson, Thomas: 265, 266

Jellico, Admiral Sir John R.: 44

Jews: none appointed to Root Commission because of bitterness in Russia toward, 62; Wilson confers on serious situation of, in Palestine; plans for American Congress of, 135; Cecil asks Wilson's view on declaration of sympathy with Zionist movement, 256; Wilson concurs in British formula, 305; Balfour's statement on national home for, in Palestine; Cecil hopes U. S. will be protecting power, 336–7; Wilson receives committee on plans for aiding Polish, Lithuanian Jews, 356; endorses Jewish War Relief campaign, 371; rejoicing among, as British occupy Jerusalem, 402; Wilson receives committee from American Union of Rumanian Jews, 405; petition to abolish restrictions on, in Rumania, 434

Joffre, Madame: 37

Joffre, Marshal Joseph: 35, 37, 46, 48, 333, 501

Johns, George S.: Wilson to, 36, 492

Johnson, Congressman Ben, Ky.: 236

Johnson, Charles F.: 276

Johnson, Senator E. S., S. D.: 46, 117, 154, 566

Jones, Senator A. A., N. M.: 153, 187, 515, 521

Jones, David B.: Wilson to, 398

Jones, E. Lester: 144

Jones, Richard L.: 22

Jones, Rufus M.: Wilson to, 241

Jones, Thomas D.: Wilson to, 154, 193, 196, 433. Also 336, 356, 358, 362, 363, 365, 372, 378, 397, 398

Jowett, Frederick W.: 91

Judson, Gen. W. V.: 373

Jusserand, J. J., French Ambassador, Washington: 17, 43, 52, 67, 79, 153, 166, 171, 176, 203, 244, 254, 290, 322, 391, 418, 432, 436, 456, 493, 513, 527, 540, 561, 569, 572

Kahn, Alexander: 149, 356

Kahn, Congressman Julius, Cal.: 60, 113, 484

Kahn, Otto H.: 4, 344

Kaledine, Gen. Alexis M.: 367

Kansas City Star: 418

Kaye, Lady Lester: 46

Keating, Congressman Edward, Cal.: 196

Keller, Kent E.: 200, 355

Kellogg, Senator F. B., Minn.: 61, 112, 216, 242, 427

Kelly, Congressman M. Clyde, Pa.: 113

Kelly, R. Lincoln: 384

Kelsey, Albert: Wilson to, 110

Kendrick, Senator J. B., Wyo.: 16, 104, 122

Kenley, J. R.: Wilson to, 374, 378, 384

Kennerley, Mitchell: Wilson to, 288

Kent, Sir Stevenson H.: 351

Kent, William: Wilson to, 170, 517, 574. Also 200, 210, 216, 408

Kenyon, Senator W. S., Iowa: 133

Kerensky, A. F.: Wilson to, 234. Also 139, 177, 236, 342

Kern, A. E.: 314

Kern, John W.: 70, 243

Kern, Mrs. John W.: 241

Kerwin, James C.: 404

Kettner, Congressman William, Cal.: 94

Kilpatrick, Major: 558

Kincaid, Earle H.: 434

King, Congressman E. J., Ill.: Wilson to, 202

King, Stanley, 446

King, Senator W. H., Utah: 16, 60, 101, 140, 217, 307, 462, 515

Kirkwood, Robert O.: 515

Kitchener, Lord H. E. C.: 72

Kitchin, Congressman Claude, N. C.; Wilson to, 13. Also 14, 200, 484

Klaw, Marc: 311, 475

Knox, Senator P. C., Pa.: 60, 73, 220, 221

Koltchak, Admiral A. V.: 309

Koo, V. K. W., Chinese Minister, Washington: 351

Kruttschnitt, Julius: 407

Kuhlmann, Richard von, German Secretary of State for Foreign Affairs from August 5, 1917: 292, 297

Labor: representation of, on Root Commission, 28–9, 62; standards of, during war, 52; Wilson receives British Labor Commissioners, 57, 71; addresses labor committee of Advisory Commission, Council of National Defense, 69; advises retention of laws safeguarding, during war, 100; receives committee representing organized, who urge food legislation, retention of half holidays in wartime, 107; Wilson urges co-operation of Alabama coal operators, miners in emergency, 111–12; Baker, Gompers agree on creation of adjustment commission, 120; Wilson receives Railroad Brotherhood representatives, 122, 370–1, 407, 430–2; asks Governor of Arizona to mediate between copper miners, operators, 142; strikes; men out at Remington Arms, 158; I. W. W. deportations, Arizona, 160–1,

Labor—*Continued*

242–3; Wilson watches labor situation with anxiety, 190; United Mine Workers of America ask help in arranging conference with Alabama coal operators, 206; Wilson confers with Covington on labor situation in California, 206–7, 262; resents harsh message from Arizona State Federation of, 208–9; government shipyard mechanics around New York strike, 224; Shipbuilding Labor Adjustment (Macy) Board created, 227; Wilson requests Georgia, Florida & Alabama Railroad accept mediation, 242–3, 244, 259–60; confers on situation in West, 244, 271; message to Gompers, 247–9; American Alliance for Labor and Democracy approves Wilson's war aims, 263; walkouts in San Francisco shipbuilding plants; Wilson approves labor representatives on industrial boards during war, 272; commission to investigate conditions of, in West, 277, 284; urges co-operation of West Coast leaders, 280–1; hopes investigation of Mooney case will soften labor troubles, 282; Baker suggests Wilson urge labor not to make "inelastic ultimatum", 316; Mediation, Conciliation Board tries for railroad agreement; Wilson threatens to take over roads rather than permit interruption of traffic, 327–8; receives Housing Committee, 334; addresses A. F. of L. convention; many threatened strikes called off as result, 350, 354; Kent memo. on U. S. labor situation, 351–2; A. F. of L. convention pledges support to Wilson, 374; Wilson asks Atlantic Coast Line Railroad to reinstate returning clerks, 374, 378, 384–5; suggests Gompers might influence Henderson in British labor's fight on Lloyd George, 385–6; street railway strike at Minneapolis, St. Paul, 399, 404; labor situation in shipyards favorable, 415; safeguards for labor of women, children, 422; Secy. Wilson, War Labor Administrator, 451; Pres. Wilson receives committee of National Women's Trade Union League, 456; sends message to United Mine Workers of America, 458; asks Sen. Bankhead's help in Alabama coal mining situation; fears must take over mines, if owners do not accept settlement, 465; requests postponement of execution of Mooney's sentence, 488–9; British Labor Mission in New York, 536; shipyard strikes, 540; Hurley calls on shipyard carpenters to resume work; Secy. Wilson appeals for volunteers; Shipping Board threatens to commandeer badly managed yards; Pres. Wilson opposes compulsory labor, 545–6; notifies striking ship carpenters of duty to return at once, 550–1; Inter-Allied Labor, Socialist conference meets, London; memo. on war aims, 558

Lafayette, the Marquis de: Wilson to, 17

Lafayette Escadrille: see War

La Follette, Senator R. M., Wis.: 213, 296, 390, 492

La Guardia, Congressman F. H., N. Y.: 127–8

Lammasch, Heinrich: 547, 570

Lamont, Thomas W.: Wilson to, 466, 514

Lane, Anne Wintermute: see *Letters of Franklin K. Lane, The*

Lane, Franklin K., Secretary of the Interior: (see also *Letters of Franklin K. Lane, The*): Wilson to, 197, 438–9. Also 4, 24, 46, 119, 126, 133, 138, 140, 408, 552

Lanier, Charles D.: 92

Lansdowne, Lord: 379, 383

Lansing-Ishii Conferences: see Japan; China

Lansing, Robert, Secretary of State (see also *War Memoirs of Robert Lansing*): Wilson to, 12, 16, 17, 25, 26, 27, 28, 32, 47, 54, 55, 58, 61, 65, 86, 89, 90, 95, 144, 215, 233, 257, 282, 298, 322, 324, 335, 342, 343, 376, 379, 380, 477, 483, 506, 542, 548, 550, 561. Also numerous other references

Lansing, Mrs. Robert: 125

Latin America: Lansing announces all republics of, except Mexico, Chile, Argentina, have supported U. S. stand, 40; Wilson on relations between U. S. and, 413–14; thinks participation of U. S. in war has strengthened bond between democracies of; approves efforts toward better news interchange between North, South America, 473–4

Lauder, Harry: 425

Law, Andrew Bonar: 133, 176, 267, 366, 383

Lawrence, David (see also *True Story of Woodrow Wilson, The*): Wilson to, 86, 293, 508. Also 187, 294

Lawrence, F. W. Pethick: 91

Lazaro, Congressman Ladislas, La.: 277

League for National Unity: 295–6, 298, 525–6

League of Nations: Bryce committee plan for, published, 52; Wilson thinks League to Enforce Peace activities unwise, but concurs in general idea, 53; French Chamber of Deputies adopts resolution favoring, 101; D. J. Lewis's plan for a, based on U. S. constitution; Wilson thinks too much to hope for, but agrees with general purposes, 155; French government impressed with Wilson's desire for, will convene commission on, desires suggestions, 176; Wilson fears commission premature, might turn up differences of view; thinks league matter of evolution, 203; Cecil suggests U. S., English commissions examine prevention-of-war schemes, 255; Lloyd George says military caste must not represent Germany in, 422; Bryce suggests international committee to prepare joint plan for, 424–5; Crosby on maintenance of peace without competitive armament, 427–8; Hertling, Czernin, sympathetic with idea of, 497; Wilson tells Italian ambassador league will make strategic considerations less important, 506–7; Phillimore Committee formed, Cecil suggests co-operation with Inquiry, 548

Le Clerque, General: 375

Lee, Blair: Wilson to, 232

Lee, Congressman Gordon, Ga.: 484

Leffingwell, R. C., Assistant Secretary of the Treasury: 412

Lenin, Nikolai: 47, 168, 341, 342, 381, 405, 459, 469, 536

Lenin, Red Dictator, George Vernadsky (Yale University Press): 341, 342, 480, 552

Lenroot, Congressman I. L., Wis.: 23, 60

Leonard Wood, Hermann Hagedorn (Harper & Bros.): 72

Letters and Friendships of Sir Cecil Spring Rice, The, edited by Stephen Gwynn (Constable & Co.): 143, 449

Letters of Franklin K. Lane, The, edited by Anne Wintermute Lane and Louise Herrick Wall (Houghton Mifflin Co.): 46

Leslie, Shane: 462

Lever, Congressman A. F., S. C.: Wilson to, 185. Also 14, 61, 70, 102, 110, 116, 199, 209, 290, 484, 552

Levy, Samuel D.: 71

Lewis, David J.: 155

Lewis, Senator J. H., Ill.: Wilson to, 106. Also 126, 135, 207, 288, 350, 415, 419, 458

Libbey, William: 277

Liberia: 57, 206

Liberty Loans: McAdoo announces 1st, 46; early subscriptions pour in, 51; Wilson will reserve fire for later issues, 84; approves suggestion that factory workmen campaign among themselves for, 90; invests $10,000 in, 93, 119; J. P. Morgan & Co. subscribe $50,000,000, 105; campaign for 1st Loan closes, with oversubscription, 113; Wilson receives 2nd Liberty Loan Committee; Woman's Liberty Loan Conference; new Loan announced, 284; Wilson thinks address in behalf of, may be more needed later, 299; proclaims Liberty Day, 304; feels unwise to himself address "lukewarm" New York in behalf of; country banks taking insufficient interest, 307–8; Wilson refuses statement in behalf of, for use in army, 312; thinks Interstate Commerce Commission statement that railroad rates should be increased would help Loan, 315, 316; invests $13,500 in; his appeals to mayors of 28 cities in behalf of, dropped by airplanes, 316; Mrs. Wilson attends lighting of first bonfire in celebration of, 320; 2nd Loan "overwhelming success", 328; Wilson consults Gregory on "outrageous utterances" about, 333

Liberty Motor: see Air Force, American

Life and Letters of Walter H. Page, The, Burton J. Hendrick (Doubleday, Page & Co.): 13, 40, 86, 124, 133, 138, 247, 407

Lincoln, Abraham: 43, 185, 246, 266, 327, 345, 353, 383, 543, 571

Lincoln, Charles M.: 247

Lincoln, Robert Todd: 327

Lind, John: 404–5

Lindley, Curtis H.: 435

Lindsey, Benjamin B.: 408

Lippmann, Walter: 33, 275, 383

Lister, Ernest, Governor of Wash.: 57

Literary Digest: 8, 273, 305

Littlepage, Congressman A. B., W. Va.: 140, 161, 191, 295, 555

Litvinov, Bolshevik agent, London, 459

Lloyd George, David, British Prime Minister (see also *War Memoirs of David Lloyd George*): Wilson to, 445. Also 8, 12, 16, 24, 25, 123, 134, 136, 179, 214, 271, 277, 278–9, 291, 292, 297, 317, 351, 355, 357, 361, 364–5, 366, 369–70, 372, 379, 382, 385, 388, 409, 415, 422, 452, 453, 455, 456, 475, 488, 497, 500, 509, 510, 527, 529, 535, 540, 549, 561

Lockhart, Robert H. B.: 459

Lodge, Senator H. C., Mass. (see also *Senate and the League of Nations, The*): 60, 70, 73, 220, 221, 486

London *Daily Chronicle*, 67; *Daily Mail*, 366; *Daily News*, 379; *Daily Telegraph*, 379; *Morning Post*, 355–6; *Times*, 8, 314, 364–5, 456

London, Treaty of: see Secret Treaties

Long, Breckinridge, Third Assistant Secretary of State: Wilson to, 56, 367–8, 420. Also 154, 458, 463

Longino, Andrew H.: 227

Longworth, Congressman Nicholas, Ohio: 493

Love, Thomas B.: 105

Lovett, R. S.: Wilson to, 225, 335, 416, 486. Also 197, 217, 226, 227, 233, 324

Lowrie, Walter: Wilson to, 283. Also 560

Ludendorff's Own Story, Erich von Ludendorff (Harper & Bros.): 200, 317–18

Lunn, Congressman G. R., N. Y.: 388, 464

Luxburg, Count, German Chargé, Buenos Aires: 255, 264

Macchi di Cellere, Count V., Italian Ambassador, Washington: 171, 373, 484, 492, 507, 562

Macchi di Cellere, Countess: 492

MacDonald, J. Ramsay: 91, 195, 224

Macfarland, Charles S.: 262

MacFarland, G. S.: Wilson to, 313, 556. Also 346, 408, 541

Mack, Julian W.: 356

Mackaye, Percy: 284

Macmillan, Sam: 312

Macmillen, Francis: 284

MacRae, Hugh: 24

Macy, V. Everit: 227, 281

Madden, Congressman M. B., Ill.: 10, 290

Malone, Dudley Field: Wilson to, 268. Also 35, 140, 168

Manchester Guardian: 379, 408

Mann, Congressman James R., Ill.: 23

Manufacturers Record: 292

Marburg, Theodore: 69
March, Gen. Peyton C.: see *Nation at War, The*
Marsh, Wilbur: 471
Marshall, Louis: 356
Marshall, Thomas R., Vice President of the United States: 1, 79, 544
Martin, Senator T. S., Va.: Wilson to, 163, 552. Also 46, 53, 60, 99, 113, 135, 137, 158, 199, 220, 251, 378, 408, 484
Martinez, Edmundo E.: 171
Masses, The: 165
Matthews, M. A.: 126
Maurice, Maj. Gen. Sir Frederick: 510
Maury, the Misses, nieces of Mrs. Wilson: 432
Mayo, Rear-Admiral H. T.: 217, 314
McAdoo, Mary Synon (Bobbs-Merrill Co.): 127, 394
McAdoo, William G., Secretary of the Treasury (see also *McAdoo*, by Mary Synon; *Crowded Years*): Wilson to, 90, 93, 119, 126, 127, 134, 359, 373, 427, 431–2, 438, 459, 472, 538, 556, 558, 559, 562, 568, 574. Also numerous other references
McAdoo, Mrs. William G. (Eleanor Randolph Wilson), daughter of Woodrow Wilson: 8, 61, 125, 186, 195, 209, 238, 241, 242, 287, 294, 356, 425, 452, 554
McAllister, F. W.: Wilson to, 232
McAneny, George: 566
McCall, S. W., Governor of Mass.: 290, 346
McCormick, Cyrus H.: Wilson to, 39, 507. Also 18, 28, 62, 244, 274, 291
McCormick, Congressman Medill: 267, 488
McCormick, Robert R.: 33
McCormick, Vance C.: Wilson to, 78, 141, 311, 539. Also numerous other references
McCumber, Senator P. J., N. D.: 242, 496
McDowell, W. F.: Wilson to, 102, 428
McEwan, W. L.: Wilson to, 73, 260
McGoodwin, Preston, U. S. Minister, Venezuela: 550
McIlhenny, John A.: 79
McKellar, Senator K. D., Tenn.: Wilson to, 150, 164. Also 83, 92, 226
McKelway, A. J.: Wilson to, 422
McKnight, R. J. G.: 148
McLaughlin, Congressman J. C., Mich.: 484
McLean, E. B.: Wilson to, 160, 167. Also 400
McNab, Gavin: 119, 191
McNally, James C.: 537
McNary, Senator Charles L., Ore.: 236
McRoberts, Samuel: 499
Meeker, Congressman J. E., Mo.: 23, 471
Meeker, Royal: 202
Meiklejohn, Alexander: Wilson to, 229
Memoirs, Viscount Kikujiro Ishii: 230, 284
Mensdorff, Count: 382, 443
Mexico: Wilson says U. S. has interests of, at heart; insists on proper treatment of U. S. citizens, 23; danger of pro-German party in, demanding withdrawal of U. S. oil well protection; Wilson on; Mexican government "does not contemplate" embargo on oil, 25–7; Joint Commission report; Carranza's

election to presidency declared official in Mexico, 38; laborers crossing border to escape draft, 90–1, 93; distortions of facts about, 160; Martinez of, brings message from Carranza, 171; alleged German plot to get, into war with U. S., 304
Meyer, Balthasar H.: 394
Meyer, Eugene, Jr.: 28, 39, 62
Mezes, S. E.: Wilson to, 352. Also 124, 275, 328, 356
Michaelis, Georg, German Chancellor, July 14 to November 2, 1917: 166, 173, 179, 198, 228, 230, 285, 297, 337
Michaïlovitch, Lioubomir, Serbian Minister, Washington: 179
Milner, Sir Alfred: 346
Milwaukee Journal, 170, 317; *Leader*, 312–13
Milyukov, Paul N.: 47
Mitchel, John Purroy: 178, 333, 528
Mitchell, Charles W.: 439, 440, 447
Mitchell, Mrs. Charles W.: Wilson to, 439. Also 440
Mittags Zeitung: 456
Moncheur, Baron: 213
Mongolia: 24
Monroe Doctrine: 5–6, 26–7, 413
Montague, Congressman A. J., Va.: 471
Mooney, T. J.: 65, 66, 282, 480, 488–9, 490–1
Moore, F. G.: Wilson to, 504
Morel, Edmund D.: 91
Morgan, J. P.: Wilson to, 6. Also 105, 158, 499, 514
Morgenthau, Henry: Wilson to, 312. Also 89, 107, 274, 356
Moriarity, J. D.: Wilson to, 115
Morris, Ira N., U. S. Minister, Sweden: 295, 310, 342, 382
Morris, Roland S., U. S. Ambassador, Japan: 18, 99, 281, 340, 361, 482
Morrison, Frank: 478
Morrison, H. S.: Wilson to, 376–7. Also 313, 479
Moser, Charles K., U. S. Consul, Harbin: 436
Moton, Robert R.: 246
Motono, Viscount Ichiro: 129, 418, 482, 569
Mott, John R.: 18, 28, 31, 35, 39, 61, 208, 244, 282, 475, 511
Mott, Lieut. Col. T. Bentley: 233
Moving Pictures: 100, 134–5, 305, 311
Munitions: first government-owned armorplate, projectile plant, 244; problem of alien enemies in factories making, 338; Pershing urges development of sources of supply, 359; Sen. Chamberlain favors creation of department of, 434; introduces bill to create, 451; Wilson disapproves, 464, 465–6, 515; bill providing for Director of, introduced in Senate, 479
Munroe, James P.: 51
Murdock, Victor: 326
Muscle Shoals Dam: 404
My Experiences in the World War, John J. Pershing (Frederick A. Stokes Co.): see numerous references

Myers, Senator H. L., Mont.: 140, 241, 307, 462, 484

Nansen, Fridtjof: 201, 356, 365
Naón, Rómulo S., Argentine Ambassador, Washington: 83, 89
Nation at War, The, Gen. Peyton C. March (Doubleday, Doran & Company): 88
National Guard: see Army, American
Naval Investigation Hearings (Government document): see numerous references
Navy, American (see also North Sea, Project for Barring; Ships): Admirals of, confer with British, French, on co-operation, 11; Sims outlines U. S. help needed, 21; *Mongolia* fires first U. S. gun of war, 24; aid for dependents of men in, 28, 127, 252–3, 294; Sims wants all available destroyers; destroyers sail for Queenstown, 34, 51; Walter Page urges more ships, 40; Sims, Vice-Admiral commanding U. S. destroyers operating from British bases, 88; Sims reports operations in European waters very satisfactory, 94; religious activities, 102, 184, 252, 482; Wilson on establishment of naval base, training station at Hampton Roads, 108; Sims asks all possible anti-submarine craft, 121–2; Daniels will send all possible, 126; Sims, Page, urge more anti-submarine craft before too late, 130; Balfour asks more ships; instructions governing maritime warfare, 138; British Embassy, Washington, urges more small fighting craft, 139; Wilson criticizes British naval policy, urging boldness, 140; Sims suggests steps against submarines; Daniels says everything suggested being done, except sending dreadnaughts; question of trawlers for this side of Atlantic; paramount duty of, to protect transports, 197; first U. S. man-of-war for escort duty arrives Gibraltar, 207; Wilson addresses officers of Atlantic Fleet, 211–12; first U. S. vessel lost in European waters, 296; construction program made public, 297; Wilson disapproves wartime benefit games between Army and, 321, 344; House of Representatives orders investigation into Navy Dept.'s conduct of war, 409; Daniels proud of, 420; telegraphs Sims that House committee wants any complaints against Department, 425–6; Sims deprecates criticisms but says still hampered by insufficient ships, 426–7; *Brooklyn* ordered to Yokohama, 443; chairman, House committee, reports "phenomenal" progress in warship construction, 472
Navy and the Nation, The, Josephus Daniels (George H. Doran Co.): 34
Negroes: Wilson informed few of, support administration fully, 29; race riots, East St. Louis, 140; Federal government will do all possible to check outrages, 145; investigation being made, 198; Wilson considers making statement on mob violence, 202; troops to be separately trained, 267; Wilson receives committee from National Assn. for Advancement of Colored People, 555
Nelson, Senator Knute, Minn.: Wilson to, 405. Also 61, 83, 91, 216, 242, 537
Netherlands: 24, 540–1, 555
Nevins, Allan: see *Henry White*
New Republic: 33, 275, 318, 383, 546
New South Wales: 280
New York *Evening Post*, 444, 496–7; *Evening Sun*, 321; *Globe and Commercial Advertiser*, 383; *Journal of Commerce*, 149; *Times*, see numerous references; *Tribune*, 291, 456, 481–2; *World*, 84, 98, 130, 180–1, 236, 246–7, 484, 486, 530, 546
Newlands, Senator F. G., Nev.: Wilson to, 308, 416. Also 67, 68, 70, 94, 112, 122, 194, 200, 209, 283, 290, 327, 401, 422, 432
Newman, O. P.: Wilson to, 237. Also 43, 217
Newman, William T.: 208
Newton D. Baker, Frederick Palmer (Dodd, Mead & Co.): see numerous references
Newton, James T.: 285
Nicaragua: 75
Nieman, L. W.: 170, 196, 317
Nitrates: 2, 46, 325
Nivelle, General R. G.: 22, 25
Norddeutsche Allgemeine Zeitung: 117–18
Nordvall, Axel R.: 89
Norris, G. W.: 169
North Sea, Project for Barring: Bureau of Ordnance plan, 21; Daniels, Wilson approving, suggests blockade of German coast; Sims replies "wholly impracticable", 22; U. S. opinion in favor of complete barrier, 65; Coast and Geodetic Survey studies, 80; Wilson confers with F. D. Roosevelt on, 99; Inter-Allied Naval Conference, London, discusses, 256; F. D. Roosevelt presents memo. on, 334
Northcliffe, Lord: 95, 99, 102, 104, 108, 116, 134, 138, 162, 180, 228, 235, 236
Norton, J. K. M.: Wilson to, 71
Norton, Congressman Patrick D., N. D.: 94
Norway: see Trade, Foreign
Noyes, Frank B.: 14, 558
Noyes, Theodore W.: 178
Nugent, Senator J. F., Idaho: 540

Obregon, Gen. Alvaro: 324
O'Connell, John: Wilson to, 280
O'Connor, Thomas P.: 148
Odell, Joseph H.: 515
Official Bulletin (see also Committee on Public Information): see numerous references
Official Statements of War Aims and Peace Proposals, December 1916 to November 1918, prepared under supervision of James Brown Scott. (Carnegie Endowment for International Peace): see numerous references
Oil: 25–7, 53, 119, 153, 415–16, 438–9, 458, 464, 471, 524

Olds, Frank P.: 186
Oliver, Frederick Scott: 42
Oliver, Congressman W. B., Ala.: 300, 472
Olney, Congressman Richard, Mass.: 464
One Hundred Red Days, Edgar Sisson (Yale University Press): 320, 420
Onou, C.: 46
Orlando, Vittorio E., Italian Prime Minister, Minister of Interior: 382, 499–500, 507, 527, 535, 549
Osborn, Mrs. Henry F.: Wilson to, 186
Osborne, Congressman H. Z., Calif.: 529
Our Navy at War, Josephus Daniels (Pictorial Bureau): 11, 44, 110, 197, 256
Our Presidents and Their Mothers, William Judson Hampton (Cornhill Publishing Co.): 270
Out of My Life, Marshal von Hindenburg (Cassell & Co.): 367
Outlook: 515
Overman Act: 496, 529, 537, 552–3
Overman, Senator L. S., N. C.: Wilson to, 24. Also 83, 107, 296, 496, 529, 537
Owen, Senator R. L., Okla.: Wilson to, 205, 517, 518. Also 24, 89, 95, 99, 129, 153, 171, 186, 241, 244, 326, 328, 355, 475, 492, 513, 515, 527

Pacifists: English, Russian, demand Allied statement of terms, 96; Ramsay MacDonald on views of British "sections miscalled 'pacifist'", 224; London *Morning Post* says British pacifists need look for no encouragement from House Mission, 355–6; Walter Page reports British, approve Lansdowne letter, 379; Wilson explains difficulty of discriminations, 396–7
Paderewska, Madame: 568
Paderewski, I. J.: Wilson to, 467. Also 80
Padgett, Congressman L. P., Tenn.: Wilson to, 108. Also 60
Page, Senator C. S., Vt.: 101, 244
Page, Thomas Nelson, U. S. Ambassador, Italy: 14, 86, 90, 311, 330, 331, 347, 357, 391, 499, 513
Page, Walter H., U. S. Ambassador, Great Britain (see also *Life and Letters of Walter H. Page, The*, Burton J. Hendrick): 4, 12, 24, 40, 85, 99, 102, 104, 109, 121, 123, 124, 130, 133, 134, 138, 149, 158, 176, 177, 214, 217, 228, 244, 247, 255, 273, 295, 304, 307, 310, 314, 337, 347, 379, 380, 391, 405, 407, 456, 482, 505, 506, 516, 551, 558, 559, 570
Painlevé, Paul, French Premier September 12 to November 14, 1917: 24
Palestine: see Jews; War
Palmer, A. M.: Wilson to, 335. Also 304, 331, 338, 354, 397, 558, 568
Palmer, Frederick (see also *Newton D. Baker* and *Bliss, Peacemaker*): 530
Panama: 128, 402, 413–14
Pan-American Treaty: 20, 27–8
Park, Congressman Frank, Ga.: 183, 242, 299
Parker, John M.: 71–2

Peabody, Francis S.: 133
Peabody, George Foster: Wilson to, 396, 487. Also 307
Peace, Discussions of (see also Rumania; Russia; Secret Treaties): Allied uneasiness lest Russia make separate peace, 10; Sixte negotiations, 25, 101, 191–2; Cecil on return of German colonies, 70–1; minimum terms on which Allies would enter conference, 78–9; British Union of Democratic Control urges Wilson induce all belligerents renounce aggressive aims, 91; English, Russian pacifists demand Allied statement of terms, 96; Wilson dissuades Sen. Owen from introducing peace terms resolution, 99; French Chamber of Deputies resolution on terms, 101; Italian objectives, 123; Root Commission to Russia not to discuss U. S. terms, 129; Lloyd George on war aims, 136; German Reichstag resolution, July 19, 1917; Chancellor's address on, 173; Allied conference on Balkans, 177, 191; Lloyd George finds no peace hope in German Chancellor's speech, 179; plan for New York *World*, Berliner *Tageblatt*, to present views of Allies, Central Powers, 180–1; MacDonald resolution states German Reichstag resolution expresses Great Britain's principles; calls on Allied governments to restate terms; Sen. Borah calls for statement of U. S. terms, 195; Balfour says unwise for British government to give detailed war aims policy now, 199; La Follette resolution for restatement of terms; King of Spain says Germany will soon offer terms; Moncheur discusses Belgian terms with Wilson, 213; Wilson asks House to organize Inquiry, 254; unofficial peace agents reported in Switzerland, 263; Pershing reports French desire peace, British morale lower, 270; Lansing approves Inquiry plan; Mezes named Director, 275; Michaelis says Wilson's attempt to sow discord between German people, government, hopeless, 285; press comments on Inquiry; Wilson requests no further publicity, 287, 293–4; Czernin on Austro-Hungarian terms, 289; Balfour informs Wilson Germany may make peace communication; Wilson advises on reply, 292; disapproves peace talk before Germany defeated, 295; Von Kuhlmann sees no impediment to peace except demand for Alsace-Lorraine; Lloyd George comments; Michaelis says Germany will refuse peace while enemy demands unacceptable, 297; Asquith warns against "patched up peace", 300–1; Milner hopes U. S. will not imitate Allied timidity in ignoring peace feelers, 346–7; outline of Inquiry subjects, 352; House cannot get French, British, to designate terms, 361; Lloyd George, House, Balfour, discuss British war aims, 370; U. S. military attaché, Petrograd, reports Russia may go out of war, suggests statement of

terms neither side could refuse, 373; Col. House will not be drawn into Allied controversies; Lansing requests information on men who may represent their governments at peace conference, 375-6; Col. House submits resolution on U. S. aims he proposes to offer at Inter-Allied Conference, 382; Wilson approves, 387; Lansdowne letter, 379, 383; Wilson tells Congress immediate task to win war; then peace of generosity, justice can be considered, 389-90; Lloyd George says victory necessary for world security, 409; House's unsuccessful efforts to persuade Allies to join "broad declaration of war aims", 417; Wilson uses Inquiry material in preparing 14-Points address, 426, 451; Lansing on statement of terms, 444; Wilson "kills" war progress statement because of possible international effect in midst of peace intimations, 445; thinks U. S. will welcome statement of terms, 449; suggestions that U. S. restate terms, 450; Wilson discusses 14-Points address with House, Lansing, 451-2, 454; Lloyd George makes war aims address, 452-4; Balfour is notified Wilson plans statement of terms, 452; 14-Points address delivered; Congress pleased; U. S. press favorable; European comment varied, 455-6; Wilson's comments on, 464, 466-7; Princeton trustees approve, 467; Balfour considers, "magnificent pronouncement"; Lloyd George approves, 475; Wilson interprets Point 10, 493; Hertling, Czernin, reply to Wilson, Lloyd George addresses, 497; Depew approves 14-Points address, 502; Wilson confers on reply to Hertling, Czernin; is rumored to have known contents of Czernin's speech before delivery; denied, 505-6, 516; Italy disappointed in 14-Points address, 506-7; Hahn, German liberal, favors informal, secret negotiations, 510; Wilson says must get peace by overcoming its enemies, 511; Owen resolution committing U. S. to support of aims in 14-Points address, 513; adverse comment of Supreme War Council on Hertling, Czernin speeches, 519; U. S. will have no secret negotiations, 527; Wilson, House, Lansing, discuss four-principles address, 531, 535; delivered; favorably received in U. S., Allied countries; German, Austrian comment suspicious, 536-7; Lloyd George finds Hertling, Czernin speeches disappointing; Balfour agrees, 540; Wilson not afraid of German trap, 554; war aims memo. adopted by Inter-Allied Labor, Socialist conference, London, 558; Hertling agrees with four principles, if proposed by all nations, 566; Balfour thinks proper time for peace discussion has not come, 570; secret proposals from Central Powers, 572

Austria-Hungary, Possibility of Separate Peace with: prospects of early peace with, 25; House, Balfour, on concessions to, as inducement to break with Germany, 66-7; Austrian Emperor ready for peace if honor, existence, of Central Powers not threatened, 92; Lloyd George considers present effort to detach Austria, Bulgaria, premature, 123; Ribot asks U. S. opinion on rumored Austrian desire for peace; Wilson's reply never sent, 183-4, 204; Czernin says Austria-Hungary will stay with her allies unless enemy shows willingness to understand viewpoint, 199; Austrian peace feeler; Great Britain's reply, 339-40; Great Britain authorized by Allied War Conference to ascertain Austrian terms; Smuts goes to Switzerland, 382; Czernin says Entente cannot separate Austria, Germany, 397-8; Balfour reports Smuts-Mensdorff conversations to Wilson, 443-4; reports Czernin favors separate peace, but would need financial aid from U. S., 532; U. S. inclined to give aid, 547; Austrian Emperor's proposal for conference, 551, 558; Wilson thinks Austria, not Hungary, stands in way of reasonable settlement, 560; Lansing, House on Emperor's proposal; Balfour consulted, 564-5; Spanish ambassador presents Emperor's letter, 566; Balfour advises, 569-70; Wilson replies, 572, 573

Pope's Peace Proposal: Wilson receives first intimation of; his views on, asked by British, 213-14; proposal forwarded by Page, London, 217; Wilson sends Balfour substance of possible reply, Balfour sympathizes, 218-19; Wilson confers with senators on, 220-1, 224; Allied views on, asked; replies, 226; Michaelis says not inspired by Central Powers, 228; Russian ambassador, Washington, fears it will split Russia if not liberally treated; first draft of Wilson's reply, 231; House suggests Allies accept Wilson's answer as theirs, 233, 237; Wilson's answer sent, approved in U. S., 236; cabinet hears reply, 241; approved by Allies; German comment bitter, 247; Wilson comments on his reply, 245, 253-4, 258; "great effect" of Wilson's reply in Germany, 286-7

Penfield, Frederic C., U. S. Ambassador, Austria-Hungary: 113

Penrose, Senator Boies, Pa.: 486

People's Counselor, The, 283

Percy, Lord Eustace: 54

Perkins, Mrs. Mary B.: Wilson to, 298

Perkins, Thomas N.: 331, 411

Perris, George H.: 67

Pershing, Gen. John J. (see also *My Experiences in the World War*): 26, 62, 75, 85, 88, 89, 105, 109, 144, 145, 149, 177, 270, 333, 355, 357, 372, 387, 388, 417, 428, 433, 449, 450, 456, 468, 483, 488, 501, 510, 520, 522, 529, 562, 565, 572

Persia: 463-4

Peru: 388

Pétain, General H. P.: 3, 70, 236, 333, 387, 468, 510

Phelan, Senator J. D., Calif.: 22, 24, 51, 132, 135, 148, 194, 284, 489, 515

Phelan, Congressman M. F., Mass.: 129

Philadelphia *Public Ledger:* 287, 396, 471

Philip, Hoffman, U. S. Minister, Colombia: 413–14

Philippines: 101, 128–9, 142–3, 228

Philips, August, Minister from the Netherlands, Washington, 555, 572

Phillimore Committee: see League of Nations

Phillips, William, Assistant Secretary of State: Wilson to, 105, 257, 327, 396. Also 21, 34, 116, 255, 322, 555

Pichon, Stephen: 381, 382, 537

Pickett, Mrs. George: 343

Pierce, Lieut. Col. Palmer E.: 197

Pinchot, Amos: Wilson to, 165. Also 496, 497

Pittman, Senator Key, Nev.: Wilson to, 127. Also 122, 391

Poincaré, Raymond, President of France: Wilson to, 457. Also 436

Poindexter, Senator Miles, Wash.: 78, 227, 489, 496

Policy of the United States Toward Maritime Commerce in War, Carlton Savage (Government document): 32, 138

Polish Affairs: Paderewski wants Polish unit in U. S. army, 80; U. S. formal recognition of Polish National Committee, Paris, 348; plans for aiding Polish Lithuanian Jews, 356; Wilson hopes New Year may fulfil Polish hopes, 467; day for aid to Polish urged by Madame Paderewska, 568

Politics (see also Congress; Wilson, Woodrow): Hughes says all thoughts of, laid aside, 16; Wilson will not have, influence his judgment, 72; insists exemption boards be chosen with no regard for, 115; is disgusted with tactics of Georgia senators, 154, 157; is interested in Mass. politics, 289–90, 326; on mayoralty campaign, New York, 333–4; is concerned over alleged use of draft organization for political purposes, 395; delighted with Pittsburgh support, 410; informed of Republican plan to charge his appointments mainly partisan, 424; Theodore Roosevelt's suggestion turned to account by Democrats, 460, 489; Wilson confers with chairman, treasurer, of Democratic National Committee, 471; Stone attacks Republicans in Senate, 485–6; Theodore Roosevelt arrives Washington, avoids direct attack on Wilson, 487; Roosevelt is reported to have practically assumed leadership of Republican party; Longworth dinner, 493; Wilson suggests Democratic National Committee expose organized Republican efforts to discredit administration; may have begun thinking about call for Democratic Congress, 498; McAdoo points out McRoberts of National City Bank, Stettinius of J. P. Morgan &

Co., recently elevated to important war positions, are Republicans, though "this alone" would not disqualify them, 499; Wilson on political considerations in personnel for Red Cross War Finance Committee, 523–4

Polk, Frank L., Counselor, Department of State: Wilson to, 493. Also 13, 85, 151, 153, 156, 159, 177, 183, 197, 200, 203, 207, 212, 309, 325, 482, 527, 546

Pollen, Arthur: 266

Pomerene, Senator Atlee, Ohio: 33, 70, 121, 194, 214, 220, 296, 372, 378, 438, 484, 492, 551

Pond, Allen B.: Wilson to, 169

Ponsonby, Arthur A. W. H.: 91

Pope Benedict XV: Wilson to, 221–3. Also 139, 213, 217, 218, 220, 224, 226, 228, 231, 233, 236, 241, 245, 247, 250, 258, 286, 423, 572

Portland (Oregon) *Nachrichten:* 314

Portugal: 548

Post, Louis F., Assistant Secretary of Labor: Wilson to, 399, 539. Also 378, 404

Pou, Congressman E. W., N. C.: Wilson to, 68, 81

Powell, Senator, Ky., 1863: 543–4

Pratt, Edward E.: 152

Press, Wilson's Relations with: see Wilson, Woodrow

Price, Theodore H.: Wilson to, 63

Priorities: 38, 67–8, 70, 112–13, 116, 214, 225, 227, 324, 486–7, 574

Prohibition: 126, 135, 137, 201, 369, 419

Propaganda: Wilson's war address dropped by airplanes in Austria-Hungary; over German trenches, 14, 98; Austrian, German, in Russia, 21, 117; organization of moving picture industry for, 134–5; plans for campaign of, in Russia, 151, 208, 244, 388–9, 454–5, 483; efforts to expose agitation against government, 169–70; Darrow to speak on East Side, New York, 210; campaign to enlighten rural people, 235; plan for scattering, over enemy countries, 247; Wilson approves leaving, to Committee on Public Information, 259; unofficial agents in Switzerland working at, for peace, 263; plan to send influential German-Americans to Copenhagen to spread, 267–8; T. N. Page urges, in Italy, to counteract effect of peace propaganda, 357; service of Assn. of National Advertisers in, 394; commercial travelers' assistance in, 526; responsibility of editors to bring truth to people, 534–5; plan for organizing writers to inform people about government, 572

Propaganda and the News, Will Irwin (McGraw-Hill Book Company): 21, 322, 475

Providence *Journal:* 253, 317

Public Papers of Woodrow Wilson, The, edited by Ray Stannard Baker and William E. Dodd (Harper & Bros.): see numerous references

Quezon, Manuel L., Resident Commissioner from the Philippine Islands: 101, 183

Raemakers, Louis: 242
Railroads (see also Priorities; Labor): Wilson confers on government control of, 7; executives of, name War Board, 14; Wilson requests investigation into production of rolling stock, motive power of, 194; has interests of, in mind, 325–6; Interstate Commerce Commission recommendations regarding; McAdoo urges Wilson assume control, operation of, during war, 394; situation of, acute; Wilson considers McAdoo for Director General, consults Brandeis, Sen. Newlands, Gregory, 401–2; cabinet discusses, 405; Wilson confers with War Board of, 407; situation of, demoralizing to New York security markets, 408–9; obstacles in, requiring legislation; Wilson confers on; drafts address, 412; receives memoranda on; is going through "deep waters" about, 416–17; Senate inquiry into situation of, 418; Wilson disapproves proposed bill for government ownership of, at present, 419; issues proclamation on control of, names McAdoo Director General; Garfield favors government operation of railroads, mines; control assumed December 28, 1917, 435; War Board resigns, Advisory Board appointed; Wilson has bill prepared embodying guarantees to roads, 438; hopes for permanent benefit for, 440; addresses Congress on, 451; coal order breaks congestion on, 487
Rainey, Congressman H. T., Ill.: 89
Raker, Congressman J. E., Calif.: 424
Ralston, Samuel M.: 317
Rankin, Congresswoman Jeannette, Mont.: 140, 176, 288
Ransdell, Senator J. E., La.: 22, 79, 104, 128, 195, 262, 284, 566
Rapallo: see Supreme War Council
Rappard, William E.: 335
Rappard, Chevalier W. L. F. C. van, Minister from the Netherlands, Washington: 24, 242, 530
Rathom, John R.: 317
Rea, Samuel: 407
Reading, Earl of, British Ambassador, Washington, from February 13, 1918: 235, 236, 277, 279, 304, 335, 361, 362, 370, 388, 447, 529, 537, 542, 546, 555, 561, 566, 568, 569
Reconstruction: 300
Red Cross: Wilson appeals for, gives $500 to, 2; writes Gompers to discuss aid for dependents of men in military, naval forces with Miss Boardman of, 29; committee named to head campaign of, 32; Wilson, Taft confer on, 39; Wilson confers on plans for War Council of, 46; announces creation of War Council, Davison, chairman, 61; urges Taft to retain chairmanship of

Executive Committee, 63; address at dedication of building of, 66; establishes Red Cross Week, 85; inquires judgment of State Dept. as to sending a unit of, to Russia, 105; confers with Taft, Secy. Lane on, 126; calls on Sunday schools for contributions to, 129; accepts services of sanitary corps in behalf of, 149; appoints Ryan to War Council of, 191; proclamation to school children in behalf of, 270; receives head of Special Commission of, to Russia, 326; Axson becomes national secretary of, 397; membership campaign for; Wilson issues appeal, 415; receives Finance Committee of, 455; talks with Axson about work of, in Europe, 481; National War Finance Committee of, proposed personnel, 523–4; good offices of, toward ending use of poison gas, 561
Redfield, W. C., Secretary of Commerce: Wilson to, 80, 118, 149, 151, 228, 301, 333, 437. Also 51, 100, 129, 154, 167, 195, 196, 289, 292, 324, 336, 338, 364, 438, 487
Redmore, Mrs. Alice V.: 23
Reed, Senator James A., Mo.: 85, 110, 112–13, 166, 234, 406, 435, 443, 521
Reed, John: 165
Reid, Harry Fielding: Wilson to, 15. Also 209
Reid, Mrs. Harry Fielding: 15
Reinsch, Paul S., U. S. Minister, China: 99, 338, 339, 340, 342, 482
Report of the Proceedings of the 37th Annual Convention of the American Federation of Labor (Law Reporter Printing Co.): 374
Reprisals: see War
Requa, Mark L.: 415, 464
Retrospect, Arthur James, First Earl of Balfour (Houghton Mifflin Co.): 44
Review of Reviews: 92, 391
Rhett, Robert G.: Wilson to, 258
Rhondda, Lord David A. T.: 493
Riaño y Gayangos, Don Juan, Spanish Ambassador, Washington: 551, 566, 572, 573
Ribot, A. F., French Prime Minister to September 8, 1917: 8, 25, 97, 101, 176, 183, 191, 199–200, 203
Ridder, Victor: 267
Ridley, Major: 274
Riordan, Congressman D. J., N. Y.: 71
Ritter, E. P. V.: Wilson to, 116
Ritter, Paul, Swiss Minister, Washington: 183
Robertson, Gen. Sir W. R.: 48, 414, 501
Robinson, Miss Flora L.: Wilson to, 393
Robinson, Senator J. T., Ark.: Wilson to, 530. Also 64, 112, 155, 203, 235, 300, 388, 472, 484
Rockefeller, John D., Jr.: 69
Romjue, Congressman M. A., Mo.: Wilson to, 501
Roosevelt, Franklin D., Assistant Secretary of the Navy: Wilson to, 296, 334. Also 99, 217
Roosevelt, Theodore: Wilson to, 77. Also 11, 17, 48, 54, 69, 70, 71–2, 76, 78, 88, 318, 379, 423, 424, 460, 480, 485, 487, 489, 493, 533, 539

Roosevelt, Mrs. Theodore: Wilson to, 533
Root, Elihu: Wilson to, 5. Also 10, 18, 28, 37, 39, 42, 45, 54, 61, 62, 67, 75, 109, 117, 121, 129, 151, 208, 215, 233, 244, 396, 424
Roper, Daniel C.: 241
Rosalsky, Otto A.: 356
Rosenwald, Julius: 150, 356
Rothschild (Baron), Nathan M.: 336
Rousseau, Rear-Admiral H. H.: 109
Roussos, Georges, Greek Minister, Washington, from September 21, 1917: 280
Rowe, L. S.: Wilson to, 464. Also 38
Royden, Thomas: 194
Rucker, Congressman W. W., Mo.: 281
Ruffin, Dr. Sterling: 280, 285
Rule, Henry: 145
Rumania (see also Secret Treaties): inquiry from, as to British, French, U. S. attitude in case of separate peace between Russia and Central Powers, 363; statement of U. S. determination to support, after war, 376; Wilson receives committee of American Union of Rumanian Jews, 405; petition to abolish restrictions on Jews in, 434; Wilson receives first minister from, makes address, 470; U. S. has no knowledge of understanding between, and Allies, re peace terms; is herself committed to safeguard integrity, freedom of smaller nations, 493; Allies, to prevent separate peace, assure Rumania will adhere to convention of Bucharest, 540; U. S. will not join, makes separate assurances, 560
Rumania, Ferdinand I, King of: Wilson to, 157. Also 363, 560
Russell, C. E.: Wilson to, 349. Also 19, 62
Russell, C. W.: Wilson to, 421, 463
Russia (see also Finance; Peace, Discussions of; Propaganda; Secret Treaties; War): welcomes U. S. into war, 8; statement on war aims, 10; war aims transmitted, with declaration of intent to continue in war, 46-7; Stevens Railway Commission to, 54-5, 57, 61, 108, 215; Wilson unwilling to receive retiring ambassador from, 57; on rights of women in, 59; fears Stockholm Conference will do harm in connection with, 65; requests suspension of Mooney's sentence because of situation in, 65-6; plans statement on U. S. policy to correct misapprehensions in, 75-6; coalition government formed in; declaration renouncing separate peace, 77; Wilson's message to provisional government of, 81, 106; aims of provisional government of, declared by British Union of Democratic Control to embody ideas of democracies of world, 91; Wilson comments on aims of, 95; pacifists in, 96; Wilson considers sending Red Cross unit to, 105; Commission to U. S. from, 120-2, 128; Wilson will not designate day for relief of, lest he offend sensibilities, 128; new ambassador from, presents credentials, 148; Russia proposes early peace conference,

149; Bolshevik uprising put down, 168; Kerensky, Prime Minister, 177; mutiny in army, 183; Russia will stay in war, 205; Wilson thinks unwise to send troops to, 214; former Czar, family, removed to "unnamed place", 215; Wilson's message to National Council of, 234; Kerensky opens National Council Assembly, 236; rumors of Bolshevik demonstration, 263; Gompers' message to people of, 272; French wish U. S. represented at conference on prevention of disintegration in, 290-1; Wilson receives Admiral Koltchak of, 309; receives Sisson, Hutchins, who are leaving for, 320; on principles to be followed in, 323; receives head of Red Cross Commission to, 326; Bolsheviks overturn provisional government, 341-2; Wilson on difficulty of dealing with; Soviet Congress calls on belligerents to begin peace negotiations, 349; Wilson dismayed over news from, 350; has not lost faith in, 355; U. S. press rumors about, 367; Trotsky proposes armistice, 371; charges U. S. entered war under stock exchange influence; British consider Russian situation hopeless at present, Clemenceau agrees, 374; elections for Constituent Assembly, 375; U. S. press statements favoring treatment of Russia as enemy have bad effect; Lansing publicly deprecates, 379, 386; Russian military operations cease; Trotsky asks Allies to join in negotiations; replies, 381, 387, 388; Trotsky removes diplomats not in sympathy with Bolsheviks, 386; Lansing proposes declaration of policy toward Russia; Wilson thinks unwise at present; peace negotiations postponed so Allies can define attitude, 395; Wilson disapproves suggestion for second mission to Russia, 396; U. S. inquires as to British, French policy toward; replies, 405; armistices signed between Russia, Central Powers, 412, 420; Sisson's relations with Bolsheviks disapproved, 420; Supreme War Council policy regarding Russia; peace negotiations begun, 426; Central Powers offer terms, 429-30; Trotsky repeats invitation to Allies to share negotiations, 436; Lansing advises no direct reply, 444; U. S. urged not to desert Russia, restatement of war aims suggested, 450; Wilson confers on situation in, 454-6; British policy in, 459; Wilson hopes to help people of, 468; attempted assassination of Lenin, 469; U. S. will recognize no independent governments in, until will of people more definitely expressed, 471; members of Congress present plan for dealing with, 475; Bolsheviks dissolve Constituent Assembly, 479-80; will hold U. S. ambassador responsible for lives of Mooney and others, 480; Wilson distressed over situation in, 486, 529; Wilson requests postponement of execution of Mooney sentence, 488-9; Francis consulted as to moderation of U. S. attitude toward, 515–16; sends "Sisson documents"; treaty between Ukraine, Central Powers, 536; German-Russian peace negotiations terminated, Trotsky declares war has ceased, 538; Walling warns against encouraging Bolsheviks, 542; $1,000,000 for purchase of supplies in; closer informal touch with Bolsheviks; Finance Section, Inter-Allied Council, recommends no recognition of new states in, without adoption of part of debt, 544–5; German advance begins, 551–2; France promises financial aid if advance is resisted, U. S. will not join, 555–6; first German terms accepted, advance continues, 556; Soviet government demoralized; Allied ambassadors agree to support resistance if offered, 558, 562; U. S. cannot interfere in form of Russian government, 564–5; new German terms accepted, worse than old, 565; advance continues; diplomatic, Red Cross missions leaving, 567

Root Commission to: Wilson approves, 16–17; personnel, 18, 28–9, 42, 61–2, 69; Wilson confers with Root on, 37; objects of, 39; announced to U. S. ambassador, Russia, purposes stated, 45; Commission calls on Wilson, 67; leaves Washington, 75; arrives Petrograd, 109; Wilson confers with, on return; report, supplementary report of, 208; Root, Mott, McCormick of, on plans for educational campaign in Russia, 244; Colcord thinks, never had sympathetic understanding of Russian situation, 396

Siberia: unwise for U. S., Japan, to send troops to Vladivostok, 432–3; Irkutsk reported in flames, 436–7; British favor force at Vladivostok to guard military stores; U. S. asked to send contingent; Brooklyn ordered to Yokohama, 442–3; Russian ambassador, Washington, urges Allies take combined action in Far East; fears Japan will act alone; Lansing instructs U. S. ambassador, Japan, to investigate, 463; U. S. hopes Vladivostok will not be occupied by foreign force, 482; disapproves intervention now; if necessary later, favors international co-operation, 532–3; military advisers, Supreme War Council, favor Japanese intervention in, specifying Japanese guarantees, creation of joint allied commission, 556; Wilson confers with House, Lansing on possible intervention; Bliss reports view of military men that intervention necessary, himself disagrees, 566–7; Balfour proposal, 568–9

Ryan, J. D.: Wilson to, 191. Also 262
Ryan, T. F.: 499

Sabath, Congressman A. J., Ill.: 73, 521
Saint-Gaudens, Louis: 353
St. Jean de Maurienne: see Secret Treaties
St. Louis Post-Dispatch: 36, 106, 492
Salter, James A.: 194

Saltzgaber, Gaylord M.: 320
Salvation Army: 378
Sargent, John Singer: Wilson to, 172, 302, 345, 403. Also 122, 310, 312, 315, 317, 320, 324, 328, 334, 335, 337, 353, 525
Sato, Aimaro, Japanese Ambassador, Washington: 107, 114, 144, 171, 298, 313, 432, 436, 438
Saturday Evening Post: 91–2, 309
Saulsbury, Senator, Del., 1863: 543–4
Saulsbury, Senator Willard, Del.: 280, 417
Saunders, William L.: 109
Savage, Carlton: see Policy of the United States Toward Maritime Commerce in War
Sayre, Francis B.: Wilson to, 6. Also 8, 45, 105, 106, 124, 181, 238, 425, 426
Sayre, Mrs. Francis B. (Jessie Woodrow Wilson), daughter of Woodrow Wilson: Wilson to, 124, 181, 238–9. Also 6, 8, 106, 183, 265, 269, 393, 425, 426, 468
Sayre, John N.: Wilson to, 45
Scheidemann, Philip: 132, 267
Schiff, Jacob H.: Wilson to, 371. Also 356
Schmedeman, A. G., U. S. Minister, Norway: 295, 310
Scott, Frank A.: 169, 197, 366
Scott, Maj. Gen. Hugh L.: 35, 62, 281
Scott, James Brown: see Official Statements of War Aims and Peace Proposals
Scribner, Charles: Wilson to, 534. Also 567
Scribner's Magazine: 384
Scudder, Edward W.: 355
Secret Service: protection of President in wartime, 71, 305, 323–4, 397; Wilson takes up overlapping functions of, in different departments, 159; W. B. Hale alleges persecution by; Wilson orders investigation, 335
Secret Treaties: U. S. ambassador, Russia, reports probable existence of, 11; conference of St. Jean de Maurienne, 25, 90; House advises Balfour to avoid discussion of peace settlements, Balfour concurs, 33; Wilson will discuss peace terms unofficially with Balfour, instructs House to inquire about, 37; House does so, suggests Wilson, State Department be supplied with copies of, 40; Wilson discusses bases of peace with Viviani, sees England, France have not same views as U. S., 43; Wilson, Balfour, House discuss, 43–4; Balfour sends Wilson copies of certain of, with main points of statement on foreign policy to British Imperial War Council, 74–5, 80; Ribot repudiates secret diplomacy charges, 101; Germany alleges Allied, 118; Walter Page suggests U. S. be represented at Allied war conferences, to get insight into ambitions for territory, 124; statement before Japanese Diet, 129–30; Balfour fears embarrassing controversies about conflicting Allied aims, 149; Wilson refers to probable Allied "undertakings among each other", 162; McAdoo submits proposed letter to governments borrowing from U. S., pointing out

February 19, 1918.

My dear Mr. Hoover,

May I not call your attention to this important point:

There is pressing need of the full
co-operation of the packing trade, of every
officer and employee, in the work of hurrying provisions abroad.   Let the packers
understand that they are engaged in a war
service in which they must take orders and
act together if the Food Administration re-
quires.

W. W.

under the direction of the Food Administration

LETTER TO HERBERT HOOVER

Original letter written by the President to Herbert Hoover, the
Food Administrator, February 19, 1918, urging the co-operation of
the packing trade.

Secret Treaties—*Continued*

loans not to be construed as approval of national objectives, 168; Serbian minister warns of "political determinations" among Allies, 179; Wilson says U. S. terms not now acceptable to France, Italy, 180; Ribot asks U. S. opinion on certain aspects of; Wilson's replies never sent, 184, 204; Michaelis alleges Allied; Ribot denies, 198–9; State Dept. telegraphs for information on Allied agreements about Asia Minor, 200; Sharp consults Cambon, reports, 202; Polk, Lansing disapprove McAdoo's proposed letter to borrowing governments; best not to have "anything on record"; McAdoo presents further arguments, 212–13, 227; Michaelis refers to Allied, again, before Reichstag, 230; Japan intends return Kiaochow to China, will retain German islands in Pacific north of equator, 263; hints of, by Milner, 346–7; All-Russian Congress of Soviets votes to publish, declaring null, void, 349; Sharp sends hints of, 350; U. S. special agent, Cairo, sends information about, 351; Rumania inquires intention of Italy, France, Great Britain, to confirm engagements, 363; New York *Times* reports certain of, recently published in Russia, 375; Wilson refers to "bargains of the Allies with regard to Asia Minor", 379–80; Lansing sends for substance of all, published in Russia, 382; U. S. will not fight for "divisions of territory such as . . . contemplated in Asia Minor", 387; Francis telegraphs translations of, 391, 418; Wilson cites Treaty of London as instance of British self-interest, 407; *Manchester Guardian* publishes texts of, 408; Italian government fears 14-Points address will interfere with Treaty of London, 456; U. S. has no knowledge of understanding between Rumania and other Allies as to peace terms, 493; publication of texts of certain, begun in New York *Evening Post*, 496–7; U. S. ambassador, Italy, sees copy of Treaty of London; Orlando seeks its reaffirmation, 499–500; Balfour writes Wilson on Treaty of London, 512; Allies assure Rumania they will adhere to convention of Bucharest, 540; U. S. will not join, 560; Balfour finds Treaty of London "regrettable" but Great Britain, France are bound by it; thinks premature discussion dangerous, 570–1

Seibold, Louis: Wilson to, 130, 148

Selections from the Correspondence of Theodore Roosevelt and Henry Cabot Lodge (Charles Scribner's Sons): 70

Senate and the League of Nations, The, Henry Cabot Lodge (Charles Scribner's Sons): 73, 224

Serbia (see also Secret Treaties): 423, 424, 492

Seventy Years of Life and Labor, Samuel Gompers (E. P. Dutton & Co.): 62

Seymour, Charles: see *Intimate Papers of Colonel House, The*

Shafroth, Senator J. F., Colo.: Wilson to, 243. Also 16, 121, 462

Shallenberger, Congressman A. C., Neb.: 464

Sharp, W. G., U. S. Ambassador, France: 90, 99, 183, 191, 200, 202, 347, 348, 350, 405, 482, 561

Shaw, Albert: Wilson to, 353, 403. Also 391

Shaw, Anna Howard: 346, 527

Sheldon, E. W.: Wilson to, 314. Also 559

Shepherd, Major: 492

Sheppard, Senator Morris, Tex.: 101, 451, 551

Sherley, Congressman Swagar, Ky.: 60, 61, 203, 295, 398, 438, 537

Shields, Senator J. K., Tenn.: 92, 226, 408, 515, 560

Ships (see also Army, American; Germany; Labor): Wilson approves wooden fleet, Goethals to direct construction of, 15; Lloyd George says victory depends on ships, 16; Emergency Fleet Corporation organized, Goethals manager, 22; Hoover reports alarming shipping conditions, 32; Council of National Defense Shipping Committee named, Denman head, 33; cabinet discusses French, British needs, 38; Wilson confers on building plans, 55–6, 60; Goethals says original wooden ship program hopeless, 86; Denman defends, 88; protection of merchant vessels, 109; controversy in Shipping Board, 117, 123–4, 172–5; Shipping Board desires recognition in formation of exports control council, 135; Wilson disapproves statement that government may requisition U. S. ships, 149–52; proposed agreement between U. S., Great Britain, to allow building of destroyers, light-craft, instead of capital ships, 152, 161, 266; Goethals, Denman, White, Brent resign, 187–90, 192, 193; Wilson writes incoming Shipping Board members, expressing confidence, 192; British government hopes U. S. will not take ownership of British ships building in U. S. yards, 228; Wilson favors public rebuke to ship owners not co-operating in safety measures, 243; contracts for first 3 government yards, 268; applications for sale of U. S. ships to foreign interests, 285–6; Wilson sends House shipping memo. to take abroad, 331; Hurley hopes 1918 shipbuilding goal will be reached; Lloyd George nervous about, 415; Senate to inquire into shipping situation, 418; Hurley says program working out well, 425; Crosby suggests Inter-Ally Shipping Board, McAdoo endorses, 427; Wilson confers at Shipping Board offices, 438, 468, 551; urges mandatory War Instructions for ships, 460–2; International Mercantile Marine Co. desire to sell British shipping securities, 494–5; Shipping Control Committee established, 509; Stevens will represent U. S. on Inter-Allied Shipping Council,

516; questionable conditions at Hog Island, 533, 541–3; Wilson on relation of Inter-Allied Shipping Board to Supreme War Council, 538; Wilson approves liquor, vice zones in areas around yards, 541

Shotwell, James T.: see *At the Paris Peace Conference*

Shouse, Congressman Jouett, Kan.: Wilson to, 240, 460. Also 397

Siam: 183

Siddons, Frederick L.: 207

Simmons, Senator F. M., N. C.: Wilson to, 251. Also 24, 83, 117, 158, 163, 296, 481, 484

Sims, Congressman T. W., Tenn.: 127, 200, 407, 438

Sims, Rear-Admiral W. S. (see also *Victory at Sea, The*): 10, 21, 22, 34, 44, 65, 88, 94, 121, 122, 124, 126, 130, 138, 144, 146, 151, 156, 177, 179, 197, 217, 425, 426, 514

Sinclair, Upton: 318–19

Sinnott, Congressman N. J., Ore.: 92

Sisson Documents: see Russia

Sisson, Edgar G. (see also *One Hundred Red Days*): 320, 323, 388, 420, 536

Sixte Negotiations: see Peace, Discussions of

Slattery, Michael J.: Wilson to, 202

Slemp, Congressman C. B., Va.: 468

Slenim, S.: Wilson to, 468

Small, Congressman John H., N. C.: Wilson to, 31. Also 22, 85, 131, 217, 284, 405, 468, 540

Smith, Congressman A. T., Idaho: 140

Smith, Alva A.: 304

Smith, Atwood: 464

Smith, Senator E. D., S. C.: 2, 33, 71, 101, 140, 209, 283, 515

Smith, Sir Frederick: 438

Smith, George M.: 321

Smith, Senator Hoke, Ga.: Wilson to, 154. Also 24, 112–13, 157–8, 484

Smith, Miss Lucy M.: Wilson to, 470, 553

Smith, Senator M. A., Ariz.: Wilson to, 207. Also 288, 462

Smith, Miss Mary R.: 470, 553

Smith, Senator W. A., Mich.: 10

Smoot, Senator Reed, Utah: 60

Smuts, Gen. Jan C.: 107, 382, 443

Snowden, Philip: 91

Socialists (see also Stockholm Conference): representation of, on Root Commission to Russia, 28–9; Wilson on "almost treasonable utterances" of certain American, 65; rejects proposed peace efforts of, 132–3; thinks bulk of, in U. S. have not "revolutionary temper", 170; circulation of Socialistic papers, 210, 319; Hillquit's "outrageous utterances" on Liberty Loans, 333; Wilson will not ask Debs' help, 419; requests excerpts from press, speeches of, in enemy countries, 505; Inter-Allied Labor, Socialist conference meets, London; memo. on war aims, 558

Somers, Orlando A.: 529

Sonnino, Baron Sidney, Italian Minister of

Foreign Affairs: 25, 90, 123, 192, 273, 382, 512, 513, 562

Spain: see Peace, Discussions of

Spain, Alphonso XIII, King of: 213, 551, 558, 565

Speeches and Literary Contributions at Fourscore and Four, Chauncey M. Depew: 502

Sprague, Frank J.: 202

Spreckels, Claus A.: 409

Spreckels, Rudolph: 24

Spring Rice, Sir Cecil A., British Ambassador, Washington: 26, 95, 134, 143, 171, 207, 263, 284, 436, 447, 458, 459, 475, 546, 547

Spring Rice, Lady: 458

Springfield *Republican*: 236, 301, 450, 505

Sprunt, John D.: Wilson to, 49

Squier, Maj. Gen. G. O.: 123, 446

Stack, Edmund J.: Wilson to, 280

State, Department of: Wilson wants "genuine expert" for Solicitor of, 24; Lansing forbids officials of, to give out information, 54, 57; R. S. Baker appointed Special Assistant of, to report conditions in England, France, Italy, 546–7

Stedman, Congressman C. M., N. C.: 288

Steed, Wickham: 565

Steel: 5, 86, 121, 159, 280

Steenerson, Congressman Halvor, Minn.: 142

Steffens, Lincoln: 128

Stephens, W. D., Governor of Cal.: Wilson to, 65, 488–9. Also 66, 207

Sterling, Senator Thomas, S. D.: 242

Stettinius, Edward R.: 499

Stevens, John F.: 28, 57, 61, 215, 569

Stevens, Raymond B.: 121, 505, 516, 538

Stewart, Duncan M.: 339

Stewart, S. V., Governor of Mont.: 241

Stimson, F. J., U. S. Ambassador, Argentina: 264, 343

Stockholm Conference: 65, 83, 104, 213, 224, 262, 542–3

Stone, M. E. (see also *Fifty Years a Journalist*): 43

Stone, Senator W. J., Mo.: 390, 475, 485

Story of the Woman's Party, The, Inez Haynes Irwin (Harcourt, Brace & Co.): 67, 121

Stovall, Pleasant A., U. S. Minister, Switzerland: Wilson to, 200. Also 92, 173, 263, 295, 310, 322, 529

Straight, Willard D.: 18

Stratton, Samuel W.: 438

Straus, Oscar S.: 18, 356

Strong, Benjamin: 308

Strunsky, Simeon: 564

Stuart, Henry C., Governor of Va.: 11

Sulzer, Hans, Swiss Minister, Washington: 45, 236, 427

Summers, Maddin, U. S. Consul General, Moscow: 488

Sunday, Mr. and Mrs. William A.: 530

Supreme Court: 80, 288

Supreme War Council (see also Army, American): British, French, Italian representatives at Rapallo agree upon, 342; House

Supreme War Council—*Continued*
reports agreement, and desire that U. S. be represented, 354; French Cabinet resigns following debate on power of, 355; Wilson insists on a, 361–2; House will attend first meeting of, 363–4; foresees trouble in workings of; Clemenceau agrees, wants U. S. to take initiative, 372–3; Council convenes at Versailles, 386; Wilson favors "most effective", obtainable, 387; Wilson, House on Bliss as military adviser, 414; Council on policy regarding Russia, 426; U. S. will participate in Council, 431; Bliss instructed to discuss co-operation of U. S., French troops with, 457–8; Foch, Pétain, Haig agree on desirability of amalgamating U. S. troops with French, British, 509–10; Council discusses use of American troops, 512; Bliss reports anxiety, fear in Council, 516; 1918 campaign plan of, includes Inter-Allied reserve, 518; issues statement containing political paragraph; Wilson, House disturbed, 519, 521; Council is notified U. S. objects to political statements by, 527–8, 549, 555, 561–2; Wilson on relation of, to other Inter-Allied boards, 538; Wilson fears "*any* expression of policy framed jointly at Paris", 561

Survey Graphic: 445

Swanson, Senator Claude A., Va.: 14, 60, 61, 220, 274, 378, 439, 458, 484, 560

Swanwick, Helena M.: 91

Sweeney, Bo, Assistant Secretary of Interior: 198

Swem, Charles L.: 182, 333, 535

Switzerland: 183, 217, 236, 244, 335

Swope, Herbert B.: 540

Synon, Mary: see *McAdoo*

Taft, Charles P.: 327

Taft, William H.: Wilson to, 63, 209. Also 20, 39, 126, 407

Talbott, Congressman J. F. C., Md.: 304

Talcott, Charles A.: 384

Tardieu, André, French High Commissioner, Washington (see also *France and America*): 79, 166, 180, 200, 228, 257, 462

Tariff Commission: 71, 408

Taussig, Frank W.: 71, 244, 328, 408, 419, 561

Taylor, Alonzo E.: 331, 358, 362

Taylor, Congressman E. T., Cal.: Wilson to, 524. Also 458

Taylor, Admiral M. M.: 123, 344

Tedcastle, A. W.: Wilson to, 421

Tener, John K.: 202

Teusler, Rudolf, cousin of Mrs. Wilson: 324

Thanksgiving Day, 1917: 300, 306, 341–2, 381

Thiel, W. A.: 492

Thomas, Senator C. S., Col.: 515, 529, 540, 541

Thomas, Monsignor: 300, 306

Thomas, W. E.: 157–8

Thompson, Huston, Assistant Attorney General: Wilson to, 383. Also 11

Thompson, W. B.: 323, 454, 467, 492, 514

Thompson, Senator W. H., Kan.: 264, 299, 443

Tillman, Senator B. R., S. C.: Wilson to, 172. Also 186, 194

Tipple, Bertrand M.: 184

Todd, G. C., Assistant to Attorney General: 412

Todd, Miss Helen: 226

Trade, Foreign (see also Economic After-War Policy): need for legislation on embargoes, 17; Wilson discusses export limitation with Netherlands minister, 24; regulation of food exports to northern neutrals; Lansing endeavors allay alarm about, in Denmark, 31; Wilson given full embargo powers; Balfour offers British commercial information, 54; Exports Council established, 124, 126; cabinet discusses exports, 135; Wilson approves McCormick's appointment to administrative committee, Exports Council, 141; Houston, Hoover urge wheat, corn embargo, 151; proclamation on exports control, explanatory statement; neutral commissions sent to U. S. to confer on, 153; policy regarding Norway, 167; Denmark, 197; Wilson confers with Nansen of Norway, 200–1; Swiss Commission on embargoes arrives, 217; Exports Council superseded by Administrative Board, Council, 228–9; proclamation, statement on exports control, 237; U. S. embargo policy, 295, 310; British wish extreme demands made on neutrals, 307; Wilson's views on policy as to Norway, Denmark, 356–7, 362, 365; confers with Nansen, T. D. Jones on, 365; further restricts exports; imports, 379; inquires Shipping Board progress on control of imports, 539; entire U. S. foreign commerce subjected to control by license, 544

Trading with the Enemy Act: 195, 294, 324

Trammell, Senator Park, Fla.: 85

Treaty of Peace with Germany, Hearings Before the Committee on Foreign Relations, United States Senate, 66th Congress, 1st session, 1919 (Government document): 263

Trevelyan, Charles P.: 91

Trimble, South, Jr.: 381

Trotsky, Leon D.: 371, 374, 381, 386, 387, 395, 436, 444, 455, 459, 536, 538

True Story of Woodrow Wilson, The, David Lawrence (George H. Doran Co.): 211

Tucker, Randolph: 266

Tumulty, Joseph P., Wilson's Secretary (see also *Woodrow Wilson As I Know Him*): Wilson to, 4, 34, 91, 98, 112, 127, 132, 135, 145, 178, 179, 196, 202, 235, 272, 286, 299, 300, 306, 312, 318, 321, 332, 346, 362, 364, 372, 400, 404, 405, 407, 412, 419, 423, 430, 434, 441, 471, 490, 492, 515, 519, 541, 564. Also 11, 57, 115, 130, 236, 298, 333, 349, 350, 353, 369, 385, 401, 451, 462, 476, 491, 495, 536

Turkey: U. S. severs relations with, 31; House, Balfour, agree on wisdom of concessions to, if will break with Germany, 66–7; practical destruction of, one of British objects, 74;

property of, not to be taken over unless used in enemy interest, 335, 338; Wilson considers attempt at separate peace with, of questionable advantage, 379–80; declaration of war on, unnecessary; Wilson tries to hold Congress back, 390, 392–3

Tuscania: 429

Udine, Prince: 83, 120, 133
Underwood, Frederick D.: 304
Underwood, Senator O. W., Ala.: 46, 60, 101, 176, 300, 515
Unity of Control: Page, London, on Allied failure to work together, 214; Lloyd George says one cause of Allied failures lack of, 277; Sharp, Paris, finds no Allied singleness of purpose, 350; Lloyd George publicly deplores lack of, 351; his statement criticized, 355; Wilson insists on single war council, 361; House announces Wilson considers unity essential; misunderstanding follows, 363–4, 366, 369; French want French "Generalissimo", 372–3; Bliss favors unified command; pessimism in House Commission reports over lack of unity, 410–11; Wilson, Clemenceau, favor unity of command, 462
Universal Military Training: 502, 507–8
Untermyer, Samuel: 435
Urueta, Carlos A., Colombian Minister, Washington: 106
Uruguay: 295

Vail, Theodore N.: Wilson to, 525
Vanderbilt, Mrs. George: 46
Van Dyke, Henry: 99, 104
Vardaman, Senator James K., Miss.: 501
Vaughan, Crawford: 566
Venezuela: 550
Vernadsky, George: see *Lenin, Red Dictator*
Vesnitch, M. R., head of Serbian War Mission: 424, 492, 496
Victory at Sea, The, Rear-Admiral William Snowden Sims (Doubleday, Page & Co.): 40, 44, 51, 94, 179
Viereck, George S.: 171
Villard, O. G.: 178
Viviani, René: 43, 46, 67, 180
Vopicka, Charles J., U. S. Minister, Rumania, Serbia, Bulgaria: 363, 376, 493, 560
Vorwärts: 330
Vreeland, Hamilton, Jr.: Wilson to, 216
Vreeland, Mr. and Mrs. W. U.: 267

Wade, Martin J.: 264
Wadsworth, Eliot: 61
Wadsworth, Senator J. W., Jr., N. Y.: 104, 155, 335
Walcott, C. D.: Wilson to, 571. Also 496
Wald, Lillian D.: Wilson to, 40. Also 52
Waldron, J. M.: Wilson to, 29
Wall, Louise Herrick: see *Letters of Franklin K. Lane, The*
Wallace, Hugh C.: 266
Wallace, Mrs. Hugh C.: Wilson to, 319

Waller, James B.: 172
Walling, William E.: 39, 73, 76, 145, 383, 542
Walsh, Senator T. J., Mont.: Wilson to, 240. Also 51, 60, 101, 143, 291
Walters, Henry: 438
War (see also Navy, American; North Sea, Project for Barring): Wilson signs proclamation of, 2; country approves, 5; Wilson prepares legislative program for, 9; appeals to people for co-operation, 22; on responsibility of German military for, 110, 350; says U. S. has no agreement with Allies, 221; says U. S. unwilling to continue indefinite trench warfare, 271; thinks people are back of administration, 356, 404; prefers "Our Associates" to "Our Allies", 402–3; pessimism in House Mission war reports, 410–11; Wilson favors co-ordination, unification of war administration, 416; says U. S. has not been so united for years, 447; kaleidoscopic changes in Europe react on U. S. war preparations, 508–9; Balfour thinks victory likely for nations having most endurance, political stability; since U. S. came in, has never doubted result, 512; Wilson disapproves plan to bring German, Austrian prisoners to work in America, 518; proposal for war workers' emblem, 531

Aerial: raid on England, 86; Lafayette Escadrille, 93; Smuts says decision of war lies in air, 107; raids on England continue, 109; reprisals demanded, 117; worst aerial fighting on French front since beginning of war, 163; Paris raided, 196; British airplanes drop explosives on enemy establishments, 226; first moonlight raid on London, 256; newspapers clamor for reprisals; French airplanes bomb Stuttgart, 288; Lloyd George will "bomb Germany with compound interest", 291; Paris raided, German account says reprisal, 511

Eastern, Western Fronts: situation when U. S. enters, 3; Rheims evacuated under bombardment, 8; British offensive around Arras, Vimy Ridge taken, 10; British astride Hindenburg line, 17; Nivelle launches offensive between Soissons, Rheims, 22; desperate fighting in Arras sector, 34; German attacks succeed along Aisne, 45; Italians begin drive against Austrians, 66; Pétain becomes Commander-in-Chief of French armies operating on French front, 70; Austro-Hungarian counter-attacks on Italian line begin, 95; British win Messines Ridge and other fortified positions held for 2½ years by Germans, 104; Canadian troops penetrate German lines south of Lens, 105; Italians resume offensive in Trentino, 122; Russian advance begins, 139, German attack launched, Western Front; north of Nieuport, 154; German troops pierce Russian lines, 177; London houses shaken by Flanders cannonading, gigantic

War—*Continued*

infantry attack follows, 199, 200; Canadian troops take Hill 70, 217; new Italian offensive begins, battle of Julian Alps, 226; French deliver smashing blow in Verdun sector, 227, 236; Russians surrender Riga, 255–6; French launch new offensive on right bank of Meuse, 265; Pershing reports failure to stop Germans, revolt among Russian troops, have depressed Allies, 270; Canadians pour poison gas into Lens, 274; U. S. 1st Division goes into quiet sector of trenches; British, French strike in Flanders, 277, 317–18; deliver smashing blow northeast of Soissons, 320; German, Austrian forces strike at Caporetto, beginning disastrous defeat for Italy, 322; Page telegraphs Allied cause at stake, England, France rushing to Italy's support, 331; 3 Americans killed in German raid; first U. S. prisoners taken, 338; Austro-German forces in close pursuit of Italian armies, 344; Passchendaele Ridge passes into British hands, 348; Italian resistance on Piave front stiffens, with Allied help, 349; British forces penetrate Hindenburg line, led by tanks, 367; military operations on Russian front cease, 381; Germans on Western Front begin counter-attacks before Cambrai, 383; Pershing reports emergency, 387; British occupy Jerusalem; advance farther, 402, 517; Germans fail to smash Ypres salient, 407; American casualties begin to come in, 408; reports vague as news gets worse, 409, 422; armistices between Russia, Central Powers, 412, 420; Germans drive in British advanced posts northeast of Ypres, 427; Belgium, northern France, Italian front under deep snow, 436, 457, 517; U. S. troops take over small section of Western Front, 509; German advance on Russia begins again, 551–2, 556

Naval: situation when U. S. enters, 10; Lloyd George says victory depends on ships, 16; Sims reports situation critical, 34; U-boat activity serious, 35, 108, 117; urgent requests for more U. S. anti-submarine craft, 40, 121–2, 130, 138, 139; Wilson suggests British convoy merchant ships; system to be tried; first convoy arrives; British will adopt, 44, 124, 179; Walter Page sends confidential report on crisis, 121; shipping being sunk around British Isles faster than new ships can be built, 139, 411; Wilson criticizes British use of navy, says U. S. must make own plans, 140; interested in nets as protection against submarines, 144; Jusserand, Wilson confer on blockade, 153; Sims says war will be decided by submarine campaign, 156; Allied merchant shipping losses, 201; British memo. on submarine situation, part U. S. can play, 207; German submarines reported operating off New England coast, 270;

U-boat toll less, 284; Inter-Allied Naval Council formed, 409

War Department: Senate inquiry into, 406; Crozier testifies, 407; Military War Council created, 410; Sen. Frelinghuysen issues statement about delays, blunders, 418; Baker testifies before Senate committee, 463; critical editorials on his testimony, 469; Wilson's controversy with Sen. Chamberlain over charges against War Dept., 480, 484–5, 496; Baker gratified at Wilson's support, 485; Gorgas testifies on overcrowding in cantonments, etc.; Baker requests permission to appear again, 498–9; speaks 5 hours in packed hearing room; statement approved by many; Wilson delighted, 503–4, 511

War Industries Board: Wilson suggests formation of, 168–9; establishment of, announced, Scott at head, 197; Wilson receives members of, 207, 262, 280, 300, 339; thinks price-determining power cannot be lodged with, 219; members of, confer with heads of big steel industries on price fixing, 280; Willard succeeds Scott as head, 366; resigns, 468, 477–8; Baruch considered for chairman of, 522–3

War Memoirs of David Lloyd George, David Lloyd George (Little, Brown & Co.): see numerous references

War Memoirs of Robert Lansing, Robert Lansing (Bobbs-Merrill Co.): see numerous references

War Savings Campaign: 360

War, the World and Wilson, The, George Creel (Harper & Bros.): 11, 17

War Trade Board: Wilson asks T. D. Jones to serve on, 196; draft executive order creating, 290; established, McCormick chairman, 304; issues first U. S. black list against enemy firms, 391; Jones resigns, 433; report of Board, 537

Warburg, Felix W.: 356

Warren, Charles, Assistant Attorney General: Wilson to, 543. Also 7

Warren, Senator F. E., Wyo.: 60, 101, 199

Washburn, Stanley: 62

Washington *Evening Star*, 178; *Post*, 160, 167–8, 368, 379, 400–1; *Times*, 178, 258

Washington, George: 266, 343

Water Power: 209, 271–2, 408, 451

Waterways: 22, 131–2, 290

Watterson, Henry: 528

Webb, Congressman E. Y., N. C.: Wilson to, 81. Also 8, 67, 380, 450

Webster, J. Edwin: Wilson to, 323

Weeks, Senator J. W., Mass.: Wilson to, 216. Also 10, 172

Weeks, R. S.: 93

Wellman, Walter: 229

Wells, John M.: 282

Wheeler, Benjamin I.: 18

Wheeler, Post, U. S. Chargé d'Affaires, Japan: 129

White, Andrew D.: Wilson to, 48–9
White, Cyrus E.: 378
White, Edward D., U. S. Supreme Court: 80
White, John B.: 187
White, William A.: 326
Whitehouse, J. H.: 21
Whitehouse, Mrs. Norman de R.: 282, 324, 362
Wilbur, Ray L.: 53
Wiley, Louis: Wilson to, 185. Also 409
Willard, Daniel: Wilson to, 477. Also 5, 14, 68, 366, 427, 468, 472
Willard, Joseph E., U. S. Ambassador, Spain: 213, 295, 310
Willcox, William R.: 424
Williams, John Skelton, Comptroller of the Currency: Wilson to, 105, 303. Also 312, 315, 438
Williams, Senator John Sharp, Miss.: Wilson to, 171, 214, 245, 251, 402, 529, 554. Also 121, 191, 220, 221, 264, 277, 296, 356, 484, 501, 521, 558
Williams, Walter: Wilson to, 38
Willis, Irene Cooper: 91
Wilson, Alice, niece of Woodrow Wilson: 99, 391, 429
Wilson, Ellen Axson: 326, 335, 354
Wilson, Field-Marshal Sir Henry: 372
Wilson, Hugh R., U. S. Chargé d'Affaires, Switzerland: 286, 533, 547
Wilson, John A., cousin of Woodrow Wilson: 8, 129, 271, 317
Wilson, John M.: 143
Wilson, Joseph R., brother of Woodrow Wilson: Wilson to, 186, 356. Also 8, 197, 282, 391, 429, 558
Wilson, Mrs. Joseph R.: 8, 391, 429
Wilson, Joseph Ruggles, father of Woodrow Wilson: 49, 110
Wilson, Mrs. Joseph Ruggles, mother of Woodrow Wilson: 269
Wilson, Margaret W., daughter of Woodrow Wilson: Wilson to, 23, 284. Also 8, 105, 106, 182, 186, 265, 316, 422, 470, 553
Wilson, William B., Secretary of Labor: Wilson to, 435. Also 53, 57, 71, 94, 111, 137, 190, 199, 206, 244, 246, 284, 451, 478, 490–1, 521, 536, 545
Wilson, Woodrow:
   Addresses: 23, 46, 66, 69, 92, 100–1, 110, 117, 148, 149, 211–12, 295–6, 324, 350, 360, 389–90, 398, 451, 455–6, 462, 470, 531, 536–7
   Congress, Personal Relations with: discourages members from enlisting, 10–11; writes Rep. Garner his services appreciated, 63–4; comments on "so-called 'courtesy'" of Senate, 78; considers Smith of Georgia, Reed, Hardwick "distinctly hostile", 112–13; Sen. Pittman has been invited only to public receptions at White House, Wilson says omission not personal, 127; thanks Sen. Chamberlain for attack on Gore's obstructionist tactics, 209; will not volunteer advice, but when asked, urges suffrage

cause, 458; controversy with Chamberlain over charges against War Department, 480, 484–5, 496, 502; battle with Congress, 486; unwilling to make deposition for La Follette trial, 492; does not wish Congress to think they can control him, 505; asks Robinson to run again for Senate, 530; is grateful for "whole-hearted champions", 555; is surprised that so many senators still suspect "necessary proposals of power", 563
   Criticisms of: Lodge attacks, 70, 73, 224; J. M. Parker criticizes Wilson, 71–2; "violent and unfair" attacks on administration, 280; Boston a hotbed of criticism, 511; Wilson reads attacks on Lincoln, thinks publication might help, 543–4
   Leadership of Allied, Associated Cause: Morgenthau brings word of desire in Europe for; Wilson feels responsibility, 274; Lloyd George says Wilson's speeches have given European peoples fresh courage, hope, 277, 279; London *Morning Post* says Wilson has given "forthright, unflinching lead" needed, 355–6; Wilson thinks address by himself may prove moral turning point, 417; T. N. Page reports fear of Italian leaders that U. S. is becoming "too potent", 513; Wilson disturbed over political paragraph in Supreme War Council statement, 519, 527–8; fears *any* expression of policy framed jointly at Paris", 561
   Personal: health, recreation, family life, 4–5, 8, 397, 481–2; is lonely for friends, 15; keeps Sunday in old-fashioned way, 21, 323; writing plans after retirement, 42–3, 534, 567–8; appointments, 64, 105, 126–7, 157–8, 197–8, 207–8, 225, 230, 243, 424; protection of, 70, 305, 323–4, 397; White House only place to "get things done", 71; on Day of Prayer, 73, 260, 314; Pershing finds him "cordial and simple"; Balfour gets on with him "tremendously", 85–6; degree from University of Bologna, 86, 265; investments, 93, 119, 169, 175, 316; memorial to his father, 110; Sargent portrait of, 122, 172, 302, 310, 403–4, 525; "over head and ears in work", 125; says opposition does not change his opinion of a man, 130; takes trip on *Mayflower* to escape "madness" of Washington, 181, 182; is well but "*very* tired", 182, 238; has become "soft-hearted" about inventions to help in war, 194; thinks it unwise to leave Washington for long, 202; will not ask draft exemptions on personal grounds, 220; is doing too much, pace is telling, 231; can get no "emotional power" into his voice, speaking into phonograph, 235; takes brief vacation trip to North Shore, Nantucket, 264–71; describes himself as a democrat with aristocratic tastes, 266; describes his mother, 269–70; signs Pocket Testament League card, 274; celebrates Mrs. Wilson's birthday, 307; can do "consecutive work" now that Congress

Wilson, Woodrow—*Continued*
adjourned, 308–9; says was never better in his life, 314; on Barnard statue of Lincoln, 327, 345–6, 353; finds Col. House a comfort, 331; McAdoo reports "genuine affection" for, among people, 334–5; Wilson receives medal from Committee of Verdun, 339; votes, 341; denies rumors of disloyalty in administration, 353; designates Bible Week, 377; is still interested in college matters, 384; thinks interruption of missionary activities would be unfortunate, 393; speaks confidentially at Gridiron dinner, 398; Christmas, birthday celebrations, 427, 428–9, 434, 437; mourns death of his old friend, C. W. Mitchell, 439–40, 446–7; his job to "keep things properly co-ordinated", 459–60; feels himself "entrusted with directing the foreign relations of the Nation", 477; urges reverent observance of Sabbath on men of army, navy, 482; congratulates a mother who has 6 sons in army, 496; sympathizes with parents who have lost their son in service, 503; can't afford personal feelings, 508; is passing through times that "try the soul", 525; weathering "storms—from Capitol Hill", 553; makes "terrible fist" of talking about himself, 571–2

Press, Relations with: Wilson appreciates editorials in support of administration, 22–3; American Newspaper Publishers Assn. passes resolution of support, 35; Wilson on "extravagant inferences" drawn by press, 60; Lawrence suggests correspondents be invited to White House on censorship situation, Wilson thinks unwise, 86–7; suggestions for advisory committees to consult with Creel; Wilson thinks unworkable, 257, 367–8, 420–1; is anxious over treatment of foreign language publications, 314; says newspaper no place to express official judgment, 321; considers handling of disloyal newspapers "thorny business", 330; deplores war publicity matter dumped on newspapers, 439; approves efforts to establish better news interchange between North, South America, 473–4; explains why cannot guide writers, 508–9; reminds editors of responsibility to publish truth, 534–5
Wilson, Mrs. Woodrow: see daily references
Wimpfheimer, Mr. and Mrs. C. A.: Wilson to, 503
Winchell, Benjamin La Fon: 230
Winchell, Major Wallace: Wilson to, 378
Winslow, Erving: 554
Wisconsin *State Journal:* 22–3, 492
Wise, Rabbi Stephen S.: Wilson to, 42, 467, 526. Also 135
Wiseman, Sir William: 96, 97, 102, 108, 128, 134, 161–3, 213, 231, 255, 296, 307, 361, 492, 520, 521, 550
Wishard, Luther D.: 339
Wolcott, Senator J. O., Del.: 60, 546
Woman Suffrage: Wilson thinks his endorsement of suffrage bill, Maryland, would harm cause, 34–5; immediate passage of amendment for, urged, as part of war program, 67; Wilson approves appointment of House committee on, 68–9, 109; Commission from Russia is confronted by suffrage banner saying America not a democracy, 121; Wilson thinks demonstrators bent on making cause obnoxious, 125; police patrol of White House increased because of disturbances; arrests made; Occoquan sentences, 128, 166, 168, 226, 321, 347, 362; Wilson asks no further arrests without notifying him, 171; pardons suffragettes, 172; thinks "colorless chronicle" of their actions should be printed, 178; Malone resigns to fight for suffrage, Wilson displeased, 268–9; Wilson hopes New York will adopt suffrage, 306; receives committee from New York State Woman Suffrage Party, makes address, 324; receives group of leaders of, 346; receives Arkansas suffragettes, 408; confers with Democratic congressmen in regard to; will not volunteer advice, but when asked urges suffrage, 458, 460; Theodore Roosevelt advocates woman member from every suffrage state on Republican National Committee; suggestion turned to account by Democratic National Committee, Wilson delighted, 460, 489; House adopts suffrage amendment, 463
Wood, Maj. Gen. Leonard: 71–2, 218, 488, 529, 565
Woodbridge, S. I.: Wilson to, 229
Woodrow, James, uncle of Woodrow Wilson: 440
Woodrow, Mrs. James, aunt of Woodrow Wilson: Wilson to, 440–1
Woodrow, James, nephew of Woodrow Wilson: 8
Woodrow Wilson and World Settlement, Ray Stannard Baker (Doubleday, Page & Co.): 75, 453, 454
Woodrow Wilson As I Know Him, Joseph P. Tumulty (Doubleday, Page & Co.): 476
Woodrow Wilson's Scrapbooks, compiled by John Randolph Bolling: 37
Woods, Hiram: Wilson to, 440
Woods, Lawrence C.: Wilson to, 409
Woods, Robert A.: 511
Woolley, R. W.: Wilson to, 84. Also 401
Woolsey, L. H., Solicitor for the Department of State: 24, 367
Wright, Theodore: Wilson to, 220

Yager, Arthur, Governor of Porto Rico: 475
Yale, William, U. S. Special Agent, Cairo: 351
Yangko, Teodoro R.: Wilson to, 142
York-Steiner: 547
Young, Congressman G. M., N. D.: 94
Young, Warren: 369

Zimmermann, Artur, German Secretary of State for Foreign Affairs to August 5, 1917: 255